Studien zur italienisch-deutschen Musikgeschichte IX

ANALECTA MUSICOLOGICA

VERÖFFENTLICHUNGEN DER MUSIKGESCHICHTLICHEN
ABTEILUNG DES DEUTSCHEN HISTORISCHEN
INSTITUTS IN ROM

BAND 14

1974
ARNO VOLK VERLAG HANS GERIG KG KÖLN

STUDIEN ZUR ITALIENISCH-DEUTSCHEN MUSIKGESCHICHTE IX

Herausgegeben von

FRIEDRICH LIPPMANN

1974
ARNO VOLK VERLAG HANS GERIG KG KÖLN

AV 222
© 1974 by Arno Volk Verlag Hans Gerig KG Köln
Alle Rechte vorbehalten
Gesamtherstellung: Druckerei Karl Hart KG, Volkach
Printed in W.-Germany · ISBN 3-87252-059-8

INHALT

NOTIZEN ZUR MUSIKALISCHEN IKONOGRAPHIE (I)
GESTIMMTE INSTRUMENTE ALS HARMONIE-ALLEGORIE

von *Volker Scherliess* (Rom)

In ihren Tagebuch-Aufzeichnungen entwirft Marie Luise Kaschnitz die Skizze einer ihr besonders nahestehenden Verwandten und beschreibt sie unter anderem mit den Worten, sie sei *»ein gut gestimmtes Instrument, das Wohlsein verbreitete, Harmonie«*[1]. Die Dichterin verwendet mit diesem Bilde — bewußt oder intuitiv — einen seit der Antike gebräuchlichen Topos: Ein Musikinstrument symbolisiert musikalische Harmonie, die dann ihrerseits auf etwas drittes Harmonisches, in diesem Falle einen ausgeglichenen, »in sich stimmigen« Charakter bezogen wird. Im platonischen Dialog *Laches* heißt es von jemandem, *»der nicht nur seine Lyra aufs beste stimmt, sondern sein eigenes Leben, indem er nämlich Worte und Taten harmonisch übereinstimmen läßt«*, er sei *»erst recht ein μουσικός«*[2]. Bei Shakespeare bittet Cordelia für den irrsinnigen Lear zu den Göttern:

> O you kind gods,
> Cure this great breach in his abused nature!
> The untuned and jarring senses, o, wind up
> Of this child-changed father. (*King Lear* IV, 7)

und auch Dante verwendet — freilich in anderer Beziehung — das Bild vom Instrument, dessen Saiten untereinander abgestimmt sind (*Par.* XIV, 118/9):

> E come giga ed arpa, in tempra tesa
> Di molte corde, fa dolce tintinno
> . . .

Nicht nur in der Literatur begegnet das »gut gestimmte Musikinstrument« als Metapher für Harmonie, sondern, mit derselben zugrundeliegenden symboli-schen Bedeutung, auch in der bildenden Kunst. Diese Tatsache — man mag sie für selbstverständlich und nicht weiter frag-würdig angesehen haben — ist bisher, so-

---

[1] Marie Luise KASCHNITZ, *Tage, Tage, Jahre. Aufzeichnungen*, Frankfurt/Main-Hamburg 1971, p. 140.

[2] PLATON, *Laches* 188 c—d: καὶ κομιδῇ μοι δοκεῖ μουσικὸς ὁ τοιοῦτος εἶναι ἁρμονίαν καλ-λίστην ἡρμοσμένος οὐ λύραν οὐδὲ παιδιᾶς ὄργανα, ἀλλὰ τῷ ὄντι αὐτὸς αὑτοῦ τὸν βίον σύμφωνον τοῖς λόγοις πρὸς τὰ ἔργα. Dieselbe Metapher: *Gorgias* 482 b—c.

weit ich sehe, kaum beachtet worden[3]. Sie ist aber wohl doch wesentlich und, gerade angesichts des sowohl in der Kunst- als auch in der Musikgeschichtsforschung wachsenden Interesses für Fragen der musikalischen Ikonographie, einer Betrachtung wert. Dabei beschränken wir uns auf solche Darstellungen, in denen die reine Stimmung eines Instrumentes sichtbar dargestellt ist, d. h. auf dem es gerade gestimmt wird; aus der Fülle dazu vorliegender Beispiele wird hier nur eine kleine Anzahl gezeigt und erörtert.

Ältestes mir bekanntes Bildzeugnis dieser Art ist die Zeichnung in einer 1023 datierten Hrabanus Maurus-Handschrift[4]; sie zeigt drei Männer, von denen einer sein dreieckiges harfenförmiges Instrument stimmt, während die beiden anderen auf einem Beckenpaar und einer Zupffidel spielen. Die dargestellte Gruppe gehört als Illustration zu Hrabanus' Buch XVIII, 4 *De musica et partibus eius*. Ob wir in ihr lediglich die lose Zusammenfügung verschiedener musikalischer Bildmotive sehen können oder ob sie als eine Allegorie der Musik zu deuten wäre, ist schwer zu entscheiden. Für die allegorische Deutung sprächen, wie wir sehen werden, das Akkordieren sowie die Beschriftung *m-u-s-i-c-a* zwischen den Saiten eines weiteren — ohne Spieler am unteren Bildfeld dargestellten — Instrumentes[5].

Im allgemeinen wurden als Allegorien der Musik allerdings Einzelfiguren dargestellt: einer der traditionellen »Erfinder der Musik« Tubalcain oder Pythagoras[6] oder, am häufigsten, eine junge Frau mit Musikattributen, oft mit einem Portativ, vielfach aber auch mit einem gestimmten Saiteninstrument. So

---

[3] Kurze Hinweise etwa bei Patricia EGAN, »Concert« Scenes in Musical Paintings of the Italian Renaissance, Journal of the American Musicological Society XIV, 1961, p. 184—195. Cfr. auch A. P. DE MIRIMONDE, L'Accord retrouvé de Gerrit van Honthorst, La Revue des Arts X, 1960, p. 109—116.

[4] Montecassino, Abtei, Codex 132, f. 444. Abb. bei Roger BRAGARD/Ferdinand J. DE HEN, Musikinstrumente aus zwei Jahrtausenden, Stuttgart 1968, p. 70; Ambrogio Maria AMELLI, Miniature sacre e profane dell'anno 1023, illustranti l'enciclopedia medioevale di Rabano Mauro, Montecassino 1896, Tafel CXXIII. Zu der Handschrift cfr. Janine WETTSTEIN, Sant'Angelo in Formis et la Peinture médiévale en Campanie, Genf 1960 (Université de Genève, Thèse No. 167), p. 109/10 (frdl. Hinweis von Frau Dr. H. Giess, Rom).

[5] Eine vergleichbare Darstellung in der Bibel von Velislav, um 1340 (Prag, Univ.-Bibl., Ms. XXIII, c. 124, f. 129v. Abb. MGG X, col. 1713/4): Eine glockenschlagende Frau — die Musica — hat links einen stimmenden, rechts einen spielenden jungen Mann mit Psalterium zur Seite. Von den überaus zahlreichen ähnlichen Darstellungen aus späterer Zeit seien genannt: Jacopo Bertoia (1544—1574), Zeichnung mit drei Personen, Typus einer »Vorbereitung zum Konzert« (cfr. Anm. 56). Florenz, Uffizien Gab. Dis. 2024 F. (Luisa MARCUCCI/Luigi PARIGI, Mostra di strumenti musicali in disegni degli Uffizi, Katalog, Florenz 1952, Abb. 10). — Abraham Bosse (1602—1676), Stich mit spielenden und stimmenden Putti (MGG VIII, Art. Laute, col. 362). — Pieter de Hooch (1629 — nach 1684), Musikalische Szene. Honululu, Academy of Arts (The Art Quarterly XXXIV, 1971, p. 379).

[6] Z. B. das Relief vom Campanile des Florentiner Domes (Werkstatt des Andrea Pisano). Cfr. Martin STAEHELIN, Pythagoras und Jubal als »Erfinder« und »Bewahrer« der Musik, Neue Zürcher Zeitung 26. 3. 1972, p. 51/2.

zeigt eine Miniatur des Nicolò da Bologna von 1354 (Abb. 1)[7] die *Frau Musica* sitzend, halb nach rechts gedreht und mit einer Laute. Sie zupft eine Saite und akkordiert sie; auf ihrem Schoß liegt ein anderes Instrument; vor ihr, in kleinerem Maßstab, schlägt Tubalcain mit zwei Hämmern auf seinen Amboß. Dieser Typ einer Musikallegorie war im Trecento offenbar verbreitet. Wir finden dieselbe Formulierung sowohl in einem Fresko von Serafino Serafini (Abb. 2)[8] als auch in einer Florentiner Handschrift derselben Zeit[9]. Das dem Giusto da Menabuoi (Ende 14. Jh.) zugeschriebene Skizzenbuch im römischen Gabinetto delle Stampe enthält eine ähnliche Zeichnung (Abb. 3)[10]: Die Musica — von zahlreichen Instrumenten und dem zu ihren Füßen hämmernden Tubal umgeben — stimmt ihre Laute; aus ihrem Munde steigen die Solmisationssilben *ut re mi fa sol la* auf[11].

Alle genannten Allegorien der Musik stehen im selben größeren Zusammenhang, nämlich der Darstellung der *Septem artes liberales,* und haben eine literarische Vorlage. Die Einteilung der Künste (Grammatik, Dialektik, Rhetorik, Geometrie, Arithmetik, Astronomie, Musik), die ursprünglich auf das antike System der propädeutischen — auf die Philosophie vorbereitenden — Fächer zurückgeht, war im ersten Viertel des 5. Jahrhunderts durch das Werk *De nuptiis Mercurii et Philologiae* des Martianus Capella kanonisiert worden. Diese romanhaft aufgebaute, in Prosa und Verspassagen abwechselnde Beschreibung der Hochzeitsfeier von Merkur und Philologia, während derer die sieben Artes in jeweils einem Buch präsentiert werden, wurde maßgeblich für das enzyklopädische Bildungssystem des Mittelalters und hatte durch lange Schultradition und Kommentierungen Auswirkungen bis in die Renaissance und darüber hinaus[12]. Die Musik — bei

---

[7] Johannes ANDREAS, *Novella in libros decretalium* (460 × 270 mm). Mailand, Bibl. Ambrosiana Ms. B 42 inf., f. 1. Cfr. Renata CIPRIANI, *Codici miniati dell'Ambrosiana*, Mailand 1968, p. 171/2.

[8] Serafino Serafini (um 1324 — ca. 1393), aus einem Freskenzyklus für die Capp. Marinetti in S. Andrea (Ferrara), datiert 1378. Ferrara, Pinacoteca Nazionale (Inv.Nr. 8).

[9] Anonyme Miniatur. Florenz, Bibl. Naz. ms. B.R. 38, f. 34 (Mitte 14. Jh.). Cfr. Katalog der Mostra storica nazionale della miniatura, Rom 1953 (Florenz, Sansoni), Tafel LXI a, Kat. Nr. 421, p. 267.

[10] Vorzeichnung für Giustos (tätig um 1370—90) zerstörtes Fresko in der Eremitani-Kapelle, Padua. Cfr. Julius von SCHLOSSER, *Giusto's Fresken in Padua und die Vorläufer der Stanza della Segnatura,* Jahrbuch der Kunsthistorischen Sammlungen des Allerhöchsten Kaiserhauses XVII, Wien 1896, p. 13—100.

[11] Von den zahlreichen erläuternden Texten in der Zeichnung und am Rande interessieren in unserem Zusammenhang vor allem die Verse *Ob loquitur numeris septem discrimina vocum/ Instat leta suis melisque thonisque canora,* mit denen die Tatsache der unterschiedlichen Stimmung der einzelnen Saiten, aus der die Harmonie hervorgeht, ausgedrückt wird. — Die Texte vollständig bei Adolfo VENTURI, *Il libro di Giusto per la Cappella degli Eremitani in Padova,* in: Le Gallerie Nazionali Italiane IV, Rom 1899, p. 371/2.

[12] Cfr. etwa die zusammenfassende Darstellung bei Ernst Robert CURTIUS, *Europäische Literatur und lateinisches Mittelalter,* Bern/München, 6. Aufl. 1967, p. 46/9. Ausführlicher: *Arts libéraux et philosophie au Moyen Age* (Actes du quatrième congrès international de philoso-

Martian heißt sie in den meisten Handschriften *Harmonia* — wird als letzter Hochzeitsgast eingeführt (Buch IX): ihr Haupt ist von glitzernden Goldplättchen umgeben, ihr Gewand strotzt von dünnen Metallscheiben, alles funkelt und klingt. In der Rechten hält sie ein tönendes, aus kreisförmig ineinander verwobenen Saiten bestehendes Instrument, Abbild der himmlischen Sphären und Symbol der *musica mundana*. Von ihm geht ein solches Strahlen und erhabenes Tönen aus, daß sich alle Götter in Verehrung seiner *extramundana intellegentia* erheben[13].

Diese Schilderung bot als Bildprogramm, im Gegensatz zu den Beschreibungen anderer *artes liberales*, nur wenige Anknüpfungspunkte[14]. Eine junge Frau im strahlenden Gewand — das ließ sich malen; aber wie sollte das seltsame Sphäreninstrument dargestellt und sein Klingen symbolisiert werden?[15] Man ersetzte es einfach durch ein bekanntes mehrstimmiges (harmonisches) Musikinstrument, das nun seinerseits die *musica mundana* symbolisieren sollte, so wie umgekehrt ein Kommentar zu Martians Text entsprechend erläutert: »*tangit in hoc loco non*

phie médiévale, Université de Montreal, 27. 8.–2. 9. 1967), Montreal/Paris 1969. — Richard McKeon, *The Transformation of the Liberal Arts in the Renaissance*, in: Developments in the Early Renaissance, Papers of the Second annual conference of the Center for Medieval and Early Renaissance Studies. State University of New York at Binghamton 4–5 May 1968, ed. Bernard S. Levy, Albany 1972, p. 158–223.

[13] Martianus Capella ed. Adolf Dick, Leipzig 1925, Nachdruck Stuttgart 1969, p. 482/3: »*Tandem inter Phoebum Pallademque media Harmonia sublimis ingreditur, cuius sonorum caput auri coruscantis bratteis comebatur, caeso etiam tenuatoque metallo rigens vestis, et omnibus ad motum gressumque rata congruentia temperatum blandis leniter crepitaculis tinniebat. cuius incessum mater Paphie, ut eam contigue sequebatur, licet pulchris rosea numeris ac libratis passibus moveretur, vix tamen poterat imitari. dextra autem quoddam gyris multiplicibus circulatum et miris ductibus intertextum velut clupeum gestitabat, quod quidem suis invicem complexibus modulatum ex illis fidibus circulatis omnium modorum concinentiam personabat. laeva autem virginis quamplures ex auro assimulatae parvaeque effigies theatralium voluptatum religatae aeque pendebant. verum ille orbis non chelys nec barbiton nec tetrachordon apparebat, sed ignota rotunditas omnium melodias transcenderat organorum. denique mox ingressa atque eiusdem orbis sonuere concentus: cuncta illa, quae dissona suavitas commendarat, velut mutescentia tacuerunt, ipseque tunc Iuppiter caelestesque divi superioris melodiae agnita granditate, quae in honorem cuiusdam ignis arcani ac flammae insopibilis fundebatur, reveriti intimum patrimumque carmen paululum in venerationem extramundanae omnes intellegentiae surrexerunt.*«

[14] Darauf wies bereits Werner Bachmann hin: *Bilddarstellungen der Musik im Rahmen der artes liberales*, in: Kongreßbericht Hamburg 1956, Kassel/Basel 1957, p. 48.

[15] Zuweilen findet man es abgewandelt als eine blaue sternenübersäte Himmelskugel oder einen sphärischen Globus mit den Planetenbahnen, so in dem Gemälde von Antonio Cavalucci (1752–1795), *L'origine della Musica*, 1786/7, Rom, Pal. Caetani (Staehelin, a. a. O. Abb. 4). — Hier dürfte sich der Maler an die weitverbreitete *Iconologia* des Cesare Ripa (Rom 1603, p. 344) gehalten haben, der unter dem Stichwort *Musica* Martians Angaben variiert, indem er die Musik als *donna giovane* auf einer *palla di color celeste* beschreibt: »*la palla scuopre che tutta l'armonia della Musica sensibile si riposa e fonda nell'armonia dei Cieli conosciuta da Pittagorici, della quale ancora noi per virtù d'essi participiamo e pero volontieri porgemo gli orecchi alle consonanze armoniche e musicali.*« (Auch der Amboß mit einigen Hämmern ist als Attribut genannt, wird allerdings nicht auf Tubal, sondern Avicenna bezogen.)

solum musicam cordarum verum etiam celestium musicam«[16]; dabei liegt die spätantike (plotinische) Auffassung zugrunde, der Weg zur kosmischen Harmonie führe über die irdische Musik[17].

Ein gestimmtes Musikinstrument als Symbol für Harmonie — die Deutung einer solchen Darstellung ist klar: Eine einzelne Saite wird auf die im Verhältnis zu den anderen richtige Tonhöhe gebracht (akkordiert); es entsteht ein stimmender, stimmiger Zusammenklang aus mehreren, einzeln verschieden klingenden Saiten. »*In cythara varietas cordarum uniformem reddit concentum.*«[18] Das entspricht genau der traditionellen Definition »*concors dissonantia, quae proprie harmonia nominatur*« (Johannes Afflighemensis)[19] oder, bei Cassiodor: »*Harmonia est enim diversarum rerum in unam convenientam redacta copulatio.*«[20] In einer um 1100 entstandenen nordfranzösischen Martianus Capella-Handschrift in der Laurenziana lesen wir am Anfang des IX. Buches über der — hier nicht stimmend, sondern beim Spiel auf ihrem Instrument dargestellten — *Frau Musica* einen Titulus, mit dem sie sich vorstellt und dessen beide mittlere Verse ebenfalls die Metapher »Harmonischer Klang durch verschieden klingende, aufeinander abgestimmte Saiten« enthalten:

> Prebens solamen luctus mihi musica nomen,
> Me natura cupit, sine me quia vivere nescit,
> Consona discretis, producens carmina chordis,
> Diverso tractu, fero concordia cantu,
> Curas artifices, per me solantur manes,
> Obliti fletus pueri, dulcedine cantus[21].

Viele ähnliche Zeugnisse ließen sich anfügen.

---

[16] Mailand, Bibl. Ambrosiana, Cod. M. 37 sup., f. 13 (12./13 Jh.). Im Kommentar des Remigius von Auxerre: »*Ab hoc loco musicam coelestem describit.*« (Zitiert nach BACHMANN, a. a. O. p. 48, Anm. 9.)

[17] Günter BANDMANN, *Melancholie und Musik*, Köln/Opladen 1960, p. 127. — Es sei betont, daß BACHMANNS Auffassung (a. a. O. p. 49), es handele sich darum, daß die *musica instrumentalis* im Vordergrund stehe, wohl nicht zutrifft, sondern daß die Instrumente als Abbild der *musica mundana* zu verstehen sind.

[18] Aus einer mittelalterlichen Heiligenlegende; zitiert nach Reinhold HAMMERSTEIN, *Die Musik der Engel*, Bern/München 1962, p. 86.

[19] Martin GERBERT, *Scriptores ecclesiastici de Musica*, II, St. Blasien 1784, p. 234. Dieser Harmoniebegriff geht zurück auf die vorsokratische Philosophie (cfr. z. B. Hermann DIELS, *Die Fragmente der Vorsokratiker*, Heraklit 10) und wurde etwa in der Eryximachos-Rede in PLATONS *Symposion* (187 a) zitiert. Er begegnet in allen Bereichen, so auch bei VASARI, der die Harmonie der Farben (*unione dei colori*) mit musikalischen Termini definiert als »*una discordanza di colori diversi accordati insieme*« und »*una discordanza accordatissima*«. (Zitiert nach Stanislaw MOSSAKOWSKI, *Raphael's »St. Cecilia«. An Iconographical Study*, Zeitschrift für Kunstgeschichte XXXI, 1968, p. 21, n. 88.)

[20] In *Psalterium expositio* (zu Ps. 150,5). J. P. MIGNE, *Patrologia Latina* LXX, col. 1053.

[21] Florenz, Bibl. Med. Laur., Cod. S. Marco 190, f. 108 c (11./12. Jh.). Abb. der Seite bei BACHMANN, a. a. O. Abb. 4. Mostra del Poliziano, Florenz 1954, Katalog Nr. 38, p. 47. Cfr. Ludwig H. HEYDENREICH, *Eine illustrierte Martianus Capella-Handschrift des Mittelalters und*

Die auf solche Weise symbolisierte *Harmonie* bezeichnete, wie wir sahen, in den behandelten Musikallegorien im Rahmen der Sieben freien Künste die Musik, speziell die *musica mundana*. Dieselbe Zuordnung eines Instruments zur Sphärenharmonie begegnet aber auch anderswo. So beschreibt Vincenzo Cartari in seinem weitverbreiteten mythologischen Handbuch *Le Imagini degli Dei degli Antichi* den Jupiter mit seinen königlichen Attributen Krone und Adler, aber auch mit einer Lira da braccio »*significante . . . da lui provenire l'armonia delli orbi celesti*«[22]. Und in ganz anderem Zusammenhang finden wir die Bedeutung ebenfalls: Ein Altarbild des Cima da Conegliano in der Mailänder Pinacoteca di Brera zeigt in einer zentralperspektivischen, nach hinten zur Landschaft hin offenen Architektur die Heiligen Petrus Martyr, Nikolaus und Augustin (Abb. 4 und 5)[23]. Das Kompositionsschema ist das der »sacra conversazione«, wie es in den großen Altartafeln der Hochrenaissance immer wiederkehrt, nur daß hier anstelle der thronenden Madonna mit dem Kinde ein Märtyrer im Mittelpunkt steht. Zu diesem Typus gehört die Darstellung eines oder mehrerer musizierender Engel; und so sitzt auch in Cimas Bilde auf der Thronstufe unter Petrus Martyr ein Engel, ohne Flügel und Nimbus, in kostbarem Gewande und mit einem Streichinstrument, einer neunsaitigen Art Fidel, beschäftigt. Ein Bogen fehlt, und der Engel spielt auch gar nicht, sondern akkordiert eine Saite. Dabei blickt er mit dem Ausdruck intensiven Horchens (der uns unten noch beschäftigen wird) aus dem Bilde heraus. Er allegorisiert Harmonie, hier jedoch nicht nur verstanden als *musica mundana*, Harmonie der sphärischen Klänge, sondern ins Theologische erhoben zur *musica coelestis*[24]. An ihr haben die drei Heiligen teil, sie erleben in ihrer *contemplatio*, ihrer Schau Gottes die Harmonie der *civitas Dei*[25], von der Tinctoris, wörtlich Augustin zitierend, sagt: »*Diversorum sonorum rationabilis moderatusque concentus concordi varietate compacta bene ordinatae Dei insinuat unitatem civitatis.*«[26] Dasselbe gilt für etliche andere Bilder, so etwa

---

ihre Kopien im Zeitalter des Frühhumanismus, in: Kunstgeschichtliche Studien für Hans Kauffmann, ed. Wolfgang Braunfels, Berlin 1956, p. 59—68. — Derselbe Titulus zu einer *Musica* in der Handschrift Rom, Bibl. Vat., Urb. lat. 329, f. 149 (Ende 15. Jh.).

[22] Padua 1608, p. 140. Abb. MGG VIII (Art. *Lira da braccio*), col. 946.

[23] Cima da Conegliano (um 1479—1517), Mailand, Pinacoteca di Brera (Inv. Nr. 176).

[24] Der Begriff begegnet, zunächst synonym, um 1300 bei Jacobus von Lüttich. Cfr. Gerhard PIETZSCH, *Die Klassifikation der Musik von Boetius bis Ugolino von Orvieto*, Halle 1929, p. 118.

[25] Das entspricht der Erweiterung der traditionellen Musikklassifikation bei Ugolino von Orvieto (Anf. 15. Jh.), der über *musica instrumentalis, musica humana* und *musica mundana* als vierte Kategorie die *musica coelestis* stellt: »*Ecce caelestis musica omnis mundanae principium, omnis humanae ac instrumentalis initium et origo.*« (Zitiert nach PIETZSCH, a. a. O. p. 122.)

[26] Augustin, MIGNE PL XLI, col. 547. TINCTORIS: *Complexus effectuum musices*, cap. IV, Edmond de COUSSEMAKER, *Scriptorum de Musica medii aevi* IV, Paris 1876, p. 194. — In ähnlicher Weise deutet Charles DE TOLNAY die Darstellung, ohne allerdings auf die Symbolik des Stimmens hinzuweisen: *The Music of the Universe, Notes on a Painting by Bicci di Lorenzo*, The Journal of the Walters Art Gallery, Baltimore/Maryl. VI, 1943, p. 99/100.

Abb. 1: Nicolò da Bologna, *Allegorie der Musik* (Miniatur)
Mailand, Biblioteca Ambrosiana

Abb. 2: Serafino Serafini, *Allegorie der Musik* (Fresko)
Ferrara, Pinacoteca Nazionale

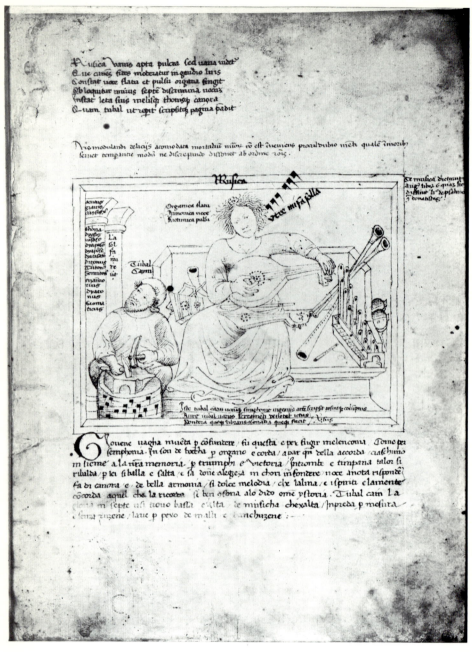

Abb. 3: Giusto da Menabuoi, *Allegorie der Musik*
Rom, Gabinetto delle Stampe

Abb. 5: Detail aus Abb. 4

Abb. 4: Cima da Conegliano, *Petrus Martyr, Nikolaus, Augustin*
Mailand, Brera

Abb. 7: Bonifazio Veronese, *Christus und Heilige* (Detail)
Venedig, Accademia

Abb. 6: Giovanni Antonio Pordenone, *Thronende Madonna und Heilige*
Susegna, Chiesa Parrocchiale

Abb. 9: Bernardino Cavallino, *Hl. Cäcilie*
Rom, Privatbesitz

Abb. 8: Florentinische Miniatur, *Christus und David*
Florenz, Laurenziana

Abb. 11: Jan Vermeer, *Lautenstimmerin*
New York, Metropolitan Museum of Art

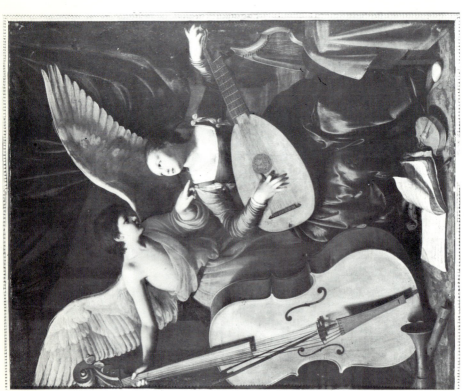

Abb. 10: Carlo Saraceni, *Hl. Cäcilie*
Rom, Palazzo Corsini

Abb. 13: Hendrik Terbrugghen, *Lautenstimmerin*
Hamburg, Kunsthalle, Kupferstichkabinett

Abb. 12: Anonym (Caravaggio-Nachfolger), *Lautenstimmerin*
Ort unbekannt

Abb. 15: Bernardo Strozzi, *Lautenstimmer*
Wien, Kunsthistorisches Museum

Abb. 14: Venezianisch, *Lira da braccio-Stimmer*
Wien, Kunsthistorisches Museum

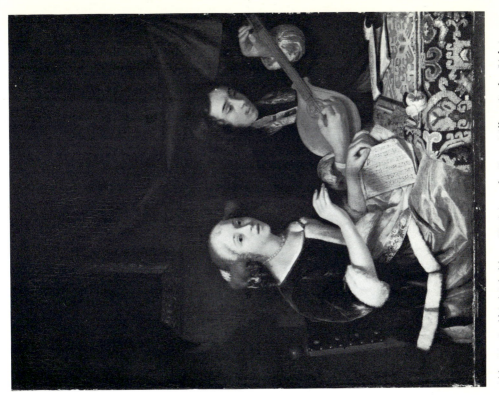

Abb. 17: Godfried Schalken, *Musizierendes Paar (Allegorie der Liebe)*
London, National Gallery

Abb. 16: Antoine Watteau, *Mezzetin*
Paris, Louvre, Cabinet des Dessins

Abb. 19: Lucas van Leyden, *Musikanten*

Abb. 18: Adriaen Hannemann, *Allegorische Darstellung*
Braunschweig, Herzog Anton Ulrich-Museum

den Altar Giovanni Antonio Pordenones in Susegna (Friuli) (Abb. 6)[27] oder Bonifazio Veroneses *Thronenden Christus mit Heiligen* in der venezianischen Accademia (Abb. 7)[28]. Hier tritt die Bedeutung des lautestimmenden Engels besonders augenfällig zutage, indem er zu Füßen des segnenden Christus neben der Himmelskugel, also in analoger äußerer Beziehung zur *musica coelestis* dargestellt ist[29].

An dieser Stelle sei darauf hingewiesen, daß auch König David mit seiner Harfe in zahlreichen mittelalterlichen Handschriften nicht spielend, sondern stimmend dargestellt wurde. Er galt als »*Mentor der Sphärenharmonie*«; »*das Bild Davids, der sein Instrument stimmt, wird in Bezug gesetzt zum Weltharmoniebild, und es wird ein vorläufiger Standort Davids als Typus in Verbindung mit Christus gewonnen.*«[30] David, der durch den Klang seiner Harfe den bösen Geist Sauls besiegt hatte (I. Sam. 16, 23), als Personifikation der ordnenden, harmonisierenden Kräfte der Musik und als alttestamentarischer Vorläufer des Erlösers Christus: so zeigt ihn z. B. eine florentinische Miniatur um 1400 (Abb. 8)[31].

Eine wiederum in der Brera befindliche *Sacra conversazione* von Bartolomeo Montagna zeigt die thronende Madonna mit vier Heiligen und vor dem Thron drei Engel[32]; einer spielt Lira da braccio, ein anderer Laute, der dritte stimmt seine Laute. Die Vermutung liegt nahe, er stimme sein Instrument mit den ande-

---

[27] Giovanni Antonio Pordenone (um 1483–1539), Susegna (Friuli), Chiesa Parrocchiale.

[28] Bonifazio dei Pitati (Veronese) (1487–1533), Venedig, Accademia (Inv. Nr. 284), 1530.

[29] Die Abhängigkeit der *musica coelestis* von Christus wird zuweilen durch das Motiv ausgedrückt, daß der Jesusknabe sich vom Schoß Mariens herabbeugt und an dem Instrument eines Engels zupft, so bei Vincenzo Foppa (1427 – um 1515), Mailand, Brera (Inv. Nr. 307). Abb. bei Angela OTTINO DELLA CHIESA, *Die Gallerie Brera in Mailand*, München 1955, p. 3.

[30] Hugo STEGER, *David Rex et Propheta*, Nürnberg 1961, p. 71 und 73. Steger gibt p. 72 eigens eine zusammenstellende Abbildung von 16 verschiedenen Stimmwerkzeugen der Davidsharfe! Eine unerwartete Bestätigung dieser Deutung bringt Wilhelm STAUDER, *Asinus ad lyram* (in: Helmuth Osthoff zu seinem siebzigsten Geburtstag, ed. Ursula AARBURG/Peter CAHN, Tutzing 1969, p. 31): Ein musizierender Esel ist nach altorientalischen Vorbildern in der mittelalterlichen Auffassung u. a. als »Gegenpol des Göttlichen«, »höllisches Gegenbild« von *David Rex et Propheta* aufgefaßt worden. Stauder gibt eine Darstellung in Meillers, wo der Esel sein Instrument stimmt (Abb. 3). »Wie David symbolisch die Harmonie der himmlischen Welt einstimmt, so stimmt der Esel die Mißharmonie der Unterwelt.« — Auch die griechische Mythologie kannte die Vorstellung, »*wonach der Kosmos das Musikinstrument ist, auf dem Apollon spielt*«. (Nach Olof GIGON, *Zum antiken Begriff der Harmonie*, in: Studium generale XIX, 1966, p. 545) — Der Engländer Robert Fludd (1574–1637) vergleicht die Welt mit einem Saiteninstrument, das von Gott gestimmt wird. (Nach Manfred LURKER, *Der Kreis als symbolischer Ausdruck der kosmischen Harmonie*, ibid., p. 531).

[31] Antiphonar, Florenz, Bibl. Med. Laur. cor. 7, f. 20. Andere Darstellungen cfr. STEGER, a. a. O. Tafel 14 (Pommersfelden, Graf von Schönbornsche Schloßbibl. Nr. 334, f. 148), Tafel 19,3 (London, Brit. Mus. Harley Ms. 4951); MGG V, Tafel 65 (Art. *Harfe*), Abb. 6 (englische Hs., München Clm 835), Abb. 8 (Relief Toulouse, Musée des Augustines).

[32] Bartolomeo Montagna (um 1450–1523), *Sacra conversazione*, signiert und datiert 1499, Mailand, Brera (Inv. Nr. 165). OTTINO DELLA CHIESA, a. a. O. p. 23; Detail MGG VIII, Tafel 40 b.

ren ab und symbolisiere dadurch auch Harmonie, ebenso wie die beiden Engel auf Veroneses *Immaculata* in Rom[33] oder auf einer Tafel von Giovanni Speranza[34]. Schon die beiden Putti mit Lauten zu Füßen der Madonna auf Mantegnas S. Zeno-Altar[35] — der linke stimmend, der rechte spielend und singend — lassen hieran denken. In diesen Bildern vermischt sich allerdings die Harmonie-Symbolik mit dem Motiv der feierlichen Ausschmückung und Erhöhung einer heiligen Szene durch Musik, wie wir sie gewöhnlich antreffen[36].

Alte, aus dem System der freien Künste überkommene Vorstellungen der personifizierten *Musica* und theologischer Inhalt sind verbunden in den Darstellungen der *Hl. Cäcilie*. Sie war von einer frühchristlichen Märtyrerin zur Patronin der Musik geworden; wie sich dieser Wandel vollzog, welche äußeren Anlässe ihn beförderten, ist noch nicht im einzelnen erforscht[37]. Nur soviel läßt sich sagen: Seit dem Anfang des 16. Jahrhunderts wird die Heilige üblicherweise mit musikalischen Attributen dargestellt, und ein Bild markiert diese Wende, die *S. Cecilia* von Raphael[38]. Dieses — von Gurlitt[39] eingehend beschriebene und gewürdigte — Gemälde wurde »epochemachend« insofern, als sich fast alle späteren Darstellungen an ihm bewußt orientierten oder zumindest durch sekundäre Vermittlung etwas von seiner »Idee der Musik« übernahmen. Raphael hatte die Heilige, nach Art einer sacra conversazione von anderen Heiligen umgeben, im Moment ihrer Ekstase dargestellt; sie wendet sich von den irdischen, am Boden liegenden Instrumenten ab und gehört nun ganz der himmlischen Musik

---

[33] Paolo Veronese (1528—1588), *Immaculata*, Rom, Kapitolinische Museen. Guido PIOVENE, *L'opera completa del Veronese*, Mailand 1968, Abb. 304.

[34] Giovanni Speranza (um 1480 — vor 1532), *Madonna mit Heiligen*, S. Giorgio d'Astico (Veneto), Chiesa di S. Giorgio. Lionello PUPPI, *Giovanni Speranza*, Rivista dell'Istituto Nazionale d'Archeologia e Storia dell'Arte, n. s. XI und XII, Rom 1963, p. 377, Abb. 4.

[35] Andrea Mantegna (1431—1506), Hochaltar, Verona, S. Zeno. Eva TIETZE-CONRAT, *Mantegna*, London 1955, Abb. 37.

[36] Cfr. Volker SCHERLIESS, *Musikalische Noten auf Kunstwerken der italienischen Renaissance bis zum Anfang des 17. Jahrhunderts* (Hamburger Beiträge zur Musikwissenschaft VIII), Hamburg 1972, p. 21 ff. — Inwieweit in den Musikdarstellungen der *sacre conversazioni* grundsätzlich (ob die Instrumente nun gestimmt, gespielt oder — auch das begegnet häufig — nur in der Hand gehalten werden) b e i d e Elemente zu sehen sind, kann hier nicht untersucht werden.

[37] Cfr. dazu ausführlicher SCHERLIESS, a. a. O. p. 23/24.

[38] Raphael (1483—1520), Pinacoteca Nazionale Bologna, um 1516.

[39] Wilibald GURLITT, *Die Musik in Raffaels Heiliger Cäcilia*, Jahrbuch der Musikbibliothek Peters 1938, p. 84 ff. (= *Musikgeschichte und Gegenwart*, Beihefte zum Archiv für Musikwissenschaft I, 1966, p. 31 ff.). Nach diesem grundlegenden Aufsatz haben sich auch Günter BANDMANN (*Melancholie und Musik*, Köln und Opladen 1960, p. 127—132) und Reinhold HAMMERSTEIN (*Die Musik der Engel*, Bern und München 1962, p. 225—257) mit der musiktheoretischen Deutung des Raphael-Bildes befaßt. Wichtigste ikonographische Arbeit ist Stanislaw MOSSAKOWSKI, *Raphael's »St. Cecilia.« An Iconographical Study*, in: Zeitschrift für Kunstgeschichte XXXI, 1968, p. 1—26. Ein weiterer Interpretationsversuch mit Ausblicken auf die späteren Cecilia-Darstellungen wird für unsere »Notizen zur musikalischen Ikonographie« vorbereitet.

an, die durch einen Chor singender Engel in den Wolken dargestellt wird. Es ist »als sänge sie: ›*musica nostra vale, coelestis musica, salve!*‹« (Gurlitt, p. 45). Dieselbe Aussage finden wir über ein Jahrhundert später bei Bernardino Cavallino (Abb. 9)[40]: Cäcilie hat Violine und Notenbücher abgelegt, erhebt den Blick und lauscht der himmlischen Harmonie. Diese wird, anders als bei Raphael, durch einen im Hintergrund sitzenden, lautenstimmenden Engel sichtbar gemacht. Hier symbolisiert also das Stimmen wiederum *musica coelestis*. Ein anderer Engel bringt Kranz und Palmzweig; so ist Cäcilie eindeutig als Heilige der Musik ausgewiesen. Carlo Saraceni bedient sich desselben »Vokabulars« (Abb. 10)[41]: Engel, Stimmen der Laute, Notenbuch und Instrumente am Boden (u. a. frühe Darstellung einer Baßgabe in Form des modernen Kontrabasses). Hier aber ist es Cäcilie selbst, die ihre große 15-saitige[42] Laute akkordiert. Sie blickt auf zu dem hinzutretenden und sie anredenden Engel, der überhaupt erst die ganze Darstellung zu einem Heiligenbilde macht, denn für sich genommen ist die lautenstimmende Dame weder durch ihre Kleidung noch durch sonst ein ikonographisches Indiz[43] als Cäcilie gekennzeichnet. Der Engel scheint sie auf die w a h r e Harmonie hinzuweisen und unterstreicht damit für uns Betrachter die ambivalente Rolle des Akkordierens, das einerseits zur alltäglichen Musizierpraxis gehört und andererseits Harmonie symbolisiert. »Der Weg zur kosmischen Harmonie führt über die irdische Musik«[44] — diese Vorstellung ist in Saracenis Bild sinnfällig wiedergegeben.

In allen bisher betrachteten Beispielen war die Musik integrierender Bestandteil der Bildaussage; ihre ikonographische Funktion ließ sich klar deuten, indem wir das Akkordieren als Harmonie-Symbol erkannten. Nun soll natürlich nicht in Bausch und Bogen einer jeden Darstellung gestimmter Instrumente dieser Sinn unterstellt werden; in vielen Fällen dürfte das Motiv einfach dem alltäglichen Musizieren abgeschaut, als »erzählende« Bereicherung eines Bildes aufzufassen sein. Das gilt sicher für Werke wie Luca Signorellis Orvietaner Fresko

---

[40] Bernardino Cavallino (1622—1654), datiert 1645, Rom, Privatbesitz. Dazu Ölstudie in Neapel, Museo Nazionale di Capodimonte (Alfred MOIR, *The Italian Followers of Caravaggio*, Cambridge/Mass. 1967, II Abb. 222). Andere Fassungen: Florenz, Palazzo vecchio, und Lyon, Musée des Beaux Arts (Photos im Kunsthistorischen Institut Florenz).

[41] Carlo Saraceni (1585—1620), Rom, Galleria Nazionale d'Arte Antica, Palazzo Corsini.

[42] Bei Fragen der Zahlensymbolik ist zwar Zurückhaltung geboten, und es ist durchaus möglich, daß Saraceni einfach eine fünfzehnsaitige Laute abgemalt hat. Es sei aber wenigstens erwähnt, daß bei RIPA, a. a. O. p. 26 (s. v. *Armonia*) die Harmonie als »*una vaga, e bella donna con una lira doppia di* quindici *corde in mano*« vorgestellt wird und der Maler sich möglicherweise daran orientiert hat.

[43] Auch in der äußeren Darstellung war Raphaels Bild für viele seiner Nachfolger maßgebend: goldenes Gewand, Haartracht, Sandalen (etwa bei Cavallino, Abb. 9). Zu Raphaels literarischen und ikonographischen Vorlagen cfr. Stanislaw MASSAKOWSKI, op. cit., p. 10/11.

[44] Cfr. Anm. 17. — Man könnte überdies sagen, daß der Maler hier das alte »*cantantibus organis in corde suo soli Deo decantabat*« der Legende, jenen Augenblick der Konversion einer römischen Edeldame »im modernen Gewande« dargestellt habe.

Berufung der Auserwählten, wo von neun musizierenden Engeln zwei ihre Instrumente stimmen[45], ebenso für den lautenstimmenden Engel auf Carpaccios
Altar in Pirano[46] und viele andere.

Betrachten wir aber im folgenden einige Bilder, bei denen eine klare Entscheidung für oder gegen die allegorische Deutung nicht auf Anhieb möglich ist.
Vermeers *Dame mit Laute* in New York (Abb. 11)[47] rechnet im allgemeinen zur
Genremalerei. Dargestellt ist das Interieur eines holländischen Bürgerhauses; eine
Dame sitzt hinter dem Tisch, stimmt die Laute und blickt zum Fenster. In dieser Weise beschreibt sie auch A. P. de Mirimonde: »*Elle écoute la note émise,
mais elle regarde aussi avec insistance la fenêtre. Elle guette la passage d'un visi-
teur . . . Toute l'attitude de la femme . . . reflète une tension inquiète.*«[48] Sicher, diese Beschreibung wird der dargestellten Szene äußerlich schon gerecht, aber »*die bloße Sachhaltigkeit jedes Gegenstandes in der Erzählung und in der Schilderung des
17. Jahrhunderts geht aus der bedeutungserfüllten Gegenständlichkeit
des Cinquecento hervor*«[49] und wir müssen fragen, ob nicht in Vermeers Bilde
doch ein tieferer Sinn verborgen liege und ob das Stimmen der Laute etwas mit
ihm zu tun habe. Während die Dame ihr Instrument akkordiert, blickt sie ver-
sonnen in Richtung des aus dem Fenster einfallenden Lichtes. Diese Art zu
schauen, die kein sichtbares Gegenüber hat, nichts Konkretes »ins Auge faßt«,
begegnet häufig im Zusammenhang mit musikalischen Darstellungen[50]. So blickt
jemand, der intensiv horcht! könnte man sagen, und ich möchte diesen Blick,
der gewissermaßen dem klingenden Ton nachsinnt, als sichtbaren Ausdruck einer
Contemplatio vestehen, die sowohl »verinnerlichtes Hören« als auch »innere
Schau«: Wahrnehmung von Harmonie bedeutet[51]. Stellen wir Vermeers Bild und

---

[45] Luca Signorelli (um 1445—1523). Abb. bei Emanuel WINTERNITZ, *Musical Instruments and
their Symbolism in Western Art,* London 1967, Tafel 37 b; dasselbe Detail MGG VIII,
Tafel 41, 2.

[46] Vittore Carpaccio (vor 1460 — vor 1526), *Thronende Madonna,* Pirano, S. Francesco. HAM-
MERSTEIN, a. a. O. Abb. 142.

[47] Jan Vermeer (1632—1675), um 1664. Metropolitan Museum of Art, Bequest of Collis P.
Huntington, 1925.

[48] A. P. DE MIRIMONDE, *Les sujets musicaux chez Vermeer de Delft,* Gazette des Beaux-Arts
1964, p. 37/38.

[49] Kurt BAUCH, *Zur Ikonographie von Caravaggios Frühwerken,* in: Kunstgeschichtliche Studien für Hans Kauffmann, ed. Wolfgang Braunfels, Berlin 1956, p. 260.

[50] So etwa auf Cimas Bild (Abb. 4) sowohl beim Engel als auch bei den Heiligen; ebenso bei
der Magdalena auf Raphaels *S. Cecilia,* Rubens' *Hl. Cäcilie* (Berlin, Gemäldegalerie. Abb.
MGG IX, Tafel 62,2) und den mittleren Knaben in Caravaggios *Musica.* Dazu cfr. Volker
SCHERLIESS, *Zu Caravaggios ›Musica‹,* Mitteilungen des Kunsthistorischen Institutes in Florenz XVII, 1973, p. 141—148.

[51] Kontemplation und Musik stehen in enger Verbindung; dazu ließen sich unendlich viele Belege anführen, cfr. etwa PIETZSCH, a. a. O. p. 112 (Theodoricus de Campo), MIGNE PL LXX,
col. 1053 (Cassiodor, *In Psalterium expositio,* zu Ps. 150,5). — Ich bin mir klar, daß das hier
Gesagte nur eine vorläufige — hoffentlich zutreffende — Andeutung ist und daß das Phänomen des ekstatischen Blickens einmal im größeren Zusammenhang gründlich untersucht werden müßte, ehe sich meine Vermutung bestätigen ließe.

Saracenis lautenstimmende Dame (ohne den Engel zu betrachten) nebeneinander (Abb. 10 und 11), so ist ihre motivische Verwandtschaft evident. Wollten wir nun die Vermeersche Harmoniesymbolik christlich verstehen, was angesichts der Beziehung zwischen Blickrichtung und einfließendem Licht naheliegen mag, dann handelte es sich auch in seinem Bild um eine *Hl. Cäcilie.* Aber andere Deutungen wären ebenfalls möglich: etwa *Allegorie der Musik, Allegorie des Gehörs.* Endgültiges läßt sich hierzu wohl nicht feststellen, weil signifikante Merkmale für die einzelnen Interpretationsmöglichkeiten (wie die dominierende Gestalt des Engels bei Saraceni) fehlen. Es sei hier nur darauf hingewiesen, daß die Darstellung eines gestimmten Instruments auch bei zunächst genrehaft scheinenden Motiven einen allegorischen Sinn haben kann. Dies gilt für eine Fülle ähnlicher Bilder aus dem 17. Jahrhundert; stellvertretend zeige ich die *Lautenstimmerin* eines unbekannten italienischen Caravaggio-Nachfolgers (Abb. 12)[52] und Hendrik Terbrugghens Zeichnung einer *Dame mit Penorcon* (Abb. 13)[53], für die ebenfalls die Frage einer allegorischen Bedeutung offen bleibt.

Derartige Darstellungen von männlichen Einzelpersonen sind seltener. Aus dem Ende des Quattrocento stammt das Dubliner Bildnis eines Mannes, der seine Lira da braccio stimmt[54]; hier wird es sich, der Kleidung und dem Ambiente nach, um das Porträt eines Musikers handeln, ebenso bei dem venezianischen Bild eines anderen Lira da braccio-Stimmers (Abb. 14)[55] und bei Laurent Fauchiers Porträt eines Mannes, der eine Laute akkordiert[56]. Das Stimmen dürfte als Berufsattribut auf die Kenntnisse der Harmonie und die kompositorischen Fähigkeiten des Dargestellten anspielen. In derselben Weise möchte ich auch Bernardo Stroz-

---

[52] Ort unbekannt. Unsere Abbildung nach dem Institutsnegativ 4827 des Kunsthistorischen Institutes Florenz.

[53] Hendrik Terbrugghen (1588—1629). Kunsthalle Hamburg, Kupferstichkabinett (25,8 × 20,3 cm; Inv. Nr. 22048). (Penorcon ist ein Instrument des Cister-Familie.) Das Blatt wird bei Walther BERNT (*Die Niederländischen Zeichner des 17. Jahrhunderts*, Band I, München 1957, Nr. 305) dem Gerard Honthorst (1590—1656) zugeschrieben.

[54] Filippino Lippi (um 1457—1504) oder Raffaellino del Garbo (um 1470 — um 1525) zugeschrieben. Dublin, National Gallery. MGG VIII, Tafel 37,2 (links beschnitten). WINTERNITZ, a. a. O. Tafel 32 b. (Die links unten auf dem Instrument angebrachte Inschrift, die wohl näheren Aufschluß über den Dargestellten bringen könnte, habe ich nicht entziffern können.)

[55] Wien, Kunsthistorisches Museum (Inv. Nr. 317), um 1510. Palma vecchio (um 1480—1528) und Domenico Mancini (1. Hälfte 16. Jh.) zugeschrieben.

[56] Laurent Fauchier (1643—1672). Abb., leider ohne Ortsangabe, bei Lucienne COLLIARD, *Un ›tabelau de musique‹ de François Puget*, Gazette des Beaux-Arts LXV, 1965, p. 287. Auch das Louvre-Bild *Die Musiker Ludwigs XIV.* von François Puget (1651—1707, datiert 1687) läßt sich so deuten; in ihm ist allerdings vom Typus her eine *Vorbereitung zu einem Konzert* (cfr. SCHERLIESS, *Zu Caravaggio*, Anm. 21), von seiner Funktion her eine *Huldigungsdarstellung* für den König zu sehen. (Die klar wiedergegebenen Noten enthalten einen vierstimmigen Satz »*Celebrate col canto di Luigi immortal la gloria e 'l vanto*«.) Cfr. COLLIARD, a. a. O. p. 283—292 (Gesamt- und Detailabb.). Abb. auch in François LESURE, *Musik und Gesellschaft im Bild*, Kassel usw. 1966, Tafel 70.

zis Darstellungen höfischer Musikanten deuten (ein Beispiel Abb. 15)[57]. Ob allerdings noch für Watteaus *Mezzetin* (Abb. 16)[58] diese attributive oder eine andere Bedeutung gilt oder ob hier das Akkordieren wirklich zum Genre gehört, kann ich nicht entscheiden.

Ebenso wie Darstellungen von Einzelpersonen sind mehrfigurige Bilder, auf denen ein Musikinstrument gestimmt wird, im Hinblick auf einen möglichen allegorischen Bildsinn zu prüfen. So konnte Caravaggios New Yorker Gemälde mit vier Knaben, von denen einer eine Laute stimmt, u. a. aus diesem Grunde als Allegorie der Musik gedeutet werden[59]. Andere ähnliche Gruppenbilder lassen sich wahrscheinlich auch vom musikalischen Sujet her erklären. Bei Darstellungen dieser Art warten die Kunsthistoriker meist mit dem Etikett »Concerto« oder »Musizierende Gesellschaft« auf und analysieren sie nicht weiter, während die Musikwissenschaftler in ihnen, ebenfalls ohne längere Prüfung, nur allzu gerne Belege für historische Aufführungspraxis sehen möchten. Hier ist für beide Seiten Vorsicht geboten; es muß von Fall zu Fall untersucht werden, ob eine nur die äußerliche Erscheinung eines solchen Bildes betrachtende Deutung nicht seinen eigentlichen Sinn verfehlt.

Halten wir fest: Ein gestimmtes Instrument k a n n Harmonie symbolisieren. Worauf sich im einzelnen Fall die Harmonie bezieht, ist nicht immer leicht zu sagen. Abgesehen von der oftmals durch sie bezeichneten Musik (als *musica mundana*, bzw. *musica coelestis*) begegnet uns eine Fülle anderer Deutungsmöglichkeiten in den Emblembüchern des 16. und 17. Jahrhunderts, in denen traditionelle wie neue, gelehrt-allegorisierende Sinnbilder ihre prägnante Formel fanden. So gibt etwa eine *impresa* bei Camillo Camilli die Darstellung zweier Lire da braccio — eine mit, eine ohne Bogen —, dazu das Motto *Aliis pulsis resona-*

---

[57] Bernardo Strozzi (1581—1644), Wien, Kunsthistorisches Museum. Cfr. die Bilder Strozzis in Hampton Court (Luisa MORTARI, *Bernardo Strozzi*, Rom 1966, Abb. 345), andere Fassungen New York, Privatbesitz (MORTARI, Tafel 8), Tarbes, Musée Massey (MORTARI, Abb. 305), Moskau, Museum der Schönen Künste (MORTARI, Abb. 347); Bergamo, Galleria Lorenzelli (MORTARI, Abb. 348); Rom, Privatbesitz (MORTARI, Abb. 357). Cfr. u. a. Carnelisz Duyster (1599—1635), »Il maestro di musica«, Museum Douai (Delfino NAVA, *Dizionario Musicale Larousse* II, Milano 1961, Tafel XI bei p. 432). Als Beispiele dafür, wie häufig noch bis in viel spätere Zeit hinein das Stimmen als Berufsattribut auf Musikerbildern dargestellt wurde, seien die anonymen Porträts von James Cervetto (1682—1783) und Jean Joseph Bott (1826—1895) genannt (*MGG* XV, Supplement, Tafel 36 und Sp. 1411/2).

[58] Antoine Watteau (1684—1721), Paris, Louvre (Cabinet des Dessins). Das Motiv des Mezzetin, eines Gitarrespielers in Komödienkostüm, kehrt bei Watteau häufig wieder. Cfr. Hélène ADHÉMAR, *Watteau, sa vie — son oeuvre*, Paris 1950: Abb. 61 (Troyes), 76 (Chantilly, Musée Condé: ausgeführtes Ölbild nach unserer Zeichnung), 95 (London, Buckingham Palace), 112 (Dresden, Gemäldegalerie), 87 und 92 (London, Wallace Collection. Dazu A. P. DE MIRIMONDE, *Les sujets musicaux chez Antoine Watteau*, Gazette des Beaux-Arts LVIII, 1961, p. 249—288, Abb. 13 und 14).

[59] Michelangelo Merisi da Caravaggio (um 1573—1610), New York, Metropolitan Museum of Art. Walter FRIEDLAENDER, *Caravaggio-Studies*, Princeton 1955, Tafel 5. Zur Deutung FRIEDLAENDER, Catalogue raisonné Nr. 5, und SCHERLIESS, *Zu Caravaggio* a. a. O.

bunt, und der Autor führt erklärend aus: »*Perche oltre al metter gl'instromenti per simbolo dell'unione, & della concordia per l'armonia, che risulta da ciascuna delle corde, quando tutte sono accordate ... & è che nei giorni della bruma se due instrumenti accordati sono vicini, mentre si toccano le corde d'uno, quelle dell'altro à tal suono si sentono risonare. Il che non in tali giorni soli, mà d'ogni tempo accade (come sperimentano tuttavia i musici) per cagione della simpathia, la quale opera mirabilmente in tutte le cose. Onde vuol dire, che per esser quegli animi tutti ben composti, al voler dell'uno sarebbe stato conforme il voler dell'altro, come dal suono d'una corda si sente risonar l'altra che sia accordata al medesimo tuono.*«[60] In dieser Quelle wird also expressis verbis unsere Deutung eines dargestellten einzelnen Saiteninstrumentes als Harmonie-Symbol bestätigt; und ebenso erklärt der Autor die akustische Tatsache des Resonierens als Ausdruck für Simpathia. Dasselbe Bildmotiv erscheint bei dem Holländer Jacob Cats als Emblem für *Harmonie der Liebenden*[61], aber auch als *Anteilnahme*[62] und *Freude von Gott*[63].

---

[60] Camillo CAMILLI, *Imprese illustri di diversi, coi discorsi,* Venedig 1586, I p. 1 (Impresa des Alcibiade Lucarini), Textzitat p. 3. — Das Phänomen der Resonanz war von Hieronymus CARDANUS (*De subtilitate libri XXI,* Basel 1553, p. 514, im Absatz *Cur nervi lirae aequaliter dum tenduntur, et si non tangatur, alterum subsilit, reliquo edente sonum*) erklärt worden.

[61] Jacob CATS, *Proteus ofte Minne-beelden verandert in Sinne-beelden,* Rotterdam 1627, Nr. 43,1. Cfr. Richard PIGOT, *Moral Emblems ... from Jacob Cats and Robert Farlie,* New York 1860, p. 117. Dazu bringen Arthur HENKEL/Albrecht SCHÖNE (*Emblemata,* Stuttgart 1967, col 1300) das Gedicht:

> *Gleichgestimmte Saiten*
> *Gleichen Klang andeuten.*
> Als zu der Rosemund ich einsmahls war gekommen,
> Hatt' ich zwey Lauten auch dahin mit mir genommen;
> Auff einer hatt' ich nun ein Endgen Stroh gelegt,
> Daß durch denselben Thon der andern auch bewegt.
> Ich sprach: mein liebstes Kind hierbey könnt ihr verspühren,
> Wie euer Hertz mein Hertz auch ohnberührt kan rühren;
> Weil beyde gleichsam sind auff einen Thon gestimmt,
> Eins auch des andern Leid und Freude bald vernimmt.

[62] CATS, a. a. O. Nr. 43,2; PIGOT, a. a. O. p. 119; HENKEL/SCHÖNE, a. a. O. col. 1301.

> *Freut einer sich*
> *Freu ich auch mich.*
> Wann man zwey Lauten hat, daß ihre Saiten eben
> Denselben gleichen Thon zusammen von sich geben,
> Und man auff einer spielt, so macht derselbe Thon,
> Daß auch die andre klingt, mitspielt und hüpfft davon.
> Die Ehr und Freude, die der andern wiederfähret,
> Nimmt sie als ihr geschehn und sie für gut erklähret,
> Sie trauret auch mit ihr. Mensch thu auch du also,
> Daß wie dein Nächster du auch traurig oder froh.

[63] CATS, a. a. O. Nr. 43,3; HENKEL/SCHÖNE, a. a. O. col. 1301:

> Erfahrung lehrt, wann man auff einer Lauten spielet,
> Daß des die andre auch, die gleich gestimmt, bald fühlet:
> Der einen Lauten-Klang der andern auch erregt,

In der Malerei wurde besonders häufig die Harmonie der Liebenden dargestellt, so etwa in einem Gemälde von Godfried Schalcken (Abb. 17)[64], wobei »gleicher Klang« zwischen Singstimme und Cister herrscht und eine Rosenblüte die Deutung als Allegorie der Liebe unterstreicht[65]. Dieses Beispiel, das gewöhnlich als »Singstunde« bezeichnet wird, mag für die vielen vergleichbaren holländischen halb- oder ganzfigurigen Doppelporträts stehen. Auf die beiden linken Figuren der sogenannten *Musizierenden Gesellschaft* (keiner musiziert tatsächlich!) von Adriaen Hannemann (Abb. 18)[66] dürfte dieselbe Aussage zu beziehen sein.

Schon ein über hundert Jahre früher entstandenes Beispiel, der 1524 datierte Stich des Lucas van Leyden (Abb. 19), läßt sich mit diesem Thema in Verbindung bringen: Eine alte Frau spielt Rebec, ein Mann stimmt dazu seine Laute. Gezeigt wird die alltägliche Erscheinung eines Bettelmusikantenpaares in einer »ungeschminkten« Darstellungsweise, wie sie später durch Pieter Breughel und seine Nachfolger zu einem Hauptfeld der niederländischen Malerei werden sollte. Lediglich genrehaft, so scheint mir, kann man bereits dieses frühe Blatt nicht sehen; dazu stehen die grotesken, übertreibenden Elemente zu stark im Vordergrund. »*Aus der sachlichen Betrachtung der gemeinen Wirklichkeit löst sich pointierende und karikierende Komödienschärfe heraus*«, sagt Max Friedländer über dies und andere Genreblätter des Leideners[67]. Wenn wir das Stimmen der Laute in solcher Richtung interpretieren wollten, dann wäre in der Tat das ironische Element der Darstellung unübersehbar und wir müßten sie als Parodie auf den »Gleichklang der Seelen« betrachten. Diese Vermutung zu Lucas' Stich ließe sich allerdings erst nach eingehenden ikonographischen Untersuchungen zu ähnlichen Szenen in seiner Zeit bekräftigen.

Ein Narr, der versucht seine Laute zu stimmen, erscheint in einem französischen Emblembuch als Symbol für die *Nutzlosigkeit des Narren für das Gemeinwohl*[68]; damit ist gewissermaßen ex contrario die alte, in der platonischen Philo-

---

Wiewohl man mit der Hand nur auff der einen schlägt.
Gott läßt den Seinen hier offt Freude wiederfahren,
Die ihnen wunderlich sich weiß zu offenbaren:
Dann ob man äuserlich schon nichtes hört und sieht:
Hupfft doch für Freuden fast ihr Hertz, Sinn und Gemüth.

[64] Godfried Schalcken (1643—1706), London, National Gallery (Inv. Nr. 998).
[65] RIPA, a. a. O. p. 26, s. v. *Amicizia*: »*La Rosa significa la piacevolezza quale sempre deve essere tra gl'amici, essendo fra di loro continua unione di volontà.*«
[66] Adriaen Hannemann (1601—1672), Braunschweig, Herzog Anton Ulrich-Museum (Kat. Nr. 223). Wie hier allerdings die anderen Figuren allegorisch zu erklären sind, weiß ich nicht.
[67] Lucas van Leyden (1494—1533). Max J. FRIEDLÄNDER, *Lucas van Leyden* (= Meister der Graphik XIII), Leipzig 1924, p. 28.
[68] Guilleaume de la PIERRIÈRE, *La Morosophie*, Lyon 1533:
    C'est bien en vain, quand d'accorder poursuys
    Mon Luc, voyant que ie suys frenetique:
    Si sot et fol en ma mayson ie suys,
    Seray ie sage au fait du bien publicque?

sophie wurzelnde und stets lebendig gebliebene Vorstellung von der Verwandtschaft zwischen musikalischer und staatlicher Harmonie ausgedrückt, wie wir sie
positiv z. B. bei Johann Mannich, *Sacra emblemata,* finden: eine Laute, deren
Saiten gestimmt werden, bezeichnet *gute Regierung*[69]. Ein Bild von Jean Garnier,
die *Allegorie der Regierung Ludwigs XIV*[70], wird in diesem Sinne durch einen
Zeitgenossen beschrieben: *»Le Roi est peint dans un ovale et parait entouré de
fruits e de plusieurs instruments de musique pour signifier, dans un sens allégori-
que, l'abondance du royaume et l'harmonie des perfaits accords qui se rencon-
trent dans le Gouvernement de l'Etat.«*[71] Ein Staatsvertrag wird in den
Emblemata des Andrea Alciati, dem weitestverbreiteten Werk dieser Art, durch
Laute und Notenbuch symbolisiert. In den entscheidenden Zeilen seiner Erklärung gibt Alciati unsere Harmonie-Metapher wieder:

> Difficile est, nisi docto homini, tot tendere chordas:
> Unaque si fuerit non bene tenta fides,
> Ruptave (quod facile est) perit omnis gratia conchae,
> Illeque praecellens cantus, ineptus erit[72].

(Zitiert nach HENKEL/SCHÖNE, a. a. O. col. 1129.) Cfr. das bei HENKEL/SCHÖNE abgebildete Beispiel oder den Holzschnitt aus Sebastian Brants *Narrenschiff,* Paris 1498, f. 70 (Abb. in
MGG XIII, Tafel 60,2).

[69] Johann MANNICH, *Sacra emblemata . . .* Nürnberg 1624, p. 78. Cfr. ebenso Julius Wilhelm
ZINCGREFF, *Emblematum ethico-politicum centuria,* Frankfurt/Main 1698, Nr. 97 mit der
Erklärung: *»Ut in fidibus ac tibiis atque cantu ipso ac vocibus concentus est quidam tenen-
dus ex distinctis sonis, sic existimetis juventutem ac senectutem, alteram sine altera nihil
posse, sed si infimus et inedius et summus ordo sit simulpermixtus, maximas vires habere.«*
Cfr. ferner Giulio Cesare CAPACCIO, *Delle Imprese,* Neapel 1592, p. 23: *»La Lira, significò
la Concordia«.* (Aus der Beschreibung des Emblems der Stadt Neapel; cfr. BANDMANN, op. cit.,
p. 110, Abb. 53.) — Bei Diego SAAVEDRA FAJARDO (FACHARDO), *L'idea di un principe politico
christiano* (1640, aus dem Span. von Paris CERCHIERI, Venedig 1654, p. 244) wird eine bekrönte
Harfe mit dem Emblemband *»Maiora minoribus consonant«* abgebildet. Erklärung: *»Forma
l'Arpa una perfetta Aristocratia, composta del governo Monarchicho & Democratico. Presiede
un'intelletto, governano molte dita, & ubbidisce un popolo di corde: tutte temperate, & tutte
conformi nella consonanza, non particolare, mà commune, & publica, senza che le maggiori
sono dalle minori discrepanti. Simile all'Arpa e una Republica«* etc. bis p. 247.

[70] Jean Garnier (1632—1705), Versailles, Schloß. A. P. DE MIRIMONDE, *Les allégories de la
Musique,* Gazette des Beaux-Arts LXXII, 1968, Abb. 46.

[71] Zitiert nach MIRIMONDE, *Les allégories,* p. 314.

[72] Andrea ALCIATI, *Emblemata,* Padua 1661, p. 60 (*Emblema X*). Italienische Ausgabe (*Diverse
imprese . . .* tratte da gli *Emblemi,* Lyon 1551, p. 12):

> *Per far, che suon disordinato e strano*
> *Non esca fuor di si diverse corde,*
> *Bisogna dotta e ben esperta mano.*
> *Perche una sola, che non ben s'acorde,*
> *O che si rompa, fa che quel concento,*
> *Che prima grato fu, tutto si scorde.*
> *Cosi qualhor più d'un Signor è intento*
> *Per commun bene a convenir insieme,*
> *S'Amor gli regge, ogni timor è spento.*
> *Ma s'un discorda, e altrove inchina e preme,*

Schließlich ein letztes Emblem: eine Laute symbolisiert *ausgeglichenen Charakter*[73]. Hier schließt sich der Kreis zu den eingangs zitierten literarischen Zeugnissen.

Das gut gestimmte Instrument — Symbol der Harmonie — ist uns als Topos in einigen Beispielen durch die Jahrhunderte begegnet; es stand für verschiedene allegorische Inhalte. Für alle angesprochenen ikonographischen Typen ließen sich zahlreiche zusätzliche Beispiele anführen. Es kam hier nur darauf an, an einem oft dargestellten musikalischen Bildmotiv verschiedene Deutungsmöglichkeiten zu zeigen und damit möglicherweise weitere Überlegungen zu den reichen Wechselbeziehungen zwischen bildender Kunst und Musik anzuregen.

Abbildungsnachweis: Museumsphotos (1, 4, 5, 11, 13, 14, 15, 17, 18) — Photothek des Kunsthistorischen Institutes Florenz (2, 6, 7, 8, 12) — Gabinetto Fotografico Nazionale, Rom (3, 9, 10) — Buchvorlagen (16, 19).

      Alhor quell'harmonia tutta perisce,
      Onde una parte impera, e l'altra geme.
Deutsche Ausgabe *(Liber emblematum, Kunstbuch,* Frankfurt/Main 1566, p. 17):
      Diß Laut so hat eins Schiffleins gstalt
      Das dFischer brauchen manigfalt
      Welche die Studenten so glehrt
      Für eigen halten on gewehrt
      Schick euwr Fürstlich gnad ich zum gschenck
      Dieweil die ein neuwen bundt anfengt
      Mit andern Fürsten Welsches Lands
      Bitt wolt solchs zgnaden annemmen zhand
      Gleich wie vil Seiten recht richten zwar
      Braucht grosse kunst klugheit fürwar
      Dann so eine nit zogen recht
      Oder abspringend glat auß schlecht
      Wie es sich dann leichtlich zutregt
      So ist alsbald all freudt erschreckt
      Und endt sich die süß Melodey
      In ein mißlautend unlieblich geschrey
      Also die Welschen Fürsten zmal
      Machen ein Bundt jetzund mit schal
      So einigkeit/lieb/glaub und treuw
      Gehalten wird bringt es kein reuw
      So aber einer abfelt und weicht
      (Wie dann leyder daselb gschicht leicht)
      So nimpt ein end solch enigkeit
      Und wirt auß aller freud ein leidt.
[73] Juan DE BORIA, *Empresas morales*, Prag 1581, p. 92, Nr. 91 (nach HENKEL/SCHÖNE, a. a. O. col. 1298).

HEINRICH ISAAC'S *PALLE, PALLE*: A NEW INTERPRETATION

by *Allan Atlas* (New York)

The subject of symbolism in music has long been a popular one, with the field of inquiry being well nigh unlimited both with respect to the many types of symbolism discussed and the musical repertories that have served as hunting grounds[1]. Recently, however, a growing number of scholars have increasingly focused their attention on one type of symbolism and one body of music: number symbolism, often with cabalistic overtones, and the music of the fifteenth- and early sixteenth-century Franco-Netherlanders. To cite only a few studies that have dealt with this subject, we may mention Van Crevel's analyses of the Obrecht Masses *Sub tuum praesidium* and *Maria zart*[2], Vellekoop's and Buning-Jurgens's discussions of the same composer's *Parce Domine*[3], Lowinsky's interpretation of Ockeghem's canon for thirty-six voices[4], Henze's comments on a number of Masses by that composer[5], Heikamp's observations about Josquin's *Missa L'homme armé super voces musicales*[6], Warren's very recent discoveries concerning Dufay's *Nuper rosarum flores*[7], and, of course, the full-scale mono-

---

[1] For a comprehensive bibliography on the subject, see Edward A. LIPPMAN, *Symbolik*, in: MGG, XII (Kassel, 1965), cols. 1801—1803.

[2] Marcus van CREVEL (ed.), *Jacobus Obrecht: Opera Omnia. Missae*, VI (Amsterdam, 1959), pp. vii—xxv; VII (1964), pp. vii—cxlvi. Van Crevel's methods and conclusions are controversial and have been criticized by Ludwig FINSCHER, *Spekulationen über eine Obrecht-Messe*, in: Musica, XIX (1965), p. 228; on the other hand, they are seemingly accepted by Edgar H. SPARKS, *Cantus Firmus in Mass and Motet, 1420—1520* (Berkeley and Los Angeles, 1963), p. 473, fn. 51. For a strictly musical analysis of the *Missa Sub tuum praesidium*, see Lewis LOCKWOOD, *A Note on Obrecht's Mass »Sub Tuum Praesidium«*, in: Revue belge de musicologie, XIV (1960), pp. 30—39.

[3] Kees VELLEKOOP, *Zusammenhänge zwischen Text und Zahl in der Kompositionsart Jacob Obrechts*, in: TvNM, XX (1964—1965), pp. 97—119; J. E. BUNING-JURGENS, *More About Jacob Obrecht's Parce Domine*, in: TvNM, XXI (1970), pp. 167—169.

[4] Edward E. LOWINSKY, *Ockeghem's Canon for Thirty-Six Voices: An Essay in Musical Iconography*, in: Essays in Musicology in Honor of Dragan Plamenac on his 70th Birthday, edited by Gustave Reese and Robert J. Snow (Pittsburgh, 1969), pp. 155—180.

[5] Marianne HENZE, *Studien zu den Messenkompositionen Johannes Ockeghems* (Berlin, 1968), pp. 191—226.

[6] Dieter HEIKAMP, *Zur Struktur der Messe »L'omme armé« super voces musicales von Josquin Desprez*, in: Mf, XIX (1966), pp. 121—141.

[7] Charles W. WARREN, *Brunelleschi's Dome and Dufay's Motet*, in: MQ, LIX (1973), pp. 92—105. For another treatment of the same subject, see Gerhard CROLL, *Festmusiken der Renaissance* (Salzburg, 1969), pp. 38—39.

graph on Franco-Netherlandish symbolism by Elders, much of which is devoted to various aspects of number symbolism[8]. The present essay, though more modest in its claims than most of those just cited — and this is fitting in view of the very elementary nature of the symbolism involved (see fn. 23) — treats of the presence of number symbolism in a work by yet another Franco-Netherlander: Heinrich Isaac, the work in question being the celebrated canzona, *Palle, palle*[9].

In a recent article about Isaac, Federico Ghisi states that *Palle, palle* was composed as »*un atto certo di omaggio e devozione a Papa Leone*...«[10], that is, as »an act of hommage and devotion to Pope Leo X.« Inherent in this statement is also the assertion that *Palle, palle* dates from no earlier than 1513, the year in which Leo, the former Giovanni de' Medici, ascended the papal throne.

Although Ghisi offers no reasons for his conclusion, it seems plausible to assume that they are the same as those that he gave when, in his study of the canti carnascialeschi, he associated with Leo's election to the papacy yet another work that contains the word »palle« in its title, the anonymous *Canto delle palle* (»*Ecco dea admirata*«) that comes down to us in Florence, Biblioteca Nazionale, Banco rari, Ms. 230, fols. 93[v]—94[r][11]. Here, Ghisi's attempt to connect music and history was based on Luca Landucci's account of the events that occurred in Florence on the night of 11 March 1513. In his *Diario fiorentino*, Landucci wrote that upon hearing of Leo's election the Florentines went through the streets shouting »*palle, palle*«, this being the party of the »*palleschi*«, the loyal supporters of the Medici[12]. Thus, Ghisi, as have a number of scholars before him[13], would see the origins of Isaac's *Palle, palle* in the political cry that

---

[8] Willem ELDERS, *Studien zur Symbolik in der Musik der alten Niederländer* (Bilthoven, 1968).

[9] The piece comes down to us in five sources, which are here listed in their probable chronological order: (1) Rome, Biblioteca Apostolica Vaticana, C.G.XIII.27, f. 0v—2r (7v—9r); (2) Washington, D.C., Library of Congress, Ms. M 2. 1 M 6 Case (Wolffheim Chansonnier), f. lxxxiv—lxxxiiiir; (3) Florence, Biblioteca Nazionale, Magl., Ms. XIX.107 bis, f. 43r (altus and bassus only; second half of piece only); (4) Cortona, Biblioteca del Comune e dell'Accademia Etrusca, Mss. 95—96 (altus and superius)/Paris, Bibliothèque nationale, nouv. acq. fr., Ms. 1817 (tenor), No. 40 (bassus lacking); and (5) Florence, Biblioteca Nazionale, Magl., Ms. XIX.117, f. 82v—83r (altus and bassus wanting for second half of piece). Modern editions of the work may be found in Benvenuto DISERTORI (ed.), *Le frottole per canto e liuto intabulate da Franciscus Bossinensis. Istituzioni e monumenti dell'arte musicale italiana*, Nuova serie, III (Milan, 1964), pp. 188—192, and Johannes WOLF (ed.), *Heinrich Isaac: Weltliche Werke*. DTÖ, 28 (Vienna, 1907), pp. 98—99. Wolf's publication, p. vii, also contains a facsimile after C.G.XIII.27.

[10] *Arrigo il Tedesco, musicista fiorentino*, in: Chigiana, XXIV (1967), p. 10.

[11] See *I canti carnascialeschi nelle fonti musicali del XV e XVI secolo* (Florence, 1937), pp. 70—71, and *Feste musicali della Firenze medicea* (Florence, 1939), p. x. Isaac's *Palle, palle* and the anonymous *Canto delle palle* are not related musically.

[12] *Diario fiorentino dal 1450 al 1516*, annotated by Iodoco DELLA BADIA (Florence, 1883), pp. 335—336.

[13] See, for example, André PIRRO, *Leo X and Music*, in: MQ, XXI (1935), p. 1; REESE, *Music in the Renaissance*, rev. ed. (New York, 1959), p. 170; Nanie BRIDGMAN, *La Vie musicale au*

began with precisely the same words and that referred to the »palle« on the Medici coat-of-arms[14].

Unfortunately, the various attempts to associate Isaac's canzona with the *»palle, palle«* cry rest on no discernible evidence. Moreover, since there were many occasions on which *»palle, palle«* echoed through the streets of Florence[15], any endeavor to pair Isaac's work with any one, specific historical event without firm documentary evidence must remain purely conjectural. And, finally, to connect Isaac's composition with Leo's election in 1513 is absolutely untenable, since the piece already appears in the Vatican chansonnier, C.G.XIII.27, fols. 0ᵛ–2ʳ (7ᵛ–9ʳ), a manuscript that I believe to have been compiled c. 1492–1494, approximately twenty years before Giovanni de' Medici became Leo X.[16] And even should our date for C.G.XIII.27 eventually prove to be too early, that *Palle, palle* still could not have been composed in honor of Leo's election is evident from its appearance in Francesco Spinacino's *Intabulatura de liuto, libro secondo*, fols. 16ʳ–17ʳ, published by Petrucci in 1507, six years prior to Leo's attaining the papacy[17].

If, then, Isaac's *Palle, palle* cannot be associated with either Leo's election in particular or the cry of the »palleschi« in general, just what significance does the piece have and why did Isaac affix to it its terse, epigrammatic title? The answer seems to lie in the rather striking structural relationship between the cantus firmus that unfolds slowly in the tenor of this four-part work and the Medici coat-of-arms, both of which, therefore, warrant brief description.

As is well known, by the latter part of the fifteenth century the Medici coat-of-arms consisted of five red »palle«, that is, balls or roundels, and one blue one, this last »palla« containing the three »gigli« or »fleurs-de-lys« that had been adopted for the Medici stemma by Piero di Cosimo, permission to do so having

---

Quattrocento (Paris 1964), p. 160; and DISERTORI, op. cit., p. 75. Disertori also believes that *Palle, palle* was *»eseguito espressamente per Leone X.«*

14 We should note that, in pointing to a possible relationship between Isaac's composition and the *»palle, palle«* cry, both PIRRO, op. cit., p. 1, and REESE, op. cit., p. 170, refer specifically to Isaac's tenor voice. That this is the key voice will become clear presently.

15 For example, on 16 September 1512, Giuliano de' Medici and his armed supporters shouted *»palle, palle«* as they entered the »Palagio de' Signori« (LANDUCCI, op. cit., p. 328). The cry was also heard on the eventful night of 9 November 1494, when the Medici were forcefully driven from Florence (LANDUCCI, op. cit., p. 74).

16 On the date of C.G.XIII.27, see the present author's *Rome, Biblioteca Apostolica Vaticana, Cappella Giulia XIII.27, and the Dissemination of the Franco-Netherlandish Chanson in Italy, c. 1460–c. 1530*, unpublished Ph.D. Dissertation, New York University, 1971. The dissertation is scheduled to appear in the Musicological Studies series of the Institute of Mediaeval Music.

17 This rather obvious proof against there being any connection between the origins of *Palle, palle* and the celebrations of 1513 has only recently been noted by Wolfgang OSTHOFF, *Theatergesang und darstellende Musik der italienischen Renaissance*, I (Tutzing, 1969), p. 111, fn. 66. For modern editions of the intabulation, see DISERTORI, op. cit., pp. 188–192, and WOLF, op. cit., pp. 161–162.

been granted by Louis XI of France in 1465[18]. The six palle are arranged in three ranks: the lowest one consists of one ball, the second, of two balls, and the third, of three, with the blue palla that contains the three gigli standing at the center of this uppermost row, usually ever so slightly higher than the two palle on either side of it.

Turning to Isaac's cantus firmus, which is not based on any known, pre-existent melody, we find an eight-note motive that is stated three times in ostinato fashion:

The cantus firmus of *Palle, palle* (after Paris 1817).

Actually, the eight notes may be divided into two distinct motivic units, the first of which consists of the five notes that are transposed up a whole step upon each repetition, the second, of the three notes that are always sounded at their original pitch level. The two motivic units are always separated by a three-measure rest.

How, then, are these two seemingly disparate items — the Medici coat-of-arms and Isaac's cantus firmus — related? To begin with, and taking into account only one of the three statements of the ostinato figure, we should like to suggest that the five-note motivic unit represents the five unadorned, red palle, while the second motivic unit, that consisting of three notes, represents the blue palla that contains the three gigli:

[18] See Adriana MARUCCHI, *Stemmi di possessori dei manoscritti conservati nella Biblioteca Vaticana*, in: Mélanges Eugène Tisserant, VII. Studi e testi, 237 (Rome, 1967), p. 94. On the origins and development of the Medici stemma, see Raymond de ROOVER, *The Three Golden Balls of the Pawnbrokers*, in: Bulletin of the Business Historical Society, XX (1946), pp. 117—124.

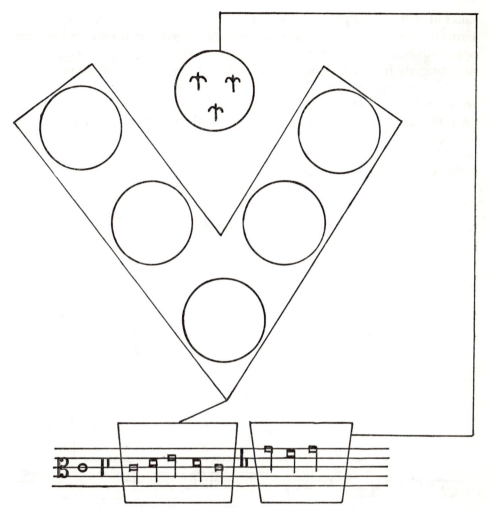

The structural relationship between the coat-of-arms and a single statement
of the ostinato figure.

Moreover, just as the sixth palla is set off from the others by three features:
(1) its inclusion of the gigli, (2) its different color, and (3) its generally raised
position, so the second motivic unit is set off from the first motivic unit by three
features: (1) the three measures of silence that precede it, (2) its different
melodic contour, which actually inverts the contour of the first melodic motive
and at the same time outlines the position of the three gigli, and (3) its higher
pitch level, which corresponds to the raised position of the sixth palla.

With respect to the cantus firmus in its entirety, we propose that each of the
three statements of the five-note motivic unit represents another of the three

ranks of palle on the coat-of-arms. For, just as the ostinato figure — simply by virtue of its melodic ascent — grows in musical intensity as it rises a whole step upon each occurrence, so the three successive ranks of palle grow weightier as they progress from a row of a single ball to a row of two balls and then to one of three (see fn. 23). Furthermore, only upon its third statement, which corresponds to the uppermost rank of palle, does the first motivic unit finally reach the note g′, a pitch hitherto reserved for the second motivic unit, the one that represents the palla with the three gigli. Similarly, it is only upon reaching the third rank of palle on the coat-of-arms that we attain the height of the palla decorated with the three fleurs-de-lys:

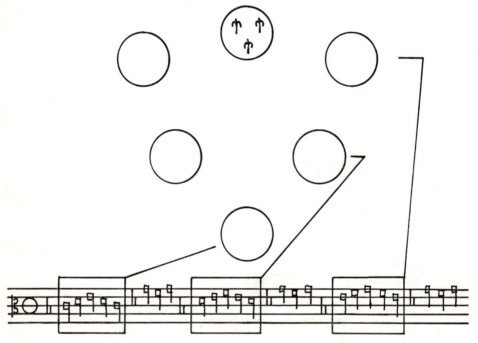

The structural relationship between the coat-of-arms and the cantus firmus as a whole.

There are still other instances of numerical correspondence between Isaac's cantus firmus and the Medici stemma that must be noted. We have already remarked that the two motivic units of the ostinato figure are separated by a three-measure rest. However, a three-measure rest also precedes each statement of the first motivic unit, so that an entire statement of the eight-note ostinato figure contains six measures of rest in all. Thus, the number of rests in the ostinato figure is equal to the number of palle on the coat-of-arms. Reverting once again to the higher level and considering the cantus firmus as a whole, we find first that there are a total of eighteen measures of rest, this number being equal to that obtained by multiplying the number of palle by the number of gigli. And upon adding the number of rests in the cantus firmus — eighteen — to the number of notes in the cantus firmus — twenty-four (admittedly, we are »mixing« breves and longs; yet this seems to be justified on the ground that they are equal to one another when considered purely as notational characters) — we obtain the sum forty-two, a number that turns out to be extremely significant. For, by applying the age-old cabalistic device of gematria in its most simple and straightforward form to the Latin alphabet — »a« = 1, »b« = 2, »c« = 3, and so on —[19], we find that the number forty-two represents the sum of the numbers that corresponds to the letters that are needed to spell out the name MEDICI (12 + 5 + 4 + 9 + 3 + 9 = 42).

Finally, *Palle, palle* contains one example of non-numerical symbolism. Isaac has written the piece in tempus perfectum, a mensuration so rare in Isaac's secular output that, among the somewhat more than one-hundred pieces (intabulations excluded) found in Wolf's edition of Isaac's secular works, only five other pieces are written in that mensuration, and two of these — *Le serviteur* and *Tart ara mon cueur* — have tempus perfectum in only one voice part of the polyphonic complex, the voice that quotes a cantus prius factus that is itself in tempus perfectum. Yet Isaac had good reason to employ that mensuration in *Palle, palle*: the mensuration sign for tempus perfectum is simply a circle, that is, a palla.

Naturally, our observations — as do those in all the essays cited in our opening paragraph — prompt the following question: Are the instances of symbolism the product of the composer's invention or do they simply reflect the workings of our own fanciful imagination? While the lack of documentary evidence does not permit us to prove our case beyond a doubt, various threads of circumstantial evidence do seem to favor our interpretation of *Palle, palle* as a piece laden with symbolism. First, we may consider the very nature and treatment of the cantus firmus itself. Not only was the cantus firmus contrived by Isaac himself — and this alone is significant — but he disposed it in a rather constructivistic manner, something that is not typical of his style in general. Surely, Isaac must have had a special reason for first having composed his own very distinctive, rather unmelodious — dare we say unmusical — cantus firmus and then having disposed it with such unyielding precision. And this reason is, we believe, best explained in terms of the symbolism noted above, which, at the very least, is far more concrete than the attempt to pair the cantus firmus with a political cry that we have never heard. Our interpretation also gains

---

[19] On gematria, see Vincent F. HOPPER, *Medieval Number Symbolism: Its Sources, Meaning, and Influence on Thought and Expression* (New York, 1938), pp. 60 ff., and Caspar LEVIAS, *Gematria*, in: The Jewish Encyclopedia, V (New York, 1903), pp. 589—592.

support from the sheer number of instances in, and levels at, which the structu-
res of the cantus firmus and the coat-of-arms mirror one another. And simply
to consider the numerous and varied points of structural parallelism mere
coincidence strains even the Renaissance concept of Fortune. As for Isaac's use
of cabalistic number symbolism, it is important to remember that it was precisely in that period during which Isaac must certainly have composed *Palle,
palle* (see below) that Pico della Mirandola was present in Florence, where he
was engaged in the very task of introducing the cabala to the Christian world[20].
And, since Isaac and Pico were both members of the intellectual and artistic
coterie that revolved around the Medici, it seems quite likely that the two men
knew one another, and that Isaac could have been influenced, if only to a
small extent, by Pico's thought. Given these circumstances, Isaac's almost
»parlor-game« use of the simple cabalistic device of gematria does not seem at
all far fetched. Finally, another piece of evidence appears in the form of a
sixteenth-century motet that survives in Verona, Società Accademia Filarmonica,
Ms. 218. The piece, which begins with the words *Vidit dominus* (Deut. 32:19)
and which was composed by an uncertain »Charlet«, has been interpreted as
being an anti-Medici motet that rails against Clement VII (Giulio de' Medici)
in particular[21]. What is important is that the tenor primus of this seven-voice
motet is cast in the form of a cantus firmus that parodies the one used by Isaac
in *Palle, palle*:

The tenor primus of *Vidit dominus*[22] (after Böker-Heil, op. cit., p. 74).

Now, it would simply make no sense at all for Charlet, in order to express his
own anti-Medici feeling, to have borrowed and thus distorted Isaac's original

---

[20] On Pico and the cabala, see Eugenio ANAGNINE, *G. Pico della Mirandola* (Bari, 1937), pp.
74 ff., and Joseph Leon BLAU, *The Christian Interpretation of the Cabala in the Renaissance*
(New York, 1944), pp. 19 ff. On the subject of Hebrew thought in Florence in general, see
Umberto CASSUTO, *Gli Ebrei a Firenze nell'età del rinascimento* (Florence, 1918).

[21] For information about both the motet and the manuscript in which it appears, see Norbert
BÖKER-HEIL, *Zu einem frühvenezianischen Motettenrepertoire*, in: Helmuth Osthoff zu seinem siebzigsten Geburtstag (Tutzing, 1969), pp. 73—77. Böker-Heil points out that the composer could not be Charles d'Argentille on political grounds. I should like to thank Professor Albert DUNNING for having called my attention to this piece.

[22] The cantus firmus appears with the following inscription: *Canon maximus maximus psalit/in
principio tamen tamquam surdus existet/In fine duplicando pillas cum liliis/requiescat in
pace.*« Ibid., p. 75. The relationship between the two cantus firmi has already been noted
by Böker-Heil (p. 77).

cantus firmus if the latter melody were not itself a symbol of pro-Medici sentiment in the first place. And the nature of that symbolism — naive and primitive and even atypical as it may be when one compares it with the highly sophisticated use of symbolism that one finds, for example, in the works of Obrecht[23] — has, we hope, been demonstrated.

In all, Isaac's *Palle, palle* does more than, to use Ghisi's term, »extol« the Medici stemma[24]. Rather, the composition should be regarded as yet another example of fifteenth-century musical iconography, the structural properties of its cantus firmus being parallel — in such ways as to rule out coincidence — to those of the Medici coat-of-arms, the object that it symbolically represents.

One loose end remains, that concerning the date of *Palle, palle*. Although we are unable to determine the precise date of composition, it seems apparent that Isaac must have composed the piece no earlier than the autumn of 1484 and no later than c. 1492—1494. The terminus ante quem is provided by the date that we have established for the compilation of C.G.XIII.27, while the terminus post quem seems to be evident from the fact that it was not until the autumn of 1484 that Isaac arrived in Florence[25], and it seems reasonable to assume that Isaac wrote *Palle, palle* only after he had established his close association with the Medici. In fact, since C.G.XIII.27 was written for a Medici and since *Palle, palle* occupies the opening folios of that manuscript (the Medici stemma appears within the capital initial »P«), a position often reserved for a piece of special significance, it may be that Isaac composed *Palle, palle* specifically for the compilation of C.G.XIII.27. Though this is, to be sure, pure speculation, it would, in view of our interpretation of the piece, certainly have been a most appropriate gesture.

---

[23] We use these terms on the ground that Isaac has not availed himself of a number of the more sophisticated devices that the Franco-Netherlanders usually employed in order to represent numerical relationships. For example, rather than expressing the three ranks of palle, which stand in a 1:2:3 relationship to one another, by means of proportional augmentation of the cantus firmus upon each successive statement of the five-note motivic unit, Isaac retains the initial rhythmic configuration throughout and expresses the ranks of palle by upward transposition. Similarly, there is no attempt to express the 1:2:3 relationship by first having canon at the octave and then canon at the fifth, although the use of canon to represent symbolically things numerical was a favorite device of the fifteenth-century Franco-Netherlanders and was in fact employed by Isaac in his motet *Angeli Archangeli* (see ELDERS, op. cit., p. 99). Even the device of gematria is applied in its most simplistic form. It is in these respects that Isaac's use of symbolism can fairly be called unsophisticated and even atypical. It is also interesting to note that in the literature on Franco-Netherlandish musical number symbolism Isaac, of all the major composers of the period, appears to be the one who is mentioned the least of all. We are probably justified in concluding that number symbolism held little fascination for Isaac and that its appearance in *Palle, palle* was occasioned by the special function of the piece.

[24] GHISI, op. cit., p. 10.

[25] Frank A. D'ACCONE, *Heinrich Isaac in Florence: New and Unpublished Documents*, in: MQ, XLIX (1963), p. 465.

LA VAG'ANGIOLETTA (AND OTHERS)*

by *Stuart Reiner* (Rome)

Part I

The intended protagonist of this study is elusive; research and reflection initially aimed at recapturing her traces have caused the study to ramify as it progressed, and to become more truly a composite of studies. Sometimes her name alone unites their subject matter; sometimes, it is her personal but humble connection with an event that has induced me to review the event itself: the separate sections of the work therefore are held together only loosely, as heterogeneous items assembled momentarily around a single magnet.

The title, too, is a composite: when first conceived, it was meant to be recognized as a quotation; but it was born a misquotation, helplessly open to challenge on the question of its legitimacy. I hope the reader will agree, though, that even a bastardized quotation can be well born if it springs from two illustrious parents. For on the one hand my title was engendered by that of Ademollo's noted account of a seventeenth-century virtuosa and the musicians and patricians among whom she moved[1]; although the breadth and stature of *La bell'Adriana* are features I dare not claim have been reproduced here, some links beyond the likeness of titles will confirm that this work and Ademollo's are related. As to the other parent:

> Mentre vaga Angioletta / Ogni anima gentil cantando
> alletta, / ...
> (While the fair Angioletta / Is luring with her song
> all noble spirits, / ...)

* While preparing this study I learned that Professor Arthur Mendel would soon retire from the Music Department of Princeton University, where I had had the privilege of being his student. For »privilege«, I might as appropriately write: honor, joy, utmost good fortune. Throughout my schooling I have been genuinely blessed with excellent teachers; but none has bestowed more lucid guidance, greater stimulation, or more generous and amiable friendship than has Professor Mendel. I therefore offer these pages particularly to him, together with my wish that his works, and his pastimes, may continue always to bring him: honor, joy, and utmost good fortune!

[1] Alessandro ADEMOLLO, *La bell'Adriana ed altre virtuose del suo tempo alla corte di Mantova: Contributo di documenti per la storia della musica in Italia nel primo quarto del Seicento*, Città di Castello 1888, S. Lapi.

Thus begins a poem by Battista Guarini which served as the text for one of Claudio Monteverdi's »madrigali amorosi«[2]. In a special sense, the poem seems made for such service: the remainder of it is largely a catalogue — with Monteverdi's music one might say it became an illustrated catalogue — of vocal effects »the fair Angioletta« is said to command. This circumstance, together with a plausible inference that Monteverdi as well as Guarini may have been personally acquainted with her enchanting and agile voice, has prompted Professor Denis Stevens to speculate on the identity of the Angioletta thus so impressively commemorated[3].

In the three paragraphs he devotes to this speculation, Stevens' single specific guess is that our »vaga Angioletta« and Ademollo's »bell'Adriana« are one: that is, that Guarini and Monteverdi both probably meant to celebrate the much celebrated protagonist of Ademollo's book, Adriana Basile. Stevens' basic clue is a well known passage in one of Monteverdi's letters, comparing Adriana's talents favorably with those of two other leading performers[4]. It should be remarked that although that comparison may have truly reflected Monteverdi's overwhelming predilection for Adriana (as Stevens supposes), it may on the other hand have owed something to the fact that the two other ladies worked respectively for princely patrons in Rome and Florence, whereas Monteverdi's letter was directed to a son of the Duke of Mantua, Adriana's (and Monteverdi's) proud employer at the time[5].

---

[2] In *Madrigali gverrieri, et amorosi con alcuni opuscoli in genere rappresentatiuo, che saranno per breui episodij frà i canti senza gesto. Libro ottavo*, Venetia 1638, Alessandro Vincenti.

[3] Denis STEVENS, *Madrigali Guerrieri, et Amorosi*, in *The Monteverdi Companion*, ed. Denis Arnold and Nigel Fortune, New York 1968, W. W. Norton & Company, pp. 251—253. (Stevens' essay originally appeared in The Musical Quarterly, LIII, No. 2 [1967], pp. 161—187; in the present article, however, all citations of page numbers for the essay will refer to its second printing.)

[4] Letter of 28th December 1610, partially published in Stefano DAVARI, *Notizie biografiche del distinto maestro di musica Claudio Monteverdi desunte dai documenti dell'Archivio Storico Gonzaga*, Mantova 1885, G. Mondovi, p. 25. The other two divas mentioned in Monteverdi's letter are »Signora Hippolita«, i. e. Hippolita Recupito, who at that time was in the service of Cardinal Alessandro Damasceni Peretti, called Montalto; and a »daughter of Signor Giulio Romano« (generally assumed to mean Francesca Caccini) evidently employed at the Medici court.

[5] The letter usually is said to have been written to Alessandro Striggio, for such is the indication given by G. Francesco MALIPIERO (*Claudio Monteverdi*, Milano 1929, Fratelli Treves, p. 145). According to DAVARI, p. 25, the addressee was »the Duke's ambassador in Rome«; and the same opinion was repeated by Emil VOGEL (*Claudio Monteverdi: Leben, Wirken im Lichte der zeitgenössischen Kritik und Verzeichniss seiner im Druck erschienenen Werke*, Vierteljahrsschrift für Musikwissenschaft, III, No. 3 [1887], p. 357). But although the original document bears no address or endorsement, its content shows that the addressee must have been Monteverdi's fellow composer Cardinal (later, duke) Ferdinando Gonzaga. This emerges most explicitly in a passage immediately following Monteverdi's praise of Adriana, as he goes on:

»I was compelled to assure her how highly Their Most Illustrious Lordships Cardinals Montalto [see n. 4, above] and Peretti [by adoption (born Andrea Baroni)] honor and

Stevens seems to find a precedent for his guess, though, in Alfred Einstein's essay on the published letters of the Abbot Angelo Grillo[6], a contemporary and, apparently, a devotee of the singer or singers in question. Stevens writes: »In a footnote to Grillo's tribute to Adriana Basile, Einstein cites yet another reference to the angelic voice (›Angioletta‹) in another of the Abbot's letters«[7]. Actually, this is not true. Stevens' information is based on a posthumous translation of Einstein's article[8]; the translation is in many places so grossly inept that it may well be — indeed, I hope it is — without equal among »scholarly« texts[9]. To enumerate its flaws here is neither practical nor necessary (some of the ruined passages should in any event call attention to themselves through their glaring incoherence); what concerns us is that the translator, dealing with Einstein's note about »Angioletta«, misrepresented the content, the placement, and thus inevitably the point of the note, which in the original essay is not connected,

----

esteem her, and how much the more Your Most Illustrious Lordship does; in reply to which [report of] Your Most Illustrious Lordship's good opinion she said, ›Signora Hippolita [see n. 4, above] has qualities more prepossessing than mine, in this gentleman's eyes: for, to be sure, I have heard the endless praises he bestows on her‹. Upon which I labored greatly to make her believe differently; but it seems to me I did not achieve the result I had wished, for she added, ›If His Lordship Cardinal Gonzaga held me in the esteem you say, he would have found me worthy of one of his lovely arias, for me to sing‹. Dear sir, favor me with one, so that through this proof I may undeceive her« — translated from the original document (Mantova, Archivio di Stato: Archivio Gonzaga, Autografi, cassetta 6, ff. 108ᵛ—109ʳ); cf. the transcription in Malipiero, p. 146.

Equally unmistakable are the flattering tone of the letter and the probability that this was not inadvertent: for Monteverdi's most pressing objective (signified earlier in the letter) was to obtain for his son a sizable favor that depended on the Cardinal's pleasure. A companion to this document is Monteverdi's letter of 22nd June 1611 (in Davari, pp. [57]—58; in Malipiero, pp. 151—152), which deals with several of the same topics and was apparently meant for the same reader: in the case of this second letter both Davari and Malipiero recognized the unnamed addressee as Cardinal Gonzaga. (Ferdinando Gonzaga also was surely the recipient of Monteverdi's letter of 26th November 1608, which addresses him by his ecclesiastical title, »Illustrissimo et Reuerendissimo«, but also refers to him as a »Prencipe«; the first to publish this letter, MALIPIERO [p. 134, n. 1] opines merely that it was »probabilmente a un ecclesiastico«.)

[6] Originally printed as: Alfred EINSTEIN, Abbate Angelo Grillo's Briefe als musikgeschichtliche Quelle, Kirchenmusikalisches Jahrbuch, XXIV (1911), pp. [145]—157 (cited hereinafter as: Einstein, Briefe).

[7] STEVENS, p. 252.

[8] Abbot Angelo Grillo's Letters as Source Material for Music History, first published in Alfred EINSTEIN, Essays on Music, New York 1956, W. W. Norton & Company, pp. 153—173. Although STEVENS (p. 252, n. 2) gives inaccurate publication data for his source it is clear that he used the revised edition of this book (ed. Ralph LEAVIS, London 1958, Faber and Faber), pp. 159—178; unfortunately, the reviser did not work from Einstein's German publication but from the posthumous American edition (see his preface, ibid., pp. 7—8): consequently, the revisions most needed in the translated version of the essay have never been made.

[9] The end result is all the more unfortunate since Einstein's original translations of Grillo's letters into German (Briefe, passim) already contain more than a few notable errors.

typographically or otherwise, with the passage mentioning Adriana[10]. On the contrary, from what Einstein reported in that note it would seem impossible that Grillo's Angioletta could have been Adriana: for the Abbot's letter about Angioletta is addressed to a man in Venice named Perazzo Perazzi, who (as Einstein's brief quotation makes clear) was Angioletta's patron when Grillo wrote to him; and although all of Grillo's published letters were printed without their dates[11], Einstein asserts that this one was written sometime prior to 1613.[12] Now, Adriana Basile seems not to have left Naples for northern Italy until 1610,[13] from which time until at least the latter part of November 1616 she was continuously in the service of the Gonzagas, the ducal family of Mantua[14]. How, then, can she have been the musician Grillo knew in Venice as Perazzi's protégée?

While we are on the subject of datings it will not be amiss to consider as closely as we can the date of Guarini's poem. Stevens' source for Guarini's verses (apart from their appearance in a modern publication of Monteverdi's madrigal book[15])

---

[10] EINSTEIN, *Briefe*, p. 156: the note reporting Grillo's letter about the »vertuosa Angioletta« is introduced — somewhat later than the American and English editions introduce it — simply to demonstrate the Abbot's familiarity with the musical life of Venice.

I think it advisable to add here that the foregoing remarks, and all other passages in the present essay bearing on Denis Stevens' work, already were in typescript when Stevens, prompted by one of my book reviews (Journal of the American Musicological Society, XXIII, No. 2 [1970], pp. 343—349), presented himself as a spokesman for greater discernment in the making and judging of translations (ibid., XXIV, No. 2 [1971], pp. 320—323). My reply to his commentary is by now in print (ibid., XXV, No. 2 [1972], pp. 283—285), and nothing in the present article is meant to extend or to revive our discussion. Indeed, to preclude any such inference by the reader I had considered revising or eliminating a substantial portion of this article; I hope I have been right to rely instead on the reader's acceptance of the present disclaimer, and of my good faith in making it.

[11] A suggestion to the contrary seems to emerge in two passages of EINSTEIN's essay (*Briefe*, pp. 148 and 155) — and is incorporated into STEVENS' work (*Madrigali Guerrieri*, p. 252) — but is solely the result of awkwardnesses in Einstein's presentation.

[12] I shall dispute Einstein's dating later on (in Part III of this study); however, it is manifest and, for the moment, sufficient that the letter must have been written before 12th August 1616, the dedication date of the volume in which it was published (*Delle lettere del Reverend.mo Padre Abbate D. Angelo G r i l l o, volume primo . . .*, Venetia 1616, Gio. Battista Ciotti).

[13] See ADEMOLLO, p. 118.

[14] Ibid., pp. 221—222.

[15] G. Francesco MALIPIERO (ed.), *Tutte le opere di Claudio Monteverdi*, VIII, Bologna 1929, Enrico Venturi (cf. STEVENS, *Madrigali Guerrieri*, p. 251, n. 2). Monteverdi's setting, incidentally, departs slightly from the original text of *Mentre vaga Angioletta*, although Stevens does not say so. Guarini's poem, having pictured the poet's heart as transformed by Angioletta's song into a companionably singing nightingale, ends, »E spiega già per non star meco il volo« — freely, »And then, quite leaving me, it wings toward Heaven«. In the musical version »meco« is replaced by »mesto«, yielding (freely): »Then, to escape its grief, it wings toward Heaven«. It is not clear whether Monteverdi introduced this variant, deliberately or inadvertently, or whether it originated as an error of his printer's; in any case, it is not a product of Malipiero's transcription but appears in all relevant part

was a collected edition issued a century-and-a-quarter after the poet's death[16], and which, among its many deficiencies in scholarly apparatus, omits to indicate the original publication dates of the works it reproduces. Lacking a more accurate guide, Stevens ventures only to intimate that the poem probably was written either in 1610 or shortly thereafter — as it would have to have been if Adriana's was the voice that inspired it. (As already mentioned, Adriana appears to have come north from Naples no earlier than 1610; and Guarini, who died in 1612, seems never to have traveled farther south than Rome[17].) Another source for Guarini's work, presumably known to Ademollo, is the much earlier but equally posthumous edition of 1621.[18] Ademollo evidently assigned the poem to the same period as Stevens does, but was no more precise: observing a pronounced mimetic resemblance between *Mentre vaga Angioletta* and a number of literary tributes specifically addressed to Adriana Basile at the height of her career in the north, he merely remarked that one would think these tributes were copied from Guarini's poem if Guarini had written his composition before all the other authors wrote theirs[19]. As a matter of fact, *Mentre vaga Angioletta* appears in all editions of Guarini's *Rime,* including the first, which was published in 1598.[20] Thus it presumably did serve as the model for all markedly similar tributes dedicated to Adriana; but by the same token Guarini's poem itself cannot have been dedicated to her.

This objection, to be sure, does not necessarily apply to the musical setting of *Mentre vaga Angioletta,* which Monteverdi published in 1638, long after he had first heard Adriana and professed his admiration for her. Stevens thoughtfully points out that he may have had her in mind as he set Guarini's text even if (as we find to be the case) the text itself originally was meant to refer to some other singer[21]. One might of course express the reservation that although Guarini seems clearly to have written with a particular singer in mind, Monteverdi need not have been thinking of anything but Guarini's words while he set them; but

---

books of the 1638 print: *Tenore primo,* pp. 67, 68; *Tenore secondo,* pp. 39, 40; *Basso continvo,* p. 49. (A complete set of part books is in Bologna, Biblioteca del Museo Civico: collocation BB8.)

[16] *Delle opere del Cavalier Battista G u a r i n i,* Verona 1737—1738, Giovanni Alberto Tumermani (cf. Stevens, *Madrigali Guerrieri,* p. 251, n. 3).

[17] Cf. art. *Guarini, Battista,* in *Enciclopedia italiana di scienze, lettere ed arti,* 2nd printing, Roma, Istituto della Enciclopedia Italiana, XVIII (1951), pp. 25—26.

[18] In *La bell'Adriana* references to Guarini's works are made without citations of any specific edition. Throughout his book, however, Ademollo drew extensively on Pietro Canal's *Della musica in Mantova* (Venezia 1881, Giuseppe Antonelli); there, the 1621 edition (Venezia, Ciotti) is the only one mentioned (Canal, p. 101, continuing n. 1 of p. 100).

[19] Ademollo, p. 154. As Stevens notes, Ademollo did not infer from this resemblance that Guarini's own poem might concern Adriana (Stevens, *Madrigali Guerrieri,* p. 252, n. 3).

[20] *Rime del Molto Illvstre Signor Caualiere Battista G v a r i n i,* Venetia 1598, Gio. Battista Ciotti, ff. 130v—131r.

[21] Stevens, *Madrigali Guerrieri,* p. 253.

if we put aside this quibble we must allow that Stevens' conjecture is fairly unassailable. Even to call it in question one ought to be ready with a strong alternative candidate to suggest in place of Adriana: that is, some singer who might have had both the opportunity and the talent to impress Monteverdi (and perhaps Guarini or Grillo, or both), and to whom Monteverdi (et al.) might reasonably have applied the designation »Angioletta«. It is time, then, to consider the sense of that designation.

As my earlier quotation from his essay will suggest, Stevens appears not to have had a very exact idea of what »Angioletta« means (for it does not mean »the angelic voice«). If, like Stevens, we take it as involving a common noun — which in the sixteenth and seventeenth centuries might be capitalized, and sometimes was — we easily find that the word is a diminutive of the feminine form of »angiolo« (alternatively spelled »angelo«), which means »angel«. We find, besides, that at least one clearly identifiable musician of Guarini's and Monteverdi's time was described by contemporaries, more than once, as a little angel; and that the word used was »Angioletta«, capital initial and all. Two such descriptions, which Stevens seems not to have noticed, are reprinted in Ademollo's book — for, oddly enough, they refer precisely to Adriana Basile[22]. In view of what has been said above, of course, this cannot persuade us that Adriana was either Guarini's or Grillo's Angioletta; but it can lend strength to Stevens' surmise that she may nevertheless have been the lady Monteverdi had in mind, insofar as we infer that the word »Angioletta« might be applied as a common noun to any sufficiently attractive virtuosa. (That we readily find it applied to Adriana may be due chiefly to Ademollo's zeal in making documents about her so plentifully and conveniently accessible.) According to this interpretation, then, Monteverdi — or, for that matter, Guarini — may have intended »Angioletta« simply as an epithet, »little angel«, affectionately or eulogistically conferred upon whatever singer had inspired his composition, and whom the composition leaves otherwise anonymous.

If, on the other hand, »Angioletta« may be interpreted as a proper noun, the singer's anonymity is considerably modified: in that usage the word is a diminutive of »Angiola«, which, again, is a standard alternative spelling of »Angela«. Hence the subject of Guarini's poem, Monteverdi's music, Grillo's letter, or any combination of these, may have been a musician named Angela, who (as the diminutive suggests) was young or petite — or, very likely, both young and petite — when first she was called »Angioletta«.

---

[22] They are quoted in ADEMOLLO, pp. 14 and 286, respectively from Michelarcangelo Alfonso Gaetano d'Aragona, Duke of Laurenzana, and Domizio Bombarda, both in Bombarda (ed.), *Il teatro delle glorie della Signora Adriana Basile . . .*, 2nd ed., Napoli 1628. Ademollo did not attempt to relate these quotations (nor, hence, the person of Adriana) to Guarini's use of the word »Angioletta«.

Is there any reason to think the »Angioletta« in question may indeed be a
proper noun? There is of course the fact that a poet rendering public homage to
a gifted lady's public charms ordinarily is not too reticent to mention the lady's
name. Stevens himself observes that one of Guarini's poems is inscribed to
»Vittoria [Archilei] cantatrice«[23] (in fact, not one but two of Guarini's poems
are so inscribed)[24]: one might suppose, then, that when Guarini referred to
another singer solely as »Angioletta« he did so because that noun seemed to him
a sufficient identification — quite possibly because it was a recognizable form
of her accustomed name. However, any singer as talented as the one described
in *Mentre vaga Angioletta* might be expected to leave a record of her career
approximately as conspicuous as that left by Adriana (or, before her, by Vittoria); and the awkward truth is that no singer named Angela, of either great
or little renown, is known to have flourished in Guarini's time.

Stevens can hardly be blamed, then, if »Angioletta« did not suggest to him a
hypothetical Angela whose very existence he would have found undocumented.
Nor perhaps, by the same token, could he be expected to close his ears to the
siren song of Adriana, whose triumphs, by contrast, have been documented in
such tempting abundance. Ademollo's book after all is only a crowning tribute,
prompted and pervaded by the many tributes Adriana received in her own day.
Indeed, as we are about to usher her definitively out of these pages it will be
fitting, in deference to her splendor, that we do so by publishing here still
another tribute to her, which Ademollo had not the fortune to see. This quaint
homage appears in a letter written by the secretary of Count Francesco Martinengo, to the Dowager Marchesa Isabella Bentivoglio[25] (mother-in-law of the
Count's daughter) in Ferrara:

I have used ... a bit of diligence to obtain one of these little birds that Your Most Illustrious Ladyship commissioned me to find, and I have come up with a goldfinch (»cardelino«, as it is called here), which I have kept in my house for several days. I find this not at all unpleasant; indeed, I dare say that just as among the Angelas and Lucias	Hò usato ... un poco de deligenza per hauere uno de questi ucelletti che VS Ill:ma mi diede comissione di trouare et mi è capitato un cardelino, cosi qui nominato, che hò tenuto alcuni giorni in casa, che non mi riesce cosa ingrata, anzi ardirei di dire, che se trà le An- gele, et le Lucie, si trouano anco delle Adriane, che eccedono a quelle nel can-

---

[23] STEVENS, *Madrigali Guerrieri*, p. 251.

[24] In the edition used by Stevens (see n. 16, above), madrigals 149 and 151 (pp. 115—116; the
dedications to Vittoria are shown only in the table of contents, respectively on pp. 392
and 388). The earliest edition of the *Rime* in which I have seen these poems is dated 1602
(Venetia, Gio. bat. [sic] Ciotti, f. 74r—74v, as madrigals 159 and 161).

[25] In an earlier article I mistakenly gave the name of this same marchesa as Laura, confusing
her with another member of the Bentivoglio family (Stuart REINER, *Preparations in Parma
— 1618, 1627—28*, The Music Review, XXV, No. 4 [1964], p. 285, n. 61); I welcome the
opportunity of restoring to Isabella Bentivoglio the title rightfully hers.

one finds also some Adrianas, who sur-
pass them in song, so among [the members of] this other species, of irrational
animals, one might in the matter of
talent almost attribute to this one I
have here a certain preëminence over
others. . . . Venice, 18th July 1612.
      Giovan Antonio Scorzoli

to; cosi trà quest'altra spetie de ani-
mali irationali si potrebbe quasi dare
qualche preminenza di uirtù trà gl'altri
a questo, che tengo qui. . . . Venetia li
18 Luglio 1612
      Giovan Antonio Scorzoli.
      [X.66, *238*; A][26]

A music lover's fancy, and a lovely thought. In expressing it, the reader will
observe, Scorzoli found it convenient to refer not only to Adriana but also to
two other ladies, both apparently singers, and one of whom was called Angela.
The Bentivoglio Archive, which has yielded up this trace of a singing Angela,
will in fact provide enough documentation to give a fuller account of her. To
make the account clearer, though, we shall do well to begin with some documents from another archive, that of the Gonzaga family in Mantua.

Duke Vincenzo Gonzaga prided himself on the sufficiency of his musical staff;

---

[26] Throughout this study, letters from the Archivio Bentivoglio (Ferrara, Archivio di Stato)
will be identified by bracketed symbols placed at the ends of the transcriptions or citations. A
Roman numeral and an ordinary Arabic numeral will signify respectively the shelf (*scaffale*)
and packet (*mazzo*) numbers; an italicized number will indicate foliation within the
packet. For Bentivoglio documents and for others, when shown in the main text of the
article, descriptive information generally will be added after the location of the document,
by means of the following characters: A (the body of the letter is autograph), S (the body
of the letter is scribal), N (the addressee is named in the document), C (the city to which
the letter was sent is named in the document). The symbols following Scorzoli's letter, for
instance, signify that the quoted passage is transcribed from: Archivio Bentivoglio, scaffale
X, mazzo 66, folio 238; and that the letter is in Scorzoli's own hand. From the absence of
the symbols »N« and »C« the reader will understand also that my identification of Scorzoli's addressee as »Isabella Bentivoglio . . . in Ferrara« is based on information not explicit in the document; in this and all similar cases such facts have been derived from
other documents, whether or not those documents are cited in the present study: in no case
is the information based on casual guesswork. It should be added that even scribal letters
ordinarily have autograph signatures (exceptions will be noted); and that autograph
postscripts often are appended to scribal letters — for such cases the symbol »S« will be
used, and the postscripts, if quoted, will be separately identified as autograph. (All desig-
nations of letters as autograph or scribal are based on my own observations.)
Procedures used in the transcriptions: Elisions will be indicated in the standard manner,
except that no indication will be made of the omission of closing salutations. Common
abbreviations of some personal titles will be shown as they appear; all other abbreviated
words will be spelled out in full, their missing elements supplied in italic characters. (In the
original of the foregoing letter, for example, Scorzoli signed his Christian name »Gio.
Antō«.) Letters omitted within words will more rarely be supplied in brackets: this will
be done only where the original shows no standard sign for abbreviation but is simply a
misspelling; since spelling throughout these documents is largely idiosyncratic, this procedure (like the indication »[sic]«) will be confined to cases in which a suspicion of error
would otherwise inevitably fall upon the present writer (as transcriber) or his printer. In
every other respect (and, indirectly, in these respects as well) the orthography, no matter
how unorthodox it may at times look to Italian-speaking readers, will faithfully reflect
that of the original documents.

when, in 1608, he made acknowledged use of borrowed singers, he allowed an
official account to imply that he had accepted their services as a favor to their
patrons[27]. Actually, he had on that occasion been compelled to seek just such
reinforcements, and had gone to some trouble to find them. The court had
scheduled a lavish program of entertainments to celebrate the wedding of Vincenzo's son and heir apparent, Prince Francesco; among these entertainments,
several (including Monteverdi's *Arianna,* his *Ballo delle ingrate,* and the *intermedii* that would be performed with Guarini's *Idropica*) gave Vincenzo's
musicians more than enough to do. In fact, there were more roles to fill than
singers to fill them, and Vincenzo, as well as his duchess, Eleonora, had written
to the Grand Duke of Tuscany (Eleonora's uncle) appealing for help; the Grand
Duke's negative replies, respectively dated 4th and 11th December 1607, are
in the Gonzaga Archive, and have been published[28]. Other documents, not
heretofore reported, show that Vincenzo did not limit his hopes to the coöpera-
tion of the Grand Duke Ferdinando. For example, we find that on the day
Ferdinando was issuing his second refusal, Vincenzo's secretary was writing to
a colleague in Mantua, the ducal counsellor Annibale Iberti, as follows:

His Lordship the Duke forgot to tell Your Lordship to write to Genoa, to get that woman who sings to come to Mantua, if His Highness cannot have the singers for whom the Grand Duke has been asked. ... Casette di Comacchio, 11th December 1607. Alessandro Striggio	Il Sig.r Duca s'è dimenticato di dire à .V.S. che scriua à Genoua per far uenire à Mantoua quella che canta, non potendo S.A. hauere i cantori richiesti al Gran Duca. ... Dalle Casette di Comacchio il di 11 di Xbre 1607. Alessandro Striggio[29]

We do not know who the woman from Genoa was, nor is there any sign that
her services were obtained. Before long, though, Striggio himself received from

---

[27] »The musicians who here appeared, men and women alike, were ... all servitors of the
Duke; only excepting two who, with a view to gratifying other persons, were made use
of along with the rest. For the Duke has, among many distinguished servitors in all sciences
and in every kind of art, exquisite musical forces: in addition to men of talent in that
profession, many women who, haply, have few equals in Italy« — translated from [Fe-
derico FOLLINO], *Compendio delle sontvose feste fatte l'anno M.DC.VIII. nella città di
Mantova, per le reali nozze del Serenissimo Prencipe D. Francesco Gonzaga, con la Serenissima Infante Margherita di Savoia,* Mantova 1608, Aurelio & Lodouico Osanna, p. 74.
(The Italian text is reprinted in Angelo SOLERTI, *Gli albori del melodramma,* Milano
[1904—1905], Remo Sandron, III, p. 208.)

[28] In DAVARI, p. 13, n. 1.

[29] Mantova, Archivio di Stato: Archivio Gonzaga, busta 1265 [A, N, C]. It sometimes is reported that Striggio became a ducal secretary only in 1622: e.g. in Denis ARNOLD,
Monteverdi, »The Master Musicians Series«, London 1963, J. M. Dent and Sons, p. 199;
also ARNOLD and Nigel FORTUNE, *The Monteverdi Companion,* p. 29. I do not know
what evidence underlies that assumption; but I find »sig.r Segretario striggio« so called in a
dispatch from Mantua dated 30th November 1607 (see n. 146, below).

his duke a letter that brought him thirty-two miles back along the road toward
Mantua, to Ferrara. Shortly afterward, the Duke had the following commu-
nication:

Signor Striggio has delivered to me
Your Most Serene Highness' very kind
letter of the 14th instant. ... I have let
the aforementioned Signor Striggio listen
to this young woman who sings; if, on
the basis of the report he gives you,
Your Highness considers her suitable
for the purpose you wish to have her
serve, then — as you are the master of
our lives and our goods — any time
you care to let me know your wishes
I shall be awaiting them.... Ferrara, 18th
December 1607.
    The Marchesa Bentivoglio

Il s^r striggi mha reso la benigniss*i*ma
littera di vAs degli 14 del presente. ...
al deto s^r strigi ho fatto sentir questa
giouane che canta et dalla relacione che
egli fara a vA se la giudicara a proposito *per* Il bisogno che ella se ne uol
seruire si come e patrona delle uite e
sostanze nostre senpre che ella si de-
gnara farmi saper la sua uolonta la
staro atendendo. ... di ferrara agli 18
decenbre 1607
    la Marchese [sic] Bentiuoglia[30]

Meanwhile the Marchesa's daughter-in-law, Caterina Martinengo Bentivoglio,
wrote to her husband, Enzo, who was temporarily in Rome:

Your Lordship will have learned from
Her Ladyship [the Marchesa Isabella]
what the Duke of Mantua is planning
to do with Angela[31] — about which, it
is clear that if he should want her it
will be necessary to provide clothes for
her; so Your Lordship may let me
know what I am to do. ... Ferrara,
19th December 1607.
    Your Caterina

VS auera inteso dalla sig^{ra} quelo che
il ducha di mantoua disegna di fare della angiola si che se la uolese bisognerebe
uestirla siche VS puotra auisarmi quelo
ho da fare. ... da ferara li 19 desembre 1607
    Caterina sua
    [IX.42, *760*; A]

If Enzo's mother did write him about the Duke's plans for Angela, her letter
has disappeared. Caterina herself wrote Enzo again about the girl; but her
words, far from making matters clear, invite us to wonder whether her Angela

---

[30] Archivio Gonzaga, busta 1265 [A, N].

[31] In the series of documents on which this study is based, proper names recur in varied
spellings: the variants do not appear only among spellings by different writers, but were
sometimes produced, on different occasions, by a single writer — sometimes, indeed, in the
spelling of his or her own name. In most cases therefore it has seemed to me no abuse,
but a probable service to the reader, to settle upon one easily recognizable spelling per
name and to use it throughout the English translations; the reader will in any case be able
to observe the extent of this liberty, since the original spellings are shown in the accompanying transcriptions. (The liberty itself is not a new one — adjustments of the sort have
been practiced for decades, in many widely read historical texts. All that is unusual here
is that the reader is being allowed to know and witness the procedure.)

was after all identical to the Marchesa's »young woman who sings«. Certainly,
Angela here seems to have had a different occupation in the Bentivoglio household:

Angela will leave for Mantua the day
after tomorrow, accompanied in the
manner that Your Lordship will learn
of from Her Ladyship. ... We have
completed another bolt of cloth. Right
after the holydays we shall start another one, but Angela's departure will
hamper me; however, I have formed
an intention of getting Madonna Barbara's Caterina and having her work
in her [Angela's] stead. ... This wedding ... will not take place until the
end of Carnival. ... Ferrara, 25th December 1607.
        Your Caterina

puosdimane partira langiola per mantoua acompagnata come VS intendara
dalla sig.ra ... abiamo finito una altra
lista subito fate le feste ne cominsiare-
mo una altra ma mi dara dano landa-
ta dela angola ho pero pensato che
uoglio tor la Caterina di madona barbara et farla lauorare in suo canbio.
... queste noze ... non si fano sino
alultimo di Carneuale. ... da ferara li
25 desembre 1607
        Caterina sua
        [IX.42, *807–808*; A, N, C]

The wedding to which Caterina referred presumably was Prince Francesco's,
although her prediction of the wedding date does not agree with what is reported
in familiar modern accounts; we shall have to deal with that discrepancy later.
Meanwhile, having noted that Angela appears to have been a weaver or an
embroiderer, let us assure ourselves that she also was the singer whose services
had been offered to Vincenzo Gonzaga. Here is another letter to Enzo Bentivoglio in Rome:

His Lordship the Duke of Mantua has
sent to fetch Angela; I am sending her
to him tomorrow morning, accompanied
by a [serving-]woman, by a brother
of hers, and by Ercole Zenzignoli: thus
I trust she will have a safe trip. And
also as to her stay in Mantua I believe
all will go well, considering what His
Highness writes me about having her
handed over at once to Madam [the
Duchess] (as you will see from his letter)[32]. Truly, if His Lordship the Duke
were not so beneficent a patron of ours
as you yourself know him to be, I
should not have become involved in this
vexatious matter. I do trust, though,
that you are not going to suffer any
sort of annoyance on this account —

Il s.r Duca di Mantova hà mandato à
pigliare l'Angella, la quale glila inuio
domattina accompagnata da una donna, da uno suo fratello, da Ercole Zenzignoli, cosi uoglio sperare andarà sicura, et quanto poi al suo stare à
Mantova credo anco che le cose siano
per passare bene, stando quello mi scriue S.A. come dalla sua lettera uedrete
di farla consignare subito à Madam-
ma; ueramente se il s.r Duca non ci
fosse quell'amoreuole padrone che uoi
stesso sappete io non sarei entrato in
questa briga, uoglio pero sperare che
di questo fatto uoi non siate per riceuere
alcun disgusto. ch'è quanto in questo particolare m'occorre dirui.
[PS. (autograph):] In uio domatina

---

[32] The Duke's letter is not now in the Bentivoglio Archive.

which is all I have to say to you on the subject.

[PS. (autograph):] Tomorrow, St. John's Day, I am sending this pretty singer of ours; [*crossed out:* you will see from the*] I hope she will conduct herself well — and I shall say no more about that. Here, wherever one goes [literally, »in all the shops«] people are saying that you will be ambassador. ...

Your loving mother,
The Marchesa Bentivoglio

che [=ch'è] Il giorno di sangiouani questa nostra bella cantora [*crossed out:* uoi uedrete da dalla] et spero si portera bene e sopra cio non diro altro qui si dice per tute le botege che uoi andate anbasiatore. ...

Amoreuolissima mat[r]e la
Marchese Bentiuoglia
[IX.43, *43*; S, N, C]

It is helpful to know that Enzo Bentivoglio's election to the post of Ferrarese Ambassador to the Holy See took place on 8th February 1608;[33] for the foregoing letter is undated, and its mention of St. John's Day (which in colloquial usage now most often refers to 24th June) might, if taken by itself, confuse matters. (A postponement? A second trip? Perhaps a second Angela?) Actually the letter must have been written on 26th December 1607, and simply confirms what Caterina had announced in hers of the preceding day. Accordingly, »this pretty singer of ours«, released from textile tasks, must have left for Mantua on 27th December, the feast of St. John the Apostle and Evangelist. On the 26th, in fact, the Marchesa entrusted the Duke's messenger with a letter to the Duchess:

I am about to send this ugly singer to His Lordship the Duke, my supreme master. He writes me that through Your Highness' courtesy she will be watched over while she is there. I know it is unnecessary for me to commend her to Your Highness, for I am certain it would be superfluous, considering Your Highness' infinite goodness. ... Ferrara, 26th December 1607.

The Marchesa Bentivoglio

Hora inuio questa bruta cantora al s\u02b3 Ducha mio sopremo patron Il qual mi scriue che dalla begnita [sic] di VA sara fata cosdodire mentre stara costi so che non occore che io la racomandi a VA sapendo molto bene eser superf[l]uo alla infinita bonta di VA. ... di ferrara agli 26 decembre 1607
la Marchese Bentiuoglia[34]

and another, to the Duke himself:

I am sending you this young woman of ours who sings; she is accompanied by two [serving-]women of our household, by an elderly manservant of mine, and by a brother of hers. This brother would appreciate it — and the girl

gli mando questa nostra giouane che canta acconpagnata da dua done qui di casa e da un mio huomo atenpato e da un fratelo dalla [sic] deta giouane Il qual suo fratelo auerebe desiderio ella [= e la] giouane gusto che egli restassi

---

[33] It was immediately reported to him in two letters of that date [IX.43, *341, 351*].

[34] Archivio Gonzaga, busta 1265 [A].

would be pleased — if he might remain there as long as she stays. ...

About the young woman: I must tell Your Highness that it is roughly eighteen months since she became a member of our household, and that [when she arrived] she not only was unable to read but did not know so much as a syllable or note of song, possessing no valuable quality other than her voice. Since then, to be sure, we have had her taught to understand written words and musical notation [literally, »letter characters and notes of music«], with the result that she is beginning to read a bit and, in a groping fashion, to sight-sing. ([So far,] the pieces she sings have all been learned by rote.) Your Highness accordingly may [wish to] impart all of this to whoever shall have charge of teaching her. Nor should I neglect to bring to Your Highness' attention that it takes hard work and great endurance for her own [accustomed] teacher to get his teachings into her head; hence, what with changing teachers, there can be no doubt that she will not make the showing that — solely in order to serve Your Highness exquisitely — I should like. I beg you to forgive me for this lengthy discourse I have written you; but it has been necessary to tell you everything, by way of apology for the girl (and for myself as well). May it please God that her voice give satisfaction — her face, at all events, will be no liability.

...Ferrara, 26th December 1607.

The Marchesa Bentivoglio

costi fin che ella si tratenira. ...

Della giouine e forza che io dichi a vA che sono da diciote mesi incircha che si ritroua qui in casa et lei non sapeua non sollo legere ma nonche conose[va] silaba ne nota di musicha per cantare non hauendo di buono solo la uoce E uero che in questo tenpo se gli e fato insegnare di conosere i carateri di letera e note di musica onde comincia a leger alquanto et a cantare a tastone le note, tuto quelo che ella canta sono tute cose inparate alla mente et pero tuto questo potra vA far sapere a chi auera cura dinsegnarle non restando di poner in consideracione a vA che il proprio maestro dura fatica e pacienza grande col farla capazze di quelo che glinsegna e pero non sera dubio che col mutar maestro non facesse quella riusita che desiderarei tuto per seruir esquisitamente a vA la qual suplico a perdonarmi di questa longa diceria che io le scriuo ma per far la schusa della giouane et ancor mia e stato necesario a dirgli Il tuto piacia a dio che riescha la uoce che del uiso non fara pecar

... Di ferrara agli 26 decenbre 1607
la Marchese Bentiuoglia[35]

Here, we must pause to acknowledge that if Angela's vocal training began only in 1606, she cannot after all have been the melodious Angioletta of Guarini's poem published in 1598. It of course is possible to adopt Stevens' approach and to argue that our singer may nonetheless have become the subject of Monteverdi's *madrigale amoroso*; equally, she may have been the Angioletta mentioned in Grillo's letter. Later, indeed, certain facts will favor such conjectures; but to spare

---

[35] Ibid. [A].

the reader's patience it is fair to announce that the evidence for those conjectures is slight, and that the conjectures themselves will remain, at last, moot. We shall find, though, that there are better reasons for pursuing what we can of Angela's story.

Having for the moment interrupted that story, we may prolong the interruption briefly to consider the anonymity of Guarini's Angioletta, which so far has resisted both Stevens' curiosity and our own. I have suggested that there is something out of the ordinary in Guarini's having left her anonymous despite his evident relish in advertising her abilities; I would now add that his failure to advertise her name as well may have been due to considerations of taste: specifically, it might have seemed vulgar of Guarini to blazon the singer's name if that name happened to be his own. Let us note that Guarini's immediate family included at least one accomplished singer, and perhaps two. The poet's wife, Taddea, was a sister of the renowned Lucrezia Bendidio, or Bendedei, one of the celebrated »three ladies« whose vocal prowess was a pride of the Ferrarese court in the time of its last duke, Alfonso II d'Este[36]; and another of the Bendidio sisters, Isabella, was hardly less esteemed as a singer at the same court[37]. (In the foregoing pages, incidentally, we have been examining some of the letters this Isabella wrote in her later years, long after the marriage rite and the investiture that had made her »la Marchese Bentiuoglia«[38].) It would not be surprising if Taddea Bendidio, like her sisters, possessed a pleasing and practiced voice.

To be sure, no such fact has been reported; but information of the sort generally comes to us from court chronicles, court correspondence, and prefaces to the published music of court composers: it tends to leave out of account singers not employed at court — that is, non-professionals. But in suggesting that Taddea, while not a professional singer, may yet have been a singer of some ability, I do not mean to argue from silence; for there is some indication — albeit less conclusive than the evidence of chronicles — that she commanded the kind of vocal skill that could move her husband to flights of verse. One of his sonnets (distinctly a love poem) in fact celebrates »the beauty and the song of his admirable lady«[39]; although the poem purports »to make her fair and noble name

---

[36] See Remo CESERANI, Bendidio, Lucrezia, in Dizionario biografico degli italiani, Roma, Istituto della Enciclopedia Italiana, VIII (1966), pp. 234—235.

[37] See Luigi Francesco VALDRIGHI, Cappelle, concerti e musiche di casa d'Este (dal sec. XV al XVIII), Atti e memorie delle RR. Deputazioni di Storia Patria per le provincie modenesi e parmensi, Serie III, Vol. II (1883), pp. 426, 465—466.

[38] Isabella married Cornelio Bentivoglio in 1573: see CESERANI, p. 235. Bentivoglio was not, as Ceserani indicates, a marchese at the time, but he received that title three years later: cf. Pompeo LITTA, Le famiglie celebri italiane, [Milano] 1819—1848, P. E. Giusti: Bentivoglio di Bologna, tavola VI (Ramo di Ferrara).

[39] The poem is headed »Bellezza, & canto della sua Donna mirabile« (Rime, 1598, f. 5r).

immortal«[40], the name itself — just like the real name of Angioletta in the madrigal — is omitted. Oddly, though, it is possible to detect what may have been the justification of that line: the seeming vestiges of an acrostic, perhaps abandoned as the muse took freer flight. An early edition of the poem shows its first lines thus:

> TAccia il cielo, e la terra al nouo canto
> Di lei, c'ha l'armonia celeste, e'l volto,
> E con doppio valor vincendo hà tolto
> Il pregio al Sole, à le Sirene il vanto.[41]

Is it merely fanciful to see in the capital letters beginning these lines a trace of the name the poet meant »to make ... immortal«? It may be, since the first editor of the *Rime* used a different printing scheme, capitalizing the entire first word of the poem[42]. Besides, if Guarini had intended an acrostic on his wife's name he might easily have achieved a more passable one by rearranging the fourth line of the sonnet — *Al Sole il pregio, à le Sirene il vanto* — at no expense to syntax, rhyme, or scansion[43]. The most that can be said, perhaps, is that Guarini's »admirable lady« was a singer; but then, the least that can be said is that Taddea was, after all, Guarini's lady.

The facts are more straightforward in the case of the poet's daughter. Anna Guarini, along with her aunts Lucrezia and Isabella, definitely did sing at the court of Alfonso d'Este[44]. She died — murdered by her husband, in collusion with her brother — almost before the echoes of her songs. The murder occurred on 3rd May 1598;[45] twenty-five days later, the printer Ciotti signed the dedication of the volume in which *Mentre vaga Angioletta* first appeared[46]. Was Anna the subject of that poem, whom the poet found it more fitting to call by a term of endearment than by her proper name? I think this would not be remarkable; rather, it would be remarkable if Guarini, whose muse was so

---

[40] The tenth and eleventh lines of the poem read: »L'anima sueglio addormentata, e tarda, / Per far eterno il suo bel nome, e chiaro« (ibid.).

[41] *Rime*, 1602, f. 10ʳ.

[42] *Rime*, 1598, f. 5ʳ.

[43] Whether such a rearrangement would have undermined more subtle poetic values is a question beyond my competence — perhaps nowhere more so than in connection with Guarini's verses. For this reason, I cannot evaluate the merit of a suspicion I find tempting: that the hypothetical rearrangement I have shown may in fact have been part of an original draft, replaced by the published reading for the sake of a poetic nuance.

[44] See Giuseppe CAMPORI, *La figlia del Guarini, narrazione del secolo XVI (da documenti inediti dell'archivio governativo di Modena)*, Nuova antologia di scienze, lettere ed arti, XII, Fasc. 10 (1869), p. 326.

[45] See Vittorio ROSSI, *Battista Guarini ed il Pastor fido*, Torino 1886, Ermanno Loescher, pp. 115—116.

[46] *Rime*, 1598, f. [iii]ʳ.

susceptible to the charms of song, had never produced any lines in praise of the expert young voice to which he himself had given life.

Meanwhile, we have left our own Angioletta on the eve of her departure for Mantua; let us resume her story.

A week after Angela set out from Ferrara, Prince Francesco Gonzaga wrote to Isabella Bentivoglio:

Most Illustrious Madam:
Your Ladyship's two [serving-]women are coming back with your manservant; the girl is staying, with her brother. As Your Ladyship well foresaw, she will not be able to manage in time for the work that was desired of her; but she will, nonetheless, perform her assignment in the *intermedii* of the long comedy, for which less study is required. ... Mantua, 3rd January 1608.
The Prince of Mantua

Molt'Ill.re Sig.ra Se ne ritornano le due donne di V.S. col suo huomo, et resta la giouane col fratello, la quale per l'opera ch'ella era desiderata, non potrà riuscire à tempo come V.S. beni*ssimo* hà preuisto, mà farà però la sua parte negl'intermedij della Comedia grande, doue si ricerca minor studio. ... Di Mantoua, a' 3 di Genaro 1608.
Il Prin*cipe* di Mant[ova]
[VIII.17, *201*; S, N]

Some years ago I published this letter in another context, and guessed that the *intermedii* it mentions must have been those written by Gabriello Chiabrera for the première of Guarini's *Idropica*[47]; that guess will be substantiated by further documentation in the present article. First, though, we ought to consider the work Angela originally had been desired to perform — for, notwithstanding the pessimism of Francesco Gonzaga and Isabella Bentivoglio, there is reason to think the girl did »manage in time« for that work. Here is part of a letter from an officer of the Mantuan court, the Commendator Langosco, to Enzo Bentivoglio:

Owing to the foretaste she has given of the good results we may expect, in the play already sung, I have found Their Highnesses so well disposed to-ward the young woman about whom you write me, that not only do they agree to have Rasio or some other vir-tuoso keep her in training but, when His Lordship the Prince's wedding is over, Most Serene Madam is thinking of sending her to Florence, to the house-hold of Zazarina, for at least a year in

Hò trouato cosi buona uolontà nelle Alt.ze loro uerso la Giouane di che mi scriue per il saggio che hà dato della buona riuscita che si può sperare, nella Comedia già cantata, che non solo si contentano che il Rasio, ó, altro Vir-tuoso la tenghino essercitata, ma Mad.a Ser.ma hà pensiere, finite che saranno le nozze del s.r Prencipe di mandarla, á, Fiorenza *per* un anno al meno in Casa del Zazarina, accioche possa me-glio affinare quel talento, che con la

---

[47] REINER, *Preparations in Parma*, p. 285, n. 61.

order that she may the better refine that
talent which, through judicious guidance,
nature aided by study will grant her.
Her Highness also said to me that if
Your Most Illustrious Lordship were
agreeable, she would greatly like to
keep her in her service: Your Most
Illustrious Lordship therefore will o-
blige me by letting me know whether
that would suit you. ... Mantua, 18th
February 1608.

Brother Orazio Langosco

scorta di persona giudiciosa le sarà
concesso dalla natura aiutata dal studio,
hauendomi soggionto S.A. che quando
fosse con sodisfattione di V.S. Ill.ma
desideraria grandemente di tenerla al
suo seruizio; però V.S.I. mi farà gratia
di darmi auiso se ciò le sarà di gusto. ... Di Mantoua li 18 Febraro
1608.

Frate oratio Langosco.
[IX.43, *392*; S, N]

Let us clarify a few points. The »long comedy« with *intermedii,* to which the
Prince of Mantua had referred, was not itself sung; nor, as we shall see, had
it been presented by 18th February. Angela had demonstrated that she could be
expected to do well in that production, by doing well in another one which
Langosco's letter calls »la Comedia già cantata«[48]: a work that would fit the

---

[48] »Comedia« is the word used both in the Prince's letter and in Langosco's; meticulous readers
may observe that in the one case I have translated it as »comedy«, but in the other, as
»play«. This is not a matter of so-called »free« translation, but of legitimate — indeed,
obligatory — interpretation: for the word admits more than one definition, and its meaning varies from one document to another. It will become clear on a later page that the
Prince's »Comedia« was Guarini's *Idropica,* specifically a comedy. About the work mentioned by Langosco, however, no such specification can be made: for his phrase, therefore,
a more generic translation of »Comedia« seemed prudent. But the question that really may
appear troublesome is whether the two definitions embodied in these non-synonymous
translations truly were both available to Mantuans writing in 1608: from Professor Nino
Pirrotta's recent discussion of the term »commedia«, some readers might think not. For
Pirrotta has seemingly suggested that one of these definitions (the one I have rendered as
»play«) came into Italian usage after 1625, in Rome, and only then spread elsewhere;
his remarks also can suggest (though I wonder whether the suggestion was intended) that
when this occurred »commedia« no longer was used to mean »comedy«. I have in mind
the following:
   »Opera [during the ascendancy of the Barberini family] ... became the main form
   of theatrical activity in Rome, and as such it expanded the scope of its plots and the
   range of its subjects. ... [A series of examples is given, the earliest dated 1626.] One
   external indication of change was the gradual abandonment of such names as ›favola‹
   or ›pastorale‹ in favor of ›commedia per musica,‹ or even simply ›commedia.‹ [footnote:]
   For instance, in the *Argomento et allegoria della commedia musicale Chi soffre speri*
   (Rome, 1639).... The habit of referring to operas as comedies, an intriguing and often
   confusing feature of Roman chroniclers, occasionally spread outside Rome. ... [main
   text:] Under the growing influence exerted on Italian theatrical activity by the Spanish
   theatre, the term had lost its connotation of a precisely defined comic genre; it meant rather
   any kind of theatrical action developed mainly through dialogue« — Nino PIRROTTA,
   Early Opera and Aria, in *New Looks at Italian Opera: Essays in Honor of Donald
   J. Grout,* ed. William W. Austin, Ithaca, New York 1968, Cornell University Press,
   pp. 95—96; the same material, in Italian, is in PIRROTTA and Elena POVOLEDO, *Li due
   Orfei: Da Poliziano a Monteverdi,* Torino 1969, Edizioni RAI Radiotelevisione Italiana,
   p. 347 and p. 367, n. 113.
As I have intimated, I am not certain of having correctly interpreted, on all points,

case is Marco da Gagliano's *Dafne*, which had lately received its première in the course of Carnival festivities held in Mantua[49]. Next, the »Rasio« mentioned in the letter as a prospective vocal coach for Angela certainly was Francesco Rasi, a composer, poet, instrumentalist, and highly esteemed tenor who was in the Gonzagas' service at that time; it was he, in fact, who had performed the leading role of Apollo in Gagliano's opera[50]. (As Nigel Fortune has plausibly suggested, Rasi may also have sung the title role of Monteverdi's *Orfeo* at its première in 1607.)[51] »Zazarina«, finally, can be deciphered without difficulty as a mis-spelling of »Zazzerino«, the well known nickname of Iacopo Peri. (Partly because the Duchess of Mántua was a Medici, partly because her son Ferdinando had been studying in Tuscany and meeting its celebrities, Peri found it easy in those days to maintain close ties with the Mantuan court[52].) Peri's excellence as a singer is praised, among other places, in Gagliano's preface to the score of the aforementioned *Dafne*[53].

Regarding other details directly and indirectly connected with Gagliano's opera, it would be an understatement to say that some conspicuous stones have been left unturned; several that might easily serve as steppingstones for our narrative will in consequence present themselves as stumbling blocks if we proceed without setting them straight. Unfortunately, this means that it will be necessary to suspend once more the progress of Angela's story, for the embarrassing purpose of correcting a few errors apparently too innocuous to have ever troubled anyone; for in the present context they turn out to be a great nuisance indeed.

In his preface to *Dafne*, Gagliano named three of the six soloists who had

---

Pirrotta's views as expressed in this passage; but I have no reason to assume that any reader will receive from the same material impressions different from my own. Therefore, since Pirrotta's assumptions seem to me to conflict with those I am applying to the recurrent word »commedia« in the present article, I shall append to this article a short note at the end of Part I, devoted to a few historical illustrations that may be helpful.

[49] See the preface to the published score: Marco da GAGLIANO, *La Dafne*, Firenze 1608, Cristo-fano Marescotti, p. [v] (first reprinted in Emil VOGEL, *Marco da Gagliano: Zur Geschichte des florentiner Musiklebens von 1570—1650*, Vierteljahrsschrift für Musikwissenschaft, V, No. 4 [1889], p. 558). (Vogel's study, in two parts, is in Nos. 3 and 4 of the 1889 volume: respectively, pp. [396]—442 and pp. [509]—568; it will be cited hereinafter simply as Vogel, *Gagliano*, followed by the appropriate page number.)

[50] Ibid.

[51] See FORTUNE, letter to the Editor, in The Music Review, XV, No. 1 (1954), p. 88. For further information Fortune's article on Rasi in *Die Musik in Geschichte und Gegenwart* (Kassel, Bärenreiter, XI [1963], cols. 4—6), together with its bibliography, is recommended.

[52] Covering just the twelve-month period roughly bisected by the date of Langosco's letter (i.e. August 1607—July 1608), ten letters from Peri have been published from originals in the Archivio Gonzaga (in DAVARI, pp. 14—15, 17, 103—106; ADEMOLLO, pp. 58—59, 64—65; and Angelo SOLERTI, *Musica, ballo e drammatica alla corte medicea dal 1600 al 1637*, Firenze 1905, R. Bemporad & Figlio, p. 39, n. 1).

[53] GAGLIANO, pp. [v]—[vi] (reprinted in VOGEL, *Gagliano*, p. 559).

portrayed the characters of his opera at its première; and historians have managed to attribute to those three singers no less than four of the six roles in question (leaving unattributed only the roles of Ovid — the prologue — and Venus). Of the four attributions, however, two are unwarranted and almost certainly incorrect; they must be the first topic of our enforced digression.

Concerning Caterina Martinelli, Gagliano's preface records only that she gave an effective rendition of the song *Chi da lacci d'Amor*[54]. Music historians who have occasion to refer to this passage of Rinuccini's text unfailingly mention that it belongs to the role of Cupid (*Amore*)[55]; and those who refer to Martinelli's connection with Gagliano's setting customarily specify, accordingly, that she sang the part of Cupid[56]: which is to say that on these points the historians have consistently written in contradiction to the evidence (indeed, with never so much as a remark to indicate why they do so). In Gagliano's score, a recitative for Venus beginning »Vanne pur lieto« — quite properly introduced by the character cue »Venere« — is directly followed, with no new character cue, by the aria *Chi da lacci d'Amor*[57]: that is, the single cue, »Venere«, evidently applies not only to the recitative but also to the ensuing aria. It is true that an inattentive reader might be misled by a different sort of visual cue shown in this passage: for throughout the score fresh character cues are accompanied by fresh clefs; and a new clef does appear on the staff devoted to the vocal line, midway through a system, as *Chi da lacci d'Amor* is about to begin (or, more accurately, the soprano clef already in force is there reiterated). Like Venus, Cupid is a soprano, so it might be possible at first glance to imagine that this fresh soprano clef, at the close of Venus' recitative, heralds a vocal entry for Cupid. (In that case, of course, one would have to suppose that the appropriate character cue was omitted through an oversight; since errors are not lacking elsewhere in the print, this one might in itself seem plausible.) Actually, as happens elsewhere in Gagliano's score[58] and quite commonly in later ones, the clef in this instance is reiterated simply in conjunction with the appearance of a new key signature. That nothing more is involved — that is, no new entry for Cupid — ought in fact to be perfectly clear, since the first note following the new soprano clef corresponds to the last syllable of Venus' recitative: »[... ritor]no«.

The same confusion, though, can arise just where it ought most easily to be

---

[54] GAGLIANO, p. [v] (reprinted in VOGEL, *Gagliano*, p. 558).

[55] Cf. e.g. VOGEL, *Gagliano*, p. 439, and William V. PORTER, *Peri and Corsi's Dafne: Some New Discoveries and Observations*, Journal of the American Musicological Society, XVIII, No. 2 (1965), pp. 178, 179.

[56] Cf. e.g. ADEMOLLO, p. 41, and VOGEL, *Gagliano*, p. 426, n. 2.

[57] GAGLIANO, pp. 18—19.

[58] Ibid., pp. 31, 45, 49.

eliminated: in an examination of the original edition of Rinuccini's libretto. In that first printing the recitative *Vanne pur lieto* and the ensuing *Chi da lacci d'Amor* a r e furnished with separate character cues; the two cues, however, are identica — in each instance, »Ven.«[59]. But if all those lines were to be sung by Venus, why reiterate her cue? I imagine, precisely to signal the demarcation between recitative and aria. (Not, of course, to signal it as a suggestion to composers, for the text had been set to music some years before it was printed[60];

---

[59] *La Dafne d'Ottavio R i n v c c i n i rappresentata alla Sereniss. Gran Dvchessa di Toscana dal Signor Iacopo Corsi*, Firenze 1600, Giorgio Marescotti, pp. [8], [9].

[60] Peri's preface to his *Euridice* recounts that Rinuccini and Iacopo Corsi had invited him in 1594 to suggest or devise a musical idiom suitable for setting the *Dafne* text (*Le mvsiche di Iacopo P e r i nobil fiorentino sopra l'Euridice del Sig. Ottavio Rinuccini rappresentate nello sponsalizio della Cristianissima Maria Medici Regina di Francia e di Navarra*, Firenze 1600 [1601], Giorgio Marescotti, p. [v], reprinted in Angelo SOLERTI [ed.], *Le origini del melodramma: Testimonianze dei contemporanei*, Torino 1903, Fratelli Bocca, p. 45); GAGLIANO, p. [v] (reprinted in VOGEL, *Gagliano*, pp. 558—559) reports that the product, a setting by Peri and Corsi, received its première in Carnival of 1597; PERI, p. [vi] (reprinted in Solerti, *Origini*, p. 48) adds that the work was presented at Carnival time for three consecutive years. It now is generally assumed that problems connected with these early specifications are clarified in Oscar G. SONNECK's often cited article »*Dafne«, the First Opera: A Chronological Study* (Sammelbände der Internationalen Musikgesellschaft, XV [1913—1914], pp. 102—110). Actually, I believe, some of the problems Sonneck raised were imaginary; more to the point, some of his solutions were careless: most notably, those based on his inconsistent recourse to data regarding the Florentine calendar. In order to minimize what he conceived to be a problem — the long interval between Peri's »1594« and Gagliano's »1597« — Sonneck (pp. 106, 107) pointed out that according to the tradition still followed in Florence in that period, »1594« included the first months of what we should call 1595. That point (an unnecessary one, since Sonneck rightly understood that Peri's »1594« was in no case meant to be a performance date) would not have served Sonneck's purpose — to narrow the gap between »1594« and »1597« — had Sonneck applied the same bit of lore to both dates. Accordingly, he did not apply it to Gagliano's »Carnouale dell'anno 1597«, although for several obvious reasons it is more relevant in that connection. (For one thing, only six days of Carnival fall in December; the bulk of it belongs to what we should call the new year.) Owing to this quite arbitrary omission Sonneck's conclusion had to be, and was, that the première took place in 1597 (i.e. in the early months of the year to which we assign that number) and that the further performances specified in Peri's »tre Anni continui« were given in Carnival of 1597/8 and early in 1599 (Sonneck, pp. 107—108). That Sonneck's article has done more to confuse than to clarify the matter is evident in PORTER, pp. [170]—172, which purports to repeat Sonneck's findings but actually departs significantly, albeit unwittingly, from them: Porter gives the date of the première as 1598, even though he concludes the series of Carnival performances with those of 1599. Although — or, rather, because — Porter's account is not an accurate résumé of Sonneck's, it probably dates the première correctly: adding a third consecutive Carnival to Porter's two (in accordance with Peri's indication), we may presume that the earliest performances took place in the Carnivals of 1597/8, 1598/9, and 1599/1600 — i.e. most likely in the first months of 1598, 1599, and 1600. I note that a similar suggestion is offered in Alfred LOEWENBERG, *Annals of Opera, 1597—1940*, 2nd ed. rev., Genève 1955, Societas Bibliographica, I, col. 2; but Loewenberg, compounding a small error derived from Sonneck's article (p. 106), gave as his basis the information that in Florence, during the period in question, »the Julian Calendar was still in force by which the new year began on 1 March«. In effect, this is triply erroneous. At no time in its history had the Julian calendar

rather, to apprise the audience that a formal song would begin at the words
»Chi da lacci d'Amor«.) To be sure, character cues in libretti are most often
used to mark the first words of characters just previously silent; and the thought
expressed in *Chi da lacci d'Amor* could as appropriately be uttered by Cupid
as by Venus. Consequently Rinuccini's seemingly redundant repetition of the
cue »Ven.«, although not a unique case, can easily be mistaken for a printer's
error — especially if the music is not at hand to suggest a different interpretation. Perhaps that is why Gaetano Poggiali, when he produced the first modern
edition of Rinuccini's text, departed from the author's indication and assigned
Chi da lacci d'Amor to Cupid[61]. But it seems entirely improbable that Rinuccini's printer was at fault, for when a second printing appeared (and it is the
only other print of the libretto issued in the poet's lifetime) it was, in this
regard, identical to the original edition[62].

Angelo Solerti, who was acquainted with the early sources, may nevertheless
have been guided by Poggiali's unexplained revision; for, also without explanation or comment, his own edition of the text presents *Chi da lacci d'Amor* as a
speech of Cupid's[63]. This is especially disappointing since Solerti had seen a
further document — a copy of Gagliano's printed score containing manuscript
additions in an evidently contemporary hand[64] — that might easily have helped
to put matters right. The handwritten annotations include a good many stage
directions, and among them is an exit cue for Cupid five verses before the start

---

begun its year on any day other than 1st January; the Julian calendar was not used in
Florence during any year ever mentioned in connection with *Dafne*; and, both before and
after abandonment of the Julian calendar (which, in short, is totally irrelevant in this
context), the Florentine practice was to begin the civil year on 25th March. But Loewenberg himself seems not to have attached much importance to his own suggestion: Sonneck's
date, 1597, is the one he ultimately assigned to the *Dafne* première (Loewenberg, col. 1;
and, implicitly, in the title of his book).

[61] Gaetano POGGIALI (ed.), *Drammi musicali di Ottavio Rinuccini ora per la prima volta
insieme raccolti, ed accuratamente ripubblicati*, Livorno 1802, Tommaso Masi e Compagno,
p. 10. Poggiali's publication was to have included a preface; in it, no doubt, his reason for
departing from the original character cue would have been explained. But although Poggiali's preface is listed in his table of contents, the page on which it is there said to be,
or to begin, is not present in any known copy of the volume (see Luigi CLASIO's commentary in P. Leopoldo RICASOLI [ed.], *La Dafne di Ottavio Rinuccini nuovamente stampata*,
Firenze 1810, Stamperia di Borgognissanti, p. 61; and SOLERTI, *Albori*, II, pp. ix and 98).
It may be that Poggiali's alteration consequently has never been recognized as such.

[62] *La Dafne d'Ottavio Rinvccini rappresentata al Sereniss. Duca di Parma dalla Serenissima
Grandvchessa di Toscana*, Firenze 1604, Cristofano Marescotti, pp. [8], [9]; since nothing
on these pages needed revision they in fact were printed — like most pages of the second
edition — from the original plates (see CLASIO in RICASOLI, p. 46; and SOLERTI, *Albori*, I,
p. 66, and II, pp. vi—vii).

[63] SOLERTI, *Albori*, II, p. 84. Poggiali's work in fact is among those Solerti consulted (ibid.,
p. ix).

[64] See ibid., p. xi; p. [77], n. 1; and pp. [77]—98 passim.

of *Chi da lacci d'Amor*[65]. (The exact moment for obeying the exit instruction is shown as clearly as possible by a line drawn from that instruction [»Amore si parta«] to the note being sung at that moment by Venus.) Had the cue not been written, Cupid's exit at that point still would seem called for, inasmuch as he is Venus' obedient son: for she begins her aforementioned recitative precisely by ordering him to leave her for a while alone[66]. Left to herself, then, Venus obviously is the one that must sing *Chi da lacci d'Amor*.

Nor is there any contrary suggestion in other early sources. Solerti reported just one contemporary manuscript of Rinuccini's text, which he found »altogether devoid of special interest [*affatto inconcludente*]«[67]; I have seen for myself that the relevant character cues in it are identical to those in the early prints[68]. And, in the single manuscript copy in which it is known, the setting of *Chi da lacci d'Amor* attributed to Peri carries no indication at all of the role to which it belongs[69]. In short, the only conclusion that can reasonably be drawn from the evidence is that the song belongs, and always has belonged, to the role of Venus. In Gagliano's opera, then, Caterina Martinelli, who sang *Chi da lacci d'Amor*, must have portrayed Venus; accordingly — since Venus and Cupid appear together and so cannot be impersonated by one performer — Cupid must have been played not by Martinelli but by some other singer, as yet unidentified.

I acknowledge, dear reader, that the four preceding paragraphs have somewhat the character of a sledge hammer manufactured expressly to slay a mosquito; but since the information at issue has been consistently misrepresented for a hundred and seventy years[70], let us admit that the mosquito was an abnormally robust one.

Another ephemera that has cheated death is the notion that Martinelli, in addition to her alleged role of Cupid, sang that of Daphne in Gagliano's work. This

---

[65] Firenze, Biblioteca Nazionale: Fondo Magliabechi, Mus. ant. 36, p. 19. SOLERTI (*Albori*, II, p. 84) reported the exit cue (slightly misread) but incorrectly placed it a f t e r the ottava rima *Chi da lacci d'Amor*.

[66] »Vanne pur lieto, ò figlio / ... / Per queste selue intanto / Farò dolce soggiorno« — RINUCCINI, *Dafne*, 1601 and 1604, pp. [8]—[9]; GAGLIANO, pp. 18—19; cf. SOLERTI, *Albori*, II, pp. 83—84.

[67] SOLERTI, *Albori*, II, p. vi.

[68] Firenze, Biblioteca Nazionale: MS. Magliabechi VII.562, f. 5v.

[69] Ibid.: MS. Magliabechi XIX.66, f. 154r—154v. The manuscript also omits to name the composer; nevertheless, Federico GHISI, who identified the piece as a fragment of the Peri-Corsi *Dafne*, attributed it to Peri (Ghisi, *Alle fonti della monodia*, Milano 1940, F.lli Bocca, pp. 12, 22). Ghisi did not explain his attribution, nor has anyone else brought evidence to support it (or to refute it). Presumably worth noting, then, is a letter in which Peri did mention having set *Chi da lacci d'Amor* to music (see his letter of 23rd April 1608, published in DAVARI, pp. 105—106); but let us note also how far this is from guaranteeing that the piece in the Florentine manuscript is Peri's work.

[70] I know of only one (all but invisible) exception; it occurs, I am glad to say, in Stuart REINER, »*Vi sono molt'altre mezz'Arie* ...«, in *Studies in Music History: Essays for Oliver Strunk*, ed. Harold Powers, Princeton 1968, Princeton University Press, p. 252, n. 23.

idea was first advanced by Ademollo, explicitly as a conjecture[71], but it quickly achieved the status of ostensible fact in other scholars' writings[72] and has been thriving nicely ever since in standard reference works[73]. A document does indeed exist which can be — and was — erroneously construed to support Ademollo's guess; I shall mention it a bit later, in what I consider to be its proper context. Here, it may suffice to review Ademollo's primary assumptions: i.e. that Gagliano would not have neglected to name in his preface the performer who had sung the title role in his opera; and that since Martinelli was the only woman he did name (albeit in another connection), she must have sung that role[74]. Actually, the facts warrant an exactly opposite interpretation: if Martinelli truly had sung two principal roles in his opera, Gagliano, who clearly was disposed to praise her, would hardly have neglected to cite that proof of her versatility. What Ademollo may have failed to consider is that when a composer selected names to mention in a preface he was less likely to be influenced by the prominence of a singer's role than by the prominence of the singer, or of the singer's patron: for the well known performer and the powerful patron (who, of course, generally were associated with one another) could most effectively demand such puffs; besides, it was precisely by flaunting their names that the composer himself reaped his greatest share of reflected glory. (Thus Peri, although he named several singers in the preface to his *Euridice,* omitted the one who, in t h a t work, had performed the title role; but he made a point of mentioning the Medici favorite Vittoria Archilei, who had had no part at all in his opera.)[75] Martinelli, a Gonzaga protégée, probably would have been named in Gagliano's preface no matter what role she had played; but even if Gagliano

---

[71] ADEMOLLO, pp. 41—42.

[72] E.g. in VOGEL, *Gagliano,* pp. 426, 430.

[73] E.g. in C. STAINER and Alfred LOEWENBERG, *Gagliano, Marco da (Zenobi),* in *Grove's Dictionary of Music and Musicians,* 5th ed., London 1954, Macmillan & Co., III, p. 542.

[74] As Rinuccini's libretto nowhere requires Cupid and Daphne to appear together, there was nothing in it to rule out Ademollo's conjecture; nor does any such conflict arise from our attributing to Martinelli the part of Venus (who, like Cupid, is never seen with Daphne).

[75] PERI, pp. [v]—[vi] (reprinted in SOLERTI, *Origini,* pp. 47—48). It has been asserted, on the basis of this passage, that Archilei »sang the role of Eurydice at the first performance« (Oliver STRUNK [ed.], *Source Readings in Music History from Classical Antiquity through the Romantic Era,* New York 1950, W. W. Norton & Company, p. 371, n. 5); but Peri offered no such indication. (The passage in fact does not concern *Euridice* at all; it refers to Archilei's connection — not very clearly specified at that — with the first samples of Peri's music for *Dafne.*) What Peri's preface does report about the role of Eurydice is that it was one of the parts taken, at the première, by protégés of Giulio Caccini (Peri, p. [vi], reprinted in Solerti, *Origini,* pp. 48—49; cf. Strunk, p. 376); and, from an assortment of evidence, Claude V. PALISCA has cogently inferred that it probably was Caccini's sister-in-law who played Eurydice on that occasion, as she apparently did in a later production (Palisca, *The First Performance of »Euridice«,* in *Queens College Department of Music Twenty-Fifth Anniversary Festschrift,* ed. Albert Mell, New York 1964, Queens College Press, pp. 10—11, 17—18).

had meant to hand out credit solely on the basis of conspicuous service he still might have singled out the performer of Venus, a longer and vocalistically showier role than Daphne. All in all, there is no reason to attribute to Martinelli any part in *Dafne* other than the one Gagliano indicated she had played.

Having resolved these misunderstandings, we at last are in a position accurately to summarize the credits in Gagliano's preface, and to add to this purged account of them such conjectures of our own as may seem appropriate. I already have mentioned that Gagliano named Francesco Rasi in connection with the role of Apollo; and, as we have now seen, he commended Caterina Martinelli for her portrayal of Venus; in addition, he specified that Antonio Brandi (whose prized services had finally been lent, after initial refusals, by the Grand Duke of Tuscany) had played the messenger Thirsis[76]. This leaves a further three roles unaccounted-for. The soprano role of Cupid, far from being suited to Caterina Martinelli, almost certainly was assigned to a young boy, for such was the standard practice in casting that ubiquitous part[77]; this in fact may have something to do with Gagliano's failure to name the performer (who most likely was too young to have attained any wide reputation)[78]. Ovid, the prologue, is a tenor role; in this instance Gagliano may have omitted the performer's name in deference to the customary dictates of modesty, for I think it

---

[76] GAGLIANO, p. [vii] (reprinted in VOGEL, *Gagliano*, p. 561).

[77] An exception to this custom seems implicit in one account of the annotated *Dafne* score mentioned earlier (n. 65, above). The annotations in that score include the names of some performers, and VOGEL (*Gagliano*, p. 438) reported that the role of Cupid is there assigned to »Tonina« (i.e. »little Antonia«); according to Vogel's résumé the same singer and another called »Cecchina« (whom, on the basis of this nickname, Vogel identified as Francesca Caccini) played two of the nymphs in the chorus. (In the same résumé Vogel conjecturally added to »Tonina«'s assignment the role of Daphne, which the annotations leave unattributed; he gave no explanation for his guess, but his reasoning may be inferred from what has been said above regarding Cupid and Daphne as supposed halves of a dual role.) SOLERTI's account of the same score, however, shows these names as »Tonino« and »Cecchino« (*Albori*, II, pp. [77]—98 passim): i.e. »little Antonio« and »little Francesco«. In this respect I am able to verify Solerti's readings (and thus to confirm that Cupid in this instance too was played by a boy). »Cecchino« and »Cecc.o« appear in the annotations a total of eight times (on pp. 2, 4, 21, 42, 47, and 54 of the score); »Tonino« and »Ton.o«, a total of seven times (ibid., pp. 2, 4, 15, 42): in every case the ending is masculine. (It is well to add that the singers named in the annotations for the roles of Apollo and Venus are not the ones mentioned in Gagliano's preface: hence it is clear that these annotations were not made in connection with the première. The relevant performance probably was that given in Florence, at the home of Don Giovanni de' Medici, on 9th February 1611, on the occasion of a visit paid by Ferdinando Gonzaga; this performance is recorded in the well known diary of Cesare Tinghi: in SOLERTI, *Musica, ballo*, pp. 60—61.)

[78] In fact, a letter dated 21st January 1608 reports that a little boy had been sent to Mantua from Florence several days earlier, in the company of »Messer Santi« (presumably Santi Orlandi, sometime *maestro di cappella* of Ferdinando Gonzaga): see the letter from Pandolfo Stufa quoted in DAVARI, p. 14, n. 2.

quite possible that he had sung the part himself[79]. Finally, excluding the unlikely chance that our Angela had been brought to Mantua merely to portray one of the nymphs in the chorus, we arrive, by elimination, at the part she must have played in *Dafne* if she appeared in it at all: that is, the title role.

If she appeared in it at all: I add the conditional clause advisedly, for the question is complicated by the fact that another musical stage work was performed in Mantua in the same season. Moreover, it is impossible to determine the relevance of this other work to our story; for what we know about it is negligible, and what we can reasonably guess is, I think, less than some estimable scholars have imagined. A letter from Iacopo Peri to Ferdinando Gonzaga, dated 8th April 1608, offers congratulations on the success of »the two entertainments acted in music, to the applause of all Mantua — especially, *Dafne* [*le due feste recitate in musica con plauso di tutta Mantova, e in particolare la Dafne*]«[80]. What was the title, or the subject, of the other entertainment? Who was its librettist, and who its composer? Neither Peri's letter nor any other document now known answers these questions. Ademollo surmised that the librettist may have been Ferdinando Gonzaga himself[81]; but from the evidence (or, more accurately, from the scarcity of evidence) this seems altogether improbable. Had Gonzaga been the author, Peri — and not only Peri — would surely have had what we may kindly call the generosity to pay the Prince a compliment or two on his achievement; in other instances, there is no shortage of documentation to illustrate this unsurprising kind of thoughtfulness. Peri's letter, instead, leaves us guessing exactly because it hurries past the work in question to »especially, *Dafne*«[82].

---

[79] No modern account reports that Gagliano was a singer; but a suggestion to that effect can be found in the diary of Cesare Tinghi, in an entry of 15th January 1621: »S.A. ... si trattenne a sentire cantare di musica dalla Cecchina, dalla Settimia sua sorella venuta da Lucca, dalla Arcangiola et *dal maestro di cappella*« (i.e. Gagliano) — published in SOLERTI, *Musica, ballo*, p. 158; italics mine.

[80] Published in DAVARI, p. 14.

[81] ADEMOLLO, p. 59 and p. 54, n. 1.

[82] This is not to suggest that Ademollo's guess was haphazard. It was based on a letter of 23rd July 1607 in which Gagliano, addressing Gonzaga, mentioned having delivered »the choruses of Your Excellency's play [*i cori della Commedia di V.E.*].«. But this phrase may signify merely that Gonzaga was sponsoring the play, not necessarily that he had written it; the same is true of other phrases, in other documents, that have been adduced to show Gonzaga's multiple artistic talents (e.g. in ADEMOLLO, p. 65, regarding another letter from Gagliano; and in Domenico DE' PAOLI, *Claudio Monteverdi*, Milano 1945, Ulrico Hoepli, p. 106, interpreting — but without citation — documents shown in SOLERTI, *Musica, ballo*, p. 38). I do not deny that Gonzaga did write at least one play, for that much is clear from Monteverdi's letter of 11th February 1615 (published in MALIPIERO, *Claudio Monteverdi*, p. 157). I would suggest, though, that the play for which Gagliano sent choruses to him in July of 1607 may easily have been the *Giudizio di Paride* of Michelangelo Buonarroti the Younger: Gonzaga had commissioned that work and, until August of 1607, expected to have it performed in Mantua. His plan had to be changed when the Medici family, Buonar-

In a more elaborate attempt to decipher Peri's allusion, Solerti cited a letter Gagliano had written in December 1607, to the same Ferdinando Gonzaga (Solerti, following an indication of Vogel's, named Francesco Gonzaga as the addressee, but I believe Vogel's assertion was based on a misunderstanding[83]). Gagliano, preparing to come to Mantua, offered to bring along a »favoletta per recitar cantando« — not better identified — which, he said, could be got ready for performance in short order. Vogel, the first to publish this letter in its entirety[84], had assumed it referred to *Dafne*[85]; Solerti proposed, instead, that the *favoletta* must have been some libretto of Gabriello Chiabrera's — thus, our »other« entertainment — for according to Solerti the term »favoletta da recitar cantando« was virtually a Chiabrera trade-mark[86]. But this term (whether

---

roti's (and Gagliano's) regular patrons, laid claim to the work; Buonarroti explained this development — and in effect withdrew from Gonzaga's commission — in a letter dated 31st July 1607 (published in SOLERTI, *Albori*, I, pp. 75—76); and the play was given the following year in Florence, on 25th October (see SOLERTI, *Musica, ballo*, pp. 46—47, 55—56) and again on 19th November (ibid., p. 54; Solerti's n. 1 is confused: he may have misread a »19« as »17« in the date of the auxiliary document cited there). Apart from the musical *intermedii* with which Buonarroti's play came to be performed, the contemporary edition of the text shows that each of its five acts closed with (or was followed by) a formal »CORO« for nymphs, shepherds, or cupids (*Il givdizio di Paride favola del S. Michelagnolo B v o n a r - r o t i. rappresentata nelle felicissime nozze del Sereniss. Cosimo Medici Principe di Toscana e della Seren. Principessa Maria Maddalena Arciduchessa di Austria*, Firenze 1608, Sermartelli, pp. 13—14, 29—30, 40—41, 55—56, 63).

[83] VOGEL (*Gagliano*, p. 550, n. 1) named Francesco Gonzaga as the addressee of five of Gagliano's letters; all five, though, probably were written to Francesco's brother Ferdinando. Vogel apparently reasoned from the honorific titles used in most of Gagliano's letters, for addressees not otherwise identified: thus he recognized that Ferdinando must have been the recipient addressed as »Illustrissimo et Reverendissimo« in twenty letters (ibid., p. 550, n. 1, and pp. 552—557, 562—564), for that form of address was appropriate to Ferdinando's station as a cardinal. But those letters all were written after 24th December 1607 — the date on which Ferdinando received the announcement of his cardinalate (see DAVARI, p. 14) — whereas the five letters here in question all were written before that date: in these five, the form of address is »Illustrissimo et Eccellentissimo«, which then suited Prince Ferdinando as properly as Prince Francesco. The content of the five early letters repeatedly suggests they were written to Ferdinando; and if this were not so, it still would be odd to think (as Vogel must have thought) that Francesco was Gagliano's sole patron in Mantua until December of 1607 but never was in touch with him thereafter: the likelihood instead is that Francesco never was directly a patron of Gagliano's at all.

[84] VOGEL, *Gagliano*, p. 552: letter of 3rd December 1607.

[85] Ibid., p. 425. DAVARI (p. 14, n. 3) already had quoted the relevant portion of Gagliano's letter, but had not declared any opinion as to the identity of the »favoletta«; from the context in which he placed the quotation, however, it seems probable that he, too, assumed it concerned *Dafne*.

[86] Angelo SOLERTI, *Le »favolette da recitarsi cantando« di Gabriello Chiabrera*, Giornale storico e letterario della Liguria, IV, Nos. 7—9 (1903), p. 231. Solerti somewhat overstated his case; in Chiabrera's known writings, the closest counterpart of Gagliano's phrase is »Favolette . . . da rappresentarsi cantando«, the collective title of some works published in 1615 (see Solerti, *Le »favolette . . .«*, p. 229). Comparable locutions — »favolette per doversi rappresentare cantando«, »favoletta da cantarsi in su le scene« — do appear in letters

with »da« or with »per«) simply means »a little story to be acted out in song«[87]; and Solerti's premise that the term belonged to Chiabrera is, I should say, easily overruled by one of Chiabrera's own statements: »Ottavio Rinuccini ... fu il primiero che in sulla scena conducesse *a rappresentarsi favole cantate*, ... e trasse altri a seguire i suoi trovamenti«[88] (»Ottavio Rinuccini ... was the first man that caused sung stories to be acted on the stage; ... and he led others to imitate his discoveries«). Certainly, Gagliano was expecting material from Rinuccini at the very time he proposed to bring Ferdinando Gonzaga a »favoletta«: eight days later, Rinuccini confessed to Gonzaga that his own tardiness in completing that material was delaying Gagliano's trip[89]. (In this connection it should be recalled that although the libretto of *Dafne* dates back to the 1590's,[90] Rinuccini made alterations and additions for the 1608 production, amounting to more than 150 new verses[91].) Solerti's assumption, then, seems as farfetched as Vogel's seems natural: the chances are that Gagliano's letter did concern *Dafne,* and can tell us nothing about the mysterious other entertainment[92].

Since we cannot identify that other entertainment (as we see, even its authorship remains hidden) we have no direct means of gauging the possibility that it was the one in which our Angela participated. Lacking direct evidence, we may

---

Chiabrera wrote before 1615 (quoted ibid., pp. 232—233); so it is safe to say (as, perhaps, Solerti ought simply to have said) that Chiabrera liked to call his libretti »favolette«. That alone might suggest a connection with Gagliano's »favoletta«, especially since Solerti tells us that Chiabrera's use of the word can be traced back as far as 1595 (ibid., p. 229, n. 2); but Solerti's alleged source for this claim — Achille Neri, *Gabriello Chiabrera e la corte di Mantova,* Giornale storico della letteratura italiana, VII, Fasc. 21 (1886), pp. 332—333 — does not support it. Neri neither quotes nor mentions any use of the word prior to its appearance in a letter of Chiabrera's dated 28th September 1608 (published ibid., p. 323) — i.e. nearly ten months l a t e r than Gagliano's offer of a »favoletta« for use in Mantua (cf. n. 84, above).

[87] I am aware that some colleagues are accustomed to translate the root word, »favola«, with its most familiar cognate, »fable«; this can be misleading, since the best known definition of »fable« will not fit most »favole«. Of the several potential meanings of »favola«, the one usually applicable to Renaissance texts can be expressed most clearly as »story«, or »tale«.

[88] Gabriello Chiabrera, eulogy on Ottavio Rinuccini, published by »Olimpio Fenicio« in *Alcune poesie di Gabriele Chiabrera non mai prima d'ora pubblicate,* Genova 1794, Caffarelli, p. 92. (Italics shown in the quotation are mine.)

[89] Rinuccini, letter of 11th December 1607 (quoted in Davari, p. 15, continuing n. 3 of p. 14).

[90] See n. 60, above.

[91] These modifications of the earlier, 445-line text are shown in Solerti, *Albori,* II, pp. 76—97 passim.

[92] Gagliano (pp. [v]—[vi], reprinted in Vogel, *Gagliano,* pp. 558—559) in fact did apply the term »favola« to *Dafne,* as well as to *Euridice* and *Arianna,* all three of which of course were written »to be acted out in song«. The diminutive »favoletta«, in Gagliano's letter as in Chiabrera's usage, seems intended not as a refinement of technical terminology but simply as a way of announcing that the *favole* in question were short ones — or, quite possibly, as an expression of the ostensible modesty with which those *favole* were being proffered.

pardonably look about for circumstantial clues. One such clue does seem to present itself, and to point toward Angela's having appeared in this other work — at least, inasmuch as it points away from Gagliano's opera and its title role: I am referring to the accepted dating of the première of *Dafne*. We have seen that Angela came to Mantua only toward the end of December 1607; and *Dafne* is universally acknowledged to have been presented sometime in January 1608;[93] in the few weeks (at most) that intervened, how could Angela have learned, or been expected to learn, so central a role as the one she must have played if she appeared in that opera? Besides, Langosco's letter reporting the success of Angela's performance was written on 18th February: a bit late, we might think, if that performance had taken place in January; and if it took place later than January, we presumably ought to infer that it had nothing to do with *Dafne* but must have been part of the elusive »other« work. This reasoning, though, would be ill founded. First of all the title role of *Dafne*, although obviously essential to the plot, is neither long nor difficult: Daphne appears just once in the work, and all her utterances (amounting to thirty lines of poetry) are shown on just seven pages of the fifty-five-page score[94]; the part involves no ensembles; nor does it entail any coloratura singing (in fact, Daphne's music never departs from a one-note-per-syllable style of declamation)[95]; and the vocal line rarely exceeds the compass $e'-d''$ (for a maximum range of $d'-f''$). Briefly, there seems no reason why the role could not be learned in relatively little time.

Moreover, the time available must have been more generous than has been suggested above; for the accepted dating of the *Dafne* première is thoroughly unsound. The error again has to do with Caterina Martinelli, whose career is

---

[93] »Universally« is meant to cover all the ground any reader might find relevant, whence a comprehensive listing of citations is as unnecessary as it would be impractical. Allowing that even what is called universal often has exceptions, it might be more appropriate to list these; but the only one I know in this connection derives from an unfortunate slip in the work of an estimable scholar: »*Dafne*, performed at Mantua in 1607 and published in 1608«. For the rest, January 1608 seems to be unanimously accepted as the date of the première.

[94] GAGLIANO, pp. 22—23, 25—29.

[95] Some readers may suppose it is not possible to determine from the score how much coloratura actually was used in performance, for various documents of the period (most prominently, Giulio Caccini's well known preface to his *Nuove musiche* of 1602) indicate that singers were accustomed to improvise embellishments at discretion. Like Caccini, however, Gagliano opposed this practice, and in his preface to *Dafne* he admonished: »Where the story does not require it let all ornamentation be quite eschewed [*doue la fauola non lo ricerca, lascisi del tutto ogni ornamento*]« (GAGLIANO, p. [v]; cf. VOGEL, *Gagliano*, p. 558). His preface cites examples of the places in his opera that do call for ornamented singing (ibid.); examining those pieces (none of which belongs to the title role), one finds that the composer has in fact written out their ornamentation. Gagliano himself came to Mantua from Florence in time to attend — and probably to superintend — rehearsals (ibid., and DAVARI, p. 14, n. 3); so it can be assumed that his singers all sang their parts as he wished them sung, and as we find them written.

now most often recalled in connection with its untimely end — untimely not only because she died, full of promise, at the age of seventeen, but also because her death occurred very shortly before she was to have performed the title role of Monteverdi's *Arianna,* for which she had been preparing under the composer's guidance[96]. Contemplating some details of this catastrophe, Davari reasoned as follows: Martinelli was known to be seriously ill as early as 2nd February 1608,[97] and her illness must have worsened during the ensuing weeks, since she died on 9th March[98]; hence she cannot have made her appearance in *Dafne* any later than the end of January — during which month, accordingly, that opera must have had its première[99]. Davari's conclusion has always been accepted, although its basis is decisively refuted by a document Ademollo published three years later. The document, a letter reporting Martinelli's death, makes it quite clear that she had appeared on the stage sometime around the middle of February 1608; for it refers to the acclaim she had earned »in the performances she gave at the end of Carnival [*nelle ationi che fece nell'ultimo di Carnevale*]«[100], and Carnival in 1608 ended on 19th February[101].

The aforementioned document, incidentally, is the one Ademollo used to substantiate (as he thought) his thesis that Martinelli played more than one role in *Dafne*: for the letter does mention her »performances«. That plural, however, has an entirely different significance, as we learn from a further document, previously unpublished. This is a dispatch from Mantua, dated 8th March 1608 (a day before the supposed date of Martinelli's death):

---

[96] See VOGEL, *Claudio Monteverdi*, p. 346. (Vogel mistakenly gives Martinelli's age at her death as eighteen; actually, she died »in her eighteenth year«: see n. 98, below.)

[97] A letter of that date from Ferdinando Gonzaga (quoted in DAVARI, p. 14, n. 1) contains the earliest known report of Martinelli's illness.

[98] Her epitaph, formerly to be seen in Mantua's Carmelite church (long ago abolished), was first published in Francesco Saverio QUADRIO, *Della storia e della ragione d'ogni poesia,* III², Milano 1744, Francesco Agnelli, p. 534. Quadrio's quotation ends: »Obiit adolescentiae suae anno XVIII., die VIIII. Martii. M. DC. VIII.«.

[99] DAVARI, p. 16.

[100] Letter from Annibale Chieppio dated 9th March 1608, as published in ADEMOLLO, p. 42, n. 1. On the same page Ademollo's main text quotes the phrase differently (». . . nell'ultimo carnevale«), making it seem to refer only to »the recent Carnival«, rather than to »the end of Carnival«: perhaps this is one reason no-one has ever noticed that the document proves Martinelli was active after January. (Ademollo himself cannot have noticed it; for, like everyone else, he assigned the *Dafne* performance to January: ibid., p. 53.) Since the tiny difference between Ademollo's two quotations obviously makes more than a tiny difference to the history involved, I have been to see the document itself (Archivio Gonzaga, busta 2711); the crucial »di« is indeed present, although I find that in other respects neither of Ademollo's versions is faithful to the original, which reads: »nelle attioni che fece al-l'ultimo di Carneuale«. (Of Ademollo's two transcriptions, the less accurate one may have derived from CANAL, p. 85, where the letter was first reported and misquoted.)

[101] Other writers have reported that this Carnival ended on 17th February (e.g. SOLERTI, in *Albori,* I, p. 91); a traditional tendency to emphasize Carnival Sunday — the antepenultimate day of the season — may be responsible for their error.

»La Romanina«[102], an extraordinary singer, has died of smallpox; she was buried yesterday evening, with some pomp, in the Carmelite church. This loss is deplored by everyone in the entire city, on account of her having been so exceptionally gifted, and on account of the ineffable pleasure she gave [us] in the two plays performed during the recent Carnival. His Highness must be dismayed about her dying at the very time of these nuptials, considering the [resultant] disruption of the new and regal plays that are being prepared (in one of which she impersonated Ariadne wonderfully well); and these overseers are quite badly disconcerted. Another girl already has arrived, sent from Florence, but I understand she will not do[103], and negotiations are afoot to obtain a different one who is in the service of His Lordship Cardinal Montalto[105]; but she cannot possibly prepare in time, as the moment for the nuptials here is drawing very close.

La Romanina cantatrice rara è morta delle Varole, et hieri sera fù sepolta nel Carmine con qualche honoreuolezza; La perdità [sic] è dispiacciuta uniuersalmente à tutta la Città, per esser [stata] così singo*larmente* uertuosa, et per la indicibile sodisfattione, ch'ella diede nelle due Comedie recitate il Carneuale prossimo passato; S. Alt. ne sentirà dispiacere, per esser mancata nella congiuntura di q*ueste* nozze per lo sconcerto delle nuoue, et Regali Comedie, che si preparano, in una delle quali ella rappresentaua Ariana mirabil*mente*, et q*uesti* sopraintendenti sono in grandissima confusione; Di già n'è uenuta un'altra mandata da Fiorenza, ma intendo, che non riesce; Et si tratta, di farne uenir' un'altra, che hà il sig.r Card.le Montalto; ma non potrà esser' in tempo all'ordine, stringendosi assai il tempo delle nozze quà.[104]

---

[102] »La Romanina« (»the little Roman girl«) was a nickname of Martinelli's: see DAVARI, p. 23, and ADEMOLLO, p. 46.

[103] In a letter of 20th December 1607 (published in DAVARI, pp. 12—13) Ottavio Rinuccini mentioned that he had been counting on having Settimia Caccini portray Venus in *Arianna*; although it then seemed that Settimia's patrons would not let her leave Florence (ibid., p. 13, n. 1) it is generally agreed that they eventually did send her to Mantua, for a letter of 10th March 1608 reports that »the Florentine girl will play Venus« (ADEMOLLO, p. 75). But it never has been clear at what point her services finally were lent (see SOLERTI, *Albori*, I, p. 91). From the document shown above it seems likely that Settimia — always assuming she was indeed »the Florentine girl« in question — was sent around 6th or 7th March, as a prospective substitute for the dead or dying Martinelli; I imagine that when she was found unsuitable for the role of Ariadne, Rinuccini reasserted his original wish to have her play Venus: thus the aforementioned letter of 10th March relates that another potential stand-in was being sent for »*poichè* [since] la Fiorentina farà Venere« (italics mine). (Obviously, still another singer must in that case have been released from the assignment of playing Venus; but there is nothing to tell us who she was.)

[104] Biblioteca Vaticana: MS. Urb. lat. 1076, I, 171r—171v.

[105] There is no telling whether this singer would have been sent, nor whether she could have prepared in time, for within a few days Virginia Andreini had been successfully auditioned for the vacant role (see CANAL, pp. 111—112). It is not difficult, though, to guess the identity of the Cardinal's virtuosa: presumably she was the well known Hippolita Recupito (about whom, see nn. 4 and 5, above, and Alberto CAMETTI, *Chi era l'»Hippolita«, cantatrice del cardinal di Montalto*, Sammelbände der Internationalen Musikgesellschaft, XV [1913—1914], pp. 111—123). In another article I improperly allowed this lady's name to appear as »Ippolita ne' Cleria di Camilluccia« by failing to translate in its entirety a

A minor surprise afforded by this document is the news that Martinelli (who, as we have seen, was active later than is generally supposed) died somewhat earlier than has previously been reported[106]. But what chiefly concerns us is the notice that she had appeared »in the t w o plays performed during the recent Carnival«: for it seems clear enough that these must have been »the two entertainments« we read of in Peri's letter — i.e. *Dafne* and the »other« one — and that Martinelli's involvement in these two works accounts for the separate performances ascribed to her in Ademollo's document mentioned above. Not only does this eliminate the one remaining reason for attributing to Martinelli a dual role in the première of Gagliano's *Dafne*; it gives us a substantial reason to revise the dating of that première: for Ademollo's document shows that Martinelli's »performances« b o t h took place »at the end of Carnival« — thus, very likely around 13th to 19th February.

This of course is anything but helpful to our guessing which of the two productions involved Angela. Langosco's letter of 18th February, so far as we can tell in the light of our new information, may have been written a day or two after either of those productions, and thus may as plausibly refer to the one as to the other. And even if Angela appeared in *Dafne* she may have had seven weeks or more to study her part: enough time, presumably, to learn the less than seven pages of music that constitute the title role of that opera.

The relative easiness of such an undertaking may in itself suggest that it cannot have been Angela's assignment; for the work desired of Angela was one that Prince Francesco (according to his letter of 3rd January) had not expected her to accomplish within the allotted time: from this hint we might suppose it was not the part of Daphne with which Angela was concerned, but some more demanding role in the »other« entertainment. This line of reasoning, though, is

---

phrase referring to her (REINER, *Preparations in Parma*, p. 277); the translation should have read: »I do not suggest to Your Most Illustrious Lordship Signora Ippolita, *nor Camilluccia's Cleria*«. To make full amends I should add that »Camilluccia's Cleria« probably was the »Sig. Cleria Agazzarri [sic]. Romana« who sang two roles in Iacopo Cicognini's *Amor pudico*, presented in Rome on 9th February 1614 (*Copia d'vna lettera del Sig. Romolo P a r a d i s o. con la quale dà auuiso dell'apparato, e grandezza, con che si è rappresentato il festino dell'Eccellentiss. Sig. Principe Peretti*, Roma 1614, Girolamo Discepolo, p. 66); »Camilluccia« (»little Camilla«) — evidently Cleria's personal patroness — must have been Camilla Peretti, daughter of the Prince of Venafro, Michele Damasceni Peretti, who sponsored the 1614 production. Cleria's surname and occupation are enough to suggest that she may have been the wife or — notwithstanding the appellative »Romana«, which, for one thing, sometimes was applied loosely — a sister of the composer Agostino Agazzari.

[106] The news may seem suspect, since the epitaph transcribed by Quadrio (see n. 98, above) is not the only documentation that has been reported to show Martinelli died on 9th March: cf. ADEMOLLO, p. 44, n. 2. I cannot account for the conflict in the evidence, but can affirm that the date of the dispatch quoted above is written quite legibly, and the dispatch as a whole is too short to suggest that more than one sitting was spent on writing it.

virtually invalidated by some obvious considerations. For one thing, someone would have to learn whatever part the Prince thought Angela unable to manage; if the part did pass to another performer, Angela may have been asked to lighten that performer's burden by taking over an easier part in exchange — quite conceivably, the role of Daphne. Perhaps more to the point, we cannot exclude the possibility that one or both of »the two plays« had originally been scheduled for presentation several weeks earlier than the time in which both came to be performed; for, as we have seen, Martinelli had a role in each of them: her illness accordingly may have delayed either or both of the two productions. We do not know exactly when Martinelli was found to be ill, but we do know that her condition caused less alarm just before her death than it had elicited in an earlier stage, when — too briefly — her life was considered to be in danger[107]. Delays brought about by that initial alarm may have given Angela her chance to master an assignment for which time originally had seemed (and would have been) too short — again, quite conceivably to learn the role of Daphne. Conceivably — but, of course, not necessarily.

Once more, then, we find ourselves without a reliable clue as to the work and the role in which Angela was heard. In our uncertainty we might resort — as to some extent Ademollo did — to an argument from silence: specifically, from Gagliano's silence about the performer who had played Daphne in his opera. From what has been said earlier it will at least be clear that there must have been particular criteria behind Gagliano's silence (covering, as it did, just three of the six soloists who had performed in *Dafne*); and that these criteria probably were such that even if Angela performed the title role of his opera Gagliano might well omit her name from his preface. In 1608 she had barely begun to be a singer at all — apparently she was just making her début — and so had no reputation that could either oblige or entice the composer to mention her. Nor could her patron's standing matter much in this connection, for he was not a sponsor of Gagliano's or of Rinuccini's, and he was not a guest of honor — in fact, he was not a guest at all — at the Carnival festivities[108]. Thus we might consider that Gagliano's uncommunicativeness about the performer of Daphne in a sense fits Angela especially well. But even so desperate a hypothesis has, like *Dafne* itself, an imponderable counterpart close at hand; for, as I

---

[107] Three letters, presented together in ADEMOLLO, p. 43, n. 1, show that although Martinelli's survival was considered uncertain on 2nd February 1608, she was displaying hopeful signs of recovery by the 28th, and by 5th March was thought to be out of danger.

[108] He had of course been invited, but as Ferrarese Ambassador to the papal court he was diligently at work advancing the financial interests of the Bentivoglio family, and was reluctant to suspend his business activities for a jaunt to Mantua; in letters of 29th December 1607 [IX.42, 835] and 2nd January 1608 [IX.43, 50—51] he made this clear to his brother and his mother, and asked them to help him decline the invitation with suitable tact.

also have suggested earlier, Gagliano's silence would be equally understandable where a role had been played by a young boy. It should be remarked that boys were cast not only as Cupids but, sometimes, as nymphs[109]; Daphne is a nymph, and one Daphne — the messenger in Peri's *Euridice* — had in fact been portrayed by a boy[110]. From my earlier description of the music assigned to Gagliano's Daphne it will be evident that a boy could indeed have sung the role — for precisely the same reasons that entitle us to believe Angela could have sung it.

Let us hope our exertions in the preceding paragraphs have been in some way beneficial; for the question on which they have centered not only remains unsolved but at present appears unsolvable. We cannot be certain whether Angela played Daphne in *Dafne* or a different, undiscoverable role in a different, unidentifiable work.

Whatever role our singer did play, in whatever work, it apparently had given her scope to distinguish herself: according to Langosco's letter the Duchess now wanted Angela on her own musical staff, and proposed to have her tutored for at least a year by Iacopo Peri, one of the most eminent musicians of the time. Pietro Canal once pointed out that Guglielmo Gonzaga (the Duchess' late father-in-law) favored this training-program approach to the hiring of musicians, presumably on account of its economic benefits to the employer[111]. Those benefits need not be explained here, as they are no less familiar in our own day and have never been restricted to the field of music. The nature of this policy, however, helps us to understand Langosco's labored suggestion that talent was something Angela had yet to attain. Enzo Bentivoglio seems to have been unmoved by the ploy, as we learn from a letter written to him by Langosco's brother, Count Baldassare:

I have not omitted to intercede with Most Serene Madam, to the end that Your Lordship may be granted the	Io non hò mancato di fare Vfficio con madama Ser.ma à fine, che V.S. resti consolata di Mad.na Angela per con-

---

[109] Cf. the case of »Cecchino« and »Tonino« reported in n. 77, above; also SOLERTI, *Albori*, I, p.83; and FORTUNE, letter to the Editor cited in n. 51, above.

[110] PERI, p. [vi] (reprinted in SOLERTI, *Origini*, p. 49). Eurydice herself is a nymph, and although she had been impersonated by a woman in one or more productions of *Euridice* (see n. 75, above) it ought to be pointed out that she undoubtedly was played by a boy in Monteverdi's *Orfeo*: cf., in a letter to the Duchess of Mantua from Gabriele Bertazzuolo, the allusion to »quel Pretino che fece da Euridice nel Orfeo del Ser.mo S.r Prencipe« — »that priestling [i.e. boy seminarist] who portrayed Eurydice in His Most Serene Lordship the Prince [Francesco Gonzaga]'s *Orfeo*«. (Bertazzuolo's letter, dated 28th October 1608, is published entire in SOLERTI, *Musica, ballo*, pp. 54—57; the fleeting but informative mention of the »priestling« appears on p. 55.)

[111] CANAL, pp. 36—37.

satisfaction of taking Madonna Angela with you to Rome. Her Highness has willingly agreed to accommodate you in this respect, but not until the occasion of the wedding is over, in [the festivities for] which this young woman has a theatrical role and is already so far advanced with it that to take her away now, when there is so little time, would upset everything. Rest assured though, Your Lordship, that you shall not be deprived of her; however, it would be opportune for you to oblige Her Highness on this occasion. ... Mantua, 19th March 1608.

    Baldassare Langosco

dursela à Roma: S.A. uolontieri hà accettato di sodisfarnela, ma non prima, che sia spirata quest'*occasione* delle Nozze, nelle quali questa Giouane hà una parte di Comedia, et è già tanto introdotta, che il leuarla addesso, che u'è più poco tempo, sconcertaria ogni cosa. Però V.S. s'assicuri, che non ne resterà impedita, ma conuiene, ch'ella compiaccia S.A. per questa *occasione*. ... Di Mantoua li 19 di Marzo 1608.

    Baldassar, [sic] Langosco.

    [IX.43, *653*; S, N]

As the reader may recall, Caterina Bentivoglio had forecast that the wedding would be held at the end of Carnival (that is, by 19th February); but when Count Baldassare signed the foregoing letter, that time was a month past. Quite apart from the Duchess' wish to make Angela a permanent member of her court, Bentivoglio must have felt he had cause for uneasiness concerning the speedy return of his singer. It is likely that he replied to the Count's letter in terms that made clear his altogether justifiable misgivings; for on 26th March, in another letter to Bentivoglio, the Count — probably with a view to reassuring his correspondent — added an autograph postscript saying:

When the wedding is over, Most Serene Madam will send your young woman; but she does not wish to do so until then, as she has great need of her for the nuptials — which will take place shortly, for the bride is to arrive here fifteen [days] after Easter.

Madama Ser^ma, fatto le nozze, mandarà la sua giouane, má prima non uolle, auendone gran bisogno per le nozze, qualle nozze si farano inbreue, poiche la Sposa deue esser quà quindeci [giorni] doppo paschua.

    [IX.43, *700*; S]

»Quindici giorni« usually is idiomatic and means just two weeks; since Easter in 1608 would fall on 6th April, the Count was in effect predicting that Francesco Gonzaga's bride, the Infanta Margherita of Savoy, would arrive on 20th April. Thus, by inference, he was suggesting that Angela might be free to leave Mantua approximately a month after Bentivoglio received his letter (which, nonetheless, would be more than two months later than Caterina had foreseen).

As that time too drew nearer, and passed by, Bentivoglio was kept notified about the projected celebrations, and about his singer. Neither, he must have observed, seemed any closer to arriving; we can learn about both, though, from letters he received while waiting. Here is one sent in reply to two of his own:

As to learning, I am learning. My role is the prologue, whom I represent as being Mantua [i.e. Manto, the mythical founder of Mantua] coming from underneath the ground; and I am to say (singing) that she built the aforesaid city, and to end by praising to the skies all those sovereigns. My other part is the ending, [in] which they present me as the goddess of joy, in a cloud; and I dismiss them [saying] that they should go with »the art, unfamiliar to them, of rejoicing well«[112]. I regret only that Your Most Illustrious Lordship, Her Ladyship the Marchesa, and Signora Caterina are not going to hear whether I perform my part[s] well: for I already know them and have rehearsed them on the stage. Yesterday evening His Lordship the Prince issued a challenge to two tourneys — one on foot and the other on horseback, in full armor [literally, »in the armed man«] — and His Lordship the Duke then went to accept the challenge[113]. This week His Lordship the Prince is leaving for Turin [the capital of the duchy of Savoy], and they say he will come back with the Infanta at the end of this month; others say it will drag on until Ascension [15th May] — whence, not knowing the facts about this, I can say no more to Your Most Illustrious Lordship, except to close. ... Mantua, 11th April 1608.

Angela Zanibelli

Del'imparare io imparo, et la mia parte e il prologo il quallo io fingo desero [= d'essere] mantoa che uenga di soto terra et ch'io dica cantando de auere adificata detta Citta con ludare in ultimo tuti quelli prencipi ecelsamente; laltra mia parte e lultima qual me fing[o]no la dea della leticia in una nuuola et gli licencio che uada con lartenuta fra lor del ben guire[112] a me rincreso sollo che V.S. Ill.ma con la sig Marchesa et la sig.ra Caterina non sia a sentire se io facio bene la mia parte che gia le so et le ho prouato in sena; Ero [= ieri] sera il sig.r Prencipe fece una desfida de dua tornei, uno a piede, laltro a cauallo, nel homo armato, et il sig duca ando poi ad acetare la desfida, Questa sitimana parte il sigr Prenci[p]e per turino et se dice che trornara [sic] con la infante alla fine di questo meso, et alt[r]i dicano che si andera in longo sino alla sensa doue che non sapendo la certeza di questo non poso diro altro a V.S. Ill.ma senon far fino. ... Di mantoa alli 11 Aprillo 1608

Angola [sic] Zanibellj
[IX.44, *100*; A]

---

[112] Angela's spelling of the Italian text turns it into gibberish; I have necessarily based my translation on the original — as will appear presently — rather than on her sub-linguistic rendering of it.

[113] According to [FOLLINO], pp. 1—3, this challenge was delivered on the Wednesday after Easter — one day earlier than Angela's letter indicates. But official *descrizioni* must often have been written (at least, in part) before the events had taken place that they purport to describe — written, that is, on the basis of what was planned to happen. Outdoor events (such as the Prince's challenge) of course were particularly subject to postponements on account of bad weather; when such postponements occurred, the chronicler who was ahead with his work would naturally be expected to go back and revise his indications in conformity to the facts. (In his coverage of the wedding entertainments Follino indeed report-

Whatever Angela's merits were as a vocalist, she cannot yet have been one of those singers who reputedly moved their hearers by grasping and conveying poetic refinements in the texts they sang: since (like many of her »betters«) she was barely literate, we find that she garbled as much as she quoted of the text assigned to her. The quotation nevertheless can be identified as a line from Chiabrera's *intermedii* for Guarini's *Idropica*[114]; and the rest of her description corresponds to elements of the Chiabrera work. Later we shall consider some details regarding that work, and regarding Angela's assignment in it. For the moment let us simply note that Angela had two roles in the production, and that these were respectively in the prologue and in the finale — episodes that, between them, framed not only Chiabrera's *intermedii* but Guarini's comedy. She would therefore be especially conspicuous, and the quality of her performance proportionately critical, in the evening's entertainment: we probably will be right, then, to season with an additional grain of salt — as someone in Mantua apparently did — Commendator Langosco's thesis that Angela would acquire true talent only after a period of further study.

Enzo Bentivoglio did in fact intend to have his protégée continue studying, but he too seems to have shown more faith than Langosco in the abilities she already possessed: this much emerges from another of her letters to Bentivoglio (again in reply to one from him). In the same letter, too, we find some further news about the ever receding date of the Infanta's arrival[115]:

About singing: I remember what I learned there [in Ferrara], and I believe I shall articulate my runs [literally, »beat the passages«] better than I formerly did, even though I never practiced them with the instruments [i.e. with orchestral accompaniment; literally, with »sound«]. Then, as to singing with proper breath control [literally,

del cantare quello che sapeua costi io me la reco[r]do et credo che batero meglio gli pasagi di quelo che faceuo benche non gli abbia mai studiato con il suono; poi del cantar sicura V.S. Ill.ma sa benisimo che in cosi pochi giorni non poso auerlo imparato pero del studiare io studio, V.S. Ill.ma dice che uol tore in casa una giouane che

---

ed that windy weather had caused the postponement of a mock naval battle [ibid., p. 65] and that rain had delayed a tourney [ibid., pp. 72, 99].) But undoubtedly there were slip-ups: a case in point has been detected in Marcello Buttigli's *Descrittione* of the nuptial festivities held in Parma in 1628 (see Paolo MINUCCI DEL ROSSO, *Le nozze di Margherita de' Medici con Odoardo Farnese Duca di Parma e Piacenza*, La rassegna nazionale, XXII, No. 4 [1885], p. 557). In the present case I imagine Angela's letter provides the true date of the Prince's challenge — and indirectly tells us that on 9th April 1608, it rained in Mantua.

[114] »Hor dunque al mio venire / Apprendete mortali / L'arte ignota frà voi del ben gioire« (in [FOLLINO], p. 99; cf. SOLERTI, *Albori*, III, p. 232).

[115] In translating this letter I have necessarily interpreted on a basis of personal judgment some phrases that I take to be obsolete technical terms, or colloquial substitutes for such terms.

singing »securely«, or »with sureness«]: Your Most Illustrious Lordship is quite well aware that in so few days I cannot have learned it; but as to studying, I am studying. Your Most Illustrious Lordship writes of resolving to take into the household a young girl who is learning to sing: for what little judgment I have, I believe you have done very well. But about your saying that she must then be my pupil: to this I can only reply that I do not consider myself qualified for such service; however, she too might study with the teacher [from] whom I shall be learning. I believe the nuptials will not be delayed much longer, for His Highness of Savoy, His Most Serene Lordship [the Prince] of Mantua, and the Infanta are leaving [Turin] today, and will make their [ceremonial] entry next Monday [12th May]. ... Mantua, 5th May 1608.

Angela Zanibelli

impara cantare per quel poco g[i]udicio ch'io ho credo che abbia fato benisimo ma in dire che abbia poi esere mia desipola non poso rispondere in questo se non dire che io non mi conosco buona in tal effeto pero da quel maestro che impararo io potra inpararare [sic] anco ella; le nozze credo che andara in longo poco per che .S.A di sauoglia con il sere.^{mo} di mantoa et la infante parteno ogi, et farano la intrata lune prosimo. ... di mantoa alli 5 magio 1608

Angola Zanibella
[IX.44, *339*; A, N]

How could Angela, herself a fledgling musician, be expected to teach another beginner? Bentivoglio must have set great store by the competence she was displaying, and the experience she was acquiring, in Mantua. There, less than two years after her first music lesson, her singing had satisfied an audience of nobles, accustomed to excellence; at Carnival, she had performed in a theatrical work; soon, on a more stately occasion, she would appear in another one. Most important, the preparations for these assignments had brought her into contact with many first-rate musicians — an advantage not so easily to be had in Ferrara since the dissolution of the d'Este court, ten years earlier. In Mantua, Angela had had the opportunity to observe, and to associate with, leading singers of two courts — regulars in the Gonzagas' service such as Francesco Rasi and Caterina Martinelli; and equally renowned visitors from Florence, Antonio Brandi and Settimia Caccini — all of them famous throughout Italy for their vocal skill. Bentivoglio may not have been wrong, then, to hope his singer would return with some modicum of professional polish — with some sophistication, or some lore, worth imparting to the new colleague she would find in her master's household.

How soon, though, would Angela herself be free to rejoin that household? In April, she had heard and reported that the Infanta was due to arrive in Mantua at the end of that month; on 5th May, that the arrival would take place in another week; but, ten days later:

Here there is no more news, except that Ascension Day has been postponed until the [time of the] wedding. Ambassadors from various places, and other gentry, are arriving every day; but concerning the arrival of the sovereigns and cardinals that are in Turin[116], nothing is known except that they are expected daily. Now, as I have no more to say, I pray the Lord God that Your Most Illustrious and Most Excellent[117] Lordship's trip here to Mantua may be a pleasant one for you. ... Mantua, 15th May 1608.

Angela Zanibelli

Qui non ui è altro di nouo se non che il giorno della sensa lano trasferito sino alle noze; Ogni giorno ariua Ambasia-[to]ri di diuersi loghi et altri sig.ri ma de la uenuta delle [sic] Prencipi et Card.li che si troua in turino non se sa se non che se aspeta di giorno in giorno; Ora non mi ocorendo altro prego il sig.r iddio che la uenuta di V.S. Ill.ma et Ecce.ma qui a mantoa sia con sua felicita. ... di mantoa alli 15 maggio 1608

Angola Zanibelli

[IX.44, *402*; A]

Despite its appearance, the first sentence of the foregoing quotation can involve no slip of Angela's pen[118]: for it was written precisely on Ascension Day (or, at least, on the day that feast was celebrated throughout the rest of Christendom). What Angela probably meant to report was that in Mantua the festivities normally connected with Ascension Day had been postponed, so as not to diminish the effect of those that would begin upon the bride's arrival, »expected daily«. We note in passing that the repeated delay of that arrival had gone on so long that Bentivoglio, who Angela had formerly understood would miss the celebrations, now would attend them.

The considerable difference between the schedule originally proposed and the one finally observed is worth attention for some other reasons. Nino Pirrotta has recently cited the Mantuan festivities of 1608, along with those held in Parma twenty years later, as instances supporting his belief that in the early seventeenth century even the simplest musical plays were accorded plenty of rehearsal time[119]. For »the long preparations in Parma« Pirrotta drew on an article which unfortunately sheds no light on the extraordinary reason for their

---

[116] Two cardinals who had joined the bridal party in Turin are identified in a dispatch from Venice dated 3rd May 1608: »Scriuono di Milano delli 30. pass*ato* ... che teneu*ano* di Turino l'arriuo iui delli Ill.mi card.li Aldobrand*ino* et s*an* cesareo [respectively, Pietro and Silvestro Aldobrandini, uncle and nephew], alli quali insieme col P*rincipe* di Mantoua ueniuano dal ser.mo di sauoia dati regij trattenim*enti*« (Biblioteca Vaticana: MS. Urb. lat. 1076, I, f. 311r).

[117] By birth, Bentivoglio was entitled to be called »Most Illustrious Lordship«, and that is how he usually is addressed in the letters shown here; Angela added »Most Excellent« in recognition of the ambassadorial post her patron currently held in Rome.

[118] In fact a dispatch from Mantua, sent to the Duke of Urbino on 16th May 1608, similarly reports: »Si è prorogata la festa della Sensa« (Urb. lat. 1076, I, f. 340v).

[119] Pirrotta, *Early Opera and Aria*, pp. 71—72 and n. 73. Pirrotta expresses the same claim still more forcefully in the Italian version of his essay (in *Li due Orfei*, p. 329 and p. 363, n. 73).

extraordinary length. In an article of my own it is demonstrated that those preparations — entailing among other things the overhauling of a derelict theatre and the construction of an entirely new one with a full set of elaborate stage machines — originally were planned to take no more than about three months, during which time libretti and music also would have had to be written, and performers chosen and rehearsed[120]. That those three months were prolonged into seventeen had nothing to do with the exigencies of art, but (as I also showed) was a fortuitous result of diplomatic machinations aimed at dissolving the wedding arrangements that were to be celebrated, and reassigning the bride to a different groom (and the groom to a different bride, the younger sister of his original fiancée)[121]. Oddly enough, a comparable maneuver had some place in what we might well call »the long maunderings in Mantua«. We recall that when Angela set out for that city, Prince Francesco's wedding was expected to take place by 19th February; but at the very time Caterina Bentivoglio was relaying that information to her husband, Enzo was in possession of a letter from one of his close friends, the Marchese of Scandiano, which offered a somewhat different forecast:

Concerning the nuptials of Mantua: although these Most Serene sovereigns of Savoy and Mantua suppose that they will perform them during the coming Carnival season; and that they have entirely dissuaded the Emperor's ambassador from seeking to delay them any further; and that they decidedly will not agree to [a marriage with] the second[-born] girl (as His Majesty had been urging in order that he might [have] more time to think the matter over), I believe nevertheless that if the Emperor insists in earnest that they postpone them [the nuptials] until Easter, they will do so. (The departure of His Highness and His Lordship the Prince for Turin, escorted by 60 of the most distinguished cavaliers — all of them guests from abroad — was to have taken place on 12th January.) ... Ferrara, 22nd December 1607.
     Giulio Thieni

Le Nozze di Mantova se bene questi ss.mi di Sauoia, et di Mantova tengano di farle questo Carnevale et di hauer' escluso l'Ambasciatore totalmente dell'Imperatore di uolerle allongare più, é risolutamente di non uoler concludere con la seconda come la M.tà sua ne faceua instanza per [aver] egli tempo ancora da pensarui, nondimeno credo, che se l'Imperatore farà instanza da uero perche le differiscano fin a Pasca, che ló faranno, la partita per Turino di SA. et del s.r Prencipe, con la Compagnia di 60. Caualieri Principali, et tutti Forastieri, doueua essere alli 12 di Gennaio. ... Di Ferrara li 22 Xbre 1607.
     Giulio Thieni
     [IX.42, *790ᵛ–788*; A, N]

The Prince had been scheduled to leave on 12th January, presumably to marry in Turin and to fetch his bride back to Mantua; but the bride still was in

---

[120] REINER, *Preparations in Parma*, pp. 291, 294—295, 297.
[121] Ibid., pp. 291—292.

Turin, and the Prince still planning to fetch her, when Angela mentioned the matter in her letter of 11th April: as of that time, then, a delay of at least three months had occurred in the proceedings. Since Thieni's letter predicts just such a delay, we may be tempted to attribute the slowdown to the Emperor's intervention. In part, this would be correct; but in a broader sense the Emperor's need for »more time to think« can best be understood as one result, and the delay in Mantua as another result, of a common cause — namely, the political aims of Duke Carlo Emanuele I of Savoy, father of the prospective bride. As these aims and their immediate consequences are explained, the significance of Thieni's letter — and of the slowdown in Mantua — will become clearer.

Carlo Emanuele's uneasiness about foreign encroachments in Italy was well known. One of his typical declarations (according to the Venetian ambassador who reported it) was: »When all is said and done, I am Italian; and it is essential that we [Italians] come to terms with one another: for these foreigners offer their friendship not in our interest but simply in order to take from us everything we own, and to compel us to serve their purposes, so that they may the more easily subjugate us all«[122]. His mistrust of foreigners doubtless was sharpened by their proximity to his own domain: to the west, his border lands interlocked with those of France; the northern frontier of Savoy touched Switzerland; and to the east lay Milan and its territories, ruled by Spain. Obviously, it would be reassuring to Carlo Emanuele to see the Italian states »come to terms with one another« in a confederation that would stand off foreign influences and drive out those already present; obviously, too, the reassurance for him would be greatest if Savoy were the leader of such a confederation. Nationalistic aspirations, dynastic ambitions, and xenophobic growlings thus came to be recognizable features of Carlo Emanuele's political personality. When it became known that Savoy and Mantua were planning an alliance through marriage, the news could easily be — and surely was — understood in that light; accordingly, it was understood to carry menacing implications. For one thing, both duchies were fiefs of the Holy Roman Empire; an increase of solidarity between them, by virtue of a direct union, did not necessarily augur well for the German Emperor, Rudolf II. And another Habsburg, Philip III

---

[122] »Sua Altezza [Carlo Emanuele] ... più volte mi ha detto: io sono alla fine italiano e bisogna che fra noi c'intendiamo bene, perchè l'amicizia di questi forestieri non è procurata da loro per bene nostro, ma solo per levarci quanto possediamo, e per obbligarci di servire ai loro fini, per poter tanto più facilmente assoggettarci tutti« — report delivered to the Venetian senate on 26th January 1609 by Pietro Contarini (published in Nicolò BAROZZI and Guglielmo BERCHET [eds.], *Relazioni degli stati europei lette al senato dagli ambasciatori veneziani nel secolo decimosettimo*, Venezia, Pietro Naratovich, Serie III, Vol. I [1862], p. 102).

of Spain, needed no cartographer to remind him that his North Italian holdings lay between Savoy and Mantua — clearly an awkward position if those two states should unite in fact and in anti-foreign policy. Moreover, if as a sequel to such a union Milan should find itself in armed struggle against Mantua and Savoy, not only would its troubles be troubles for Spain, but Savoy's and Mantua's losses would be losses for their feudal landlord and military liege, the Emperor Rudolf. Thus the Habsburg cousins both had reason to deplore the prospect of a marriage between Francesco Gonzaga and Margherita of Savoy.

Rudolf probably undertook his own courtship of Margherita (let us agree to call it that) principally or solely to forestall the Mantua-Savoy alliance; indeed, he may have been prodded into doing so by his Spanish cousin, for their common good. The Dukes of Savoy and Mantua no doubt suspected as much; but once the Emperor had expressed a notion of marrying Margherita they were obliged, as his vassals, to give him the opportunity to make a firm proposal — which meant, in effect, the chance to dicker with his prospective father-in-law concerning terms for a marriage contract. If the terms he proposed should prove as acceptable as those already made on Francesco Gonzaga's behalf, he, the Emperor, would have to be given right of way to claim the bride; perhaps more important, no-one else could claim her until Rudolf had received a reasonable opportunity to exercise his prerogative as a wooer. The Mantua-Savoy marriage was held back while Rudolf went through the motions of enticing Carlo Emanuele to become his father-in-law.

Clearly, there was small chance of those negotiations' being speeded to fruition even if Carlo Emanuele took them seriously. An additional tie with Germany would be as little conformable to his nationalist aims as an Italian in-lawship would be dear to them; insofar as it lay with him to make proposals or counterproposals regarding a marriage agreement, his terms for such an agreement with Rudolf cannot have been modest. And Rudolf himself must have been more eager to keep the negotiations going than to bring them to a conclusion by plighting his troth to Margherita. His courtship, at any rate, was not of the whirlwind variety and, since Savoy and Mantua were able in fairness to claim a previous engagement, the Emperor was given a deadline by which to declare definite intentions or to stand aside. The deadline, 31st July 1607, passed without any declaration, but Rudolf quite naturally was disinclined to stand aside, and he went right on negotiating[123]. Perhaps he managed to persuade Carlo

---

[123] Dispatch dated 6th August 1607, from Prague: »Si intende che il matrimonio che trattaua l'imperatore con le [sic] prima Principessa di Sauoia ... non sia per hauer piu loco essendo passato il termine di tutto il mese di luglio che lei [Sua Maestà] prese a risoluersi tuttauia hauendo .S.M. scritto a quell'Altezza come si intende potrebbe essere che il negocio non fosse totalmente escluso« (Biblioteca Vaticana: MS. Urb. lat. 1075, II, f. 524r).

Emanuele that his intentions were honorable; perhaps he persuaded himself (or Philip of Spain persuaded him) that as a last resort he might really have to marry the girl he was ostensibly courting: at all events, he succeeded in obtaining a new time limit. It was agreed that if Rudolf claimed Margherita's hand by 20th January 1608, Francesco Gonzaga would defer to him; but Francesco in that case would marry Margherita's next-oldest sister, Isabella[124]. This compromise, obviously, would not eliminate the Habsburgs' worries; Rudolf's best course still was, to procrastinate. He professed to favor Francesco's marrying Isabella, so that the Gonzagas' arrangements and his own might proceed without hampering one another; but it was clear enough that Carlo Emanuele would not marry off Isabella while her older sister's prospects remained indefinite: so all progress continued to await the Emperor's decision. That decision, as before, continued to be withheld; Rudolf still refused to drop the matter, but his emissary to Savoy seemed mysteriously unable to secure an agreement he could accept[125]. This state of affairs of course could not go on indefinitely, and as the new deadline drew near, messengers passed with increasing frequency between Italy and the imperial court in Prague[126]; one of their errands on Rudolf's behalf involved an attempt to persuade the Duke of Mantua, quite bluntly, »not to hurry the marriage« — an admonition delivered toward the beginning of January 1608.[127] As we know, Mantua in fact did not hurry the marriage — for it did not avail itself of the deadline of 20th January — whence we might suppose that the Emperor's courtship was headed at last toward a definite marriage agreement. Actually, though, Rudolf's liberation from the January deadline was an incidental result of a move that had, finally, been devised by Spain.

This Spanish stratagem was aimed directly at the marriage agreement that had already been worked out between Savoy and Mantua. On the occasion of their

---

[124] Dispatch dated 30th November 1607, from Mantua: »le nozze future ... si sono publicate di sicuro; et stabilito, che alli .20. di Gennaio il Ser.mo s.r Prencipe nostro debba esser colà [in Turin] per isposare; et sposerà la prima, caso non la truoui sposata à nome dell'Imperatore (ilche creda V.S., se le pare) et, se ciò fosse seguito, sposerà la seconda« (ibid., f. 754v).

[125] Dispatch dated 24th December 1607, from Prague: »Il s.r Consigliero Eghemiller non è anco ritornato da Turino, et quì habbiamo per sicuro, che S. M.tà non sia per maritarsi« (ibid., f. 829r).

[126] Dispatch dated 7th January 1608, from Prague: »La Corte non ragiona al presente se non di staffette, et Corrieri che si mandano di quà in Italia, et d'Italia qua per certi interessi di matrimonij, se ben' nessuno ardisce di parlarne chiaro« (Urb. lat. 1076, I, f. 46v).

[127] Letter dated 7th January 1608, from Prague, quoted in the dispatch shown above (n. 126): »quì la Settimana passata il s.r Marchese di Castiglione inuiò corriero, dicesì [sic], con lettere per dar conto à S. M.tà d'hauer trattato co'l s.r Duca di Mantoua, che non affretti il matrimonio conforme l'ordine datoli di quà« (ibid., f. 47v). (The Marchese of Castiglione, Francesco Gonzaga, was a counsellor of the Emperor's, and, later, his ambassador to the Spanish court. Vincenzo Gonzaga was the Marchese's third cousin once removed.)

alliance those two states were to exchange certain intervening lands with one
another, in such a fashion that the holdings of each duchy would be better
consolidated: the plan, which suited both households, was assumed to be a
basic condition of their union[128]. But in January 1608 Philip III declared that
the intended exchange was not legally possible, since Spain — and Milan, as
Spain's deputy — had a latent claim on some of the lands in question[129]. Those
lands had been ceded to Savoy by the Holy Roman Emperor Charles V (Philip's
grandfather, Charles I of Spain); but if Savoy attempted to dispose of them
they would automatically revert to Spanish control: for they had been given —
so Philip asserted — as i n a l i e n a b l e properties, not legally transferable to
any third owner. The Governor of Milan explained this to the Dukes of
Savoy and Mantua; whereupon it became quite needless for the Emperor
Rudolf to fear Mantua would »hurry the marriage«[130]: it was now the Gonzagas
who needed »time to think the matter over«, for it appeared they could not
receive the Savoy lands that were to have been given them along with the
Savoy bride. They announced that the wedding would be postponed until after
Easter, but knowledgeable observers wryly wondered what Easter they had in
mind[131]. The reason officially given for the postponement was the imminence of
Lent (during which season entertainments ordinarily could not be presented)[132]:
this might seem to accord with Professor Pirrotta's assumptions, for the
implication was that more time was needed to perfect the preparations in
Mantua. But a reliable informant at the Gonzaga court confided (as far as he
dared):

---

[128] Dispatch dated 29th September 1607, from Venice: »Scriuono di Turino ... che'l Ser.º di
Mantoua ... era stato alquanti giorni a Turino riceuuto con gran magnificenza dall Alt.ª
di Sauoia sendo seguita la conclusione del parentado altre uolte scritto tra queste Alt.ᵉ ...
con le conditioni altre uolte scritte del baratto dalcune terre nel Monferato« (Urb. lat.
1075, II, f. 616r); and, later in the same dispatch: »Scriuono di Milano di 26 stante che ...
di Turino teneuano che quell Alt.ª hauesse Deputato il Pressidente Monzo, Il Senator
Goueano et il Secretario Roncasio a terminare [= determinare] li confini col Piemonte et
il baratto delle terre che si tramerano tra luno e laltro stato con li ministri dell Altª di
Mantova auanti che s'effettuino le nozze tra i figliuoli« (ibid., f. 618r).

[129] Dispatch dated 19th January 1608, from Venice: »Si hà auiso da buona banda, ... ch'esse
Nozze non habbino da seguire senon fatto Carneuale, mostrandosi la M.ta Cattolica [Philip
of Spain] non esser contenta, per non hauer hauuto raguaglio della permuta delle terre, che
queste Altezze fano, prettendendo S. M.ta, che parte di esse terre siano Membri, ò giurisdi-
tioni dello Stato di Milano« (Urb. lat. 1076, I, f. 42r).

[130] Dispatch dated 4th February 1608, from Prague: »hauendo il Conte di Fuentes fatto
intendere alle Alt.ᵉ di Sauoia, et di Mantoua, che non intendeua, che la permuta fra loro
trattata andasse innanti, come pregiuditiale alla Inuestitura, che diede del Contado d'Asti
Carlo quinto alli Duchi di Sauoia, di non alienar quei beni, nè farne contratto, pare che
questo matrimonio si e stato differito à Pasqua« (ibid., f. 114r).

[131] Dispatch dated 23rd January 1608, from Ferrara: »Anco quì s'è intesa la proroga delle nozze
di Mantoua sino à Pasqua; ma non si dice, di quale Pasqua s'intendano« (ibid., f. 54r).

[132] Dispatch dated 12th January 1608, from Mantua: »Le Nozze Serenissime sono differite à
dopo Pasqua per la strettezza del tempo del Carneuale« (ibid., f. 29r).

I should like to say something about the wedding, but my lips are being kept closed; I shall say to you only that a postponement has occurred which, to those who know, is very different from what people take it for. I do not know what to expect; I am afraid, afraid, a-fraid—and I could say a thousand times, I am afraid — for it is not merely a matter of the wedding, but is something worse. Somehow, someone will have to untangle this Gordian knot! But then, I personally suppose it may already have been cut; and when it is possible to speak, I shall speak. Meanwhile, if you wish me well, consent that for the present I keep silent.

Vorrei dire alcuna cosa delle Nozze, ma mi uien chiusa la bocca; le dico solo, che si è fatta una proroga, laquale, à chi sà, è molto differente da quello la crede la piazza: Io non sò che mi dire, temo, et temo, et temo, et potrei dire mille uolte; temo; Perche ciò non è solo delle nozze, ma di peggio; non può fare, che non si snodi questo groppo Gordiano, seben, quanto à me, tengo, c'horamai sia tagliato, et quando si potrà dire, dirò; In tanto si contenti come mi ama, così ch'io taccia per adesso.[133]

Obviously, something more serious was at stake than a shortage of rehearsal time. We may guess what strands composed the Gordian knot: clear intimations of prompt military action by Spain and Milan if Savoy and Mantua should carry out their territorial contract (for Mantua, this would mean having to fight for a gift immediately upon receiving it); and, very likely, a threat that Carlo Emanuele would make war against Mantua if the Gonzagas did n o t go through with the agreement. Probably it was the Emperor Rudolf's matrimonial negotiations with Savoy that were hopefully thought to be cutting the knot; but no joyful tidings came from Prague or Savoy. Fear grew more widespread, and Mantuans soon were writing on the walls around their city, »God help us!«[134].

How long could such an unnerving deadlock be permitted to continue? The answer of course is implicit in the date on which Francesco Gonzaga finally did marry Margherita of Savoy; but whoever seeks that date in scholarly books will find a bewildering array of conflicting answers. To mention just a few: the

---

[133] Quoted in a dispatch dated 5th January 1608, from Mantua, under the subheading »Da un'altra persona pur di Mantoua, che sá qualchecosa« (ibid., ff. 15v—16r). The informant must in fact have had access to the court's secrets, for the postponement itself was not announced officially until nearly the middle of January (see n. 134, below); we see, though, that it had been decided upon in the very first days of the month.

[134] Dispatch dated 14th January 1608, from Mantua: »Si è finalmente publicata la dilatione delle Nozze sino à Pasqua, ma chi ne parla tace il meglio; et quanto à me tengo per certo, che non se ne faccia altro; perche in somma li spagnuoli non sentono bene la congiuntione di questi due Prencipi. Si ueggono nel Padrone [Duke Vincenzo] gran pensieri, ma maggiori nel s.r Prencipe; et non è mancato chi hà uoluto dar loro anco occasione di pensare coll'andare scriuendo sopra tutti i cantoni della Città, et in mille luoghi di Corte; Dio ci aiuti« (Urb. lat. 1076, I, f. 30r).

wedding took place on 25th May 1608, according to Angelo Solerti[135]; »at the
beginning of May [*ai primi di maggio*]«, according to Vittorio Rossi[136]; »during
the carnival of 1608«, according to Henry Prunières[137]. Solerti's documentation,
which he mistook for an account of the wedding, describes only the Mantuan
court's attendance at Mass on Pentecost Sunday[138]; Rossi cited no documentation
at all (and was equally mistaken); and Prunières reasoned from the performance
date of Gagliano's *Dafne*, which he erroneously supposed was presented as part
of the wedding festivities[139]. Oddly enough Prunières' dating, vague and ill
founded as it is, happens to be at least partially correct: as will presently be
explained, the matrimonial requisites were fulfilled in part on 17th February,
and completed some three weeks later. The reader no doubt will marvel at
this; for we have seen that documents written well after Carnival of 1608 refer
to »le nozze« (»the nuptials«, or »the wedding«) as a coming event, impatiently
awaited. Similar expressions, in other documents, may have led to the incorrect
datings given by Rossi and others. This is no paradox; rather, the term »nozze«
appears in these documents in a secondary sense, referring not to the marriage
ceremony itself but to the attendant festivities[140]. Still, why did Mantua not
perform those festivities immediately, once the marriage itself had been performed? Was there some truth in the official allusion to Lenten restrictions? Hardly; for both Savoy and Mantua had been released from those restrictions, by a
papal dispensation[141]. During Lent, in fact, the Savoy court did offer its wedding guests a variety of entertainments, in which neither the dignity of the season nor that of the court was at all times manifest. (On the fourth Lenten
Saturday, for example, a lion, a lioness, a pair of tigers, a wild boar, two bulls,
a mule, a monkey, and a pack of hounds were penned up together so as to

---

[135] *Albori*, I, p. 98, continuing n. 2 of p. 97.

[136] *Battista Guarini*, p. 154.

[137] *A New History of Music: The Middle Ages to Mozart*, ed. and trans. Edward Lockspeiser,
2nd printing, New York 1944, Macmillan, p. 189.

[138] [FOLLINO], p. 19: »Il giorno seguente, che fù la Domenica della Pentecoste, essendo stata
la Chiesa di Santa Barbara in Corte addobbata ... alla presenza di tutti i Prencipi, e con
l'interuento del Cardinale [i.e. Ferdinando Gonzaga], fù dall'Abbate di quella Chiesa cele-
brata Messa solenne; passandosene dipoi quei Serenissimi, per esser l'hora già tarda, à desinare«.
(I have elided only a description of the decorations.)

[139] PRUNIÈRES, p. 189.

[140] This application of »nuptials« and »wedding« is perhaps familiar to the reader. (If not,
cf. e.g. the relevant entries in *Webster's New Collegiate Dictionary*, Springfield, Massachu-
setts 1949, G. & C. Merriam Co., pp. 577, 970.) The pertinent usage in Italian is illustrated clearly in the *Vocabolario degli Accademici della Crusca*, 5th printing, Firenze 1863—1923, Tipografia Galileiana, XI, p. 264, in a quotation referring to a marriage
held without *nozze*.

[141] Dispatch dated 23rd February 1608, from Rome: »quanto alle feste, et solennità dello
sponsalitio si faranno anco di Quaresima, così dispensati dal Papa« (Urb. lat. 1076, I, f.
126ᵛ).

provide a spectacle of bloody and unbridled strife; the animals, characteristically saner than their masters, decided on a course of peaceful coexistence, to the express disappointment of their noble observers[142]. These ladies and gentlemen, though, were resourceful at finding their own outlets for their high spirits: the day before, they had brought a court banquet to a rousing close with a general, impromptu hurling of tableware[143].)

Yet in Mantua, as we know, festive impulses were held in check not only throughout the traditionally austere season of Lent but until Ascension itself had passed (or, as reported, had been »postponed«). Would it be correct after all to suppose that the entertainment schedule in Mantua was deliberately slowed down to allow more time for rehearsals? Again, the answer must be negative: the grandeur of the festivities could not, and did not, compensate the Gonzagas for the expense and embarrassment that resulted from their postponement. A famine had been going on in Mantua since the preceding autumn[144]; the court nevertheless had begun at that time to collect food supplies for the invited throng of wedding guests[145]. Those supplies of course were not expected to remain sound until late spring, when the delayed festivities at last began; the inevitable spoilage was all the more distressing on account of the famine. And in order to provide accommodations for the guests, many officers of the court had moved out of their homes by the end of November[146]: certainly, the guests

---

[142] Dispatch lacking the customary date line, but written in Turin on 22nd March 1608: »Il Sabbato [15th March] si fecero entrare in uno steccato due Leoni Maschio, e femina, due Tigri, un Cinghiale, due Tori, una Mula, una Simia, e molti Cani con pensiere che douessero azzuffarsi insieme, mà se ne stettero tutti taciti sino à sera, lasciando tutti gli spettatori mal sodisfatti« (ibid., f. 216r).

[143] Letter of Massimiliano Montecuccoli, dated 26th March 1608, from Turin: »Il desinare fu allegrissimo et si fecero molti brindisi che fu cagione che qualcheduno s'alterasse per il souerchio bere. Nel leuar delle Tauole furno gettate le confettioni delle quali non n'era grandissima quantita per la sala et non finì la burla che insieme con li confetti uolauano i piatti. Finalmente ogn'uno andò al suo alloggiamento chi da se et chi con l'aiuto d'altri. La sera non si cenó et la mattina seguente ogn'uno si leuò tardissimo« (Roma, Biblioteca Vallicelliana: MS. M.19, f. 310r—310v).

[144] Three dispatches from Mantua: 21st September 1607: »La carestia, ch'è quì d'ogni cosa, et in superlatiuo grado, farà tanto più memorabili queste nozze« (Urb. lat. 1075, II, f. 613v); 23rd November 1607: »gli spettatori resteranno sodisfatti, ma non già essi, che faranno la spesa; perche certo questo non è l'anno di allargare la mano« (ibid., f. 742r); 28th December 1607: »ogni cosa è piena di allegrezze [on account of Ferdinando Gonzaga's being made a cardinal], non ostante la estrema carestia di tutto, et di danaro più che del resto« (ibid., f. 820v).

[145] Dispatch dated 28th September 1607, from Mantua: »si sono dati certi ordini in questo stato per proueder di uini, et di cose magnatiue per le nozze« (ibid., f. 629r).

[146] Dispatch dated 30th November 1607, from Mantua: »S'attende alli preparamenti nuttiali. Il s.r Massimiliano Capriano Cameriere di S. Alt. è deputato ad andar' alle case, per dessignar le stanze essendo stato sin' in casa del sr Consigliero Chieppio à dessignarne cinque, ilquale s.r Consigliero hà detto, che questa sarà una delle gran Foresterie, che sia mai stata à Mantoua. ... Già molti Cortigiani prencipali, come il s.r Conte Valeriano Cattaneo Aio

must have been invited for Carnival. (As we have seen, the wedding at one point was expected to take place on or near 20th January.) Indeed, I believe it is possible to detect a note of wistfulness in Gagliano's report that when the wedding festivities (again, »le nozze«) were postponed, his *Dafne* was presented so as not to let the Carnival season pass without some diversion[147]: had the delay not occurred, his work probably would have had the honor of being one of the wedding entertainments; instead, it must have been offered as a sop to the bored and disappointed guests who had assembled in Mantua for nuptial festivities that seemed increasingly imaginary as the days passed. The necessity of detaining those guests was, beyond all doubt, harmful both to the Gonzagas' prestige and to their purse — for some of the visitors were in Mantua at the court's expense, and some (perhaps not the same ones) left in irritation when the delay had gone on until the middle of May[148]. In short, it is quite implausible that the Gonzagas created these inconveniences for their guests, their courtiers, and themselves in an effort to guarantee a high level of performance in their theatrical productions. To understand why they continued to postpone those productions even after the wedding, we must turn again to the story of the wedding itself; and, once more, we must view that story in terms of its essentially political nature.

As explained earlier, Spain feared that Savoy and Mantua, once they were allied, would pose a significant threat to the Spanish forces in and around Milan. That fear was not groundless, and all the interested parties knew it was the true motive behind the Spanish attempt to obstruct the Savoy-Mantua marriage plans. But as Spain had considered it impolitic to openly voice its fear and mistrust, it had instead raised a legalistic cavil concerning the territorial exchange ordained by the two dukes to coincide with their children's wedding[149]. Although the Spanish maneuver did succeed in suspending progress for a while, Savoy and Mantua soon saw their way round this interference: they

---

d'esso s.ʳ Prencipe, e'l sig.ʳ Segretario striggio si sono ritirati fuora di Corte per dar luogo à' forestieri« (ibid., ff. 754ᵛ—755ʳ).

[147] GAGLIANO, p. [v] (reprinted in VOGEL, *Gagliano*, p. 558).

[148] Dispatch dated 16th May 1608, from Mantua: »concorrono molti forastieri chi à spese di S.A., et chi alle proprie, et molti di questi stracchi di tante dilationi se ne partono« (Urb. lat. 1076, I, f. 340ᵛ).

[149] The Spanish King's objection can rightly be called a cavil, for it was based on a willful misreading of the entailment clause to which it referred. Actually, the clause limited ownership of the entailed lands not to Savoy but to the descendants of the original grantee, Carlo Emanuele's grandmother (see Lino MARINI, *Beatrice di Portogallo, duchessa di Savoia*, in *Dizionario biografico degli italiani*, VII [1965], p. 365). Margherita could receive those lands; and she could hand them down to her own descendants, even though those descendants would belong to the ducal line of Mantua. If the limiting clause had had the force Philip III pretended to see in it, he probably would have cited it only after the alleged violation had been committed: then (according to his thesis), Spain could have repossessed the lands in question. His true purpose, obviously, was to complicate the issue, and to

eliminated from their formal agreement those portions of their territorial contract that Spain had contested, and — before any further protests could be devised by Philip III or by the German Emperor — hastened to solemnize the marriage (against which, after all, no direct objection had ever been officially
raised)[150]. They were not indeed satisfied to forgo the territorial arrangements
they originally had envisioned; rather, they must have foreseen that it would
be easier to effectuate those arrangements once they were securely allied. (If they
behaved peaceably toward Milan, the Spanish King might eventually drop his
legalistic objections, which, as they knew, had been no more than a pretext in
the first place; and if peaceable behavior did not seem opportune — as to Carlo
Emanuele it sometimes did not[151] — the two duchies, after they had united,
would be better able to achieve or defend by force the disputed territorial
exchange, in defiance of Spain's alleged authority over the lands at issue.) For
the moment, Savoy's and Mantua's first concern had to be the enactment of the
marriage; accordingly, they went ahead with it, and there was nothing
Spain, Milan, or the Emperor Rudolf could do but extend congratulations,
although — again, as all parties knew — they were edgier than ever at the turn
affairs had taken. Carlo Emanuele in fact found means of redoubling both the
congratulations and the edginess: announcing his intention of accepting the
twenty-one-year-old Gonzaga as a bridegroom for his eighteen-year-old
daughter, he simultaneously announced, as a surprise, the engagement of
Margherita's sixteen-year-old sister, Isabella, to the sixteen-year-old Prince of
Modena, Alfonso III d'Este[152]. Clearly, all of the Emperor's supposed wishes
regarding the two Savoy princesses had been overridden by Carlo Emanuele
in his campaign for Italian unity[153]. Rudolf himself simply settled back into

---

intimate that it might serve Milan as an excuse — however spurious — to make trouble; for
it seemed likely that if either Savoy or Mantua could be made to back down from the territorial agreement they had reached, their entente itself might founder.

[150] Dispatch dated 16th February 1608, from Venice: »Di Turino habbiamo, che quel Ser.mo
habbi scritto al Principe di Mantoua, che con sole 12 Persone se ne passasse in quella Città
à cellebrare le Nozze con là [sic] sua Figliuola, terminate per li 17 del corrente, sebene non
si sà se ui sia l'intiera sodisfattione delle Maestà Cesarea [the Emperor Rudolf] et Cattolica [Philip of Spain]« (ibid., f. 107v).

[151] Cf. this obituary, from a contemporary diary: »Alli 5. di Agosto 1630. si hebbe nova della
morte di Carlo Emanuele Duca di Savoja, il quale in vita sua era stato homo inquietissimo, et
al presente bona causa delle guerre, et romori, che si sentono grandissimi nell'Italia« — Giacinto
Gigli, Diario romano (1608—1670), ed. Giuseppe Ricciotti, Roma 1958, Tumminelli, p. 116.

[152] Dispatch incorrectly dated 13th February (actually written on 16th February) 1608, from
Mantua: »... e'l medesimo corriero [from Turin], che portò l'auuiso d'andare à sposare,
portò anco nuoua della conchiusione del matrimonio della secondogenita co'l Prencipe di
Modona, et qui si è publicata, et che sarà anco sposata nel medesimo tempo; ... È passato
questo negozio con tanta segretezza, che non se n'hà hauuta pur' ombra; nè in Modona
istessa si è saputa cosa alcuna« (Urb. lat. 1076, I, f. 106r).

[153] Dispatch dated 1st March 1608, from Mantua: »il matrimonio di Modona ... dà fastidio à
qualche persona per le conseguenze, che ne ponno risultare; et parendo ch'esso matrimonio non
sia d'intiera proportione mette qualche gelosia de' fini segreti« (ibid., f. 151r).

his accustomed bachelor existence; he still was single four years later when, at the age of sixty, he died of the effects of »an oil procured from far-off lands, [applied] for the purpose of helping in coitus«[154].

As the world still discovers to its sorrow, political nervousness tends to be contagious, and the first to come down with it are seldom reluctant to pass it on to their presumed adversaries. Carlo Emanuele had made no secret of his uneasiness about foreigners in Italy; consequently, Spanish Milan saw cause for uneasiness at the Savoy-Mantua alliance. And there are signs that at the moment of that alliance the Gonzagas, aware of the strain their move was imposing on Milanese nerves, felt their own share of nervousness as to what the Milanese might do by way of nervous reaction. Thus we find that Francesco Gonzaga did not attend his own wedding, but arranged to be married by proxy[155], thereby temporarily avoiding a trip that would have taken him through or past Milanese lands; for it was not inconceivable that on such a trip he might find trouble waiting along the way. The ceremony was held in Turin on 17th February; only when he was assured that it had taken place did Francesco himself set out for that city[156]. He of course had to join his bride there eventually, if only to ensure the contractual value of their marriage, which clearly was of great importance to both households: for the marriage could not be considered indissoluble in all circumstances until it had been consummated[157]. But in the meantime the proxy wedding united the two states officially enough: they now

---

[154] I imagine this obituary does not agree with official announcements; the notice, transmitted privately from Prague shortly after the Emperor died there (on 20th January 1612), is quoted in a letter of 20th February: »Dice della Morte del Imperatore et anco la cagione che sia stata per causa d'essersi Unto dun Oglio hauuto da paesi lontani fatto per Intentione di aiutar al Coito, qual è stato tanto potento [sic] che l'ha conquassato tutto, e mosso li humori che l'hano fettidamente ricercato per tutta la Vita da Capo à Piedi et al fine condottolo à Morte, et per la Vergogna non ha conferito Il male a persona alcuna sin al fine ridutto al estremo et miserabile« [X.63, 664].

[155] Two dispatches from Mantua: 9th February 1608: »Si uà discorrendo, che sia accertato il tempo delle nozze Serenissime fra pochissimi giorni, et che si farà il matrimonio per procuratorem colla primogenita« (Urb. lat. 1076, I, f. 96r); »13th« (recte 16th) February 1608: »Mercore, che fù alli .13. del presente partì per Turino il s.r Marchese [of Vescovado] Carlo Gonzaga [a third cousin of Vincenzo's] con l'annello sposalitio, et la procura fatta dal Ser.mo s.r Prencipe in persona del s.r Duca [Henri] di Nemurs [a second cousin of Carlo Emanuele's], ilquale deue sposare à nome di S.A. Domenica l'ultima di Carneuale [17th February] la Ser.ma Infante Donna Margarita primogenita di Sauoia« (ibid., f. 106r).

[156] Dispatch dated 22nd February 1608, from Mantua: »Hoggi alle 20. hore è arriuato un corriero spedito dal s.r Duca di Nemurs da Turino con la nuoua dello sposalitio seguito li .17. domenica di carneuale alle 22. hore; ... et alle 24. hore queste Alt.e [Francesco and Vincenzo] tutte consolate partirono per Turino« (ibid., f. 129r).

[157] Cf. e. g. E. L. HESTON, subsection 11 of art. Marriage, Canon Law of, in New Catholic Encyclopedia, New York 1967, McGraw-Hill Book Company, IX, pp. 286—287; or (more exhaustive historically) Pietro PALAZZINI, subsection 7 of art. Matrimonio in Enciclopedia cattolica, Città del Vaticano, Ente per l'Enciclopedia Cattolica e per il Libro Cattolico, VIII (1952), cols. 463—468.

could be expected to respond jointly to any untoward gesture Milan might make to the bridegroom in his nuptial passage. Nor did the Gonzagas wish to overestimate this deterrent; planning Francesco's trip, they initially chose a route that would by-pass Milan[158], presumably so as to eliminate any occasion for diplomatic gestures (or undiplomatic ones) on the part of the Spanish Governor, de Fuentes. But the Governor showed himself unwilling to let this opportunity pass without a demonstration of his cordiality[159]; and perhaps the Gonzagas, or their new in-laws, decided that it would not do to seem fearful or hostile. The Mantuans changed their minds and their itinerary, and friendly appearances were kept up: de Fuentes received Francesco and Vincenzo Gonzaga, and their retinue, as guests in his city[160]. In the course of their visit the Governor arranged to confer with one of Vincenzo's agents; but the agent brought back no report, for he died, »of a sudden«, during the interview[161]. Not long afterward the d'Este family revised its own travel plans: Duke Cesare was to have gone along on his son's wedding journey (not preceded by a proxy ceremony), with a stopover in Milan; instead, young Alfonso was sent in the company of his uncle — and by another route[162].

Both bridegrooms claimed their brides in due course: Francesco and Margherita received an archbishop's blessing on 10th March, and were lodged together that night[163]; Alfonso and Isabella were wed six days later[164]. But we can easily

---

[158] Dispatch dated 23rd February 1608, from Rome: »Et con lettere di Milano ... scriuono che le nozze si doueuano fare per li 17 del Corrente, douendo il Duca di Mantoua co'l Prencipe suo figliuolo et con solo 15, ò 20 gentilhuomini passare à Turino per la uia di Pauia senza toccar milano à fine di consummare il matrimonio« (Urb. lat. 1076, I, f. 126v).

[159] Dispatch dated 22nd February 1608, from Mantua: »Hoggi ... è arriuato un corriero del s.r Conte di Fuentes, che inuita S.A. à Milano« (ibid., f. 129r).

[160] Two dispatches from Venice: 23rd February 1608: »Di Milano delli 20 stante scriuono ... Che'l Fuentes haueua mandato molti Vffitiali et titolati alli Confini di Cassano [d'Adda] per riceuere il Ser.mo di Mantoua, et alloggiare li Caualieri, che l'accompagnerano« (ibid., f. 133r); 1st March 1608: »Scriuono di Milano delli 27 passato l'arriuo iui del Ser.mo di Mantoua, incontrato fuori di Porta orientale dal Fuentes con tutte le sue guardie, et grandissimo numero de Caualieri« (ibid., f. 146r).

[161] Dispatch dated 8th March 1608, from Rome: »Di Milano con lettere delli 28 passato, [scrivono] che era morto d'Improuiso mentre staua all'audienza del Conte di Fuentes, l'Agente del Duca di Mantua« (ibid., f. 161v).

[162] Dispatch dated 15th March 1608, from Venice: »di Milano ... s'ha ... Che il Duca di Modena si doueua riceuer con ogni magnificenza nel passaggio, che farà per Milano nell'andar à Turino per le Nozze del figliuolo« (ibid., f. 182r); but, later in the same dispatch: »Scriuono di Milano di 12. stante, che'l Principe di Modena era passato à Turino col Card.le [Alessandro] d'Este suo zio ... senza toccar Milano« (ibid., f. 183v).

[163] Dispatch without date line, but written in Turin on 11th March 1608: »La mattina seguente [Monday, 10th March] furono ad udir la Messa in Domo, et à riceuer la beneditione dell'Arciuescovo per i Ser.mi Sposi. ... Finito il desinare ... si ritirarono, ne per quella sera si fece altro per dare agio alli sposi, et hoggi ch'è il martedi ... Il s.r Prencipe si tratiene con la sua sposa« (ibid., f. 215r—215v).

[164] Dispatch without date line, but written in Turin on 22nd March 1608: »La Domenica [16th March] il Prencipe di Modona sposò l'infante D. Isabella« (ibid., f. 216r).

imagine that some sinister shadows hung over the gaiety duly exhibited in Turin — shadows deliberately cast by Spain and by de Fuentes. The result, I believe, can be seen in some facts already described; a few not very recondite guesses will now suffice to give those facts the coherent meaning that probably belongs to them. One guess is that Vincenzo Gonzaga, sufficiently persuaded that Spain and Milan were prepared to shed blood if further provoked, was unwilling to resume the suspended part of the territorial pact he originally had made with Savoy: in fact, he did no more about it. Another guess is that the Duke of Savoy was of a different mind, and was more displeased and impatient at the timorousness of his new ally than fearful of offending the foreigners he regarded as, in any case, his natural foes; that Carlo Emanuele was unafraid to wage war for the lands he had been promised is indeed clear, for he did so — against Mantua — five years later. I hope the reader will agree, then, that neither of these guesses greatly strains belief; for if both conjectures are accepted the rest of the story explains itself easily enough.

The territorial and the matrimonial proceedings were to have moved forward together; when, contrary to Carlo Emanuele's wishes, Vincenzo Gonzaga opted to accept the new, limited version of the territorial transaction, Carlo Emanuele simply and tacitly confronted him with a new, limited version of the matrimonial transaction. In the matter of territorial concessions, Vincenzo stood firm on the contractual sufficiency of what had been arranged at the time of the wedding ceremony: he made no move to hand over the further lands that originally had figured in his share of the agreement, and which Savoy still coveted[165]. In the matter of matrimonial formalities, Carlo Emanuele in effect stood firm on the contractual sufficiency of what h e had conceded at the time of the wedding — solemnization, and due consummation, of his daughter's marriage to a Gonzaga: he made no move to hand over the daughter herself to her husband's keeping. As we have seen, her departure for Mantua was post-

---

[165] The territory of Monferrato had lost its autonomy in 1533, and, thereupon, had immediately become an object of controversy between Savoy and Mantua: each of those states was able to assert a seemingly valid hereditary right to the vacant fief. When their dispute had gone on for three years, an imperial decree awarded the lands to Mantua; but Savoy was unwilling to renounce its own claim, and the matter continued for generations to be a source of discord between the two duchies. (See Annibale BOZZOLA, *Il marchesato e il ducato di Monferrato*, in *Enciclopedia italiana*, XXIII [2nd printing 1951], p. 659.) A stipulation aimed at adjusting this conflict, then, probably was the most significant feature of the territorial plan drafted by Vincenzo Gonzaga and Carlo Emanuele (see n. 128, above); but, owing to Spain's protest, the adjustment did not take place. Carlo Emanuele's vexation over this defeat can be inferred from the fact that during the next two decades he waged two wars (neither of them successful) to obtain control of Monferrato (see Walter MATURI, *Lo stato sabaudo*, in *Enciclopedia italiana*, XXX [2nd printing 1949], pp. 944—945).

poned time after time; as we also have seen, the ever mounting delay was both costly and humiliating for the Gonzagas — at a time when cost was an especially serious consideration for them, and prestige almost a visible element of the elaborate festivities awaiting (or, to the general displeasure, being awaited by) their wedding guests.

But the bride's failure to appear had still another, even less agreeable aspect. We must bear in mind that the status of a bride in such marriages was to a considerable extent that of a hostage: her presence in her husband's domain ensured — as well as anything could ensure — that his family would receive only amicable treatment from hers. For, once she was housed within the walls of her in-laws' city, not only her tenor of life but her tenure of it was largely in their hands; and one need only read the annals of a few noble families to be impressed at how little their relatively sheltered mode of existence served in those days to protect them against such misadventures as sudden, fatal bouts of indigestion, short but no less fatal falls, and the like. Viewed in this light, Carlo Emanuele's delay about sending his daughter to Mantua might be seen (and, I believe, was meant to be seen, by the Gonzagas) as the sign of a sudden reluctance to offer guarantees of amicability; more bluntly, the delay could be taken to signify that Savoy was preparing to go to war against Mantua, precisely in order to obtain the lands that Vincenzo Gonzaga, in the interests of peace, no longer wished to trade. After all (Carlo Emanuele may have reasoned), if a hint of Milanese belligerency could frighten Vincenzo away from their plan, might not a hint of Savoiard belligerency frighten him back to it?

The bride's delay thus neatly achieved several familiar objectives of what people unwincingly call diplomacy: it made Carlo Emanuele's nominal but overly independent ally at once the victim of a public embarrassment, an economic hardship, and an indefinite but undoubtedly disquieting threat of war — nuisances the victim might terminate (or at least mitigate) at his own discretion, by simply surrendering to his tormentor's will. Allowing that diplomacy of this sort differs from outright coercion, its distinguishing feature of course is a polite pretense that the deliberately created ills are accidents and the deliberately exhibited threat imaginary; in this respect, too, Carlo Emanuele's diplomacy was impeccable. Accounting for his daughter's peculiar immobility he mentioned neither territorial projects nor, certainly, martial ones: Margherita (though many said otherwise) was staying on in Turin only to mourn the death of the Archduchess of Graz[166]. An innocent excuse indeed, but also a transparent one:

---

[166] Dispatch dated 24th May 1608, from Rome: »Scriuono ... di Turino, ... che delle nozze della sposa di Mantua non sene parlaua et si credeua non sene farebbe altro fino à Settembre et la causa se bene multi multa dicunt uogliono sia per causa della morte dell'Arciduchessa di Gratz« (Urb. lat. 1076, I, ff. 359v—360r).

for, archduchesses notwithstanding, it could hardly be denied that Margherita's newly wed sister was by now securely installed in h e r husband's home[167]. In fact, the Archduchess of Graz had been no member of Margherita's family circle, and might as aptly be mourned by any Habsburg vassal (for instance, by any of the Gonzagas — who, far from letting grief get the better of them, were as eager as ever to get on with their celebrations). But a transparent excuse too can be effective diplomacy: the more easily it is seen through, the more perceptible is the threat it pretends to veil. Vincenzo Gonzaga must have understood what he was meant to understand, even though it behooved him to reply in terms as inconsequential (thus, as diplomatic) as Carlo Emanuele's. Never questioning the personal sorrow purportedly detaining Margherita, Vincenzo managed just the same to express and to explain diplomatically — i.e. non-politically — his own impatience: he too was motivated by a purely personal affliction. His knee, he averred, was troubling him, and required hydrotherapy; a trip to Spa was called for, but he could not think of leaving Mantua until the wedding festivities were out of the way and the guests homeward bound: surely his daughter-in-law might oblige him by hastening her arrival, on which the entire schedule depended[168].

In Turin, pangs over a departed archduchess; in Mantua, pangs of a resurgent arthritis. Such messages, barely significant in their content, meaningful enough in their context, measured out the awkward pause in the two dukes' carefully planned gesture of brotherhood — a pause peculiarly fertile in those unbrotherly phenomena we now associate with the term »cold war«. My conviction, in short, is that this final delay, like the other delays in the matrimonial program, was inspired by a precise political motive, perfectly consistent with the motives that, in the first place, had inspired the marriage agreement itself. Carlo Emanuele, inconvenienced by Vincenzo Gonzaga's willingness to receive and give less than had been planned, sought to improve matters by waging against Vincenzo a deliberate war of nerves; the total weaponry and the solitary plan of action for that war consisted in the mere postponement of his daughter's trip to Mantua.

---

[167] Dispatch dated 12th April 1608, from Rome: »Del Principe di Modena con lettere delli 2. stante habbiamo la partita da Turino di questo Seren.mo con l'Infanta sua sposa. ... All'ultimo di Marzo giunsero per il Pò à Piacenza ... et alli .8. stante andarono à Parma. ... Alli .9. poi questi Serenissimi doueuano fare l'entrata in Reggio [scil. Reggio Emilia, ruled by the Duke of Modena]« (ibid., f. 247r—247v).

[168] Two dispatches: 16th May 1608, from Mantua: »Non si sà ancora il preciso tempo della uenuta della Ser.ma Prencipessa, et per la instanza, che ne fà ultimamente il Ser.mo sig.r Duca ... si spera, che fra pochi giorni sarà quì; Volendo S.A. nel principio di Giugno partir per Fiandra, à pigliar l'acqua dei bagni di Spà« (ibid., f. 340r); 24th May 1608, from Venice: »Le lettere di Mantova de 20 portano ... [che] quel Duca aggrauato di male in un ginocchio ... disegnaua andare à Bagni di spaha, et perciò richiamaua il figliuolo con la sposa ... quanto prima« (ibid., f. 368r).

A notable advantage of this tactic was that even though it produced genuine trouble and worry for Vincenzo, the delay could be explained away — was in fact continuously being explained away — with a colorable semblance of innocence: Carlo Emanuele therefore was free to discontinue the harassment, without loss of face, any time he judged there was more to gain through amity than through intimidation. But, for this very reason, Vincenzo may have remained unintimidated throughout his ordeal: that is, he may have perceived that if his ally-antagonist chose to cloak a threat in veils of diplomacy rather than in gales of bluster, the threat itself probably was indeed illusory, and had been designed to be withdrawn — not implemented — if it proved ineffective. Bearing the delay with fortitude, Vincenzo could not stem its rising toll of embarrassment and expense; but if he feared that graver troubles were to follow, he did not show it: his only acknowledged cause for a plaintive expression was his aching knee.

The knee prevailed: finding Vincenzo firm, Carlo Emanuele relinquished his daughter at last, leaving further settlements to be achieved as outcomes, rather than conditions, of Margherita's move to Mantua. (She was going there in the virtual certainty of becoming duchess upon Vincenzo's death; it seemed equally certain that her first male child would be a future duke of Mantua — presumably, with the benefit of her guidance, a duke more sympathetic than Vincenzo to Savoy's views and designs. Committing Margherita to her husband's care, Carlo Emanuele could consider that he was merely mortgaging for a time some of his political hopes.)[169] And so the disgruntled Duke of Savoy after all had attained nothing through his miniature, one-sided cold war — except perhaps a measure of spiteful satisfaction at having discomfited the Gonzagas. In his pique he may indeed have relished their discomfiture, for he managed to conclude the episode with an unmistakable public snub. He was to have

---

[169] His grudging patience was not rewarded. Francesco Gonzaga did become duke of Mantua, and Margherita its duchess, in February 1612; by that time, too, they had produced a son; but before the year was out, both the child and Francesco had died of smallpox. The ducal authority passed to Francesco's brother Ferdinando — and Carlo Emanuele found himself deprived of the chance to wield any fatherly or grandfatherly influence over the conduct of Mantuan affairs. He demanded the return of his daughter, and, after several months of hesitation, Ferdinando allowed Margherita to leave Mantua. With that hostage safely back in Savoy, Carlo Emanuele promptly sent troops to occupy several towns in Monferrato, thus launching, in April 1613, the first of his wars over the lands Vincenzo Gonzaga had been dissuaded from giving him in 1608 (see n. 165, above; and Lodovico Antonio MURA-TORI, *Annali d'Italia dell'era volgare sino all'anno 1749*, Milano 1744—1749, Giovambatista Pasquali, XI, pp. 41—43). For all his scheming, and for all his battling, his craving for those lands was thwarted throughout the remainder of his lifetime; but the most ambitious of his cravings was fulfilled nine generations later, when his descendants began ruling, as kings, a united Italy.

escorted Margherita to Mantua[170], where he naturally was expected to attend the festivities offered in honor of her wedding and his own new alliance; but, at the last, he resolved to keep aloof from the proceedings: a little way out of Turin he bade his daughter farewell, and headed back home[171]. His conspicuous absence from the celebrations surely dampened the already compromised spirit of the occasion; but even so, after the vicissitudes described above, enthusiasm in Mantua must have been lively and heartfelt when, from that city's lacustrine shore, »on the Saturday before Pentecost — 24th May — ... the ceremonial barge carrying the Most Serene bride ... was sighted«[172], and the overdue revels finally were permitted to begin.

Within the next fifteen days, all the postponed festivities were held. Ascension Day was hurriedly given place on the Monday after Pentecost (just eleven days past its proper time)[173]; the tourneys announced on 10th April came to be fought after an interval somewhat less than two months long[174]; the varied program of musical stage works was presented in its dazzling entirety between 28th May and 5th June, inclusive[175]; and the last wedding banquet was consumed on 8th June, bringing the happy proceedings to a close[176]. By 9th June Vincenzo Gonzaga was free to do whatever he pleased, wherever he liked, about the knee he had found so difficult to bend.

---

[170] Dispatch dated 5th April 1608, from Venice: »Di Turino auisano ... Che ... quella [Infanta sposa] di Mantoua ... sarà accompagnata dal Duca suo Padre sino à Mantoua« (Urb. lat. 1076, I, f. 235r).

[171] Dispatch dated 24th May 1608, from Venice: »Scriuono di Milano delli 21. stante tener di Turino, che quel Duca risoluto non passar à Mantoua, haueua accompagnata la primagenita sposa sino à Chiuasso, [the bride] seguitando di là il suo uiaggio accompagnata dalli Principi fratelli, et s.A. tornò subito à Turino« (ibid., f. 364r).

[172] »Il Sabbato precedente alla Pentecoste, & ventesimo quarto di Maggio, ... fù veduto ... il Bucintoro, che conduceua la Serenissima Sposa« — [FOLLINO], pp. 6—7.

[173] »La mattina ... del Lunedì, secondo giorno della Pentecoste [26th May], si trasferirono ... i Prencipi tutti, e le Prencipesse nella ... Chiesa di S. Andrea, doue si mostrò ... il pretioso sangue del Redentor nostro, con l'occasione di vna procession solenne, che in altro tempo suol farsi il giorno dell'Ascensione, ma per all'hora trasferita nel dì sodetto« — ibid., pp. 26—27. (The traditional and festive character of the procession is described at some length.)

[174] »Il Duca con nuouo trattenimento recò ... il Martedì [3rd June] nuouo diletto, col far il Torneo« (ibid., p. 99); and, about the same event, »Era di già molto alto il Sole [i.e. on the morning of 4th June], quando si diede fine ... al Torneare« (ibid., p. 124). »Il giorno seguente per esser la festa del santissimo Sacramento [5th June] ... si fece la mattina la solita processione, ... Riducendosi dopò il pranzo le genti ... à veder la giostra dell'huomo armato« (ibid., p. 134). (The résumé of Follino's indications given by SOLERTI [Albori, I, p. 98, continuing n. 2 of p. 97] is deficient with respect to these datings.)

[175] SOLERTI, ibid., gives the correct dates for these works, derived from [FOLLINO], passim: Arianna, 28th May; L'idropica with Chiabrera's intermedii, 2nd June; Ballo delle ingrate, 4th June; Balletto d'Ifigenia, 5th June.

[176] »La Domenica [8th June] ... il Duca con superbo banchetto chiuse la pompa delle sontuose Feste« — [FOLLINO], p. 149.

But for the impediments I have described, he might have enjoyed the same liberty approximately four months sooner. Official obstructions to his son's marriage had been removed on 20th January: between that date and the end of Carnival, 19th February, all the scheduled events might easily have been accommodated — the wedding ceremony itself; the performances of *Dafne* and the other, unidentified Carnival play; and the two weeks' worth of pageantry finally offered as wedding entertainment[177]. Instead, the Mantuan court had spent the early months of 1608 anxiously revising and re-revising its schedules, in circumstances not at all conducive to merrymaking[178].

What had all this to do with music and musicians? My point is precisely that music and musicians, normally the subjects of music history, must not be mistaken for its rulers: their fate was often shaped (as, certainly, in this case) by persons and policies beyond their immediate influence and not especially responsive to their needs. During the period here in question, for example, the last thing likely to have troubled Vincenzo Gonzaga was the convenience of his entertainment staff (or, as we prefer to say, his artists). Monteverdi, composing *Arianna* for production among the wedding entertainments, was rushed nearly to death — literally, according to his own report[179]. I doubt that his

---

[177] To be sure, not all the wedding works actually were ready in Carnival: the score for Chiabrera's *intermedii* was not even begun until sometime around the beginning of March (see Carlo Rossi's letter quoted in CANAL, pp. 114—115). Guarini's *Idropica* could of course have been performed without those *intermedii* if it had truly been impossible to have them ready in time. Even if that expedient had seemed unacceptable, and the Gonzagas had had to sacrifice the entire production to get their celebrating done in Carnival, the program of wedding fêtes would have betrayed no sign of abbreviation; on the contrary, it presumably would have appeared somewhat longer: for *Dafne* and the other, unidentified Carnival play would then have been part of a single, amalgamated Carnival-wedding festivity (as, obviously, I believe had originally been desired). It would be vain, therefore, to imagine that the state of the Chiabrera *intermedii* in any way affected the date set for the wedding celebrations. Rather, the postponement of those celebrations can explain the late start on the music for Chiabrera's text: the postponement was decreed in the first days of the year (see n. 133, above); from then on, there simply was no cause to hurry the inception of new works for the wedding program.

[178] The lengthy recital of those clearly extra-musical circumstances was not originally part of my plan for this study. Rather, I had hoped to avoid such an undertaking (and so long a digression) by supplying references to historical works which, I supposed, would recount the necessary facts. Casting about for suitable references, however, I found no publication, or group of publications, that conveyed as much information as I believe transpires from the contemporary dispatches I already had seen. That is why I have chosen, reluctantly, to reconstruct the relevant history primarily from those dispatches, and to present their testimony in the accompanying footnotes.

[179] »La brevità del tempo fu cagione ch'io mi riducessi quasi alla morte nel scrivere l'Arianna« (Monteverdi, letter of 1st May 1627, as published in DAVARI, p. 75). Several other documents refer to the composer's prolonged illness after his exhausting labors connected with the wedding celebrations: see the two letters from his father, dated 9th and 27th November 1608, published in VOGEL, *Claudio Monteverdi*, respectively on p. 353 (in a partial translation into German) and p. 428; and Monteverdi's own letter of 2nd December 1608, first published in DAVARI, pp. 18—21.

frantic haste was dictated principally by a wish to leave more time for rehearsals; rather, he must have been spurred by an order to have his opera ready
for presentation in Carnival, in conformity with the court's all too transitory
hopes about the wedding itself (and, presumably, about the timing of all related
celebrations). He probably saw no line of Rinuccini's libretto before the latter
part of October 1607;[180] yet a letter of 2nd February 1608 in fact indicates
that by that date the bulk of the music was complete[181]. And one of Monteverdi's
own letters mentions that the opera — eventually performed on 28th May —
had required five months of rehearsal[182]: even allowing for some inexactness,

---

[180] On 9th October Monteverdi asked for the text he was to set, and urged that it be given
him within the following seven or eight days (see Francesco Gonzaga's letter of 10th October 1607, quoted in DAVARI, p. 12, n. 2); but he may have been kept waiting at least an
additional week, for it was not until 23rd October that Rinuccini himself arrived in Mantua, presumably to collaborate with Monteverdi (see Alessandro Striggio's letter of 25th
October 1607, quoted ibid.). (To prepare the libretto of *Dafne* for Gagliano, who was in
Florence, Rinuccini returned there: see his letter cited in n. 89, above.)

[181] The letter, from Ferdinando Gonzaga, is quoted in DAVARI, p. 14, n. 1.

[182] Monteverdi, letter of 9th January 1620: »*non* sono cose da farle cosi alla sfuggita, et lo sa
l'Arianna, che ci uolsero cinque mesi di proua co*n* molta instanza, dopo finita et inparata
a mente« — Archivio Gonzaga, Autografi, cassetta 6, f. 183ᵛ. (Earlier transcriptions of the
passage are available — in CANAL, p. 107; DAVARI, p. 66; VOGEL, *Claudio Monteverdi*,
p. 347, n. 3; SOLERTI, *Albori*, I, p. 97; MALIPIERO, *Claudio Monteverdi*, p. 186 — but each,
in one respect or another, is defective.) Monteverdi's statement has been discounted in some
recent publications; and indeed there is reason to doubt its full reliability. The letter was
written with an explicit motive, which may be relevant: a patron had offered a commission
that Monteverdi considered too ambitious to be fulfilled satisfactorily in the time available;
to illustrate how impractical the plan was, Monteverdi called attention to the long preparation *Arianna* had needed. Obviously, he wished to stress the length of that preparation,
and he may have been willing to do so even at the cost of some inaccuracy. Another letter
(cited above, n. 181) indicates that the opera had still to be finished as of 2nd February 1608;
yet Monteverdi's claim is that it received five months' rehearsal a f t e r the music had
been »completed and learned by heart«: ARNOLD and FORTUNE (in *The Monteverdi Companion*, p. 47) are right, therefore, to characterize that claim as an exaggeration. Still
another letter (quoted in SOLERTI, *Albori*, I, p. 92) makes it appear that *Arianna* cannot in
fact have been »completed and learned by heart« until sometime around mid-March; for
that letter reports that the Duchess of Mantua had declared the work »exceedingly arid
[*assai sciutta*]« in its lack of action, and that Rinuccini had therefore promised, on 26th
February, to »enrich« the libretto. (Perhaps this is why PIRROTTA [in *Early Opera and
Aria*, p. 71, n. 73; in *Li due Orfei*, p. 363, n. 73], referring to the lengthy preparation of
Arianna, cites no rehearsal date earlier than March.) Did Monteverdi, then, exaggerate to
the extent of approximately doubling the correct tally of rehearsal months? Apart from
questions of honor, this would be odd, since his assertion was addressed to an officer of the
Mantuan court, for transmission to the current duke: both of those gentlemen were in a
position to recognize, or easily to uncover, so gross an overstatement of the facts. A
different conclusion is possible, in the light of what has been said above. We have seen
evidence that the preparation of the wedding entertainments must initially have been
pursued in considerable haste: the wedding was at one time expected to take place around
20th January — certainly, sometime in Carnival — and Monteverdi was rushed »nearly to
death« composing *Arianna* for the occasion. It seems likely that in such circumstances the

we may conclude from this that a sizable part of the score was ready early in January[183]. That twenty weeks or more of rehearsal time was truly necessary may have been Monteverdi's view; that such time was allowed, after the feverish hurry imposed on the writing of the work, was almost certainly a surprise to everyone — a fortuitous result, that is, of the difficulties that slowed down the matrimonial proceedings themselves, quite against the court's wishes.

The slowdown, with its bonus of rehearsal time, unquestionably was a welcome boon for the performers; from their master's viewpoint, they had simply become the unexpected beneficiaries of a bitter and enervating series of political misfortunes that, among other things, had reduced the value of his son's marriage and the level of his own exchequer. There is every reason to suppose that if those misfortunes had not intervened, *Arianna* and all the other wedding pieces would have been produced, not after an extended period of rehearsal befitting their status as works of art, but in the haste that suited their function as incidental accessories of an urgent political act. No doubt the artists' burden would in that case have been colossal; this was indeed foreseen[184], but there was more than a grain of truth in the contention of one observer that »just the same, when mighty rulers so desire, their works appear, all complete, in a

---

various sections of the opera would be put into rehearsal as soon as they were composed; and the letter that reports the work unfinished on 2nd February states that very little was lacking, and that the score was substantially complete, at that date. Accordingly, I imagine that various portions of the work — together, amounting to nearly the whole of it — had begun to be rehearsed on various dates at least as early as January (see n. 183, below). Monteverdi's reference to five months may have seemed to him no more than an excusable »rounding-off« of some interval closely approximating that length — or, conceivably, an approximate average, based on the disparate lengths of rehearsal time devoted to separate sections of the work, separately »completed and learned by heart«. Then, the Duchess expressed her wish for improvements in *Arianna* well after the wedding program had been postponed (see n. 133, above) and time had unexpectedly become available for such refinements; there seems to be no question that the »enrichments« Rinuccini provided after 26th February were additions to an already complete, original version (see Pirrotta, *Early Opera and Aria*, p. 90, n. 103; *Li due Orfei*, p. 366, n. 103). I would suggest that the Duchess' criticism occurred to her after she had become acquainted with that original version in at least one fully staged rehearsal. In short, there may be more to Monteverdi's claim than has lately met the eye — but there still is nothing to suggest that his »five months« were the willing gift of a patron eager to improve the lives of artists or the quality of artistic offerings.

[183] Unless most of *Arianna* was written before the end of 1607, it is unclear why Monteverdi should have been rushed »nearly to death« writing it: the prime incentive to hurry — the prospect, that is, of an early wedding — had vanished before the new year was more than a few days old (see n. 133, above).

[184] Dispatch dated 8th November 1607, from Mantua: »Le Nozze son concluse al sicuro, et il Ser.mo Padrone spera di farle à Carneuale; . . . In tanto quì si uanno preparando gran cose, . . . Ma à i preparamenti diuisati temo che'l tempo non serua« (Urb. lat. 1075, II, f. 706r).

trice«[185]. It is well to add that mighty rulers took this for granted: all documents I have seen bearing on the preparation of seventeenth-century musical plays tend to suggest that hasty preliminaries were the rule, and lengthy ones the exception — not at all the other way round[186].

Were the musicians of that time so nimble, then, that they could be counted upon to produce consummate results »in a trice«? Perhaps through necessity they were: singers employed in operas, for example, not only had usually to learn their roles quickly; they seldom could expect to repeat any role in a second season (or even, necessarily, within a single season). Since opera itself was new, the basis for compiling a handy repertoire of repeatable roles of course was lacking; by the same token, there was more incentive to fill out than to replay the scanty stock of available works, and as a rule audiences rightly expected novelties, not revivals. Thus, extended study of any given role was as much a rarity after as before its first performance. For the performer as for the composer, each production was likely to be a venture as new, risky, and exacting as its predecessors. Yet contemporary accounts of performances — not only official *descrizioni* but less partisan reports, such as are found in courtiers' periodic newsletters to their principals — generally amount to what we should call rave notices: the word »squisito« — »exquisite« — is as commonplace in those reviews as is hand-clapping in modern theatres. That tribute, »squisito«, is indeed so nearly omnipresent as to justify (in my opinion, at least) some skepticism: like hand-clapping, it may seem less often the product of an individually reasoned critique than of a widespread conditioned tic. Perhaps, in short, the portrayals given by seventeenth-century opera singers, seldom based on more than a few weeks' study, in many cases appeared »exquisite« only in comparison with one another, at an over-all level that we should now find a good deal less praiseworthy. Certainly, the case of *Arianna*, considered in the context supplied above, can suggest that when an opera of those times received all the prepara-

---

[185] Dispatch dated 9th November 1607, from Mantua (in the same hand as the dispatch cited in the preceding note): »Alcuni sperano le nozze à questo carneuale, il tempo mi par brieue, et gli apparecchi, se ben si mouono, non mi pare però, che sieno accelerati; Tuttauia le cose de' Prencipi grandi compariscano perfettamente ad un tratto, quando uogliono« (ibid., f. 708ʳ).

[186] The case of Chiabrera's *intermedii* for *L'idropica*, if not typical, may nevertheless be pointed out as indicative. The musical setting for those *intermedii* was begun while the politico-nuptial situation was at a standstill, and preparations did not have to be carried on at top speed. Even so, the task of supplying music for the *intermedii* was apportioned in such a way as to get the writing done quickly: Chiabrera's six playlets were assigned, individually, to six composers. The composers set to work at about the beginning of March (see n. 177, above); quite soon afterward — within, at most, six weeks — the score must have been not only completed, but taught to the singers and put through at least one general rehearsal: for on 11th April, Angela was able to report that she already had learned her roles in the prologue and the finale, and had »rehearsed them on the stage«.

tion its composer thought necessary, the composer might owe his luck not to the generosity of his patron's arrangements but to their failure.

In that respect (and practically no other) Monteverdi was lucky in 1608 — as he would be, owing to similar circumstances, in Parma twenty years later. Still luckier were the performers: they cannot have been subjected to the kind of pressure that had beset Monteverdi in his harrowing race to complete *Arianna*. Before all of them can have even received their parts, the illusion of a need for hurry was ended by the political deadlock[187]; the resultant abundance of rehearsal time may, indeed, have allowed them to make the Mantuan wedding fêtes genuinely »exquisite«.

And for one of them, Angela Zanibelli, the Gonzagas' altered schedule must have had some further consequences: as I shall explain, it probably accounts for the most noteworthy aspects of her service at the ducal court.

(To be continued)

Appendix on the term »commedia«[188]

There can be no doubt that theatrical works other than comedies were called »commedia« in Rome after 1625. Some instances that can illustrate the practice (although they have not hitherto been called upon to do so) are:

Ottavio Tronsarelli, *La catena d'Adone* favola *boschereccia* (title of the printed libretto, Roma 1626, Francesco Corbelletti), to which a contemporary diary refers in the phrase »le commedie delli S.ri Conti«[189];

Michelangelo Rossi, *Erminia svl Giordano* dramma *mvsicale* (title of the printed score, Roma 1637, Paolo Masotti), to which a letter of 1633 refers as one of several »commedie«[190];

Stefano Landi, *Il S. Alessio* dramma *mvsicale* (title of the printed score, Roma 1634, Paolo Masotti), which its librettist, in letters as yet unpublished, twice called »la Commedia«[191].

---

[187] See n. 133, above.

[188] This appendix relates to a question set forth in n. 48, above; it is not intended to be a comprehensive résumé of the meanings »commedia« has temporarily assumed or lastingly accumulated in the long history of the Italian language. For present purposes most of those usages would be irrelevant; some, in any case, are too familiar to need comment, while others (e.g. Dante's in the title of his famous trilogy) already occupy the special places they merit in the hearts and works of lexicographers. Just two definitions can make or receive any contribution here: they alone will be considered.

[189] See Reiner, »*Vi sono molt'altre mezz'Arie . . .*«, p. 248, n. 15.

[190] See the letter from Fabio Almerici quoted in Alfredo Saviotti, *Feste e spettacoli nel Seicento*, Giornale storico della letteratura italiana, XLI, Fasc. 121 (1903), p. 70.

[191] In one, for example: »Mando un'Argomento della Commedia rappresentata al Principe di Polonia, in un teatro molto nobile, con habiti ricchi, e con macchine di qualche considera- tione, mà sopra*tutto* cantata, e rappresentata con esquisitezza. . . . Roma 21 Gennaio 1634. Giulio Rospigliosi«.

But the same practice can be documented, outside of Rome, at least as far back as the beginning of the century:

A »Comedia che si fa in Musica« is mentioned in a letter sent from Florence on 29th August 1600. Solerti, who published the letter[192], placed it in a context that has led other writers to connect it with Rinuccini's *Euridice*; Claude V. Palisca has shown that Chiabrera's *Rapimento di Cefalo* may more plausibly have been the work meant[193]. In either case, the piece was not a comedy: *Euridice* was generically described as a *favola*[194], and Chiabrera's libretto was published during his lifetime as a *dramma*[195].

Rinuccini's *Dafne*, too, was a *favola*, in the terminology of both Peri[196] and Gagliano[197]; but a dispatch from Mantua dated 8th March 1608 (published on p. 55 of the present study) refers to it as one of »le due Comedie«.

The same poet printed his *Arianna* as a *tragedia*[198], but Gagliano called it a *favola*[199], and in the aforementioned dispatch from Mantua it figures among the »nuoue, et Regali Comedie, che si preparano«: a goodly gamut of epithets, applied to a single work in a single year.

Other examples surely could be added to both of the foregoing groups, and the half-dozen cases I have cited could themselves be enlarged upon by reference to further documents about them. I have chosen these illustrations solely because I found them readily at hand and suitably explicit. In all of these instances — whether from Rome after 1625 or from northern Italy earlier in the century — any seeming contradiction in terminology will vanish when it is understood that »commedia« was used to mean »play« (and that »favola« meant simply »tale«, or »story«)[200].

Surely n o t indicative of this usage, however, is the *Argomento et allegoria della*

---

[192] In *Musica, ballo*, p. [23].

[193] Palisca, *The First Performance of »Euridice«*, p. 8; relevant information is given also on pp. 3—5.

[194] E.g. by Caccini, in *L'Evridice composta in mvsica in stile rappresentatiuo da Giulio Caccini detto Romano*, Firenze 1600, Giorgio Marescotti, p. [iii] (reprinted in Solerti, *Origini*, p. 50); and by Gagliano (see n. 92, above).

[195] *Il rapimento di Cefalo dramma musicale di Gabriello Chiabrera*, Venezia 1625, Combi: see Solerti, *Albori*, III, p. 7.

[196] Peri, p. [v] (reprinted in Solerti, *Origini*, p. 45).

[197] See n. 92, above.

[198] *L'Arianna tragedia del Sig. Ottavio Rinvccini. gentil'hvomo della camera del Re Cristianissimo. rappresentata in musica nelle reali nozze del Serenissimo Principe di Mantoua, e della Serenissima Infanta di Sauoia*, Firenze 1608, Giunti. The title page of another edition (Venetia 1608, Bernardo Giunti, Gio. Battista Ciotti, & Compagni) shows only minor variants; it, too, presents the work as *L'Arianna tragedia*.

[199] See n. 92, above. Elsewhere, it has been made to appear that Rinuccini himself called *Arianna* a »Favola«: an excerpt from the poet's letter of 20th December 1607, beginning and ending with advice about *Arianna*, has been published both by Davari (pp. 12—13) and by Solerti (*Albori*, I, pp. 89—90); and each of those scholars has introduced his quotation in such a manner as to indicate that everything in it — including the word »Favola« — has to do with *Arianna*. But only a momentary change of subject can account for the mention of »Mes.r Marco« (i.e. Gagliano) midway through the passage: the nearby reference to a »Favola« must concern *Dafne*. (So must everything else in that part of the excerpt, shown in Solerti's transcription — though not in Davari's — as a separate paragraph.)

[200] See n. 87, above.

comedia mvsicale intitolata Chi soffre speri (first published 1637; revised, 1639)[201]. For the second edition of this *argomento* the title page was largely recast, but the description »comedia mvsicale« was not altered; these two editions are the only cases I know in which a printed *argomento* shows the term »commedia« (however spelled) juxtaposed to the title of an opera[202]. The surviving score of *Chi soffre speri* also includes »comedia« on its title page, prominently placed before the title of the opera, and in larger letters[203]. Nino Pirrotta has more than once pointed out that the typographic prominence of the word »tragedia« on the title page of Rinuccini's *Arianna* is symptomatic — that it was meant to call attention to a new development in the character of opera texts[204]. I would say that the prominence of the word »comedia« on the title page of *Chi soffre speri* — supported by the titles of its two *argomenti* — reflects a parallel aim on the part of its librettist, Giulio Rospigliosi. Nor has Rospigliosi's intent generally been missed: Ulderico Rolandi found scholarly opinion unanimous in declaring *Chi soffre speri* »the first musical *commedia* presented in Rome«[205]. Rolandi was not unaware that musical plays had been seen and heard in Rome long before *Chi soffre speri* appeared; nor for that matter was I unaware of it when I proposed that a work of 1635 may more truly have been the first Roman *commedia musicale*[206]. What Rolandi and I (and Rolandi's unanimous scholars) had in mind of course was that *Chi soffre speri* is, specifically, a comedy; and I imagine we all assumed — as I mean here to assert — that when the term »commedia« was applied to it, even in the seventeenth century, that is what was expressed. Similarly, when Guarini presented his *Idropica* he was aware (as one who had written lengthily on the relationships and differences among theatrical genres[207]) that what he had wrought was neither a pastoral, a tragedy, nor a tragicomedy, but, precisely, a comedy; and although there may somewhere be a document that calls *L'idropica* by an epithet other than »commedia«, I know of none[208]. The point of this paragraph, briefly, is

---

[201] Regarding the two editions, see Stuart REINER, *Collaboration in* Chi soffre speri, in The Music Review, XXII, No. 4 (1961), pp. [265], 273, 281.

[202] Printed *argomenti* for operas of this period, even including the *argomenti* sometimes given in scores or libretti, are fairly rare among surviving documents; but I am acquainted with fourteen separately printed ones, spanning a period of over twenty years.

[203] COMEDIA / CHI SOFFRE SPERI / POESIA / DELL'ILLVSTRISSIMO MŎN. / RVSPIGLIOSI / Posta in Musica / DALLI SIGNORI / VERGILIO MAZZOCCHI, E MARCO / MARRAZZOLI [sic] (Biblioteca Vaticana: MS. Barb. lat. 4386, f. 1r).

[204] In *Early Opera and Aria*, p. 50, n. 34; in *Li due Orfei*, p. 359, n. 34; and in the »Discussione« following Nino PIRROTTA, *Teatro, scene e musica nelle opere di Monteverdi*, in *Claudio Monteverdi e il suo tempo*, ed. Raffaello Monterosso, Verona 1969, Stamperia Valdonega, p. 66.

[205] ROLANDI, *La prima commedia musicale rappresentata a Roma nel 1639*, Nuova antologia, Serie VII, Vol. CCLV, Fasc. 1334 (1927), p. 523: »Per unanime consenso di studiosi la prima commedia musicale rappresentata a Roma fu appunto *Chi soffre speri*«.

[206] REINER, *Collaboration in* Chi soffre speri, p. 275, n. 30.

[207] In *Il Verrato ovvero Difesa di qvanto ha scritto M. Giason Denores* [sic]. *contra le tragicomedie, et le pastorali, in vn svo discorso di poesia*, Ferrara 1588, Vincenzo Galdura; and *Il Verato* [sic] *secondo ovvero Replica dell'Attizzato accademico ferrarese in difesa del Pastorfido* [sic], *contra la seconda scrittura di Messer Giason de Nores intitolata Apologia*, Firenze 1593, Filippo Givnti.

[208] The play was first printed as *La idropica commedia del M. Ill. Sig. Caualier Battista* G u a r i n i (Venetia 1613, Gio: Batt: Ciotti). Although this first edition is posthumous, the presence of the word »commedia« on the title page seems consonant with the author's inten-

that even in times and places in which '»commedia« could mean, simply and generically, »play«, it also could — and necessarily did — serve to signify »comedy«, as
distinct from other kinds of play. If this double sense seems too inherently bewildering
to be viable (or, consequently, to be credible), I may add that it still is verifiably
current in Italian usage, and can be encountered from one end of Italy to the other[209].
To be sure, conversations into which the word falls do sometimes eddy a bit in its
wake of potential ambiguity, but no more often than conversations in which »Lei«
(»you«) and »lei« (»she«) both need to be used.

For the scholar or the translator (or the innocent but curious bystander) concerned with
such words, the only suitable course is to evaluate each case as it arises — if possible,
on the basis of auxiliary evidence. »Commedia« certainly calls for such treatment: for
(as I hope will now be apparent) it has been capable since at least as long ago as
1600, and probably throughout Italy, of meaning alternately »comedy« and »play«.
If in the intervening years there has been any temporal or geographic break in the
continuity of this double usage, I submit that it remains to be demonstrated.

---

tion: a prologue he had written for a Venetian production of the work is, precisely, a
commentary on the history of *commedie*. Moreover, the commentary supports the view
that »commedia« here meant »comedy«, rather than simply »play«: »la Commedia Greca,
& Latina ... deposta la loro antica scurilità, & sordidezza, ... più costumate, & più
nobili diuentassero: La doue per il contrario, quella de' nostri tempi ... è stata indegna-
mente costretta ... à diuenire ancora vagabonda, & publica meretrice: ... vestita da
giuocolare, non sà far altro, che ridere« (ibid., f. [vi]^r—[vi]^v).

[209] Italian radio and television broadcasts all are produced by a government-franchised agency
called the RAI. In the announcements of the RAI, »commedia« will sometimes refer to a
work by Goldoni, but is just as likely to be applied to the dramatization of a Kafka story.
Since this agency, which is a monopoly, transmits its programs on a network basis throughout
Italy, I need not perform a direct survey — it is enough to turn on the radio — to obtain
convincing evidence that the two meanings of »commedia« both »can be encountered from
one end of Italy to the other« and are both accepted in current usage. The works most
likely to escape this equivocal classification (or these homonymous classifications) are — as
in the past they generally have been — plays whose authors have bestowed on them sub-
title epithets of deliberately individualistic character (in the manner of Da Ponte's
»dramma giocoso«).

THE *ANTIPHONAE, SEU SACRAE CANTIONES* (1613) OF GIOVANNI FRANCESCO ANERIO: A LITURGICAL STUDY[1]

by *James Armstrong* (Waterville, Maine)

The student of Italian Baroque Vesper music confronts a mountainous body of works, still largely unexplored[2]. While one is most grateful for the contributions of a few scholars, notably Laurence Feininger, whose editions have illuminated the development of polychoral Vesper music in Italy[3], the bulk of Italian Vesper music in the seventeenth century remains covered by the »deep shade« that Alfred Orel lamented nearly fifty years ago[4].

In fact, the only work from this repertory to have become widely known and to have been studied in considerable detail is Monteverdi's Marian Vespers of

[1] The research for this study was undertaken in Rome during the academic year 1970—71, thanks to generous financial assistance from Connecticut College, where I was then teaching.

[2] The relative importance of Vesper music in the seventeenth century can be gauged by a comparison of types of music offered for sale by an important Italian publishing firm, the VINCENTI of Venice, in four catalogues issued between 1591 and 1662:

	1591	1621	1649	1662
Vesper Psalms	10	54	89	102
Masses	22	77	106	120
Motets	12	182	216	274

While one's attention is drawn immediately to the spectacular growth of the motet repertory, the table also shows that a 2 : 1 advantage of masses over Vesper psalms in 1591 had dropped to a 6 : 5 ratio by 1662. The seventy-odd composers whose Vesper music was offered for sale in 1662 form an impressive company of seventeenth-century masters, including Claudio MONTEVERDI, Ignazio DONATI, Stefano BERNARDI, Francesco CAVALLI, Antonio CIFRA, Alessandro GRANDI, Tarquinio MERULA, Giovanni ROVETTA, Giovanni LEGRENZI, Marco UCCELLINI, and Maurizio CAZZATI. The Vincenti catalogue of 1591 has been reprinted by G. THIBAULT, *Deux catalogues de libraires musicaux: Vincenti et Gardane (Venise 1591)*, in: Revue de musicologie 13, 1929, pp. 177—183. The 1649 catalogue has been reprinted by F. X. HABERL and R. EITNER in: Beilage zu Monatshefte für Musikgeschichte 15, 1883, pp. 19—40, together with an otherwise unknown Vincenti catalogue of 1619 (pp. 1—18) that appears to be nearly identical with the 1621 catalogue cited below. The two remaining catalogues, *Indice di tutte le opere di musica, che si trovano nella Stampa della Pigna*, Venezia 1621, Alessandro Vincenti; and *Indice di tutte le opere di musica...*, Venezia 1662, Alessandro Vincenti, have not been reprinted. The 1591 catalogue is preserved at the Bibliothèque Mazarine (Paris); the 1621, 1649, and 1662 catalogues are at the Civico Museo Bibliografico Musicale (Bologna). The Vesper music listed in the Vincenti catalogues is the subject of a study (now in progress) by the present author.

[3] *Monumenta liturgiae polychoralis Sanctae Ecclesiae Romanae: Psalmodia cum duobus choris [... cum tribus choris concertata; ... cum quatuor choris]*, Trento and Roma 1950.

[4] Alfred OREL, *Die katholische Kirchenmusik von 1600—1750*, in: *Handbuch der Musikgeschichte*, ed. Guido Adler, Frankfurt am Main 1924, p. 445.

1610[5]. The controversy surrounding this work gives ample evidence of the rudimentary state of our present knowledge of Vesper music and of the liturgical requirements which the music is intended to fulfill[6]. The Monteverdi controversy concerns five non-liturgical compositions inserted among the Marian psalms, hymn, and *Magnificat: Nigra sum, Pulchra es, Duo Seraphim, Audi coelum,* and the *Sonata sopra Sancta Maria.* These five works do not conform textually to any known Marian office, but they occur in Monteverdi's collection in positions normally occupied by psalm antiphons.

The Roman Breviary provides for antiphons to be repeated before and after each of the five psalms and the *Magnificat* on feasts of Double rank. On lesser occasions the complete antiphon is said only after the psalm; the initial statement is confined to an incipit[7]. While the *Caeremoniale Episcoporum* forbids the substitution of other texts, the antiphons which follow the psalms and *Magnificat* may be played on the organ, provided the proper texts are recited aloud at the same time[8]. Since only the antiphons are missing from the 1610 Vespers, it is tempting to suppose that their position in the liturgy was to be occupied by

---

[5] Claudio MONTEVERDI, *Sanctissimae Virgini missa senis vocibus, ac vesperae pluribus decantandae, cum nonnullis sacris concentibus, ad sacella sive principum cubicula accommodata,* Venezia 1610, Amadino. The Vesper music occupies the second half of the print, introduced (in the *Bassus generalis*) by the rubric: *Vespro della B. Vergine da concerto, composto sopra canti fermi.*

[6] In addition to the literature cited in Denis STEVENS, *Where Are the Vespers of Yesteryear?,* in: The Musical Quarterly 47, 1961, pp. 315—330, and Stephen BONTA, *Liturgical Problems in Monteverdi's Marian Vespers,* in: JAMS 20, 1967, pp. 87—106, the following authors have made valuable recent contributions to the discussion of this work in its liturgical context: Giuseppe BIELLA, *La »Messa« il »Vespro« e i »Sacri Concenti« di Claudio Monteverdi,* in: Musica sacra 88, 1964, pp. 104—115; Wolfgang OSTHOFF, *Unità liturgica e artistica nei »Vespri« del 1610,* in: Rivista italiana di musicologia 2, 1967, pp. 314—327. Useful studies on other aspects of Monteverdi's church music (including the 1610 collection) may be found in two important collections of essays commemorating the Monteverdi anniversary in 1967: *Atti del convegno di studi dedicato a Claudio Monteverdi, Siena, 28—30 aprile 1967,* in: Rivista italiana di musicologia 2, 1967, pp. 201—389; and *Claudio Monteverdi e il suo tempo,* ed. Raffaello MONTEROSSO, Verona 1969, Stamperia Valdonega. See the review of the latter publication by Stuart REINER, in: MLA Notes 26, 1969—1970, pp. 747—748. The reader is also referred to Bjørn HJELMBORG, *Omkring Monteverdis Vesper-cyklus,* in: Dansk Musiktidsskrift 33, 1958, pp. 39—43; and to Guido Pannain's analysis in Guglielmo BARBLAN, Claudio GALLICO, and Guido PANNAIN, *Claudio Monteverdi nel quarto centenario della nascita,* [Torino 1967], Edizioni RAI Radiotelevisione italiana, pp. 332—344.

[7] *Brev 1618,* fol. ****1: »*In Duplicibus ad Vesperas, Matutinum, & Laudes tantùm, Antiphonae dicuntur ante Psalmos integrae, & post Psalmos integrae repetuntur: in aliis Horis, & in Officio non Duplici, in principio Psalmi inchoatur tantùm Antiphona, deinde in fine integra dicitur.*«

[8] *Caeremoniale Episcoporum Clementis Papae VIII. et Innocentii X. iussu recognitum,* Roma 1670, p. 140: »*... &, si placuit, finito quolibet Psalmo, poterit Antiphona per organum repeti, dum tamen per aliquos Mansionarios, aut alios ad id deputatos eadem Antiphona clara voce repetatur. Et, si quis esset, qui cum organo cantare vellet, nihil aliud cantet, quam ipsam Antiphonam ...*«

the five non-liturgical pieces, some of whose texts resemble actual antiphons. Is it merely coincidence that the five pieces are printed in the partbooks precisely in those places where one would expect to find the missing antiphons[9]?

On the other hand, no evidence has yet come to light that the Church's prohibition against altered texts, clearly stated in the *Caeremoniale Episcoporum* and restated at intervals thereafter[10], was ever so flagrantly violated as Monteverdi appears to have done. If his intention was to compose a set of antiphon-substitutes, why was none provided after the *Magnificat*? Indeed, the reference to »*nonnullis sacris concentibus*« on the title page has suggested to some scholars that Monteverdi intended the five pieces as devotional motets, not necessarily to be performed at Vespers; their musical style is also quite distinct from the style of the canonical pieces[11].

Up to the present time the controversy has seemed incapable of resolution to general satisfaction. Monteverdi has left too few clues, and supporting evidence from other composers has been lacking. Denis Stevens's question remains: Where are the Vespers of yesteryear? More specifically, is there any evidence that other seventeenth-century composers wrote non-liturgical vocal music for performance at Vespers, as Monteverdi seems to have done? Could such motets have been performed as antiphon-substitutes? Our study of Giovanni Francesco Anerio's *Antiphonae*, prompted by the controversy sketched in the preceding paragraphs, is addressed to these questions.

The title of the collection follows:

CANTVS. / ANTIPHONAE, / SEV SACRAE CANTIONES, / QVAE IN TOTIVS ANNI / VESPERARVM AC COMPLETORII / SOLEMNITATI-BVS DECANTARI SOLENT; / IN TRES PARTES DISTRIBVTAE; / Quarū prima Natiuitatis Domini, Circumcisionis, Epiphaniae, & omniū Sanctorū / Secunda, Festa mobilia, & Communia Sanctorum. / Tertia, Praecipua Mendicantium Religionum festa complectitur. / Binis, Ternis, & Quaternis vocibus concinendae. Vna cum Basso / ad Organum. / AVCTORE, IO: FRANCISCO ANERIO ROMANO. / In Ecclesia Sanctissimae Virginis ad Montes

---

[9] The arguments for considering these pieces antiphon-substitutes are summarized in BONTA, *Liturgical Problems*, p. 97.

[10] James ARMSTRONG, *The Vesper Psalms and Magnificats of Maurizio Cazzati*. Unpublished Ph. D. dissertation, Harvard University 1969, I, pp. 403—406.

[11] These arguments are best summarized in BIELLA, pp. 111—114. Non-liturgical vocal music could have been added at the end of Vespers; see ARMSTRONG, I, p. 34, footnote 22. In the eighteenth century it was a Venetian custom to conclude Vespers with a group of solo motets, followed by one of the Marian antiphons; see Sven Hostrup HANSELL, *Sacred Music at the Incurabili in Venice at the Time of J. A. Hasse*, in: JAMS 23, 1970, p. 290.

Capellae Magistro. / PRIMA PARS. / Romae, Apud Io: Baptistam Roblectum.
M. DC. XIII. / Superiorum permissu[12].

Each of the three volumes is dedicated to one of three brothers of the Alaleoni
family of Rome; the dedications, which are dated at Rome on September 3, 5,
and 13 (1613), respectively[13], are signed by a certain Robertus Belandus[14]. The
complete set consists of the following partbooks: *Cantus, Tenor, Altus,* and
Bassus ad Organum (Prima Pars); Cantus, Tenor, Bassus, and *Bassus ad Organum (Secunda Pars); Cantus, Tenor, Altus,* and *Bassus ad Organum (Tertia
Pars)*[15]. Pagination is continuous in the *Prima* and *Secunda Pars*; the *Tertia Pars*
is paginated separately[16].

The *Antiphonae* were published during Anerio's first year of tenure as maestro
di cappella of the Jesuit church of S. Maria dei Monti in Rome, where he served
until 1621[17]. This Baroque church, built in 1582[18], is located on a modest little
piazza in the valley at the base of the Viminal, Quirinal, and Esquiline hills.
The small organ gallery above the main entrance is large enough for only a few
singers but would be entirely suitable for the performance of Anerio's *Antiphonae*. It has not been possible to inspect the organ at close range, but the

---

[12] »Canto. Antiphons, or sacred songs, which are to be sung at the solemn celebration of
Vespers and Compline throughout the year; divided into three parts; of which the first
[comprises the feasts] of the Nativity of the Lord, of the Circumcision, of the Epiphany,
and of all the saints[;] the second, movable feasts and the Common of Saints. The third
includes special feasts of the mendicant orders. To be sung with two, three, and four voices.
With a bass for organ. Composed by Giovanni Francesco Anerio romano. Maestro di cappella in the church of S. Maria dei Monti. First part. In Rome, [printed] by Giovanni
Battista Robletti [?]. 1613. With the permission of the authorities.«

[13] *Tertio Non., Nonis,* and *Idibus Septembris. Anno M. DC. XIII.*

[14] Concerning the contents of the dedications, see F. X. HABERL, *Giovanni Francesco Anerio,*
in: Kirchenmusikalisches Jahrbuch 1, 1886, pp. 54—55. See also Gaetano GASPARI, *Catalogo
della Biblioteca del Liceo Musicale di Bologna,* II, Bologna 1892, pp. 157—158.

[15] The copy consulted was that preserved in the Biblioteca di S. Cecilia (Rome), under the
catalogue number GCS.1.A.15 (bound in one volume). The parts contain numerous corrections and emendations in pen, probably the work of a seventeenth or eighteenth-century
hand; some of these additions are discussed in this article. I am grateful to the directress
of the library, Signorina Emilia Zanetti, for many kindnesses during my sojourn in Rome,
and in particular for permission to microfilm this work for the present study.

[16] The *Bassus* of the *Secunda Pars* is also paginated separately.

[17] Karl Gustav FELLERER, *Anerio,* in: MGG 1, 1949—1951, col. 470; see also MGG Supplement, col. 216. For further information on the life of G. F. Anerio, see HABERL, *Anerio;*
Hellmuth FEDERHOFER, *Ein Beitrag zur Biographie von Giovanni Francesco Anerio,* in: Die
Musikforschung 2, 1949, pp. 210—213; id., *Nochmals zur Biographie von Giovanni Francesco
Anerio,* in: Die Musikforschung 6, 1953, pp. 346—347; Raffaele CASIMIRI, *Disciplina musicae
e mastri di capella dopo il Concilio di Trento nei maggiori istituti ecclesiastici di Roma,*
in: Note d'archivio 15, 1938, pp. 6—10.

[18] HABERL, *Anerio,* p. 54.

appearance of the case suggests that the original instrument may still be in place.

Part I of Anerio's collection is devoted to Vesper antiphons for the Proper of Saints for important feasts throughout the year, together with the Proper of the Time from Advent to the Epiphany. Part II includes Vesper antiphons for the Proper of the Time from Easter to Corpus Christi and for the Common of Saints; at the end of Part II we find the three antiphons for Compline to which the title page refers. Part III contains Vesper antiphons from special offices (including rhymed offices) of the principal saints of four mendicant orders: Augustinian, Franciscan, Dominican, and Carmelite.

TABLE I

Index Antiphonarum, & Cantionum quae in prima parte continentur[19].

In Aduentu, & vigilia Natiuitatis Domini[20].
1. Orietur sicut sol. à 2. Canti. à carte		3
2. Cum ortus[21] fuerit a 2. bassi.		3
3. Montes, & colles, a 2. tenori.		4
4. Hierusalem. a 2. alti.		4

In festo S. Andreae Apostoli [Nov. 30]. In primis, & secundis Vesperis.
5. Salue Crux. a quattro, 2. canti, & 2. alti.		5
6. Beatus Andreas, a 2. alto, & tenore.		5
7. Andreas Christi famulus, a 2. bassi.		6
8. Maximilla, a 2. canti.		6

In festo S. Nicolai [Dec. 6], vt in Comm. Conf Pont. vide in 2 parte[22].

In festo S. Ambrosij [Dec. 7], vt in Com. Conf. Pont. vide in 2. parte[23].

In festo Conceptionis B. Virginis [Dec. 8], vt in Natiuitate eiusdem mutato nomine Natiuitatis in nomen Conceptionis. à carte.   50[24]

In festo S. Damasi Papae [Dec. 11], vt in Com. Conf. Pōt. vide in 2. parte[25].

---

[19] »Index of antiphons and songs [i.e., motets] which are contained in Part I.« Table of contents from *Bassus ad Organum*, Part I, pp. 64—67; Anerio's page numbers refer to that partbook only. In a few instances the rubrics in the Index differ from those in the body of the partbook; these differences are noted below. Instances in which the order of the pieces changes from partbook to partbook are also noted below. The number preceding each title has been assigned by this writer; Anerio does not number the pieces. Unless otherwise indicated, the dates of the feasts are supplied from *Brev 1606*.

[20] Rubric within the partbook: *In Aduentu Domini*.

[21] Corrected from original: *ortu*.

[22] See No. 168—172.

[23] See No. 168—172.

[24] »In the feast of the Conception of the Blessed Virgin, as in the Nativity of the same [Sept. 8], the name *Nativitas* changed to the name *Conceptio*.« See No. 93—96.

[25] See No. 168—172.

In festo S. Luciae [Dec. 13]. In primis, & secundis Vesperis.

     9. Orante sancta Lucia, à 2. Tenore, e cāto.   7

    10. Per te Lucia, a 2. baritono, & basso.   7

    11. Lucia virgo, a 2 canto, & tenore[26].   8

    12. Benedico te, a 2. alto, & basso[27].   8

In festo S. Tomae Apostoli [Dec. 21], vt in commune Apostolorum. vide in 2. parte[28].

In Natiuitate Domini [Dec. 25]. In primis, & secundis Vesperis.

    13. Tecum principiū, a 2. canto, & tenore[29].   9

    14. Exortum est, a 2. bassi.   9

    15. Apud Dominum, a 2. alti.   9

    16. Facta est cum Angelo, a 2. canto, e ten[30].   10

In festo SS Stephani, Ioannis, Innocentium [Dec. 26, 27, 28]. vt in die Natiuitatis [Dec. 25] à Carte.   9[31]

In festo S Thomae Cantuariensis [Dec. 29], vt in Comm. mart vide in 2. parte[32].

In festo S. Siluestri Papae [Dec 31], vt in Comm. Conf. Pont vide in 2 parte[33].

In Circumcisione Domini [Jan. 1]. In primis, & secundis Vesperis.

    17. O admirabile, a trè. 2. canti, & basso.   10

    18. Quando natus, a 2 tenori.   11

    19. Rubrum[34], a 2. alti.   11

    20. Germinauit, a 2. bassi.   12

In Epiphania Domini [Jan. 6]. In primis, & secundis Vesperis.

    21. Omnes de Saba venient, a 2. canto, & basso.   13

    22. Venit lumen, a 2. alti.   13

    23. Stella ista, a 2. canti.   14

    24. Tria sunt munera, a trè, due canti, & basso.   14

In festo S. Antonii [Jan. 17], vt in Commune Confessorum non Pontificum. vide in 2. par[35].

In Cathedra S. Petri [Jan. 18], vt In Commune Confessorum Pontificum. vide in 2 parte[36].

In festo SS. Fabiani, & Sebastiani [Jan. 20][37], vt in commune Martirum. vide in 2. parte[38].

In festo S. Agnetis [Jan. 21]. In primis, & secundis Vesperis.

    25. Stans beata Agnes, à 2. cāto, & tenore.   15

    26. Anulo[39] suo, a 2. alto, & Tenore[40].   15

---

[26] Added instruction within the partbook: *Alla quarta.*

[27] Added instruction within the partbook: *Alla quarta.*

[28] See No. 143—150.

[29] Added instruction within the partbook: *Alla 4.*

[30] Added instruction within the partbook: *Alla quarta.*

[31] See No. 13—16.

[32] See No. 156—159.

[33] See No. 168—172.

[34] Corrected from original: *Rubum.*

[35] See No. 173—177.

[36] See No. 168—172.

[37] Original punctuation: two commas.

[38] See No. 160—167.

[39] Corrected from original: *Annulo.*

[40] Added instruction within the partbook: *Alla quarta.*

27. Ecce quod concupiui, a due bassi.   16

28. Ipsi sum desponsata, a due canti.   16

In Conuersione S. Pauli [Jan. 25], vt in die Commemorationis eiusdem
[June 30].   52[41]

In festo Purificatione B. Virginis [Feb. 2]. In primis Vesperis. Vt in die
Circumcisionis [Jan. 1][42].

In secundis Vesperis.

29. Simeon iustus, a 2. canto, & basso.   17

30. Responsum, a 2. canto, & tenore[43].   17

31. Accipiens, a 2. bassi.   18

32. Cum inducerent, a 3. 2. canti, & basso.   18

In festo S. Agatae [Feb. 5]. In primis, & secundis Vesp.

33. Quis es tu, à 4. trè canti, & basso.   19

34. Medicinam à 3. Alti.   19

35. Agatha à 3. bassi.   20

36. Domine Iesu à 3. doi canti, e basso.   20

In Cathedra S. Petri Antiochiae [Feb. 22] vide in commune Confess. Pont.
in 2. par[44].

In festo S. Matthiae Apostoli [Feb. 24], vide in commune Apostolorum,
in 2. par[45].

In festo Sancti Thomae de Aquino [Mar. 7] vide in com. confess. non Pont.
in 2. parte[46].

In festo S. Gregorij Papae [Mar. 12] vide in com. Confess. Pont. in 2. parte[47].

In festo S. Ioseph [Mar. 19] vide in com. Confess nō Pont. in 2. parte[48].

In festo S. Benedicti [Mar. 21] vide in com. Confess. non Pont. in 2. parte[49].

In Annunciatione B. V. [Mar. 25] in primis & secundis Vesperis.

37. Missus est, à doi canto, e Tenore[50].   21

38. Gaude, à doi alto, e tenore.   21

39. Quomodo, a 3. doi canti, e basso.   22

40. Gabriel, a 2. bassi.   22

In festo S. Leonis Papae [Apr. 11] vide in com. Confess. Pont. in 2. parte[51].

In festo S. Marci [Apr. 25], vide in comm. Euangelistarum tempore Paschali[52]

In festo ss. Apostolorum Philippi, & Iacobi [May 1].

41. Domine ostende, a 2. canti.   23

42. Tanto tempore, à 2. alti.   23

43. Non Turbetur, à 2. tenori.   24

44. Si mansuetis[53], à 2. canto, e basso.   24

---

[41] See No. 61—64.

[42] See No. 17—20.

[43] Additional instruction within the partbook: *sonate come stà*.

[44] See No. 168—172.

[45] See No. 143—150.

[46] See No. 173—177.

[47] See No. 168—172.

[48] See No. 173—177.

[49] See No. 173—177.

[50] Additional instruction within the partbook: *sonate come stà*.

[51] See No. 168—172.

[52] See No. 151—155.

[53] Corrected from original: *manseritis*.

In festo S. Athanasij [May 2], vide in comm. Confess. Pont. in 2. parte[54].

In Inuentione S. Crucis [May 3], in primis, & secundis Vesperis.

45. O magnum, à 2. canto, e basso.	25
46. Salua nos, à 2. alto, e tenore.	25
47. Ecce Crucem, à 2. canti.	26
48. Per lignum, à 2. canto, e tenore[55].	26

In festo S. Io. ante Portam Latinam [May 6], vide in comm Apostolorum, tempore Paschali[56].

In Apparitione S. Michaelis Archangeli [May 8], vide in festo dedicationis eiusdem die 29. Septembris[57].

In festo S. Gregorij Nazianzeni [May 9], vide in com. Confess. Pont. in 2. par[58].

In festo S. Barnabae Apostoli [June 11], vide in comm. Apostolorum, in 2. parte[59].

In festo S. Basilij [June 14], vide in comm. Confess. Pont. in 2 parte[60].

In Vigilia Natiuitatis S. Io. Baptistae [June 24] in primis Vesperis[61].

49. Ipse peribit[62], à 2. canto, e tenore.	27
50. Ioannes, a doi bassi.	27
51. Ex[63] vtero, a doi alti.	28
52. Iste puer, à doi canti.	28

In secundis Vesperis.

53. Elisabet, à 2. canto, e tenore[64].	29
54. Innuebant, a doi Tenori.	29
55. Inter natos, à doi canti.	30
56. Tu puer, à doi bassi.	30

In festo ss. Apostolorum Petri, & Pauli [June 29] in primis Vesperis[65].

57. Petrus, & Ioannes, a 2. canto, e tenore[66].	31
58. Argentum, & aurū, à 2. alto, e tenore.	31
59. Dixit Angelus, à 2. canti.	32
60. Si diligis me, à 2. canto, e basso.	32

In 2. Vesperis, vt in comm. Apostolorum[67].

In commemoratione S. Pauli Apostoli [June 30] in primis Vesperis.

61. Ego Plantaui[68], à 2 canto, e tenore[69].	33
62. Libenter, à doi, alto, e basso.	33

---

[54] See No. 168—172.
[55] Additional instruction within the partbook: *alla 4.*
[56] See No. 151—155.
[57] See No. 97—100.
[58] See No. 168—172.
[59] See No. 143—150.
[60] See No. 168—172.
[61] Rubric within the partbook: *In Natiu. S. Io. Baptistae. In primis Vesp.*
[62] Corrected from original: *praeibit.*
[63] Corrected from original: *In.*
[64] Additional instruction within the partbook: *Alla quarta.*
[65] Rubric within the partbook: *In festo SS. Apostolorum Petri, & Pauli. In primis & secundis Vesperis.*
[66] Additional instruction within the partbook: *sonate come stà.*
[67] Within the partbook this rubric is crossed out in pen. See also No. 147—150.
[68] Corrected from original: *Plantani.*
[69] Additional instruction within the partbook: *Alla quarta.*

---

70 Corrected from original: *Vespris*.
71 Within the partbook this rubric is crossed out in pen. See also No. 147—150.
72 Additional instruction within the partbook: *Alla quarta*.
73 Additional instruction within the partbook: *sonate come stà*.
74 See No. 168—172.
75 Corrected from original: *Apestoli*.
76 See No. 143—150.
77 See No. 69—72.
78 Additional instruction within the partbook: *sonate come stà*.
79 Additional instruction within the partbook: *Alla quarta*.
80 Additional instruction within the partbook: *Alla quarta*.

In festo S. Bernardi Abb. [Aug. 20] vide in com. Confess. non Pontific. in 2. parte[81].

In festo S. Bartholomaei Apostoli [Aug. 24 or 25] vide in com. Apostolorum in 2. parte[82].

In Decollatione S. Io Baptistae [Aug. 29] in primis & secundis Vesperis.

In Natiuitate B.V. [Sept. 8] in primis, & secundis[85] Vesperis.

In festo Exaltationis S. Crucis [Sept. 14], vide vt in inuentione eiusdem [May 3][87].

In festo S. Matthaei Apostoli [Sept. 21], vide vt in com. Apostolorum in 2. parte[88].

In Dedicatione S. Michaelis Archangeli [Sept. 29] in primis, & secundis Vesperis.

In festo S. Hieronymi [Sept. 30], vide in com. Confess. non Pontifi. in 2. parte[91].

In festo S. Francisci [Oct. 4], & Stigmatum eiusdem [Sept. 17[82]], in primis, & secundis Vesperis.

In festo S. Lucae Euangelistae [Oct. 18], vide in com. Apostolorum, in 2. parte[94].

---

[81] See No. 173—177.
[82] See No. 143—150.
[83] Additional instruction within the partbook: *sonate come stà.*
[84] Additional instruction within the partbook: *Alla quarta.*
[85] Corrected from original: *secuudi.*
[86] Corrected from original: *Gioriosae.*
[87] See No. 45—48.
[88] See No. 143—150.
[89] Additional instruction within the partbook: *Alla quarta.*
[90] Additional instruction within the partbook: *Alla quarta.*
[91] See No. 173—177.
[92] The feast of the Imprinting of the Holy Stigmata on St. Francis is not included in the *Brev 1606* calendar; date supplied from the modern Roman calendar.
[93] Additional instruction within the partbook: *sonate come stà.*
[94] See No. 143—150.

FINIS.

Index Antiphonarum, & Cantionum quae in secunda parte continentur[101].

---

[95] See No. 143—150.
[96] See No. 189—193.
[97] Corrected from original: *59*.
[98] See No. 189—193.
[99] Additional instruction within the partbook: *A due Soprani*.
[100] See No. 178—181.
[101] »Index of antiphons and songs [i.e., motets] which are contained in Part II.« Table of contents from *Bassus ad Organum*, Part II, pp. 122—123; Anerio's page numbers refer to that partbook only.

---

[102] Additional instruction within the partbook: *Alla 4.*

[103] In the *Cantus* and *Tenor* partbooks, this piece is inserted after No. 193, with the rubric: *Residuum in Ascensione Domini.*

[104] In the Index the word *tenori* is added in pen to the title. Additional instruction within the partbook: *A due Cāti. Alla 4.*

[105] Additional instruction within the partbook: *Sonate come stà.*

[106] Additional instruction within the partbook: *Sonate come stà.*

[107] Additional instruction within the partbook: *Alla quarta.*

[108] Rubric within the partbook: *In Commune Apostolorum, in secundis Vesperis.*

[109] Additional instruction within the partbook: *A 2. Soprani. Alla quarta.*

[110] This piece is actually composed for alto and bass.

[111] Additional instruction within the partbook: *Alla quarta.*

---

[112] In the Index the word *tenori* is added in pen here.
[113] Additional instruction within the partbook: *A 3. doi Soprani, e Basso.*
[114] Additional instruction within the partbook: *Alla quarta.*
[115] Corrected from original: *49.*
[116] Additional instruction within the partbook: *A due Soprani.*
[117] Additional instruction within the partbook: *Alla quarta.*
[118] Additional instruction within the partbook: *Alla quarta.*
[119] Corrected from original: *Quid.*
[120] Additional instruction within the partbook: *A due Soprani. Alla quarta.*
[121] Additional instruction within the partbook: *Alla quarta.*
[122] Corrected from original: *eanto.*
[123] Additional instruction within the partbook: *sonate come stà.*

FINIS.

Index Antiphonarum, & Cantionum, quae in tertia parte continentur[137].

In festo S. Augustini [Aug. 28].

---

[124] This title is crossed out in pen.   [125] See No. 69.   [126] This title is crossed out in pen.

[127] This page number is crossed out in pen. See also No. 70.

[128] Additional instruction within the partbook: *A trè, due Soprani, e vn Basso.*

[129] »When, however, the office of the Blessed Virgin should occur, the following [pieces] may be sung.« Rubric missing within the partbook.

[130] In the Index the words *à due canti* are added in pen. In the *Tenor* partbook this piece is inserted after No. 196 without rubric; in the *Bassus* partbook, after No. 193 with the rubric: *Residuũ in Commune Mulierũ Sanctarũ.* The rubric in the *Bassus* is crossed out in pen.

[131] Rubric missing within the partbook.

[132] In the Index the words *ò tenori* are added in pen. Within the partbook the following instruction is added in pen: *à 2. canti, ò tenori.*

[133] In the Index the word *tenori* is added in pen. Additional instruction within the partbook: *A due Soprani.* Within the partbook the following instruction is also added in pen: *à 2. Tenori.*

[134] Within the partbook the title has been emended in pen to the following: *Bene Fundata est.*

[135] In the Index the words *2. canti, Alto, & Tenore* are added in pen. Additional instruction within the partbook: *Sonate come stà. A 4. due Canti, Alto, e Tenore.*

[136] Within the partbook this piece is preceded by the rubric: *Tempore Paschali.* Additional instruction within the partbook: *Alla quarta.*

[137] »Index of antiphons and songs [i.e., motets] which are contained in Part III.« Table of contents from *Bassus ad Organum*, Part III, p. 32; Anerio's page numbers refer to that partbook only.

---

[138] Additional instruction within the partbook: *Alla quarta.*
[139] Additional instruction within the partbook: *Alla quarta.*
[140] Additional instruction within the partbook: *Alla quarta.*
[141] Additional instruction within the partbook: *sonate come stà.*
[142] Additional instruction within the partbook: *Alla Quarta.* This piece is scored for soprano, alto, tenor, and bass.
[143] Additional instruction within the partbook: *A due, Contralto, e Ten.*
[144] Additional instruction within the partbook: *Alla Quarta.*
[145] In the Index the words *Canto, Tenore* have been changed in pen to *Canti, dui* [i.e., *due Canti*].
[146] Additional instruction within the partbook: *A Trè, due Canti, e Basso.*
[147] Additional instruction within the partbook: *Alla quarta.*
[148] Additional instruction within the partbook: *Alla quarta.*
[149] Additional instruction within the partbook: *Alla quarta.*

In festo S. Catharinae Senensis[150].

225. Immortali laude. a due, Cāto, e Tenor.	20
226. O Virgo maxima. a 3. due Cāti, & Bas.	20
227. Det Catharina, à quattro[151].	21
228. Maxima est. à trè, due Cāti, & vn Ten[152].	22

In festo S. Thomae de Aquino [Mar. 7].

229. Faelix Thomas a due, Cāto, e Tenore.	22
230. Faelix doctor. a 3. due Canti, & Basso.	23
231. Beati Thomae. a 3. Canto, Alto, e Ten[153].	24
232. Adsunt doctoris[154], a 4. due Soprani, vn Contralto, & vn Tenore[155].	24

In festo S. Eliae[156].

233. Zelo zelatus. a due, Canto, e Tenore.	25
234. Vsquequo. a due Tenori.	25
235. Si homo Dei. a due, Canto, e Basso.	26
236. Ascendens Elias, à 3. due Soprani[157], & vn Basso[158].	26

In festo S. Elisei[159].

237. Postula quod vis. a due, Canto, e Ten.	27
238. Cum transissent. a due Tenori.	27
239. Clamauerūt filii, à 3. due Cāti, e Basso.	28
240. Rem difficilem, a 4 due Soprani, vn Contralto, Baritono, ouero Tenore[160].	28

In festo S. Alberti[161].

241. O Alberte norma, a 4 due Soprani, vn Contralto, & vn Baritono[162].	29
242. Puro corde, à 3. due Soprani, & vn Baritono[163].	30
243. Tua sancta dextera. a due Bassi[164].	30
244. Excellentem dominū, a 3. Contralti[165].	31

FINIS.

---

[150] The feast of St. Catherine of Sienna is not included in the *Brev 1606* calendar. According to the calendar in *BrevDom 1615*, the feast was then celebrated on the »*Dominica proxima post Festum S. Crucis*«, that is, the Sunday next after May 3. In the modern Roman calendar the feast falls on April 30.

[151] Additional instruction within the partbook: *Alla quarta, A. 4. Canto, Alto, Tenore, & Basso.*

[152] Additional instruction within the partbook: *Alla quarta.*

[153] Additional instruction within the partbook: *Alla quarta.*

[154] Corrected from original: *doctores.*

[155] Additional instruction within the partbook: *Sonate come stà. A 4. Canto, alto, tenore, & basso.*

[156] The feast of St. Elias is not included in the *Brev 1606* calendar. According to the calendar in *BrevCarm 1672*, the feast was then celebrated on July 20.

[157] Corrected from original: *Sopranoi.*

[158] Additional instruction within the partbook: *A 3. due Cāti, e Basso.*

[159] The feast of St. Eliseus is not included in the *Brev 1606* calendar. According to the calendar in *BrevCarm 1579*, the feast was then celebrated on June 14.

[160] Additional instruction within the partbook: *Alla quarta. A 4. due Canti, un Alto, & un Tenore, ouero Baritono.*

[161] Rubric missing within the partbook. The feast of St. Albert of the Carmelites is not included in the *Brev 1606* calendar. According to the calendar in *BrevCarm 1579*, the feast was then celebrated on August 7.

[162] Additional instruction within the partbook: *A 4. Due Canti, Alto, & Baritono. Sonate come sta.*

[163] Additional instruction within the partbook: *A 3. due Canti, e Baritono.*

[164] Additional instruction within the partbook: *Alla quarta.*

[165] Additional instruction within the partbook: *A trè Alti.*

The forces required are very modest: two, three, or four voices supported by organ. All the pieces are composed in a dignified and unassuming Seconda Prattica style; no extraordinary burdens have been placed on the singers[166]. It is assumed that soloists are required, not a chorus, and that only the organ is needed for accompaniment, since the set includes only one copy of each partbook.

Anerio's terminology and choice of clefs for the various voices are what one might expect: *Canto* (alternatively called *Soprano*) in the soprano C-clef; *Alto* (alternatively called *Contralto*) in the alto C-clef; *Tenore* in the tenor C-clef; *Baritono* in the baritone F-clef; *Basso* in the bass F-clef. Where these clefs appear in the voice parts, Anerio customarily notates the figured bass in the bass F-clef. On occasion the figured bass is notated in the tenor C-clef below normal clefs in the voice parts; whenever this situation occurs, Anerio warns the organist against transposition: »*Sonate come stà*«[167]. At other times Anerio uses the so-called chiavette (high clefs): *Canto* notated in the violin G-clef; *Alto* in the mezzo-soprano C-clef; *Tenore* in the alto C-clef; *Basso* in the tenor C-clef[168]. To accompany these high clefs the figured bass is written alternatively in the tenor C-clef, the alto C-clef, or the baritone F-clef, with the rubric »*Alla quarta*« (»At the fourth« [below notated pitch]). Transposition down a fourth is therefore apparently indicated for these pieces in chiavette[169].

---

[166] For Hugo LEICHTENTRITT's rather harsh judgment of the Seconda Prattica motet style of G. F. Anerio, see his *Geschichte der Motette*, Leipzig 1908, p. 242.

[167] »Play as it is.« This warning appears 14 times; see Table I, above.

[168] The terms *Soprano* and *Contralto* do not appear in the pieces written in the high clefs.

[169] The names of the clefs are those given in Gustave REESE, *Music in the Renaissance* (revised edition), New York 1959, p. 249. The following exceptions to the clef combinations given above should be noted: No. 12 (high clefs): The *Basso* part (T clef) is called *Tenore* in the partbook, but *Basso* in the Index.

No. 16 (high clefs): The *Tenore* part (A clef) is called *Alto* in the partbook, but *Tenore* in the Index.

No. 38 (normal clefs): The *Tenore* should be read in the T clef, not in the A clef as notated (typographical error).

No. 42: The two *Alto* parts are notated in the M clef with a signature of one flat, but the figured bass is notated in the B clef without a key signature. It is necessary to transpose the voice parts down a fourth, leaving the figured bass at pitch.

No. 43 (normal clefs): The two *Tenore* parts should be read in the T clef, not in the A clef as notated (typographical error).

No. 46 (normal clefs): The *Tenore* part should be read in the T clef, not in the A clef as notated (typographical error).

No. 61: The *Tenore* is notated in the T clef, although the high clefs are used in the other parts, and Anerio requires transposition down a fourth. (Ordinarily the A clef is used for the *Tenore* in such cases.)

No. 88 (high clefs): The instruction »*Alla quarta*« is missing from this piece. Probably transposition is required, nevertheless.

No. 157: The two *Tenore* parts are notated in the A clef with a signature of one flat, but the figured bass is notated in the B clef without a key signature. It is necessary to transpose the voice parts down a fourth, leaving the figured bass at pitch.

Anerio's mensural practice is well described by Adriano Banchieri in his *Cartella musicale* (3rd edition, 1614): pieces in duple meter are notated in what Banchieri calls *tempo perfetto minore* (C), in which two minims receive one *battuta* (tactus). Banchieri cautions us that it has become customary in his time to beat this tempo slowly (*adagio*) because of the small note values used (*note negre*). In fact, the croma (eighth note) is the smallest note value to appear frequently in this collection. As Banchieri points out, passages in triple meter in Anerio's music are notated in *tripla proportione di equalità* (C $\frac{3}{1}$), in which three semibreves take the place of one semibreve in *tempo perfetto minore*[170]. Anerio's mensuration is typical of modern practice in his time, and stands in contrast to the white notation of the Prima Prattica.

Both the title page and the index refer to *cantiones* or *sacrae cantiones* in addition to *antiphonae*. (*Sacrae cantiones* is a common term for motets in this period.) Is it possible that Anerio's collection comprises two types of compositions: antiphons (liturgical pieces) and motets (non-liturgical pieces)? Within the partbooks themselves, we find, Anerio makes no distinction between pieces intended for liturgical and for non-liturgical use; all are grouped together under the appropriate feast. For this reason, and for other reasons that will be put forth shortly, we believe that all the pieces except No. 194—196 (the Compline antiphons) should be considered as Vesper antiphons or antiphon-substitutes. The term *sacrae cantiones* may be merely a warning that not all the »antiphons« are based on Breviary antiphon texts[171].

No. 193 (normal clefs): The *Tenore* (T clef) is called *Tenor siue Baritonus* in the partbook, but *Tenore* in the Index.

No. 231 (high clefs): The *Tenore* part (A clef) is called *Alto* in the partbook, but *Tenore* in the Index.

No. 232 (normal clefs): The *Tenore* part (T clef) is called *Baritono* in the partbook, but *Tenore* in the Index. In the *Bassus ad Organum* partbook the four voices are erroneously labeled *Canto, Alto, Tenore,* and *Basso;* for the correct terms see Table I, above.

No. 240 (high clefs): The *Tenore* part (A clef) is called *Baritono, ouero Tenore* in the partbook and also in the Index.

No. 241 (normal clefs): The *Tenore* part (T clef) is called *Baritono* in the partbook and also in the Index.

No. 242 (normal clefs): The *Tenore* part (T clef) is called *Baritono* in the partbook and also in the Index.

A few of the pieces marked »*Alla quarta*« carry signatures of one flat (the only signature Anerio uses in this collection); most are notated without any key signature. For further information on transposition practice and other aspects of pitch, see Arthur MENDEL, *Pitch in the 16th and Early 17th Centuries*, in: The Musical Quarterly 34, 1948, pp. 336-357.

[170] Adriano BANCHIERI, *Cartella musicale nel canto figurato[,] fermo, & contrapunto . . . novamente in questa terza impressione ridotta dall'antica alla moderna pratica*, Venezia 1614, Giacomo Vincenti, p. 167. Banchieri's terms are defined on pp. 29-32. No. 71 in Anerio's collection uses what Banchieri calls *sesquialtera*: blackened notes grouped in triplets in *tempo perfetto minore*.

[171] One wonders if Monteverdi did not use a similar term for the same purpose in his 1610 collection: »*cum nonnullis sacris concentibus.*«

The three Compline antiphons in Part II of Anerio's collection are easily identified in the Sunday Office[172]. *Miserere mihi* (No. 194) is the psalm antiphon
throughout the year, replaced in Paschal Time by *Alleluia* (No. 195). *Salva nos*
(No. 196), the antiphon at the *Nunc dimittis,* is invariable throughout the year;
during Paschal Time an Alleluia is added to the body of the antiphon. The
Compline texts used by Anerio are perfectly proper from a liturgical point of
view.

Of the 59 sets of Vesper antiphons contained in the three books of Anerio's collection, however, only 12 sets are liturgically impeccable. These 12 sets comprise
the first four Vesper antiphons of the feast in question, set forth in the proper
liturgical order without significant textual alterations.

TABLE II

SETS OF VESPER ANTIPHONS OF COMPLETE LITURGICAL PROPRIETY
(comprising the first four antiphons for each feast, in the proper order)[173]

COMPOSITION	ANERIO'S RUBRIC
No. 5–8	In festo S. Andreae Apostoli. In primis, & secundis Vesperis. [Ant. 1–4][174]
No. 17–20	In Circumcisione Domini. In primis, & secundis Vesperis. [Ant. 1–4][175]
No. 49–52	In Vigilia Natiuitatis S. Io. Baptistae in primis Vesperis. [Ant. 1–4][176]
No. 93–96	In Natiuitate B. V. in primis, & secundis Vesperis. [Ant. 1–4][177]
No. 117–120	In festo S. Clementis, in primis, & secundis Vesperis. [Ant. 1–4][178]
No. 121–124	In Resurrectione Domini. [Ant. 1–4][179]

---

[172] See *Brev 1606*, p. 110.

[173] Minor variations in spelling and punctuation have been disregarded in compiling this table.

[174] Source of texts: *Brev 1606*, p. 696.

[175] Source of texts: *Brev 1606*, p. 194. The same antiphons are used at 1st Vespers on the Purification of the Blessed Virgin (Feb. 2); see *Brev 1606*, p. 733.

[176] Source of texts: *Brev 1606*, pp. 798—799.

[177] Source of texts: *Brev 1606*, pp. 910—911. The same antiphons are used at 1st and 2nd Vespers
on the Conception of the Blessed Virgin (Dec. 8), by substituting the word *Conceptio* for the
word *Nativitas*; see *Brev 1606*, p. 703.

[178] Source of texts: *AntR 1572*, fol. 159ᵛ; slight differences in *Brev 1606*, p. 990.

[179] Source of texts: *Brev 1606*, p. 384.

No. 143—146   In Commune Apostolorum, & Euangelistarum.
                   In primis Vesperis.
                   [Ant. 1—4][180]

No. 147—150   [In Commune Apostolorum, & Euangelistarum.]
                   In secundis Vesperis.
                   [Ant. 1—4][181]

No. 156—159   In Commune vnius Martiris.
                   In primis, & secundis Vesperis.
                   [Ant. 1—4][182]

No. 201—204   In festo S. Monicae.
                   [Ant. 1—4][183]

No. 205—208   In festo S. Nicolai de Tollentino.
                   [Ant. 1—4][184]

No. 213—216   In festo S. Clarae Virginis.
                   [Ant. 1—4][185]

These 12 sets of antiphons establish a standard of liturgical propriety against which the others may be judged. But why has Anerio provided only four antiphons for both First and Second Vespers, when the Breviary requires six for each service? Moreover, in liturgical practice the *Magnificat* antiphon regularly changes from First Vespers (the eve of the feast) to Second Vespers; and on a few great feasts, such as the Nativity of St. John the Baptist, the five psalm antiphons also change from First to Second Vespers. In Anerio's collection we never find more than five; four settings are normal[186]. Even such feasts of First Class as Christmas and Easter receive only four antiphons to the set. Taking Table II as a guide to Anerio's customary practice, it appears that on most feasts only

---

[180] Source of texts: *Brev 1606*, pp. 1000—1001.

[181] Source of texts: *Brev 1606*, pp. 1001—1002.

[182] Source of texts: *Brev 1606*, p. 1016.

[183] Source of texts: *Brev 1559*, fol. 491ᵛ.

[184] Source of texts: *Brev 1559*, fol. 507ᵛ. The first word of No. 208 is *Suscitavit* in this source, instead of Anerio's *Suscitans*.

[185] Source of texts: *Analecta hymnica medii aevi*, ed. G. M. Dreves with C. Blume and H. M. Bannister, V, Leipzig 1889, p. 157 (antiphons for 1st Vespers only).

[186] Five antiphons are provided only for the Ascension of Our Lord (No. 125—129), Pentecost (No. 130—134), the Common of Apostles, Evangelists and Martyrs in Paschal Time (No. 151—155), the Common of Confessor Bishops (No. 168—172), the Common of Confessors not Bishops (No. 173—177), the Office of the Blessed Virgin (No. 184—188), and the Common of the Dedication of a Church (No. 189—193). In all these instances Anerio evidently intends all five antiphons for performance in order at both 1st and 2nd Vespers, as we shall see. Occasionally Anerio has provided two complete sets of four antiphons each, one set for 1st Vespers and another for 2nd Vespers. The following feasts are represented by these double sets: the Nativity of St. John the Baptist (No. 49—52 and No. 53—56), the Common of Apostles and Evangelists out of Paschal Time (No. 143—146 and No. 147—150), and the Common of Two or More Martyrs (No. 160—163 and No. 164—167).

the first four antiphons were performed at Vespers, whatever the rank of the feast.

Were the remaining antiphons merely omitted? A brief reconsideration of evidence presented earlier suggests a possible solution to this problem, on which Anerio is silent. As we have seen, on great feasts (such as the principal feasts of the Blessed Virgin) each antiphon is to be sung twice, before and after the associated psalm or canticle[187]. The *Caeremoniale Episcoporum* mentions the antiphons before the psalms to ensure that they will be sung with care and to establish the order of precedence of the clergy assigned to their intonation; the possible omission of these antiphons is not mentioned[188]. It is only the repetition of the antiphons after the psalms that requires special legislation to avoid abuses[189]. We should like to advance the hypothesis that Anerio's antiphons and antiphon-substitutes were intended for performance following their associated psalms. The antiphons before the psalms may have been intoned to their Gregorian melodies, if they were not omitted altogether.

It seems clear that non-liturgical vocal and instrumental pieces of various kinds were inserted among the liturgical items at Vespers in seventeenth-century Italy. Paul Hainlein, in describing Vespers at the church of S. Francesco, Venice, on the feast of the Conception of the Blessed Virgin in 1647, tells us about the decorations of the church, the number of musicians and their disposition (35 musicians divided into concerto and ripieno groups; Cavalli was among the performers), the Vesper items performed (the five Marian psalms, the hymn *Ave maris stella,* and the *Magnificat* are mentioned), and the name of the composer (Rovetta). But Hainlein reserves his most enthusiastic and detailed descriptions for the »motets or sonatas« (»*ein Motetten oder Sonata*«) that were performed »between each psalm« (»*zwischen jedweter psalm*«). One piece, performed by soprano and bass soloists, was dedicated to the confounding of the Turks. Another was a violin solo played by a *Frate* whose equal, in

---

[187] See above, p. 90. STEVENS, p. 320, is somewhat misleading on this point.

[188] *Caeremoniale Episcoporum,* pp. 139—140: »*Subdiaconus pręintonat primam Antiphonam; & donec per Episcopum non fuerit praeintonatio repetita, Cęremoniarius, & Subdiaconus pręintonator expectant ibidem stantes; ea autem repetita intelligibili voce, siue ex 'libro, siue memoriter, prout magis Episcopo placuerit ... Episcopus verò sic perstat, donec expleta per chorum Antiphona, inceptus fuerit primus Psalmus ... Reliquae quatuor Antiphonae iuxta debitum, & condecentem ordinem, ritumque antiquum, per eundem Subdiaconum, seu alterum, ad quem spectat, praeintonari debent, hoc ordine; videlicet, secunda Diacono assistenti à dexteris Episcopi; tertia Presbytero assistenti; quarta primo Canonico in choro manenti, siue ille sit Archidiaconus, siue Archipresbyter; quinta Diacono assistenti à sinistris Episcopi. Eadem omnia etiam in praeintonatione aliarum Antiphonarum obseruantur, quae in prima seruari debere dictum est. ...*«

[189] See above, p. 90. Significantly, the instrumental antiphon-substitutes mentioned in BONTA, *Liturgical Problems,* pp. 98—100, are all intended to follow (not precede) their associated psalms or *Magnificat.* See also BONTA, *The Uses of the Sonata da Chiesa,* in JAMS 22, 1969, pp. 79—82.

Hainlein's opinion, was not to be found outside the Imperial Court Chapel[190]. If we can trust Hainlein's description — and he seems to know the Roman liturgy — these special pieces, which were clearly not antiphons, were inserted in the place of the antiphons between the psalms. Since there are five psalms at Vespers, four such inserted pieces would suffice, even at Solemn Vespers on a great feast.

What of the remaining two antiphons? Perhaps they were to be replaced by instrumental music, as the *Caeremoniale Episcoporum* permits[191]. It is interesting to find a possible answer in Monteverdi's 1610 Vespers, if we accept the theory that *Nigra sum* and the other »sacred songs« are antiphon-substitutes. Monteverdi has provided only four (not six or seven) motets, inserting them in the print between the five psalms. The other non-liturgical composition, following the fifth psalm, is an instrumental *Sonata* with vocal cantus firmus, not a motet[192]. Since, as we shall see, there are other similarities between Monteverdi and Anerio in the matter of antiphon-substitutes, it is tempting to cite Monteverdi's print in support of our arguments that Anerio's antiphons ought probably to be performed between the five psalms. At the present time, unfortunately, this question cannot be answered with certainty[193].

All but 12 of the remaining sets in Anerio's collection include at least one composition that can be identified as a genuine antiphon. These individual antiphons also present a canonical text and appear in the correct liturgical order for the feast in question, although other pieces in the same set may not pass the same tests. Sixty-eight antiphons can be accounted for in this manner, making a total of 116 antiphons of unimpeachable propriety (Table II added to Table III).

---

[190] Hainlein's letter, dated December 13, 1647, is printed in Wilibald Gurlitt, *Ein Briefwechsel zwischen Paul Hainlein und L. Friedrich Behaim aus den Jahren 1647—48*, in: Sammelbände der Internationalen Musikgesellschaft 14, 1912—1913, p. 497. See also Osthoff, p. 319.

[191] See above, p. 90.

[192] Both Biella, pp. 113—114, and Bonta, *Liturgical Problems*, p. 93 (footnote 23), have taken note of this significant fact to support their very different conclusions.

[193] Another reason might be advanced for Anerio's failure to provide a full set of antiphons for each feast. It was not considered essential in Anerio's time to sing all five psalms in elaborate settings; especially on lesser feasts, time and effort could be saved by employing falsobordone or Gregorian psalm-tone recitation for one or more of the psalms. Casimiri, *Disciplina musicae*, in: Note d'archivio 19, 1942, pp. 160—161, quotes from the diary of Rector Michele Lauretano of the German College of Rome, concerning Vespers in the church of S. Apollinare on June 9, 1583: »*Il Vespero ha da spedirsi presto, e l'Organo soni poco per star tutti in piedi. Il Primo S a l m o si cantò in g r e g o r i a n o ... l'altri [salmi] in f a l s o b o r d o n e, et uno sopra l'organo.*« This diary entry is also discussed in Thomas J. Culley, S. J., *Jesuits and Music, Vol. I. A study of the musicians connected with the German College in Rome during the seventeenth century and of their activities in Northern Europe*, St. Louis and Roma 1970, Jesuit Historical Institute, p. 81. Similar practices have been observed at S. Maria Maggiore (Bergamo) in 1623, and at S. Petronio (Bologna) in 1658; see Jerome Roche, *Music at S. Maria Maggiore, Bergamo, 1614—1643*, in: Music and Letters 47, 1966, p. 298, and Armstrong, I, pp. 52—62. Perhaps the performance of polyphonic settings of antiphons could be curtailed as well.

TABLE III

INDIVIDUAL VESPER ANTIPHONS OF COMPLETE LITURGICAL PROPRIETY
(mixed among other compositions of doubtful propriety)[194]

COMPOSITION	ANERIO'S RUBRIC
No. 9, 12	In festo S. Luciae. In primis, & secundis Vesperis. [Ant. 1, 4][195]
No. 22	In Epiphania Domini. In primis, & secundis Vesperis. [Ant. 2][196]
No. 29, 31	[In festo Purificatione B. Virginis.] In secundis Vesperis. [Ant. 1, 3][197]
No. 34	In festo S. Agatae. In primis, & secundis Vesp. [Ant. 2][198]
No. 41	In festo ss. Apostolorum Philippi, & Iacobi. [Ant. 1][199]
No. 45, 46, 47	In Inuentione S. Crucis, in primis, & secundis Vesperis. [Ant. 1, 2, 3][200]
No. 53, 54	[In festo Natiuitatis S. Io. Baptistae] In secundis Vesperis. [Ant. 1, 2][201]
No. 57, 59	In festo ss. Apostolorum Petri, & Pauli in primis Vesperis. [Ant. 1, 3][202]
No. 62	In commemoratione S. Pauli Apostoli in primis Vesperis. [Ant. 2][203]
No. 65, 66, 67	In festo Visitationis B. V. in primis, & secundis Vesperis. [Ant. 1, 2, 3][204]

---

[194] Minor variations in spelling and punctuation have been disregarded in compiling this table. See also Table II, above.
[195] Source of texts: *Brev 1606*, p. 706.
[196] Source of text: *Brev 1606*, p. 212.
[197] Source of texts: *Brev 1606*, p. 737.
[198] Source of text: *Brev 1606*, p. 740.
[199] Source of text: *Brev 1606*, p. 765.
[200] Source of texts: *Brev 1606*, p. 772.
[201] Source of texts: *Brev 1606*, p. 805.
[202] Source of texts: *Brev 1606*, p. 815.
[203] Source of text: *Brev 1606*, p. 820.
[204] Source of texts: *Brev 1606*, p. 825.

No. 69	In festo S. Mariae Magdalenae, in primis, & secundis Vesperis. [Ant. 1][205]
No. 73, 74, 75	In festo S. Petri ad vincula in primis, & secundis Vesperis. [Ant. 1, 2, 3][206]
No. 77, 78, 79	In festo Transfigurationis Domini in primis & secundis Vesperis. [Ant. 1, 2, 3][207]
No. 87, 88	In Assumptione B. V. in primis, & secundis Vesperis. [Ant. 3, 4][208]
No. 89, 92	In Decollatione S. Io Baptistae in primis & secundis Vesperis. [Ant. 1, 4][209]
No. 98, 99	In Dedicatione S. Michaelis Archangeli in primis, & secundis Vesperis. [Ant. 2, 3][210]
No. 105, 107	In festo omnium Sanctorum in primis & secundis Vesperis. [Ant. 1, 3][211]
No. 109, 111, 112	In festo S. Martini Episcopi, in primis, & secundis Vesperis. [Ant. 1, 3, 4][212]
No. 125	In Ascensione Domini. In primis, & secundis Vesperis. [Ant. 1][213]
No. 133	In festo Pentecostes. [Ant. 4][214]
No. 135, 136	In festo Sanctissimae Trinitatis. [Ant. 1, 2][215]
No. 139, 140	In Solemnitate Corporis Christi. [Ant. 1, 2][216]
No. 151, 152, 153, 154	In Commune Apostolorum, Euangelistarum, & Martirum, tempore Paschali. In primis, & secundis Vesperis. [Ant. 1, 2, 3, 4][217]

[205] Source of text: *Brev 1606*, p. 839.
[206] Source of texts: *Brev 1606*, p. 851.
[207] Source of texts: *Brev 1606*, p. 868.
[208] Source of texts: *Brev 1606*, p. 887.
[209] Source of texts: *Brev 1606*, p. 906.
[210] Source of texts: *Brev 1606*, pp. 942—943.
[211] Source of texts: *Brev 1606*, p. 961.
[212] Source of texts: *Brev 1606*, p. 979.
[213] Source of text: *Brev 1606*, p. 444.
[214] Source of text: *Brev 1606*, p. 472.
[215] Source of texts: *Brev 1606*, p. 488.
[216] Source of texts: *Brev 1606*, p. 493.
[217] Source of texts: *Brev 1606*, p. 1008.

No. 160, 161, 162   In Commune plurimorum Martirum.
                    In primis Vesperis.
                    [Ant. 1, 2, 3][218]
No. 164, 165, 166   [In Commune plurimorum Martirum.]
                    In secundis Vesperis.
                    [Ant. 1, 2, 3][219]
No. 169, 170, 171   In Commune Confessorum Pontificum.
                    In primis, & secundis Vesperis.
                    [Ant. 2, 3, 4][220]
No. 173, 175   In Commune Confessorum non Pontificum.
                    In primis, & secundis Vesperis.
                    [Ant. 1, 3][221]
No. 189, 191   In Commune Dedicationis Ecclesiae.
                    In primis, & secundis Vesperis.
                    [Ant. 1, 3][222]
No. 197   In festo S. Augustini.
                    [Ant. 1][223]
No. 217   In festo S. Antonii de Padua.
                    [Ant. 1][224]
No. 221   In festo S. Dominici.
                    [Ant. 1][225]
No. 225   In festo S. Catharinae Senensis.
                    [Ant. 1][226]
No. 229   In festo S. Thomae de Aquino.
                    [Ant. 1][227]
No. 233, 234, 235   In festo S. Eliae.
                    [Ant. 1, 2, 3][228]
No. 237   In festo S. Elisei.
                    [Ant. 1][229]

The rest of the pieces in the collection present serious difficulties from a liturgical point of view. It will be helpful to consider the least irregular works first. Twenty-eight compositions are Vesper antiphons with canonical texts — but out of order, assigned to the wrong Vespers (e.g., Second Vespers instead of First Vespers), or even transferred from another feast. These treacherous antiphons are mixed in among the others without a word of warning.

---

[218] Source of texts: *Brev 1606*, pp. 1031—1032.
[219] Source of texts: *Brev 1606*, p. 1032.
[220] Source of texts: *Brev 1606*, p. 1041.
[221] Source of texts: *Brev 1606*, p. 1049.
[222] Source of texts: *Brev 1606*, p. 1075.
[223] Source of text: *Brev 1559*, fol. 473 (1st Vespers only).
[224] Source of text: *Analecta hymnica*, V, p. 126 (1st Vespers only).
[225] Source of text: *Analecta hymnica*, XXV, p. 239 (antiphon for all the psalms at 1st Vespers).
[226] Source of text: *BrevDom 1615*, p. 866 (antiphon for all the psalms).
[227] Source of text: *Analecta hymnica*, V, p. 230 (antiphon for all the psalms at 1st Vespers).
[228] Source of texts: *BrevCarm 1672*, p. 1042 (antiphons at 1st Vespers).
[229] Source of text: *BrevCarm 1672*, p. 978 (antiphon at 2nd Vespers).

It is natural to assume, for example, that a set of four pieces bearing the rubric
»*In Commune plurimorum Martirum. In primis Vesperis*« (No. 160—163) consists
of the first four antiphons at First Vespers on feasts of Two or More Martyrs
out of Paschal Time. In fact, only the first three pieces make use of the appropriate antiphon texts. The fourth piece (No. 163) is *Absterget Deus*, the
fourth antiphon from Second Vespers, rather than *Martyres Domini,* the proper
fourth antiphon from First Vespers[230].

In other cases it appears that Anerio simply chose antiphon texts at will from
the seven normally provided in the Breviary for each important feast, disregard-
ing the correct sequence. For example, the first two pieces in the set for the
feast of St. Agnes (No. 25—26) are *Stans beata Agnes,* actually the *Magnificat*
antiphon at Second Vespers, and *Anulo suo,* the third psalm antiphon at First
and Second Vespers[231].

In the set for the feast of SS. Philip and James the first piece, *Domine ostende*
(No. 41), is in fact a setting of the proper first antiphon, followed by *Tanto
tempore* (No. 42), the third antiphon, and *Non turbetur* (No. 43), the *Magnificat*
antiphon at First Vespers[232]. In view of the fact that Anerio's basic plan seems
to be the provision of music for the first four antiphons, one might reasonably
expect a word of warning when the composer is about to alter the order of the
texts. Unfortunately, no warning is ever given.

As Table IV makes clear, these wandering antiphons are inserted in Anerio's
sets at any point, replacing the proper first, second, third, or fourth antiphon.
The only common characteristics of these antiphons are that the texts are taken
from Vesper antiphons found in the Breviary; that the texts are unaltered; and
that the pieces are liturgically out of place in Anerio's collection.

TABLE IV
VESPER ANTIPHONS WITH BORROWED TEXTS
(out of proper liturgical order in Anerio's collection)[233]

COMPOSITION	ANERIO'S RUBRIC	ACTUAL LITURGICAL SOURCE
No. 2	In Aduentu, & vigilia Natiuitatis Domini. [Ant. 2]	Nativity of Our Lord 1st Vespers Ant. to *Magnificat*[234]

---

[230] The same text appears in a different musical setting as Anerio's fourth antiphon on the feast of All Saints (No. 108).

[231] The third and fourth pieces in this set, *Ecce quod concupivi* and *Ipsi sum desponsata* (No. 27—28) are not Vesper antiphons at all; these pieces are included in Table V, below.

[232] The fourth piece in the set, *Si mansuetis* (No. 44), sets an altered version of the *Magnificat* antiphon at 2nd Vespers; see Table VI, below.

[233] Minor variations in spelling and punctuation have been disregarded in compiling this table. For source of rubrics, see Table I, above. The position of the composition within each of Anerio's sets of antiphons is supplied in brackets.

[234] Source of text: *Brev 1606*, p. 151.

No. 10	In festo S. Luciae.	St. Lucy
	In primis, & secundis Vesperis.	1st and 2nd Vespers
	[Ant. 2]	Ant. 3[235]
No. 11	Ibid.	St. Lucy
		1st and 2nd Vespers
	[Ant. 3]	Ant. 2[236]
No. 13	In Natiuitate Domini.	Nativity of Our Lord
	In primis, & secundis Vesperis.	2nd Vespers
	[Ant. 1]	Ant. 1[237]
No. 14	Ibid.	Nativity of Our Lord
		2nd Vespers
	[Ant. 2]	Ant. 3[238]
No. 15	Ibid.	Nativity of Our Lord
		2nd Vespers
	[Ant. 3]	Ant. 4[239]
No. 23	In Epiphania Domini.	Epiphany of Our Lord
	In primis, & secundis Vesperis.	1st and 2nd Vespers
	[Ant. 3]	Ant. 5[240]
No. 25	In festo S. Agnetis.	St. Agnes
	In primis, & secundis Vesperis.	2nd Vespers
	[Ant. 1]	Ant. to *Magnificat*[241]
No. 26	Ibid.	St. Agnes
		1st and 2nd Vespers
	[Ant. 2]	Ant. 3[242]
No. 42	In festo ss. Apostolorum Philippi, & Iacobi.	SS. Philip and James
		1st and 2nd Vespers
	[Ant. 2]	Ant. 3[243]
No. 43	Ibid.	SS. Philip and James
		1st Vespers
	[Ant. 3]	Ant. to *Magnificat*[244]
No. 56	[In festo Natiuitatis S. Io. Baptistae]	Nativity of St. John the Baptist
	In secundis Vesperis.	2nd Vespers
	[Ant. 4]	Ant. 5[245]
No. 82	In festo S. Laurentij	St. Lawrence
	in primis, & secundis Vesperis.	1st Vespers
	[Ant. 2]	Ant. to *Magnificat*[246]

---

[235] Source of text: *Brev 1606*, p. 706.
[236] Source of text: *Brev 1606*, p. 706.
[237] Source of text: *Brev 1606*, p. 162.
[238] Source of text: *Brev 1606*, p. 162.
[239] Source of text: *Brev 1606*, p. 162.
[240] Source of text: *Brev 1606*, p. 212.
[241] Source of text: *Brev 1606*, p. 722.
[242] Source of text: *Brev 1606*, *p. 721*.
[243] Source of text: *Brev 1606*, p. 765.
[244] Source of text: *Brev 1606*, p. 763.
[245] Source of text: *Brev 1606*, p. 805.
[246] Source of text: *Brev 1606*, p. 871.

No. 101   In festo S. Francisci, & Stigmatum   Imprinting of the Holy Stigmata
               eiusdem,   on St. Francis
           in primis, & secundis Vesperis.   1st Vespers
           [Ant. 1]   Ant. 1[247]
No. 102   Ibid.   Imprinting of the Holy Stigmata
                                                      on St. Francis
                                                   1st Vespers
           [Ant. 2]   Ant. 2[248]
No. 103   Ibid.   Imprinting of the Holy Stigmata
                                                      on St. Francis
                                                   1st Vespers
           [Ant. 3]   Ant. 3[249]
No. 104   Ibid.   Within the Octave of the Feast of
                                                      St. Francis
           [Ant. 4]   Ant. to *Magnificat*[250]
No. 108   In festo omnium Sanctorum   Common of Two or More Martyrs
                                                      out of Paschal Time
           in primis, & secundis Vesperis.   2nd Vespers
           [Ant. 4]   Ant. 4[251]
No. 116   In festo Sanctae Ceciliae   St. Cecilia
           in primis, & secundis Vesperis.   2nd Vespers
           [Ant. 4]   Ant. to *Magnificat*[252]
No. 126   In Ascensione Domini.   Ascension of Our Lord
           in primis, & secundis Vesperis.   1st and 2nd Vespers
           [Ant. 2]   Ant. 3[253]
No. 127   Ibid.   Ascension of Our Lord
                                                   1st and 2nd Vespers
           [Ant. 3]   Ant. 4[254]
No. 163   In Commune plurimorum Mar-   Common of Two or More Martyrs
               tirum.   out of Paschal Time
           In primis Vesperis.   2nd Vespers
           [Ant. 4]   Ant. 4[255]
No. 199   In festo S. Augustini.   St. Augustine
                                                   1st Vespers
           [Ant. 3]   Ant. to *Magnificat*[256]
No. 211   In festo S. Francisci.   Imprinting of the Holy Stigmata
                                                      on St. Francis
                                                   2nd Vespers
           [Ant. 3]   Ant. to *Magnificat*[257]

---

[247] Source of text: *AntR 1572*, fol. 195; compare *Analecta hymnica*, XXVI, p. 45.
[248] Source of text: *Analecta hymnica*, XXVI, p. 45.
[249] Source of text: *Analecta hymnica*, XXVI, p. 46.
[250] Source of text: *AntR 1572*, fol. 189; compare *Analecta hymnica*, V, p. 178.
[251] Source of text: *Brev 1606*, p. 1032.
[252] Source of text: *Brev 1606*, p. 989.
[253] Source of text: *Brev 1606*, p. 444.
[254] Source of text: *Brev 1606*, pp. 444—445.
[255] Source of text: *Brev 1606*, p. 1032.
[256] Source of text: *Brev 1559*, fol. 473ᵛ.   [257] Source of text: *Analecta hymnica*, XXVI, p. 46.

No. 223	In festo S. Dominici.	St. Dominic
		2nd Vespers
	[Ant. 3]	Ant. to *Magnificat*[258]
No. 226	In festo S. Catharinae Senensis.	St. Catherine of Sienna
		2nd Vespers
	[Ant. 2]	Ant. to *Magnificat*[259]
No. 239	In festo S. Elisei.	Within the Octave of the Feast of St. Eliseus
	[Ant. 3]	Ant. to *Magnificat*[260]
No. 241	In festo S. Alberti.	St. Albert of the Carmelites
		1st Vespers
	[Ant. 1]	Ant. to *Magnificat*[261]

Moving still further out of the bounds of liturgical propriety, we encounter in Table V 22 compositions whose texts, taken without alteration from the Breviary, are nevertheless not Vesper antiphons at all. Most of the texts, in fact, prove to be antiphons for Lauds or Matins, or great responsories at Matins (generally using only the initial respond, omitting the verse and second respond)[262]. Certainly we can reject the notion that Anerio may have intended some of these pieces for Matins or Lauds, since the rubric that introduces each set is unambiguous: this is Vesper music. The only pieces for which another office than Vespers is specified, as we have seen, are the three Compline antiphons at the end of Part II[263].

---

[258] Source of text: *Analecta hymnica*, XXV, p. 241.

[259] Source of text: *BrevDom 1615*, p. 871.

[260] Source of text: *BrevCarm 1672*, p. 979.

[261] Source of text: *BrevCarm 1579*, fol. 357; compare *Analecta hymnica*, V, p. 102.

[262] *Duo Seraphim*, the third of the »motets« in Monteverdi's 1610 collection, has similarly been identified with a Matins responsory; see Leo SCHRADE, *Monteverdi, Creator of Modern Music*, New York 1950, p. 251. See also STEVENS, p. 321.

[263] Seventeenth-century lists of obligations for church musicians provide further evidence on this point. Choirs were generally required to sing at Mass and Vespers on Sundays and most important feast days; the rank of the feast (and local custom) determined the amount of music to be performed in canto figurato. The musicians sang at Matins only on the greatest feasts (typically Christmas Eve, the last days of Holy Week, the Eve of Easter and Pentecost, and perhaps one or two other feasts). See, for example, CASIMIRI, *Disciplina musicae*, in: Note d'archivio 12, 1935, pp. 7—14 (on the musical obligations of the Seminario Romano, 1586—1640); ROCHE, p. 298 (on S. Maria Maggiore, Bergamo, 1622); Sr. Mary Nicole [Anne] SCHNOEBELEN, *The Concerted Mass at San Petronio in Bologna: ca. 1660—1730. A Documentary and Analytical Study*. Unpublished Ph. D. dissertation, University of Illinois 1966, pp. 54—57 (on S. Petronio, Bologna, 1658); Francesco PASINI, *Notes sur la vie de Giovanni Battista Bassani*, in: Sammelbände der Internationalen Musikgesellschaft 7, 1905—1906, pp. 592—594 (on the Duomo of Ferrara, 1688). The feasts included in Anerio's collection are representative of seventeenth-century Italian practice.

TABLE V

TEXTS BORROWED WITHOUT ALTERATION
FROM LITURGICAL SOURCES OTHER THAN VESPER ANTIPHONS[264]

COMPOSITION	ANERIO'S RUBRIC	ACTUAL LITURGICAL SOURCE
No. 1	In Aduentu, & vigilia Natiuitatis Domini. [Ant. 1]	Christmas Eve Lauds Ant. to *Benedictus*[265]
No. 21	In Epiphania Domini. In primis, & secundis Vesperis. [Ant. 1]	Epiphany of Our Lord Matins Resp. 5 (respond only)[266]
No. 27	In festo S. Agnetis. In primis, & secundis Vesperis. [Ant. 3]	St. Agnes Lauds Ant. to *Benedictus*[267]
No. 28	Ibid. [Ant. 4]	St. Agnes Matins Resp. 7 (respond only)[268]
No. 39	In Annunciatione B. V. in primis & secundis Vesperis. [Ant. 3]	Annunciation of the Blessed Virgin Lauds Ant. to *Benedictus*[269]
No. 63	In commemoratione S. Pauli Apostoli in primis Vesperis. [Ant. 3]	Commemoration of St. Paul 1st Vespers Chapter[270]
No. 64	Ibid. [Ant. 4]	Commemoration of St. Paul Matins Ant. 2 in 3rd Nocturn[271]
No. 70	In festo S. Mariae Magdalenae, in primis, & secundis Vesperis. [Ant. 2]	Common of Holy Women Matins Ant. 2 in 1st Nocturn[272]

---

[264] Minor variations in spelling and punctuation have been disregarded in compiling this table. For source of rubrics, see Table I, above. The position of the composition within each of Anerio's sets of antiphons is supplied in brackets.

[265] Source of text: *Brev 1606*, p. 150.

[266] Source of text: *Brev 1606*, p. 209. A shortened version of the text appears in *Brev 1606*, p. 221, as the Ant. to *Magnificat* on the 5th day within the Octave of the Epiphany.

[267] Source of text: *Brev 1606*, pp. 721–722.

[268] Source of text: *Brev 1606*, p. 721.

[269] Source of text: *Brev 1606*, pp. 755–756.

[270] Source of text: *Brev 1606*, p. 816.

[271] Source of text: *Brev 1606*, p. 819.

[272] Source of text: *Brev 1606*, p. 1064. This text also appears in *Brev 1606*, p. 1092, as Ant. 2 at Vespers in the Little Office of the Blessed Virgin out of Advent, and in other Marian offices.

No. 71	Ibid.	Common of Holy Women
		Matins
	[Ant. 3]	Ant. 1 in 3rd Nocturn[273]
No. 81	In festo S. Laurentij	St. Lawrence
	in primis, & secundis Vesperis.	Matins
	[Ant. 1]	Resp. 2 (respond only)[274]
No. 97	In Dedicatione S. Michaelis Archangeli	Dedication of the Church of St. Michael, the Archangel
	in primis, & secundis Vesperis.	Matins
	[Ant. 1]	Resp. 2 (respond only)[275]
No. 100	Ibid.	Dedication of the Church of St. Michael, the Archangel
		Lauds
	[Ant. 4]	Ant. to *Benedictus*[276]
No. 114	In festo Sanctae Ceciliae	St. Cecilia
	in primis, & secundis Vesperis.	Lauds
	[Ant. 2]	Ant. to *Benedictus*[277]
No. 128	In Ascensione Domini.	Ascension of Our Lord
	In primis, & secundis Vesperis.	Matins
	[Ant. 4]	Ant. 3 in 2nd Nocturn[278]
No. 138	In festo Sanctissimae Trinitatis.	Feast of the Blessed Trinity
		Matins
	[Ant. 4]	Resp. 7 (complete)[279]
No. 172	In Commune Confessorum Pontificum.	Common of a Confessor Bishop
	In primis, & secundis Vesperis.	Matins
	[Ant. 5]	Resp. 1 (respond only)[280]
No. 174	In Commune Confessorum non Pontificum.	Common of a Confessor Bishop
	In primis, & secundis Vesperis.	Matins
	[Ant. 2]	Resp. 1 (respond only)[281]
No. 177	Ibid.	Common of a Confessor, not a Bishop
		Matins
	[Ant. 5]	Ant. 1 in 3rd Nocturn[282]

---

[273] Source of text: *Brev 1606*, p. 1058. This text also appears in *Brev 1606*, p. 1092, as Ant. 3 at Vespers in the Little Office of the Blessed Virgin out of Advent, and in other Marian offices.

[274] Source of text: *Brev 1606*, p. 872.

[275] Source of text: *Brev 1606*, p. 937. A shortened version of the text appears in *Brev 1606*, p. 942, as Ant. 1 at Vespers.

[276] Source of text: *Brev 1606*, p. 943.   [277] Source of text: *Brev 1606*, p. 988.

[278] Source of text: *Brev 1606*, p. 441.   [279] Source of text: *Brev 1606*, p. 487.

[280] Source of text: *Brev 1606*, p. 1036. Similar but not identical texts may be found in *Brev 1606*, p. 1041, as Ant. to *Benedictus* at Lauds and as Ant. 5 at Vespers.

[281] Source of text: see footnote 280, above. In No. 174 the words *in pauca* are changed to *super pauca*, and an Alleluia is added for Paschal Time; otherwise the two texts are identical. The proper text for Ant. 2, »*Euge . . . in modico*«, may be found in *Brev 1606*, p. 1049.

[282] Source of text: *Brev 1606*, p. 1039.

No. 219	In festo S. Antonii de Padua.	St. Anthony of Padua Lauds
	[Ant. 3]	Ant. to *Benedictus*[283]
No. 228	In festo S. Catharinae Senensis.	St. Catherine of Sienna Lauds
	[Ant. 4]	Ant. to *Benedictus*[284]
No. 242	In festo S. Alberti.	St. Albert of the Carmelites Lauds (and for Vespers?)
	[Ant. 2]	Ant. 2[285]
No. 244	Ibid.	St. Albert of the Carmelites Lauds (and for Vespers?)
	[Ant. 4]	Ant. 4[286]

We find in Table V our first important clues to Anerio's practice in the alteration of antiphon texts, for some of his borrowed texts prove to be paraphrases of genuine Vesper antiphons. *Stetit Angelus* (No. 97), the first piece in the set for the Dedication of the Church of St. Michael, the Archangel, is a setting of the second responsory at Matins (omitting verse and second respond)[287]. The genuine first antiphon at Vespers, however, is a truncated version of the same text[288]:

> *Stetit Angelus iuxta aram templi,*
> *habens thuribulum aureum in manu sua:*
> & data sunt ei incensa multa: Et ascendit
> fumus aromatū de manu Angeli in conspectu Dñi.[289]

Anerio has simply substituted a longer text for the short one provided in the liturgy. This does not mean that he has composed a piece for Matins; the rubric »*in primis, & secundis Vesperis*« is perfectly clear. Is *Stetit Angelus* a non-liturgical Michaelmas Day motet, and not an antiphon at all? Perhaps. But it seems more likely that the piece was composed as a substitute for the proper first antiphon at Vespers, especially since the second and third pieces in this set (No. 98 and 99) are settings of the genuine second and third antiphons for this feast.

Anerio's two compositions entitled *Euge serve bone* (No. 172 and 174) appear under the rubrics, »*In Commune Confessorum Pontificum. In primis, & secundis Vesperis*« and »*In Commune Confessorum non Pontificum. In primis, & secundis Vesperis*«, respectively. The texts of the two are nearly identical except

---

[283] Source of text: *Analecta hymnica*, V, p. 128.

[284] Source of text: *BrevDom 1615*, p. 871.

[285] Source of text: *Analecta hymnica*, V, p. 103. It is not clear whether this antiphon is intended to serve at 2nd Vespers as well as Lauds.

[286] Source of text: *Analecta hymnica*, V, p. 103. It is not clear whether this antiphon is intended to serve at 2nd Vespers as well as Lauds.

[287] Source of text: *Brev 1606*, p. 937.

[288] Antiphon text in italics.

[289] Antiphon text may be found in *Brev 1606*, p. 942.

that an optional Alleluia for Paschal Time has been added to the second. In the Breviary this text appears as the first responsory (omitting the verse) at Matins on feasts of Confessor Bishops:

> Euge serue bone & fidelis, quia in pauca
> fuisti fidelis, supra multa te constituam:
> Intra in gaudium Domini tui[290].

The proper Vesper antiphons which Anerio ought to have set are these:

> Ant. 5 at Vespers, Common of a Confessor Bishop:
> Serue bone & fidelis, intra in gaudium
> Domini tui[291].

> Ant. 2 at Vespers, Common of a Confessor, not a Bishop:
> Euge serue bone, in modico fidelis, intra
> in gaudiū Domini tui[292].

In these two cases Anerio has chosen a substitute text which paraphrases at greater length the meaning of the original antiphons.

An example of a freer kind of text substitution is provided by *Quomodo fiet istud* (No. 39), Anerio's third antiphon in the set for the feast of the Annunciation. Anerio's text, which appears in the Breviary as the *Benedictus* antiphon at Lauds, takes the form of a dialogue between the Blessed Virgin, who asks how she can conceive a child, »seeing that I know not a man«, and the Angel Gabriel, who explains the miracle to her. The Vesper antiphon, on the other hand, simply announces the miracle in the Angel's words to Mary. The two texts, then, are related in subject but not in language:

> Ant. to *Benedictus* at Lauds (Anerio's text):
> Quomodo fiet istud, Angele Dei, quoniam virū non cognosco?
> Audi Maria virgo: Spiritus sanctus superueniet in te, & virtus
> Altissimi obumbrabit tibi[293].

> Ant. 3 at Vespers:
> Ne timeas Maria: inuenisti gratiam apud
> Dominum: ecce concipies & paries filium[294].

Many of Anerio's borrowed texts are quite unrelated to the Vesper antiphons they presumably replace. The first piece in the set composed for the feast of the Epiphany (No. 21) is a setting of a Matins responsory:

> Resp. 5 at Matins (omitting the verse):
> Omnes de Saba venient, aurum & thus
> deferentes, & laudem Dño annuntiantes,
> Alleluia, alleluia, alleluia[295].

---

[290] Source of text: *Brev 1606*, p. 1036. For differences between No. 172 and 174, see footnote 281, above.

[291] Source of text: *Brev 1606*, p. 1041.

[292] Source of text: *Brev 1606*, p. 1049.

[293] Source of text: *Brev 1606*, pp. 755—756.

[294] Source of text: *Brev 1606*, p. 755.   [295] Source of text: *Brev 1606*, p. 209.

The proper first antiphon at Vespers is entirely different:

> *Ante luciferum genitus, & ante saecula,*
> *Dominus Saluator noster hodie mundo apparuit*[296].

In the arrangement of Anerio's collection it is clear that *Omnes de Saba* is intended to take the place of the first antiphon, for the second piece in the set (No. 22) is *Venit lumen*, the proper second antiphon for the feast. It is difficult to justify substitutions like this one. One might observe merely that *Omnes de Saba* is an appealing and joyful text that vividly portrays the occasion being celebrated, while *Ante luciferum* is a sober reflection upon the significance of the feast, as the absence of an Alleluia makes plain. In any event, the source of Anerio's text is to be found among the responsories of Matins, where many other antiphon-substitutes also originated, as we have seen. No doubt compositions like *Omnes de Saba* could be performed as non-liturgical motets on any suitable occasion; the important point is that they seem to have a liturgical function as antiphon-substitutes, even when the texts are quite dissimilar from those of the Breviary.

The next group of compositions consists of 31 antiphons with altered or expanded texts. These texts are based on genuine Vesper antiphons, not borrowed from elsewhere in the Divine Office. More than one-third of the pieces are out of proper liturgical order for their feast, however. Unlike the compositions discussed previously, the present works exhibit significant differences between Anerio's texts and those of the Breviary, as Table VI makes clear.

TABLE VI

Vesper Antiphons with Altered or Expanded Texts[297]

Compos.	Anerio's Rubric	Liturgical Source and Text
No. 3	In Aduentu, & vigilia Natiuitatis Domini.	2nd Sunday of Advent
		Vespers
	[Ant. 3]	Ant. 4
		Montes & colles cantabunt coram Deo laudem, & omnia ligna siluarum

---

[296] Source of text: *Brev 1606*, p. 212.

[297] To facilitate comparison between Anerio's text and that of the Breviary, both are given in full in the following manner: Breviary (or other source) text in italics; text omitted by Anerio in italics and set within brackets; Anerio's added text in roman type. Spelling and punctuation are taken from the Breviary (or other source); minor variations in spelling and punctuation have been disregarded. When essential punctuation is lacking, the texts are divided by slashes corresponding to Anerio's cadences. When Anerio's text seems to be a composite of two or more Breviary texts, his text is given in the table; the corresponding Breviary texts appear in the footnotes.

		plaudent manibus: quoniam veniret [*veniet*] *dominator Dominus in regnum aeternum.* [*alleluia, alleluia.*][298]
No. 4	Ibid.	3rd Sunday of Advent
		Vespers
	[Ant. 4]	Ant. 2
		Ierusalem gaude gaudio magno, quia veniet tibi Saluator tuus/ haurietis aquas in gaudio/ de fontibus Saluatoris. [*allel.*][299]
No. 30	[In festo Purificationis B. Virginis.] In secundis Vesperis.	Purification of the Blessed Virgin 2nd Vespers
	[Ant. 2]	Ant. 2
		Responsum accepit Simeon à Spiritu sancto, nō visurum se mortem, nisi videret Christū Domini [*Dominum*][300].
No. 33	In festo S. Agatae. In primis, & secundis Vesp.	St. Agatha 1st and 2nd Vespers
	[Ant. 1]	Ant. 1
		Quis es tu, qui venisti ad me curare vulnera mea? Ego sum Apostolus Christi: nihil in me dubites filia. Ipse me misit ad te/ & in nomine eius curata es[301].
No. 36	Ibid.	St. Agatha
		Composite of various Vesper antiphons
	[Ant. 4]	
		Domine Iesu Christe magister bone/ gratias tibi ago/ quia memor es mei/ qui me carnificum tormenta superare fecisti/ qui me per Apostolum tuum dignatus es ab omni plaga curare/ & mammillam meam meo pectori restituere[302].

---

[298] Source of text: *Brev 1606*, p. 126.

[299] Source of text: *Brev 1606*, p. 134. Compare *Isaias* XII.3: »*Haurietis aquas in gaudio de fontibus salvatoris.*«

[300] Source of text: *Brev 1606*, p. 737. Compare *Ev. sec. Lucam* II.26: »*Et responsum acceperat a Spiritu Sancto, non visurum se mortem, nisi prius videret Christum Domini.*«

[301] Source of text: *Brev 1606*, p. 740. Compare *Brev 1606*, p. 739 (Resp. 3 at Matins): »*Quis es tu, qui venisti ad me curare vulnera mea? ego sum Apostolus Christi: nihil in me dubites filia: ipse me misit ad te, Quem dilexisti mente & puro corde. [V.] Nā & ego Apostolus eius sum, & in nomine eius scias te esse curandam.*«

[302] Compare *Brev 1606*, p. 738 (Ant. to *Magnificat*): »*Stans beata Agatha in medio carceris, expansis manibus orabat ad Dominum: Domine Iesu Christe, magister bone, gratias tibi ago, qui me fecisti vincere tormenta carnificum: iube me Domine ad tuam immarcescibilem gloriam feliciter peruenire.*« Compare also p. 740 (Ant. 3): »*Gratias tibi ago, Domine Iesu Christe, quia memor es mei, & misisti ad me Apostolum tuum curare vulnera mea.*« Compare also p. 740 (Ant. 4): »*Benedico te Pater Domini mei Iesu Christi: quia per Apostolum*

No. 37   In Annunciatione B. V.   Annunciation of the Blessed Virgin
          in primis & secundis Vesperis.   1st and 2nd Vespers
          [Ant. 1]   Ant. 1
                                                    Missus est Angelus Gabriel [*Ga-*
                                                briel Angelus] *ad Mariam virginem*
                                                desponsatam Ioseph. & expauescit Vir-
                                                go de lumine/ Ne timeas Maria Inueni-
                                                sti gratiam apud Dominum/ Ecce con-
                                                cipies & paries Filium[303].

No. 40   Ibid.   Annunciation of the Blessed Virgin
                                                2nd Vespers
          [Ant. 4]   Ant. to *Magnificat*
                                                    Gabriel Angelus locutus est Marię,
                                                dicens: Aue gratia plena, Dominus te-
                                                cum: benedicta tu in mulieribus. & be-
                                                nedictus fructus ventris tui[304].

No. 44   In festo ss. Apostolorum Philippi,   SS. Philip and James
          & Iacobi.

                                                2nd Vespers
          [Ant. 4]   Ant. to *Magnificat*
                                                    Si mansuetis [*manseritis*] *in me,*
                                                & verba mea in vobis manserint,
                                                quodcumque petieritis patrem in no-
                                                mine meo fiat [*fiet*] *vobis, alleluia,*
                                                alleluia[305].

No. 55   [In festo Natiuitatis S. Io. Bap-   Nativity of St. John the Baptist
          tistae]
          In secundis Vesperis.   Composite of two Vesper antiphons
          [Ant. 3]
                                                    Inter natos mulierum nō surrexit
                                                maior Ioanne Baptista/ & multi In
                                                natiuitate eius gaudebūt[306].

---

tuum mamillam meam meo pectori restituisti.« Compare also p. 740 (Ant. 5): »*Qui me dig-*
natus est ab omni plaga curare, & mamillam meam meo pectori restituere, ipsum inuoco
Deum viuum.«

[303] Source of text: *Brev 1606*, p. 755. Compare *Brev 1606*, p. 753 (Resp. 1 at Matins, omitting
   verse): »*Missus est Gabriel Angelus ad Mariam virginem desponsatam Ioseph, nuntians ei*
   verbum: & expauecit Virgo de lumine. Ne timeas Maria: inuenisti gratiā apud Dominum:
   Ecce concipies & paries, & vocabitur Altissimi filius.« Compare also *Ev. sec. Lucam* I.31:
   »*Ecce concipies in utero, et paries filium, et vocabis nomen ejus JESUM.*«

[304] Source of text: *Brev 1606*, p. 756; 6th word corrected from original: *diceas.* Compare
   AntR 1572, fol. 128v: »*Gabriel angelus locutus est marię dicens: aue gratia plena dominus*
   tecum: benedicta tu inter mulieres: & benedictus fructus ventris tui.«

[305] Source of text: *Brev 1606*, p. 766. Compare *Ev. sec. Joannem* XIV.13: »*Et quodcumque*
   petieritis Patrem in nomine meo, hoc faciam . . .«

[306] Compare *Brev 1606*, p. 805 (Ant. 4 at 2nd Vespers): »*Inter natos mulierum non surrexit*
   maior Ioanne Baptista.« Compare also p. 805 (Ant. 3 at 2nd Vespers): »*Ioannes, vocabitur*
   nomen eius: & in natiuitate eius multi gaudebunt.«

No. 58   In festo ss. Apostolorum Petri, &   Holy Apostles Peter and Paul
         Pauli
         in primis Vesperis.   1st Vespers
         [Ant. 2]   Ant. 2

Argentum & aurū non est mihi: quod autem habeo, hoc tibi do. In nomine Iesu Christi Nazareni/ Surge & ambula[307].

No. 61   In commemoratione S. Pauli   Commemoration of St. Paul
         Apostoli
         in primis Vesperis.   1st Vespers
         [Ant. 1]   Ant. 1

Ego plantaui, Apollo rigauit, Deus autem incrementum dedit, [alleluia.][308]

No. 72   In festo S. Mariae Magdalenae,   St. Mary Magdalen
         in primis, & secundis Vesperis.   1st and 2nd Vespers
         [Ant. 4]   Ant. 3

Iam hiems transijt, imber abijt, & recessit: surge amica mea, & veni. Alleluia[309].

No. 76   In festo S. Petri ad vincula   St. Peter's Chains
         in primis, & secundis Vesperis.   1st and 2nd Vespers
         [Ant. 4]   Ant. 4

Misit Dominus Angelum suum, & liberauit me de manu Herodis, & de omni expectatione plebis Iudeorum. [alle.][310]

No. 80   In festo Transfigurationis Domini   Transfiguration of Our Lord
         in primis & secundis Vesperis.   1st and 2nd Vespers
         [Ant. 4]   Ant. 4

Respondens autem Petrus dixit ad Iesum: Dñe, bonum est nos hic esse. faciamus hic tria tabernacula/ tibi vnum/ Moysi vnum/ & Hellę vnum/ Alleluia[311].

---

[307] Source of text: *Brev 1606*, p. 815. Compare *Act. Apost.* III.6: »*Petrus autem dixit: Argentum et aurum non est mihi; quod autem habeo, hoc tibi do. In nomine Jesu Christi Nazareni, surge, et ambula.*«

[308] Source of text: *Brev 1606*, p. 820.

[309] Source of text: *Brev 1606*, p. 839. This text appears also in *Brev 1606*, p. 1093, as Ant. 4 at Vespers in the Little Office of the Blessed Virgin out of Advent, and in other Marian offices.

[310] Source of text: *Brev 1606*, p. 851. Compare *Act. Apost.* XII.11: »*Et Petrus ad se reversus, dixit: Nunc scio vere quia misit Dominus angelum suum, et eripuit me \de \manu Herodis, et de omni exspectatione plebis Judaeorum.*«

[311] Source of text: *Brev 1606*, p. 869. Compare *Ev. sec. Matthaeum* XVII.4: »*Respondens autem Petrus, dixit ad Jesum: Domine, bonum est nos hic esse; si vis, faciamus hic tria tabernacula, tibi unum, Moysi unum, et Eliae unum.*«

No. 85	In Assumptione B. V. in primis, & secundis Vesperis. [Ant. 1]	Assumption of the Blessed Virgin 1st and 2nd Vespers Ant. 1 *Assumpta est Maria in caelum, gaudent Angeli, laudantes benedicunt Dominum.* Alleluia[312].
No. 86	Ibid. [Ant. 2]	Assumption of the Blessed Virgin 1st and 2nd Vespers Ant. 2 *Maria virgo assumpta est ad aethereum thalamum, in quo Rex regum stellato sedet solio.* Alleluia[313].
No. 90	In Decollatione S. Io Baptistae in primis & secundis Vesperis. [Ant. 2]	Beheading of St. John the Baptist Composite of two Vesper antiphons Domine mi Rex da mihi in desco caput Ioannis Baptistae/ & contristatus est Rex/ propter iusiurandū[314].
No. 91	Ibid. [Ant. 3]	Beheading of St. John the Baptist 1st and 2nd Vespers Ant. 3 *Puellae saltanti imperauit mater: nihil aliud petas, nisi caput Ioannis* Baptistae[315].
No. 106	In festo omnium Sanctorum in primis & secundis Vesperis. [Ant. 2]	All Saints 1st and 2nd Vespers Ant. 2 *Et omnes Angeli stabant in circuitu throni, & ceciderunt [in conspectu throni] in facies suas, & adorauerunt Deum*[316].
No. 113	In festo Sanctae Ceciliae in primis, & secundis Vesperis. [Ant. 1]	St. Cecilia 1st and 2nd Vespers Ant. 1 *Cantantibus organis Caecilia* virgo soli *Domino decantabat, dicens: Fiat cor meum* & *corpus meum immaculatum, vt non confundar*[317].
No. 115	Ibid. [Ant. 3]	St. Cecilia 1st Vespers Ant. to *Magnificat*

---

[312] Source of text: *Brev 1606*, p. 887.

[313] Source of text: *Brev 1606*, p. 887.

[314] Compare *Brev 1606*, p. 906 (Ant. 2 at 1st and 2nd Vespers): »*Domine mi rex, da mihi in disco caput Ioannis Baptistae.*« Compare also pp. 906—907 (Ant. 5): »*Da mihi in disco caput Ioannis Baptistae: & contristatus est rex propter iusiurandum.*«

[315] Source of text: *Brev 1606*, p. 906.

[316] Source of text: *Brev 1606*, p. 961.

[317] Source of text: *Brev 1606*, p. 988.

Est secretum Valeriane, quod tibi volo dicere: Angelum Domini [*Dei*] *habeo amatorem, qui nimeo zelo custodit corpus meum*[318].

No. 176	In Commune Confessorum non Pontificum.	Common of a Confessor, not a Bishop
	In primis, & secundis Vesperis.	1st and 2nd Vespers
	[Ant. 4]	Ant. 4

Beatus ille seruus, quem cum venerit dominus eius, & pulsauerit ianuam, inuenerit vigilantem. Amen dico vobis/ super omnia bona constituet eum. [P.T.] Alleluia[319].

No. 178	In Commune Virginum.	Common of Virgins
	In primis, & secundis Vesperis.	Composite of two Vesper antiphons
	[Ant. 1]	

Haec est Virgo sapiens/ & vna de numero prudentum/ quē dominus vigilantem inuenit. [P.T.] Alleluia[320].

No. 186	[Officium de B. V.]	Office of the Immaculate Conception of the Blessed Virgin
		Composite of three Vesper antiphons
	[Ant. 3]	

Sicut lilium inter spinas/ sic amica mea Inter filias Hyerusalem/ Tota pulchra es Maria/ & macula non est in te/ Tu gloria Hyerusalē/ Tu laetitia Israel/ Tu honorificentia populi nostri. Alleluia[321].

No. 190	In Commune Dedicationis Ecclesiae.	Common of the Dedication of a Church
	In primis, & secundis Vesperis.	1st Vespers
	[Ant. 2]	Ant. to *Magnificat*

Sanctificauit Dominus tabernaculum suum: quia haec est domus Dei, in qua inuocabitur nomen eius, de quo

---

[318] Source of text: *Brev 1606*, p. 985.

[319] Source of text: *Brev 1606*, p. 1049. Compare *Ev. sec. Matthaeum* XXIV.46—47: »*Beatus ille servus, quem cum venerit dominus ejus, invenerit sic facientem.* [47.] *Amen dico vobis, quoniam super omnia bona sua constituet eum.*«

[320] The Alleluia has been crossed out in pen. Compare *Brev 1606*, p. 1060 (Ant. 1 at 1st and 2nd Vespers): »*Haec est virgo sapiens, & vna de numero prudentum.*« Compare also p. 1060 (Ant. 2): »*Haec est virgo sapiens, quam Dominus vigilantem inuenit.*«

[321] Compare *AntR 1572*, fol. 183 (*Officiũ immaculate cõceptionis beatę virginis Marię editum per Reuerendum patrem dominum Leonardum nogarolum proto notarium ˈapostolicum: artium ac sacre theologie doctorem famosissimũ*: Ant. 1 at 1st Vespers): »*Sicut lilium inter spinas: sic amica mea inter filias Ade alleluia.*« Compare also fol. 183 (Ant. 2): »*Tota pulchra es maria: & macula originalis nõ est in te: alleluia.*« Compare also fol. 183 (Ant. 3): »*Tu gloria hierusalē: tu lętitia israel: tu honorificentia populi nostri alleluia.*«

scriptum est: *Et erit nomen meum ibi, dicit Dominus.* [P.T.] Alleluia[322].

No. 198   In festo S. Augustini.

Office of St. Augustine
1st Vespers

[Ant. 2]   Ant. 2

Augustini [*Huius*] *mater deuotissima, quem carne prius pepererat mundo, caritatis visceribus postmodum, multo semine lacrymarum genuit Christo*[323].

No. 209   In festo S Francisci.

Office of St. Francis
1st Vespers

[Ant. 1]   Ant. 1

Franciscus, vir catholicus
Et totus apostolicus,
   Ecclesiae Romanę [*teneri*]
Fidem teneri [*Romanae*] *docuit,*
Presbyterosque monuit
   Prae cunctis revereri[324].

No. 210   Ibid.

Office of St. Francis
1st Vespers

[Ant. 2]   Ant. to *Magnificat*

O stupor et gaudium
O judex homo mentium,
   Tu nostrae militiae
      Currus et auriga;
Ignea praesentibus
Transfiguratum fratribus
   In solari specie [*facie*]
      Vexit te quadriga;
In te signis radians,
In te ventura nuntians
   Requievit spiritus
      Duplex prophetarum;
Tuis asta [*adsta*] *posteris,*
Pater Francisce, miseris nostram
   Nam increscunt gemitus
      Ovium tuarum[325].

No. 218   In festo S. Antonii de Padua.

Office of St. Anthony of Padua
1st Vespers

---

[322] Source of text: *Brev 1606*, p. 1068.

[323] Source of text: *Brev 1559*, fol. 473: *Officia ad vsvm fratrum eremitarum sancti Augustini. In sancti patris Augustini ep[iscop]i & confessoris.*

[324] Source of text: *Analecta hymnica*, V, p. 175.

[325] Source of text: *Analecta hymnica*, V, p. 176. Compare *AntR 1572*, fol. 187: »*O stupor & gaudiũ: o iudex homo mentium: tu nostrę militię currus & auriga: ignea pręsentibus transfiguratum fratribus in solari specie vexit te quadriga. in te signis radians: in te ventura nũcians requieuit spũs duplex p[ro]phetarũ. tuis asta posteris pater francisce miseris: nã increscũt gemitum ouium tuarũ.*«

[Ant. 2]

Ant. 2
Sapienti filio
*   Pater gloriatur,*
Hoc et in Antonio
*   Digne* demonstratur [*commenda-*
*   tur*][326].

No. 236   In festo S. Eliae.

Office of St. Elias
2nd Vespers

[Ant. 4]

Ant. 5
*   Ascendens [Ascendit] Elias per*
turbinem in caelum, Eliseus autem vi-
debat, & clamabat: Pater mi, pater
mi, currus Israel, & auriga eius[327].

No. 240   In festo S. Elisei.

Office of St. Eliseus
Composite of two Vesper antiphons

[Ant. 4]

    Rem difficilem postulasti/ attamen
si videris me quando tollarate [sic]/
erit tibi quod petisti/ Eliseus autem
videbat & clamabat/ Pater mi/ Currus Israel/ & auriga eius[328].

Anerio's licenses in this group of altered texts fall into three categories. The first, and easiest to dispose of, consists of Breviary texts which are substantially intact in Anerio's version, although a word or two may have been changed here and there. Sometimes the only change is the addition or omission of the Alleluia, as in No. 61 and No. 72. Such small changes hardly seem worth mentioning, except for the fact that to the Church the strict adherence to the canonical text of the Divine Office is essential to the proper celebration of the liturgy[329]. The Alleluia itself is not to be added to an antiphon ad libitum, but to give joyous expression to the celebration of a prescribed feast, particularly during Paschal Time, at the Church's command.

The second category in Table VI includes texts to which important new material has been added, often doubling the length of the text. In general these additions appear in the form of a coda at the end of the text. In one interesting case, that of the antiphon *Gabriel Angelus* (No. 40), the final phrase, »*et benedictus fructus ventris tui*«, absent from *Brev 1606*, is present in an earlier version of this

---

[326] Source of text: *Analecta hymnica*, V, p. 126.
[327] Source of text: *BrevCarm 1672*, p. 1048.
[328] Compare *BrevCarm 1672*, p. 978 (Ant. 3 at 2nd Vespers): »*Rem difficilem postulasti: atta-men si videris me, quando tollar à te, erit tibi quod petisti.*« Compare also p. 978 (Ant. 4 at 2nd Vespers): »*Eliseus autem videbat, & clamabat, pater mi, pater mi, currus Israel, & auriga eius.*«
[329] See p. 91, above.

antiphon published in *AntR 1572*. The suspicion grows that others of these »altered texts« may present a version from another liturgical source, as yet unknown[330]. Further study of liturgical books of the time would undoubtedly reveal sources for other antiphons-with-coda in our list, for it is plain that Anerio does not restrict himself to the official Roman Breviary of his time.

It appears that the expanded texts of the antiphons *Quis es tu* (No. 33) and *Missus est Angelus* (No. 37) are borrowed (in altered versions) from Matins responsories for the respective feasts. As we have observed[331], responsory texts are an important source of antiphon-substitutes for Vespers. It is not surprising, therefore, to discover these links between the present group of antiphons and Matins responsories.

In other cases Anerio seems to have chosen a Vulgate text in preference to that of the Breviary. In *Responsum accepit* (No. 30) the Vulgate words »*Christum Domini*« are chosen in preference to the Breviary's »*Dominum*«. The codas of *Argentum et aurum* (No. 58), *Misit Dominus* (No. 76), and other works are also taken from the Vulgate.

The third category in Table VI consists of a few texts which seem to be compilations of phrases from two or more separate antiphons. This procedure is particularly evident in *Domine mi rex* (No. 90), *Haec est virgo sapiens* (No. 178), and *Rem difficilem* (No. 240), each of which is clearly a composite of two separate antiphons. It is worthwhile observing that in *Domine mi rex* the composer brings together the second and fifth antiphons of the feast, rather than the second and third. In the case of *Inter natos* (No. 55) a portion of the third antiphon is appended to the complete fourth antiphon, reversing the order of the texts in the Breviary; while in *Sicut lilium* (No. 186) the first three antiphons at First Vespers of a special office of the Immaculate Conception are brought together in a single composition. *Domine Jesu Christe* (No. 36), on the other hand, seems to be a free compilation of phrases from four separate antiphons, put together without regard for proper liturgical order.

But we have one more group of compositions to consider (Table VII): pieces with altered texts based on sources other than Vesper antiphons, and a few works for which no source has been found. These pieces, in effect, combine all the licenses that we have previously encountered.

---

[330] Jacquelyn A. MATTFELD, *Some Relationships Between Texts and Cantus Firmi in the Liturgical Motets of Josquin des Pres,* in: JAMS 14, 1961, p. 161, draws perhaps too strong a contrast between the liturgical orthodoxy of the post-Tridentine Church and the freedom of early sixteenth-century practice. Indeed, it seems that her efforts to search out liturgical sources for supposedly non-liturgical Josquin motets can be applied with great profit to the study of the post-Tridentine motet as well.

[331] See p. 117, above.

TABLE VII

Compositions with Altered or Expanded Texts
(sources other than Vesper antiphons) or with unidentified Texts[332]

Compos.	Anerio's Rubric	Liturgical Source and Text
No. 16	In Natiuitate Domini. In primis, & secundis Vesperis. [Ant. 4]	Nativity of Our Lord Lauds Ant. 4 *Facta est cum Angelo multitudo caelestis exercitus laudantium Deum, & dicentium: Gloria in excelsis Deo, & in terra pax hominibus bonae voluntatis, [alleluia.]*[333]
No. 24	In Epiphania Domini. In primis, & secundis Vesperis. [Ant. 4]	3rd Day within the Octave of the Epiphany Lauds Ant. to *Benedictus* *Tria sunt munera* praeciosa *quae obtulerunt Magi Domino in die* ista/ *& habent in se diuina mysteria/ In auro vt ostendatur regis potentia/ in thure Sacerdotem magnū considera/ & in mirrha dominicam sepulturam [aurum, thus, & myrrhā, filio Dei, Regi magno,] alleluia*[334].
No. 32	[In festo Purificationis B. Virginis.] In secundis Vesperis. [Ant. 4]	Purification of the Blessed Virgin Lauds Ant. to *Benedictus* *Cum inducerent puerum Iesum parentes eius in templū/ accepit eum Simeon in vlnas suas, & benedixit Deum, dicens: Nunc dimittis seruum tuum in pace*[335].
No. 35	In festo S. Agatae. In primis, & secundis Vesp. [Ant. 3]	St. Agatha Matins Resp. 2 (respond only) *Agatha laetissime & glorianter ibat ad carcerem: & quasi ad epulas inuitata: agonem suum praecibus domino [Domino precibus] commendabat*[336].

---

[332] For explanation of the manner in which this table should be interpreted, see footnote 297, above.

[333] Source of text: *Brev 1606*, p. 161.

[334] Source of text: *Brev 1606*, p. 217.

[335] Source of text: *Brev 1606*, p. 737.

[336] Source of text: *Brev 1606*, pp. 738–739.

No. 38   In Annunciatione B. V.   Annunciation of the Blessed Virgin
in primis & secundis Vesperis.   Matins
[Ant. 2]   Resp. 8 (respond only)

Gaude Maria virgo, cunctas haereses sola interemisti/ in vniuerso mundo/ quae Gabrielis Archangeli dictis credidisti: Dum virgo Deum & hominem genuisti, & post partum virgo inuiolata permansisti[337].

No. 48   In Inuentione S. Crucis,
in primis, & secundis Vesperis.
[Ant. 4]

Per lignū serui facti sumus/ & per sanctā Crucē liberati sumus/ fructus arboris seduxit nos/ filius Dei redemit nos/ Alleluia[338].

No. 60   In festo ss. Apostolorum Petri, &   Holy Apostles Peter and Paul
        Pauli
in primis Vesperis.   Matins
[Ant. 4]   Resp. 2 (respond only)

Si diligis me, Simon Petre, pasce oues meas: Domine, tu scis [nosti] quia amo te, Et animam meam pono pro te[339].

No. 68   In festo Visitationis B. V.   Visitation of the Blessed Virgin
in primis, & secundis Vesperis.   Lauds
[Ant. 4]   Ant. to *Benedictus*

Cum audisset salutationem Mariae Elisabeth, exclamauit voce magna dicens [& dixit:] Vnde hoc mihi, vt veniat mater Domini mei ad me, alleluia[340].

No. 83   In festo S. Laurentij   St. Lawrence
in primis, & secundis Vesperis.   Matins
[Ant. 3]   Resp. 5 (including verse)

Noli me derelinquere pater sancte, quia thesauros tuos iam expendi. Non nego [ego] te desero, fili, neque derelinquo: sed maiora tibi debentur pro fide [Christi] certamina. [V.] Nos

---

[337] Source of text: *Brev 1606*, p. 755.

[338] No Breviary source known. The text (without Alleluia) appears in *Liber usualis*, p. 746, as Ant. 2 in the 4th part of the Afternoon Liturgy on Good Friday. Compare also *Brev 1606*, p. 772 (Ant. 5 at 1st and 2nd Vespers for the Finding of the Holy Cross): »*Per signum crucis de inimicis nostri libera nos Deus noster, allel.*«

[339] Source of text: *Brev 1606*, p. 813. Compare *Ev. sec. Joannem* XXI.15: »*Cum ergo prandissent, dicit Simoni Petro Jesus: Simon Joannis, diligis me plus his? Dicit ei: Etiam, Domine, tu scis quia amo te. Dicit ei: Pasce agnos meos.*«

[340] Source of text: *Brev 1606*, p. 825.

quasi senes leuioris pugnae cursum re-cipimus, te autem quasi inuenem ma-net gloriosior de tyranno triumphus: post triduum me sequeris Sacerdotem Leuita[341].

No. 84	Ibid.	St. Lawrence
		Matins
	[Ant. 4]	Resp. 6 (respond only)

Beatus Laurentius clamabat [*cla-mauit,*] & dixit: *Deum meū colo, & illi soli seruio, Et ideo non timeo tor-mēta tua*[341a].

No. 110	In festo S. Martini Episcopi, in primis, & secundis Vesperis.	St. Martin
		Composite of phrases from two anti-phons
	[Ant. 2]	

Sacerdos Dei Martinus/ Pastor egregius/ gemma sacerdotum/ Abra-hae sinu laetus excipitur/ Caelum di-ues ingreditur/ Hymnis caelestibus ho-noratur[342].

No. 129	In Ascensione Domini. In primis, & secundis Vesperis.	Ascension of Our Lord
		Matins
	[Ant. 5]	Resp. 6 (respond only)

Ascendens Christus in altum/ alle-luia/ *captiuam duxit captiuitatem/* Alleluia/ *Dedit dona hominibus, alle-luia, alleluia, alleluia*[343].

No. 130	In festo Pentecostes.	Feast of Pentecost
		1st Vespers
	[Ant. 1]	Chapter

Cum complerentur dies Penteco-stes, erant omnes discipuli pariter in eodem loco: & factus est repente de caelo sonus tamquam aduenientis spi-ritus vehementis, & repleuit totam do-mū, vbi erant sedentes. Alleluia[344].

No. 131	Ibid.	5th Day within the Octave of Pente-cost
		Matins

---

[341] Source of text: *Brev 1606*, p. 873.

[341a] Source of text: *Brev 1606*, p. 874.

[342] Compare *Brev 1606*, p. 978 (Ant. 3 in 3rd Nocturn of Matins): »*Sacerdos Dei Martine, pa-stor egregie, ora pro nobis Deum.*« Compare also p. 979 (Ant. 5 at 1st and 2nd Vespers): »*Martinus Abrahae sinu laetus excipitur, Martinus hic pauper & modicus, caelum diues ingreditur, hymnis caelestibus honoratur.*«

[343] Source of text: *Brev 1606*, p. 442.

[344] Source of text: *Brev 1606*, p. 467. Compare p. 472 (Ant. 1 at 1st and 2nd Vespers): »*Cum complerentur dies Pentecostes, erant omnes pariter in eodem loco, alleluia.*«

[Ant. 2]   Resp. 3 (respond only)
                                        Aduenit ignis diuinus, nō combu-
                                        rens, sed illuminans; non comburens
                                        [*consumens,*] *sed lucens: & inuenit*
                                        corda discipulorum receptacula mun-
                                        da: Et tribuit eis charismatū dona, al-
                                        leluia, alleluia[345].

No. 132   Ibid.   Feast of Pentecost
                                        Mass
             [Ant. 3]   2nd Alleluia (verse only)
                                        Veni sancte Spiritus, reple tuorum
                                        corda fidelium: et tui amoris in eis ig-
                                        nem accende. alleluia[346].

No. 134   Ibid.   3rd Day within the Octave of Pente-
                                            cost
                                        Matins
             [Ant. 5]   Resp. 2 (respond only)
                                        Loquebātur [*varijs linguis*] *Apo-*
                                        stoli magnalia Dei, Prout Spiritus
                                        sanctus dabat eloqui illis, alleluia[347].

No. 137   In festo Sanctissimae Trinitatis.   Feast of the Blessed Trinity
                                        Composite of three Matins antiphons

             [Ant. 3]

                                        Libera nos/ & salua nos/ viuifica
                                        nos/ O beata Trinitas/ Te inuocamus/
                                        Te laudamus/ Te adoramus/ O beata
                                        Trinitas/ spes nostra/ salus nostra/ ho-
                                        nor noster/ O beata Trinitas[348].

No. 141   In Solemnitate Corporis Christi.   Corpus Christi
                                        Composite of two Matins antiphons

             [Ant. 3]

                                        Cibauit nos Dominus ex adipe fru-
                                        menti/ & de petra/ melle saturauit
                                        nos/ Ex altari tuo Domine/ Christū
                                        sumimus/ in quem cor & caro nostrā
                                        exultāt[349].

No. 142   Ibid.   Corpus Christi

---

[345] Source of text: *Brev 1606*, p. 477.

[346] Source of text: *Liber usualis*, p. 880. No Breviary source known.

[347] Source of text: *Brev 1606*, p. 475. Compare p. 472 (Ant. 5 at 1st and 2nd Vespers on the feast of Pentecost): »*Loquebantur varijs linguis Apostoli magnalia Dei, alleluia, allel. allel.*«

[348] Compare *Brev 1606*, p. 484 (Ant. 3 in 2nd Nocturn of Matins): »*Libera nos, salua nos, viuifica nos, ò beata Trinitas.*« Compare also p. 483 (Ant. 1 in 2nd Nocturn of Matins): »*Te inuocamus, te laudamus, te adoramus, ò beata Trinitas.*« Compare also p. 484 (Ant. 2 in 2nd Nocturn of Matins): »*Spes nostra, salus nostra, honor noster, ò beata Trinitas.*«

[349] Compare *Brev 1606*, p. 500 (Ant. 2 in 3rd Nocturn of Matins): »*Cibauit nos Dominus ex adipe frumenti: & de petra, melle saturauit nos.*« Compare also p. 500 (Ant. 3 in 3rd Nocturn of Matins): »*Ex altari tuo Domine, Christum sumimus: in quem cor & caro nostra exultant.*«

	[Ant. 4]	Composite of phrases from two short responsories
		Panem Caeli dedit eis/ Panem Angelorum manducauit homo/ educes panem de terra/ & vinum laetificet cor hominis[350].
No. 155	In Commune Apostolorum, Euangelistarum, & Martirum, tempore Paschali.	Common of Apostles, Evangelists and Martyrs in Paschal Time
	In primis, & secundis Vesperis. [Ant. 5]	Matins Resp. 8 (including verse) *Candidi facti sunt [Nazaraei] Nazareni eius, [alleluia:] splendorē Deo dederunt, [alleluia:] Et sicut lac coagulati sunt, [alleluia, alleluia.] [V.] Candidiores niue, nitidiores lacte, rubicundiores ebore antiquo, sapphiro pulchriores. Alleluia[351].*
No. 167	[In Commune plurimorum Martirum.] In secundis Vesperis. [Ant. 4]	
		Qui diligitis Dominum/ laetamini in domino/ & confitemini memoriae sanctitatis eius/ Custodit Dominus animas sanctorū suorum/ de manu peccatoris liberabit eos[352].
No. 168	In Commune Confessorum Pontificum.	Common of a Confessor Bishop
	In primis, & secundis Vesperis. [Ant. 1]	1st and 2nd Vespers Chapter *Ecce sacerdos magnus, qui in diebus suis placuit Deo, & inuentus est iustus: & in tempore iracundiae factus est reconciliatio. [P.T.] Alleluia[353].*
No. 179	In Commune Virginum. In primis, & secundis Vesperis. [Ant. 2]	Common of Virgins Matins Resp. 7 (respond only)

---

[350] Compare *Brev 1606*, p. 502 (Short Resp. at Terce): »*Panem caeli dedit eis, Alleluia, alleluia. [V.] Panem Angelorum manducauit homo. Alleluia, alleluia.*« Compare also p. 503 (Short Resp. at None): »*Educas panem de terra, Alleluia, alleluia. [V.] Et vinum laetificet cor hominis. Alleluia, alleluia.*«

[351] Source of text: *Brev 1606*, p. 1008.

[352] No Breviary source known. Compare *Psal.* XCVI.10,12: »*Qui diligitis Dominum, odite malum; custodit Dominus animas sanctorum suorum, de manu peccatoris liberabit eos. [12.] Laetamini, justi, in Domino; et confitemini memoriae sanctificationis ejus.*«

[353] Source of text: *Brev 1606*, p. 1034. Compare p. 1041 (Ant. 1 at 1st and 2nd Vespers): »*Ecce sacerdos magnus, qui in diebus suis placuit Deo, & inuentus est iustus.*«

Haec est virgo sapiens, quam Dominus vigilantem inuenit, quae acceptis lampadibus sumpsit [*secum oleum:*] oleum secum/ *Et veniēte Domino, introiuit cum eo ad nuptias.* [P.T.] Alleluia[354].

No. 180 Ibid. [Ant. 3]
Common of Holy Women
Matins
Resp. 8 (respond only)
Regnum mundi, & omnem ornatum sęculi contempsi propter amorem Domini mei Iesu Christi: Quem vidi, quem amaui, in quem credidi, quem dilexi. [P.T.] *Alleluia*[355] .

No. 181 Ibid. [Ant. 4]
Composite of phrases from various texts

Veni electa mea/ & ponam in te trhonum meum/ quia Concupiuit rex speciem tuam/ vox enim tua dulcis/ & facies tua decora. [P.T.] Alleluia[356].

No. 182 In Commune Mulierum Sanctarum. In primis, & secundis Vesperis. [Ant. 3]

Pulchra facie/ sed pulchrior fide/ Beata es N.[357]/ respuens mundum/ Laetaberis cū Angelis/ Intercede pro nobis ad Dominum[358].

No. 183 Ibid. [Ant. 4]
Common of Holy Women Martyrs
Sext
Chapter
Liberasti me Domine/ *secundum multitudinem misericordiae nominis tui à rugientibus praeparatis ad escam, de manibus quaerentiū animam meam,*

---

354 Source of text: *Brev 1606*, p. 1060. Compare p. 1060 (Ant. 2 at 1st and 2nd Vespers): *»Haec est virgo sapiens, quam Dominus vigilantem inuenit.«*

355 Source of text: *Brev 1606*, p. 1066. Alleluia crossed out in pen.

356 Compare *Brev 1606*, p. 1055 (Common of Virgins: Resp. 1 at Matins, omitting verse): *»Veni electa mea, & ponam in te thronum meum: Quia concupiuit Rex speciem tuam.«* Compare also *AntR 1572*, fol. 183v *(Officiū immaculate cōceptionis beate virginis Marię editum per Reuerendum patrem dominum Leonardum nogarolum proto notarium apostolicum: artium ac sacre theologie doctorem famosissimū*: Ant. 4 at 1st Vespers): *»Vox enim tua dulcis: & facies illa tua decora nimis alleluia.«* Compare also *Brev 1606*, p. 1060 (Common of Virgins: Ant. 4 at 1st and 2nd Vespers): *»Veni electa mea, & ponam in te thronum meum, alleluia.«* Compare also *Cant. Cantic.* II.14: *». . . vox enim tua dulcis, et facies tua decora.«*

357 = *nomen*, that is, the name of the saint.

358 Source of text unknown.

		& de multis tribulationibus quae circumdederunt me[359].
No. 184	[Officium de B. V.]	Office of the Immaculate Conception of the Blessed Virgin
		Matins
	[Ant. 1]	4th Lesson in 2nd Nocturn (selections)

O Virgo benedicta super omnes faeminas/ Quae Angelos vincis puritate/ quę omnes sanctos superas pietate/ O Maria Mater Domini/ sicut in prima faemina abundauit delictum/ Ita & in te superabundauit omnis plenitudo gratiae/ & ideo super omnes ignara delicti/ Alleluia[360].

No. 185	Ibid.	Office of the Presentation of the Blessed Virgin
		Composite of the Chapter at 1st Vespers and the Chapter at Sext
	[Ant. 2]	

Ego quasi vitis fructificaui suauitatem odoris/ Et flores mei fructus hominis & honestatis/ Transite ad me omnes qui cōcupiscitis me/ & a generationibus meis adimplemini/ spiritus enim meus super mel dulcis/ & haereditas mea super mel & fauum/ memoria mea in generatione saeculorum/ Alleluia[361].

No. 187	Ibid.	Office of the Immaculate Conception of the Blessed Virgin
		Matins
	[Ant. 4]	Ant. 3 in 3rd Nocturn

Quę est ista quę progreditur: quasi *aurora* consurgens [*congens:*] *pulchra*

---

[359] Source of text: *Brev 1606*, p. 1067.

[360] Compare *Brev 1559*, fol. 239 (*Officium nouū immaculatę cōceptionıs. Ex dictis plurimorum sanctorum. Hilarius. Lectio quarta*): »O Virgo benedicta sup[er] omnes feminas: quę angelos vincis puritate, quę oēs sanctos superas pietate. ... Augustinus. O mater dñi, sicut in prima femina abūdauit delictū: ita & in te sup[er]abūdauit omnis plenitudo gratię: & ideo super omnes ignara delicti. ...«

[361] Compare *Brev 1559*, fol. 359 (*In festo pręsentationis virginis Marię: quod festum primo fuit celebratū in Frācia, ad instantiā christianissimi regis francorum ... nunc nouiter sanctissimus papa Sixtus quartus, ipsum publicauit: vt p[er] totū mūdū fieri d[e]beat* ...: Chapter at 1st Vespers): »Ego quasi vitis fructificaui suauitatē odoris: & flores mei, fructus honoris, & honestatis: Deo gratias.« Compare also fol. 362 (Chapter at Sext): »Transite ad me omnes qui concupiscitis me: & a generationibus meis adimplemini: spiritus enim meus super mel dulcis: & heraeditas mea super mel, & fauum: memoria in generatione seculorum.« Compare also *Ecclesiasticus XXIV.28*: »Memoria mea in generationes saeculorum.«

vt luna: electa vt sol: terribilis vt ca-
strorum acies ordinata, hall'a[362].

No. 188   Ibid.   Little Office of the Blessed Virgin
                                     out of Advent
                                     Lauds
            [Ant. 5]   Ant. 5
                                     Pulchra es amica mea/ suauis &
                                     decora, [filia] sicut Ierusalem: terri-
                                     bilis vt castrorum acies ordinata. Au-
                                     uerte oculos tuos a me/ quia ipsi me
                                     auuolare fecerunt[363].

No. 192   In Commune Dedicationis Eccle-   Common of the Dedication of a
                             siae.   Church
            In primis, & secundis Vesperis. Matins
            [Ant. 4]   Resp. 2 (respond only)
                                     Fundata est[364] *domus Domini supra*
                                     verticem montium, & exaltata est su-
                                     per omnes colles: Et venient ad eam
                                     omnes gentes, dicentes [& *dicent,*]
                                     Gloria tibi Domine. [P.T.] Alleluia[365].

No. 193   Ibid.

            [Ant. 5]

                                     O quā bene fundata est hęc domus
                                     Domini/ Cuius structura lapides prae-
                                     ciosi/ & muri eius aurū electum/ Ideo
                                     portae inferi non praeualebit aduer-
                                     sus eam[366].

No. 200   In festo S. Augustini.   Office of St. Augustine
                                            Matins

---

[362] Source of text: *Brev 1559*, fol. 240 (*Officium nouū immaculatę cōceptionis*). This text,
without Alleluia, also appears in *Brev 1606*, p. 1102, as the Chapter at Prime in the Little
Office of the Blessed Virgin out of Advent. The word *congens* is probably an abbreviation
of the word *consurgens*.

[363] Source of text: *Brev 1606*, p. 1100. Compare *Cant. Cantic.* VI.3—4: »*Pulchra es, amica mea,*
suavis, et decora sicut Jerusalem; terribilis ut castrorum acies ordinata. [4.] *Averte oculos*
tuos a me, quia ipsi me avolare fecerunt. . . .«

[364] The first two words have been corrected in pen to read: »*Bene fundata est.*«

[365] Source of text: *Brev 1606*, p. 1070. Compare p. 1075 (Ant. 4 at 1st and 2nd Vespers): »*Be-*
ne fundata est domus Domini supra firmam petram.«

[366] Source of text unknown. Compare *Brev 1606*, p. 1075 (Common of the Dedication of a
Church: Ant. 4 at 1st and 2nd Vespers): »*Bene fundata est domus Domini supra firmam*
petram.« Compare also *III Regum* VII.9: »*Omnia lapidibus pretiosis, qui ad normam quam-*
dam atque mensuram tam intrinsecus quam extrinsecus serrati erant, a fundamento usque
ad summitatem parietum, et extrinsecus usque ad atrium majus.« Compare also *Apocal.*
XXI.18—19: »*Et erat structura muri ejus ex lapide jaspide; ipsa vero civitas, aurum mun-*
dum simile vitro mundo. [19.] *Et fundamenta muri civitatis omni lapide pretioso ornata.*
. . .« Compare also *Ev. sec. Matthaeum* XVI.18: »*. . . et portae inferi non praevalebunt ad-*
versus eam.«

[Ant. 4]

Resp. 3 (respond only)
O lumen ecclesiae,
 Beate Augustine,
Nobilis prosapiae
 Doctor legis divinae,
[*Tu pie sine mora*
Pro nobis Deum ora,]
Aeremitarum pater & fundator/ pro nobis apud Deum/ esto pius aduocatus/ alleluia[367].

No. 212 In festo S. Francisci.

Office of St. Francis
Lauds

[Ant. 4]

Ant. to *Benedictus*
O martyr desiderio,
Francisce, quanto studio
 Compatiens hunc sequeris,
 Quem passum libro reperis,
  Quem aperuisti;
Tu contuens in aere
 Seraphim [*Seraph in*] *cruce positum,*
Ex tunc in palmis, latere
 Et pedibus effigiem
  Fers plagarum Christi;
Tu gregis [*gregi*] *tuo provide*
 Qui post felicem transitum
Dirae prius et lividae
 Glorificatae speciem
  Carnis praedendisti[368].

No. 220 In festo S. Antonii de Padua.
   [Ant. 4]

O lingua benedicta/ quę Deū semper benedixisti/ & alios benedicere docuisti/ nūc perspicue cernitur/ quanti meriti fueris apud Deum[369].

No. 222 In festo S. Dominici.

Office of St. Dominic
Composite of two texts

[Ant. 2]

Adsunt Dominici/
 laeta solemnia/
laude multiplici/
 plaudat Ecclesia/
adest dies laetitiae/
 Quo beatus Dominicus/

---

[367] Source of text: *Analecta hymnica*, V, p. 137.
[368] Source of text: *Analecta hymnica*, V, p. 178.
[369] Source of text unknown.

Aulam Caelestis curiae/
    Ciuis intrat magnificus[370].

No. 224   Ibid.   Office of St. Dominic
                                        Composite of two Lauds antiphons

    [Ant. 4]

                                        Scala Caeli prominens/
                                            Fratri reuelatur/
                                        Per quam pater transiens/
                                            sursum ferebatur/
                                        fulget in Choro virginum/
                                            Dominicus doctor veritatis/
                                        sertum honoris germinum
                                            gerens cū beatis[371].

No. 227   In festo S. Catharinae Senensis.   Office of St. Catherine of Sienna
                                        Composite of two antiphons

    [Ant. 3]

                                            Det Catharina frui nos vero lumi-
                                        ne Christi/ & societ superis virgo be-
                                        ata choris/ ad sedes regni faciat transi-
                                        re supernis/ virgo fouēs meritis nos
                                        Catharina suis/ alleluia[372].

No. 230   In festo S. Thomae de Aquino.   Office of St. Thomas of Aquin
                                        Matins
    [Ant. 2]   Resp. 5 (including verse and 2nd
                                            respond)
                                        Felix doctor Thomas *cujus solatio*
                                        Angelorum servit attentio,
                                        Petrus, Paulus favent obsequio,
                                        Dei mater mulcet alloquio;
                                        [V.] *Elevatus a terra cernitur,*
                                        Crucifixus eum alloquitur [*ei collo-*
                                                    quitur.]
                                        Dei mater mulcet alloquio[373].

---

[370] Compare *Analecta hymnica*, XXV, p. 239 (Invitatory at Matins): »*Assunt Dominic/ Laeta sollemnia,/ Laude multiplici/ Plaudat ecclesia.*« Compare also p. 241 (Ant. 1 at Lauds): »*Adest dies laetitiae,/ Quo beatus Dominicus/ Aulam caelestis curiae/ Civis instrat magnificus.*«

[371] Compare *Analecta hymnica*, XXV, p. 241 (Ant. 3 at Lauds): »*Scala caelo prominens/ Fratri revelatur,/ Per quam pater transiens/ Sursum ferebatur.*« Compare also p. 241 (Ant. 5 at Lauds): »*Fulget in choro virginum/ Doctor veritatis/ Sertum honoris geminum/ Gerens cum beatis.*« It is not clear whether these antiphons are intended to serve at 2nd Vespers as well as Lauds.

[372] Compare *BrevDom 1615*, p. 871 (Lauds within the Octave of the Feast of St. Catherine of Sienna: Ant. to *Benedictus*): »*Det Catharina frui nos vero lumine Christi: Et societ superis virgo beata choris, alleluia.*« Compare also p. 872 (Vespers within the Octave of the Feast of St. Catherine: Ant. to *Magnificat*): »*Ad sedes regni faciat transire superni, Virgo fouens meritis nos Catharina suis, alleluia.*«

[373] Source of text: *Analecta hymnica*, V, p. 231.

No. 231   Ibid.

[Ant. 3]

Office of St. Thomas of Aquin
Matins
Resp. 8 (respond only)
Beati Thomae gloria
   Divo fulsit miraculo,
Dum odoris fragrantia [*fraglantia*]
   Mira fluxit ex [de] tumulo,
Qui nitens pudicitia
   Vixit absque piaculo[374].

No. 232   Ibid.

[Ant. 4]

Office of St. Thomas of Aquin
Composite of two texts

Adsunt Doctoris Caelici/
   Thomae festa sollemnia/
deuotione supplici/
   laudes promat Ecclesia/
O Thoma laus & gloria/
   Prędicatorum Ordinis/
Nos transfer ad Caelestia/
   professor sacri numinis[375].

No. 238   In festo S. Elisei.

[Ant. 2]

Office of St. Eliseus
Matins
Resp. 2 (respond only)
   Cum transissent Elias, & Eliseus
Iordanem per siccum, dixit Eliseus:
Obsecro pater mi/ *vt fiat in me duplex*
spiritus tuus[376].

No. 243   In festo S. Alberti.

[Ant. 3]

Office of St. Albert of the Carmelites
Lauds
Ant. 3
Tua sancta dextera,
Jesu, nos suscipiat
Et Alberti precibus
[*Gratiose*] gloriose nos *protegat*[377].

As we should expect from our scrutiny of other Anerio texts, the present texts are borrowed mostly from the offices of Matins and Lauds. In particular, Anerio has drawn heavily on great responsories (usually omitting the verse) and *Benedictus* antiphons for his sources. Antiphons at Matins are used from

---

[374] Source of text: *Analecta hymnica*, V, p. 232.

[375] Compare *Analecta hymnica*, V, p. 230 (Invitatory at Matins): »*Adsunt doctoris coelici/ Thomae festa solemnia,/ Devotione supplici/ Laudes promat ecclesia.*« Compare also p. 232 (Vespers within the Octave of the Feast of St. Thomas of Aquin: Ant. to *Magnificat*): »O *Thoma, laus et gloria/ Praedicatorum ordinis,/ Nos transfer ad coelestia,/ Professor sacri numinis.*«

[376] Source of text: *BrevCarm 1672*, p. 974.

[377] Source of text: *Analecta hymnica*, V, p. 103. It is not clear whether this antiphon is intended to serve at 2nd Vespers as well as Lauds.

time to time, as are psalm antiphons at Lauds[378]. For the rest, the sources are widely scattered throughout the liturgy. We find readings (the chapter at Vespers, Prime, and Sext; portions of a lesson at Matins), an antiphon from the Afternoon Liturgy on Good Friday, the verse of an Alleluia from the Mass on the feast of Pentecost, short responsories from the Little Hours, and invitatories at Matins. Several texts are designated in the liturgy for use within the Octave of the feast, not (as Anerio suggests) on the feast day itself. No liturgical source has been found for four of the pieces (No. 167, 182, 193, and 220), but two of these (No. 167 and No. 193) have been traced to the Vulgate.

Several texts combine two separate antiphons in one; we have encountered such works before[379]. Anerio's *Cibavit nos* (No. 141) combines two Matins antiphons. *Libera nos* (No. 137), Anerio's third antiphon for Vespers on Trinity Sunday, is a composite of three separate antiphons for Matins, put together out of order. The rhymed text for the feast of St. Dominic, *Adsunt Dominici* (No. 222), brings together the invitatory for Matins and an antiphon for Lauds; while *Scala caeli* (No. 224), designated for the same feast, combines the third and fifth antiphons for Lauds. (Ant. 4 is not used.)

Concerning the textual alterations admitted to the pieces in Table VII, our observations of the Table VI pieces may be repeated. Some texts survive unchanged except for the addition or subtraction of a word or two (No. 16, 32, et al.); in *Felix doctor* (No. 230), a rhymed text, the added word »*Thomas*« ruins the meter, unfortunately. A few of the lengthier texts are related to genuine Vesper antiphons which Anerio probably found too brief for his purposes (No. 130, 134, 168, et al.).

In other cases no single liturgical source can be cited; the author appears to have selected phrases from several sources to compose his text. *Sacerdos Dei Martinus* (No. 110) contains phrases from antiphons at Matins and Vespers; *Adsunt Dominici* (No. 222) is a composite of an invitatory at Matins and an antiphon at Lauds. *Veni electa mea* (No. 181) draws from three different sources. The first phrase of the text is taken from Ant. 4 at Vespers in the Common of Virgins, corresponding exactly to the liturgical position to which the work has been assigned by Anerio in the print. As frequently happens, we can also trace the text to a responsory at Matins; both the first and the second phrases of Anerio's text correspond to the opening section (respond) of the

---

[378] The question arises: Are these antiphons at Lauds sometimes also usable at 2nd Vespers? The liturgical sources are often unclear on this point; see, for example, *Analecta hymnica*, XXV, pp. 239—240 (Office of St. Dominic). The Roman Breviary often provides two sets of psalm antiphons for important feasts, one for 1st Vespers, the other for Lauds »*et per horas*« (including 2nd Vespers); see, for example, *Brev 1606*, pp. 733—737 (Purification of the Blessed Virgin).

[379] See p. 130, above.

responsory. The third phrase (from the Song of Songs) has been traced to an office of the Immaculate Conception that Anerio has used elsewhere in the collection (No. 186, included in Table VI).

Our attention is drawn particularly to a few texts which differ considerably from any possible models that we have been able to discover in the liturgy. One is built upon the first two couplets of a Matins responsory from a rhymed office for St. Augustine: O *lumen ecclesiae* (No. 200). The rhymed responsory is not used in full; instead, a prose tail is grafted on to complete the sense. It is not clear why Anerio did not use the full responsory text, and we do not know the source of the added prose[380].

Pulchra es (No. 188) can be traced in part to the Vulgate (Song of Songs). In this case Anerio has selected a rather long scriptural text in preference to the shortened version of the same text that appears in the Breviary as an antiphon at Lauds[381]. *Tria sunt munera* (No. 24) is also based on an antiphon at Lauds but is clearly labeled for performance at Vespers on the Epiphany. Only the most tenuous connection has been preserved between the liturgical text and Anerio's version: the last half of the original antiphon is replaced by a lengthy new coda for which no source has been found, either in the liturgy or in scripture.

Two pieces composed for the Common of the Dedication of a Church offer a particularly interesting example of the relationship between liturgical and non-liturgical texts in Anerio's collection. *Fundata est domus* (No. 192) is taken from the respond of a Matins responsory, with minor alterations. In the copy now preserved in the Santa Cecilia Library the beginning of the text has been altered by pen to read, »*Bene fundata est domus . . .*«; the music has also been changed slightly in rhythm to fit the new text. Evidently some performer (seventeenth or eighteenth century, probably) wished to reconcile this text with that of Ant. 4 at Vespers, *Bene fundata est domus*. Even with this emendation, Anerio's text still differs considerably from the Breviary version, as Table VII demonstrates. The attempt of this unknown editor to bring the two texts closer together is significant for two reasons: first, we have evidence that Anerio's set-

---

[380] Anerio's other three antiphons in this set (No. 197—199) have been found in a prose office for St. Augustine in *Brev 1559*, fol. 473 ff.; the prose passage in No. 200 does not come from that office. As we have seen before, Anerio does not hesitate to draw from two or more unrelated liturgical sources in a single set of antiphons. In the present case, evidently, Anerio has combined both a poetic text and an unrelated prose text.

[381] The liturgical position of *Pulchra es* is open to doubt. The *Canto I* of this piece is inserted at the end of the *Bassus* partbook under the rubric »*Residuum in Commune Mulierum Sanctarum.*« In the *Bassus ad Organum* book, however, the piece appears after *Quae est ista* (No. 187), as if it were the fifth Vesper antiphon for the office of the Blessed Virgin. We therefore ascribe *Pulchra es* to the Marian office. It is significant that the second of the five inserted pieces in Monteverdi's 1610 collection is a setting of this same text; see OSTHOFF, p. 317. One suspects, therefore, that Monteverdi composed his *Pulchra es* as an antiphon-substitute, in spite of its non-liturgical text.

ting has probably been performed at Vespers as an antiphon; second, the editor was more concerned about correcting the beginning of the antiphon than its conclusion. This attitude toward Breviary texts is shared by Anerio, whose antiphons often adhere closely to the liturgical text for the first phrase or two, then introduce new material at the end.

The second piece, O *quam bene fundata est* (No. 193), follows *Fundata est domus* in the collection; the two texts are obviously related, at least in their opening phrases. Unlike the first piece, the second cannot be traced to any known liturgical source, but seems to be a pastiche of scriptural passages describing the glories of the Church[382].

Since these two compositions on similar texts are the fourth and fifth of a set of five pieces, we should certainly inquire whether the fifth piece is an addendum, to be performed at the end of the service, or possibly in place of one of the other four antiphons. In two other instances (No. 129 and 188) the final work in a set of five has been printed at the end of the vocal partbooks and marked *Residuum*[383]. However, in two of Anerio's five-antiphon sets the final works (No. 172, included in Table V; and No. 134 in the present Table) closely resemble the fifth Breviary antiphons for their respective feasts. Finally, it is by no means unknown for two successive antiphons in the same office to employ similar or even identical texts[384]. For these reasons we believe that O *quam bene fundata est* is not an addendum, but was probably intended as the fifth antiphon for the Dedication of a Church, in place of the proper *Lapides pretiosi*[385]. As we have seen, Anerio often replaces a Breviary antiphon by a substitute text that is quite unrelated to the original.

One other piece of evidence can be brought to bear on the problem of the proper liturgical role for Anerio's antiphons, including those with altered texts.

Twenty-three of the works in the collection are based on Gregorian antiphon melodies. These works and their sources are listed below in Table VIII. In each case only the first few notes of the chant appear in paraphrase at the beginning of the piece; generally the chant is imitated between the voices.

---

[382] Actually, the Old Testament passages are a description of Solomon's Temple, while those from the Revelation portray the New Jerusalem.

[383] Further information in Table I; see also footnote 381, above.

[384] *Felix Thomas*, for example, serves as the antiphon to all five Vesper psalms in the rhymed office of St. Thomas of Aquin; see *Analecta hymnica*, V, p. 230. Anerio uses this text in No. 229, as the first in a set of four.

[385] See *Brev 1606*, p. 1075.

TABLE VIII

ANERIO'S CANTUS FIRMUS COMPOSITIONS

COMPOS.	SOURCE OF CANTUS FIRMUS[386]	MODE[387]	TRANSPOSITION[388]	ACTUAL KEY OF SETTING[389]
No. 5	Fol. 120: *Salve crux pretiosa*	7	Down a whole step	F major (1 flat)
No. 6	Fol. 120: *Beatus Andreas*	8	Up a fifth	G major
No. 15	Fol. 31v: *Apud Dominum*	4		G minor (1 flat)
No. 45	Fol. 150: *O magnum pietatis*	7		G major
No. 76	Fol. 139: *Misit Dominus*	7	Down a whole step	F major (1 flat)
No. 94	Fol. 149: *Nativitas est hodie*	7	Down a whole step	F major (1 flat)
No. 95	Fol. 149: *Regali ex progenie*	6		F major (1 flat)
No. 104	Fol. 189: *Salve sancte pater*	2[390]	Up a fourth	G minor (1 flat)
No. 112	Fol. 157v: *Oculis ac manibus*	7	Up a fourth	C major
No. 120	Fol. 159v: *De sub cuius pede*	7	Down a fifth	G major
No. 122	Fol. 83: *Et ecce terremotus*	7	Down a fifth	G major
No. 124	Fol. 83: *Prae timore*	7		G major
No. 125	Fol. 91: *Viri Galilei*	7	Down a whole step	F major (1 flat)
No. 133	Fol. 94: *Fontes et omnia*	1		D minor
No. 143	Fol. 160v: *Hoc est preceptum*	8		C major
No. 145	Fol. 160v: *Vos amici mei*	1		D minor
No. 151	Fol. 128v: *Sancti tui Domine*	8	Up a fourth[391]	F major (1 flat)
No. 160	Fol. 163: *Omnes sancti*	8		G minor (1 flat)
No. 168	Fol. 165: *Ecce sacerdos*	7	Down a whole step	F major (1 flat)
No. 169	Fol. 165: *Non est inventus*	7	Down a fifth	G major
No. 175	Fol. 166v: *Fidelis servus*	3[392]	Down a fourth	F major (1 flat)
No. 176	Fol. 166v: *Beatus ille servus*	7	Up a fourth	F major (1 flat)
No. 209	Fol. 186: *Franciscus vir catholicus*	1		D minor

All but five of these compositions are settings of authentic antiphons, set forth in the order assigned by the Breviary and without significant changes of text. Such antiphons reinforce our belief that Anerio probably intended each set of pieces to be performed in the order printed, as antiphons between the psalms. *Fontes et omnia* (No. 133), for example, is a setting of the proper fourth antiphon at Vespers on the feast of Pentecost, using both words and music of the

[386] Page numbers refer to *AntR 1572*.
[387] Modes of cantus firmi as identified in *AntR 1572*.
[388] Refers to cantus firmus transposition in Anerio's setting; octave transposition is not included here.
[389] The pieces are analyzed tonally for purposes of comparison; Anerio does not use modern tonal terminology, of course. Key signatures given in parentheses.
[390] Mode not stated in *AntR 1572*.
[391] This piece carries the instruction »*Alla quarta*« (i.e., to be transposed down a fourth); see p. 105, above.
[392] Mode not stated in *AntR 1572*.

Gregorian antiphon. Even though none of the other four compositions in Anerio's Pentecost set is based on a canonical antiphon text, the composer has been careful to insert this one work exactly in the correct position required by the liturgy: fourth in the set. One assumes, therefore, that the composer intended all five pieces to be performed in order[393].

In two exceptional cases Anerio has incorporated a cantus firmus in an antiphon which appears out of proper order in his collection. Both *Apud Dominum* (No. 15) and *Salve sancte pater* (No. 104) incorporate the proper Gregorian melodies for these texts, yet both works are assigned a position different from that which they hold in the Breviary[394]. The union of text and Gregorian melody is evidently not disturbed by a shift of position in the liturgy.

Three of the cantus firmus compositions have altered texts significantly longer than those of the Breviary. *Misit Dominus* (No. 76, included also in Table VI) is based on Ant. 4 at Vespers on the feast of St. Peter's Chains. Although Anerio has added extra text from the Vulgate and omitted the Alleluia, the original antiphon melody appears as a cantus firmus. The same procedure is to be found in *Beatus ille servus* (No. 176, also in Table VI). The complete text of *Ecce sacerdos* (No. 168, included in Table VII) is taken from the chapter at Vespers on feasts of a Confessor Bishop; an Alleluia has been added. Nevertheless, Anerio has selected as his cantus firmus the Gregorian melody of the Vesper antiphon *Ecce sacerdos*, which has a considerably shorter text. It seems evident, therefore, that compositions with altered texts were indeed intended to take the place of the Breviary antiphons at Vespers, in spite of the admonitions of the *Caeremoniale Episcoporum*[395].

In summary, Anerio's collection, in its arrangement and in its selection of texts, suggests a much broader interpretation of the term antiphon than has previously been offered in the study of seventeenth-century Vesper music. It is no longer possible to dismiss settings of texts (like those in Monteverdi's 1610 Vespers) that do not conform to the antiphons of the Roman Breviary. Often the Breviary is merely a point of departure for the composer, who alters the antiphons or adds additional text. The order of the antiphons may be changed, and antiphons transposed from another office or even another feast. Short texts may be replaced by longer texts, particularly from Matins and Lauds.

Since Anerio, unlike Monteverdi, includes no psalms in his collection, we cannot be sure whether the antiphons were intended to precede or follow their associated psalms. Other evidence suggests that they should follow the psalms, or that they can be thought of as interludes between the psalms. If this is indeed

---

[393] The texts of the other four works in this set (No. 130, 131, 132, and 134) are included in Table VII.
[394] The sources of these texts are included in Table IV.
[395] See p. 90, above.

the case, then four or five antiphon-substitutes would suffice for one service. The six antiphons provided by the Breviary could be said or sung before the psalms and *Magnificat*; they need not be omitted altogether. Anerio's collection therefore includes, as its title indicates, all the antiphons or antiphon-substitutes necessary for Vespers and Compline on the major feasts of the church year. The term *sacrae cantiones* does not refer to a separate body of pieces, it would appear, but merely suggests that not all the compositions are based on the proper Breviary texts.

POSTSCRIPT

Since transposition practice at Vespers has been a matter of some controversy[396], it will be helpful to consider briefly the transpositions to which the Gregorian antiphon melodies are subjected in Anerio's collection. (See Table VIII.)

Only five of Anerio's cantus firmi are harmonized in the keys with which the respective modes were regularly associated in the seventeenth century[397]: No. 133, 145, and 209 (antiphons in Mode 1, harmonized in D minor); No. 104 (antiphon in Mode 2, transposed up a fourth and harmonized in G minor with a key signature of one flat); and No. 95 (antiphon in Mode 6, harmonized in F major with a key signature of one flat). The Mode 3 cantus firmus of *Fidelis servus* (No. 175), which we might expect to have been harmonized in A minor, has instead been transposed down a fourth and harmonized in F major (key signature of one flat). A Mode 4 cantus firmus is ordinarily harmonized in E-Phrygian in the seventeenth century; *Apud Dominum* (No. 15) is harmonized in the unexpected key of G minor (key signature of one flat).

The rest of the cantus firmi are all in Modes 7 or 8. Seven of the Mode 7 antiphons are founded on the same well-known melody[398]. Anerio uses this cantus firmus only once at normal pitch, harmonized in G major (No. 45). In three compositions he transposes the same cantus firmus down a fifth, still harmonized in G major, however (No. 120, 122, and 169). In three other works (No. 5, 94, and 168) this cantus firmus is transposed down a whole step, with harmonization in F major (key signature of one flat). The same variety of transpositions and harmonizations is exhibited in the rest of the cantus firmus settings, such as *Omnes sancti* (No. 160), in which a Mode 8 cantus firmus is harmonized in the key of G minor (key signature of one flat), rather than the expected G major.

---

[396] See, for example, STEVENS, pp. 318—320, and BONTA, *Liturgical Problems*, pp. 95—96.

[397] See Adriano BANCHIERI, *L'Organo suonarino, opera ventesima quinta*, Venezia 1611, Amadino, p. 20: *Guide secure nell'organo.*

[398] The version of this melody in use today may be seen in *Liber usualis*, p. 1307: *Salve Crux pretiosa.* The version in *AntR 1572*, fol. 120, differs somewhat from the Solesmes reading. Concerning this melody, see Willi APEL, *Gregorian Chant*, Bloomington, Indiana 1958, pp. 400—402.

Anerio's collection reminds us that a seventeenth-century composer need not limit himself to a single key in the harmonization of Gregorian melodies of the same mode.

Anerio's modal practice necessarily raises questions about the tonal relationship between antiphon and psalm. It has been generally assumed that the same key (e.g., F major) must be preserved between antiphon and psalm, since in Gregorian chant the tone of the psalm is selected to match the mode of the antiphon[399]. Considering the variety of keys in Anerio's cantus firmus compositions, we have to admit the possibility that a G-minor harmonization of an antiphon in Mode 4 (as in No. 15) might be combined with the normal E-Phrygian setting of Psalm Tone 4[400]. The two cantus firmi could be in the same mode, but harmonized in two unrelated keys with different key signatures.

It has been previously suggested, but without specific evidence, that antiphon and psalm need not necessarily fall in the same key[401]. Professor Stephen Bonta has recently brought to our attention a print by Paolo Agostino, *Salmi della Madonna[,] Magnificat a 3. voci. Hinno Ave maris stella, antifone a una 2. & 3. voci. Et motetti tutti concertati . . . Con il basso continuo per sonare. Divisa in due parti. Libro primo*, Roma 1619, L. A. Soldi[402]. Agostino provides a complete Marian office, including two or three settings of each psalm, of the hymn, and of the *Magnificat*. Following the first setting of each psalm, we find the appropriate antiphon (*Dum esset rex*, etc.) with its proper text; Alleluia refrains have been added to the antiphons[403]. The psalms illustrate the usual seventeenth-century key scheme, described by Banchieri. The antiphons are not identified as to mode in the print, and none of the antiphons contains a cantus firmus. However, a comparative analysis of the psalms and antiphons reveals that two of the antiphons do not correspond in key to any of the alternative settings of the associated psalms: *Dum esset rex* (in F major) is linked with *Dixit Dominus*, in alternative settings based on Tones 2 (G minor) and 1 (D minor); while *Iam hiems* (in C major) is linked with *Nisi Dominus*, in settings based on Tones 2 (G minor) and 8 (G major). Here is further evidence, therefore, that antiphon and psalm need not be in the same key.

---

[399] STEVENS, p. 319: »*It is one of the prime principles of psalmody that the psalm or canticle should be sung in the same tone as the antiphon specified . . . In Monteverdi's [1610] collection there is no such agreement . . .*«

[400] BANCHIERI, *L'Organo suonarino*, p. 20, shows the harmony normally associated with Tone 4.

[401] See BONTA, *Liturgical Problems*, p. 97.

[402] The copy consulted is that preserved in the Civico Museo Bibliografico Musicale (Bologna), under the catalogue number V/38.

[403] Source of antiphon texts: *Brev 1606*, pp. 1092—1093 (Little Office of the Blessed Virgin out of Advent). In addition to the antiphons Agostino has included nine non-liturgical Marian motets among the psalms. Perhaps these motets are intended as alternative antiphon-substitutes.

LIST OF ABBREVIATIONS

AntR 1572   [Antiphonarium Sacrosanctę Romanę Ecclesię: continens omnia quę cōmuniter cātantur in ecclesia: tam pro dñicali & feriali & festiuo: vc3 Natiuitate dñi: & solēnitatibus intra eandem octa. Epiphania quoq3 & Resurrectione dñi. Ascensio. Pēteco. trinita. Corpore christi: &c. Cum proprio etiam atq3 cōmuni sanctorū. Et toto officio defunctorū: ac Añis beatę Virginis post Cōpletorium decantandis: &c. VENETIIS. M D LXXII.]

BrevCarm 1579   BREVIARIVM antiquae professionis Regularium Beatissimae DEI genitricis semperq3 virginis MARIAE de monte Carmelo, Ex vsu & consuetudine approbata Hierosolymitanae Ecclesiae, & Dominici Sepulchri: nuperrimè iussu Ampliss. P. D. IOAN. BAPTISTAE CAFFARDI SENENSIS Proprioris, Promagistriq[ue]; Generalis Apostolici totius Ordinis, reformatum, & excusum. VENETIIS APVD IVNTAS, 1579.

BrevCarm 1672   BREVIARIVM CARMELITARUM IUXTA HIEROSOLYMITANAE ECCLESIAE ANTIQUAM CONSUETUDINEM CAPITULI GENERALIS DECRETO ad normam Romani Breuiarij directum A REVEREND^mo P. MAGISTRO MATTHAEO ORLANDO GENERALI reuisum & correctum Nouis Officijs Sanctorum à Sanctissimo Domin[o] D. Nostro CLEMENTE X. pro tota Ecclesia ordinatis, & alijs Ordini Carmelitarum nuper concessis, ET Ab Eminent. ac Reuerendiss. Domino Cardinali BONA authoritate Apostolica recognitum & approbatum. ANTUERPIAE, Typis MARCELLI PARYS, sub Turri Divae Virginis, in aureâ Claui, 1672.

BrevDom 1615   BREVIARIVM IVXTA RITVM SACRI ORDINIS FF. Praedic. S. P. N. DOMINICI. Auctorita[te] Apostolica reform[a]tum, & approbatum, jussu vero editum. R. P. Fr. Seraphini Sicci Papiensi totius pręfati Ora. Generalis Magistri. ROMAE, Ex Typographia Alfonsi Ciacco[n]i Apud Io. Paulum Profilium. M. LC. XV.

Brev 1559   BREVIARIVM ROMANVM Optime recognitum: in quo Commune sanctorum cum suis psalmis, nonnullę octauę, Tabula Roarssina, [?] Officium nominis Iesu, Desponsationis Marię, & alia multa, quę in ceteris desiderabātur, nuper sunt accommodata. VENETIIS, Petrus Bosellus excu [?] curabat, M D L I X

Brev 1606   BREVIARIVM ROMANVM EX DECRETO SACROSANCTI Concilij Tridentini restitutum, PII QVINTI PONT. MAX. iussu editum, Et CLEMENTIS VIII. auctoritate recognitum. ROMAE, Typographia Vaticana. M DC VI.

Brev 1618   [Breviarium Romanum ex decreto SS. Concilii Tridentini restitutum. Antverpiae, Ex officina Plantiniana, apud Balthasarem Moretum et viduam Jo. Moreti et Joannem Meursium, 1618]

All the liturgical books listed above except *Brev 1618* are preserved in the Biblioteca Apostolica Vaticana (Roma). *Brev 1618* was consulted in the Beinecke Rare Book and Manuscript Library (New Haven, Connecticut). References to the *Liber Usualis* are taken from the following edition: *The Liber Usualis with Introduction and Rubrics in English, edited by the Benedictines of Solesmes,* Tournai and New York 1959, Desclée. References to Scripture are taken from the following edition of the Vulgate: *Biblia sacra juxta Vulgatam Clementinam divisionibus, summariis et concordantiis ornata,* Roma 1956, Desclée.

MUSICIANS AT THE MEDICI COURT IN THE MID-SEVENTEENTH CENTURY

by *Frederick Hammond* (Los Angeles)

The volume Florence, Archivio di Stato, *Guardaroba Mediceo 664* consists of material relating to music at the court of the Grand Dukes of Tuscany between 1590 and 1669. The bulk of the contents dates roughly between 1630 and 1669 and consists of four inventories of musical instruments together with records of their loan and return, and lists of the court musicians together with their salaries and dates of service[1]. These lists were copied as appendices to a remarkable memorandum on the reform of the court musical establishment. As the numerous corrections and marginal alternatives show, the memorandum as preserved in

---

[1] Material from *Guardaroba 664* has appeared previously, e.g., Mario FABBRI and Enzo SET-TESOLDI, *Aggiunte e rettifiche alle biografie di Marco e Giovanni Battista da Gagliano*, Chigiana XXI (1964, pp. 131—142, p. 140). The present article is the first publication of all the material relating to musicians in its entirety, however. A summary of material in *Guardaroba 664* relating to musical instruments will appear in Analecta musicologica 15.
The complete contents of *Guardaroba 664* are as follows:
f. 1v—3r 1654 inventory of instruments
f. 7r—45r records of instrument loans
f. 49r letter of Carlo di Tommaso Strozzi to Federigo Gondi, 5 maggio 1646 enclosing
f. 50r—50v folio of Carlo Strozzi concerning musicians in Arte di Mercatanti
f. 51r—54v memorandum (cf. pp. 152—155)
f. 57r letter of padri of Santissima Annunziata to Grand Duke about organ pipes
f. 58r—58v letter of P. Niccolo Sapit., Firenze, 31 marzo 1662 about voices, instruments necessary for Dominica in Albis at the church of the Cavalieri di S. Stefano in Pisa
f. 59r—59v Copia/ Ruolo di Musici di S.A. Ser.ma (cf. p. 159)
f. 63r—65r documents c. 1651—54 concerning the organ of the Annunziata
f. 70r—81r Copia del Ruolo di Musica di S.A. Ser.ma (cf. pp. 161—168)
f. 82r—82v Listra di Musici di S.A. Ser.ma che si regalano per S. Giovanni (cf. p. 161)
f. 83r Nota di tutti i Musici di S.A. Ser.ma, a quali gli si fà dare le Corde dal Liutaio
f. 83v—84r lists of singers and players (cf. pp. 157—158)
f. 85r—85v 1640 inventory of instruments
f. 86r—88r records of instrument loans
f. 89r—90r 1652 inventory of instruments
f. 92r—92v records of instrument loans
f. 96r letter of Suora Maria Lisabetta Albizzi to Grand Duke
f. 97r—98r autograph receipts of instruments, 30 agosto 1669
f. 99r total of instruments
f. 100v total of wind instruments
f. 101r partial list of instruments
f. 103v—110r ledger of instruments
f. 111r—112v 1669 inventory of instruments
f. 113—114 separate sheets with miscellaneous receipts, payments etc.

Guardaroba 664 is a draft version. Unfortunately, it is neither signed, dated, nor addressed. If the Balì Saracinelli mentioned in the past tense at the end of the letter is to be identified with the *cameriere* Ferdinando Saracinelli, then his death on 26 February 1639/40[2] provides a terminus a quo, and the letter may have been addressed to a successor. The list of musicians accompanying the memorandum must have been complete some time after 1643, when Giovanni Battista da Gagliano's accession to the post of *maestro di cappella* at the Duomo is noted, and before 1650/1, when the notice of his death appears as a later addition.

The anonymous author prefaces his suggestions for the reform of the granducal *Musica* with an account of its constitution illustrated by a list of the performers comprising each of its subdivisions: singers for chapel, chamber and stage totaling five women, three castrati, three tenors and bass; instrumentalists for the same comprising two lutenists, two theorbists, a keyboard player, and a harpist; a string ensemble of six members for entertainments, meals and dances; and a wind ensemble of eight members for table music, dances, and public concerts. The proposals for musical and financial reorganization of this structure give an idea both of the complex finances of the Medici court and of the life of the average musicians employed there. This has been amplified in detail by the references to contemporary account books which are given in the notes.

The translation (see pp. 155–157) presents the corrected text of the memorandum; variants and cancellations are given in the Italian original. Abbreviations have been expanded and spelling and punctuation discreetly modernized in this and the other Italian transcriptions.

Guardaroba Mediceo, 664, f. 51r–54v[3]

Per poter meglio discorrere intorno a' modi che potessero trovarsi di migliorare il servizio della musica di S.A., sicome pare che la necessità sforzi di fare, bisogna prima che io dica informazione di quanto segue, come la Ser.ma Casa spende nelle prouvisioni de' musici, et altre spese che occorono per essi circa scudi 4250- l'anno; come si vede per l'inclusa copia del ruolo di essi, fra' quali la maggior parte o sono del tutto inabili, o poco buoni per il Ser.mo servizio. Causa di questo è che molti arrolati non perfetti, o per loro propria trascuraggine diventono peggiori, ó vero per la vecchiaia ó per altro accidente si rendono [canc.: del tutto inabili] tanto inutili che non possono servire á niente. Et non essendo solito questa corte levar ad alcuno la prouvisione una volta ottenuta; è forza per conseguenza di accrescer sempre la spesa con pigliarne di quando in quando [canc.: alcuna volta] de' nuovi, senza mai poter arrivare [canc.: in un'istesso tempo] a tener insieme un [canc.: esquisito] mediocre concerto. Si distinguono questi in quattro sorti di musici, cioè cantori e sonatori per la cappella e per camera e per scena o altro che bisogni; in donne tenute similmente per il medesimo

---

[2] Firenze, Archivio di Stato, Depositeria Generale 1527 (*Libro dei Salariati del Ser.mo Gran Duca*, 1639/40), c. 130, MS 321, p. 560.

[3] I am indebted to Prof. Gino Corti for the transcription of this document.

effetto; in [f. 51v] sonatori di viola a braccio per balli e festini o per la tavola, che si chiamano il concerto de' franzesi; et in sonatori di strumenti a fiato, detto del concerto de' franciosini, che suonano alla tavola anch'essi in occasione di feste et di forastieri et simili, et per la città publicamente in ringhiera d'estate tre volte la settimana. Onde supponendo di voler mantenere i medesimi concerti, poichè non par conveniente si deva star senza cantatrici provisionate; nè di levare il concerto de' franzesi da ballo come l'altro de' franciosini, rendendosi quello necessario per festini, et altri balli che continuamente [canc.: si fanno] occorrono, et questo se non altro per mantenere quell'honorevolezza alla città, propotrei di vedere se si potesse conseguire in gran parte l'intento sopradetto con far nel modo che segue.

Prima [canc.: stimo necessario] di levare tutti quelli che sono cattivi, acciò dieno luogo a pigliarne altri de' buoni, però che di dieci persone che sono in cappella, vi sono tre castrati che poco vagliono; il basso similmente; il Mariani tenore cattivissimo, et D. Honorato per la sua passata infermità se ne può far poco assegnamento. [in marg.: Et perchè io presuppongo, come intendo, che la Ser.ma Casa habbia di molti uffizi bassi, molte cappellanie e canonicati di S. Lorenzo, i quali continuamente si danno a questo e a quello, bisognerebbe vedere se di qua si potesse cavare il rimedio]. A questi [canc.: dunque potrebbe S.A.] far dare [canc.: bisognerebbe veder la spesa?] in cambio della lor provvisione o per parte di essa, cappellanie, [f. 52r] canonicati di S. Lorenzo; uffizi, o altri consimili, per li quali havessero la medesima [canc.: entrata] emolumento, [et restando come prima obbligati a chiese quando fussero comandati] il che crederrei che potesse seguire per questo verso con molta lor satisfazione, e nel medesimo tempo ancora il miglioramento della Cappella. Nella quale [canc.: vorrei] si potrebbe determinare che'l numero de' cantori fusse solo di cinque voci cioè due soprani, un contralto, un tenore et un basso, se possibil fosse fossero esquisiti; et un sonatore di stromento, un sonatore d'arpa; et uno di tiorba; et un compositore o maestro di cappella che voglia dirsi; perchè questo concerto potrebbe servire per le necessità, potendosi cantare le messe e vespri a cinque voci molto bene. Et quando alcuna volta occorresse cantare a sei o a otto voci, per ripieno (non importando l'altre essere così perfette) pigliare di quelle della cappella di Duomo, che sempre ve ne sono delle mediocri si come si usa ancora presentemente. A questi dovrebbero bastare di provvisione scudi 8— il mese per uno, parendomi che li cantori assai buoni, et quelli che per ordinario sono stanziati in Firenze, possino starvi, sì come il Mazzanti et simili; et a quelli che paressi meritassero più, potrebbe S.A. soccorrere nel modo sopradetto, cioè [f. 52v] à preti con cappellanie e simili, come ha D. Honorato, alli altri con farli aiutanti di canonici come sono l'Anglesi e Fabio dell'Arpa, o con uffizi come si è detto. Sichè questo concerto non costerebbe più di scudi 70- il mese, che sariano scudi 840- l'anno, poichè il sonatore di viola et violini si possono cavare da' franzesi, i quali servono in più luoghi, come fa Mons.re Pietro.

[in marg.: sc. 40- le cinque voci
8- l'organista
5- l'arpe
7- il maestro di cappella
6- la tiorba

————

sc. 66-]

Il medesimo stile si potrebbe tenere nel concerto de' franzesi da ballo, nel quale si spenderebbe molto meno se le parti più principali non havessero a servire in altri luoghi, come Mons.re Pietro suddetto che serve a tutte le musiche, in capella et in camera, a' balli e per tutto. Similmente Mons.re Gioacchino che è maestro di ballo delle Signore dame, come ancora il cappellaino de' Signori paggi. Onde se questi hanno gran provvisione, servono anche in altre cose, per le quale o bisognerebbe pagarli, o tener altri provvisionati. Sta dunque ancor questo concerto in scudi 70- il mese in circa, che sono l'anno scudi 840-, et per questo solo servizio si avrebbe facilmente con scudi 600- solamente l' anno.

Nel concerto de' franciosini si potrebbe determinare medesimamente che le provvisioni loro non passassero scudi 6- il mese per uno, perchè con questa [f. 53r] pare possono stare quei sonatori che sono ordinari, si come il Bacherelli, il Gioia et altri, et quando alcuno ve ne sia che faccia frutto più che ordinariamente (il che suol riuscire a pochi istrumenti simili) si potrebbe supplire come sopra o con uffizi, cancellerie o altre cose simili, come avviene al Gioia che tira scudi 5- per provvisione di questo concerto e di quello de' franzesi, et anche serve di sotto furiere con altri scudi — di provvisione, che starebbe ancor questo concerto a scudi 50- il mese in circa, che sono 600 l'anno.

Onde tutti questi concerti si potrebbono in questo modo tenere facilmente con poco più di scudi 2000- l'anno di provvisioni, e ci sarieno di più le donne, nelle quali si potrebbe spendere altri scudi 300- o col tenere una sola perfettissima et darli tutta la somma detta per provvisione, overo più et delle più ordinarie, per far concerto, dividendo fra esse quello che ad una sola si darebbe, et bisognando soccorrere ancor queste con le cose sopradette, com'haveva la Signora Vittoria Archilei, che tirava scudi 12- il mese di pensione sopra del fisco. Di modo con scudi 2500- in circa di provvisione di quel di più che si applicava ne' modi suddetti, crederrei che forse S.A. poteva restar meglio servito di quello che presentemente segue. Ma bisogna haver sempre mira di levar via quelli che diventono cattivi, et di farn' arrolare di buoni et trovare modo di sapere di mano in mano [f. 53v] le vacanze che seguono di canonicati o di cappellanie o altri uffizi suddetti, per poterli destinare et concedere a quelli che sono atti a poterli ricevere. Perchè tutto il fondamento di questo discorso sta nel poter remunerare tanto gli inabili quanto quelli che servono, in cambio di provvisioni, con queste simili cose supponendo che la Ser.ma Casa ne habbia moltissime da distribuire, sì come ho sempre sentito dire, et oltre a questi habbino anche molte chiese di benefizi di lor data et di buonissima rendita, sopra i quali non so se vi si potrebbe mettere pensioni per voltarle e farne pagare per supplire nella spesa a questo servizio. In altra maniera non so vedere come si possa stare con meno gente nè spender meno del sopradetto, anzi quando mancasserò i modi descritti, crederei fusse necessità d'aggravarne la borsa di S.A., poichè i professori buoni di queste scienze non possono vivere se non arrivano alli emolumenti accennati. Et quando si volessero riformare tutti, et tenerne solo due o tre buonissimi provvisionati, et il restante pagarli di mano in mano che bisogno venisse di servirsene, come molte volte è stato considerato, non crederei nè meno tornasse il conto poichè si spenderebbe quasi il medesimo, e non parrebbe che si [f. 54r] S.A. tenesse musica, poichè non si potrebbe dar per pagamento meno di uno scudo per uno per volta, et occorrerebbe servirsene, per quanto ho potuto far conto, circa di 80 volte l'anno, onde a otto voci sarebbe di spesa circa scudi 800- et di più li provvisionati. E causerebbe oltre a ciò che non ci sarebbe gente buona, mentre che il guadagno fussi incerto, sichè molto peggio seguirebbe di quello che adesso segue. [alternate version (cancelled): Non uoglio tralasciar di dire come da molti mesi in qua sono vacanti circa a sc. 50 il mese di prouuisioni: come si vede nella lista inclusa, et che molto si è auanzato nelle spese da quello che si faceua a tempo del S. Balì Saracinelli poiche a musici sino a sc. — l'anno, et a duo uiene ragguagliatamente a sc. 120 l'anno, per il che si può far conto che la spesa arrivasse in quel tempo anche a sc. 5000- l'anno.]

Non volgio già tralasciare di dire come conosco assai difficile il far questa mutazione tutta ad un tratto et resecare, per così dire, questa materia così di repente; ma perchè già da molti mesi in qua sono vacanti da scudi 50- di provvisioni come si vede nella lista, [f. 54v] crederrei che si potesse ridar queste per provvisioni a nuovi suggetti, et poi a poco a poco rimborsarne nel modo di sopra accennato, tanto più che da molti anni in qua si spende assai meno nelle cose occorrenti che non si spendeva a tempo del Balì Saracinelli.

Translation:

In order better to discuss the possible ways for improving the service of His Highness' musical establishment, as seems necessary, I must first provide the following information, that the Most Serene House spends about 4250 scudi a year on the support of musicians and on other expenses for them, as appears from the enclosed copy of the roll of musicians. Of these, the greater part are either completely incompetent or inadequate for the service of His Highness. The reason for this is that many of those on the payroll become worse through incomplete training or their own carelessness, or through old age or some other circumstance they are rendered so useless that they are no good at all. And, since this court generally does not remove anyone who is on the payroll, of necessity the expense increases through hiring new musicians from time to time without ever being able to keep together even a passable ensemble. These musicians are divided into four groups. That is, singers and players for chapel or chamber or stage or other needs; women maintained for the same purposes; string players [sonatori di viola a braccio] for dances and entertainments or for meals, who are called the ensemble of the franzesi; and wind players, called the ensemble of the franciosini, who also play at table when there are festivals and foreign guests and the like, and who play publicly for the City three times a week in the Ringhiera (Enclosure) in summer[4]. Supposing that one wishes to maintain the same ensembles (since it seems unfitting to remain without salaried female singers, or to do away with the ensemble of the franzesi for dances, or to abolish the other ensemble of the franciosini since the first is necessary for the festivals and other dances which constantly occur, and the other is necessary if only to maintain the dignity of the City), I would propose attempting to fulfill most of the above-mentioned functions in the following manner.
First, (I deem it necessary) to dismiss all the bad performers so as to have room to choose other good ones, for of the ten people in the cappella there are three castrati

---

[4] f. 83v—84r; cf. pp. 157/58. On the franciosini, cf. Florence, Archivio di Stato, Miscellanea Medicea 436 (Storia di Etichetta di Toscana dal 1600 al 1647), f. 69r: »[la sera] ... si fece musica da franzosini ...«; f. 70v: »Alla Tauola vi fù la Musica di franzosini« (both 1 Jan. 1633/4). — The Ringhiera, no longer in existence, was built into the façade of Palazzo della Signoria to accomodate the Signoria at public functions. According to an old description,
Ad essa si va con 10 scalini, 5 che portano alla platea avanti la porta principale e per altri 5 a mano sinistra si sale alla Ringhiera suddetta, la quale ha una banchina di 3 gradi di pietra da sedere rasente la muraglia, e per davanti un parapetto alto circa un braccio, sul quale posa il Leone di pietra, che era prima dorato e che stava sulla cantonata verso tramontana, con altri 3 sulle altre cantonate, quale fu rimesso nell'anno 1564 dal G. D. Cosimo I in occasione di fabbricarvi la bella Fontana, che vi è.
(Pietro GORI, Le Feste fiorentine attraverso i secoli: le feste per San Giovanni, Firenze, 1926, p. 349.)

of little worth, and the bass likewise; Mariani, a dreadful tenor; and Don Honorato through his recent illness can give little help. [in marg.: And since I suppose, as I understand, that His Highness has many minor posts, many chaplaincies and canonries of S. Lorenzo, which are constantly being given to this one and that one, one should see if some remedy could be found here.] Therefore, His Highness could give in exchange for their salary or a part of it chaplaincies, canonries of S. Lorenzo, official posts and the like, for which they would receive the same sum, which I think could be carried out this way with great satisfaction to them and, at the same time, great improvement to the cappella. For the cappella, the number of singers could be fixed at only five voices, that is, two sopranos, a contralto, a tenor and a bass, if they were excellent, and a keyboard player, a harpist and a theorbist, and a composer or *maestro di cappella* as he may be called; because this ensemble could serve for ordinary needs, being able to sing very well masses and vespers for five voices. And when there should be occasion to sing in six or eight parts, choosing the fillers-in (since they do not need to be so skilled) from the cappella of the Cathedral as is done at present, since there are always passable singers there. A provision of eight scudi per month should be enough for one of these, since it appears to me that very good singers, and those who are generally lodged in Florence, could stay there, like Mazzanti and similar cases; and His Highness could assist those who seemed to merit more in the aforesaid manner, that is, aiding priests with chaplaincies and such (as Don Honorato has), and the others by making them assistant canons as are Anglesi and Fabio dell'Arpa, or with official posts as above. So that this ensemble would not cost more than 70 scudi a month, which would be 840 scudi a year, since the viola and violin players could be obtained from the *franzesi*, who serve in several places, as Mons. Pietro does.

[*in marg.*   Sc. 40- the five voices
                          8- the organist
                          5- the harp
                          7- the maestro di cappella
                          6- the theorbo
                   ——
             sc. 66-]

One could apply the same system in the ensemble of the *franzesi* for dances, for which one would spend less if the principal players did not have to perform in other places, like the above-mentioned Mons. Pietro, who serves in all the musical organizations, chapel, chamber, dances and for everything. Similarly, Mons. Gioacchino, who is the dancing-master for the ladies-in-waiting, and also the chaplain of the pages. Whence, if these have large salaries, they serve also in other things for which they should be paid, or others would have to be paid. This ensemble therefore costs about 70 scudi a month, or 840 scudi a year, and for this service without any of the others one could pay only 600 scudi a year.

In the ensemble of the *franciosini* one could determine in the same way that their salaries did not exceed 6 scudi a month apiece, because it seems that ordinary players like Bacherelli, Gioia, and others, can manage with this, and when there is someone who produces results out of the ordinary (which happens with few such instruments), the salary could be supplemented as above or with official posts, chanceries or other similar things, as happens with Gioia, who draws 5 scudi as a salary for this ensemble and that of the *franzesi*, and also serves as underquartermaster with an additional — scudi of salary; so that this ensemble also could manage with about 50 scudi a month, which makes 600 a year.

Whence all these ensembles could be maintained easily in this manner with little more than 2000 scudi a year for salaries, and in addition there would be the women, for whom one could spend another 300 scudi, or just keep one completely accomplished one and give her the whole sum as a salary, or more of them and less accomplished ones to make an ensemble, dividing among them what one would give to a single singer. And it would be necessary to assist these also by the above means, as with Signora Vittoria Archilei, who drew a salary of 12 scudi a month from the exchequer. So that with about 2500 scudi in salaries, in addition to that applied in the above manner, I would think that perhaps His Highness could be better served than presently. But one must always have the object of getting rid of those who are getting worse and of enrolling good ones, and of finding a way of knowing constantly the vacancies of canonries or chaplaincies or the other abovementioned posts in order to appoint and assign them to appropriate recipients. For this reason, the whole basis of this discussion lies in being able to recompense not only those who serve but also those who are no longer able to, with those things which are mentioned above in place of salaries on the assumption that the Most Serene House has many of them to distribute, as I have always heard, and that in addition to these they have many beneficed churches of excellent income in their gift, although I do not know if these incomes could be diverted to supplement the expenses of this service. I do not see any way one could retain fewer people or spend less than the above, but if the means I described were lacking, I think it would be necessary to burden His Highness' purse with this expense, since the good practitioners of these arts cannot live on less than the aforesaid salaries. And if one wished to reform everything, and keep on a regular salary only two or three excellent performers and pay the rest from time to time as the need arose to use them, which has often been considered, I do not believe the bill would be any less since one would spend almost the same, and it would not appear that His Highness maintained a regular musical establishment. This because one could not pay less than one scudo a time per person, and one would need to employ them about 80 times a year, as far as I can estimate. Therefore, for eight voices one would spend about 800 scudi in addition to the regulary salaried performers. In addition, the result would be that they were not good performers, since the salary would be uncertain, so that things would go much worse than they do now.

I do not wish to omit saying how difficult I know it would be to make this change all at once and cut back, so to speak, so suddenly; but because for many months there has been a vacancy of 50 scudi in salaries as one sees from the list, I would think that this could be reassigned as salaries for new entrants, and then little by little they could be reimbursed in the manner outlined above, the more so since for many years much less has been spent on these things than was spent in the time of the Balì Saracinelli.

A list in the same hand as the other documents gives the members of the various subdivisions of the granducal musical establishment as outlined above in the memorandum:

f. 83v

Cantori della Cappella del Ser.mo Gran' Duca

S.ra Vettoria Archilei
S.ra Settimia Caccini
S.ra Catterina di Pier Maria Casselli [recte: Cappelli]

S.ra Maria Botti	
Mad.a Polisena di Domenico Poggi	
Messr. Antonio del Frate [Cinatti]	Tenore Carlo Fei soprano.
+Messr. Pier Raffaelli	Basso Alessandro Cecconi
Messr. Domenico Sarti	Soprano
Don Honorato Magi	Tenore
Messr. Gio: Antonio Mariani	Tenore
Messr. Luca Agnoletti	Soprano
Messr. Francesco Burri	Contralto Bartolomeo Mazzanti

Sonatori per la medesima Cappella di S.A.S., e Compositori

Messr. Pompeo da Modena	Liuto
Lorenzo [Allegri] del Liuto	il medesimo
Gio Batta: da Gagliano	Tiorba
+Agnolo Conti	Tiorba
Domenico Anglesi	Strumento
Fabio Oldradi	Arpa

f. 84r

Del Concerto di Ballo

Mons. Giouacchino Bianchotti	Tobbia
Mons. Giouanni Castor	Giobatta Lasignini
Mons. Pietro Asolani	Andrea Bianchotti
Gio: Batta: dell'Auca [?]	
Messr. Cosimo Gioia	
Carlo Asolani	

Del Concerto de' Franzosini

Messr. Pauolo Grazzi	Il frate della Nunziata
	[Fra Domenico Maria Brancaccini]
Messr. Jacopo del Franzosino	Lorenzo Buti
Messr. Vettorio Baldacci	
Messr. Vergilio Grazzi	
Messr. Tobbia [Crigiader] Todesco	
Messr. Gio: Batta: d'Ant.o Lassagnini	
Messr. Stefano Jacomelli	
Messr. Vincenzo Bacherelli	

Di più per comporre

S. Alfonso Peri

Strumentaio

Messr. Stefano Soldini

Guardaroba 664, f. 59r
Copia/ Ruolo de' Musici di S.A. Ser.ᵐᵃ à Carta 10:

1. Vittoria Archilei   sc. 10:—:— n° 56
2. Pauolo del Franciosino   sc. 16:—:— n° 58: 914: 2135:
3. Jacopo del Franciosino   sc. 11:—:— n° 141: 914
4. Pompeo di Girolamo da Modena   sc. 8:—:— n° 158: 914
5. Lorenzo Allegri   sc. 12:—:— n° 584:
6. Vettorio Baldacci   sc. 10:—:— n° 688: 914: 1340:
7. Virgilio Grazzi   sc. 10:—:— n° 688: 914: 1340:
8. Giouacchino Bianchotti   sc. 10:—:— n° 878:
9. Antonio del Frate Cinatti   sc. 4:—:— n° 870:
10. Giouanni Castor   sc. 16:—:— n° 221:
11. Pietro Asolanti   sc. 14:—:— n° 1374: 2105:
12. Tobbia Crigiader Todesco   sc. 16:—:— n° 1302: 1445:
13. S.re Piero Raffaelli Basso   sc. 10:—:— n° 1186: 1449:
14. M. Domenico Sarti Castratto   sc. 15:—:— n° 1500: 836: 2012:
15. Gio: Batta: dell'Auca [Accia?]   sc. 14:—:— n° 1674: 2104:
16. Gio: Batta: da Gagliano   sc. 4:—:— n° 1728:
                                                      se li augumenta scudi 3 n° 2246:
                                                      primo Agosto 163()
17. D. Onorato Magi Monaco di S. Trinita   sc. 10:—:— n° 1848: se li augumenta
                                                      scudi 7 come Cappellano
18. M.ro Stefano Strumentaio per tener' in ordine   sc. 4:—:— n° 1903:
    li strumenti di tutte l'Altezze Serenissime
19. GioBatta: d'Ant.º Lassagnini detto   sc. 9:—:— n° 1993: 2109
    il Biondino
20. Agnolo Conti Guardaroba per li Strumenti   sc. 4:—:— n° 1993: se li augumenta
                                                      scudi 3 n° 2245: primo Agosto 163()
21. Stefano di Gio: Batta: Jacomelli   sc. 4:—: n° 1995: 2135
22. Vincenzio di Bastiano Baccherelli   sc. 4:—:— n° 1995: 2135: n° 2220
                                                      se li augumenta scudi 2
23. Alfonso di Jacopo Peri   sc. 4:3:20: n° 2068:
24. Gio: Antonio Mariani   sc. 3:—:— n° 2091:

f. 59v
25. Cosimo di Gio: Gioia   sc. 4:—:— n° 2164:
26. Settimia Caccini ne Ficcizzani   sc. 15:—:— n° 2183:
                                                      24 Dicembre 1636:
27. Catterina di Pier Maria Cappelli entrò   sc. 5:—:— n° 2247:
    con prouision di scudi cinque dico   primo Agosto 1637: adi 23
                                                      Novembre 1639 scudi 3 n° 2379:
28. Fran:º Bussi in luogo di Aless.º Tatini   sc. 4:—:— n° 2282:
                                                      5 Settembre 1637:
29. Luca Agnoletti 4 Dicembre 1638   sc. 15:—:— n° 2339:
30. Domenico Anglesi in luogo di Giusto della   sc. 8:—:— n° 2347:
    Valle [16 Marzo 1638 cancelled]
31. Carlo di Pietro Assolani 25 Aprile 1639   sc. 4:—:— n° 2350:
    Fabio Oldrado sonator d'Arpa
    23 Settembre 1640: entrò con prouision di scudi 5:—: n°

The lists of musicians appended to this memorandum have been annotated from other sources in the Archivio di Stato in Florence. Unfortunately, the series of *salariati* and *pensionati* books has been broken up, so that payment records are not available for the entire period covered by the documents in *Guardaroba 664*. The supplementary materials which I have used are designated by the following sigla:

LR = *Lista de' Musici di S.A.Ser.ma che si regalano per S. Giovanni* (Guardaroba Mediceo 664, f. 82r—82v, infra, p. —);

NC = *Nota di tutti i Musici di S.A. Ser.ma, à quali gli si fà dare le Corde dal Liutaio* (ibid., f. 83r);

GR 448 = Guardaroba Mediceo 448, *Debitori e Creditori* B, 1628—1633;

GR 449 = Guardaroba Mediceo 449, *Libro di Vestiti*, 1628—1633;

GR 450 = Guardaroba Mediceo 450: *Giornale del Libro di Debitori e Creditori di Guardaroba di S.A.S.; Quaderno di Sparatimenti; Debitori e Creditori,* D, 1629—1631;

GR 454 = Guardaroba Mediceo 454, *Libro di Entrata e Uscita*, 1629/30;

GR 459 = Guardaroba Mediceo 459: *Giornale del Libro di Debitori e Creditori di Guardaroba di S.A.S., E; Quaderno di Sparatimenti, E; Debitori e Creditori,* 1631—1633;

GR 460 = Guardaroba Mediceo 460, *Entrata e Uscita del Libro di debitori, e creditori della Guardaroba di S.A.S.*, 1631—1632;

GR 465 = Guardaroba Mediceo 465: *Giornale del libro di Debitori, e Creditori di Guardaroba di S.A.S.; Giornale, A; Debitori e Creditori, F*, 1633—1635;

MS 321 = Manoscritti 321, *Cariche d'Onore concesse da S. Serenissimi GG. Duchi Tomo Secondo che contiene gl'arrolati della Corte* (abstracts of rolls 1540—1692);

1631/2 = Depositeria Generale 1524, *Libro dei Salariati da S.A.S.*, Sept. 1631—Aug. 1632;

1634/5 = Depositeria Generale, *Libro dei Salariati da S.A.S.*, Sept. 1634—Aug. 1635;

1635/6 = Depositeria Generale 1525, *Libro dei Salariati da S.A.S.*, Sept. 1635—Aug. 1636;

1636/7 = Depositeria Generale 1526, *Libro dei Salariati da S.A.S.*, Sept. 1636—Aug. 1637 (many entries, however, cover only nine months);

1639/40 = Depositeria Generale 1527, *Libro dei Salariati del Serenissimo Gran Duca,* Sept. 1639—Aug. 1640

1640 I = *Inventario delle robe che sono nella stanza degli Strumenti di S.A.S. consegnati,* 1640 (Guardaroba 664, f. 85r—87v) (further on this and 1652 I, 1654 I, and 1669 I, cf. Analecta musicologica, vol. 15);

1641/2 = Depositeria Generale 1528, *Libro dei Salariati del Serenissimo Gran Duca,* Sept. 1641—Aug. 1642

1648/9 = Depositeria Generale 1529, *Libro dei Salariati*, Sept. 1648—Aug. 1649;

1652 I = *Inventario delli Strumenti, che sono nella Guardaroba di S.A.*, 1652 (Guardaroba 664, f. 89r—92v);

1654 I = *Copia dell'Inventario, è Rassegna di tutti li Strumenti che si ritrovono nella stanza della Guardaroba della Musica*, 1654 (ibid., f. 1v—45r);

1656/7 = Depositeria Generale 1531 [*Libro di Provisionati, C*], Sept. 1656—Aug. 1657;

1657/8 = Depositeria Generale 1530, *Libro di Entrata e Uscita*, 1657—1658;

1658/9 = Depositeria Generale 1532, *Libro di Provisionati*, Sept. 1658—Aug. 1659;

1660/1 = Depositeria Generale 1533, *Provisionati di Camera di S.A.S.*, Sept. 1660—
   Aug. 1661;

1669 I = *Inventario di tutti li Strumenti che si ritrovano nella Stanza della Guardaroba
   della Musica*, 1669 (Guardaroba 664, f. 103v—112r).

In addition to f. and p., indicating folio and page, c. (*carta*) has been used to
designate a ledger opening, where left and right hand pages bear the same
number. The indications in brackets are taken from f. 83v—84r. *Franzese* deno-
tes a member of the string ensemble, the *franzesi*; *franciosino*, a member of the
franciosini, the wind ensemble.

f. 82r
Lista de' Musici di S.A. Ser.ma che si regalano per S. Giovanni

M.ro Agostino Guasconi [Vasconi] Organista, da S. Benedetto
M. Antonio Guelfi in Via Noua da S. Paolo
Andrea figlio di Monsù Giouacchino, da l'orto di S. Spirito
Baccio Baglioni, da Via S. Maria
Carlo Zucagni in sù la Costa
Curtio Diodati in Calonica
Ceseri Sabatini aiuto del   [illegible] in Via Tedesca al n° 5.
Catterina detta la Rossina Fanciulla da S. Felice in Piazza
      [cancelled in marg.: ui è altra uolta per errore.]
M.ro Domenico Saracini liutaio da Mercato Uecchio
Emilia Grazzi da S. Jacopo in Campo Corbelini
Francesco Pierozzi in Parioncino
Giouanni Caesi da orsan Michele
Gio: Batta: Grandi dal Canto del Pino
Lorenzo Buti dietro à S. Felice
Luigi Vantucci da Piazza Madonna
Lisabetta Fanciulla in Casa la Sig.ra Settimia
Maria Botti in Via S. Giovanni
M.ro Marco da Gagliano Maestro di Cappella di S.A. Ser.ma in S. Lorenzo+
Matteo Grassi in Via del Palagio
M.ro Michele Cilandri in Via dell'Amorino

f. 82v
M.ro Nicolo Baldocci da S. Jacopo in Campo Corbelini
Polisena Poggi nelle abbandonate di S.Cattarina
Tobbia Monteuerdi in Via del Cocumero
      [marg.: ui è altra uolta per errore]
Tomasso Ferrini Tauolaccino in Via del Pepe al n° 22.
Vergilio d. Pacchiano Porta di Strumenti in Palazzuolo

f. 70r
Copia/ del Ruolo de' Musici di S.A. Ser.ma
      Adì primo Giugno 1609.

Antonio del Frate Cinatti[5], [tenore] entrò con prouisione di scudi quattro come nella filza de' rescritti à Carta numero 870: sotto il dì primo Giugno 1609. sono dico

sc. 4:—:—

Adì 28 Settembre 1631:

Agnolo Conti[6] [tiorba] entrò con prouisione di scudi quattro, come in filza à Carta numero 933: dico sc. 4:—:—

E più Adì primo Agosto 1637: se li augumenta scudi tre, come in filza à Carta numero 2245: dico sc. 3:—:—

se ne dette sc. 4— à Carlo Fei, & sc. 3 all' Mazzanti

Adì 7 Settembre 1633:

Alfonso di Jacopo Peri[7] entrò con prouisione di scudi quattro, e mezzo, come in filza à Carta n° 2068: dico sc. 4:3:10

Adì 20 Dicembre 1640

Andrea di Monsù Giouacchino Biancotti[8] [franzese] entrò con prouisione di scudi dua il mese dico sc. 2:—:—

Adì 2 Marzo 1640

D. Alessandro Cecconi di Pisa Musico entrò con prouisione di ducati dieci il mese sc. 10:—:—

f. 70v

Adì 1641

Il sig.re Bartolomeo Mazzanti[9], [contralto] hebbe la prouisione di ducati quattro, che lassò M. Fran.co Burri [contralto] per hauer egli hauta la Chiesa dico sc. 4:—:—

E più Adì primo Luglio 1642, se gli augumenta ducati tre il mese della prouisione, che godeva il già M. Agnolo Conti dico sc. 3:—:—

f. 71r

Adì 22. Luglio 1636:

Cosimo di Gio: Gioia[10], [franzese] entrò con prouisione di scudi quattro dico sc. 4:—:—

E Adì 20 Dicembre 1640 l'augumento scudi uno sc. 1:—:—

Adì primo Agosto 1637.

Catterina di Pier Maria Cappelli[11] entrò con prouisione di scudi cinque dico sc. 5:—:—

E più Adì 23 Nouembre 1639: se li augumenta scudi tre dico sc. 3:—:—

Adì 25. Aprile 1639:

---

[5] 1631/2: c. 76, sc. 88; 1634/5: c. 107, sc. 92; MS 321: 1635, p. 543, sc. 11; 1635/6: c. 125, sc. 88; 1636/7: c. 134, sc. 36; 1639/40: c. 104, sc. 62 (»Andrea del frate Cinatti«); 1641/2: c. 8, sc. 80.

[6] 1631/2: c. 107, sc. 44.2.16; MS 321: 1634, p. 535, »Agnolo Conti furiere sc. 15—«; 1634/5: c. 77, sc. 48; 1635/6: c. 112, sc. 48; 1636/7: c. 141, sc. 39; 1639/40: c. 139, sc. 84; 1641/2: c. 123, sc. 35; 1654 I: f. 13r, »Monsu Agnolo . . . un Basso di Viola à Gamba«, 1666.

[7] 1634/5: c. 123, sc. 54; 1635/6: c. 92, sc. 49.3.8.; 1636/7: c. 116, sc. 58.3.10; 1641/2: c. 60, sc. 40.3.10.

[8] LR: f. 82r; NC: »Il Figliuolo di Monsù Giouacchino nel tempo, che si fa baletti, e Festini«; 1639/40: c. 95, sc. 120; 1641/2: c. 162, sc. 32.

[9] 1656/7: c. 24, sc. 48; 1658/9: c. 22, sc. 48; 1669 I, f. 106r; died 28 August 1669 (ibid., f. 111r).

[10] NC; 1635/6: c. 132, sc. 5.—10—.; 1636/7: c. 40, sc. 36; 1639/40: c. 58, sc. 48; 1640 I: f. 87r, »Due Contr'alti . . . Tre Cornetti, Vna Sordellina«; 1641/2: c. 55, sc. 64.

[11] LR: f. 82r, »Catterina detta la Rossina« (?); N.C: »Catterina detta la Rossina«; 1636/7: c. 154, sc. 5; 1639/40: c. 77, sc. 87.5.6.8; 1640 I: f. 87v, »Due Leuti«; 1641/2: c. 131, sc. 96; 1648/9: c. 148, sc. 140.

Carlo di Monsù Pietro Asolani[12] [franzese] entrò con prouisione di scudi quattro
dico   sc. 4:—:—

Adì 20. Luglio 1642.

Carlo Fei[13] Musico Castratto [soprano] entrò con prouisione di ducati quattro   sc. 4:—
f. 71v

Adì primo Febbraio 1619:

M. Domenico Sarti[14] Castratto [soprano] entrò con prouisione di scudi sei il mese,
come in filza à Carta n° 1500: sono dico   sc. 6:—:—
E più Adì 18: Agosto 1628: se li augumentò altri scudi sei, come in Filza à Carta
1838: dico   sc. 6:—:—
E più Adì 3. Marzo 1631: se li augumentorno altri tre scudi, come in Filza à Carta
2012: sono dico   sc. 3:—:—
E più Adì   dalla Dispensa scudi quattro dico   sc. 4:—:—

Adì 16: Marzo 1638:

Domenico Anglesi[15] [strumento] entrò con prouisione di scudi otto in luogo di Giusto
della Valle[16] dico   sc. 8:—:—

Adì 20 Luglio 1642.

Fra Domenico Maria Brancaccini[17] [franciosino] della Santissima Nunziata entrò con
prouisione di ducati quattro il mese   sc. 4:—:—
[f. 72r blank]
f. 72v

Adì 5. Dicembre 1637.

Francesco Burri[18] [contralto] entrò con prouisione di scudi quattro, in luogo d'Alessandro Tattini[19] dico   sc. 4:—:—

---

[12] NC: »il Figliuolo di Monsù Pietro«; 1639/40: c. 96, sc. 48; 1641/2: c. 28, sc. 48.

[13] 1641/2: c. 181, sc. 5.2.6.9. (Agosto 1641).

[14] GR 450: 1629, c. 45, sc. 27.3.10; 1630, c. 66, sc. 27.3.10; GR 454: 1629, p. xvii, sc. 27.3.10;
1631/2: c. 57, sc. 161.5.12; GR 459: *Quaderno*, f. 2v, sc. 27.3.10; f. 4v, sc. 5.5.3.4.;
f. 7v, 10v, 13v, sc. 27.3.10; *Debitori e Creditori*, c. 20, sc. 27.3.10; c. 27, sc. 5.5.1.4; c. 35,
37, 46, 54, sc. 27.3.10; GR 460: f. 23r, sc. 27.3.10; f. 27v, sc. 5.5.1.4; f. 31r, sc. 27.3.10;
GR 465: c. 38, sc. 27.3.10; 1634/5: c. 54, sc. 180; 1635/6: c. 69, sc. 180; 1636/7: c. 52, sc.
135; 1639/40: c. 122, sc. 180; 1640 I: f. 87v, »Vn' Cimbalo di Napoli..., Vna Chitarrina
alla Spagnola...«; 1641/2: c. 126, sc. 180; 1648/9: c. 35, sc. 345; 1652 I: f. 92v; 1654 I:
f. 19r; 1669 I: f. 106v.

[15] 1639/40: c. 35, sc. 138; 1641/2: c. 6, sc. 96; 1648/9: c. 159, sc. 96; Conto, Guardaroba 664,
f. 63r, 1652; 1654 I: f. 19r, »un Organo di Legno Principale, è Ottaua, ...«, 1666; 1656/7:
c. 37, sc. 96; 1658/9: c. 33, sc. 96; 1669 I: f. 108r, »Vn Organo di Legnio principale, è
ottaua...«; f. 97v, autograph receipt for »un Cimbalo con tastiera d'Auorio è d'ebano...«
and »un Organo di Legno con due registri...«

[16] 1636/7: c. 72, sc. 72.

[17] 1640 I: f. 87v, »Vn' Fagotto con' sue appartenze, Vn' Trombone senza Ciambella, Vna
Viola di Cremona con l'Arco, Vn' Cornetto chiaro alla 4.ª, Vn' Cornetto muto con' sua
Ghiera, Vna Spinetta Verde piccola«; 1648/9: c. 30, sc. 100 (sc. 64 received); 1652 I: f. 92v,
»Vn' fagotto..., Vn' trombone, Vna Viola di Cremona...«; 1654 I: f. 19r, »tre Cornetti
Chiari, è uno Muto, è un Grauicembolo à un Rigistro del' Trasontino...« 1657, »due fa-
gotti«, 1661; 1656/7: c. 128, sc. 48; 1658/9: c. 34, sc. 68; 1669 I: f. 107r, »Graue cembolo...
à due registri«, f. 97r, autograph receipt for the same.

[18] 1639/40: c. 68, sc. 48.

[19] 1631/2: c. 75, sc. 48; 1634/5: c. 56, sc. 48.

Adì primo Luglio 1641 restò il sopradetto a Ruolo, ma hauendo hauto la chiesa, si dette la prouisione al Mazzanti

Adì 23. di Settembre 1640.

Fabio Oldradi[20] Sonator d'Arpa entrò con prouisione di scudi cinque dico   sc. 5:—:—

Franc:co di   da S. Casciano Castratto tira di Camera di S.A. scudi cinque il mese dico   sc. 5:—:—

si partì senza licenzia

f. 73r

Adì primo Dicembre 1608:

Giouacchino Biancotti[21] [franzese] entrò con prouisione di scudi dieci il mese come in filza à Carta nº 878: sono dico   sc. 10:—:—

E più Adì   dalla Dispensa scudi sei dico   sc. 6:—:—

Adì primo Agosto 1614:

Giouanni Castor[22] [franzese] entrò con prouisione di scudi sei, come in Filza à Carta nº 1221: sono dico   sc. 6:—:—

E Adì   ducati quattro, hà di Camera di S.A.S.   sc. 4:—:—

Adì 19 Giugno 1623:

Gio: Batta: dell'Auca [?][23] [franzese] entrò con prouisione di scudi dieci, come in Filza à Carta nº 1674: sono dico   sc. 10:—:—

E più Adì 7 ottobre 1634: se li augumenta scudi quattro, come in filza à Carta nº 2104: sono dico   sc. 4:—:—

Adì primo Ottobre 1624 (morì di Gennaio 1650 ab incarnazione)

Gio: Batta: da Gagliano[24] [tiorba] entrò con prouisione di scudi quattro come in Filza à Carta nº 1728: sono dico   sc. 4:—:—

E più Adì primo Agosto 1637: se li augumenta scudi tre, come in filza à Carta nº 2246: dico   sc. 3:—:—

Adì 9 Giugno 1643.

Entrò Maestro di Cappella del Duomo con prouisione di ducati dieci come per Rescritto di S.A.S. sotto detto dì, et Anno ecc.   sc. 10—.—

f. 73v

Adì 2. Marzo 1633:

Gio: Antonio Mariani[25] [tenore] entrò con prouisione di scudi tre dico   sc. 3:—:—

Adì 28. Settembre 1631.

---

[20] 1641/2: c. 147, sc. 60.

[21] NC: »Monsù Giouacchino per sonare alle S.re Dame«; 1631/2: c. 55, sc. 120; 1634/5: c. 65, sc. 120; 1635/6: c. 75, sc. 130; 1636/7: c. 44, sc. 92; 1639/40: c. 95, sc. 120; 1641/2: c. 82, sc. 120; 1640 I: f. 87v, »Vn' Basso di Viola«; 1648/9: c. 48, sc. 16.

[22] 1631/2: c. 34, sc. 120; 1634/5: c. 26, sc. 120; 1635/6: c. 46, sc. 114.4.52; 1636/7: c. 32, sc. 54; 1640 I: f. 87v, »Vn' Tenore di Viola«; 1641/2: c. 82, sc. 72; 1648/9: c. 50, sc. 108.

[23] Is this one person with two functions, musician and *ballerino*, or two separate persons, as the variations in the name suggest? 1631/2: c. 59, sc. 120; 1634/5: c. 56, »maestro di ballo«, sc. 163.1.8; 1635/6: c. 66, sc. 168; 1636/7: c. 61, sc. 126; 1639/40: c. 89, sc. 168; 1641/2: c. 94, sc. 168; 1648/9: c. 52, sc. 88.1.8.— (died).

[24] The words in parentheses are a later addition. NC: »gli si dà in tempo, che si fà Cappella à Palazzo, corde, e assetare Strumenti«; 1631/2: c. 79, sc. 48; 1634/5: c. 78, sc. 48; 1635/6: c. 122, sc. 48; 1636/7: c. 74, sc. 43; 1639/40: c. 157, sc. 84; 1641/2: c. 154, sc. 84; 1648/9: c. 52, sc. 161.

[25] 1636/7: c. 27, sc. 27; 1639/40: c. 121, sc. 36; 1641/2: c. 36, sc. 36; 1648/9: c. 58, sc. 63; 1654 I: »Gio: Ant:o Mariani Orefice ... un Fagotto, et un Serpentone«; 1656/7: c. 70, sc. 56.

Gio: Batta: di Antonio Lassagnini[26] [franciosino] detto il Biondino, entrò con prouisione di scudi sei dico   sc. 6:—:—
E Adì 11. Nouembre 1634: se li augumenta scudi tre, dico   sc. 3:—:—
f. 74r

    Adì 24 Nouembre 1628.
D. Honorato Magi [tenore] Monaco di Santa Trinita[27] entrò con prouisione di scudi
dieci dico   sc. 10:—:—
E Adì 8 Ottobre 1637: se li augumenta scudi sette come Cappellano dico   sc. 7:—:—
f. 74v

    Adì primo Ottobre 1609.
Jacopo del Franciosino[28] entrò con prouisione di scudi dieci, dico   sc. 10:—:—
E Adì primo Ottobre 1609: se li augmenta scudi uno dico   sc. 1:—:—
f. 75r

    Adì 11: Aprile 1604:
Lorenzo Allegri[29], [liuto] entrò con prouisione di scudi dodici il mese dico, come in
filza à Carta n° 584   sc. 12:—:—

    Adì 4 Dicembre 1638
Luca Agnoletti[30], [soprano] entrò con prouisione di scudi quindici il mese dico
                                                                             sc. 15:—:—

    Adì 20 di Dicembre 1640.
Lorenzo di MichellAngelo Buti[31] [franciosino] entrò con prouisione di scudi dua
                                                                             sc. 2:—:—
f. 75v

    Adì
S.ra Maria Botti[32], hà della Dispensa di S.A.S. in conto della sua parte scudi dieci
dico   sc. 10:—:—
E Adì   scudi dua tira di prouisione   sc. 2:—:—
[f. 76 blank]
f. 77r

---

[26] NC; 1631/2: c. 109, sc. 66.4.14; 1634/5: c. 111, sc. 81; 1635/6: c. 57, sc. 136; 1636/7: c. 20,
sc. 81; 1639/40: c. 61, sc. 108; 1641/2: c. 91, sc. 108; 1640 I: f. 87v, »Vn' Trombone, Due
Viole à braccio«; 1648/9; c. 56, sc. 166.6.1.4; 1652 I: f. 92v, »Dua Viole abraccio«; 1654 I:
f. 25r, »un Tenore di Viola à Braccio«. Succeeded Bartolomeo Mazzanti in the Guardaroba
28 August 1669 (1669 I, f. 101r).

[27] MS 321: 1621, p. 493, sc. 10—; 1631/2: c. 8, sc. 160; 1634/5: c. 69, sc. 120; 1635/6: c. 105,
sc. 120; 1636/7: c. 59, sc. 90; 1639/40: c. 124, sc. 204; 1641/2: c. 126, sc. 204; 1648/9: c.
82, sc. 357.

[28] 1631/2: c. 51, sc. 96; 1634/5: c. 91, sc. 132; 1635/6: c. 78, sc. 132; 1636/7: c. 50, sc. 99;
1639/40: c. 140, sc. 132; 1640 I: f. 86r, »vna Viola à braccio . . ., Vn' Cornetto chiaro, Vna
Trauersa, e Tre Cornetti muti«; 1641/2: c. 139, sc. 132; 1648/9: c. 64, sc. 297; 1652 I:
f. 92r = 1640 I.

[29] MS 321: 1611, p. 387, »Suonatore di Liuto sc. 12«, 1616, p. 427, sc. 12, 1617, p. 435, sc.
12; GR 448: f. 62r, »Lorenzo Allegri Guardaroba della Musica . . . Un trombone d'argento
con suo bochetto senza storta musicale . . .«; 1631/2: c. 30, sc. 190; 1634/5: c. 15, sc. 150;
1635/6: c. 78, »maestro di Sonare«, sc. 144; 1636/7: c. 19, »maestro di Liuto«, sc. 140;
1639/40: c. 10, sc. 146; 1641/2: c. 17, sc. 144; 1648/9: c. 67, sc. 49.4.18.

[30] 1639/40: c. 94, sc. 180; 1648/9: c. 68, sc. 289.6.1.4.

[31] LR: f. 82r; 1640 I: f. 86r, »Vn' Basso di Viola . . ., e Vn' Trombone«.

[32] LR: f. 82r; 1639/40: c. 93, sc. 24; 1648/9: c. 158, sc. 24.

Adì
Pauolo Grazzi detto il Franciosino[33], entrò con prouisione di scudi sei dico   sc. 6:—:—
E Adì primo Ottobre 1609: se li augumenta scudi uno dico   sc. 1:—:—
E Adì   se li augumenta scudi tre dico   sc. 3:—:—
E più Adì 27 Agosto 1635: se li augumenta scudi quattro dico   sc. 4:—:—
E Adì   se li augumenta scudi dua   sc. 2:—:—
    Adì primo Agosto 1593:
Pompeo di Girolamo da Modena[34] [liuto] entrò con prouisione di scudi sette dico
                                                                                           s. 7:—:—
E Adì primo Ottobre 1609. se li augumenta scudi uno, dico   sc. 1:—:—
    Adì 15. Ottobre 1617.
Pietro Asolani[35], [franzese] entrò con prouisione di scudi dieci dico   sc. 10:—:—
E Adì 9. Ottobre 1634: se li augumenta scudi quattro dico   sc. 4:—:—
E più Adì   in conto della sua parte, che ha dalla Dispensa di S.A.S. scudi sei dico
                                                                                           sc. 6:—:—
f. 77v
    Adì 19 Dicembre 1613.
Piero Raffaelli[36] Basso, entrò con prouisione di scudi tre dico   sc. 3:—:—
E Adì 14. Febbraio 1618. se li augumenta scudi sette, dico   sc. 7:—:—
Si dettero al Cecconi
Mad.a Polisena Poggi[37] figliuola di Domenico Poggi tira dalla Dispensa di S.A.S. per
sua parte scudi cinque il mese dico   sc. 5:—:—
si è mancata, & la prouisione non la tira più perche gli fù dato la Dote in contanti
[f. 78 blank]
f. 79r
    Adì primo Ottobre 1629:
Stefano Soldini[38] strumentaio entrò con provisione di scudi quattro dico   sc. 4:—:—
    Adì 28. Settembre 1631.
Stefano di Gio: Batta: Jacomelli[39], [franciosino] entrò con prouisione di scudi tre
dico   sc. 3:—:—
E Adì 28 Agosto 1635: se li augumenta scudi uno, dico   sc. 1:—:—
    Adì 24 Dicembre 1636:

---

[33] NC: 1631/2: c. 75, sc. 144; 1634/5: c. 55, sc. 144; 1635/6: c. 88, sc. 192.2.8.; 1636/7: c. 48,
   sc. 144; 1639/40: c. 99, sc. 192; 1641/2: c. 132, sc. 192; 1648/9: c. 86, sc. 448.
[34] 1631/2: c. 56, sc. 96; 1634/5: c. 34, sc. 96; 1635/6: c. 46, sc. 96; 1636/7: c. 40, sc. 72; 1639/
   40: c. 138, sc. 96; 1641/2: c. 58, sc. 96.
[35] NC: »Monsù Pietro, e Monsù Giouacchino per sonare alle S.re Dame«; 1631/2: c. 61, sc. 120;
   1634/5: c. 36, sc. 193.1.8; 1636/7: c. 4, sc. 126; 1639/40: c. 15, sc. 206; 1640 I: f. 86v, »Vn'
   Serpentone, Vna Viola à sei corde, Vn' Violino, Vna muta di libri per i Violini«; 1648/9:
   c. 159, sc. 168.
[36] 1631/2: c. 83, sc. 120; 1634/5: c. 78, sc. 120; 1635/6: c. 89, sc. 120; 1636/7: c. 78, sc. 90;
   1639/40: c. 112, sc. 120.
[37] LR: f. 82v.
[38] 1631/2: c. 83, sc. 48; 1634/5: c. 47, sc. 48; 1635/6: c. 52, sc. 48; 1636/7: c. 76, sc. 36; 1639/
   40: c. 94, sc. 48; 1640 I: f. 86r, »Dua Spinette«; 1641/2: c. 95, sc. 48; 1648/9: c. 94, sc. 52.
[39] 1631/2: c. 120, sc. 30; 1634/5: c. 47, sc. 48; 1635/6: c. 56, sc. 48; 1636/7: c. 51, sc. 36; 1639/
   40: c. 68, sc. 48; 1640 I: f. 86v, »Vna Viola à braccio . . ., Vn' Cornetto chiaro, Vna Trauersa, e Vn' Trombone«; 1648/9: c. 92, sc. 60; 1652 I: f. 92r, the instruments of 1640 I plus
   »Vn' Cornetto gli si dette, e le se rifece ghiera quando si fece la festa à Camera«; 1654 I:
   f. 41r, »un Tenore di Viola«.

Settimia Caccini ne' Ficcizzani[40], entrò con prouisione di scudi quindici dico   sc. 15:—:—
E Adì primo   scudi 50. tira di Camera di S.A.S. l'anno per pigione della Casa, che
uengano il mese raguagliati   sc.
f. 79v

    Adì 25 Luglio 1642.
Il Sig.re Don Stefano Lambardi dal Monte Santa Maria, entrò al seruizio di Musico
di S.A. Ser.ma senza prouisione   sc.
f. 80r

    Adì 18 Maggio 1636:
Tobbia Crigiader Todesco[41], [franciosino] entrò con prouisione di scudi dieci dico
                                                                          sc. 10:—:—
E, Adì 15. Dicembre 1638: se li augumenta scudi sei dico   sc. 6:—:—
f. 80v

    Adì
Vittoria Archilei[42] entrò con prouisione di scudi dieci dico   sc. 10:—:—
E Adì   scudi dodici che tira dal Fisco lasciatigli à uita da S.A.S. dico sc. 12:—:—
E Adì   scudi quattro di Camera di S.A.S.   sc. 4:—:—

    Adì primo Ottobre 1609
Vettorio Baldacci[43] [franciosino] entrò con prouisione di scudi cinque sono dico
                                                                          sc. 5:—:—
e Adì primo Ottobre 1609. se li augumenta scudi uno dico   sc. 1:—:—
E più Adì 26: Gennaio 1616: se li augumenta scudi quattro, dico   sc. 4:—:—

    Adì 20 Ottobre 1606:
Virgilio Grazzi[44], [franciosino] entrò con prouisione di scudi cinque dico sc. 5:—:—
E Adì primo Ottobre 1609. se li augumenta scudi uno dico   sc. 1:—:—
E più Adì 26. Gennaio 1616. se li augumenta scudi quattro dico   sc. 4:—:—
Se ne dette sc. 4— a fra Domenico Maria Brancaccini
f. 81r

    Adì 13. Nouembre 1631:
Vincenzio di Bastiano Baccherelli[45], [franciosino] entrò con prouisione di scudi tre
dico   sc. 3:—:—

[40] MS 321: 1611, p. 386, sc. 10 (Settimia Caccini); 1636/7: c. 107, sc. 123 (Settimia Caccini, ne Ghizzanti); 1639/40: c. 110, sc. 180; 1641/2: c. 124, sc. 180 (Settimia Caccini); 1648/9: c. 163, sc. 180 (ibid.); 1657/8: f. 26v, »Settimia Ghiuizzani Musica sc. 24«, f. 31r, sc. 37.3.10 »per conto di Pigione di Casa ogni mesi sc. ventidua da cominciarsi 1 Novembre 1657«; 1660/1: p. 33, sc. 19.2.6.8 (Settimia Ghiuizzani), p. 42, sc. 36.1.15.

[41] 1631/2: c. 2 (»Tobbia Criensneider Musico«), sc. 244; 1634/5: c. 45, sc. 192; 1635/6: c. 55, sc. 192; 1636/7: c. 41, sc. 190; 1639/40: c. 5, sc. 242 (»Tubbia Todesco«); 1641/2: c. 3, sc. 192; 1648/9: c. 96, sc. 222.4.4; 1656/7: c. 120, sc. 120; 1658/9: c. 117, sc. 120.

[42] MS 321: 1600, p. 312, sc. 10; 1631/2: c. 62, sc. 120; 1634/5: c. 33, sc. 120; 1635/6: c. 74, sc. 120; 1636/7: c. 56, sc. 90; 1639/40: c. 105, sc. 120; 1641/2: c. 97, sc. 120.

[43] 1631/2: c. 50, sc. 120; 1634/5: c. 49, sc. 120; 1635/6: c. 83, sc. 120; 1636/7: c. 53, sc. 90; 1639/40: c. 117, sc.   ; 1640 I: f. 87r, »Vn' Cornetto chiaro, Vna Trauersa grossa del Concerto, Vna Viola di Cremona à braccio«; 1641/2: c. 126, sc. 120; 1648/9: c. 97, sc. 248.4 (70 received); 1652 I: f. 92r = 1640 I.

[44] NC: »in tempo de' Festini«; 1631/2: c. 74, sc. 120; 1634/5: c. 48, sc. 120; 1635/6: c. 76, sc. 120; 1636/7: c. 54, sc. 90; 1639/40: c. 121, sc. 120; 1640 I: f. 86r, »Vna Trauersa, Vn' Cornetto muto, Vna Viola di Cremona, Vna muta di Viole...«; 1641/2: c. 128, sc. 64.

[45] NC; 1631/2: c. 120, sc. 30; 1634/5: c. 39, sc. 36; 1636/7: c. 51, sc. 42.1.4; 1639/40: c. 68, sc. 72; 1640 I: f. 86v, »Vn' Serpentone, Vn' Trombone, Vn' Violino..., Dua Tenuri di Viola,

E, Adì 28 Agosto 1635, se li augumenta scudi uno   sc. 1:—:—
E più Adì   se li augumenta scudi dua, dico   sc. 2:—:—

In addition to the performers listed in the above *Ruolo* other names occur in the account books. Dancers were not included in the roll, and some musicians may have been omitted as being merely casual performers, others — trumpeters, for example — because they did not form a part of the strictly musical establishment[46].

Agnolo Ricci ballerino
     MS 321: 1601, p. 321, »Maestro del ballare del Gran Principe sc. 7—«; GR 449: c.xiii; 1635/6: c. 124, sc. 143; 1636/7: c. 121, sc. 99; 1639/40: c. 46, sc. 165.
Agostino Vasconi organista
     GR 450: 1630, p. 64, sc. 16; GR 465: c. 52, sc. 29.5——; c. 53: sc. 51.5 »tanti se li fanno buono per assett.re di dua organi di legno . . .«
Alessandro Tatini musico
     1631/2: c. 75, sc. 48, 1634/5: c. 56, sc. 48.
Andrea Benizi Trombetto
     MS 321: 1611, p. 387, sc. 10.
Angelica Sciameroni Musica
     1636/7: c. 21, sc. 144.
Antonio Archilei Musico
     MS 321: 1600, p. 312, sc. 11.
Antonio del Franciosino
     1631/2: c. 56, sc. 132; 1634/5: c. 39, sc. 6.6.15.4 (one payment).
Antonio Gai Suonatore
     MS 321: 1616, p. 425, sc. 10.

Vn' Cornetto muto, Due Trauerse mezzane, Vna Trauersa grossa, Vna Trauersa piccola, Tre Cornetti, Vn' Fagotto«; 1641/2: c. 119, sc. 72; 1648/9: c. 96, sc. 102; 1654 I: f. 45r, »un Basso di Viola grande di Cremona à 4 da Gamba . . .«; 1656/7: c. 122, sc. 57.4.4«.

[46] The festivities for the wedding of Odoardo Farnese, Duke of Parma, with Princess Margherita de' Medici in October of 1628 drew to Florence two celebrated Roman musicians, the harpsichordist Andrea Falconieri and the castrato Loreto Vittori, known as the Cavalier Loreto. I have not discovered records of payments to these two musicians. Their progress to Florence, however, can be followed in the letters of the Balì Andrea Cioli to Orazio Linati (Florence, Archivio di Stato, Archivio Mediceo del Principato, filza 179). On 5 Sept. 1628 Cioli wrote Linati: »Io scriverò dunque ad Andrea Falconieri che seguiti i Signori Cardinali Lodovisi et Aldobrandini quando si partiranno di Roma per qua . . . Io ho anche scritto a Roma che il Cav.r Loreto musico se ne venga subito a questa volta, e lo ho invitato a casa mia; sichè se V.S. Ill.ma vorrà poi sentire una villanella, io ne la potrò servire.« (n. 79). A letter of 23 Sept. 1628 records some confusion over the employment of »Lorenzino« (presumably Vittori) by the Medici and the Farnese: »Quanto a Lorenzino Musico io spero che il Ser.mo Duca lo potrà havere costà al servizio delle sue feste, perchè havendone parlato col Sig.r Principe Don Lorenzo, che lo tiene al suo stipendio . . .« Linati is expected ». . . una sera alla veglia in casa mia, per sentir sonare Andrea Falconieri e cantar il Cavalier Loreto, il quale alloggia da me, come seguì hiersera con grandissimo mio gusto.« (n. 117).
The disposition of Lorenzino is also discussed in two further letters, n. 123 of 26 Sept. and n. 131 of 30 Sept.

Emilio de' Cavalieri
    MS 321: 1589, 1591—1600, p. 243, 257, 265, 275, 282, 290, 295, 298, 302, 306, 310, sc. 25; 1601/2, p. 319: »sc. 25 + a Roma 23 Febb. 1602«.
Francesca Caccini Signorini Musica
    MS 321: 1611, p. 388, sc.10; 1614, p. 412, sc. 20; 1617, p. 434, sc. 18.
Francesco Mariani musico
    1631/2: c. 105, sc. 156.2.16.
Gio: Batista Signorini Musico
    MS 321: 1611, p. 388, sc. 13; 1614, p. 412, sc. 13; 1615, p. 420, sc. 13; 1617, p. 435, sc. 13.
Girolamo Fantini Trombetto
    GR 448 (1631): f. 66, »Girolamo Fantini da Spuleti, nuovo trombetto di S.A.S. ... Una tromba d'argento ... Una banderola da tromba ... Una banderola da tromba...«; 1631/2: c. 15, sc. 120; 1634/5: c. 61, sc. 120; 1635/6: c. 11, sc. 120; 1636/7: c. 18, sc. 90; 1639/40: c. 22, sc. 123; 1640 I: f. 87v, »Vna Viola nuoua«; 1641/2: c. 12, sc. 120.
Girolamo Frescobaldi Musico
    MS 321: p. 485—495, »Ruolo del Sereniss.mo Granduca del 1621 ... Estratto dal suo Originale esistente nell'Archivio de' Soprasindaci di S.A.S.«, p. 493, sc. 25 per month; 1628, p. 511, sc. 25; 1631, p. 524, sc. 25; 1632, p. 529, sc. 25; 1633, p. 534, »Maestro di Cappella sc. 29«; 1631/2: c. 21, sc. 300.
Giuliano del Franciosino
    1631/2: c. 30, sc. 132; 1634/5: c. 22, sc. 132; 1635/6: c. 49, sc. 138; 1636/7: c. 28, sc. 99; 1639/40: c. 66, sc. 88 +; 1640 I: f. 87v, »Quali Strumenti si sono rihauti da Messr. Giuliano del Franciosino ...«
Jacopo Peri detto il Zazzerino Musico
    MS 321: 1600, p. 313, sc. 9; 1631/2: c. 111, sc. 108.
Jacobo Rineldi tronbetta
    1636/7: c. 116, sc. 70.
Onofrio Gualfedrucci Musico
    MS 321: 1600, p. 310, sc. 15.
Orazio Benuenuti Musico
    MS 321: 1600, p. 310, sc. 8.
Ottavio Ferrini Trombetto
    1631/2: c. 3, sc. 8 per month; 1635/6: c. 48, sc. 128; 1636/7: c. 33, sc. 90.
Piero Saminiati musico
    1635/6: c. 97, sc. 24.1.8; 1636/7: c. 58, sc. 11.4.13.4.

PASQUALINI AS COPYIST

by *Gloria Rose* (Buffalo, N.Y.)

In the Barberini collection of music manuscripts at the Vatican Library, there remains much to be explored[1]. I propose here to discuss a number of manuscripts which hold certain features in common: Barb. lat. MSS. 4187, 4188, 4189, 4190, 4191, 4192, 4193, 4194, 4195, 4198, 4203, 4209, 4219, 4220, 4221, 4222, 4223, 4231 and 4296. These manuscripts date from the seventeenth century, and they consist mainly of Italian cantatas and oratorios, or sections from them, by unnamed composers. The striking feature of the manuscripts is that they were all evidently prepared, in whole or in part, by the same copyist. His hand is also found in Barb. lat. 4218 and 4199, but only on the covers and in the opening pieces of music.

Within this large group of manuscripts, a smaller group of five volumes shows particular characteristics in common. Barb. lat. 4219, 4220, 4221, 4222 and 4223 are all written on the same size of eight-stave, oblong paper; they are all thick volumes, of about 200 folios each; they are all bound in cardboard covered with parchment; they are all dated; they all have an index at the end, in the copyist's hand; and with one exception, they all have written on the flyleaf, in the copyist's hand:

MAP.

Straccia foglio
Perdimento di tempo per sfuggir lozio

The exception is Barb. lat. 4222, where the monogram MAP is lacking, the spelling is »*lotio*« instead of »*lozio*«, and the order of the two lines »*Straccia foglio*« and »*Perdimento . . .*« is reversed.

Some of these five manuscripts also give, on their front covers, a brief description of their contents; for example, »*Ariette a Solo*« in Barb. lat. 4221. All of the pieces in these five manuscripts are in the same hand, with just a few exceptions. The hand, as indicated above, is that of the copyist who was responsible for a good many other volumes in the Barberini collection.

To identify the copyist, what can we say is known about him? First, he was active around 1650, for the dates that he wrote in Barb. lat. 4219—4223 range

---

[1] My recent work there was very generously made possible by research grants from the National Endowment for the Humanities and the Howard Foundation.

from 1634 to 1683. Second, he had quite a long life, since he copied music for a period of almost fifty years. Third, he lived evidently in Rome, for the contents of the manuscripts point to a Roman repertory: the poet named most often is Giovanni Lotti; and some of the music, though anonymous here, is attributed elsewhere to Luigi Rossi. Fourth, he was employed by Cardinal Antonio Barberini, at least while he prepared Barb. lat. 4203. This manuscript shows the Barberini coat of arms, with a cardinal's hat above, on its front and back covers; and twelve of the cantatas in it are set to poems by this Cardinal Antonio Barberini. Barb. lat. 4203 shows several different hands up to folio 69v; but from folio 70 to the end of the volume, it is in the hand of our copyist.

All these clues do lead towards a possible identification of the copyist. But I think that he has identified himself by writing his initials, MAP in a monogram, on the flyleaf of the manuscripts Barb. lat. 4219—4221 and 4223. Scholars before myself have understood the initials MAP to stand for Marc'Antonio Pasqualini. They have assumed, however, that a piece headed MAP was either composed by Pasqualini or sung by him[2]. Since Pasqualini was both composer and singer, he might indeed have composed or sung any pieces headed MAP. Yet there is another possibility which arises from a study of the handwritings concerned. MAP may refer to Pasqualini as copyist.

As already mentioned, dates are marked in Barb. lat. 4219—4223 for years from 1634 to 1683. To be more specific, Barb. lat. 4220 is dated 1634 on the index at the end of the volume (fol. 161), and 1654 on the front cover. Barb. lat. 4221 is dated 1638 on the front cover, and 1638 again on the index at the end (fol. 153). Barb. lat. 4219 is dated 1656 on the index at the end (fol. 215), and 1663 on the front cover. Barb. lat. 4222 is dated 1676 on the flyleaf. Barb. lat. 4223 is dated 1683 (very faintly) on the front cover.

Now Marc'Antonio Pasqualini lived from 1614 to 1691. He was born, died, and spent most of his life in Rome. He retired in 1659 from the papal chapel, after twenty-five years of service there[3], so that he had from that time more leisure available than previously. The copyist of all these manuscripts obviously had leisure enough to prepare them, and there is even a hint that he may have had too much leisure. This is the comment in each volume of Barb. lat. 4219—4223: »Straccia foglio / Perdimento di tempo per sfuggir lozio« (Scribbling book / A waste of time so as to escape idleness). An amusing remark, no doubt; but it contains truth if the copyist was someone with rather too much time on his hands.

To fill in his time, then, the copyist wrote out a great deal of music. He not only

---

[2] See Eleanor CALUORI, Introduction to the *Wellesley Edition Cantata Index Series*, Fascicle 3a, Luigi Rossi (Wellesley, 1965), pp. viii—xi; and the further references given there.
[3] Alberto CAMETTI, *Musicisti celebri del Seicento in Roma: Marc'Antonio Pasqualini*, Musica d'oggi, III (1921), p. 99.

copied it; he may have recomposed some of it. In Barb. lat. 4219 and 4222 (prepared by our scribe) there are pieces for two, three or four voices which are found as solo pieces in Barb. lat. 4201, 4204 and 4205 (not prepared by our scribe). In Barb. lat. 4219, some pieces appear in different settings; for example, *»Spargete sospiri«* is notated for four voices and basso continuo, then for four voices without continuo, then for three voices with continuo, then with a different text. These same pieces, from Barb. lat. 4219, occur in another manuscript copied by our scribe, Barb. lat. 4188; here each piece occurs in one setting only. It is possible that these arrangements were made by the composer(s) and then merely copied by our scribe. But it is just as likely that the copyist — himself a musician, after all — took up the pieces and reworked them for various combinations of voices.

The monogram MAP, written at the start of Barb. lat. 4219—4221 and 4223, also appears at the head of many individual pieces in the manuscripts, and at the head of all pieces in Barb. lat. 4223. In addition to MAP, *»Un Infelice Core amò, servì penò«* in Barb. lat. 4223, fols. 116—123v, is headed *»Del S.ʳ Marco Antᵒ Pasqualini«*; and *»Di gioir speranza infida«* in Barb. lat. 4223, fols. 149—152v, is headed *»Del Sigʳ Marcantonio Pasqualini«*. But these attributions are not in the hand of the same copyist; they are in a second and a third hand. They are so faint that they are hardly legible, and it even looks as though they have been rubbed out. Perhaps the two scribes who attributed these pieces to Pasqualini found out later that he was not the composer and tried then to remove their attributions.

Along with the monogram MAP, the word »Streviglio« appears at the head of some pieces. This word »Streviglio«, occasionally in the variant forms »Estreviglio« or »Striviglio« or »Estriviglio«, occurs in other Italian manuscripts of the same period, notably in Barb. lat. 4201, 4204 and 4205. In Giuseppe Baronci's handwritten catalogue of the Barberini music manuscripts, Streviglio is identified as Marc'Antonio Pasqualini. Some later writers have accepted Baronci's identification[4]. But in the music manuscripts the word »Streviglio« always appears alone; it is not preceded by the phrase »Del Sig.«, which customarily precedes the name of the composer in a manuscript attribution. Nor can the word »Streviglio« refer to a poet. When a poet's name is given, it is customarily prefixed by the words »Poesia del«. Moreover and more conclusive, an actual poet is sometimes named next to the word »Streviglio«. For example, there is the heading in Barb. lat. 4222, fol. 127: *»MAP a 2. streviglio Poesia del S. Lotti«*.

---

[4] Alberto GHISLANZONI, *Luigi Rossi (Aloysius de Rubeis): Biografia e analisi delle composizioni* (Milan and Rome, 1954), p.92 and p.112, n.5; also Oscar MISCHIATI, *Pasqualini, Marc'Antonio (Beiname: Streviglio)*, MGG, X (1962), col. 861. But the identification is rejected by Eleanor CALUORI, op. cit., p. ix, n. 40.

Starting probably from Baronci's identification, Alberto Ghislanzoni has suggested that Streviglio was a name given to Pasqualini by his friend Luigi Rossi[5]. This is surely mistaken. As we have seen, »Streviglio« is unlikely to be the name of a composer, or of any person at all. But Ghislanzoni was on to the right idea when he connected »Streviglio« with »Estribillo«, the refrain of Spanish songs then in fashion[6]. In fact, »Estribillo« is the Spanish word for refrain; it refers to a refrain in verse which is repeated after every strophe of a poem.

Now the musical pieces headed »Streviglio« which I have examined are all in rondo form, or at least they have a section which returns. This is the case in Barb. lat 4201, 4204, 4205, 4220, 4221, 4222 and 4223. In Barb. lat. 4205, there is even a piece where the word »Streviglio« occurs not at the start, but twice in the middle of the piece: it occurs at the first statement of a section and then at the return of that section. This certainly seems to indicate that »Streviglio« meant »refrain«.

In Rome, Biblioteca Casanatense, MS. 2468, fols. 39—46v, the anonymous cantata *»E qual misero e conforme allo stato d'un Amante«* is headed »Estreviglio«. Here the cantata is in the form of rondo-strophic variations, with the refrain *»E qual misero«*. In this case, too, »Estreviglio« seems to mean a refrain, or a piece with a refrain.

In yet another cantata, the word »estriviglio« occurs not as a heading, but in the text of the piece. This is in Cesti's cantata *»Aspettate, adesso canto«,* where the text reads: *»se qual ch'un gli lavora l'estriviglio e un par di stanze«*[7]. The (anonymous) author has been describing, and mocking, the various kinds of song then most popular. Here he speaks of the »estriviglio« in a context of poetry: »if someone works up the refrain for them and a couple of stanzas«.

»Streviglio« is not, however, a very common word in the musical sources generally. When Ghislanzoni associated it with Pasqualini and Luigi Rossi, he had some grounds. For »Streviglio« does occur in manuscripts which include the monogram MAP, standing for Marc'Antonio Pasqualini, and in manuscripts which have connections with Luigi Rossi. Among the manuscripts containing the word »Streviglio« are Barb. lat. 4201, 4204 and 4205; and these three volumes are, I believe, mainly in the hand of Luigi Rossi. I hope to deal with them later in a separate study, for I think that they represent actual composing books of Luigi Rossi, with some pieces in the hand of Pasqualini. Conversely, I think

[5] GHISLANZONI, op. cit., p. 92.

[6] Ibid.

[7] Antonio CESTI, *»Aspettate, adesso canto«,* in the Wellesley Edition, No. 5, The Italian Cantata, I, ed. David Burrows (Wellesley, 1963), p. 88. The sources are London, British Museum, Harley MS. 1863, fols. 69v—78, and Naples, Biblioteca del Conservatorio di Musica »S. Pietro a Majella«, MS. 33.4.11, fols. 42—51v.

that Barb. lat. 4221, which is mainly in Pasqualini's hand, begins with two pieces in the hand of Luigi Rossi. These two musicians were colleagues and friends. They were both in the service of Cardinal Antonio Barberini, and they shared the experience of many performances together. Their friendship was evidently a close one. When Luigi Rossi made out his Will of 14 November 1641, he left several paintings and a pair of gloves to »*Marco Antonio Pasqualino ... his very dear friend*«[8].

Among the other manuscripts prepared by our copyist, Barb. lat. 4194 and 4195 contain the two parts of a work titled *Gioseppe*. The composer is not named. But Luigi Rossi is known to have composed an oratorio called *Gioseppe*. This work is listed in the old, handwritten catalogue of the Magliabechi Library, now part of the Biblioteca Nazionale Centrale in Florence. The catalogue was prepared by Antonio Targoni Tozzetti sometime in the second half of the eighteenth century, before 1783, when Tozzetti died. Listed in volume 6 on folio 61, as part of MS. XIX.22, is the following work: »*Gioseppe figlio di Giacobbe opera spirituale fatta in musica da Aloigi de ROSSI napolitano in Roma.*« Apparently this MS. XIX.22 was seen by Charles Burney, who wrote in 1789: »*In the Magliabecchi library at Florence, I found the scene of an oratorio called ›Giuseppe figlio di Giacobbe, Opera spirituale, fatta in Musica da Aloigi de Rossi, Napolitano, in Roma‹.*«[9]

Unfortunately, Magl. MS. XIX.22 has been missing since 1883. But Barb. lat. 4194—4195, titled *Gioseppe*, may well be another copy of this oratorio by Luigi Rossi. The extant *Gioseppe* certainly dates from the period of Luigi Rossi, and musically it is compatible with his style.

Returning to the whole group of manuscripts under discussion here, we might review the reasons for suggesting that Pasqualini was their main copyist. He lived at the right time and place, in Rome during the decades around 1650. He lived for long enough to have copied the many volumes concerned: Pasqualini's dates are 1614—1691, and the dates in the manuscripts go from 1634 to 1683. Pasqualini was employed by Cardinal Antonio Barberini, for whom Barb. lat. 4203 was prepared. And Pasqualini, with his first names Marc'Antonio, is surely the person intended by the monogram MAP.

Now it happens that an assured, signed autograph of Pasqualini does survive. This is a manuscript at the Vatican Library, Cappella Sistina, Diari 67. It is a book of attendance of the members of the Sistine Chapel for the year 1648. The handwriting is the same throughout, and it is acknowledged to be the handwriting of Pasqualini. Written in ink on the parchment front cover is the following title: »*LIBRO / Di Punti Dell'Anno / M.D.CXLVIII. / Di / Marc-*

---

[8] GHISLANZONI, op. cit., pp. 186—187.
[9] Charles BURNEY, *A General History of Music*, IV (London, 1789), p. 155.

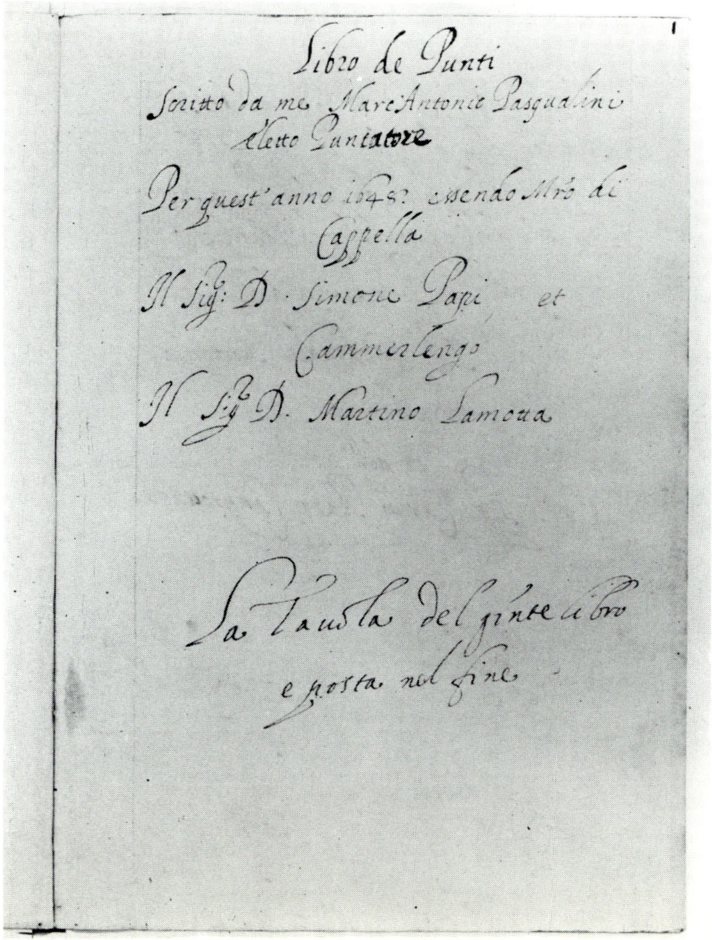

Libro de Punti

Scritto da me Marc'Antonio Pasqualini
detto Cavaliere

Per quest'anno 1643: essendo M.ro di
Cappella

Il Sig.r D. Simone Pape   et
Commer...

Il Sig.r D. Marino Lancar

La Tavola del pine è oro
è posta nel fine.

Plate I. Roma, Biblioteca Apostolica Vaticana,
Cappella Sistina, Diari 67, fol. 1.

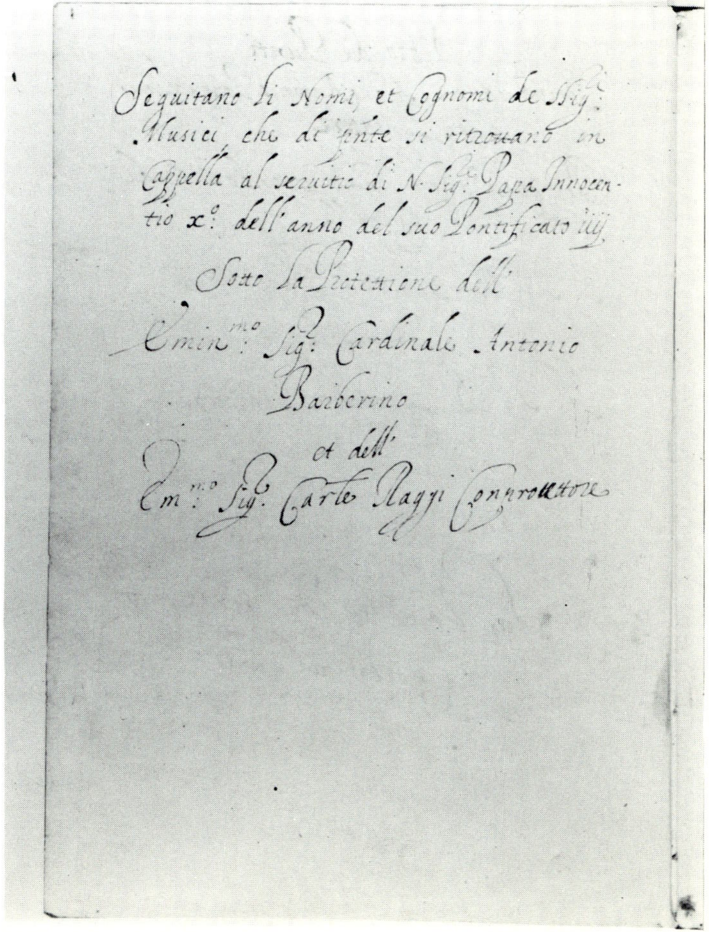

Seguitano li Nomi, et Cognomi de Sig.ri
Musici, che al fine si ritrovano in
Cappella al servitio di N. Sig.re Papa Urbano
8.o xo: dell'anno del suo Pontificato 19.

Sua S.tà Urbano 8.o

E.mo Sig.r Cardinale Antonio
Barberino

et alli
E.mo S.r Carlo Magi Commettente

Plate II. Roma, B.A.V., Capp. Sist., Diar. 67, fol. 1v.

Plate III. Roma, B.A.V., Barb. lat. MS. 4203, fol. 86v.

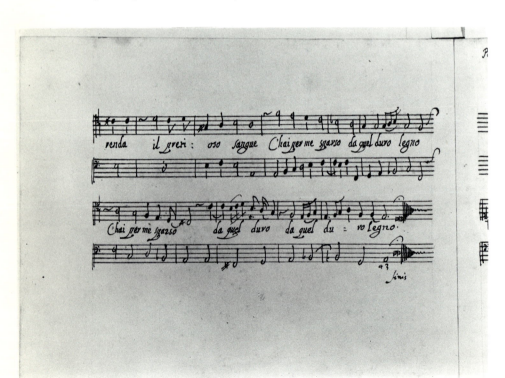

Plate IV. Roma, B.A.V., Barb. lat. MS. 4203, fol. 87.

antonio Pasqualini«. The information on folio 1 is even more explicit, and this is reproduced here on Plate I. The continuation of the title-page is shown on Plate II.

For the purpose of comparison, two folios of Barb. lat. 4203 are reproduced here on Plates III and IV. The writing in the music manuscripts is much heavier than that in the book of attendance. But the slant is the same, and the letters are similar enough to suggest that both manuscripts were written by the same person.

If Pasqualini is, as I believe, the main copyist of all these manuscripts, this strengthens the case for Luigi Rossi's authorship of the works in Barb. lat. 4187, 4188, 4189, 4190, 4191, 4192, 4193, 4194, 4195, 4198, 4199, 4209, 4218, 4231 and 4296. Ghislanzoni has already claimed these works for Luigi Rossi, but without giving very conclusive proof[10]. The fact is that the sources are problematic, and Ghislanzoni has increased the confusion by giving careless and mistaken references to attributions and supposed autographs of Luigi Rossi. Much clarification will still be needed to sort out these works, for they are preserved in rough drafts, in fair copies, and in parts for separate voices and instruments.

The identification of Pasqualini as copyist may help to clarify some questions. Or it may raise further questions, since this is an aspect of Pasqualini's work which has not yet been considered. We knew previously that he excelled as a virtuoso singer, and we have over forty-five of the cantatas that he composed[11]. But now it appears that Pasqualini was active too as a copyist. In his three capacities of singer, composer and scribe, Pasqualini contributed well to the music of his time.

---

[10] GHISLANZONI, op. cit., pp. 94—117, 217—218; and *Tre oratori e tre cantate morali di Luigi Rossi ritrovati nella Biblioteca Vaticana*, Revue belge de musicologie, IX (1955), pp. 3—11.

[11] Sources listed in my article on Pasqualini in Grove's Dictionary of Music and Musicians, 6th ed., forthcoming.

DIE *DAMIRA*-OPERN DER BEIDEN ZIANI

von *Theophil Antonicek* (Wien)

BIOGRAPHISCHES

Pietro Andrea Ziani und sein Neffe Marc'Antonio gehörten in ihrer Zeit zu den berühmtesten Repräsentanten der italienischen Musik beiderseits der Alpen. Dies bezeugen die Aufführungsdaten ihrer Werke und die ehrenvollen Berufungen, die beide erhielten, aber auch Zeitgenossen wie Johann Philipp Krieger, der den älteren Ziani in Italien aufsuchte und wohl von ihm dessen *Sacrae laudes* opus 6 erhielt, aus denen er später in Weißenfels verschiedene Werke aufführte[1], oder der Satiriker Bartolomeo Dotti, der Marc'Antonio Zianis Bedeutung als eines der führenden Opernkomponisten unterstrich, wenn er im Zuge seiner Schmähungen gegen die Textdichter sagte: »*Versi poi stroppj che solo, / Per conciarli in bocca ai musici, / Al Ziani, al Pollarolo, / Fa mestier esser cerusici.*«[2]

Zur Biographie der beiden Komponisten seien hier nur einige Berichtigungen und Nachträge gebracht[3]. Pietro Andrea Ziani muß, entgegen der geläufigen Angabe »um 1620«, spätestens am 21. Dezember 1616 geboren sein. Dies ergibt sich aus dem vorgeschriebenen Mindestalter für Diakons- und Priesterweihe, die Ziani am 19. März 1639 und 22. Dezember 1640 erhielt[4]. Zu diesem Zeitpunkt befand er sich im Kloster San Salvatore, als dessen Canonico regolare und Organist er sich am 20. Juni 1640 bezeichnet. Seine Zugehörigkeit zum Orden der lateranensischen Chorherren ist dennoch ein merkwürdiges Kapitel, das, vor allem wegen des Fehlens einschlägiger Dokumente im Archiv von San Salva-

---

[1] Johann MATTHESON, *Grundlage einer Ehren-Pforte*, Hamburg 1740, Selbstverlag, p. 148. — Max SEIFFERT, Vorwort zu Johann Philipp KRIEGER, *21 ausgewählte Kirchenkompositionen*, DDT 53/54, Leipzig 1916, Breitkopf & Härtel, p. X, XI, XL.

[2] Bartolomeo DOTTI, *Satire*, Amsterdam 1790 (ohne Verlag), p. 94.

[3] Sie beziehen sich auf meinen Artikel *Ziani* in MGG 14, 1968, c. 1253—1262. Dort auch die hier nicht weiter nachgewiesenen Angaben.

[4] Venedig, Archivio patriarcale, *Liber Ordinationum a die 31 Januarij 1638. An[no] D[omini] usque ad Diem 17. Dece[m]bris 1639* [vol. 3], fol. 126v—127v; ebendort *Liber Ordinationum 4.* (1639—1642), fol. 83r–v. — Zur Berechnung des Lebensalters vgl. Mario RINALDI, *La data di nascita di Antonio Vivaldi*, Siena 1943, Ticci, p. 18—21. — Von einem am 28. 2. 1613 in San Trovaso getauften »*Piero fi[gli]ol[o] de Bastiam de Zuani, et de Anna iugali*« ist nicht mit Sicherheit auszuschließen, daß es sich um Pietro Andrea handelt: Venedig, S. Gervasio e S. Protasio M. M. (S. Trovaso), *Registro Battesimi de 1 Gennaio 1607 al 5 Gennaio 1651*, Buchstabe P, 28. 2. 1613

tore[5], vorderhand ungeklärt ist. Einerseits erscheint in seinem opus 3 von 1641 nur noch der Organistentitel und verschwindet der des Canonicus von da an überhaupt; andererseits ersuchte am 7. März 1668 die Kaiserinmutter Eleonora Gonzaga den Kardinal Spinola um seine Hilfe, damit Ziani von Alessandro Borromeo in Padua die *»dispensatio sive derogatio clausulae«* erhalte[6], was wohl als die Entbindung von klösterlichen Verpflichtungen zu verstehen ist. Vielleicht hatte das Beispiel Antonio Cestis dazu angeregt. Das Organistenamt an San Salvatore dürfte Ziani aber jedenfalls noch eine Weile behalten haben, was auch erklärt, warum er in keinem Anstellungsverhältnis zu San Marco stand, das die besten Musiker Venedigs stets an sich zog[7]. Er mag dort trotzdem bei verschiedenen Gelegenheiten mitgewirkt haben[8]. Bis in die Fünfzigerjahre liegt sein Leben wieder im Dunkel, dann geben die Aufführungsdaten der Opern und die Anstellung als Kapellmeister in Bergamo 1657—1659 Hinweise auf seinen Aufenthalt. Seine Ernennung zum Vizekapellmeister der Kaiserinwitwe Eleonora muß bereits 1662 (nicht 1663) erfolgt sein, da er in einem Schreiben dieser Fürstin an den Auditor der Rota Romana vom 15. Dezember 1662 bereits als *»Aulicae Nostrae Capellae Musices Praefectus«* genannt wird[9]. Das Schreiben stellt zugleich einen Beweis von großer Gunst dar, betrifft es doch nicht einmal Ziani selbst, sondern seinen Bruder, den die Fürstin für das Priorat des Benediktinerklosters Santa Giustina in Padua (und den Inhaber dieser Stelle für eine Abtei) empfiehlt. Ziani hat sich also tatsächlich, wie er selbst sagt[10], für sein Familie eingesetzt. Auch sein Gesuch vom 12. März 1667 *»vmb eine[n] Paßbr[ief] auff 100 march gearbeites Silber, solches nach venedig zu vberschikhen«*[11], bezweckte wohl eine Zuwendung an seine Verwandten.

Zianis Lebensziel wird wohl die Kapellmeisterstelle an San Marco gewesen sein. Aus diesem Grunde dürfte er auch den Dienst Eleonoras wieder verlassen und den Posten des ersten Markusorganisten angenommen haben. Eleonora stattete ihn bei seiner Abreise mit einem schmeichelhaften Geleitbrief aus[12]. Das Scheitern seiner Bewerbung um die Nachfolge Cavallis als Kapellmeister nahm dem

---

[5] Ein von mir MGG c. 1253 angegebenes Profeßbuch von San Salvatore erwies sich bei nochmaliger genauer Prüfung als versprengter Bestand des Jesuitenkonvents von S. Sebastiano.

[6] Wien, Österreichische Nationalbibliothek, Handschriftensammlung Codex 7654 (handschriftliches Formularienbuch der Kaiserinwitwe Eleonora Gonzaga), p. 209—210.

[7] Vgl. dagegen Anna MONDOLFI-BOSSARELLI, *Ancora intorno al Codice napoletano della Incoronazione di Poppea*, in: Rivista Italiana di Musicologia II 2, 1967, p. 307.

[8] Auch Francesco Usper-Sponga vertrat G. B. Grillo: Sandro DALLA LIBERA, *L'arte degli organi a Venezia*, Venedig-Rom 1962, p. 43 f. — Denis ARNOLD, *Usper*, in: MGG 13, 1966, c. 1184 f.

[9] Wien, Österreichische Nationalbibliothek a. a. O. p. 88—89.

[10] An Marco Faustini, Wien, 25. 7. 1665: Venedig, Archivio di Stato, Scuola Grande di S. Marco, busta 188, fol. 83r.

[11] Wien, Hofkammerarchiv, Hoffinanz, Indices, Band 885 (1667), fol. 156v.

[12] Wien, Österreichische Nationalbibliothek, a. a. O. S. 38—39.

damals Sechzigjährigen so gut wie jede Hoffnung. Man sieht daher einen Zusammenhang zwischen dieser Enttäuschung und dem Abgang nach Neapel. Er war dort bereits 1673 gewesen und könnte überhaupt mit den »Febi armonici« zusammengearbeitet haben, so daß man in seiner Reise nach dem Süden nicht unbedingt eine Reaktion auf diesen Rückschlag sehen muß. Jedenfalls überschritt Ziani seinen Urlaub und wurde von der Procuratia de Supra von San Marco zur Rückkehr in seine Pflichten aufgefordert[13]. Caffi hat aus der sich daraus entwickelnden Korrespondenz Zianis mit seinen Vorgesetzten ein rebellierendes Verhalten des Komponisten herausgelesen und seinen Charakter in ein etwas übles Licht gebracht, was auf spätere Darstellungen nachwirkte. Ohne seine Deutung auszuschließen, muß doch darauf verwiesen werden, daß Zianis ständige Versicherungen, ausschließlich Krankheit mache ihm die Reise unmöglich, keineswegs unglaubhaft klingen und einmal auch mit einem notariell beglaubigten ärztlichen Zeugnis belegt wurden. Auch klagt er bereits in seinen Briefen aus Österreich an Marco Faustini über verschiedene Leiden[14]. Wenn die neapolitanischen Akten als zusätzliches Indiz für Zianis Intrigantentum herangezogen werden, so muß dies sicherlich ebenfalls mit einiger Vorsicht aufgenommen werden. Ziani war als Fremder zweifellos von vornherein mißliebig, und die Umstände seiner Anstellung und in der Hofkapelle der Vizekönige überhaupt konnten nicht dazu beitragen, ihm Sympathien zu erwerben.

Im Werkverzeichnis Pietro Andrea Zianis in MGG ist zu berichtigen, daß von *Circe* (Wien 1665) keine Musik überliefert ist, hingegen die dort darüber gemachten Angaben auf *L'Elice* (Wien 1666) zu beziehen sind. Ferner ist auch von *La ricreazione burlesca* (Wien 1663/68) eine Partitur in der Österreichischen

---

[13] Venedig, Archivio di Stato, Procuratia de Supra, busta 91, processo 208, fasc. 2, fol. 17r, 18r—v, 19r, 21r, 22r, 23r—v; ebendort, Procuratia de Supra, Decreti e terminazioni, vol. 147 (1675—1690), fol. 45v—46r, 50r (Abschrift Procuratia de Supra, busta 91, processo 207, fasc. 1, fol. 47r), 50v—51r (Abschrift ebendort fol. 48r—v). — Francesco CAFFI, *Storia della musica sacra nella già Cappella ducale di San Marco in Venezia dal 1318 al 1797*, Bd. I, Venedig 1854, Antonelli, p. 304 f.

[14] Dieser Briefwechsel befindet sich in einem umfangreichen Bestand von venezianischen Theaterakten (Venedig, Archivio di Stato, Scuola Grande di San Marco, buste 188 und 194), dessen Entdeckung ihr eigenes Schicksal hatte: Der erste unbeachtet gebliebene (und vom Verfasser aus purem Zufall gefundene) Hinweis dürfte 1887 erfolgt sein: »C.« [B. CECCHETTI], *Carte relativi ai teatri di San Cassiano e dei Santi Giovanni e Paolo*, in: Archivio Veneto tom. 34, 1887, p. 246. Hermann KRETZSCHMAR veröffentlichte aufgrund ihm von Taddeo von WIEL überlassener Abschriften daraus deutsche Auszüge von Briefen Cavallis, Cestis, Zianis und Pollarolis (*Beiträge* und *Neue Beiträge zur Geschichte der venetianischen Oper*, in: JbP 14/1907, 1908, p. 71—81, bzw. 17/1910, 1911, p. 61—71), ohne jedoch die Quellen anzugeben oder zu kennen, was ihm den nicht ungerechten Tadel von Henry PRUNIERES eintrug (*Cavalli et l'opéra venitien au XVIIe siècle*, Paris 1931, Rieder, p. 33). Erst in den letzten Jahren konnten die Bestände von Remo GIAZOTTO neu entdeckt werden; sie wurden von ihm mit korrekten Angaben und ausführlichen Auszügen veröffentlicht (*La guerra dei palchi*, in: Nuova RMI 1, 1967, p. 245—286 u. 465—508; dazu Ergänzungen aus anderen Beständen ebendort 3, 1969, p. 906—933, und 5, 1971, p. 1034—1052).

Nationalbibliothek in Wien vorhanden[15]. Die Libretti zu einigen bisher unbekannten Oratorien Zianis fanden sich in der Biblioteca Marciana in Venedig im
Nachlaß Apostolo Zenos, einem Bestand, auf dessen außerordentlichen Wert für
die Wiener Theatergeschichte Luigi Ferrari aufmerksam machte[16], der aber noch
(wie Ferrari selbst andeutet) über dessen Angaben hinaus unbekanntes Wiener
Material enthält. Von Pietro Andrea Ziani befinden sich dort folgende in MGG
noch nicht genannte Titel: *Oratorio dell'incredulità di S. Tomaso,* Text von Giovanni Antonio Scacchi, Wien 1665, Cosmerovius. — *Oratorio di S. Pietro pian-
gente,* Text von Pietro Guadagni, Wien 1665, Cosmerovius; Exemplar auch in
der Universitätsbibliothek Graz[17]; wahrscheinlich ist die Musik in der anonymen
Partitur 18926 der Österreichischen Nationalbibliothek erhalten. — *Gli affetti
pietosi per il sepolcro di Cristo,* Text von Domenico Federici, Wien 1666,
Cosmerovius; auch handschriftlich in der Österreichischen Nationalbibliothek[18]. —
Bei dem im alten Partiturenverzeichnis der Wiener Hofkapelle geführten und
inzwischen verlorenen *Oratorio: Lagrime della Vergine nel Sepolcro di Cristo*
(1662), Text von Aurelio Amalteo, liegt wohl Identität mit *Lagrime della
Pietà nel sepolcro di Cristo* vor, dessen Libretto (Wien 1667, Cosmerovius)
ebenfalls an der genannten Stelle und im Civico Museo Bibliografico Musicale
in Bologna erhalten ist[19].
Als Pietro Andrea Ziani 1684 in Neapel im Sterben lag, hatte er außer seinem
Schüler Cristoforo Caresana einen Neffen bei sich[20]. Es ist möglich, daß dies der
damals 31jährige Marc'Antonio gewesen ist. Er hatte am 29. Mai 1677 die
Übernahme eines Briefes der Prokuratoren an seinen Onkel bestätigt[21], stand mit
diesem also in näherer Verbindung. Zu Marc'Antonio Zianis Biographie wäre
zu ergänzen, daß er vor seiner Ehe mit Giacomina (vielleicht einer geborenen
Fantin) mit einer Ursula verheiratet war, die am 29. April 1703 mit 42 Jahren
in Wien starb, eine Woche nach ihrer sechzehnjährigen Tochter Margareta[22]. Ein

---

[15] Siehe dazu neuerdings Isolde BARTELS, *Die Instrumentalstücke in Oper und Oratorium der
frühvenezianischen Zeit. Dargestellt an Werken von Cavalli, Bertalli, P. A. Ziani und Cesti
anhand der Bestände der Österreichischen Nationalbibliothek in Wien,* mschr. Diss. Wien 1971.
[16] Luigi FERRARI, *Per una bibliografia del teatro italiano in Vienna,* in: Studi di bibliografia e
di argomento romano. In memoria di Luigi Gregori, Rom 1949, Palombi, p. 136—150.
[17] Anton MAYER, *Wiens Buchdrucker-Geschichte 1482—1882,* Bd. I, Wien 1883, Frick, p. 311.
[18] Marcus LANDAU, *Die italienische Literatur am österreichischen Hofe,* Wien 1879, Gerold, S.
18. — *Tabulae codicum manu scriptorum praeter graecos et orientales in bibliotheca palatina
Vindobonensi asservatorum,* Bd. VII, Neudruck Graz 1965, Akademische Druck- u. Verlags-
anstalt, p. 199 (13276).
[19] Gaetano GASPARI - Ugo SESINI, *Catalogo della biblioteca del Liceo musicale di Bologna,* Bd.
V/1, Bologna 1943, Azzoguidi, p. 554.
[20] Ulisse PROTA-GIURLEO, *Breve storia del Teatro di corte e della musica a Napoli nei sec.
XVII—XVIII,* in: F. de FILIPPIS - U. PROTA-GIURLEO, *Il teatro di corte del Palazzo Reale
di Napoli,* Neapel 1952, p. 38.
[21] Venedig, Archivio di Stato, Procuratia de Supra, busta 91, processo 208, fasc. 2, fol. 22r.
[22] Wien, Archiv der Stadt Wien, Totenprotokoll 20 (1701—1705), fol. 187r, 189v.

Brief Zianis an Giacomo Antonio Perti von Wien, 28. Juli 1703, läßt noch seinen Schmerz über diesen Schlag erkennen[23]. Derselbe Brief zeigt auffallende Vertrautheit mit den musikalischen Verhältnissen Bolognas, was auf einen längeren
Aufenthalt, vielleicht zu Studienzwecken, schließen läßt.

Interessant im Bezug auf Ziani ist eine leider nicht belegte Angabe Caffis, er sei
der Lehrer Caldaras gewesen[24]. Da beide von Herzog Ferdinando Carlo von
Mantua protegiert wurden, ist diese Möglichkeit nicht auszuschließen. Ziani
könnte Caldara in diesem Fall vielleicht auch die Wege zu seinen Anstellungen
bei Ferdinando Carlo und bei den Habsburgern geebnet haben.

Als Ziani nach Wien berufen wurde, war er bereits einer der am meisten geachteten Opernkomponisten. Er scheint seinen Ruhm am Kaiserhof noch vermehrt
zu haben. Die ihm hier entgegengebrachte Schätzung zeigt sich in der Gewährung
einer Gnadenpension nach seinem Tod nicht nur für seine Gattin, sondern auch
für seinen Bruder Francesco, ein singulärer Fall[25]. Des Ablebens Zianis wurde in
seiner Heimatstadt mit einer großen Trauermusik unter Mitwirkung Senesinos
in San Salvatore gedacht[26].

Die Familienverhältnisse der beiden Ziani haben sich bisher nicht klären lassen.
Wohl gibt es im 17. Jahrhundert Träger des Namens in Venedig, darunter den
Komponisten Alessandro und die Sängerin Margherita[27]. Ein Verwandtschaftsverhältnis ist aber nur bei einer Marietta Ziani und ihrem Gatten Carlo offenkundig[28]. In Mariettas Nachlaß befand sich unter anderem »Vn Retrato del
P. Ziani«, zweifellos Pietro Andrea, und »Vna Spineta con sotto li suoi piedi«,
was musikalische Interessen belegt. Einen mutmaßlichen Bruder Carlo erwähnt
Pietro Andrea Ziani am 13. Dezember 1665 als verstorben[29]. Es könnte sich um
den Gatten Mariettas handeln. Da Mariettas hinterlassene Kinder 1678 Francesco, Battista, Anna Maria und Giustina genannt werden, steht fest, daß

[23] Bologna, Civico Museo Bibliografico Musicale.
[24] Francesco CAFFI, *Storia della musica teatrale in Venezia* IV, Manuskript in Venedig, Biblioteca Marciana, Cod. It. IV 748 = 10466, fol. 78r, 326v.
[25] Wien, Haus-, Hof- und Staatsarchiv, Obersthofmeisteramt, Akten, Karton 13, fol. 196r, 362r,
372r—v, 381r; ebendort Protokolle Band 8, fol. 400r. — Ludwig von KÖCHEL, *Johann Joseph
Fux*, Wien 1872, Hölder, p. 302 f., 305, 379 f.
[26] Eberhard PREUSSNER, *Die musikalischen Reisen des Herrn von Uffenbach*, Kassel-Basel 1949,
Bärenreiter, p. 66.
[27] Von Alessandro Ziani, Camaldulensermönch, gibt es eine Sammlung *Harmonie di Strumenti
Musicali* opus 1, Venedig 1683, Gardano (Exemplare in Bologna, Oxford, Münster), s. u. a.
Claudio SARTORI, *Bibliografia della musica strumentale italiana stampata in Italia fino al
1700*, Florenz 1952, Olschki, p. 506 f. u.v.a. — Alessandro und der unten und in MGG
genannte Geiger Pietro Ziani erwähnt von Sir Jack Allan WESTRUP in: Mf 22, 1969, p. 225.
Zu Margherita Ziani siehe Francesco FLORIMO, *La scuola musicale di Napoli e i suoi conservatori*, Bd. IV, Neapel 1882, Morano, p. 18 f.
[28] Nachlaßverhandlung der Marietta Ziani: Venedig, Archivio di Stato, Ospedali e luoghi pii,
busta 420, Nr. 13, processo 417, fol. 1r, 4r, 8r.
[29] Venedig, Archivio di Stato, Scuola Grande di S. Marco, busta 194, fol. 116r.

Marc'Antonio nicht von diesem möglichen Bruder Pietro Andreas stammen kann. Einen namentlich nicht genannten Bruder empfiehlt Pietro Andera Ziani in dem erwähnten Brief dem Theaterunternehmer Marco Faustini, vielleicht zum Einsatz in einer musikalischen Funktion. Ein Musiker namens Pietro Ziani ist aus späterer Zeit bekannt. Er steht jedenfalls in naher Beziehung zum jüngeren Ziani, könnte vielleicht dessen Vater gewesen sein. Die beiden waren zusammen im Dienst von San Marco und des Mantuaner Hofes und gehörten zu den Gründungsmitgliedern der venezianischen Cäcilienbruderschaft[30]. 1706 wird Pietro Ziani unter den besten Geigern Venedigs genannt[31]. Wenn er wirklich Marc'Antonios Vater war, müßte er damals gut siebzig Jahre gewesen sein, was eine Erklärung dafür wäre, warum er nicht auch mit an den Kaiserhof ging.

Die »Damira«-Opern

Pietro Andrea Zianis Oper *Le fortune di Rodope e di Damira* wurde erstmals im Karneval 1657 im Teatro Sant'Apollinare als das letzte dort gegebene Drama und die einzige Oper dieses Jahres in Venedig (wegen des Krieges um Candia) gegeben[32]. Pächter des Theaters war noch Marco Faustini, der jedoch den Vertrag mit den Besitzern von S. Apollinare damals eben löste oder gelöst hatte und die Pacht von San Cassiano übernahm. Hier standen ihm in nicht ganz geklärter Weise Marc'Antonio Corraro und Alvise (Luigi) Duodo zur Seite[33]. Diesen beiden ist das Textbuch der *Fortune* gewidmet. Der Text war die »*favola terza*« Aurelio Aurelis. Die Ausführenden waren Anna Maria Volta (Rodope), Giacinto Zucchi (Creonte), Anna Renzi (Damira), Carlo Macchiati (Nigrane), Filippo Manini (Breno), Carlo Manelli (Lerino), Raffaele Caccialupi (Sicandro), Antonio Draghi (Bato), Pietro Cefalo (Nerina) und Antonio Formenti (Erpago). Die Namen Mannelli und Draghi stechen natürlich hervor. Draghi scheint hier ein Jahr früher auf als in der gängigen Literatur und außerdem in der bisher nicht erwähnten Funktion als Opernsänger. Seine Verbindung mit Ziani, die zumindest einige Jahre später eine sehr freundschaftliche war, könnte dessen Berufung nach Österreich veranlaßt haben. Draghi befand sich bereits seit 1658 im Dienste Eleonora Gonzagas. Beide Komponisten traten hier übrigens in komischen Rol-

---

[30] F. Caffi, *Storia della musica sacra* a. a. O. Bd. II, 1855, p. 62. — Angelo Bertolotti, *Musici alla corte dei Gonzaga in Mantova*, Milano 1890, Ricordi, p. 114. — *Matricola del sovvegno de' Signori Musici sotto l'invocazione di S. Cecilia Vergine, & Martire Nella Chiesa di S. Martino*, Venedig 1691, p. 10—11.

[31] M. Coronelli, *Guida de' Forestieri sacro-profana per osservare il più ragguardevole nella Città di Venezia . . .*, Venedig 1706, p. 20.

[32] Textbuch Venedig 1657, Andrea Giuliani.

[33] Giazotto, a. a. O. 1, 1967, p. 257 f. — Cristoforo Ivanovich, *Minerva al tavolino*, Venedig 1681, Pezzana, p. 400.

len auf. Ein weiterer derartiger Part, Batos Gattin Nerina, wurde von einem Mann gesungen.

Aureli unterläßt es in seinem an den Leser gerichteten Vorwort nicht, dem Komponisten eine Verbeugung zu machen: »*Aggradisci le mie debolezze, honorate di Musica da la somma virtù del Signor Padre Ziani. Questi con la soavità del suo stile, & con l'inuentione dell'arie supplirà dolcemente à l'imperfettioni del Drama*«[34].

Weitere Aufführungen des Werkes gab es im Teatro Guastavillani in Bologna im Karneval 1658, wobei der Creonte von Agostino Trombetti gesungen wurde[35]. Ferner 1660 in Bergamo mit Anna Felicita Chiusi (Rodope), Pellegrino Canneri (Creonte), Virginia Camuffi (Damira), Francesco Maria Rascarini (Nigrane), Giacomo Filippo Biella (Breno), Antonio Rossi (Lerino), Antonio Secondo (Sicandro), Giovanni Battista Ferrari (Bato), Giovanni Botti (Nerina) und Antonio Franceschini (Erpago). In gleicher Besetzung fand die Aufführung 1661 in Mailand statt[36]. Im selben Jahr kam das Werk an das Nuovo Teatro in Livorno, 1662 an das Teatro di S. Lorenzo in Ferrara[37] und an das Teatro Regio in Turin. Hier wirkten zwei der eben genannten Sänger wieder mit; die Besetzung war Antonio Cavaglieri (Notte im Prolog und Erpago), Francesco Antonio Bertino (Aurora im Prolog), Anna Felicita Chiusi (Rodope), Francesco Galli (Creonte), Silvia Manni (Damira), Francesco Maria Rascarini (Nigrane), Angelo Maria Lesma (Breno), Carlo Lesma (Lerino), Giovanni Battista Pizzalla (Sicandro), Giovanni Antonio Borretti (Bato) und Giovanni Battista Righino detto Lucidano (Nerina)[38]. 1667 wurde die Oper auf dem Teatro de' Signori Accademici Filergiti in Forlì, 1669 auf dem des Unternehmers Rodino in Palermo, 1670 am Teatro Formagliari in Bologna, 1674 auf dem Teatro dell'Illustrissima Comunità in Reggio Emilia aufgeführt[39].

Von Marc'Antonio Zianis *Damira placata* lassen sich so umfangreiche Angaben nicht erbringen[40]. Die Aufführung — die einzige bekannte — fand in der Inverno-Stagione 1680 im Teatro San Moisè statt und zwar mit Holzpuppen. Die Sänger befanden sich hinter der Bühne. Von derartigen Aufführungen gab es in San Moisè noch mehrere[41], wobei die Texte immer von Filippo Acciajuoli

---

[34] p. 9 f.

[35] Textbuch bei Giacomo Monti. — Gaetano GASPARI, *Catalogo della Biblioteca del Liceo musicale di Bologna*, Bd. IV, Bologna 1905, Merlani, p. 176.

[36] Textbücher beider Aufführungen Milano s. a., Giulio Cesare Malatesta.

[37] Textbücher Livorno 1661, Gio. Vincenzo Bonfigli; Ferrara 1662, Gio. Battista Maresti.

[38] Textbuch bei Bartolomeo Zavatta.

[39] Textbücher Forlì s. a., Giovanni Saporetti; Palermo 1669, Bua e Camagna; Bologna 1670, Herede di Benacci; Reggio 1674, Prospero Vedrotti.

[40] Textbuch Venedig 1680, Francesco Nicolini.

[41] Alfred WOTQUENNE, *Catalogue de la Bibliothèque du Conservatoire de Musique de Bruxelles*, Ann. I: *Libretti d'Opéras et d'Oratorios italiens du XVIIe siècle*, Brüssel 1901, Schepen und Katto, p. 49. — Livio Niso GALVANI, *I teatri musicali di Venezia nel secolo XVII*, Milano 1878, Ricordi, p. 61 f.

stammten, der auch die Überarbeitung des Aurelischen Textes für Ziani vornahm. Das Libretto ist »*consacrato al genio de' Curiosi*«; an die »*Curiosi*« ist auch das hübsche Widmungsgedicht gerichtet, welches die stehende Figur des »*Bell'vmore*« unterzeichnet.

Von beiden Opern sind handschriftliche Partituren in der Biblioteca Marciana in Venedig überliefert. Pietro Andreas Drama hat die Signatur Cod. It. IV 450 = 9974, das Marc'Antonios Cod. It. IV 405 = 9925. Von Pietro Andrea Zianis *Fortune* sind außerdem Partituren in Modena (Biblioteca Estense Mus. F. 1301) und Neapel (Conservatorio S. Pietro a Majella 33.6.6.) vorhanden[42]. Die nachfolgenden Untersuchungen fußen auf den venezianischen Partituren.

DER TEXT

Da die vorliegenden Ausführungen sich mit der Musik der beiden Opern beschäftigen wollen, wurde auch für den Text jener der beiden Partituren der Biblioteca Marciana zugrundegelegt. Er zeigt teilweise recht erhebliche Unterschiede gegenüber den Libretti. Namentlich trifft dies für Pietro Andrea Zianis Drama zu. Hier muß dies wenigstens zum Teil auch bei der Aufführung so gewesen sein, da der Inhalt von Szenen, die in der Partitur fehlen, im Textbuch aber enthalten sind, in der ersteren in späteren Szenen nacherzählt wird. Da dies vor allem im letzten Akt der Fall ist, ist anzunehmen, daß die Notwendigkeit des raschen Fertigwerdens drastische Verkürzungen erzwungen hat. Die Partitur hat im dritten Akt nur 12 Szenen gegen 22 des Libretto. In den letzten beiden Szenen der Partitur fehlt auf weite Strecken auch die Textunterlegung, ferner weisen die Szenen des dritten Aktes keine durchlaufende Numerierung auf.

Die Dichtung Aurelis handelt von der schönen ägyptischen Dame Rodope, zu welcher König Creonte so sehr in Liebe entbrannte, daß er, um sie besitzen zu können, sich seiner Gattin Damira entledigen wollte. Er lockte diese unter dem Vorwand einer Lustfahrt auf dem Nil auf ein Schiff und ließ sie darauf unversehens allein abtreiben. Da das Schiff an einem Felsen scheiterte, glaubte er die Königin tot und holte Rodope an seinen Hof. Damira war es jedoch gelungen, sich schwimmend zu retten. Der Bauer Bato fand sie — sie gab sich als Waise Fidalba aus, welche aus Verzweiflung den Tod gesucht habe —, brachte sie zu seiner Frau Nerina und nahm sie als Tochter an.

So stehen, nach dem *Argomento* des Textbuches, die Dinge beim Beginn der Oper. Der eigentlichen Handlung geht ein Prolog voraus, der in der »Reggia del Diletto« spielt. Diletto stellt sich als der Regent des bevorstehenden Vergnügens vor. Auf sein Geheiß öffnet sich der Vorhang. Man sieht Diletto selbst mit Lascivia, wie sie Himeneo

---

[42] Pio LODI, *Catalogo delle Opere Musicali . . . Città di Modena, R. Biblioteca Estense*, Parma s. a., Fresching, p. 141. — Guido GASPERINI u. Franca GALLO, *Catalogo delle Opere Musicali . . . Città di Napoli, Biblioteca del R. Conservatorio di Musica di S. Pietro a Majella*, Parma 1934, Fresching, p. 313.

einschläfern, um ihm Fackel und Kette zu rauben und damit den Bund Rodopes und Creontes zu schließen. Giunone erscheint in macchina, hält sie auf und weckt Himeneo, der erschreckt das Geschehene bemerkt. Auf Geheiß Giunones erhält er seine Attribute zurück, muß aber dieser die Wiedervereinigung Damiras und Creontes und den anderen beiden einen geliebten Mann für Rodope versprechen. Lascivia und Diletto bejubeln die Lösung in einem Schlußduett, in welchem Diletto wieder aus der Rolle des stehlenden Intriganten heraustritt und sich als der beherrschende Lenker angenehmer Unterhaltung präsentiert: »*Del diletto / sol ricetto / quest'albergo hoggi sarà…*«.

Die handelnden Personen der Oper selbst sind die beiden Rivalinnen Rodope und Damira (beide Sopran), Creonte (Baß), sein Gefolgsmann Sicandro (Tenor), das Bauernpaar Bato (Baß) und Nerina (Alt), Rodopes beide Anbeter Nigrane und Breno (beide Alt), ihr Diener Lerino (Sopran) und die Episodenrolle des Hofmalers Erpago (wechselt zwischen Tenor- und Baßschlüssel). Creonte hat keine einzige Arie zu singen, was vermutlich auf Besetzungsschwierigkeiten bei der Aufführung zurückzuführen ist.

Die Handlung beginnt in der Nähe von Batos Behausung in einer »Campagna di Vendemia«, vielleicht einer Anspielung auf Gegenden der venezianischen Terraferma. (I 1) Creonte ist bei der Jagd unter sein Pferd gestürzt, Bato hat ihn für tot hervorgezogen und trägt ihn auf den Schultern weg. So trifft ihn Sicandro, der Creonte nachgefolgt ist. Als Sicandro Creonte atmen sieht, eilt er um Wasser. (2) Der alleingelassene Bato will seine Angst durch Singen bekämpfen. Als Creonte zu sprechen beginnt, läuft er davon, (3) wird jedoch von Sicandro aufgehalten. Dieser überzeugt ihn mit Mühe, daß er es nicht mit einem Geist, sondern mit einem Lebenden zu tun habe. Als Bato erfährt, wen er gerettet hat, ändert er sein Verhalten und erinnert deutlich an Creontes Dankesschuld ihm gegenüber. Creonte lädt ihn mit Frau und Tochter an den Hof. (4) Kaum ist Bato weg, erkundigt sich Creonte nach Rodope und befiehlt eilige Rückkehr.

(5) Damira beklagt ihr Los. (6) Nerina kommt dazu und warnt sie vor dem Alleinsein und den dabei drohenden Gefahren für ihre Keuschheit. (7) Bato bringt die Nachricht von der Einladung.

(8) In den Gemächern Rodopes versichern sich diese und Nigrane ihre Liebe. Rodope hofft, bald Königin zu werden und für sein Wohl wirken zu können. Nach zärtlichem Abschied Nigranes (9) kommt Lerino und meldet Breno. An diesem, meint Rodope, liege ihr nicht viel, doch sei sie ihm als ihrem ersten Liebhaber schuldig, Liebe zu heucheln, (10) was sie in der nächsten Szene auch tut. (11) Lerino meldet Creontes Ankunft, Rodope vertröstet Breno zärtlich, (12) um sich nach seinem Abgang über ihn lustig zu machen und ein fröhliches Lied von Amor, der mit den Herzen spiele, zu singen. Beim Nahen des Königs lehnt sie sich zurück, um Trauer vorzuschützen. (13) Creonte, davon betroffen, wird von ihr mit Vorwürfen überfallen und endlich dazu gebracht, in die Ehe einzuwilligen. In diesem Augenblick fällt ein Gemälde von der Wand, auf welchem der Untergang Damiras dargestellt ist. Entsetzt entfernt sich Creonte. Rodope beschließt, nicht nachzugeben. (14) Lerino, ärgerlich über das Bild, bleibt allein zurück.

(15) Breno und Nigrane treffen zusammen und prahlen mit ihrer Liebe. Eben als sie erkennen, daß sie dieselbe, Rodope, lieben, (16) fährt Creonte dazwischen und gebietet ihnen bei Todesstrafe, die Residenz bis abends zu verlassen.

(17) Damira begrüßt die ihr wohlbekannten Mauern des Palastes, (18) gefolgt von Bato und Nerina. (19) Sie treffen Sicandro, der sie zu Creonte bringen will.

(20) Lerino spottet auf die Liebenden, die mit Seufzern anstatt mit Gold werben. (21) Da kommt Nerina, die die Ihrigen verloren hat, und bittet ihn, sie zu Creonte

zu bringen. Sie gehen, geraten aber in ein Maskentreiben — eine direkte Bezugnahme auf den ja während der Aufführung im vollen Gang befindlichen venezianischen Karneval.

(II 1) Damira erblickt das Bild ihres Unterganges. (2) Sicandro, von Bato zu Damiras Schutz geschickt, während Bato selbst Nerina suchen will, kommt und erklärt ihr die auf dem Bild dargestellten Umstände. Von Schmerz überwältigt, fällt ihm Damira ohnmächtig in die Arme. (3) Dies sieht die immer argwöhnische Nerina, die mit Lerino daherkommt, und wird dadurch in ihrer Ansicht bestärkt, daß das einzige Heilmittel für ihre Tochter ein Mann sei; Sicandro und Lerino bieten sich sofort dafür an. (4) Nigrane verabschiedet sich von Rodope, die ihm jedoch Rettung verspricht, da sie noch heute Königin zu werden hoffe. (5) Lerino bringt eine Rose für Rodope, in der Nigrane ein Symbol seines Schicksals sieht. Er sieht Breno kommen und geht zum Schein, um ihn und Rodope heimlich zu beobachten. (6) Rodope verlangt von Lerino einen Spiegel und erblickt darin Creonte, der ebenfalls herbeischleicht. Breno erklärt ihr seine Liebe, sie weist ihn schroff ab, flüstert ihm aber zu, daß Creonte lausche. Alle drei Liebhaber sind von ihrer Treue überzeugt. (7) Lerino, der zugesehen hat, meint, er würde nur lieben, wenn er sicher vor solchem Verrat wäre.

(8) Creonte übergibt Bato und Nerina die Aufsicht über den königlichen Garten.

(9) Rodope entzündet Creontes Liebe und ringt ihm das Eheversprechen ab, (10) da tritt Damira dazwischen. Sie hat beschlossen, sich wahnsinnig zu stellen, und verflucht und feiert das Paar in dauerndem Wechsel, bis sich Creonte schließlich, von der Ähnlichkeit Fidalbas mit der toten Damira und ihren Reden erschüttert, entfernt, um nicht selbst verrückt zu werden. (11) Sicandro berichtet Nerina und Bato von der Szene.

(12) Der von Gewissensbissen geplagte Creonte ist beim Denkmal Damiras, (13) als Lerino erscheint, um ihn zu Rodope zu rufen. (14) Da kommt Damira und beginnt wieder ihr Spiel, entfernt sich aber wieder und läßt den König verzweifelt zurück. Es fehlt an dieser Stelle in der Partitur Creontes Äußerung (vor seinem Abgang), er habe den Eindruck, der Schatten Damiras rufe ihm ständig zu: »*Se Damira morì Rodope mora.*« (15) Diese Worte hört Rodope, wiederholt sie und beschließt, ihm zuvorzukommen. (16) Sie verspricht Breno die Ehe für die Ermordung Creontes (17) und gleich darauf Nigrane, er werde König und sie Königin sein, wenn er den Mörder Creontes töte. (18) Nigrane bleibt ratlos zurück.

(19) Nerina verfolgt Bato mit Eifersucht. (20) Damira kommt und stellt sich auch ihnen gegenüber von Sinnen. (21) Da eilt Sicandro herbei und warnt vor einer Schar von Narren, welche der Spur der einen Närrin folgten. Bato flüchtet zu langsam und wird von den Narren eingekreist.

(III 1) Rodope befiehlt dem Hofmaler Erpago, Damiras Bild aus ihren Zimmern zu entfernen und durch ein anderes zu ersetzen, auf dem eine Wütende einen Hartherzigen töte. Erpage rät ihr, lieber einen neuen Liebhaber zu suchen. Sie gehen und lassen das Bild stehen. (2) Der ohnehin aufgewühlte Creonte findet es (3) und ist noch mehr erschüttert, als die vermeintliche Doppelgängerin Damiras erscheint und ihn, nachdem sie ihn wieder gequält hat, alleine läßt. Im Libretto folgt nun das Attentat Brenos auf Creonte, das Nigrane verhindert, der jedoch, da Breno flüchtet, selbst für den Täter gehalten und von Creonte zu Kerker und Tod verurteilt wird; in der Partitur erfährt man dies erst später (8. Szene) aus Nigranes Mund. (4) Der gefangene Nigrane hat nur noch den Wunsch nach einem letzten Blick Rodopes (5) und trägt dem vorüberkommenden Bato seine Abschiedsworte an die Geliebte auf. (6) Dieser bestellt sie und erhält als Lohn eine goldene Kette, (7) was von der dazutretenden Nerina für einen Liebeslohn gehalten wird. Streitend gehen die Eheleute auseinander.

(8) Zu Nigrane in den Kerker kommen Rodope und Lerino in Masken. Nigrane erhält von Rodope deren Kleider und entfernt sich mit Lerino. (9) Rodope, über den Fehlschlag Brenos ärgerlich, bleibt zurück.
(10) Breno bemerkt Vorbereitungen zu einem Karnevalsfest und will im Schutze der Masken seinen Anschlag wiederholen. (11) An der Ausführung dieser Absicht wird er jedoch abermals von Nigrane gehindert, der eben mit Lerino auf dem Weg aus dem Kerker auf Creonte getroffen ist. Nigrane gibt sich zu erkennen, erklärt dem König, er habe ihm schon zum zweiten Mal das Leben gerettet, und teilt ihm mit, daß Rodope im Kerker sei. Die übrigen Personen und (12) Rodope erscheinen. Alles wird aufgeklärt. Creonte kehrt reumütig zu Damira zurück, auf deren Fürsprache Rodope und Breno Verzeihung erlangen. Nigrane und Rodope werden vereinigt. Damira wird von allen gefeiert.

Bei Acciajuoli und Marc'Antonio Ziani haben vier der handelnden Personen andere Namen: Rodope heißt hier Fillide, Bato Silo, Nerina Lerina und Lerino Nerillo. Zwei andere, Sicandro und Erpago, fallen überhaupt weg; die Funktionen des ersteren übernimmt weitgehend Nerillo mit, eine seiner Arien geht auf Creonte über («*Che non può donna che bella*», in beiden Opern I 4), der hier zum Unterschied von Pietro Andrea Ziani auch einige Arien zu singen hat. Andere Stimmlagen als bei Pietro Andrea haben Silo (Tenor), Breno (Sopran) und Nerillo (Alt). Die Gesamtzahl der Arien ist trotz der Einschränkung der Personen höher als beim älteren Ziani (45 gegen 38).

(I 1) Die Oper beginnt hier mit der Szene Damiras (2) und ihrem Dialog mit Nerina (bei Pietro Andrea Ziani I 5—6). (3) Silo schlägt im Walde Holz und beklagt sein hartes Los, (4) als Creonte mit seiner Jagdgesellschaft kommt und über heftigen Durst klagt. Silo tritt hervor, gibt ihm zu trinken und erhält dafür die Einladung an den Hof (entspricht ungefähr Pietro Andrea I 3—4). (5) Auf Fillides Liebesszene mit Nigrane (P.A. I 8) folgt hier noch (6) eine Arie Fillides auf diesen. Die Szenen 7—13 entsprechen P.A. I 9—11 und 13—16. Dem Bannurteil Creontes folgt eine Szene (14), in welcher sich Nigrane und Breno freundschaftlich einigen, die Entscheidung ihrer Konkurrenz Amor zu überlassen. 15—17 sind inhaltlich die gleichen wie I 17—19 bei Pietro Andrea, nur übernimmt Nerillo die Rolle Sicandros.
II 1 entspricht P.A. II 4, in der folgenden Szene (2) versichert Fillide Breno ihre Liebe. (3) Nerillo, dem Breno leidtut, besingt die betrogenen Liebhaber. (4) Damira erblickt das Gemälde, (5) Nerillo kommt dazu, um sie in Silos Auftrag zu beschützen, und erklärt ihr die Bedeutung des Bildes. Als er ihr von der bevorstehenden Hochzeit Creontes mit Fillide erzählt, verlangt sie, zu Creonte gebracht zu werden. 6—9 entsprechen P.A. II 8—11 (mit Rollentausch Sicandro-Nerillo in der letzten), 10 bringt die Reue Creontes mit den schicksalhaften Worten (P.A. II 14), 11—14 korrespondieren mit P.A. 15—16 und 20—21.
(III 1) Creonte betrauert Damiras Tod am Nil als an ihrem Grab und schläft ein. (2) Breno sieht ihn und will ihn töten, wird aber von Nigrane aufgehalten und flieht. (3) Creonte erwacht, hält Nigrane für den Schuldigen und befiehlt seine Hinrichtung. Die folgenden vier Szenen (4—7) sind die gleichen wie bei Pietro Andrea Ziani.
(8) Breno fühlt sich vom Schicksal verraten und wirft verzweifelt die Mordwaffe weg. (9) Damira findet sie und beschließt, Fillide damit zu töten.

(10) Zu Nigrane im Kerker (11) kommt Fillide mit Nerillo. (12) Während die Liebenden nebenan ihre Kleider tauschen, besingt Nerillo das harte Los, Verliebten zu
dienen.

(13) Nerina, welche sich wegen der Verführung Silos an Fillide rächen will, hinter-
bringt Creonte, sie habe diese mit Nerillo maskiert aus dem Kerker kommen sehen.
Sie verbergen sich in Fillides Zimmern. (14) Nigrane kommt mit Nerillo. Er legt sich
nieder um zu schlafen, und auch Nerillo, der versprochen hat, ihn zu bewachen, schläft
sofort ein. (15) Damira erscheint mit Brenos Schwert, erblickt Nigrane in Fillides Kleidern und will die Rivalin töten. (16) Creonte stürzt mit Nerina aus dem Versteck hervor und hält sie auf. Da gibt sich Damira zu erkennen. Creonte bittet reumütig um
Verzeihung. Auch Nigrane offenbart sich. (17) Endlich tritt auch Fillide auf und be-
zichtigt Creonte, ihr nach dem Leben getrachtet zu haben. Alles löst sich wie bei Pietro
Andrea Ziani. Damiras Freudengesang beschließt die Oper.

Die Musik

Man könnte vermuten, daß der Überarbeitung des Textes Aurelio Aurelis durch
Filippo Acciajuoli auch eine solche der Musik entspräche, noch dazu wo es sich
um Onkel und Neffen, womöglich auch Lehrer und Schüler handelt. Davon
kann jedoch nicht die Rede sein. Marc'Antonio Ziani hat das Werk völlig neu
komponiert und zeigt in seiner Partitur so wenige Anklänge an jene des Onkels,
daß man meinen möchte, er habe solche absichtlich vermieden. Indes ist es ziemlich unsicher, ob er Pietro Andreas *Fortune* überhaupt kannte, war er doch zur
Zeit ihrer Aufführung in Venedig noch ein Kind und befand sich der ältere Ziani
längst in Neapel, als Marc'Antonio den Stoff bearbeitete.

Zeigen sich bei Vergleichen, auch bei solchen textgleicher Stellen der beiden
Opern, zunächst wenige direkte Gemeinsamkeiten, so ist es umgekehrt auch wieder nicht so, daß prinzipielle Unterschiede in der Weise der Vertonung auf
Schritt und Tritt in die Augen sprängen. Gerade bei den Textübereinstimmungen
sind die gewählten Arten der musikalischen Konzeption oft nicht mehr als zwei
Möglichkeiten auf derselben Ebene. Dennoch besteht ein Unterschied sowohl in
der Haltung gegenüber dem Drama als auch in den Eigenheiten der Komposition,
wobei diese letzteren zum Teil eine gewisse Entwicklung vom älteren zum jüngeren Meister zeigen.

Bei Pietro Andrea Ziani ist die Hauptgestalt des Dramas Rodope, der Typus der
schönen und klugen Frau, der Meisterin in den Freuden des Daseins, denen sie
nicht anheimfällt, sondern die sie mit überlegener Kunst der Lebensführung zu
genießen und zu steuern weiß. Diese Ausrichtung tritt im Drama selbst — Rodope, in den Personenverzeichnissen stets an erster Stelle, hat von den Haupt-
figuren die meisten (6) Arien —, noch mehr aber durch den Prolog hervor. Dieser wäre für die eigentliche dramatische Handlung entbehrlich, und Aureli mag
mit ihm vielleicht zunächst auch nur einer Konvention Genüge getan haben. Es

ist auch nicht auszuschließen, daß der Prolog zusätzlich durch Bezugnahme auf historische Ereignisse (aktuell wäre der Seesieg bei den Dardanellen 1656 gewesen) oder andere Begebenheiten der Zeit in Venedig motiviert wurde. Die Widmung an die beiden Theaterpächter, welche eben gemeinsam mit Faustini den neuen Kontrakt an San Cassiano geschlossen hatten, legt den Verdacht nahe, daß die im Geiste des »Diletto« spielende Geschichte von der Eheschließung Rodopes diese neue Theaterehe mitmeint. Ob dem nun so ist oder nicht, es ist jedenfalls verständlich, daß man bei der Aufführung in Reggio 1674 den Prolog offensichtlich nicht genügend begründet fand und ihn bearbeitete. Die Handlung wurde auf einen Prolog und zwei Intermedien zwischen den Akten ausgedehnt, inhaltlich verändert und ausgebaut. Die drei Akte erscheinen dadurch immer als die Folge der Ereignisse in den vorhergegangenen Rahmenepisoden. Diese bestanden aus dem Streit zweier Götterparteien, Venus (welche hier an die Stelle Junos trat), Himeneo und Amor auf der einen Seite, der einmal sogar Jupiter zu Hilfe kam, und Pluto und Lascivia auf der anderen.

Nun kommt aber, wie angedeutet, der ursprünglichen Fassung des Prologs zwar keine unmittelbare dramatische Funktion zu, doch hat sie sehr wohl einen inneren Bezug zum Drama, gibt eigentlich sogar dem Zuhörer den Schlüssel, wie er dieses aufzunehmen habe. Die Verkörperung des den Prolog beherrschenden »Diletto« in der Oper selbst ist Rodope. Um sie geht es im Prolog ja fast ausschließlich: ob sie ihr Glück mit Creonte, als Königin also, oder mit einem anderen findet, ist nicht wichtig, wenn es nur ein *»gradito e bel consorte«* ist — eine frivole Variante des barocken Motivs von der Hinfälligkeit von Ehre und Rang. Dieser leichtfüßige Charakter ist von Acciajuoli 1680 stark zurückgedrängt worden. Jetzt tritt Damira nicht nur im Titel, sondern auch in der Gesamtkonzeption in die führende Stellung. Mit zehn Arien hat sie weitaus die meisten von allen handelnden Personen. Möglicherweise war diese Modifikation durch die Umstände der Aufführung bestimmt, die sich an ein mehr exklusives Publikum gewandt haben könnte.

Für die Betrachtung der Komposition ist es aber von großer Wichtigkeit, daß bei Pietro Andrea Ziani der Zuschnitt des Dramas auf Rodope die musikalische Gestaltung des ganzen Werkes grundlegend bestimmt. Die Welt des Diletto, Rodopes, der Liebe findet in der Musik ihren Ausdruck in einer starken Bevorzugung pastoraler Thematik. Sie beherrscht den Prolog weitgehend und kommt in der Oper mehrfach bedeutsam zum Durchbruch. Neben dem pastoralen treten auch noch andere musikalische Typen in mehrfacher Verwendung auf. In dieser Abhängigkeit von der Typik der barocken Musiksprache unterscheidet sich Pietro Andrea Ziani deutlich von seinem Neffen. Selbstverständlich sind auch bei diesem die Thementypen nicht völlig verschwunden, doch werden sie von einer starken Tendenz zu individueller Gestaltung der einzelnen Stücke zurückgedrängt. Dabei kommt der kunstvollen thematischen Arbeit besondere Bedeutung zu, auch dies möglicherweise im Hinblick auf ein anspruchsvolleres Publikum, wennschon sich Marc'Antonio Ziani auch sonst als Meister gediegener Satzkunst zeigt.

Es versteht sich, daß die musikalische Typik bei Pietro Andrea Ziani nicht zu einer starren Schematik führt. Hingegen erreicht er damit eine Abrundung des musikalischen Geschehens, die sich in dieser Form beim Neffen nicht findet. Bei Marc'Antonio liegt eben das Hauptgewicht auf der subtilen Gestaltung jeder Nummer. Kunstgriffe wie die von Hermann Kretzschmar[43] hervorgehobene Geschlossenheit einer Szene durch Wiederaufnahme der ersten Zeile der Eingangsarie am Schluß des dieser folgenden Rezitativs (Damiras *»Che mi giova esser reina«*, I 5) gibt es bei dem Jüngeren nicht. Wohl aber zeigt Pietro Andrea Ziani in der formalen Disposition seines Prologes eine noch dichtere, an Monteverdi gemahnende Geschlossenheit der Gestaltung, welche die von Kretzschmar erwähnte Szene weit übertrifft. Der Prolog zerfällt in zwei Teile, einen statischen, mehr lyrischen, und einen vorwiegend rezitativischen, in welchem sich die kleine Handlung abspielt. Durch den recht einfachen Kunstgriff der Wiederholung zweier Stücke nach den ihnen jeweils folgenden erhält der erste Teil große musikalische Dichte: die Sinfonia wird nach dem einleitenden Rezitativ des Diletto (Bevorzugung von Dreiklangsschritten und mehrmaliges Erreichen des Spitzentones d^1 unterstreichen den Charakter des Heroldsrufes) wiederholt. Es folgt eine Arie des Diletto *»Lieto Dio«* und sodann ein Duett Diletto-Lascivia, dessen Text aus dem achtmaligen Absingen des Wortes *»Dormi«* besteht und das von einem mit ihm musikalisch identischen Instrumentalritornell eingeleitet und beschlossen wird. In derselben Form wird es nach einem zweiteiligen ariosen Gesang der Lascivia *»Vaghe stelle«* ebenfalls wiederholt. Derartige wörtliche Entsprechungen gibt es in dem nun folgenden zweiten Teil nicht, doch wird auch er von einem Duett Lascivia-Diletto beschlossen, so daß auch hier eine formale Beziehung besteht. Sie wird noch dadurch verstärkt, daß zwischen den beiden Duetten zwei Rezitative stehen, die ihrerseits eine musikalisch sehr dicht gearbeitete Arie Giunones umschließen.

Der planmäßigen Formgebung entspricht die Einheitlichkeit der musikalischen Gestaltung durch die bevorzugte Verwendung pastoraler Melodik. Unverhüllt repräsentiert den Pastoraltypus[44] freilich nur Dilettos *»Lieto Dio«*,

---

[43] *Weitere Beiträge,* a. a. O. p. 63.
[44] Herbert SEIFERT, *Einige Thementypen des Barock bei Beethoven,* in: Beethoven-Studien, Festgabe der Österreichischen Akademie der Wissenschaften zum 200. Geburtstag von Ludwig van Beethoven, Wien 1970, Böhlau, p. 144 ff.

1

während die übrigen Stellen Varianten darstellen. Von den drei Abschnitten der Sinfonia kommt dem Typus der dritte am nächsten:

2

Etwas weiter entfernt tritt er in Lascivias »Vaghe stelle« auf, mit der immer wieder zu beobachtenden punktierten Schlußwendung, der Quintabstieg auch am Anfang der Sinfonia:

3

Die Sekundvorhalte (im letzten Beispiel nur einer) treten betont in dem Einschläferungsduett »Dormi« auf; ihr Wiedererscheinen in Giunones Arie auf die Worte »Apri gl'occhi, incauto dio« nimmt vielleicht absichtlich darauf Bezug (Rückgängigmachung des »Dormi«):

4

Auch der Mittelteil der Sinfonia zeigt mit Quinte und nachfolgender Sext sowie stufenweisem Abstieg von dieser, der im weiteren Verlauf nochmals mit den Sekundvorhalten auftritt, Verwandtschaft zum Grundschema. Die hier auftretende gleichlaufende Achtelbewegung aller Stimmen findet sich auch als Struktur, jedoch ohne thematischen Bezug, im Schlußduett des Prologes, so daß allenthalben Fäden zwischen dem Prolog und der Sinfonia bestehen, die man somit als Vorahnung einer Programmsinfonie bezeichnen kann.

5

Im Verlauf der Oper tritt der Typus in verschiedenen Varianten auf. In der Gestalt, welche bei Ziani seine reinste Verkörperung darstellt, erscheint er außer in der Arie des Diletto noch zweimal. Zuerst bezeichnenderweise als Liebesarie Rodopes auf Nigrane (I 8), der ja von Anfang an ihre eigentliche Wahl ist und am Schluß ihr *»gradito e bel consorte«* wird. Das zweite Mal bedient sich dieses Typs Lerinos einigermaßen zynische Arie *»Donne, mi rassembrate simil a la pittura«*, womit er auf leichtsinnige Frauen wie seine Herrin Rodope anspielt (I 14):

6

In einer Stilisierung eigener Art verwendet ihn eine dreistrophige Arie (II 3), in welcher zuerst Nerina Damira als einziges Heilmittel ihres Leidens einen Gatten empfiehlt und dann sich Lerino und Sicandro nacheinander zu diesem Zweck sofort anbieten. In derselben Gestalt beginnt bald darauf eine Arie Lerinos, in welcher er versichert, er wolle zwar gerne lieben, aber sich nicht betrügen lassen (II 7):

7

Während aber im letzten Fall eine freie Weiterentwicklung folgt, bleibt der aufsteigende phrygische Tetrachord in der Strophenarie als Ostinato ständig präsent, nur mit Überleitungsfloskeln zwischen den Zeilen und, in der Mitte der Arie, mit Wechsel der Tonhöhe (dis—e—fis—gis). Damit kommt zum Ausdruck, daß die an Damira gerichtete Rede aller drei Personen nur ein- und dieselbe leichtfertige Gesinnung offenbart, die beharrlich immer wieder vorgetragen wird. Allerdings bestehen doch gewisse kleine Unterschiede zwischen den Personen. In Nerinas und auch noch in Lerinos Strophen herrschen plappernde Tonwiederholungen und die mit Absprung erreichte pointierte Kadenz von Nerinas erster Zeile vor. Hingegen tritt bei dem seriöseren Sicandro die oft bei empfindsamen Stellen auftretende Folge von fallender Quarte und steigender Sekunde (wie am Anfang von Lerinos und Sicandros Strophe) in den Vordergrund.

Einen engeren Sinn hat ein ebenfalls sehr häufig anzutreffender Typus, der für Verstrickung, vor allem Liebesverstrickung, steht. Breno (I 15), Lerino (I 20), Nerina (II 11), Rodope (III 9) bringen ihn in Dur, Sicandro (I 4) in Moll:

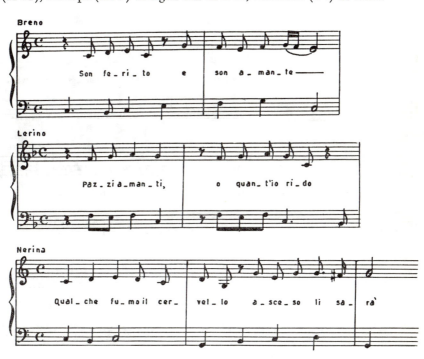

Auch hier gibt es eine spezielle Stilisierung, in welcher gleichmäßige Achteln das ausweglose Getriebenwerden charakterisieren; so vor allem bei Nerinas Warnung vor den Gefahren der Liebe, vor denen niemand gefeit sei (I 6), anfangs auch in Brenos Arie von seinem völligen Gefangensein durch den *Crin amato* Rodopes (III 10) und schließlich auch als Bato hilflos im Gewühl der Narren steckt (II 21):

9

Weitere derartige, auf allgemein gebräuchliche Floskeln zurückgehende Entsprechungen finden sich natürlich. So etwa die Dreiklangsmotivik, die durch wiederholte Wechselnoten charakterisierte Trompetenmelodik oder auch der schon innerhalb des Pastoraltypus beobachtete stufenweise Abgang der Oberstimme, meist von der Quint der Tonart und gerne mit Sekundvorhalten, und gleichzeitiger stufenweiser Aufwärtsbewegung des Basses. Ein Beispiel sei noch herausgegriffen, das zwar in den *Fortune* nur einmal (II 9) vorkommt, wegen der Parallelität zu einem anderen Werk des Komponisten jedoch Interesse erweckt. Es ist Rodopes Liebesarie auf Creonte »*O vita gradita*«:

10

Der Anfang der Arie entspricht wörtlich einer solchen in Zianis *Annibale in Capua*. Die lustige Person Gilbo — sie gleicht im Charakter dem Bato der *Fortune* — erteilt dort den Liebenden den Rat, nicht nur eine, sondern mehrere zu lieben[45]. Und an eben dieses Rezept hält sich ja Rodope in den *Fortune*. Bezeichnend, daß sie den Typus Creonte gegenüber verwendet, den sie ja nur im Sinne Gilbos liebt, während sie ihrer Liebe für Nigrane mit dem Pastoraltypus Ausdruck gibt.

Treten in der Verwendung der Thementypen und auch in der Auffassung des Dramas im besonderen und im allgemeinen Unterschiede zwischen den beiden Komponisten zutage, so finden sich in der Kompositionstechnik Übereinstimmungen, zum Teil auch Weiterentwicklung von Prinzipien des älteren durch den jüngeren Komponisten. Dies trifft vor allem auf die Verbindung der einzelnen Abschnitte der Arien zu, die »Kunst des Überganges« also. Ein von Pietro Andrea Ziani gebrauchtes, von Marc'Antonio aber zu einem der wichtigsten seiner Ariengestaltung erhobenes Prinzip ist das der Verknüpfung aller oder der meisten Abschnitte mit dem Beginn durch dasselbe Motiv. Dieses liegt zumeist im Baß und wird oft, aber nicht immer vom folgenden Singstimmeneinsatz wörtlich oder variativ imitierend aufgenommen. Dies ist sehr häufig auch dann der Fall, wenn es sich nicht um ein stehendes Motiv handelt. Bei Marc'Antonio Ziani fin-

[45] Hellmuth Christian WOLFF, *Die venezianische Oper in der zweiten Hälfte des 17. Jahrhunderts*, Berlin 1937, Klinz, p. 167, und Notenanhang Nr. 52. Wolff verweist auf den Correntencharakter und das Vorkommen des Typus (in Moll) auch in Cavallis *Giasone* (Abdruck in Robert EITNERS *Publikationen Aelterer Praktischer und Theoretischer Musikwerke*, Bd. XII, Leipzig 1883, Breitkopf & Härtel, p. 29).

det sich noch als Variante dieser Vorimitationen, daß die Singstimme nicht sofort, sondern erst in der nächsten Phrase auf das einleitende Baßmotiv zurück-
greift, zum Beispiel in der Renommierarie Brenos und Nigranes (I 14) gleich am
Anfang:

11

Das Prinzip der Verbindung aller Abschnitte durch dasselbe Motiv ist bei Pietro
Andrea Ziani noch nicht so ausgebildet wie bei seinem Neffen, immerhin aber
deutlich vorhanden. In Rodopes Arie »Luci belle« (I 8, Notenbeispiel 6), die sich
in einen Abschnitt im Tripel- und einen im geraden Takt gliedert, eröffnen im
ersteren die vier auftaktigen Achtel alle Zeilen, zunächst in der stufenweise auf-
steigenden Form wie anfangs, dann melodisch modifiziert. In Brenos ebenfalls
oben zitierter Melodie »Son ferito« (I 15, Notenbeispiel 8), welche die Seicento-
form a—b—b′ hat, steht das punktierte Wechselnotenmotiv des Basses am Anfang aller drei Teile, beim Übergang zum zweiten überdies durch den sich auf
den Beginn der Singstimme beziehenden Terzaufstieg (hier augmentiert und
punktiert) eingeleitet. Auch Giunones Arie im Prolog »Sorta è l'alba«, mit
welcher die Göttin Himeneo aus seinem Schlaf holt, zeigt solche verbindenden
Elemente. Diese Arie weist eine stetige Steigerung auf: Giunones erst sanftes,
ja wiegendes Wecken wird zusehends immer drängender, die zuerst vorwiegend
in engen Intervallen und abwärts sich bewegende Melodik wird weiter und steigt
auf; die Instrumente, die zunächst nur wiederholende Einwürfe vorbringen, beteiligen sich am thematischen Geschehen, um am Ende nochmals Giunone allein
das Wort zu lassen für eine letzte Steigerung bis zum entschiedenen »non dormir
più«. Im ersten Takt dieser Arie treten drei melodische Elemente auf: in der
Singstimme ein Wechselnotenmotiv und ein Oktavsprung, im Baß eine aufsteigende Skala in jambischem Rhythmus. Erste und zweite Verszeile werden dadurch verbunden, daß der Baß nacheinander das Oktav-, Wechselnoten- und
Skalenmotiv bringt, wobei die ersten unter einem Halteton, das letzte unter Re-
zitation auf e i n e r Tonhöhe erklingen, also alle drei deutlich hörbar hervor-
treten. Die Weiterführung der Singstimme in der zweiten Textzeile wird aus
dem Skalenmotiv entwickelt und schließt mit dem Wechselnotenmotiv, das
nun in eine Halbenote ausmündet. In dieser dezidierten Schlußform kehrt es
als Schlußpointe der Arie, in dem erwähnten »non dormir più«, wieder, das
zweimal den Höhepunkt von Sequenzsteigerungen bildet:

12

Am konsequentesten ist das Prinzip bei Pietro Andrea Ziani in den beiden Arienstrophen der Streitszene zwischen Bato und Nerina befolgt. Und dies ist insofern interessant, als hier der einzige Punkt ist, wo die beiden Opern wirklich eine überzeugende Parallele aufweisen (in beiden III 7). Diese besteht nicht nur in der Anwendung des gleichen Bauprinzips, sondern auch in der in den beiden Strophen jeweils verschiedenen Aufteilung der Textzeilen auf die musikalischen Abschnitte (Bato bzw. Silo 2—4—1, Nerina bzw. Lerina 3—2—1; der letzte ist immer die Wiederholung der ersten Textzeile; die Strophe der Gattin hat eine Textzeile weniger) und nicht zuletzt in der melodischen Übereinstimmung des Motivs selbst:

13

Beispielhaft läßt sich die Anwendung des Prinzips bei Marc'Antonio Ziani an Fillides von Instrumenten begleiteter Dacapo-Arie »*Fa quanto sai, fortuna perfida*« beobachten (I 10):

14

Dem Einsatz der Singstimme geht ein längeres instrumentales Zwischenspiel voraus. Dieses beginnt wie die Singstimme mit einem imitatorischen Einsatz des Themenkopfes, hier auf die beiden Oberstimmen aufgeteilt. Erst dann bringen die 2. Violine, vom Baß mit dem Themenkopf kontrapunktiert, und die 1. Violine das ganze Thema, von dessen Fortspinnung, dem Sechzehntelmotiv, dann Material abgespalten wird. Vor dem Beginn der Singstimme bringt der Baß, wie im Beispiel zu sehen ist, nochmals das ganze Thema und wiederholt es auch nach der ersten Zeile. Das »*Fa quanto sai*« wird zweimal in Eigenimitation vorgebracht, ehe mit einer neuen Wendung die Adressatin, »*fortuna perfida*«, angesprochen wird. Daß derselbe Text zweimal oder zwei kongruierende Zeilen musikalisch übereinstimmend (wörtlich, sequenzierend, imitierend), normalerweise mit Zwischenimitation des Basses (wie oben), vorgebracht werden und dann der Zielpunkt der Rede akzentuiert herausgestellt wird, ist ein innerhalb von Arien und Rezitativen häufig anzutreffender Vorgang. In der hier behandelten Arie bringt der Baß sofort nach »*fortuna perfida*«, noch in Engführung dazu, den Themenkopf und beantwortet ihn selbst auf der Dominante. Die dritte Textzeile »*ti rivincerò*« arbeitet schließlich wie der Schluß der Instrumentaleinleitung mit dem abgespalteten Material der Themenfortspinnung. Die Überleitung zum Mittelteil bildet ein Zwischenspiel der Instrumente mit den Partikeln des Themas. Die ersten beiden Zeilen des Mittelteils (»*a dispetto d'empio fato / del diadema sospirato / questo crin cinto vedrò*«) beginnen mit Tonwiederholungen der Singstimme zu stufenweise absteigenden Bässen, ein allgemein gebräuchliches Verfahren, das in diesem Fall aber außerdem an die Stufengänge von »*fortuna perfida*« anknüpft; an den Zeilenenden stehen kurze imitierende Einwürfe der In-

strumente mit dem Sechzehntelmotiv des Themas. Die letzte Zeile der Arie
nimmt in der Singstimme nicht mehr Bezug auf das Hauptthema; wohl aber
erfolgt die Überleitung zu ihrer Textwiederholung im Baß mit der Themenfortspinnung, bedient sich ein kurzer Instrumentaleinwurf in der Wiederholung des
Themenmaterials und wird schließlich zur wörtlichen (bis auf die Kadenz) Reprise wieder mit der variierten Themenfortspinnung übergeleitet.

Ein Charakteristikum dieser Arie bildet auch die schrittweise Entfernung vom
thematischen Material des Anfangs, was einen bei Marc'Antonio sehr oft zu
beobachtenden Zug darstellt. Oft wird dabei bis zum völligen Verlassen des Zu-
sammenhangs gegangen, oft bleibt der Ausgangspunkt aber auch, wie hier, bis
zum Schluß spurenhaft wirksam.

Eine einfachere Form der Anwendung eines stehenden Motivs für sämtliche Abschnitte besteht darin, eine geschlossene Baßphrase am Beginn und Ende und
zwischen den Zeilen wörtlich oder nicht gestaltverändernd variiert vorzubrin-
gen. So ist es in Silos »*L'esser povero*« (I 3), wo eine kolorierte Form des Baß-
themas auch dem ersten Abschnitt der Singstimme zugrundeliegt, oder in Brenos
Arie »*Per ciglio sì vago*« (II 12), deren Baßformel eine Variante der eben genannten ist:

15

Hier bildet die erste Zeile der Singstimme eine verkürzte Fassung der Baßformel. Bei der Überleitung zum Mittelteil wird der Skalenabstieg der Formel bis
zum a verlängert und dann die Kadenz angeschlossen, wodurch sich eine Modu-
lation nach F-Dur ergibt. Im Mittelteil, der in der Singstimme ebenfalls mit dem
Hauptthema beginnt, steht als vorletzter Unterabschnitt ein Solo der Singstimme; dasselbe ist auch im entsprechenden Abschnitt der auf das Da capo folgenden Coda der Fall. Die Geschlossenheit der Arie wird somit durch die Beziehung von Anfang bzw. Schluß des Mittelteils auf Anfang bzw. Schluß der
ganzen Arie noch verstärkt.

Nur am Anfang, als Baß der ersten Zeile und als ihr Schluß, wird in Creontes Devisenarie »*Pensieri molesti*« (III 1) eine Allerweltsfloskel gebracht:

16

Bei konsequenter Durchführung nähert sich diese Form dem Ostinato. Sie ersetzt ihn bei Marc'Antonio Ziani auch gewissermaßen, da sich bei ihm im Gegensatz zu Pietro Andrea kein Stück mit strengem Ostinato findet. Von dem Ostinato der Strophenarie »*So ben io*« bei Pietro Andrea Ziani wurde bereits gesprochen (II 3, Notenbeispiel 7). Nicht starr durchgeführt, mit dem Prinzip der sukzessiven Entfernung vom Thema kombiniert ist der Bau von Sicandros Klagearie »*Dolore ch'il core struggendo mi vai*« (I 1). Das vor und nach der Arie zu spielende Ritornell bringt eine Baßlinie, die zweimal variiert wiederholt wird (a–b–b'; der Anfang mit stufenweisem Quintaufstieg im Baß und gegenzügiger Bewegung der Oberstimmen mit Sekundvorhalten knüpft an oben besprochene Stellen des unmittelbar vorausgehenden Prologs an). Dieser Baß und seine erste variierte Wiederholung liegen auch der Arie zugrunde, die dann frei weitergeführt wird, jedoch mit weitgehender Beibehaltung der vorherrschenden Stufenbewegung des Basses. Da das Ritornell auch nach der Arie erklingt, hört man den Baß und seine Varianten insgesamt achtmal, was auch bei nicht völliger Konsequenz im Ostinato einen diesem entsprechenden Höreindruck erweckt. Eine richtige Passacaglia ist aber Nigranes Lamento (mit Instrumenten) »*Rodope dove sei*« (III 4). Der Baß teilt sich in einen chromatischen und einen diatonischen Teil:

17

Singstimme und Instrumente stehen im ganzen Stück in engem Wechselspiel. Die durch den Text geforderte Wiederholung der ersten Zeile findet bis auf den Anfang »Rodope« keine musikalische Entsprechung, auch das eine in solchen Fällen nicht seltene Erscheinung.

Dem Ostinato stehen die Formen mit gehenden Bässen, quasi ostinato, nahe. Sie kommen in Situationen vor, in welchen die jeweilige Person einer überwältigenden Tatsache gegenübersteht, die sich in dem unaufhaltsam vorrückenden Baß verkörpert, über dem das fühlende Herz seinen Affekten Ausdruck gibt[46]. Diese können positiv oder negativ sein, Brenos hingerissene Bewunderung des Liebreizes Rodopes ebenso wie Nigranes hoffnungslose Verzweiflung im Kerker. Die erstgenannte Szene findet sich in beiden Dramen (der Arientext ist allerdings nur anfangs identisch), und beide Komponisten haben hier zum gehenden Baß gegriffen. Der Singstimme in der ersten Zeile der Arie Pietro Andrea Zianis liegt ein stufenweiser Aufstieg zur Quint und ebensolcher Abstieg von der Terz als Gerüst zugrunde. In weniger verhüllter Form tritt diese Linie am Schluß des Ritornells zutage (mit Beginn in der 2. Violine und Rollentausch — in Ritornellen häufig — nach dem ersten Takt; die parallelen Oktaven im 2. Takt des Ritornells sic):

18

In der vokalen Fassung erfolgt also eine affektgerechte Stilisierung der Quintlinie mit empfindsamer Synkope auf dem zweiten »care« und Melisma auf »sembianze«. Was aber Marc'Antonio Ziani mit etwa gleichen Mitteln daraus macht, ist symptomatisch für die Steigerung des Affektausdruckes gegenüber dem Onkel, die in der ganzen Oper ständig zutagetritt und einen weiteren Unterschied zwischen den beiden im Sinne steigernder Weiterentwicklung ausmacht.

---

[46] Vgl. Wolfgang Osthoff, *Das dramatische Spätwerk Claudio Monteverdis*, Tutzing 1960, Schneider, p. 72 ff.

19

Die Baßformel des Arienanfangs tritt auch fernerhin des öfteren auf und erfüllt die besprochene Funktion als Überleitungsmotiv, hier jedoch eingebettet in den Fluß der gleichmäßigen Bewegung. Das zweimalige devisenhafte, durch »Suspiratio« getrennte Vorbringen des »care« erregt zusammen mit dem beharrlich schreitenden Baß eine Spannung, welche sich mit dem vollständigen Vortrag der ersten Zeile zwar löst, aber keinen Ruhepunkt findet: nicht nur behält der Baß seine Bewegung selbstverständlich bei, sondern es wird durch die Anfügung des absteigenden Melismas auf *belle* die Schlußwirkung der Kadenz aufgehoben. Diese Wendung tritt auch in den beiden folgenden Abschnitten (»*dell'acceso mio cor dolce ristoro / voi mi struggete*«) bei »*dolce*« und »*struggete*« auf. Nachdem die daran anschließende Zeile im Sinne des Prinzips der schrittweisen Entfernung vom Thema keine direkten Beziehungen dazu aufweist, nähert sich der nach ihr stehende Abschnitt wieder stark dem ersten, dessen Reprise anschließt. Eine Coda bringt die Wiederholung des Textes der ersten Zeile in neuer musikalischer Fassung und den Schluß im Baß mit einer gerafften Form jenes der ersten Zeile.

Schließlich sei noch auf das Phänomen der Devisenarie hingewiesen, die sich in der hier behandelten Oper Pietro Andrea Zianis selten findet (zum Beispiel Rodopes »*Opri il fato*« III 9, Notenbeispiel 8), während Marc'Antonio ausgiebigen Gebrauch von ihr macht.

Die oben getroffene Feststellung einer merkbaren Steigerung des Affektiven in Marc'Antonio Zianis Oper gegenüber der seines Onkels trifft auch auf die Rezitative zu. Hier kommt es dadurch bei dem jüngeren Komponisten einerseits zu interessanteren und musikalisch ansprechenderen Einzellösungen, andererseits aber auch zu einem gewissen Hintanstellen der größeren Zusammenhänge. Bei Pietro Andrea Ziani hält sich das Rezitativ auf weite Strecken im Rahmen der eingebürgerten Formeln, als da etwa sind Rezitationstöne, die von Takt zu Takt (oft auch seltener) wechseln; dabei im Falle des Aufsteigens gerne ein solches in die höhere Stufe des jeweiligen Dreiklanges, welche durchgängig erreicht wird; der Abstieg geschieht häufig zur Untersekund mit der oberen Wechselnote des verlassenen Rezitationstones, etc. Dazu kommen stehende Wendungen für bestimmte Inhalte, wie fallende Terz für Anrede, steigende Sekund für Frage usw. Es ist also ein gewisser Rahmen von Möglichkeiten — die angeführten sind natürlich nur einige — vorhanden, den man als Erzähl- oder Gesprächston charakterisieren könnte (oder mit Doni, wenn man ihn dieser späteren Zeit anpassen darf, als »*stile semplice*« oder »*narrativo*«[47]). Dieser Rahmen kann durchbrochen werden, wenn bestimmte Inhalte hervorgehoben werden sollen, die von madrigalesken Schilderungen von Einzelworten (»*volare*« etc.) bis zu Gefühlsausbrüchen reichen. In diesen Fällen erleidet der Normalverlauf des Rezitativs gewissermaßen affektive Deformationen. Kennzeichnend für Pietro Andrea Ziani sind die Rezitative Rodopes. Sie entfernt sich von allen Personen der Oper am wenigsten weit vom Gesprächston, bleibt sie doch immer die souveräne Beherrscherin der Szene, die auch schwierigen Situationen ohne Erregung gegenübersteht. Einmal verliert sie aber doch die Fassung: als ihr nämlich Bato die Botschaft bringt, Nigrane sei dem Tode geweiht und sende ihr das letzte Lebewohl; kaum hat sich Bato des Auftrages erledigt, will er davoneilen; doch Rodope hält ihn auf (III 6):

20

Die Pausen, Synkopen und der offene Dominantschluß, dem keine Tonika folgt (statt dessen bricht die eifersüchtige Nerina mit D-Dur herein), zeigen, daß Rodope hier auch musikalisch aus dem Gleichgewicht gekommen ist. Die sparsame Verwendung solcher Effekte macht sie natürlich um so wirkungsvoller.

Wie für Rodope lassen sich auch für andere Personen Pietro Andrea Zianis gewisse Charakteristika beobachten, ohne daß diese jedoch unbedingt auf die eine Figur beschränkt blieben. Die stets um Damiras Jungfräulichkeit besorgte und auf Bato eifersüchtige Nerina führt meist eine recht drastische Sprache, die eigentlich eher den Gemütsbewegungen der seriösen Personen zuständе und in ihrem Munde einen komischen Effekt hervorgebracht haben wird, zumal die Rolle ja von einem Mann gesungen wurde. In Creonte wird der empfindsame

---

[47] Giovanni Battista DONI, *Trattato delle musica scenica*, in: Lyra Barberina, Florenz 1763, Gorius, Bd. II, p. 33.

Liebhaber vom gebieterischen Herrscher geschieden. Die Sprache des letzteren, Unisoni mit dem Baß und deutliche Quintabsprungskadenzen, nimmt auch Bato auf, wenn er mit Creonte plump-vertraulich spricht (II 8). Der schwankende Charakter Creontes läßt ihn gelegentlich auch lächerlich werden, etwa wenn er die beiden ertappten Liebhaber Rodopes zwar zur Rede stellt und verbannt, aber doch nicht so recht den Despoten hervorkehren kann und immer wieder bei Nennung Rodopes in schwärmerische Epitheta ausbricht (»mio foco«, »mia cara«); hier bleiben die entschiedenen Töne aus (I 15). Ähnlich auch, als er den bohrenden Quälereien der vermeintlich verrückten Fidalba recht hilflos und unköniglich gegenübersteht (II 10). Unterschiedliche Personencharakteristik zeigt sich auch in der Szene, als Creonte und Nigrane, beide versteckt, der Abweisung Brenos durch Rodope lauschen (II 6). Auf Brenos glühende Liebeserklärung reagiert Creonte trocken-formelhaft, Nigrane dagegen aufgeregt und empfindsam:

21

In dieser Szene kommt jeder der drei Liebhaber zu dem Eindruck, Rodope sei nur ihm treu. Auch hier ist Nigrane der empfindsamste, Creonte der kühlste, während Breno (er glaubt, Rodopes Abweisung sei Verstellung) etwa die Mitte hält:

22

Auch rein musikalische Gliederungsfaktoren treten innerhalb des Rezitativs bei entsprechenden Textstellen auf. So korrespondieren oft Frage und Antwort bzw. überhaupt Rede und Gegenrede oder auch aufeinanderfolgende Sätze gleichen Sinnes wörtlich oder in deutlicher Entsprechung. In Damiras und Nerinas Dialog (I 6) steht die gleiche Formel dreimal hintereinander (Damira: »Honore, e continenza contro tali nemici sanno far resistenza« / Nerina: »È ver, ma chi ha *bellezza dura gran fatica in conservarla, / l'hor è una fortezza a cui per espugnarla più di un insidiator già mai non manca«*). Dieses Gliederungsmittel findet sich ebenso bei Marc'Antonio Ziani, so beim Wutausbruch Creontes über den vermeintlichen Attentäter Nigrane und dem darauffolgenden Dialog (III 3):

23

Bei beiden Komponisten geht das Rezitativ bei gefühlsbetonten Stellen in die üblichen kantablen oder überhaupt musikalisch gestalteten Partien, vorwiegend im Tripeltakt, über. Der Gegensatz zwischen diesen und den eigentlich rezitativischen Passagen wird von Pietro Andrea Ziani (II 20) zur Unterscheidung der scheinbar verrückten von den scheinbar normalen Äußerungen Damiras (vom Blickpunkt der Bühnenpersonen) eingesetzt. Marc'Antonio Ziani markiert diesen Unterschied ebenfalls deutlich, aber mit Mitteln der Gestik (II 8):

24

Diese beiden Pole verkehren sich in der Szene, als Rodope/Fillide zum ersten Mal Creonte zu einer raschen Eheschließung drängt (I 13 bzw. 10). Die wachsende Erregung wird bei Pietro Andrea Ziani durch ein immer stärkeres Umsichgreifen gehender Bässe illustriert, während Marc'Antonio an den entsprechenden Stellen ariose Führungen einschaltet. In der zweiten derartigen Szene, einem weiteren Anlauf Rodopes also, erscheint bei Pietro Andrea Ziani am Höhepunkt der Steigerung die unverblümte Forderung Rodopes mit Imitationen eines tonrepetierenden Motivs in komplementären Rhythmen (II 9):

Das Rezitativ seinerseits bricht bei Pietro Andrea Ziani auch gelegentlich in Arien oder ariose Partien ein, und zwar in der Rolle des Lerino. In dessen beiden Arien »Donne mi rassembrate« (I 14) und »Pazzi amanti« (I 20) — die dritte »S'io son buon« kommt für diese Technik als eine von drei Strophen nicht in Frage (II 3) — stehen rezitativische Einschübe, nach denen jeweils wieder in den Arienton zurückgegangen wird (im zweiten Fall mit Taktwechsel C — 3/4), worauf ein aus diesem letzten Abschnitt gewonnenes Ritornell folgt. An einer weiteren Stelle im Part Lerinos, als er Rodope die Rose bringt (II 5), beginnt er arios mit fließenden Achteln, unterbricht mit einer rezitativischen Passage und geht wieder in die erste Bewegung zurück. Bei Lerino könnten diese Einschübe ein Mittel der Personencharakteristik sein: daß nämlich der durch seine dauernden Blicke hinter die Kulissen illusionslos und pessimistisch gewordene Diener das dauernde Beharren in der gezierten Sprache seiner Umgebung einfach nicht durchhält. Bei Marc'Antonio Ziani findet sich ebenfalls ein rezitativischer Einschub in einer Arie, hier jedoch an einer völlig ernstgemeinten Stelle, als Damira zu dem Schluß kommt, daß sie das Verrücktspielen nicht weiterbringe (»Suol de' pazzi«, III 9): eben an diesem Punkt ihrer Überlegung geht sie mitten in der Arie für die Dauer einer Zeile ins Rezitativ über (»stolta fingermi non giova«).

Marc'Antonio Zianis Rezitativ sticht von Pietro Andreas deutlich ab. Er ist mit großen Intervallen, raschem Durchlaufen großer Tonräume in beiden Richtungen, empfindsamen Stilisierungen vielerlei Art, Wortmalereien viel schneller zur Hand als sein Onkel. Dadurch wird sein Rezitativ stets pathetischer, sozusagen deutlicher, aber im ganzen doch weniger differenziert. Durch das im wesentlichen doch unterschiedslose Eingehen auf den jeweiligen beschränkten Zusammenhang

tritt auch die Personencharakteristik kaum hervor. Ein kleines, nur wenige Takte
umfassendes Meisterstück des jüngeren Ziani sei aber noch erwähnt. Es steht am
Anfang der Szene, in der Damira mit dem Schwert Brenos in der Hand kommt,
um Rodope zu töten und diese plötzlich schlafend erblickt (in Wirklichkeit
Nigrane in Rodopes Kleidern). Die Spannung wird hier mit einem dauernd
wiederholten Baßmotiv erzeugt, im gegebenen Maßstab dieselbe Methode, der
sich Mozart im Finale des zweiten *Figaro*-Aktes bedient (III 15):

26

HÄNDELS PASTICCI

von *Reinhard Strohm* (München)

Die künstlerische und wissenschaftliche Auseinandersetzung mit Händels Opernschaffen ist gerade heute von der Art, daß sie zur Anteilnahme einlädt. Es ist derzeit gar nicht abzusehen, welchen Platz in unserem historischen Bewußtsein Händels Opern noch einnehmen werden. Je mehr man sich mit ihnen beschäftigt hat, desto deutlicher wurde allerdings auch der Abstand, der uns von jener Opernwirklichkeit trennt[1].

Ein Stück jener Wirklichkeit sind Händels Pasticci: die Opern also, die er aus Werken italienischer Komponisten für seine Londoner Bühne zusammenstellte. Die Händelforschung hat ihnen bisher nicht viel Aufmerksamkeit geschenkt, zumal es wichtigere Probleme gab[2]. Ein Grund für das geringe Interesse dürfte auch die verachtete Form des Pasticcio gewesen sein. Aber die Pasticcio-Praxis ist nicht nur bei Händel, sondern allgemein in der italienischen Oper des 18. Jahrhunderts eine ernstzunehmende Tradition.

Der Name »Pasticcio« (»Pastete«) findet sich weder auf Titelblättern noch in Textbüchern der Händelzeit. Umgangssprachlich war er jedoch vorhanden. Er bezeichnete Opern (oder Oratorien), welche aus Kompositionen verschiedener Autoren zusammengesetzt sind. In dieser Bedeutung erscheint er, bezogen auf das Jahr 1725, in Quantz' Lebensbeschreibung[3]. Während er in Italien damals vielleicht schon üblich war, muß er dem Ausländer aufgefallen sein. Für eine Abgrenzung des Begriffs scheinen zwei Merkmale wesentlich:

1. Die einzelnen Stücke (zumeist Arien) des Pasticcio sind überwiegend aus anderen Aufführungszusammenhängen herausgerissen und zu einem neuen Ganzen vereinigt. Nicht von derselben Art sind die Opern, die von vornherein unter

---

[1] Ein wichtiger Versuch, diesen Abstand bewußt zu machen und zu überbrücken, ist das Buch von Winton Dean, *Handel and the Opera Seria*, University of California Press 1969. Grundlegend zur Londoner Opernbühne: Joachim Eisenschmidt, *Die szenische Darstellung der Opern Händels auf der Londoner Bühne seiner Zeit*, 2 Bde., Wolfenbüttel 1940/1941 (= Schriftenreihe des Händelhauses Halle, Heft 5 und 6).

[2] Was wir bisher über die Pasticci wissen, ergibt sich aus folgenden Werken: Friedrich Chrysander, *G. F. Händel*, Bd. II, Leipzig 1860; Sesto Fassini, *Il melodramma italiano a Londra nella prima metà del Settecento*, Torino 1914, Bocca; Otto Erich Deutsch, *Handel. A Documentary Biography*, New York (1954); William C. Smith, *Catalogue of Works*, in: *Handel. A Symposium*, hrsg. von Gerald E. Abraham, Oxford University Press 1954, p. 275—310.

[3] Johann Joachim Quantz, *Lebenslauf, von ihm selbst entworfen*, in: Friedrich Wilhelm Marpurg, *Historisch-kritische Beyträge zur Aufnahme der Musik*, Bd. I, 5. Stück, Berlin 1755.

mehreren Komponisten aufgeteilt wurden (gewöhnlich aktweise), denn bei diesen »Gemeinschaftswerken« sind alle Stücke für die gleiche Aufführung bestimmt. Wo ferner ein Arrangeur eine geschlossene Vorlage ausschließlich mit eigenen Zusätzen modifizierte, sollte man eher von »Bearbeitung« sprechen; auch hier erscheinen die Stücke ungefähr in dem Zusammenhang, für den sie ursprünglich bestimmt waren.

2. Das Pasticcio enthält Kompositionen mehrerer Autoren. Sehr oft kam es vor, auch bei Händel, daß ein Komponist ältere eigene Arien in einen neuen Zusammenhang einführte[4]. Wo die bereits früher verwendeten Stücke überwiegen, könnte man den Nebenbegriff »Pasticcio aus eigenen Werken« gebrauchen. Der ungeschmälerte Autoranspruch, der sich an solche Opern noch knüpft, war aber für die damalige Zeit wichtig.

Der ästhetischen Problematik des Pasticcio-Verfahrens wird an anderer Stelle mehr Platz zu widmen sein. Es sei aber darauf hingewiesen, daß ein geschickt zusammengestelltes Pasticcio musikalisch und dramatisch nicht uneinheitlicher sein muß als eine ungeschickt »komponierte« Oper.

Im Italien des früheren 18. Jahrhunderts und auch in London wurde keine Opernaufführung unverändert wiederholt, außer an der Bühne, von dem Ensemble und vor dem Publikum, für das sie konzipiert war. Konnte man keine fähigen Komponisten zu einer Neuanfertigung verpflichten, so war man zu Bearbeitung oder Pasticcio-Arrangement gezwungen. An den italienischen Provinztheatern, und auch in London vor Händel, beauftragte man den ortsansässigen Kapellmeister lieber mit der Zusammenstellung von Arien berühmterer Zeitgenossen als mit ganz eigenen Produktionen. Bedeutende Komponisten haben sich nur unter bestimmten Voraussetzungen als Pasticcio-Arrangeure betätigt. Drei von ihnen sind Keiser, Vivaldi und Händel, und sie hatten alle drei einen ähnlichen Grund: Der wirtschaftliche Erfolg einer Bearbeitung oder eines Pasticcio schien ihnen, bei geringerer Eigenanstrengung, ebenso gesichert wie der eines selbst komponierten Werkes. Keiser und Vivaldi waren zeitweise ihre eigenen Impresari; Händel bekam seit 1729 für Opern eigener wie fremder Produktion zumindest dasselbe Honorar[5].

In den Jahren nach 1729 führte er auch fast alle seine Pasticci auf; nur eines hat er für die (erste) Royal Academy 1725 geliefert, in der Zeit vor 1720 gar keines[6]. Die Londoner Pasticcio-Tradition, von der er zunächst ganz abseits ge-

---

[4] Vgl. zu diesem Verfahren bei Gluck: Klaus HORTSCHANSKY, *Parodie und Entlehnung im Schaffen Chr. W. Glucks*, Analecta musicologica 13, 1973; ferner id., *»Arianna« — ein Pasticcio von Gluck,* in: Die Musikforschung 24, 1971, p. 407—411.

[5] Vgl. DEUTSCH, a. a. O. p. 236.

[6] Das Pasticcio *Ernelinda* (Text von Silvani), welches am 26. 2. 1713 am Haymarket aufgeführt wurde, hat entgegen SMITH, *Catalogue of Works,* a. a. O., mit Händel nichts zu tun. — Vgl. auch *Opera Register from 1712 to 1734 (Colman Register),* bearbeitet von

standen hatte, trug er in der Zeit seiner Alleinherrschaft am Haymarket-Theater
selbst weiter.

Die Londoner Opernbühne war ja in der ersten Zeit ihres Bestehens trotz Händel — und zumal vor dessen Auftreten — Provinz, verglichen etwa mit Rom,
Venedig oder auch Wien. Das Pasticcio nach Werken italienischer Autoren, zu
dem ortsansässige Musiker wie Clayton oder Haym mehr oder weniger umfangreiche Teile beisteuerten, war bis gegen 1720 die quantitativ überwiegende Opernform; überhaupt nur Händel hat bis dahin ganz eigene Kompositionen geliefert. Die Hörgewohnheiten des Londoner Publikums, das anfangs partiell, seit
1710 völlig auf die Verwendung der Nationalsprache in den Haymarket-Opern
verzichtete, waren »pasticciohaft«. Offenbar schätzte man geistige Auseinandersetzung mit dem Opernstoff sogar geringer ein als anderswo und ließ sich in der
Unkenntnis der Sprache auch dramatisch unpassende Arientexte gefallen[7]. Seit
etwa 1720 dürfte sich doch unter der Einwirkung Händels, aber wohl auch
Rollis und Bononcinis, ein Begriff von dramatischer Einheit der Oper gebildet
haben (dem die Pasticcio-Form nicht unbedingt entgegenstehen muß), oder sogar
von musikalischer Kohärenz und Ausgewogenheit. Immerhin hat Giuseppe Riva,
der Freund Rollis und später Metastasios, seinen *Avviso ai compositori ed ai
cantanti*, welcher in seinen Vorstellungen von musikalischer und dramatischer Einheit der Oper auch der italienischen Praxis der Zeit vorauseilt, auch in London in englischer Sprache veröffentlicht (1727)[8]. Es standen der Royal Academy
von 1720 bis 1728 ja mehrere Komponisten zur Verfügung, die ein ganz eigenes
Werk über die Bühne gehen lassen konnten.

Ein wichtiger Grund für die Pasticcio-Form hat jedoch unverändert fortbestanden: Sie eignete sich vortrefflich für die Präsentation neuer Sänger mit Favorit-

---

K. Sasse, in: Händel Jb. 5, 1959, p. 199—223, Anm. 4. — Heidegger stellte das Pasticcio
nach Vorlagen von F. Gasparini und Orlandini zusammen; einzelne Arien stammen wahrscheinlich von G. Bononcini und F. Mancini. Der 2. Akt einer *Ernelinda*-Oper befindet sich
durch Zufall in der Hamburger Sammlung Händelscher Handexemplare (vgl. Anm. 9 und
10); er ist aber ein norditalienisches Original, um 1710, in dem ich ein Autograph F. Gasparinis vermute. Er stimmt mit dem Londoner Libretto von 1713 nicht überein, dürfte vielmehr
einer deutschen (Braunschweiger?) Aufführung als Vorlage gedient haben und ist eng verwandt mit F. Gasparinis *La fede tradita e vendicata*, Torino 1719. Auf diese oder eine
ähnliche Vorlage stützt sich auch die Hamburger *Ernelinda*-Aufführung von 1730, deren Zusammenstellung Telemann zugeschrieben wird: Vgl. Paul Merbach, *Das Repertoire der Hamburger Oper von 1718 bis 1750*, in: AfMW 6, 1924, p. 363. Irrig ist jedenfalls Matthesons
Zuschreibung an Händel: Vgl. Friedrich Chrysander, *Mattheson's Verzeichniss Hamburgischer
Opern von 1678 bis 1728 . . .*, in: AMZ XII, 1877, Sp. 198 ff., Nr. 228. Für die Hamburger
Ernelinda benützte man außerdem Arien aus einem Florentiner Pasticcio von 1723, *Flavio
Anicio Olibrio*, hauptsächlich von Gasparini, von dem eine Ariensammlung in Rostock, Univ.
Bibl., erhalten ist.

[7] Vgl. Addisons Polemik in *The Spectator*, Nr. 18, zitiert bei Fassini, a. a. O. p. 14 f.

[8] Vgl. Francesco Degrada, *Giuseppe Riva e il suo »Avviso ai compositori ed ai cantanti«*, in:
Analecta musicologica 4, 1967, p. 112—132.

arien ihres Repertoires, und gerade den Wünschen italienischer Gesangsvirtuosen ist man in London stets bereitwillig entgegengekommen. Das gilt ohne Zweifel auch für Händel selbst und für seine Pasticci der Jahre 1730—1734. Danach hat er sich, mit einer Ausnahme von 1737, vom Pasticcio wieder abgewandt, während die Opera of the Nobility nicht nur den Import italienischer Sänger und Komponisten, sondern auch die Tradition der Pasticcio-Aufführungen in London weiterführte.

Die vorliegende Untersuchung gilt den neun Pasticci Händels, die fast ausnahmslos zu der oben gegebenen Begriffsbestimmung passen. Es sind folgende: *Elpidia* (1725), *Ormisda* (1730), *Venceslao* (1731), *Lucio Papirio Dittatore* (1732), *Catone* (1732), *Semiramide* (1733), *Caio Fabricio* (1733), *Arbace* (1734) und *Didone abbandonata* (1737). Von allen neun Opern sind die Partituren erhalten, die Händel für seine Aufführung anfertigen ließ oder selbst mit anfertigte. Die Mehrzahl von ihnen befindet sich in der ehemals Chrysanderschen Sammlung Händelscher »Handexemplare« in Hamburg[9]. Diese Sammlung ist seit kurzem quellenkritisch erschlossen durch eine Arbeit von Hans Dieter Clausen[10]. Diese Untersuchung der »Handexemplare« (es handelt sich um Dirigierpartituren, im Folgenden kurz «Handexemplare», sowie um »Cembalopartituren« für den zweiten Cembalisten; sie umfassen die Opern, die Pasticci und die Oratorien) ist die wichtigste Voraussetzung für den vorliegenden Beitrag. Clausens Ergebnisse und Methoden sind hier so vielfach verwendet, daß nicht überall einzeln auf sie zurückverwiesen werden kann; auch für das Studium quellenkritischer Details sei dieses Buch generell empfohlen. Das Hauptgewicht meiner Ausführungen liegt auf der Mitteilung der von Händel für die Pasticci verwendeten Vorlagen (eine Gesamtübersicht findet sich am Ende des Beitrags). Die Überlegungen, die sich an die bibliographische Erschließung unmittelbar anknüpfen, betreffen im wesentlichen drei Bereiche:

1. Die Biographie. Händel hat Pasticci aufgeführt, um seinen Spielplan mit italienischen Opern aufzufüllen, von denen er sich eine zusätzliche Anziehungskraft auf das Publikum erhoffte. Wie er sich die Vorlagen beschafft hat und welche Rolle dabei außer den beteiligten Sängern etwa seine Agenten in Italien und Londoner Opernsammler gespielt haben, dies könnte vielleicht noch genauer ermittelt werden.

2. Händels Pasticcio-Verfahren. Es weicht nicht nur grundsätzlich von seinem Vorgehen bei eigenen Opern ab, sondern auch von der italienischen und sonstigen Londoner Praxis, vor allem darin, daß Händel, trotz starker Schwankungen, viel weniger Bearbeitungen und eigene Zusätze anbringt. Hier sind die wichtig-

---

[9] Hamburg, Staats- und Universitätsbibliothek, im Folgenden mit dem RISM-Sigel BRD-Hs bezeichnet.

[10] Hans Dieter CLAUSEN, *Händels Direktionspartituren* (*»Handexemplare«*), Hamburg 1972 (= Hamburger Beiträge zur Musikwissenschaft Bd. 7, hrsg. von Georg von Dadelsen).

sten Fragen noch offen. Durch genaue Vergleiche aller Stücke mit ihren Vorlagen
müßte der Anteil Händels noch gesichert werden; seine Bearbeitungspraxis wäre
der Behandlung eigener Kompositionen gegenüberzustellen (wichtig ist vor allem
die Transpositionsfrage). Vergleiche mit der Pasticcio-Technik etwa Keisers und
Vivaldis drängen sich auf; dringend erscheint eine weitere Erforschung von
Händels Zusammenarbeit mit seinen Textdichtern.
3. Händels Verhältnis zur italienischen Oper seiner Zeit. Es fällt immerhin auf,
daß er Kompositionen von Vinci, Hasse und Leo (in dieser Rangfolge) bevor-
zugt hat; die Textvorlagen stammen ausschließlich von Zeno (5) und Metastasio
(4). Händel, und nicht der Opera of the Nobility, gebührt das Verdienst, London mit der Opernproduktion der sogenannten »Neapolitanischen Schule« ver-
traut gemacht zu haben. Welche Anregungen er selbst für seine Werke aus Italien bezog, könnte nunmehr anhand von Texten und Partituren studiert werden,
die er sicher gekannt und benützt hat. Dabei wäre zu unterscheiden zwischen
dem, was er für aufführenswert hielt, und dem, wodurch er sich selbst anregen
ließ. Insgesamt scheint seine Wertschätzung für Vinci und Hasse oder auch Zeno
und Metastasio weitaus größer gewesen zu sein als sein Bedürfnis, ihre Manier
zu übernehmen.

ELPIDIA (1725)

L'Elpidia, overo li rivali generosi wurde erstmalig am 11. 5. 1725 im Haymarket-Theater aufgeführt. Elf Vorstellungen erfolgten bis zum 19. 6. 1725 (Ende
der Saison). Die nächste Spielzeit wurde am 30. 11. 1725 mit *Elpidia* in teilweise
neuer Besetzung eröffnet; fünf Aufführungen erfolgten bis zum 14. Dezember[11].
Besetzung:

Belisario (Baß): Giuseppe Maria Boschi
Olindo (Mezzosopran): Francesco Bernardi detto Senesino
Ormonte (Alt): Andrea Pacini. Später Antonio Baldi
Elpidia (Sopran): Francesca Cuzzoni
Vitige (Tenor): Francesco Borosini. Später Luigi Antinori
Rosmilda (Alt): Benedetta Sorosina[12]. Später Anna Dotti.

Die Zugehörigkeit der Partitur[13] zu den Handexemplaren und damit die Zugehörigkeit der *Elpidia* zu den von Händel aufgeführten Pasticci hat Clausen
nachgewiesen[14].

---

[11] Sämtliche Aufführungsdaten in diesem Beitrag nach Allardyce NICOLL, *A History of early
Eighteenth Century Drama 1700—1750*, Cambridge 1925, Appendix C: Handlist of Plays,
II. Italian Operas, Oratorios and Serenatas, p. 387—400.
[12] Nicht Leonora D'Ambreville (DEUTSCH, a. a. O. p. 181).
[13] GB-Lbm add. 31606. Bibliothekssigel in diesem Beitrag stets nach RISM.
[14] CLAUSEN, a. a. O. p. 136 f.

Das Libretto der Erstaufführung[15] gibt als Textautor Zeno an, als Komponisten »*Leonardo* Vinci *except some few songs by Signor Gioseppe* Orlandini«. Textgrundlage sind Zenos *Rivali generosi* (erstmalig aufgeführt in Venedig 1697 mit Musik von M. A. Ziani) in einer stark bearbeiteten Fassung. Der Textbearbeiter könnte Haym gewesen sein, der auch drei andere Operntexte der Saison nach Originalen von Zeno und Salvi adaptiert hatte. Die relativ exakte Komponistenangabe entspricht dem usus der (ersten) Royal Academy, während bei den späteren Händel-Pasticci die Komponisten nicht mitgeteilt werden, ebensowenig wie in der Regel bei seinen eigenen Werken. Da das Handexemplar hinsichtlich der Sinfonia und einiger gestrichener Arien unvollständig ist, müssen einige Londoner Drucke der Zeit zur Ergänzung hinzugezogen werden[16]. Händel und sein Textbearbeiter haben offensichtlich nicht eine ältere Partitur der *Rivali generosi* verwendet, sondern nur Zenos Text, von dem nur das dramatische Gerüst und Teile des Rezitativs sowie zwei Duette stehengeblieben sind. Eine Person (Alarico) wurde ersatzlos gestrichen. Die zwei Duette sowie zwei Akkompagnatorezitative des Originaltextes könnte Händel neu komponiert haben, während das Schlußduett (-quartett) und vermutlich auch das dritte Akkompagnatorezitativ aus Vincis *Ifigenia* stammen. Es scheint auch sicher, daß Händel die Sekkorezitative neu geschrieben hat. Selbst wenn er die Partitur einer früheren Vertonung besessen hätte, so wäre sie wegen der hier besonders einschneidenden Textänderungen kaum verwendbar gewesen. In seinen späteren Pasticci hat er selbst bei weniger gravierenden Änderungen die Rezitative neu geschrieben: eine Arbeit, auf die sich den damaligen Vorstellungen nach kaum ein Autoranspruch gründete. Auch für die Sinfonia wird eine Beteiligung Händels vermutet. Ihr Kopfsatz und eine viertaktige Adagio-Überleitung gehören zu Vincis *Eraclea* (Neapel Herbst 1724), während der Schlußsatz abweicht. In der in der *Elpidia* überlieferten Form könnte die Sinfonia jedoch mit der nicht erhaltenen Sinfonia zu Vincis *Ifigenia* identisch sein[17].

Text und Musik der meisten Arien entnahm Händel den drei neuesten und berühmtesten venezianischen Opern, die in der Saison 1724/1725 am Teatro San Giovanni Grisostomo aufgeführt worden waren: Vincis *Ifigenia* (sieben Arien und das Schlußensemble), Orlandinis *Berenice* (drei Arien) und Vincis *Rosmira fedele* (sechs Arien). Diese wurden auf die fünf Sänger Cuzzoni, Senesino, Pa-

---

[15] Die Libretti der Pasticci Händels befinden sich, wo nicht anders angegeben, in GB-Lbm.

[16] Vgl. *The British Union-Catalogue of Early Music,* hrsg. von E. B. SCHNAPPER, 2 Bde., London 1957, Bd. I, p. 315 f. Unvollständig sind im Handexemplar außer einigen später ersetzten und teilweise entfernten Arien die Sinfonia und Senesinos Arie »*Un vento lusinghier*«, die beide nach den Drucken ergänzt werden können.

[17] Vgl. Helmut HELL, *Die neapolitanische Opernsinfonie in der ersten Hälfte des 18. Jahrhunderts,* Tutzing 1971 (= Münchner Veröffentlichungen zur Musikgeschichte Bd. 19), p. 452 f. Hell spricht den Schlußsatz aus stilistischen Gründen Vinci ab und vermutet in ihm eher eine Komposition Händels.

cini, Sorosina und Borosini so verteilt, daß jeder im wesentlichen die Arien seines nach Stimmlage und Rollencharakter entsprechenden venezianischen Kollegen
erhielt. Dies hatte nicht nur den Vorteil, daß kaum transponiert werden mußte,
sondern es kam auch dem Rollenehrgeiz der Sänger entgegen. So konnte die
mittelmäßige Altistin Sorosina mit zwei Erfolgsstücken der berühmten Antonia
Merighi glänzen, und vor allem sang die Cuzzoni schon in der ersten Aufführung fünf Arien, die für ihre Rivalin Faustina Bordoni komponiert worden
waren. Händels Textbearbeiter verstand es, alle diese Arien fast ohne Veränderung der Worte in Zenos Drama einzupassen (Händels späterer Mitarbeiter,
Giacomo Rossi, hat viel öfter zum Mittel der Parodie gegriffen), während er die
nötigen Adaptierungen im Rezitativtext vornahm.

Noch vor dem Druck des Librettos wurde eine Pacini zugedachte Arie aus der
Berenice gestrichen und durch eine andere ersetzt, die er im Vorjahr in G. M.
Cappellis *Venceslao* gesungen hatte. Aus derselben Oper brachte er eine zweite
Arie mit, die allerdings nicht für ihn selbst komponiert worden war. Nach dem
Druck des Librettos wurden drei Arien für den sechsten Sänger, den Bassisten
Boschi eingefügt, von denen zwei noch in der Partitur erhalten sind. Von wem
sie stammen, war bisher nicht zu ermitteln.

Über die restlichen vier unidentifizierten Arien gibt ein Librettoexemplar des
British Museum Auskunft, in das bei fast allen Musiknummern handschriftlich
der Komponistenname eingetragen ist. Leider sind diese Eintragungen in vier
der siebzehn nachweisbaren Fälle falsch, so daß auch bei den übrigen Vorsicht
geboten ist.

Als mit der *Elpidia* die Saison 1725/1726 eröffnet wurde, waren an die Stelle
von Borosini (der nach Wien zurückging), Pacini und Sorosina neue Sänger getreten, von denen nur Anna Dotti dem Londoner Publikum bekannt war. Sie
wollten bezeichnenderweise nicht einfach die Rolle ihrer Vorgänger übernehmen,
sondern verlangten zur besseren Präsentation beim Publikum neue Ersatzarien
aus ihrem eigenen Repertoire oder dem berühmterer Kollegen. Auch Senesino
und Cuzzoni nützten die Chance und erhielten je eine zusätzliche (nicht ersetzte)
Arie. Bei der »aria aggiunta« der Cuzzoni, die aus dem neuesten Repertoire der
Faustina stammte, ist die Einlegstelle in der Partitur noch zu erkennen, während bei Senesinos Arie Provenienz und Einlegstelle unbekannt sind[18].

Das Besondere an der Pasticciotechnik der *Elpidia* ist zum einen, daß Arien
aus der neuesten venezianischen Produktion verwendet wurden, unter Bevorzugung des damals in London völlig unbekannten Leonardo Vinci, und zum
anderen die strikte Trennung von Textgrundlage und musikalischen Vorlagen,
die den Textbearbeiter vor eine schwierige Aufgabe gestellt haben muß. Mehrere

---

[18] Sämtliche sieben für die Spielzeit 1725/26 neu eingelegten Arien sind abgedruckt in *The
Quarterly Collection of Vocal Musick . . . (British Union-Catalogue,* a. a. O. p. 316).

Opern derselben Saison nach Favoritarien auszubeuten, war später Händels Technik nicht mehr, wenn sich auch eine Trennung von Text- und Musikvorlage noch im *Ormisda* findet. Vinci allerdings ist auch für die späteren Pasticci der bevorzugte Autor geblieben.

Mit dem Pasticcio *Elisa*, das am 15. 1. 1726 aufgeführt wurde, hat Händel wohl nichts zu tun. Davon sind außer dem Libretto sechs bei Walsh gedruckte Arien mit der handschriftlichen Angabe »Porpora« sowie zwei anonyme Baßarien in einem Sammelband mit ansonsten Händelschen Baßarien erhalten[19]. Die letzteren stammen, der Musik nach zu schließen, sicher nicht von Händel (auch der Schreiber des Sammelbandes ist nicht J. Chr. Smith, wie Chrysander annahm); hingegen sind 17 von den insgesamt 25 Arien- und Duett-Texten der *Elisa* in Opern Porporas aus den Jahren 1719 bis 1725 nachweisbar, in mehreren Fällen auch die Musik. Porpora hat das Sujet der *Elisa*, das an Zenos *Scipione nelle Spagne* erinnert, nicht komponiert; da die Arien aus mindestens acht seiner zum Teil wenig bekannten Werke zusammengeholt sind, dürfte der Arrangeur der Musik mit dem Komponisten selbst Verbindung gehabt haben. Der Textbearbeiter der *Elisa* ist Nicola Haym, während Händel in dieser Spielzeit wieder mit Rolli zusammenarbeitete. Da Händels *Scipione* (aufgeführt am 12. 3. 1726) von Rolli einem ähnlichen Drama nachgebildet ist[20], haben wir gewissermaßen eine verdeckte Konkurrenz zwischen Händel und Porpora mit Opern ähnlichen Sujets vor uns und damit einen seltsamen Parallelfall zu den bekannten Ereignissen der Spielzeit 1733/1734.

HÄNDELS REISEN 1728—1729 UND DAS PASTICCIO »ORMISDA« (1730)

Zwischen dem vorläufigen Ende der Royal Academy im Juni 1728 und der Wiedereröffnung des Theaters am 2. Dezember 1729 unternahm Händel zwei Reisen nach dem Festland. Das einzige Zeugnis für die erste Reise ist ein Brief Rollis vom 21. Dezember, ohne Jahresangabe, aber mit Sicherheit von 1728[21]: Händel sei zurück von seinen Reisen, habe Farinelli gehört und sei voll des Lobes; trotzdem sollten wieder Cuzzoni, Faustina und Senesino engagiert werden. Farinelli sang im Oktober 1728 in München (in Torris *Nicomede*), hielt sich aber wohl seit Dezember zur Vorbereitung der Karnevalssaison in Venedig auf. Wo Händel ihn getroffen hat, bleibt ungewiß.

---

[19] Vgl. CHRYSANDER, a. a. O. Bd. II, p. 140; DEUTSCH, a. a. O. p. 193. Der Walsh-Druck in BRD-Hs, 14 in M B/2620: *The / favourite SONGS / in the new OPERA / Call'd ELISA / as also / the Additional Songs / in the OPERA of / RODELINDA / . . .,* London (1726). Das Exemplar enthält nur die sechs *Elisa*-Arien; vier von ihnen lassen sich mit Gewißheit Porpora zuweisen. Die beiden Baßarien in BRD-Hs, M B/1654, Nr. 1 und 9.

[20] Vorlage nicht Zeno; vgl. EISENSCHMIDT, a. a. O. Bd. II, p. 12 Anm. 2.

[21] DEUTSCH, a. a. O. p. 229 f.

Am 18. Januar 1729 nahm Händel an der Versammlung der Academy teil, in
der mit ihm und Heidegger ein neuer Vertrag geschlossen wurde. Entgegen der
Vermutung Chrysanders sicherte ihm dieser die Benützung des Haymarket-Thea-
ters nicht nur bis 1733, sondern für fünf Jahre, so daß er sich von vornherein auf
fünf Spielzeiten bis einschließlich 1733/1734 einstellen durfte[22]. Um diese zu bestreiten, engagierte er nun auf seiner zweiten, vielfach belegten Reise[23] nicht nur
Sänger für die Saison 1729/30, sondern er verschaffte sich auch Partiturmaterial,
um fremde Werke aufführen zu können, sowie Libretti zur eigenen Vertonung.
Er wird damals für jede der fünf Spielzeiten je ein fremdes Werk zur Aufführung vorgesehen haben. Dieser Plan wurde erst 1733/34 mit *Caio Fabricio* und
Arbace überschritten, die 1730 und 1732 komponiert sind; für die übrigen fünf
Pasticci konnte sich Händel das meiste Material schon 1729 beschaffen. Im Folgenden werden einige Opern genannt werden, von denen er den Text oder auch
Teile der Musik in London dann verwendet hat, außerdem die Namen von Sängern, die er entweder sofort oder später engagiert hat. Diese Angaben erweisen,
zusammen mit den erhaltenen Dokumenten, Händels Reisestationen in Italien.
Venedig war das erste Ziel. Er traf dort außer mit Senesino auch mit Farinelli
zusammen, den er am Teatro S. Gio. Grisostomo in Leos *Catone in Utica* hören
konnte. Durch Farinellis Auftreten wurden damals die Konkurrenztheater beein-
trächtigt[24], auch S. Cassano, wo Faustina Bordoni, Senesino und der 1736 nach
London engagierte Domenico Annibali in Orlandinis *Adelaide* auftraten. Die
Musik dieser Oper hat Händel teilweise in *Ormisda* (allerdings erst 1730/31),
den Text schon für seinen *Lotario* (2. Dezember) verwendet[25]. An Partituren und
Libretti früherer Produktionen dürften verfügbar gewesen sein: *Ezio* (Metasta-
sio/Porpora), *Argeno* (Leo) und *Ormisda* (Cordans) von 1728, *Orlando furioso*
(Braccioli/Vivaldi) von 1727[26].
Ein Brief Händels vom 28. Februar (= 11. März) 1729 zeigt ihn noch in Venedig[27]: Er hatte jedoch einen Besuch in Neapel vor sowie ein weiteres Zusammen-
treffen mit Senesino (auf der Rückreise in Siena[28]). Zu letzterem ist es wohl nicht

[22] Vgl. CHRYSANDER, a. a. O. Bd. II, p. 326. Die auf Chrysander zurückgehende Periodisierung
    des Händelschen Schaffens, welche die mit 1729 begonnene Periode schon 1733 enden läßt,
    ist in dieser Einseitigkeit nicht mehr haltbar; vgl. zu dem 5-Jahres-Vertrag das Dokument
    bei DEUTSCH, a. a. O. p. 234, sowie Rollis Brief vom 7. (bzw. 4.) Februar 1729, DEUTSCH,
    a. a. O. p. 236 f.
[23] Vgl. DEUTSCH, a. a. O. p. 236 ff.
[24] Vgl. Rollis Brief vom 7. 2. 1729 bei DEUTSCH, a. a. O. p. 237. Rollis Bemerkung wird bestä-
    tigt durch eine Notiz zum Jahre 1729 in dem handschriftlichen *Catalogo de' Drammi musicali
    fatti in Venezia dal 1637 al 1778*, I-Mb Racc. Dramm. 6007.
[25] Vgl. Rollis Brief an Riva vom 20. 12. 1729 bei DEUTSCH, a. a. O. p. 249.
[26] Dieser *Orlando furioso* ist nicht die Textvorlage für Händels *Orlando*; Händel verwendete
    aber eine Arie aus Vivaldis Vertonung für das Pasticcio *Catone* (vgl. unten).
[27] DEUTSCH, a. a. O. p. 239.
[28] Vgl. Rollis Brief an Senesino vom 16. 5. 1729, DEUTSCH, a. a. O. p. 242 f.

mehr gekommen. In Neapel wurde Händel im März Zeuge einer Auseinandersetzung zwischen Carestini einerseits und Bernacchi und Merighi andererseits, die
eine für die primavera-Saison geplante Oper an S. Bartolomeo platzen ließ[29];
Carestini wendete sich dann nach Venedig, Bernacchi nach Parma. Alle drei
hatten noch in Hasses Karnevalsoper *Ulderica* zusammen gesungen, die Händel
nicht mehr gehört haben kann (Aschermittwoch war der 9. März). Mit Hasse
selbst kann er jedoch zusammengetroffen sein, der 1729 in Neapel wohnte (nicht
in Venedig). Ferner waren in Neapel anwesend der Theaterarchitekt Aurelio
del Pò mit seiner Gattin Anna Maria Strada[30], die vor ihrer Verheiratung in
Venedig, Milano, Livorno, Lucca und Neapel aufgetreten war (1719—1726), sowie die Buffo-Sopranistin Celeste Resse (-Gismondi?)[31]. Folgende neapolitanische
Opern haben Händel unter anderen interessiert: *Gerone* (Hasse, 1727), *Siroe*
(Sarri, 1727), *Attalo* (Hasse) und *Flavio Anicio Olibrio* (Vinci) von 1728, dazu
Hasses neue *Ulderica*[32]. Von einem Aufenthalt Händels in Rom weiß Mainwaring
Einzelheiten zu berichten[33]; er dürfte auf der Rückreise von Neapel (etwa über
die Karwoche) eingelegt worden sein. In zwei Karnevalsopern war Carlo Scalzi
aufgetreten; Rom war zudem die Heimat von Francesca Bertolli (ein Engagement von 1729 ist nicht bekannt; sie hatte 1728 in Livorno und Bologna gesungen). Händel hat sie wohl persönlich kennengelernt — gerade dieser Sängerin
kann weder ihre Stimme noch ihr Spiel, sondern nur ihr Aussehen zu einem Londoner Engagement verholfen haben[34]. Von der römischen Produktion der vergangenen Jahre hat Händel später Folgendes benützt: *Berenice* (D. Scarlatti und
Porpora, 1718), *Faramondo* (Gasparini, 1720)[35], *Giustino* (Vivaldi, 1724), *Didone*
(Metastasio/Vinci, 1726), *Semiramide* (Metastasio/Vinci, 1729), *Arianna e Teseo*
(Pariati/Leo, 1729). Im Mai 1729 dürfte Händel kaum versäumt haben, die einzige bedeutende Opernbühne außerhalb Venedigs zu besuchen, die jetzt eine
Neuproduktion brachte: Parma. Mit Farinelli, Bernacchi und der Faustina wurde
dort Giacomellis *Lucio Papirio Dittatore* gespielt, den Händel dann am
23. Mai 1732 am Haymarket aufführte, und zwar unter Benützung einer Parti-
turkopie, die am 15. Mai 1729 in Parma fertiggestellt worden war[36]. Das Engagement Bernacchis kann in Parma noch erfolgt sein, vielleicht nach einer letzten,

---

[29] Vgl. Lodovico FRATI, *Antonio Bernacchi e la sua scuola di canto,* in: RMI 29, 1922, p. 479.
ROLLI schreibt am 16. 5. (zitiert nach DEUTSCH, vgl. Anm. 28): »*Handel has written that Carestini was emulating Bernacchi.*«
[30] Vgl. Benedetto CROCE, *I teatri di Napoli, secolo XV—XVIII,* Napoli 1891, p. 294.
[31] Vgl. unten zum Pasticcio *Catone.*
[32] Aus diesen Opern verwendete Händel einzelne Arien in den Pasticci.
[33] John MAINWARING, *Memoirs of the Life of the late George Frederic Handel...,* London
1760, p. 113.
[34] Vgl. die Berichte über die Bertolli bei DEUTSCH, a. a. O. p. 247 und 249 f.
[35] Für *Berenice* und *Faramondo* gilt dies vorbehaltlich einer möglichen, noch zu ermittelnden
Zwischenvorlage.
[36] Vgl. unten zum Pasticcio *Lucio Papirio Dittatore.*

vergeblichen Bemühung um Farinelli. Erst Anfang Juli verbreitete sich in Bernacchis Heimat Bologna das Gerücht, er werde für 1500 Louisd'or nach England gehen[37]. Rolli weiß in seinem Brief vom 16. Mai[38] noch nichts von Bernacchis Verpflichtung — hingegen vom Ehepaar Fabri (Annibale Pio Fabri sang Anfang 1729 am Teatro della Pergola, Florenz) und von einem italienisch-deutschen Bassisten. Sollte Händel schon vor Mai 1729 mit Riemschneider in Verbindung getreten sein? Es hätte dann einer Reise nach Hamburg nicht mehr bedurft[39].

Aus Parma stammen folgende von Händel benützte Opern: Capellis *Venceslao* (1724), Vincis *Medo* (1728) und R. Broschis *Bradamante nell'isola d'Alcina* (Karneval 1729), die jedoch schon als *L'isola d'Alcina* 1728 in Rom gespielt worden war[40]. Bei der Reise von Rom nach Parma mußte Bologna berührt werden; dort wohnten außer Bernacchi das Ehepaar Fabri und das Ehepaar Pinacci-Bagnolesi. Orlandinis berühmte Oper *Ormisda* (Bologna 1722) muß Händel freilich nicht an Ort und Stelle erhalten haben. Weitere Stationen von Händels Italienreise lassen sich mit den hier verwendeten Kriterien nicht erschließen.

Das Pasticcio *Ormisda* ging am 4. April 1730 am Haymarket in Szene. Es sangen:

Artenice (Sopran): Anna Maria Strada
Ormisda (Tenor): Annibale Pio Fabri
Arsace (Alt): Francesca Bertolli
Erismeno (Baß): Riemschneider
Palmira (Alt): Antonia Merighi
Cosroe (Mezzosopran): Antonio Bernacchi. Später Francesco Bernardi detto Senesino.

Zenos *Ormisda* war in der Vertonung durch Caldara erstmalig am 4. November 1721 in Wien aufgeführt worden. Die zweite Vertonung durch Orlandini (Bologna, Teatro Malvezzi, Mai 1722) dürfte Händel als Vorlage verwendet haben. Einer irrigen Überlieferung zufolge liegt dem Pasticcio die Oper von B. Cordans zugrunde (Venedig 1728)[41], von der Händel vielleicht das Libretto eingesehen, aber nichts verwendet hat, was er nicht auch Orlandinis Fassung hätte entnehmen können. Ein weiterer Irrtum ist die Zuschreibung an Francesco Conti: Während das Handexemplar des *Ormisda* ohne Zuschreibung ist, lautet der Kopftitel der Cembalopartitur: *Ouverture del S.ʳ Conti*[42]. Dieser Titel kann sich

[37] Vgl. FRATI, a. a. O. p. 478.
[38] Vgl. oben Anm. 28.
[39] Vgl. CHRYSANDER, a. a. O. Bd. II, p. 232 f. Einen Besuch Händels in Hamburg 1729 konnte Chrysander außer aus dem Engagement Riemschneiders nur aus einer sehr undeutlichen Bemerkung Matthesons schließen, die wegen der Erwähnung Dresdens besser zu 1719 passen würde.
[40] Antonio Fanzaglias Libretto, in der Fassung von 1728, ist die Vorlage zu Händels *Alcina*-Text; vielleicht hat Händel aber erst in Parma beide Libretti kennengelernt.
[41] Vgl. CHRYSANDER, a. a. O. Bd. II, p. 239.
[42] Die Zuschreibung an Conti z. B. in GROVE's *Dictionary*, 5. Auflage, Bd. IV, p. 51. Handexemplar des *Ormisda*: GB-Lbm add. 31551; Cembalopartitur: BRD-Hs M A/1036.

nur auf die Ouverture beziehen, ist aber auch hier nicht gesichert. Die Ouverture
ist bereits die zweite, die Händel für das Werk vorgesehen hat: Eine zuvor in
beide Handschriften eingetragene und dann eliminierte Sinfonia stammt von
Vinci. Der erste Satz ist in dessen *Gismondo* (Rom 1727) nachweisbar, der
zweite nur in einem seiner neapolitanischen Oratorien, welches Händel kaum
zugänglich war[43]. Beide zusammen könnten aber die heute verschollene Sinfonia
zu Vincis *Flavio Anicio Olibrio* (Neapel, Dezember 1728) gebildet haben. Von
Orlandinis Vertonung hat Händel wahrscheinlich die — textlich weitgehend
übereinstimmenden — Rezitative verwendet, von den Arien jedoch übernahm er
höchstens vier. Da alle diese vier Arien Bernacchi gehören (er hatte sie 1722
ebenfalls in der Rolle des Cosroe gesungen), bleibt die Möglichkeit, daß Händel
nur Orlandinis Libretto benützt hat und für die Arien auf Bernacchi allein angewiesen war. Die Zuschreibung an Orlandini ist nicht bei allen vier Arien durch
direktes Quellenzeugnis gesichert (die Musik von »*Fia tuo sangue*« ist in Händels Exemplaren nicht erhalten), läßt sich jedoch indirekt erschließen. Alle übrigen Arien entnahm Händel anderen Opern. Außer Bernacchi haben auch Fabri
und die Merighi Arien des eigenen Repertoires beigesteuert. Alle drei waren
selbstbewußte und erfahrene Sänger, die sicher ihre wichtigsten Favoritarien auch
in Partitur mit sich führten und diese Händel anempfehlen konnten. Mehr auf
Händels Vorrat angewiesen war die Strada. Die Arie »*Se d'aquilon*« hatte sie
zwar selbst in einer Oper Porporas 1724 gesungen. Jedoch trägt eine englische
Abschrift der Arie außer ihrem Namen den Operntitel *Siface*[44]: In Porporas
Siface von 1726 war die Arie wiederum vorgetragen worden, aber nicht von der
Strada! Händel gab ihr also ihre eigene Arie zurück. Die Identifizierung der
Ormisda-Arien kann sich zum Teil an Zuschreibungen in sekundären Londoner
Kopien orientieren, die sich heute überwiegend im Konservatorium Brüssel befinden[45]. Die Quellen des Pasticcio selbst enthalten außer bei der Ouverture
keine Zuschreibung; trotzdem hat man in London über die Komponisten von
mindestens sechs Arien Bescheid gewußt. Händel dürfte sie aus in London vorhandenen Einzelfaszikeln kennengelernt haben. Das Interesse des Publikums
an *Ormisda* war groß; das Pasticcio erlebte schon in der ersten Saison vierzehn
Aufführungen, doppelt so viele wie Händels *Partenope*. Walsh druckte sehr bald

---

[43] Den Hinweis auf Vincis Oratorium verdanke ich Herrn Helmut HELL. Die Incipits beider
Sätze Vincis bei HELL, a. a. O. p. 540 f.

[44] Es ist die Abschrift in B-Bc, 4670.

[45] Ebendort befinden sich auch italienische Handschriften von Arien, die im Londoner *Ormisda*
gesungen wurden und die vielleicht über London nach Brüssel gewandert sind. Die Sammlung
enthält, z. T. mit Autornamen, 12 *Ormisda*-Arien (B-Bc 3975, 4101, 4446, 4448, 4670, 4678,
4946, 4950, 5079, 5360, 5369 und 5389), dazu 2 Arien, die in *Venceslao* aufgeführt wurden
(3758, 4679), sowie je eine, die zu *Semiramide*, *Arbace* und *Didone abbandonata* gehört
(5370, 4677 und 5015).

nach der Erstaufführung elf *Favourite Songs*[46]. Nicht mehr im Walsh-Druck enthalten sind die Ersatzarien, die erst später in *Ormisda* eingelegt worden sind. An
den Einfügungen in Handexemplar und Cembalopartitur läßt sich erkennen, was
nachträglich ausgetauscht wurde. Wohl schon vor der ersten Aufführung wurde
Vincis Sinfonia durch die Conti zugeschriebene Ouverture ersetzt, eine kurze
Sinfonia innerhalb des ersten Aktes eingelegt sowie die Arie für Riemschneider,
die noch im Libretto berücksichtigt ist. Die meisten Einlagen gehen auf die Bene-
fizvorstellung für die Strada am 21. April zurück. Hier bekam sie unter anderem
eine neue Schlußarie, als *The last song* bezeichnet, ähnlich wie auch Händels spätere Pasticci eine zugkräftige *aria finale* für den Protagonisten aufweisen, ganz
im Gegensatz zur italienischen Praxis der Zeit. Im Zusammenhang damit wurde
auch der Schlußchor ersetzt. Im Libretto-Exemplar des British Museum (11714
aa 20) sind die später eingelegten Arien für sich abgedruckt, die jedoch entgegen
der dortigen Angabe nicht alle auf den 21. April zurückgehen[47]. Drei Arien ent-
stammen nämlich Orlandinis *Adelaide,* von der Händel in der Spielzeit 1729/30
noch keine Musik verwendet hat; sie wurden in *Adelaide* von Senesino gesungen
und ersetzen hier jeweils die Arien Bernacchis. Zweifellos hat Senesino die Arien
für sich einlegen lassen, als er bei der Wiederaufnahme des *Ormisda* am 24. November 1730 (der noch vier Vorstellungen folgten) in die Rolle Bernacchis ein-
rückte.

Händel hat, zum Teil auf Vorschlag der Sänger, in die auf 1722 zurückgehende
Fassung des *Ormisda* 13 Arien aus der neueren Produktion von Orlandini, Hasse,
Vinci, Giacomelli, Sarri und Leo aufgenommen. Anders als in *Elpidia* mußten
dabei mehrere Arientexte parodiert werden. Für derartige Arbeiten stand Händel seit 1729 wieder der Textdichter des *Rinaldo,* Giacomo Rossi, zur Verfügung[48].

VENCESLAO (1731)

Venceslao wurde erstmalig am 12. Januar 1731 im Haymarket-Theater aufgeführt. Wie auch das »Colman-Register« bezeugt, war die Oper ein Mißerfolg[49];
sie wurde schon nach der vierten Vorstellung am 23. 1. vom Spielplan abgesetzt. (Händels *Poro* folgte erst am 2. Februar.) Vom *Venceslao* sind das Handexemplar, die Cembalopartitur, das Libretto und sieben von Walsh publizierte

---

[46] Vgl. William C. SMITH, *Handel. A Descriptive Catalogue of the Early Editions,* 2. Auflage,
Oxford University Press, 1970, p. 41 f.

[47] Diese Angabe von einer englischen Hand des 18. Jahrhunderts. Unter den gedruckten *Additional Songs* wird Stradas Arie »Agitata dal vento« als *The last song* betitelt.

[48] Vgl. Rollis Brief vom 3. 9. 1729, DEUTSCH, a. a. O. p. 245.

[49] »Venceslaus New Opera — did not take«; SASSE, *Opera Register* a. a. O., p. 219. Sasses
Anm. 64 zum *Ormisda,* der im Register chronologisch falsch eingeordnet ist, enthält den
Druckfehler »1731« statt »1730«.

Favourite Songs erhalten[50]. Die Besetzung, im Libretto nicht angegeben, läßt sich wie folgt erschließen:

Venceslao (Tenor): Annibale Pio Fabri
Lucinda (Alt): Antonia Merighi
Casimiro (Mezzosopran): Francesco Bernardi detto Senesino
Erenice (Sopran): Anna Maria Strada
Ernando (Alt): Francesca Bertolli
Alessandro (Baß): Giovanni Commano
Gismondo (Baß): Giovanni Commano.

Das Drama *Venceslao* von Apostolo Zeno, das dem Pasticcio zugrundeliegt, ist ein 7-Personen-Stück. Wie aus der Korrespondenz Händels und seiner italienischen Agenten vom Jahre 1730 hervorgeht[51], suchte Händel seit Juni 1730 Ersatz für den ausgeschiedenen Bernacchi, an dessen Stelle er schließlich den an sich nicht mehr gewünschten Senesino wieder verpflichten mußte. Zu dem geplanten zusätzlichen Engagement einer Sängerin, die sowohl in Männer- als auch in Frauenrollen auftreten konnte, kam es jedoch nicht mehr. Als Ersatz für Riemschneider hatte er wohl selbst in London den Bassisten Commano aufgetrieben, einen Sänger allerdings, dem er keine Arien anvertrauen konnte. So behalf er sich im *Venceslao* mit nur fünf Ariensängern, und zwar indem er die Nebenrollen Alessandro und Gismondo, die nur Rezitative haben, beide Commano zuteilte: Im Stück wird Alessandro im Laufe des ersten Akts ermordet. Bei Händel tritt er zum letzten Mal in der 7. Szene auf — an seiner Stelle ab der 10. Szene Gismondo.

Zenos Libretto war in Italien zwischen 1720 und 1730 etwa zehnmal in verschiedenen Vertonungen aufgeführt worden; es ist im Original fünfaktig. Die Bearbeitung durch Händel und seinen Librettisten Rossi schließt sich, obwohl dreiaktig, am engsten an das von G. M. Capelli 1724 für Parma vertonte fünfaktige Libretto an. Es ist aber nicht sicher, ob Händel auch Capellis Partitur besaß[52]: Nur eine Arie des Handexemplars stammt von Capelli, die in London auch einzeln vorhanden gewesen sein könnte (*»Del caro sposo«*); zwei weitere Arien, von denen die eine vielleicht geplant war und dann fallengelassen wurde (*«Qual senza stella«*) und die andere anscheinend in letzter Minute eingelegt wurde (*»Vado costante a morte«*), waren durch den Sänger Pacini schon in *Elpidia* eingebracht worden. Mehrere andere Arientexte Zenos, die bei Capelli stehen, wurden neuer Musik unterlegt und zum Teil geringfügig parodiert. Zwei Arien

---

[50] Handexemplar: BRD-Hs M A/1061; Cembalopartitur: BRD-Hs M A/189. Der Walsh-Druck: vgl. *British Union-Catalogue* a. a. O., Bd. II, p. 1036. Die nicht bei Walsh gedruckte Arie *»Lascia cadermi«* ist in das Hamburger Pasticcio *Circe* (1734) übernommen worden.
[51] DEUTSCH, a. a. O. p. 252—262.
[52] Ein Exemplar befindet sich heute in GB-Lbm add. 15993. Die Rezitative dieser Partitur konnte ich noch nicht mit Händels Handexemplar vergleichen.

auf Originaltexte schließlich (»*Nel seren*« und »*Balenar*«) sowie zwei Akkompagnatorezitative müssen aus einer anderen *Venceslao*-Vertonung stammen: am wahrscheinlichsten aus dem Pasticcio, das 1722 am Teatro S. Gio. Grisostomo in Venedig aufgeführt wurde. In ihm gleichen auch die Stimmlagen der fünf wichtigsten Sänger denen der Händelschen Fassung. Vielleicht konnte er auch das 1717 in London aufgeführte Pasticcio *Venceslao* heranziehen, von dem Text und Musik heute verschollen sind; die Instrumentierung des Akkompagnato »*Corrette a rivi*« mit Fagotten deutet möglicherweise auf eine Londoner Vorlage. Es ist auch nicht klar, woher Sinfonia (beim Schlußsatz wäre Händels Autorschaft denkbar), Chor und Sekkorezitative stammen — die letzteren muß Händel aber bearbeitet haben, da die Umstellung auf drei Akte wesentliche Textänderungen erzwang. Beweisen läßt sich das ebensowenig wie bei *Elpidia* und *Ormisda*, weil Handexemplar und Cembalopartitur fast ganz von Kopisten geschrieben sind. Aus diesem Grund sind in beiden Quellen auch keine nachträglichen Einlagen mehr als solche zu erkennen. Sie unterscheiden sich voneinander kaum und wurden etwa gleichzeitig angefertigt. Auch das Libretto, das wie üblich erst kurz vor der Aufführung gedruckt wurde, weicht fast gar nicht mehr ab. Trotzdem läßt sich noch ungefähr rekonstruieren, welche Arien von vornherein geplant gewesen sein müssen und welche erst im Lauf der Vorbereitungen hinzukamen. So ist z. B. die Hassesche Arie »*Lascia cadermi in volto*« im zweiten Akt, in B-Dur, für die Strada später eingesetzt worden, während die zunächst dort befindliche G-Dur-Arie »*Del caro sposo*« in den dritten Akt verlegt wurde (der vorangehende Rezitativschluß ist nämlich tonartlich von e nach g verbessert); im dritten Akt könnte dafür das bei Capelli hierher gehörige »*Qual senza stella*« ausgefallen sein, mitsamt seinem Rezitativ, welches ganz neu geschrieben werden mußte. »*Del caro sposo*« war zunächst, unter Beibehaltung der Anfangszeile, parodiert worden, da es schon in der ersten Planung in einem anderen Zusammenhang vorkam als bei Capelli; die Umsetzung in den dritten Akt ermöglichte nun, den Parodietext im Handexemplar zu streichen und den Originaltext wieder anzubringen.

Im Ganzen gesehen, hat sich jedoch an Händels ursprünglichem *Venceslao*-Konzept nicht viel geändert. Das liegt zum Teil daran, daß für einige Sänger (z. B. Merighi und Bertolli) von vornherein gut passende Arien auch aus Opern von Vinci und Hasse vorgesehen wurden: Die Merighi sang ausschließlich für sie selbst komponierte Arien, darunter drei aus Hasses *Attalo* (Neapel 1728). Gerade hier dürften ihre Wünsche mit Händels Vorstellungen zusammengetroffen sein, der diese Oper auch in späteren Pasticci noch ausbeutete und wohl eine

---

[53] *Venceslao* ist der einzige Fall in Händels Opernschaffen, daß er einen in London bereits bekannten Text wiederaufgeführt hat. Sein *Arminio* von 1737 geht zwar auf dieselbe Vorlage Antonio Salvis zurück wie das Pasticcio *Arminio* von 1713, doch sind beide Texte völlig voneinander abweichend bearbeitet.

Partitur davon besaß. Andererseits sind die noch auf Venedig 1722 weisenden
Arien des Tenors Fabri unangetastet geblieben. Musikalisch geriet *Venceslao*
überhaupt am uneinheitlichsten von allen Pasticci Händels. Dies gilt besonders
für die Rolle des *Casimiro*. Sie ist für Bernacchi geplant worden, der vier von
den sechs Arien in Vincis *Medo* (Parma 1728) gesungen hatte. Es sind charakteristische Beispiele für Bernacchis ganz eigenen Gesangsstil. Händel muß also die
Aufführung des *Venceslao* spätestens Mai 1730 — vielleicht schon 1729 — ins
Auge gefaßt haben. Als dann Senesino die Rolle übernahm, bekam er zwei neue
Arien zusätzlich aus A. Lottis *Alessandro Severo* von 1717 (!), die er in Dresden
1718/1719 kennengelernt haben mag, als er unter Lotti sang. Die erste von ihnen
wurde ganz zuletzt eingebaut, da der Übergang vom Rezitativschluß in h-moll
zur C-Dur-Arie nicht mehr tonartlich bereinigt wurde, jedenfalls nicht im Handexemplar. Die zweite Arie wurde nach dem Druck des Librettos wieder eli-
miniert. Eine der Bernacchi-Arien (»*Vado costante — della mia morte*«) scheint
für ihn durch Capellis Original ersetzt worden zu sein; zumindest steht im
Libretto wieder der Originaltext (»*Vado costante a morte*«). Bernacchi hatte übrigens den *Casimiro* schon in Venedig 1722 dargestellt, und doch ist keine seiner
damaligen Arien in den Londoner *Venceslao* gelangt. Auch die Strada hatte die
Erenice schon in Portas Vertonung (Neapel 1726) gesungen, wollte oder konnte
aber keiner jener Arien beibringen.

Auffallend ist am *Venceslao*, daß in vielen Arien gerade der Text erst zum Schluß
verbessert — und so dem Drama angepaßt — oder gar nachträglich unter die
Noten gesetzt worden ist. Einer dieser nachgetragenen Parodietexte könnte von
Händel selbst stammen, da er ihn dem Kopisten mit Bleistift in der Partitur vor-
gezeichnet hat (»*Parto e mi sento*«). Der Parodietext für die allererste Arie war
so spät zur Hand, daß er nicht mehr in die Partitur anstelle des dort stehenden
Originals eingetragen wurde, sondern nur noch ins Libretto gelangt ist. Die Restitution eines ursprünglich parodierten Textes wurde schon erwähnt.

Das Beschaffen von Parodietexten ist eine zentrale Aufgabe des Pasticcio-Arran-
geurs. Gerade dort, wo eine Arie der Vorlage durch eine neue ersetzt werden
soll, der dramatische Kontext aber unverändert bleibt (es ist der häufigste Anlaß zur Parodie), stellen sich ähnliche Probleme wie beim Übersetzen von Opern-
texten. Nicht nur muß die Substanz der »inhaltlichen Vorlage« (d. h. des Textes
der zu eliminierenden Arie) erhalten bleiben — die Parodie muß auch den Ton-
fall der »prosodischen Vorlage« (d. h. des Textes der neuen Arie) nachahmen,
damit sie zu der neuen Musik gesungen werden kann. Unter den von Händel
verwendeten Parodietexten sind des öfteren Kunststücke poetischer Technik zu
finden, die eine genaue Mittelung aus inhaltlicher und prosodischer Vorlage er-
zielen. Als ein Beispiel sei der Parodietext »*Parto e mi sento*« seinen beiden Vorlagen gegenübergestellt, unabhängig von der Frage, ob er von Rossi oder gar
von Händel selbst stammt.

1. Inhaltliche Vorlage
   (Zenos Originaltext)

Da te parto, e parto afflitto,
o mio giudice, o mio Re;
dir volea: mio genitor.

Ma poi tacqui il dolce nome,
che più aggrava il mio delitto,
e più accresce il tuo dolor.

2. Prosodische Vorlage
   (Text der Arie in Vincis
   Medo; von C. I. Frugoni)

Taci, o di morte
non mi parlar,
labbro vezzoso,
se il mio riposo
non vuoi turbar.

Più lieta sorte
fammi sperar,
se il cor dubbioso,
labbro amoroso,
vuoi consolar.

3. Parodietext
   (von Händel Vincis Arie unterlegt)

Parto, e mi sento
mancar il cor,
perchè sdegnato
ti lascio, o amato
mio genitor.

Il tuo tormento
mi fa penar;
sarò contento,
se il mio castigo
ti può placar.

Lucio Papirio Dittatore (1732)

Die Verschlechterung von Händels Lage als Opernunternehmer, wie sie in der Spielzeit 1731/1732 zum ersten Mal deutlich wurde, zeigt sich im Spielplan an der erhöhten Frequenz, mit der Händel neue oder wiedereinstudierte Opern anbieten mußte. Auf die erste Neuheit am 15. Januar (nach *Tamerlano, Poro* und *Admeto*) — kein Pasticcio wie im vergangenen Jahr, sondern Händels eigener *Ezio* — mußte schon am 1. Februar *Giulio Cesare* folgen; *Sosarme* (15. Februar), *Coriolano* (25. März) und *Flavio* (18. April) schlossen sich an. Der erste wirkliche Erfolg der Saison war das Oratorium *Esther* am 2. Mai, welches weitere Opernaufführungen an sich unnötig gemacht hätte. Trotzdem ließ Händel noch am 23. Mai *Lucio Papirio Dittatore* in Szene gehen, was sich dadurch erklären ließe, daß diese Oper bereits von früher her geplant und jedenfalls vor dem unerwarteten Erfolg von *Esther* konkret vorbereitet worden war. Sie wurde nach der vierten Vorstellung am 6. Juni wieder abgesetzt.

Lucio Papirio Dittatore, auf einen Text von Apostolo Zeno in der Bearbeitung durch den Parmenser Hofpoeten C. I. Frugoni (nicht zu verwechseln mit dem Konkurrenzdrama *Lucio Papirio* von A. Salvi, aus dem Frugoni allerdings Teile des Rezitativs hereingenommen hatte), war mit der Musik von Geminiano Giacomelli Anfang Mai 1729 in Parma aufgeführt worden. Wahrscheinlich hatte Händel die Oper damals in Parma gehört. Es ist die einzige Londoner Produktion Händels, die ein neues Werk eines Italieners fast unverändert auf die Bühne brachte (jedenfalls in bezug auf Arien, Chöre und Sinfonia). Sie kann deshalb nicht »Pasticcio« im strengen Sinn genannt werden.

Heute läßt sich nur noch eine Partitur von Giacomellis Oper nachweisen, und zwar in der Londoner Royal Academy of Music: Es ist eben diejenige, die Händel als Vorlage verwendet haben muß[54]. Ihr erster Besitzer war ein Sir John Buckworth[55], dessen Name 1726 in der Liste der Direktoren der Royal Academy und im Januar 1733 unter den ersten Direktoren der Opera of the Nobility auftaucht[56]. Buckworth, dessen Beziehungen zu Händel einer Klärung wert wären, besaß mehrere heute noch erhaltene Partituren italienischer Opern. Die Giacomelli-Partitur ist datiert »*Parma a dì 15 maggio 1729*« und wurde von einem Francesco Faelli geschrieben[57]. Offen bleibt, ob Händel oder Buckworth die Anfertigung der Kopie veranlaßt hat. In der Partitur befindet sich heute noch das Fragment eines Theaterzettels der *Beggar's Opera*:

	On MONDAY,	
	WILL BE	
	The BEGGA	
	Capt. Macheath	
	Peachume by M	
	Lockit by Mr.D	
Player		Mr. Anderson,
Beggar	by	Mr. Bennet
Mat o'th'Mint		Mr. Baker
Ben Budge		Mr. Wignel

Zu welchem Aufführungsdatum dieser Handzettel gehört, konnte ich noch nicht feststellen; Mai 1732 wäre nicht unmöglich[58]. Nun hätte zwar jeder Londoner

---

[54] GB-Lam, Ms. 71.

[55] Den Hinweis auf die Bibliothek der heutigen Royal Academy of Music sowie auf die darin befindliche Buckworth-Sammlung, die später im Besitz von William Savage gewesen ist, verdanke ich Mr. Richard ANDREWS, London.

[56] Vgl. DEUTSCH, a. a. O. p. 199 bzw. 304.

[57] In B-Bc, 2196, liegt unter der irrigen Zuschreibung an Leonardo Leo eine Partitur von Vincis *Medo,* die ebenfalls von Faelli angefertigt worden ist. Aus dieser Oper Vincis, aufgeführt in Parma, Mai 1728, hat Händel mehrere Arien in seinen Pasticci verwendet.

[58] Vgl. *The London Stage 1660—1800;* Part 2:1700—1729, 2 Bde., hrsg. von Emmett L. AVERY, Part 3:1729—1747, 2 Bde., hrsg. von Arthur H. SCOUTEN; Southern Illinois University Press, Carbondale 1960/1961. Aus diesem Werk geht keine entsprechende Aufführung hervor. In Frage käme jedoch Montag, der 22. Mai 1732, New Haymarket-Theater, wo Anderson (erst seit 8. Mai 1732) und Wignel damals auftraten; vgl. a. a. O. Part 3, Bd. I, p. 217.

Besitzer der Partitur theoretisch den Zettel einlegen können. Doch nur Händel oder sein Kopist hätte Grund gehabt, ihn genau dort einzulegen, wo eine der nur zwei von Händel hinzugefügten Arien (nämlich »*Alma tra miei timori*«) die ursprüngliche Arie ersetzen sollte: An dieser Stelle jedenfalls diente er Händel selbst oder seinem Kopisten als Merkzeichen. Da der Zettel in der Mitte durchgerissen ist, möchte man fast vermuten, die andere Hälfte habe einst bei der anderen zu ersetzenden Arie gelegen. Vielleicht hat Händel die Partitur von Buckworth ausgeliehen und wollte sie schonend behandeln, also keine schriftlichen Vermerke anbringen.

Das Handexemplar der Oper ist nicht erhalten, jedoch die Cembalopartitur[59] sowie das Libretto, aus dem für die Londoner Aufführung folgende Besetzung hervorgeht:

Lucio Papirio (Tenor): Giambattista Pinacci
Marco Fabio (Baß): Antonio Montagnana
Papiria (Sopran): Anna Maria Strada
Rutilia (Alt): Francesca Bertoldi
Quinto Fabio (Mezzosopran): Fr. Bernardi detto Senesino
Servilio (Alt): Anna Bagnolesi Pinacci
Cominio (Mezzosopran): Antonio Campioli.

Was Händel an Giacomellis Oper geändert hat, war allein durch die neue Sängerbesetzung veranlaßt; der fast ausschließliche Zweck der Bearbeitung war die Anpassung von Arien und Rezitativen an die Stimmlagen der Londoner Sänger. Die Rollenhierarchie der Originalbesetzung hingegen ließ sich auf das Londoner Ensemble übertragen — ganz im Gegensatz zu Händels nächstem Pasticcio *Catone*, bei dem ausführlicher von diesem Problem die Rede sein wird. Nur für den Bassisten, Montagnana, wurden zwei Arien aus dessen Repertoire eingesetzt. Ansonsten enthält das Pasticcio nur Originalarien Giacomellis; ihre Gesamtzahl wurde allerdings von 28 auf 21 reduziert. Von einer 22. Arie ist der Anfangsteil stehengeblieben, aber nur in instrumentaler Fassung, ohne Text: Es ist die Auftrittsarie des Q. Fabio (Senesino) im ersten Akt (der Sieger kehrt im Triumph von der Schlacht zurück), die auf diese Weise zu einer kurzen, prächtigen Sinfonia umgedeutet wurde. Eine weitere Arie der Papiria war zunächst geplant, wurde aber vor dem Druck des Librettos fallengelassen. Über Händels Vorgehen insgesamt gibt die erhaltene Cembalopartitur Aufschluß, welche anders als bei *Ormisda* und *Venceslao* vor dem Handexemplar angefertigt worden sein muß. Besonders wichtig ist, daß Händel sich bei den Arien mit einfachen Transpositionen begnügte, während er bei den Rezitativen meistens die »*tessitura*« verändert, also umgearbeitet hat. Für die Musik der Arien war es

---

[59] BRD-Hs M A/1029. In diese Cembalopartitur sind zum Teil auch die Instrumentaloberstimmen eingetragen.

offenbar nicht abträglich, wenn z. B. Senesinos Arien, die in Parma Farinelli gesungen hatte, um eine Quart oder Quint herabgesetzt wurden; eine Arie Senesinos wurde aus der Rolle Bernacchis (M. Fabio) herübergenommen, der etwa denselben Stimmumfang hatte, was die Transposition ersparte. Bernacchis Rolle ihrerseits ging vermittels Oktavtransposition an Montagnana. Sämtliche Arien der Faustina wurden für die Strada um einen Halb- oder Ganzton hinaufgesetzt; weitere Transpositionen gab es für die Bertolli und für Campioli, einen aus Dresden verpflichteten Mezzosopranisten. Daß Händel die Arienfolge selbst so wenig angetastet hat, mag auch äußere Gründe haben: Bei der fortgeschrittenen Saison fehlte vielleicht die Zeit für tiefergreifende Bearbeitungen, und außer Montagnana hatte kein Sänger mehr Ansprüche auf eigene Arien. Trotzdem müssen wir außerdem vermuten, daß Händel Text und Musik auch aus ästhetischen Gründen nicht für umarbeitungsbedürftig hielt.

Bei den Rezitativen ist er folgendermaßen vorgegangen: Der Kopist erhielt die Anweisung, unproblematische Transpositionen, teilweise mit Schlüsselwechsel, selbst vorzunehmen, so etwa die Oktavtransposition Bernacchi-Montagnana, Teile der Rollen Rutilia (in der Vorlage Antonia Negri), Cominio (Pacini) und Servilio (Lucia Lancetti) sowie die unveränderte Partie Lucio Papirio (Borosini). Diese schrieb er aus der Vorlage in die Cembalopartitur ab, während er bei den problematischeren Rezitativen nur Text und Continuo eintrug. Händel zeichnete dann die geänderten Rezitative mit Bleistift vor und ließ sie den Kopisten mit Tinte ausmalen. Manchmal hat er auch den bereits notierten Continuo noch mit Tinte geändert. Die Anweisungen, welche Rezitativteile unverändert zu kopieren seien und welche nicht, muß Händel dem Kopisten auf einer gesonderten Vorlage gegeben haben. Diese könnte eine Art Ur-Handexemplar gewesen sein oder, wahrscheinlicher, ein Manuskript des Textes, der ja von Rossi ohnehin etwas bearbeitet werden mußte. Die Transposition der Arien wurde vom Kopisten vorgenommen; Händel zeichnete in die Cembalopartitur die gewünschte Tonart ein (»ex C«, »ex F« usw.) und paßte selbst nur den Rezitativschluß tonartlich an[60].

CATONE (1732)

Die Spielzeit 1732/1733 wurde von Händel mit einem Pasticcio eröffnet: *Catone*, einer Bearbeitung von Metastasios zweiter *tragedia per musica Catone*

---

[60] Die Arie »*Vengo a darti anima bella*« ist in das Hamburger Pasticcio *Circe* (1734) übernommen worden. Mehrere Arien aus Giacomellis Oper finden sich in der Ariensammlung GB-Lbm add. 31504, die wohl gegen Ende der dreißiger Jahre von einem Londoner Dilettanten zusammengestellt wurde. Sie enthält außerdem eine Kontamination mehrerer norditalienischer Sammlungen (vor allem aus Genua, 1723–1726) sowie Londoner Arien von Bononcini und Händel.

in Utica, 1728 in Rom erstaufgeführt. Das Londoner Pasticcio erlebte vom 4. bis zum 18. November 1732 nur vier Vorstellungen, in folgender Besetzung:

Catone (Mezzosopran): Francesco Bernardi detto Senesino
Marzia (Sopran): Anna Maria Strada
Emilia (Sopran): Celeste Gismondi
Arbace (Alt): Francesca Bertolli
Cesare (Baß): Antonio Montagnana.

Metastasios Drama enthält noch eine sechste Rolle, Fulvio. Der Tenor Pinacci, dem sie hätte zugeteilt werden können, war aber 1732/33 nicht mehr in Händels Ensemble. Das in Hamburg erhaltene Handexemplar[61] bestätigt Chrysanders Vermutung, daß die musikalische Vorlage von Leonardo Leo stammt[62]. Händel muß die Oper Leos im Karneval 1729 in Venedig gehört haben, wo sie an S. Gio. Grisostomo mit Farinelli aufgeführt wurde. Wie bei *Lucio Papirio* ist auch hier die von Händel benützte Vorlage erhalten: Es ist das Exemplar der Royal Academy, in dem sich Bleistifteintragungen Händels befinden[63]. Sie beziehen sich auf die Eliminierung der Partie des Fulvio. Leos Partitur diente also zunächst dem Librettisten als Vorlage für die damit verbundene Textbearbeitung. Der früheste nachweisbare Besitzer dieser Partitur ist wieder John Buckworth. Er muß ebenfalls im Karneval 1729 in Venedig gewesen sein, da ihm das Libretto der zweiten damals an S. Gio. Grisostomo aufgeführten Oper, Porporas *Semiramide,* gewidmet ist. Selbstverständlich befindet sich auch diese Oper in Buckworths Sammlung[64]. Wahrscheinlich hat Buckworth Leos Partitur mit nach London gebracht und 1732 an Händel ausgeliehen.

Händel hat auch mit dem *Catone* im wesentlichen das Werk eines in London noch unbekannten Italieners der jüngeren Generation darbieten wollen. Zugleich nahm er Gelegenheit, nach den eigenen Vertonungen von *Siroe*, *Poro* und *Ezio* ein weiteres Drama Metastasios auf die Bühne zu bringen. Bei der Herstellung der Partitur übernahm Händel aus der Vorlage die Sinfonia[65] und von den Rezitativen so viel wie möglich; nur die zu ändernden Rezitativteile zeichnete er selbst den Kopisten im Handexemplar vor (nicht in die Cembalopartitur, wie bei *Lucio Papirio*: vom *Catone* ist keine Cembalopartitur erhalten). Den Rest der Rezitative konnten die Kopisten, einschließlich unproblematischer Transpo-

---

[61] BRD-Hs M A/1012.
[62] CHRYSANDER, a. a. O. Bd. II, p. 252.
[63] GB-Lam, Ms. 75.
[64] GB-Lam, Ms. 81. Die Sammlung enthält noch mehr venezianische Partituren der Zeit, darunter Porporas *Ezio* (Ms. 79) und Leos *Argeno* (Ms. 74), beide von 1728. Der Titel »Argeneo« erscheint in Kerslakes altem Verzeichnis Händelscher Handexemplare: Vgl. CLAUSEN, a. a. O. p. 17 f. Man könnte hier an ein nicht zur Aufführung gekommenes und heute verschollenes Pasticcio denken.
[65] Die einzige andere nachweisbare Partitur von Leos *Catone in Utica*, B-Bc 2194, hat eine andere Sinfonia. Beide Sinfonien stammen nach HELL, a. a. O. p. 462 ff., nicht von Leo.

sitionen, aus der Vorlage abschreiben. Mit den Arien verfuhr Händel jedoch diesmal anders: Schon weil *Catone* die Saison eröffnen sollte, wurde er wieder ein echtes Pasticcio. Von den 25 ganz oder teilweise erhaltenen Arien des Handexemplars (die später ersetzten eingerechnet) stammen nur neun aus Leos Oper. Die übrigen sind von Hasse (6), Porpora (4), Vivaldi (vermutlich 3) und Vinci (1); die Herkunft von 2 Arien ist noch ungeklärt. Der Arienbestand des *Catone* hat sich während der Vorbereitungen relativ stark verändert. Vor dem Druck des Librettos wurden im Handexemplar zwei Arien der Emilia (Gismondi) durch andere ersetzt, sowie zu den drei Arien des Cesare (Montagnana) eine vierte hinzugefügt. Eine Arie der Strada, wahrscheinlich Leos Originalarie, fiel dagegen aus. Nach dem Druck des Librettos, also vielleicht erst nach der Premiere, wurden für die Gismondi zwei weitere Arien ausgetauscht. Der Ersatz von allein vier Emilia-Arien bezeugt eine recht wählerische Einstellung der Gismondi. Wie schon *Elpidia* und *Ormisda* zeigen, erfüllte Händel in den Pasticci ziemlich großzügig die Arienwünsche besonders der neuengagierten Sänger.

Aus einem Brief von Lord Hervey geht hervor, daß Celeste (»Celestina«) Gismondi (seit London Mrs. Hempson) im Frühjahr 1729 in Neapel war[66]. Vielleicht hat Händel sie dort kennengelernt. Er hatte allerdings zunächst nicht sie, sondern die ebenfalls noch junge A. M. Strada engagiert. Die »Celestina« scheint identisch zu sein mit einer Sopranbuffa Celeste Resse, die 1724 bis 1732 am Teatro S. Bartolomeo regelmäßig in Intermezzi sang. (Genau seit Herbst 1732 taucht in den Libretti von S. Bartolomeo erstmalig eine neue Intermezzo-Sopranistin auf.)

Händels Bearbeitung von Leos *Catone* ist ein instruktives Beispiel für Probleme der Rollencharakteristik, der passenden Verteilung musikalischer und dramatischer Aufgaben auf die einzelnen Sänger. Hierüber hatte sich Händel bei der Adaption des *Lucio Papirio Dittatore* aus verschiedenen Gründen weniger Gedanken zu machen brauchen. Den *Catone* von Metastasio und Leo mußte er jedoch einer sehr veränderten Aufführungssituation anpassen, und er hatte dabei außerkünstlerischen Ansprüchen ebenso zu genügen wie künstlerischen. Daß er die Rezitative Metastasios stark gekürzt hat, liegt an der allgemeinen Londoner Bühnentradition, wie sie von Riva beschrieben wird[67]. Die Auswahl der Arien wurde spezifisch von Technik, Stimmlage und künstlerischer Eigenart der gerade jetzt engagierten Sänger bestimmt, sie konnte sich aber auch nicht von der Rangstellung des Einzelnen in der Hierarchie des Ensembles unabhängig machen,

---

[66] Der Brief Lord Herveys bei DEUTSCH, a. a. O. p. 296.
[67] Brief Rivas vom 3. 10. 1726 (DEUTSCH, a. a. O. p. 197). Zu diesem und einem anderen Brief Rivas vom 7. 9. 1725, der damalige Probleme der Londoner Rollenhierarchie schildert, vgl. besonders R. A. STREATFEILD, *Handel, Rolli, and Italian Opera in London in the eighteenth century*, in: MQ 3, 1917, p. 433 f.

wie sie sich schon in der Höhe seines Honorars manifestierte[68], und damit auch nicht vom Gewicht seiner Rolle im Drama.

Es hatten sich in der Opernpraxis längst gewisse Schemata eingebürgert, bei deren Beachtung man ein Minimum an äußerer und innerer Balance der Aufführung erwarten konnte; zu ihnen gehören die Rollenhierarchie von *prima, seconda* und *terza parte,* die Klassifizierung der Arien nach Affektcharakter und Kompositionstechnik, die Normierungen bezüglich Anzahl und Placierung der jedem Sänger zugeteilten Arien usw. Händel war ein Feind der Schematisierung auch in diesem Bereich. Daß er etwa die Rollenhierarchie als unerträgliche Fessel empfand, wissen wir konkret aus seinem Brief an Colman vom 19. 6. 1730[69]. Es ging ihm dort aber mehr darum, als Veranstalter freie Hand zu haben, um sich von dieser Seite Schwierigkeiten zu ersparen, während er als Künstler durchaus anpassungsbereit war. (Eine ähnliche Haltung hatte er ja schon in der Konkurrenzsituation Faustina/Cuzzoni 1726—1728 gezeigt.) Für das *Catone*-Ensemble waren fremde Schemata ohnehin kaum anwendbar.

Montagnana beispielsweise war als Bassist eine Ausnahmeerscheinung. Ihm konnte Händel nicht die — üblicherweise — unbedeutendste Partie zumuten, etwa die des Fulvio, mit der sich bei Leo immerhin ein G. M. Boschi hatte begnügen müssen. Montagnana sang die Rolle des Cäsar, von Leo für den Sopranisten Gizzi komponiert, und er bekam echte, anspruchsvolle Baßarien aus fremden Opern. Damit wurde die Intention des Textdichters ganz umgekehrt, der dem (Tenor-) Heroen und strengen Vater Cato den jugendlichen Liebhaber und Draufgänger Cäsar (Sopran) gegenüberstellt. Schon bei Leo, der zweiten Vertonung nach Vinci, war Catos Rolle auf einen Sopranisten übergegangen und so ihres patriarchalischen Einschlags spürbar beraubt worden. In diese durch Grimaldi neugeprägte Rolle konnte dafür Senesino, sein Londoner Erbe in mehrfacher Hinsicht, wie in ein fertiges Gewand schlüpfen: Er sang nur Arien der Vorlage. Unproblematisch war auch der Übergang der Primadonnenpartie von Lucia Facchinelli an die Strada. Händel gab ihr nur einen zusätzlichen *last song,* und zwar Vincis berühmtes *»Vò solcando un mar crudele«.* Der so gestaltete Schluß der Oper löst freilich die Problematik von Metastasios tragico fine mit Gewalt: Metastasio hatte zwar wegen der Publikumskritik den ersten, düsteren Schluß für Venedig etwas abgemildert, doch Cäsars Schluß-Akkompagnato belassen, in dem der militärische Sieger, durch Catos Freitod moralisch überwunden, verärgert seinen Lorbeer zur Erde wirft. Diese kritische Schlußmoral wurde in London (in Leos Vertonung) beibehalten, aber durch die aufgepfropfte Favoritarie dramatisch und musikalisch entwertet: Der Dramatiker Händel erweist sich nicht nur kon-

---

[68] Genaue Beträge sind nur für die Besetzung von 1729/1730 überliefert; vgl. Deutsch, a. a. O. p. 243 und 246.

[69] Deutsch, a. a. O. p. 256.

zessionsbereit gegenüber Sängerin und Publikum, sondern auch gleichgültig gegenüber dem Stoff.

Die Partie des Arbace, von Leo für Farinelli geschaffen, wurde in London fast bis zur Unkenntlichkeit reduziert. Francesca Bertolli konnte — und durfte! — keine einzige von Farinellis Arien singen. Celeste Gismondi hätte Leos Emilia gut verkörpern können: Ihre Arien in Händels Opern beweisen es. Die Veränderungen in ihrer Rolle gehen eher auf das Konto ihres persönlichen Ehrgeizes.

Catone wurde in London teilweise für eine Komposition Händels gehalten und als solche negativ beurteilt[70]. Walsh druckte immerhin sechs *Favourite Songs*[71].

DREI PASTICCI IN EINER SPIELZEIT:
»SEMIRAMIDE RICONOSCIUTA«, »CAIO FABRICIO« UND »ARBACE« (1733/1734)

Als Händel sich im Sommer 1733 unerwartet auf die Konkurrenz der Opera of the Nobility einstellen mußte, und als, vermutlich schon im Juni, alle Sänger bis auf Strada zur Gegenseite übergelaufen waren, blieb ihm für die notwendig gewordenen Vorbereitungen weniger Zeit als in früheren Jahren, zumal wenn man die Oxforder Oratorienaufführungen vom Juli 1733 mitberücksichtigt. Trotzdem konnte er nicht nur ein vollständiges Ensemble mit den berühmten Sopranisten Carestini und Scalzi zusammenstellen, sondern auch, außer der eigenen *Arianna*, gleich drei Pasticci nach fremden Autoren (statt bisher einem) zur Aufführung fertig machen. Wohl deshalb glaubte Hawkins, für Sommer 1733 eine neue Reise nach Italien annehmen zu müssen, was jedoch irrig ist[72]. Händel hatte eine Spielzeit 1733/34 ohnehin geplant, da sie in dem 1729 mit Heidegger auf fünf Jahre geschlossenen Vertrag enthalten war[73]. Zumindest die Partitur der *Semiramide riconosciuta* von Metastasio und Vinci konnte er sich schon auf der Italienreise 1729 beschaffen: Sie wurde im Karneval 1729 in Rom aufgeführt. Zur Produktion von *Caio Fabricio* (Zeno/Hasse; Rom, Karneval 1732) und *Arbace* (= *Artaserse*, Metastasio/Vinci; Rom, Karneval 1730) mag er sich erst wegen des Konkurrenzdrucks entschieden haben. Doch können diese sehr ver-

---

[70] Vgl. DEUTSCH, a. a. O. p. 296 f.

[71] Vgl. William C. SMITH, *Handel. A Descriptive Catalogue . . .*, a. a. O. p. 22. Der Druck enthält je drei Arien der Strada und der Gismondi. »*Vo' solcando*« ist offenbar von hier aus in das Hamburger Pasticcio *Circe* (1734) übergegangen.

[72] John HAWKINS, *A General History of the Science and Practice of Music*, New Edition, 2 Bde., London 1875, Bd. II, p. 876. Nach Hawkins habe Händel auf dieser Reise Farinelli gehört, »*a young man of astonishing talents, and also Carestini*«; außerdem sei er von J. Chr. Smith senior begleitet worden. Da der Angabe zu Farinelli offensichtlich eine Verwechslung mit der Reise von 1729 zugrundeliegt, könnten sich auch die beiden übrigen Angaben auf jene Reise beziehen. Vgl. auch CHRYSANDER, a. a. O. Bd. II, p. 332, und DEUTSCH, a. a. O. p. 331.

[73] Vgl. oben Anm. 22.

breiteten Partituren auch in London vorhanden gewesen sein. Carestini hatte
Händel 1728 oder 1729 in Neapel kennenlernen können; das Engagement Bernacchis 1729 schloß aber dasjenige Carestinis aus[74]. Nach Bernacchis Weggang
1730 hat sich Händel sofort um Carestini bemüht[75]. Scalzi war der Protagonist
auch von Vincis *Semiramide* 1729 gewesen und vielleicht schon von Rom 1729
mit Händel bekannt. Auch Carestini bekam im *Arbace* seine eigene Hauptrolle
von 1730 wieder.

Das Libretto der *Arianna in Creta* (von Pariati, nicht von Colman)[76] ist fast
identisch mit einer von Leo ebenfalls im Karneval 1729 in Rom vertonten Fassung. Nicolò Porpora hatte Pariatis Text schon 1717 für Wien vertont und
1727 neu komponiert. Daß er als Kapellmeister der Opera of the Nobility nun
eine von Rolli neugedichtete *Ariadne*-Oper präsentierte, war ein bewußtes
Konkurrenzmanöver gegen Händels *Arianna*, die schon am 5. Oktober 1733
fertiggestellt war: Eben wegen Händels Priorität mußte Porpora auf eine andere
Version ausweichen, obwohl ein Vergleich seiner beiden Partituren den Eindruck
erweckt, daß ihm die Musik von 1727 mehr Ehre gemacht hätte[77].

Aus naheliegenden Gründen mußte Händel 1733/34 mehr neue Opern anbieten
als jemals zuvor in einer Spielzeit. Doch warum erhöhte er die Zahl der fremden
Opern und nicht die Zahl der eigenen? Er hatte die Saison lange vor der Nobility
mit *Semiramide* (30. Oktober 1733), mit Wiederaufführungen seines *Ottone* (13.
November 1733) und mit *Caio Fabricio* (4. Dezember 1733) begonnen, antwortete
aber auf Porporas *Ariadne in Naxos* (1. Januar 1734) immer noch nicht mit der
längst vollendeten *Arianna*, sondern mit Vincis *Arbace* (5. Januar 1734): Nicht
das eigene Werk, sondern die Pasticci sollten die Konkurrenz in Schach halten. Er
wollte Porpora mit überlegenen Partituren aus dessen eigener Stilsphäre entgegentreten. Trotzdem scheint Händels Rechnung nicht ganz aufgegangen zu sein.
Nur *Arbace*, damals die erfolgreichste Oper Italiens, fand einigermaßen Anklang
mit acht Aufführungen; die andern beiden Pasticci wurden nur je viermal gespielt[78].

Wenn man den außergewöhnlichen Erfolg, den die Gegenoper in der Spielzeit
1734/35 mit Hasses *Artaserse* und mit Farinelli erzielte, nicht ausschließlich auf

---

[74] Vgl. oben Anm. 29.

[75] Vgl. den Brief Swineys an Colman vom 18. 6. 1730 (DEUTSCH, a. a. O. p. 258).

[76] Vgl. CHRYSANDER, a. a. O. Bd. II, p. 335; DEUTSCH, a. a. O. p. 342 f.; Alfred LOEWENBERG,
Annals of Opera, 2. Auflage, Genf 1955, Sp. 180 f.

[77] Von Porporas Fassung von 1727 ist das Autograph des 2. Akts in GB-Lbm add. 14114 erhalten; eine fast vollständige Ariensammlung dieser Fassung in GB-Cfm 23 F 3. Partituren
von Porporas *Ariadne in Naxos* (1734) u. a. in A-Wn, A-Wgm, GB-Lk.

[78] Die Eintragung im Colman-Register (Sasse, a. a. O. p. 222) »*Arbaces. a new Opera did not
take at all*« dürfte eine Verwechslung mit *Caio Fabricio* sein; die Chronologie ist in diesem
letzten Abschnitt des Registers ohnehin konfus. Ein negatives Urteil über *Semiramide* bei
DEUTSCH, a. a. O. p. 330.

den Sänger zurückführen will, sondern auch auf Hasses Musik und Metastasios Drama, so wirft es ein Licht auf das Londoner Publikum, daß ein Jahr zuvor unter Händel zwei Dramen Metastasios und eine Oper Hasses praktisch durchgefallen waren. Händels Pasticcio-Strategie ist an der Polarisierung des Geschmacks gescheitert: Seine eigenen Anhänger waren nur auf Händelsche Kompositionen eingeschworen, während diejenigen, die er mit der Musik der neueren Italiener zu gewinnen hoffte, wohl aus Parteilichkeit dem Haymarket-Theater fernblieben.

Händels Sängerensemble umfaßte von Beginn der Spielzeit an Strada, Carestini, Scalzi, Durastanti, die Schwestern Maria Caterina und Maria Rosa Negri sowie Gustavus Waltz. Aus den Handexemplaren der drei Pasticci geht nicht hervor, ob diese etwa noch für eine Besetzung berechnet waren, der einer der inzwischen abgesprungenen Sänger angehört hätte. Immerhin ist die Partie der *Semiramide* von vornherein der Durastanti zugedacht gewesen, da die für ihre Stimmlage transponierten Arien mit als erste ins Handexemplar eingetragen wurden. Falls Cembalopartituren je existiert haben, so dürften diese allerdings (wie bei *Lucio Papirio* und eventuell *Catone*) eine noch frühere Stufe der Vorbereitungen widergespiegelt haben.

Insgesamt scheint es, daß Händel etwa von August an mit der vollständigen Besetzung rechnen konnte und für diese die Pasticci vorbereitet hat. Dem steht nur die Behauptung der Satire »*Harmony in an Uproar*« entgegen, noch am Aufführungstag einer »*new opera*« seien Händel »*two very remarkable monsters*« abspenstig gemacht worden, für die er aber gleich Ersatz gefunden habe[79]. W. C. Smith meinte diese Bemerkung auf den *Ottone* vom 13. November 1733 beziehen zu müssen, weil ein *Ottone*-Libretto von 1733 noch die Besetzung Senesino—Montagnana—Bertolli angibt und nur durch zwei vorgeheftete Blätter an die neue Besetzung und deren Erfordernisse angepaßt ist[80]. Erstens war nun *Ottone* keine »*new opera*«; vor allem gibt aber das Libretto der *Semiramide* vom 30. Oktober 1733 schon die neue Besetzung an. Smiths *Ottone*-Libretto wurde nach Clausen für eine im März des Jahres geplante Aufführung gedruckt[81]. Der Autor der »*Harmony in an Uproar*« hat die Abwerbungsgeschichte jedenfalls melodramatisch ausgeschmückt und vor allem Händels Zeitnot beträchtlich übertrieben.

Spätestens im Oktober 1733 waren außer dem Autograph der *Arianna* auch die Handexemplare der ersten beiden Pasticci in ihrer ersten Form fertiggestellt[82].

[79] Vgl. DEUTSCH, a. a. O. p. 355.
[80] William C. SMITH, *Gustavus Waltz: Was he Handel's Cook?*, in: William C. SMITH, *Concerning Handel, His Life and Works*, London 1948, p. 178 f.
[81] CLAUSEN, a. a. O. p. 189, Anm. 6.
[82] Signaturen der drei Handexemplare: *Semiramide* BRD-Hs M A/1051, *Caio Fabricio* M A/1011, *Arbace* M A/1004. Libretti nur von *Semiramide* und *Caio Fabricio* in GB-Lbm.

Von da an lassen sich noch viele Änderungen erkennen, nicht nur in bezug auf einzelne Arien, sondern sogar auf die Rollenverteilung. Waltz war für alle drei Opern vorgesehen gewesen; er konnte oder sollte dann aber in *Semiramide* und *Arbace* nicht auftreten. Die Partie des Ircano in *Semiramide* übernahm an seiner Stelle Caterina Negri; diese wurde in der Rolle des Sibari von Rosa Negri ersetzt. In *Arbace* ging Waltz' Partie Artabano an die Durastanti, deren Semira an Caterina Negri und deren Megabise wieder an Rosa Negri. Diese Änderung vollzog sich beim *Arbace* erst während der Arbeit am Handexemplar: Der Anfang paßt noch zur alten Besetzung; von der fünften Szene an wurde das bereits vom Kopisten ausgeschriebene Rezitativ von Händel korrigiert; erst vom Schluß des zweiten Aktes an sind außer den Rezitativen auch die Arien schon für die definitive Stimmlage eingerichtet. Bei der *Semiramide* war die Umbesetzung erst nach der Fertigstellung auch der Rezitative erfolgt: Diese wurden nicht mehr eigens umgeschrieben, ebensowenig wie die zweite der drei in Frage kommenden Arien. Im *Caio Fabricio* tauschten Durastanti und Caterina Negri die Rollen, noch während am Handexemplar gearbeitet wurde. Hierbei war auch die Rollenhierarchie tangiert: Der Durastanti mußte die Partie der Bircenna von drei auf vier Arien aufgebessert werden, während der Negri von drei geplanten Turio-Arien sogar noch eine genommen wurde. Die ansonsten notwendigen Transpositionen sind nicht überall eingetragen worden; auch die tonartliche Veränderung der Rezitativschlüsse vor transponierten Arien gelangte nur noch dort ins Handexemplar, wo der Kopist die ganze Arie samt angrenzendem Rezitativ ohnehin noch einmal schreiben mußte. An vielen Stellen in diesen Pasticci wich also das Handexemplar, Händels Dirigiervorlage, zumindest tonartlich vom tatsächlich Erklingenden ab.

In den drei Pasticci fielen den Sängern letztlich folgende Partien zu (Libretti sind nur von *Semiramide* und *Caio Fabricio* erhalten):

Strada (Sopran):	*Tamiri*	*Sestia*	*Mandane*
Carestini (Sopran):	*Scitalce*	*Pirro*	*Arbace*
Scalzi (Sopran):	*Mirteo*	*Volusio*	*Artaserse*
Durastanti (Mezzosopran):	*Semiramide*	*Bircenna*	*Artabano*
Cat. Negri (Alt):	*Ircano*	*Turio*	*Semira*
Rosa Negri (Sopran):	*Sibari*	*Cinea*	*Megabise*
G. Waltz (Baß):	—	*Caio Fabricio*	—

In den drei Pasticci ist das Verhältnis zwischen der Vorlage und dem, was Händel daraus gemacht hat, relativ ähnlich. Jedesmal ging er von einer bestimmten Partitur aus, die er mehr oder weniger modifizierte, ohne jedoch den dramatischen Ablauf oder auch nur die Reihenfolge der erhalten gebliebenen Arien anzutasten. Daß das Ausmaß der Händelschen Eingriffe in die drei Vorlagen sukzessiv abnimmt, ließe sich erklären: Dies paßt erstens in eine Entwicklungslinie vom *Catone* an (er weicht von seiner Vorlage noch stärker ab als *Semiramide*) bis zur *Didone* von 1737 (sie ist ihrer Vorlage noch ähnlicher als *Arbace*). Zweitens bestand mit fortschreitender Saison immer weniger Grund für Präsentationsarien der neuen Sänger. Trotzdem unterscheidet sich *Semiramide* von den beiden späteren Pasticci auch prinzipiell. Sie umfaßt nämlich bereits im Grundplan auch ein Drittel Arien aus anderen Opern (die zum Teil parodiert waren), während dort die fremden Arien, bis auf einen von vornherein geplanten *last song* Carestinis in *Caio Fabricio,* durch Umbesetzungen und Sonderwünsche der Sänger nachträglich erzwungen wurden. Händel hatte wohl nicht damit gerechnet, daß Carestini, der wie Scalzi im Oktober nach London gekommen sein muß, nicht nur in der ersten Saisonoper und im *Ottone,* sondern sogar noch in den folgenden Pasticci seine Partie aus eigenem Repertoire auffrischen wollte, obwohl er den *Arbace* ja selbst kreiert hatte. Auch die Strada zog bei diesen Ansprüchen mit; in geringerem Maße auch Scalzi. Bei ihm stellte sich dafür nach der Ankunft heraus, daß seine Stimme seit 1729 so viel tiefer geworden war, daß er seine eigene Partie in *Semiramide* nicht mehr singen konnte; die Arien wurden zunächst um einen Ganzton, dann sogar um eine kleine bzw. große Terz herabtransponiert. In *Caio Fabricio* sind die nötigen Transpositionen zum Teil nicht mehr aus dem Handexemplar ersichtlich; der Rolle in *Arbace* war Scalzi stimmlich gewachsen[83]. Die abweichende Konzeption der *Semiramide*, die im übrigen mit der des *Catone* übereinstimmt, deutet auf eine frühere Planung dieses ersten Pasticcio. Dafür spricht auch, daß es als Sinfonia diejenige zu Vincis *Artaserse* verwendet: Als die Arbeit am *Semiramide*-Handexemplar begann, war also an eine Aufführung des *Arbace* vielleicht noch nicht gedacht.

Die Rezitative der drei Pasticci folgen weitgehend den Originalen. Beim *Arbace* hat Händel sie sogar zunächst aus der Vorlagepartitur abschreiben lassen (oder aus der verschollenen Cembalopartitur, die mit ihr noch übereinstimmte); erst als wegen der Umbesetzungen die *tessitura* geändert werden mußte, schrieb Händel die Rezitative selbst weiter. Dabei hat er sie nun aber auch an manchen Stellen geändert, wo es der Stimmlage wegen nicht nötig gewesen wäre. Akkompagnati setzte er überwiegend neu als Sekkorezitative aus. Die Texte sind in allen drei Opern gekürzt, und zwar in mehreren Arbeitsphasen nacheinander; die

---

[83] Genau Entsprechendes berichtet Charles BURNEY, *A General History of Music,* hrsg. von Frank MERCER, 2 Bde., London 1935, Bd. II, p. 782, über Carestinis Stimme. Diese Mitteilung stammt aber fast wörtlich von J. J. QUANTZ, *Lebenslauf,* a. a. O. (Anm. 3), p. 234, und Quantz gibt für das Tieferwerden von Carestinis Stimme keinen Zeitpunkt an. Vielleicht hat Burney die Mitteilung deshalb mit der Spielzeit von 1733/34 in Verbindung gebracht, weil er wußte, daß in Händels *Arianna* nachträglich einige zu hohe Stellen gestrichen bzw. herabtransponiert wurden — was übrigens Carestinis Ankunft in London auf die Zeit nach der Fertigstellung des *Arianna*-Autographs (5. 10. 1733) festlegt. Doch sind die Änderungen bei Scalzi viel einschneidender als bei Carestini, der damals noch ein echter Sopran war. Zu Händels Sängern, ihrem Gesangsstil und ihrem Ambitus vgl. besonders Rodolfo CELLETTI, *Il virtuosismo vocale nel melodramma di Händel,* in: Rivista Italiana di Musicologia 4, 1969, p. 77—101.

Zahl der Arien ist überall ein wenig reduziert. Neu ist in dieser Spielzeit, daß innerhalb der Arien Striche angebracht wurden. Eine entsprechende Reduktion erfuhr der Aufführungsapparat. In der zweiten Szene der *Semiramide* ist eine kurze Sinfonia weggefallen. Die zweite Szene des zweiten Aktes verlangt in der Vorlage Chor und Ballett, die im Rezitativtext angekündigt sind: »*... ognuno/ la mensa onori, e intanto/ misto risuoni a liete danze il canto.*« Händel verbesserte zunächst in perfektem Italienisch »*... e intanto/ sciolga ognuno la lingua in dolce canto*«, mit dem Effekt, das Ballett weglassen zu können. Aber auch der Chor war zuviel, so daß er seine eigene Verbesserung wieder strich und den Rezitativtext mit »*... la mensa onori*« enden ließ. Er ließ alles Folgende entfernen, dafür eine kurze Sinfonia offenbar eigener Komposition einfügen — und was von Metastasios und Vincis pompöser Szene geblieben ist, besteht aus diesem anspruchslosen Instrumentalstück, das zum Essen gespielt wird.

Händel hat in die musikalische Substanz seiner Vorlagen gewöhnlich nicht eingegriffen. Außer den erwähnten Arienkürzungen, die jedoch den Charakter des Stücks nicht ändern, sind bisher nur zwei Fälle musikalischer Bearbeitung nachweisbar: »*Se vuoi ch'io mora*« in der *Didone* von 1737 und »*Saper bramate*« in der *Semiramide* von 1733. Die beiden Fassungen von »*Saper bramate*« sind auf den Seiten 259—267 wiedergegeben: Beispiel 1 zeigt die Arie aus Vincis *Semiramide riconosciuta* nach einer fragmentarischen Partitur dieser Oper, die zwar in Dresden geschrieben wurde, jedoch Vincis Originalfassung wiedergibt[84]; Beispiel 2 die Bearbeitung. Sie ist im Handexemplar zwar nicht autograph, doch muß den Umständen nach angenommen werden, daß sie von Händel stammt. Der Anlaß zur Bearbeitung war die Oktavtransposition aus der Alt- in die Baßlage für Gustavus Waltz, der zunächst den Ircano singen sollte. Dies erforderte an vielen Stellen eine Änderung des Continuo; außerdem wurde die erste Violine um eine Oktave herabversetzt, die zweite Violine ihr in den Gesangsteilen unisono angeschlossen. Die Viola konnte nicht mehr all'ottava col basso geführt werden und fiel in den Gesangsteilen ganz weg. Händel geht aber über diese notwendigen Umstellungen weit hinaus. Nicht nur um einer konsequenter durchgeführten Zweistimmigkeit willen, sondern auch im Sinne motivischer Vereinheitlichung ändert er oftmals den Duktus von Melodie und Continuo (vgl. T. 10—16 mit Vinci T. 7—13) und ersetzt zwei größere Abschnitte, die bei Vinci eigene Motive haben (T. 23—27, 28—34), durch wiederholte Abschnitte (T. 26—31, 32—36). Er wertet den Kontrast zwischen der ersten und zweiten Textzeile — bei Vinci eher eine Vortragsnuance — architektonisch aus, indem er die kontrastierende Unisonogruppe auch in den zweiten Gesangsteil einführt (T. 26—31). Die Fermate und die Schlußwiederholung »*cangiando vò*« (T. 42—43; entsprechend im Ritornell T. 52—53) bedeuten technisch, daß dem Sänger Gelegenheit zu einer Kadenz ge-

---

[84] BRD-Hs M A/680 (2. und 3. Akt).

geben wird, die bei Vinci (T. 49—50) nicht besteht. In dem völlig neu gefaßten Schlußritornell fällt die Piano-Stelle auf (T. 47—49), deren musikalischer Charakter Vincis Konzeption der Arie widerspricht: Chromatik, tonrepetierender Orgelpunkt und übergebundene Dreiachtelnoten gehören zu der Vorstellung von Siciliano-Arie, wie wir sie von Händel auch sonst kennen. Vinci dagegen hat sich nicht nur hier, sondern auffallenderweise in seinem ganzen Schaffen vor so eindeutigen Anklängen an dieses Tanzmodell zurückgehalten. Auch den Mittelteil nähert Händel eigenen Siciliano-Vorbildern an. Hier entfernt er sich am weitesten von der Vorlage. Man hat den Eindruck, als habe er anfangs nicht viel mehr als eine transponierte Umschrift vorgehabt, die sich aber, gleichsam im Prozeß der Niederschrift, zunehmend verselbständigte. In der Tat dürfte für ihn, wie für viele Komponisten der Zeit, eine Neukomposition wesentlich bequemer gewesen sein als eine dem Original verantwortliche Umformung.

Der geringe Erfolg der drei Pasticci von 1733/1734 zeigt sich auch daran, daß Walsh nur vom *Arbace* ein Heft mit *Favourite Songs* zu drucken wagte[85]. Fünf Arien aus *Semiramide* sind jedoch auch in einem von J. C. Smith senior geschriebenen Sammelband erhalten; es handelt sich dabei wohl um Kopien nach dem Handexemplar[86]. Der Band enthält unter anderem auch zwei Arien aus *Arbace* sowie zahlreiche Nummern aus Produktionen der Opera of the Nobility, darunter sechs »Songs in Belmira«, Stücke eines Pasticcios, das am 23. März 1734 in Lincoln's Inn Fields aufgeführt wurde[87].

Händel in Covent Garden und »Didone abbandonata« (1737)

In den ersten beiden Jahren nach der Übernahme des Covent Garden-Theaters im Herbst 1734 verfolgte Händel eine neue Opernstrategie. Der Verzicht auf das Engagement neuer italienischer Sänger, die aufwendigen Chöre, Ballette und Instrumentalmusiken (noch 1733 hatte Händel aus der *Semiramide* Ballett und Chor entfernt), die vermehrten Oratorienaufführungen, vor allem aber die Beschränkung auf eigene Kompositionen: dies sind die Konsequenzen, die Händel aus dem unbefriedigenden Erfolg der Spielzeit 1733/34 zog, in der er noch auf Carestini und Scalzi, auf Opern von Vinci und Hasse gesetzt hatte. Senesino und Porpora hatte er damit noch standhalten können, aber nicht mehr Farinelli

---

[85] Vgl. William C. SMITH, *Handel. A Descriptive Catalogue ...*, a. a. O., p. 16 f.
[86] GB-Cfm 52 B 1.
[87] Das Pasticcio geht wohl auf *Belmira in Creta* von G. Giusti zurück, Musik von A. Galeazzi, aufgeführt im Herbst 1729 in San Moisè, Venedig. Zwei der *Belmira*-Arien in Smiths Sammelband ließen sich identifizieren: »Se il duol« ist die Parodie einer Arie aus Hasses *Cleofide* (Dresden 1731), »Non disperi peregrino« stammt aus Orlandinis *Adelaide* (San Cassiano, Venedig, 6. 2. 1729).

und Hasse selbst, die inzwischen ins Haymarket-Theater eingezogen waren. Das neue System ist in sich schlüssig: Die Ausgaben etwa für die Ballette, für die Ballerina Sallé, mußten an den Sängern und teilweise den Dekorationen eingespart werden, was zur Verpflichtung englischer Sänger (z. B. Cecilia Young und John Beard) und zu Oratorienaufführungen zwang. Händel konnte außerdem dem Publikum etwas qualitativ anderes bieten als die Gegenoper, welche er noch 1733/34 mit ihren eigenen Mitteln zu übertrumpfen versucht hatte.

Als Fortsetzung der Pasticci, insofern sie der Präsentation neuer Künstler zu dienen hatten, ist deshalb in gewissem Sinn das Tanzspiel *Terpsicore* mit der Sallé anzusehen, das zusammen mit *Pastor fido* die erste Covent Garden-Saison eröffnete (9. November 1734)[88], jedoch nicht Händels Pasticcio aus eigenen Kompositionen *Oreste*, welches am 18. Dezember folgte[89]. *Oreste* enthält Instrumentalsuiten und Ballett; Händel komponierte auch eine neue Ouverture dazu. *Oreste* ist zudem ein Füllsel im Spielplan: Es gibt also mehrere Gründe, ihn nicht mit den Pasticci nach fremden Autoren zusammen zu nennen, ebensowenig wie übrigens den *Alessandro Severo* von 1738[90].

Daß Händels neues System kaum als künstlerische Neubesinnung zu werten ist, sondern vor allem taktische Gründe hat, zeigt der erneute Umschwung von 1736 an. Die Konkurrenz hatte Senesino verloren, Farinellis Faszinationskraft war so gut wie verflogen. Händel indes hatte die persönliche Protektion des Prince of Wales gewonnen. Er wandte sich nun wieder radikal dem herrschenden Opernstil zu, dem immerhin noch jahrzehntelang der Publikumsgeschmack in Europa gehören sollte. Diese Wendung wird am deutlichsten illustriert durch das Engagement der Kastraten Gioacchino Conti detto Gizziello und Domenico Annibali[91] sowie durch die Aufführung der *Didone abbandonata* von Metastasio und Vinci.

Für ihre Neuauftritte mußten beiden Kastraten Präsentationsarien aus dem eigenen Repertoire zugestanden werden; doch geschah es diesmal — das ist neu — nicht nur im Zusammenhang mit dem Pasticcio, sondern auch in Händelschen Opern. Conti sang in den Wiederaufführungen von Händels *Ariodante* am 5. und 7. Mai 1736 sieben neue Arien, die nicht von Händel stammen[92]. Annibali sang in Händels *Poro* am 8. Dezember 1736 vier eingelegte Arien, von denen er zwei oder drei aus Dresden mitgebracht hatte; eine weitere Dresdener Arie in der *Didone*[93]. Insgesamt dürfte es in dieser Spielzeit noch mehr solcher Einlagen ge-

[88] Über *Terpsicore*, die Sallé, Cecilia Young und John Beard vgl. DEUTSCH, a. a. O., p. 373 f.

[89] Vgl. CHRYSANDER, a. a. O. Bd. II, p. 368 f.; DEUTSCH, a. a. O. p. 377.

[90] Vgl. DEUTSCH, a. a. O. p. 451.

[91] Annibali kam am 5. 10. 1736 von Dresden aus nach London: vgl. DEUTSCH, a. a. O. p. 416.

[92] Vgl. CLAUSEN, a. a. O., p. 116.

[93] Vgl. CHRYSANDER, a. a. O. Bd. II, p. 246 f.; DEUTSCH, a. a. O. p. 419. Die von Chrysander beschriebenen Notizblätter Händels (GB-Cfm 30 H 8, pp. 89—91) werden als Anweisungen für einen Kopisten zu verstehen sein, die betreffenden Arien — etwa für Händel selbst oder

geben haben; schon die erwähnten sind in den Partituren nicht oder nicht vollständig erhalten.

Metastasio-Vincis *Didone abbandonata* stammt aus dem Jahre 1726 (Teatro delle Dame, Rom, Karneval). Als veraltet konnte gerade dieses Werk nicht gelten; noch Algarotti hat den tragischen Akkompagnato-Schluß in höchsten Tönen gelobt. Händel wollte es möglichst unverändert aufführen, einschließlich der Akkompagnati, welche er in früheren vergleichbaren Fällen (*Semiramide* u. a.) öfters durch einfache Rezitative ersetzt hatte. Ansonsten mußten die Rezitative zum Teil umgeschrieben, zum Teil gekürzt werden. Auch einige Arien wurden gekürzt (etwa durch Streichung des Anfangsritornells) und sogar eine Arie eingreifend verändert. Diese Arie nämlich (*»Se vuoi ch'io mora«*), die im Handexemplar von der Vorlage abweicht, war in der heute verschollenen Cembalopartitur autograph[94]. Die Cembalopartitur wurde in diesem Fall wieder zuerst angefertigt, während das Handexemplar selbst schon Kopie ist. Die übrigen Änderungen an Vincis Musik, u. a. der Ersatz von 9 Arien, waren durch die Neubesetzung der Rollen und die Umschichtung der Rollenhierarchie bedingt. Das Libretto[95] gibt folgende Besetzung:

Didone (Sopran): Anna Maria Strada
Enea (Sopran): Gioacchino Conti detto Gizziello
Jarba (Alt): Domenico Annibali
Selene (Alt): Francesca Bertolli
Osmida (Alt): Maria Caterina Negri
Araspe (Tenor): John Beard.

Nicht nur mit der Musik, sondern auch mit dem Textmaterial von Vincis Vorlage ist Händel sehr ökonomisch umgegangen. In drei Fällen wurden Originaltexte einfach der dem Sänger zugestandenen neuen Musik unterlegt, was Parodien ersparte. Mit der veränderten Rollenhierarchie, die unter anderem eine Herabstufung der Rolle Beards verlangte, wurde Händel auf ähnliche Weise fertig: Er gab einfach je einen Arientext des Araspe wörtlich an Didone bzw. Enea. Einer davon (*»Sono intrepido«*) wird außerdem zu fremder Musik vorgetragen, was natürlich dem Zusammenhang zwischen Text, Musik und Szene schadet. Auffällig ist die Inkongruenz auch bei *»Cadrà fra poco«*: Die Musik dazu hatte Händel mit einem anderen Parodietext in *Semiramide* verwendet und brachte sie nun noch einmal mit einem *Didone*-Text zusammen. Dasselbe geschah bei *»A trion-*

---

für einen Bekannten — noch einmal herauszuschreiben. Von den Einlagen in *Poro* muß *»Per l'africane arene«* von Händel vorgeschlagen worden sein; sie gehört zu Vincis *Flavio Anicio Olibrio*, welcher mit Bernacchi im Dezember 1728 in Neapel aufgeführt wurde.

[94] Samuel Arnold besaß einen *»half score«*, nämlich die Cembalopartitur. Daß darin die Arie *»Se vuoi ch'io mora«* sowie die Singstimme fast des gesamten Rezitativs autograph war, bezeugt er selbst in einer Notiz auf dem Vorsatzblatt des Handexemplars: GB-Lbm add. 31607.

[95] BRD-Hs M A/401.

far«, das mit dem Originaltext in *Catone* erklungen war. Auch *»Tanto amor«*
stand ihm bereits aus *Semiramide* zur Verfügung, war aber dort nicht verwendet
worden. Händel hatte offenbar nicht nur mit der Textbeschaffung Mühe — vielleicht wirkte Rossi gar nicht mehr mit —, sondern es scheint auch sein Vorrat an
Partituren knapp geworden zu sein.

Die erste Aufführung der *Didone* fand am 13. April 1737 statt. Händel war
durch einen Schlaganfall gehindert, sie selbst zu leiten[96]. Es gab noch drei Wiederholungen. Wiederum war es Händel nicht gelungen, einer in Italien allgemein bewunderten Oper auf der Londoner Bühne zum Erfolg zu verhelfen. Bei
der Konkurrenz, die damals ebenfalls vor dem Bankrott stand, erlebten Hasses
Siroe und Pescettis *Demetrio* immerhin weit mehr Aufführungen. Händel aber
hatte sich, nicht zuletzt mit den Oratorien, inzwischen eine Anhängerschaft herangezogen, die ihm in der Wertschätzung von Vinci oder Hasse nicht zu folgen
imstande war. Händels Musik — und dies scheint die Grundproblematik seiner Pa-
sticcioaufführungen zu sein — war auf seiner eigenen Bühne eine zu erdrückende
Konkurrenz für Opern italienischer Herkunft.

Gesamtübersicht

Im Folgenden werden Sinfonia und Arien der neun chronologisch geordneten Pasticcio-Aufführungen Händels einzeln aufgezählt, und zwar in der Reihenfolge,
wie sie im Handexemplar bzw. Libretto erscheinen, einschließlich der eliminierten
oder später eingelegten Stücke. Die Spalten zeigen von links nach rechts: 1. Name des Sängers unter Händel. 2. Text der Arie bei Händel. Er ist eingeklammert,
wenn die Arie im Handexemplar nicht erhalten ist. 3. Komponist und Operntitel
der Vorlage. Der Operntitel ist eingeklammert, wo er nur aus dem Libretto
oder sekundärer Überlieferung erschlossen wurde; zusätzlich der Komponistenname, falls auch er nur erschlossen ist. 4. Originaltext der Arie, wenn sie bei
Händel parodiert ist; andernfalls »id.«. 5. Name des Sängers der Vorlage.
Wenn er die Arie auch bei Händel gesungen hat, Name in Kursiven. Die waage-
rechten Striche im Bezirk der ersten beiden Spalten bedeuten die Akttrennung.

---

[96] Vgl. Deutsch, a. a. O. p. 431 f.

ELPIDIA (11. Mai 1725)

Sinfonia

Vinci, Eraclea, Neapel 1724 (mit neuem Schlußsatz)

Besetzung	Arie	Herkunft	Neue Fassung	Sänger
Senesino + Pacini	»Il valor–il vigor«	(Vinci zugeschrieben)*		
Cuzzoni	»Dea triforme«	Vinci, Ifigenia, Venedig 1725	id.	Bordoni
Borosini	»Per serbarti«	Orlandini, Berenice, Venedig 1725	id.	Barbieri
Sorosina ersetzt durch: Dotti	»Si può ma sol«	Vinci, Rosmira fedele, Venedig 1725	id.	Antonia Me-righi
	»Sorge qual luccioletta«	Sarri, Arsace, Neapel 1718	id.	
Borosini ersetzt durch: Antinori	»Se non trovo«	(Peli zugeschrieben)*		
	»Amor deh lasciami«	(Orlandini, Lucio Papirio, Bologna 1718)	»Sì, sì, lasciatemi«	G. Paita
Cuzzoni	»D'alma luce«	Vinci, Ifigenia	id.	Bordoni
Cuzzoni	»Amante tuo costante«	Vinci, Rosmira	»Amante ch'in-costante«	Carlo Scalzi
Boschi	»Dopo il vento«	?		
Pacini ersetzt durch: Baldi	»Men superba«	Vinci, Rosmira	id.	Bernardi
Baldi	»Ahi nemico al nostro affetto«	(Giacomelli, Ipermestra, Venedig 1724?)	»Dal tuo sdegno e dal tuo amore«	(Baldi)
Senesino	»Un vento lusinghier«	(Sarri zugeschrieben)* (Merope, Neapel 1716)	id.	Senesino

* Zeitgenössischer Vermerk in einem Libretto des British Museum.

Cuzzoni + Senesino »Deh caro Olindo«	?		
Cuzzoni »Parto bell'idol mio«	?		
im Libretto:			
Senesino »Dimmi bell'idol mio«	(Fiorè zugeschrieben)*	id.	(Vittoria Tesi)
Pacini (»Qual senza stella«)	(Capelli, Venceslao, Parma 1724)		
ersetzt durch:			
Baldi »Parte il piè«	(Giacomelli, Ipermestra)	id.	Bernacchi
Cuzzoni »Dolce orror«	Vinci, Ifigenia	id.	Bordoni
Borosini »Al mio tesoro«	Vinci, Rosmira	id.	Barbieri
Senesino »Addio dille«	Orlandini, Berenice	id.	Scalzi
Cuzzoni »Pupillette«	Vinci, Ifigenia	id.	Bordoni
Senesino »Di pur ch'io sono«	(Vinci zugeschrieben)*		
Cuzzoni »Bell'alma«	Vinci, Ifigenia	id.	Giovanni Ossi
Cuzzoni »Più non sò dirti spera« (später eingelegt)	Vinci, Trionfo di Camilla, Parma 1725	»Più non sò finger sdegni«	Bordoni
Boschi »Di quel crudel«	?		
Pacini »Ad amar la tua beltade«	Orlandini, Berenice	»Ad amar varia beltade«	Bernardi
ersetzt durch:			
Pacini »Vado costante«	Capelli, Venceslao	id.	Pacini
Sorosina »Già sente il core«	Vinci, Ifigenia	id.	Merighi
ersetzt durch:			
Dotti »Con nodi più tenaci«	(Sarri, Aless. Severo, Neapel 1719)	id.	Dotti

* Zeitgenössischer Vermerk in einem Libretto des British Museum.

Senesino	»Barbara mi schernisci«	Vinci, *Rosmira*	id.	Scalzi
Cuzzoni	»Tortora ch'il suo«	Vinci, *Rosmira*	id.	Bordoni
Boschi	(unbekannte Einlage)			
Borosini	»Vanne e spera«	Vinci, *Rosmira*	id.	Barbieri
Cuzzoni + Senesino	»Stringi al sen«	Vinci, *Ifigenia*	id.	Bordoni + Scalzi

ORMISDA (4. April 1730)

	Sinfonia	Vinci (*Flavio An. Olibrio*, Neapel 1728?) (Conti zugeschrieben)		
	ersetzt durch Ouverture			
Strada	»Pupillette vezzosette«	Hasse, *Tigrane*, Neapel 1729	id.	Anna Maria Mazoni
Bernacchi	»Sino alla goccia«	(Orlandini, *Ormisda*, Bologna 1722)	id.	*Bernacchi*
ersetzt durch: Senesino	»Ricordati ch'è mio«	Orlandini, *Adelaide*, Venedig 1729	id.	Senesino
Merighi	»Infelice«	Vinci, (*F. A. Olibrio*) ?	»Tu m'offendi«	*Merighi*
Fabri	»Se non sa qual«			
Strada	»O caro mio tesoro«	Vinci, *Caduta dei Decemviri*, Neapel 1727	»Del caro mio tesoro«	Carlo Scalzi
ersetzt durch:	»Non ti confonder«	Hasse, *Sorella amante*, Neapel 1729	id.	?
Bertolli	»Tacerò se tu lo brami«	? (Text: *Didone abbandonata*)		
Fabri	»Se non pensi«	?		

ersetzt durch:	»Non fulmina ancora«	(Orlandini, Lucio Papirio, Bologna 1718)	id.	G. Paita
Bernacchi ersetzt durch:	»Vede quel pastorello«	Orlandini (Ormisda)	id.	(Bernacchi)
Senesino Merighi	»E' quella la bella« »Se quel cor con nobil vanto«	Orlandini, Adelaide Hasse (Ulderica, Neapel 1729)	»Tiranna ma bella« »Pria di darmi un sì bel vanto«	Senesino (Merighi)
Strada ersetzt durch unbekannte Arie	»Se d'aquilon«	(Porpora, Semiramide, Neapel 1724)	id.	(Strada)
Bernacchi ersetzt durch:	»Leon feroce«	(Orlandini, Ormisda)	id.	(Bernacchi)
Riemschneider (später eingelegt)	»Reo mi brami« »Come l'onda furibonda«	? Fiore (Sesostri, Turin 1717)	»Mira l'onda furibonda«	G. M. Boschi
Merighi später unterlegter Text:	»La speranza« »Nel tuo amor«	Orlandini, Antigona, Bologna 1727	»Le pupille« „	Merighi „
Fabri	»Sì sì lasciatemi«	(Orlandini, Lucio Papirio, Bologna 1718) (vgl. Elpidia) (Porta zugeschrieben)	id.	G. Paita
Bertolli ersetzt durch:	»Lasciami amico« »Tuona il ciel«	Leo, Argeno, Venedig 1728	id.	Elisabetta Uttini

Merighi	»Timido pellegrin«	(Giay, Publio Corn. Scipione, Turin 1726) Vinci, Semiramide, Rom 1729	id.	(Merighi)
Strada	»Sentirsi dire«		id.	Scalzi
Bernacchi ersetzt durch:	(»Fia tuo sangue«)	(Orlandini, Ormisda)	id.	(Bernacchi)
Senesino	»Di mia costanza«	Orlandini, Adelaide	»Vedrò più liete«	Senesino
Bertolli	»Io corro pietoso«	?		
Fabri	»Ti sento amor di padre«	? (Text: Alessandro Severo)		
Fabri ersetzt durch:	»Speranze del mio cor«	Giacomelli, Zidiana, Milano 1728	id.	Fabri
Strada	»Passagier che in selva oscura«	Hasse, Sesostrate, Neapel 1726	id.	Scalzi
Merighi	»Se mi toglie il tuo furore«	Hasse, Attalo, Neapel 1728	»Tu svenasti il mio tesoro«	Merighi
Strada ersetzt durch:	»Amico il fato«	Sarri, Siroe, Neapel 1727	id.	Maddalena Salvai
Schlußchor ersetzt durch:	»Agitata dal vento«	?		
	»D'applauso«	?		
	»Tutto rida«	?		

VENCESLAO (12. Januar 1731)

Sinfonia

		?		Anna Bagnolesi
Bertolli	»Se a danni miei«	?	id.	
später parodiert:	(»Se già di Marte«)			
Fabri	»Se tu vuoi dar«	Vinci, Stratonica, Neapel 1727		
(Bernacchi,) Senesino	»Quell'odio che in mente«	?	»Quel fiume che in monte«	Bernacchi
Merighi	»Lascia il lido«	Vinci, Medo, Parma 1728		Merighi
Strada	»Io sento al cor«	(Porpora, Amare per regnare, Neapel, 1723) Giacomelli, Lucio Pap. Ditt., Parma 1729	»Tornate ancor«	Bordoni
Fabri	»Ecco l'alba«	?	»Se morir deggio ingrato«	
Merighi	»Per mia vendetta ingrato«	Orlandini, Antigona, Bologna 1727	id.	Merighi
Strada	»Son belle in ciel le stelle«	Porta (Ulisse, Venedig 1725)	»Vengo a voi«	Carestini
(Bernacchi,) Senesino	»D'ira armato«	Vinci, Medo		Bernacchi
Fabri	»Nel seren«	(Venceslao, 1722?)	id.	Barbieri
Merighi	»Con bella speme«	Hasse, Attalo, Neapel 1728	»Con dolce frode«	Merighi
Strada	»Lascia cadermi«	Hasse, Artaserse, Venedig 1730	id.	Farinelli
(Bernacchi,) Senesino	»Parto, e mi sento«	Vinci, Medo	»Taci, o di morte«	Bernacchi

Merighi	»La vaga luccioletta«		id.	*Merighi*
Bertolli	»Vuò ritrar«	Hasse, Attalo		
Bernacchi	»Vado costante — della mia morte«	Vinci, Medo	»Nella foresta leone invitto«	*Bernacchi*
			?	
wohl ersetzt durch:				
Senesino	(»Vado costante a morte«)	?	?	
Strada	»Come nave in ria tempesta«	Porpora, Semiramide, Neapel 1724	id.	Farinelli
Merighi	»Corro, volo«	Hasse, Attalo	id.	*Merighi*
Bertolli	»Spero alfin che il cielo irato«	Hasse, Gerone, Neapel 1727	»Sappi poi che il cielo irato«	Bagnolesi
Senesino	»Da te se mi divide«	Lotti, Aless. Severo, Venedig 1717	»Da te tu mi dividi«	?
Fabri	»Balenar«	(Venceslao, 1722?)	id.	Barbieri
Strada	»Del caro sposo«	Capelli, Venceslao, Parma 1724	id.	Bordoni
Senesino (gestrichen)	»Fido amor non più lamenti«	Lotti, Aless. Severo	»Fidi amori or sì dolenti«	?

LUCIO PAPIRIO DITTATORE (23. Mai 1732)

	Sinfonia	Giacomelli, *Lucio Pap. Ditt.* Parma 1729		
Pinacci	»Dall'alta tua«	"		Borosini
Montagnana	»Chi del fato«	Porpora, *Siface*, Rom 1730		*Montagnana*
Strada	»Per dolce mio«	Giacomelli, *L. Pap. Ditt.*		Bordoni

Campioli	»Per te già forte«	»	Pacini
Bagnolesi	»Se ti ferisce«	»	Lancetti
Bertolli	»Che follia pregar«	»	Negri
Senesino	»Non ti chiedo«	»	Farinelli
Strada	»Consigliando«	»	Bordoni
Bagnolesi	»Porto nel cuore«	»	Lancetti
Montagnana	»Scostati nè più«	»	Bernacchi
Strada	»Ti lascio m'involo«	»	Bordoni
Bertolli	»Vanne e prega«	»	Negri
Senesino	»Que' begli occhi«	»	Farinelli
Strada	»Tornate ancor«	»	Bordoni
(gestrichen; vgl. Venceslao)			
Pinacci	»Fra le scuri«	»	Borosini
Senesino	»Spera sì presago«	»	Bernacchi!
Bagnolesi	»Sorge dal monte«	»	Lancetti
Bertolli	»Cor di viltà«	»	Negri
Pinacci	»Sulla tomba coronata«	»	Borsoni
Senesino	»Questa fronte«	»	Farinelli
Montagnana	»Alma tra miei timori«	(Porpora, Poro, Turin 1731) »O sugli estivi ardori«	Montagnana
Strada	»Vengo a darti«	Giacomelli, L. Pap. Ditt.	Bordoni

CATONE (4. November 1732)
Sinfonia

		(nicht von Leo)		
Senesino	»Con sì bel nome«	Leo, *Catone*, Venedig 1729	id.	Nicolino Grimaldi
Strada	»Non ti minaccio«	Leo, *Catone*	id.	Lucia Facchinelli
Bertolli	»Un raggio di speme«	(Hasse, *Dalisa*, Venedig 1730)	»*Un raggio di stella*«	(Antonio Pasi)
Senesino	»Pensa di chi«	Leo, *Catone*	id.	Grimaldi
Montagnana	»Non paventa«	Porpora, *Siface*, Rom 1730	id.	*Montagnana* (Anna Girò)
Gismondi	»La cervetta timidetta«	Vivaldi, (*Semiramide*, Mantua 1732)	id.	
ersetzt durch:	»Priva del caro sposo«	Porpora, *Germanico*, Rom 1732	id.	Angelo Monticelli
Gismondi ersetzt durch:	»Vaghe labbra voi fingete«	(Hasse, *Ulderica*, Neapel 1729)	»*Vaghe labbra voi ridete*«	(Carestini)
	»Chi mi toglie«	Hasse, *Attalo*, Neapel 1728	id.	Merighi
Strada	»E' follia se nascondete«	Leo, *Catone*	id.	Facchinelli
Senesino	»Mi conosci«	Leo, *Catone*	id.	Grimaldi
Bertolli	»Vaghe luci, luci belle«	(Vivaldi, *Ipermestra*, Florenz 1727?)	id.	(Lucia Lancetti
Montagnana	»Agitato da più venti«	?		
Strada (gestrichen)	(»Di tenero affetto«)	Leo, *Catone*	id.	Facchinelli

Gismondi ersetzt durch:	»Care faci«	?		
Montagnana (später eingelegt)	»Sento in riva«	Hasse, *Attalo*	id.	Merighi
	»Sò che nascondi«	Vivaldi, *Orlando*, Venedig 1727	»Benchè nasconda«	Gaetano Pinetti
Senesino	»Dovea svenarti«	Leo, *Catone*	id.	Grimaldi
Strada	»Sò che godendo«	Leo, *Catone*	id.	Facchinelli
Gismondi	»Fra tanti pensieri«	Hasse, *Demetrio*, Venedig 1732	id.	Bordoni
Strada	»Confusa, smarrita«	Leo, *Catone*	id.	Facchinelli
Bertolli	»Quando piomba«	Porpora, (*Poro*, Turin 1731)	id.	(Anna Bagnolesi)
Montagnana	»E' ver che all'amo« (unbekannte Arie)	(Porpora, *Poro*)	id.	(*Montagnana*)
Gismondi ersetzt durch:	»Vede il nocchier la sponda«	Hasse, *Euristeo*, Venedig 1732	id.	Caffarelli
Senesino	»Per darvi alcun«	Leo, *Catone*	id.	Grimaldi
Strada ersetzt durch:	»Soffre talor«	(Leo, *Catone*)	id.	Dom. Gizzi
	»Vò solcando«	Vinci, *Artaserse*, Rom 1730	id.	Carestini

SEMIRAMIDE RICONOSCIUTA (30. Oktober 1733)

	Sinfonia	Vinci, Artaserse, Rom 1730		
Durastanti	»Non sò se più«	Vinci, Semiramide, Rom 1729	id.	Giacinto Fontana
Carestini	»Scherza il nocchier«	Fr. Corselli (Vermerk im Handexemplar)		
Strada	»Che quel cor«	Vinci, Semiramide	id.	Gaetano Berenstadt
G. Waltz	(»Maggior follia«)	Vinci, Semiramide	id.	Domenico Annibali
ersetzt durch:				
Cat. Negri	»Trovo ch'è gran follia«	Hasse, Caio Fabricio, Rom, 1732	»Non sempre oprar«	Scalzi
Scalzi	»Bel piacer«	Vinci, Semiramide	id.	Scalzi
Rosa Negri	»Pensa ad amare«	?		
Carestini	(unbekannte Arie)			
ersetzt durch:				
	»Dal labbro tuo«	Hasse, (Antigona, Milano 1732)	id.	Carestini
Strada	»Ti credo a me pietoso«	Hasse, (Arminio, Mailand 1730)	»Potresti esser pietoso«	(Bordoni)
Durastanti	»Voi non sapete«	Vinci, Semiramide	id.	Fontana
ersetzt durch:				
	(»Se colle vostre«)	?		
Scalzi	»Rondinella«	Vinci, Semiramide	id.	Scalzi
Strada	»Mi disprezzi«	Hasse, (Arminio)	»Dolce rieda«	(Bordoni)
Carestini	(unbekannte Arie)			
ersetzt durch:				
	»Il cor che sdegnato«	Feo, Ipermestra, Rom 1728	id.	Carestini

Cat. Negri	»Saper bramate«	Vinci, Semiramide	id.	Berenstadt
Scalzi	»Sarà piacer«	Leo, Demetrio, Neapel 1732	id.	Teresa Cotti
Cat. Negri	(unbekannte Arie)			
ersetzt durch:				
Rosa Negri	»D'amor trafitto sei«	Leo, Argeno, Venedig 1728	»Mio cor tradito sei«	Farinelli
Scalzi	»Fiumicel«	Vinci, Semiramide	id.	Scalzi
Strada	»Tortorella«	Sarri, Artemisia, Neapel 1731	id.	Cuzzoni
Durastanti	»Tradita, sprezzata«	Vinci, Semiramide	id.	Fontana
Carestini	»Passagier«	Vinci, Semiramide	id.	Barbieri
ersetzt durch:				
	»Peregrin«	Hasse, Attalo, Neapel 1728	id.	Carestini
G. Waltz	(unbekannte Arie)			
ersetzt durch:				
Cat. Negri	»Qual nocchier«	Feo, Andromaca, Rom 1730	id.	Annibali
Scalzi	»In braccio a mille«	Vinci, Semiramide	id.	Scalzi
Cat. Negri	(unbekannte Arie)			
ersetzt durch:				
Rosa Negri	»Avezzo alla catena«	Hasse, Demetrio, Venedig 1732	»Non sembra ardito e fiero«	Appiani
Durastanti	»Fuggi dagli occhi«	Vinci, Semiramide	id.	Fontana
Carestini	»Se in campo«	Vinci,Catone, Rom 1728	id.	Carestini
Strada	»Per far che risplenda«	Hasse, Tigrane, Neapel 1729	»Se brami che splenda«	Mazzoni

				Carestini
Carestini	»Un'aura placida di bella speme«	(Porta, Gianguir, Milano 1732)	id.	
CAIO FABRICIO (4. Dezember 1733) Sinfonia		?		
Cat. Negri	»In così lieto«	Hasse, Caio Fabricio Rom 1732	id.	Alessandro Veroni
Carestini ersetzt durch:	(»Vedi l'amata figlia«)	Hasse, C. Fabricio	id.	Caffarelli
	»Fissa ne' sguardi«	Hasse, (Ulderica, Neapel 1729)	id.	(Antonio Bernacchi)
Strada	»Il trono, il regno«	Hasse, C. Fabricio	id.	Angelo Monticelli
Cat. Negri ersetzt durch: Durastanti	»Non ti ricuso«	Hasse, C. Fabricio	id.	Felice Salimbeni
	»Vezzi lusinghe«	Hasse, Tigrane, Neapel 1729	id.	Teresa Pieri
Scalzi ersetzt durch:	(»Scherza talor«)	Hasse, C. Fabricio	id.	A. Fontana
	»Per amor se il cor«	Vinci, Astianatte, Neapel 1725	id.	Farinelli
Carestini ersetzt durch: Durastini	»Reca la pace«	Hasse, C. Fabricio	id.	Caffarelli
	»Quando verrà«	?		
Strada	»Caro sposo«	Hasse, C. Fabricio	id.	Monticelli

Durastanti	»Amore a lei«	Hasse, C. Fabricio	id.	Salimbeni
Carestini	»Non ha più pace«	Hasse, C. Fabricio	id.	Caffarelli
Rosa Negri	»Giovani cori«	Hasse, C. Fabricio	id.	Felice Che-cacci
G. Waltz gestrichen; vgl. Semiramide	»Non sempre oprar«	Hasse, C. Fabricio	id.	Dom. Annibali
Scalzi ersetzt durch:	(unbekannte Arie) »Troppo fiere«	(Corselli, Venere placata, Venedig 1731)	id.	(Pietro Murigi)
Carestini ersetzt durch:	(unbekannte Arie) »Al foco del mio amore«	(Albinoni, La fortezza al cimento, Milano 1729)	id.	Carestini
Strada	»Non mi chiamar«	Hasse, C. Fabricio	id.	Monticelli
Scalzi	»Nocchier che teme«	Hasse, C. Fabricio	id.	Fontana
Durastanti ersetzt durch:	(»Sarà vezzosa«)	Hasse, C. Fabricio	id.	Veroni
Cat. Negri	»È grande e bella«	anonym: Neapel ca. 1725	»Non sempre torna«	
Durastanti	»Volgi a me«	Hasse, C. Fabricio	id.	Salimbeni
G. Waltz	»Quella è mia figlia«	Hasse, C. Fabricio	id.	Annibali
Carestini	»Vedrai morir«	Hasse, C. Fabricio	id.	Caffarelli
Strada	»Lo sposo va«	Hasse, C. Fabricio	id.	Monticelli
Scalzi	»Varcherò«	Hasse, C. Fabricio	id.	Fontana
Carestini	»Vorrei da lacci sciogliere«	Leo, Demetrio, Neapel 1732 (nicht von Hasse)	id.	Teresa Cotti
Schlußchor	»Con la pace«			

ARBACE (5. Januar 1734)

	Sinfonia	?		
Strada	»Conservati fedele«	Vinci, Artaserse, Rom 1730	id.	Giacinto Fontana
Carestini	»Fra cento affanni«	"	id.	Carestini
Scalzi	»Per pietà bell'idol mio«	"	id.	Raffaele Signorini
Cat. Negri	»Bramar di perdere«	"	id.	Giuseppe Appiani
Scalzi	»Deh respirar«	"	id.	Signorini
Durastanti	»Non ti son padre«	"	id.	Francis Tolve
Strada	»Impallidisci ingrato«	Hasse, Issipile, Neapel 1732	»Impallidisce in campo«	Lucia Fachinelli
Carestini	»Vò solcando«	Vinci, Artaserse	id.	Carestini
Vgl. Catone; ersetzt durch:				
	»Son qual nave ch'agitata«	(Hasse, Artaserse, Lucca 1730)	id.	(Farinelli)
Scalzi	»Rendimi il caro«	Vinci, Artaserse	id.	Signorini
Carestini	»Mi scacci sdegnato«	"	id.	Carestini
ersetzt durch:				
	»Caro padre ab forse è questo«	Porta, Lucio Papirio, Rom 1732	id.	Carestini
Rosa Negri	»Non temer ch'io«	Vinci, Artaserse	id.	Giovanni Ossi
Strada	»Se d'un amor«	"	id.	Fontana
Carestini	»Per quel paterno«	Vinci, Artaserse	id.	Carestini

Scalzi	»Potessi al mio diletto«	Hasse, Dalisa, Venedig 1730	»Se fosse il mio diletto«	Bordoni
Durastanti	»Così stupisce«	Vinci, Artaserse	id.	Tolve
ersetzt durch:				
Carestini	»Perchè tarda è mai«	"	id.	Carestini
Scalzi	(»Nuvoletta«)	"	id.	Signorini
Carestini	»Se l'amor tuo mi rendi«	Hasse, Siroe, Bologna 1733	id.	Farinelli
Carestini	»L'onda dal mar«	Vinci, Artaserse	id.	Carestini
Durastanti	»Figlio se più«	"	id.	Tolve
Strada	»Mi credi spietata«	"	id.	Fontana
Strada + Carestini	»Tu vuoi ch'io viva«	"	id.	Fontana + Carestini
Schlußchor ersetzt durch:				
Carestini	»Di te degno non sarei«	Porta, L. Papirio	id.	Carestini

DIDONE ABBANDONATA (13. April 1737)

Sinfonia		Vinci, Didone, Rom 1726		
Conti	»Ahi lasso vorrei«	?	id.	Finazzi
Bertolli	»Dirò che fida sei«	Vinci, Didone	id.	
Strada	»Son regina e sono amante«	"	id.	Fontana
Cat. Negri	»Grato rende«	"	id.	Franchi
Annibali	»Fra lo splendor«	"	id.	Berenstadt

Beard	»Se dalle stelle«	»	id.	Domenico Gizzi
Conti	»Quando saprai«	»	id.	Antonio Barbieri
Annibali	»Son quel fiume«	»		Gaetano Berenstadt
Strada	»Non ha ragione«	»		Fontana
Conti	»Tra fieri opposti«	?		
Annibali	»Leon ch'errando vada«	Vinci, Didone	id.	Berenstadt
Bertolli	»Tanto amor sì bella fede«	Vinci, Semiramide, Rom 1729	»Ei d'amor quasi delira«	Pietro Murigi
Beard	»Amor che nasce«	Vinci, Didone	id.	Gizzi
Strada	»Se vuoi ch'io mora«	Vinci, Didone	id.	Fontana
Conti	»Vedi nel mio«	»	id.	Barbieri
Conti	»Sono intrepido nell'alma«	Giacomelli, Annibale, Rom 1731	»Per te perdo il mio contento«	Angelo Monticelli
Annibali	»Chiamami pur così«	Vinci, Didone	id.	Berenstadt
Strada	»Ritorna a lusingarmi«	Vivaldi, Griselda, Venedig 1735	id.	Margherita Giacomazzi

				(Annibali?)
Annibali (verschollene Einlage)	("Quel pastor")	Ristori		
Conti	"Mi tradì l'infida"	?		
Cat. Negri	"Quando l'onda"	Vinci, Didone	id.	Franchi
Conti	"A trionfar mi chiama"	Hasse, Euristeo, Venedig 1732 (vgl. Catone)	"Vede il nocchier la sponda"	Caffarelli
Bertolli	"Ch'io resti! Ch'io viva! Ma come?"	Hasse, Issipile, Neapel 1732	"Ch'io speri! Ma come?"	Lucia Fachinelli
Strada	"Va crescendo"	Vinci, Didone	id.	Fontana
Strada	"Già si desta"	"	id.	Gizzi!
Annibali	"Cadrà fra poco in cenere"	Hasse, C. Fabricio, Rom 1732, vgl. Semiramide, C. Fabricio	"Non sempre oprar da forte"	Annibali
Strada (Schluß-Akkompagnato)	"Vado ma dove"	Vinci, Didone	id.	Fontana

Beispiel 1: Leonardo Vinci, *»Saper bramate«* *(Semiramide riconosciuta,* 1729)

Il ge_nio è stra_no, lo veg_go an_ch'i_o, lo veg_go an_ch'i _ o.

Ma ten _ to in_va_no can_giar de_si_o, can_giar de _ si _ o,

l'i_stes_so ir_ca _ _no sem _ _ pre, sem _ pre sa_

Beispiel 2: L. Vinci, *»Saper bramate«* in Händels Fassung (1733)

Dà Capo

DAGLI ARCHIVI MILANESI:
LETTERE DI RANIERI DE CALZABIGI E DI ANTONIA BERNASCONI

di *Mariangela Donà* (Milano)

Ranieri Calzabigi (o De Calsabigi, come egli stesso si firmava[1]) appartiene alla schiera di quei geniali avventurieri settecenteschi, che annovera nelle sue file anche Giacomo Casanova e Lorenzo Da Ponte. Come osserva Piero Chiara nella prefazione all'edizione delle *Memorie e altri scritti* di Lorenzo Da Ponte[2], il Settecento, *»secolo in cui la scienza e la cultura hanno un carattere di irregolarità, d'improvvisazione, di cosmopolitismo e di eclettismo«*, offriva il terreno favorevole al fiorire delle più disparate personalità, *»che passavano facilmente dalla letteratura e dall'arte al commercio, all'industria, all'attività scientifica, alla diplomazia«.* Anche il Calzabigi risponde puntualmente a queste caratteristiche: nato a Livorno nel 1714, letterato, Accademico Etrusco di Cortona, Arcade col nome di Liburno Drepanio, la sua biografia ce lo mostra a diverse riprese costretto a campare di espedienti, dapprima a Napoli, poi a Parigi, dove, col fratello minore Anton Maria e con Giacomo Casanova, impianta una lotteria regia. Versatile, colto, abile conoscitore del commercio e delle operazioni di finanza, nel 1761 lo troviamo a Vienna, segretario del Principe von Kaunitz e consigliere in materia d'economia alla Corte. E qui, com'è noto, avvenne l'incontro con Gluck, che determinò la famosa riforma del melodramma. In seguito Calzabigi scompare anche da Vienna. Fu probabilmente a Livorno (dove, nel 1774, uscì la prima edizione delle sue opere, col titolo *Poesie*, nella Stamperia dell'Enciclopedia), poi a Pisa, infine a Napoli, dove restò fino alla morte (1795).

Non tutto è noto nella biografia del Calzabigi, ed anche intorno al suo carattere e alla sua persona non si sa molto più di quanto risulti dal vivace ritratto che

---

[1] La lezione *»Calzabigi«* sembra essere quella originaria, attestata dall'atto di nascita e dai documenti fino al 1755. La forma *»Calsabigi«*, preceduta da un *»De«* certo arbitrario, fu adottata dall'autore a partire dal 1755 (nell'edizione delle opere di Metastasio curata da lui). Cfr. Ghino LAZZERI, *La vita e l'opera letteraria di Ranieri Calzabigi*, Città di Castello, Lapi, 1907, p. 7 n.

[2] Milano, Longanesi, 1971, p. 13 e seg.

ne fece Giacomo Casanova[3]. Può essere dunque interessante leggere alcune sue lettere autografe, per la maggior parte inedite, che si conservano a Milano, parte alla Biblioteca Ambrosiana e parte all'Archivio di Stato (Archivio Greppi).

In aggiunta alle lettere sue riprodurrò anche alcune lettere di una sua amica e interprete: Antonia Bernasconi, che sono del pari conservate nell'Archivio Greppi. L'accostamento mi è parso pertinente, anche perché il Calzabigi nomina più volte questa cantante nelle sue lettere al Padre Frisi. Qualche particolare biografico della Bernasconi può essere interessante, anche perché, nel 1770–71, ella si trovava a Milano per interpretare il *Mitridate re di Ponto* di Mozart.

Le lettere che qui si pubblicano sono comprese fra il 1768 e il 1772: risalgono quindi all'epoca probabilmente più fortunata e brillante dell'accidentata esistenza del Calzabigi, quella della sua permanenza alla Corte di Vienna. Qui il suo talento era riconosciuto e apprezzato da un ambiente di gusto raffinato e da un principe illuminato come il Kaunitz, né mancava al poeta una certa sicurezza economica (anche se, come vedremo, i debiti non l'abbandonavano). Ancora il Casanova, che lo rivide a Vienna nel 1767, ce lo mostra spregiudicato e brillante, anche se costantemente afflitto da quella specie di scabbia che lo tormentava anche a Parigi:

»Puis je suis allé voir Calsabigi l'aîné qui travaillait au lit. Tout son corps était couvert de dartres; le prince allait chez lui presque tous les jours [...] J'allais aux spectacles et souvent dîner chez Calsabigi, qui faisait pompe de son athéisme, et qui impudemment disait toujours du mal de Metastasio qui le méprisait; mais Calsabigi s'en moquait. Grand calculateur politique, il était l'homme du prince Kaunitz.«[4]

---

[3] Casanova conobbe a Parigi, nel 1757, i due fratelli Calzabigi: dapprima il minore, Anton Maria, e poi Ranieri, e insieme organizzarono una lotteria, che aveva lo scopo di risanare le finanze regie. Ed ecco il dialogo con Anton Maria e quindi l'incontro con Ranieri:

»— C'est donc M. votre frère qui est l'auteur du projet.
— C'est mon frère. Il est malade, mais il se porte bien d'esprit. Nous allons le voir.
J'ai vu un homme au lit tout couvert de dartres; mais cela ne l'empêchait pas de manger avec un excellent appétit, d'écrire, de converser, et de faire parfaitement toutes les fonctions d'un homme qui se porte bien. Il ne paraissait devant personne parce que, outre que les dartres le défiguraient, il était obligé à tout moment de se gratter dans un endroit ou dans l'autre, ce qui à Paris est une chose abominable qu'on ne pardonne jamais, soit qu'on se gratte à cause de maladie ou par mauvaise habitude. Calsabigi me dit donc qu'il se tenait là sans voir personne parce que la peau lui démangeait, et qu'il n'avait autre soulagement que celui de se frotter.
— Dieu, me dit-il, ne peut m'avoir donné des ongles qu'à cet fin.
— Vous croyez donc aux causes finales, et je vous fais mon compliment. Malgré cela je crois que vous vous gratteriez quand même Dieu aurait oublié de vous donner des ongles.
Je l'ai alors vu sourire, et nous parlâmes de notre affaire. Dans moins d'une heure je lui ai trouvé beaucoup d'esprit. Il était l'aîné, et il était garçon. Grand calculateur, très versé dans la finance théorique et pratique, connaissant le commerce de toutes les nations, docte en histoire, bel esprit, adorateur du beau sexe, et poète. Il était natif de Livourne; il avait travaillé à Naples dans le ministère, et il était venu à Paris avec M. de l'Hôpital. Son frère était aussi fort habile, mais il devait lui céder en tout.«
(Jacques CASANOVA de Seingalt Vénitien, *Histoire de ma vie*, Vol. 5, Chap. II. Ed. intégrale, Wiesbaden-Paris, 1960, T. III, p. 28).   [4] Op. cit., vol. X, cap. IX, p. 238–239.

I destinatari di questi due gruppi di lettere sono due personaggi entrambi importanti, sebbene per motivi diversi, nella Milano del 18° secolo: il Padre Paolo Frisi e Antonio Greppi. Nessuno dei due era letterato o musicista: scienziato l'uno, finanziere l'altro: eppure con entrambi il Calzabigi s'intrattiene su questioni di poesia, di teatro, di musica, di cultura. Questa versatilità, questa apertura ai vari aspetti della cultura e dell'arte anche da parte di chi non era del mestiere era un tratto mirabile di quel secolo giustamente detto dei »lumi«. Sia l'uno che l'altro avevano molteplici rapporti con persone e fatti del mondo musicale e teatrale milanese, come attestano i voluminosi carteggi di entrambi. Non sarà dunque inutile, anche per la storia musicale, vederne più da vicino i connotati.

Il Padre Paolo Frisi, al quale sono indirizzate le lettere che si conservano all'Ambrosiana (Y. 152 sup.), era un matematico e astronomo milanese (1728–1784). Barnabita, professore di metafisica ed etica, poi di aritmetica e algebra a Lodi, a Casale Monferrato, a Pisa e infine a Milano, era uno dei più celebri scienziati del suo tempo. Autore di molti scritti (fra i quali il principale è la *Cosmographia physica et mathematica*, Milano 1774–75), studioso dei fenomeni della luce e della meccanica celeste, era anche profondo conoscitore dell'idraulica pratica, tanto da essere incaricato dal governo austriaco di studiare il modo di regolare il corso di fiumi e canali nell'Italia settentrionale. Amico di letterati e artisti e amicissimo dei Verri, frequentava la migliore società milanese, brillandovi per la conversazione frizzante ed erudita. Era socio di tutte le principali accademie europee e intratteneva anche una corrispondenza vastissima con personalità di rilievo. Alla Biblioteca Ambrosiana (Y. 148–154 sup.) sono conservati ben 7 grossi volumi di lettere autografe dirette a lui da scienziati, artisti, uomini politici, principi, ecc. La maggior parte delle notizie su di lui sono contenute nelle *Memorie appartenenti alla vita ed agli studj del Signor Don Paolo Frisi Regio Censore, e Professore di matematica e socio delle primarie Accademie d'Europa*, scritte alla sua morte appunto dall'amico Pietro Verri (Milano, Giuseppe Marelli, 1787).

È molto probabile che il Calzabigi l'avesse conosciuto nel 1768, poiché, come scrive Pietro Verri (p. 37), in quell'anno il Padre Frisi *»passò all'Imperial Corte di Vienna dove presso le più eminenti persone venne distinto ed onorato. Fra queste debbo nominare il primo il Sig. Principe di Kaunitz, che sentì vera stima per questo nostro Concittadino; ravvisò lo spirito e il genio di lui, e conservogli sin che visse una ferma protezione«*[5]. Infatti molte sono le lettere di Kaunitz (come, del resto, anche del conte Firmian) al Padre Frisi, e tutte piene di amiche-

---

[5] Del soggiorno austriaco di Paolo Frisi dà notizie particolareggiate uno dei corrispondenti di Antonio Greppi da Vienna, Giovanni Pietro DE SORESINA, in alcune lettere conservate all'Archivio di Stato di Milano (Arch. Greppi, cart. 55, sett. e ott. 1768).

vole stima. Ritornato a Milano da Vienna, lo scienziato, evidentemente, mantenne frequenti rapporti epistolari col Calzabigi, il quale, fra l'altro, lo teneva al corrente della vita alla Corte.

Queste lettere, infatti, non vertono soltanto su argomenti attinenti all'attività di librettista del Calzabigi, ma trattano anche temi di politica e di attualità (come la soppressione dei Gesuiti, la guerra contro i Turchi, l'insurrezione dei Corsi). Scritte in uno stile vivace e sbrigliato, qualche volta mordace, da vero toscano qual era il loro autore (anche quando si esprime in elegante francese), esse danno l'immagine di un'intelligenza viva, di un uomo di corte che tributa il doveroso omaggio ai suoi protettori, ma che, nello stesso tempo, ha l'occhio critico per i risvolti negativi di quella società pur colta e aperta ai valori dell'arte e della scienza. Mentre incensa, anche nelle lettere private, »il nostro degnissimo Mecenate«, il principe di Kaunitz, e adatta a lui un'epigrafe dedicata ad Antonino Pio (epigrafe che infatti si ritrova nell'edizione delle sue Poesie), il Calzabigi ci fa intravvedere una Corte di Vienna dove »le cose del Teatro sono ridotte a tal forzosa parsimonia che convien per sempre sbandirne la spesa d'un'opera seria« (lettera del 6 maggio 1771). E ancora: »Qui non v'è filosofia. Tutto è grossolano. La superficie è in onore« (24 agosto 1772). Anche alcuni tratti autobiografici emergono da queste lettere, per esempio la sua cattiva salute, i suoi »incommodi«, che non gli permettono di accompagnare Sua Eccellenza nella villeggiatura di Austerlitz, e spesso perfino gli impediscono di partecipare alle riunioni nel palazzo. Apprendiamo poi che gli sta a cuore la cantante Antonia Bernasconi, sua amica, »scelta per rappresentar sempre le prime parti di donna nelle mie cose drammatiche« (11 ottobre 1770). (Ma della Bernasconi parleremo più avanti.)

La sua inclinazione per le belle donne è attestata anche dalla lettera del 24 agosto 1772: »Avevo abbandonato la Lira; ma impegno per bella Dama me l'ha fatta ripigliare doppo 4 anni«.

Ma naturalmente il tema principale delle lettere del Calzabigi è quello dei suoi drammi per musica. Con grande evidenza risalta la consapevolezza della novità del suo stile e della sua concezione del teatro d'opera e l'amara constatazione di quanto il pubblico italiano fosse refrattario ad accettarla.

Argomento di speciale rilievo e interesse è quello delle prime tre lettere al Padre Frisi (lettera del 15 dic. 1768; lettera senza data, ma certo della fine dello stesso anno; lettera del 12 genn. 1769): e cioè l'indignazione (legittima) dell'autore per la manomissione subìta dalla sua Alceste nell'esecuzione fattane al Teatro Ducale di Milano: deformato da insulsi allungamenti il libretto, ripudiata la musica di Gluck per farla riscrivere dal »rappezzator di note Guglielmi«. Questo argomento ci porta al secondo destinatario delle lettere di Calzabigi: Antonio Greppi, corresponsabile, insieme con gli altri direttori del Teatro Ducale, di tanto scempio, nonostante la sua buona amicizia col librettista. Al Greppi infatti il Calzabigi aveva scritto, già il 6 aprile 1768, quella lunga e importante lettera (ben nota perché pubblicata da Carlo Antonio Vianello[6]), che, nell'intento di indurlo ad abbandonare l'idea di manomettere il suo testo, contiene un'ampia ed efficace esposizione delle idee intorno al dramma per musica, che avevano fatto del Calzabigi, in unione a Gluck, appunto il consapevole riformatore del teatro d'opera.

Prima di soffermarci sull'episodio, vediamo chi fosse Antonio Greppi, del quale si conserva nell'Archivio di Stato di Milano un voluminosissimo carteggio. Di origine bergamasca (precisamente di Cazzano di Valseriana), Antonio Greppi (1722—1799), grazie alle sue qualità di abilissimo finanziere, divenne una delle persone più influenti di Milano. Istituita da Maria Teresa la »ferma generale«, incaricata della riscossione delle principali privative (sale, tabacco, dazi sulle mercanzie), Antonio Greppi, nel 1751, ne ebbe l'appalto insieme con altri quattro soci. Greppi, il più abile fra essi, era divenuto l'uomo indispensabile delle finanze milanesi, tenuto in gran conto dal cancelliere Kaunitz e dall'imperatrice stessa. Contro il sistema di appalto si battè Pietro Verri, sostenendo che lo Stato doveva provvedere direttamente all'esazione; tuttavia la ferma fu riconfermata più volte a Greppi dal governo austriaco. Giuseppe II l'abolì nel 1770. L'abile finanziere, quando comprese che non era possibile contrastare questa decisione, rinunciò spontaneamente alla sua carica, ottenendo così aperta e tangibile gratitudine da parte della Corte. Dopo essere stato nominato, nel 1770, Consigliere della Camera dei conti, nel 1778 Antonio Greppi fu nominato feudatario di Bussero e Conte. Oltre che col mondo finanziario e politico egli aveva stretti rapporti anche con gli ambienti della cultura e del teatro: era infatti uno dei gestori del Teatro Ducale e, dopo l'incendio di questo, figura tra i palchettisti che, nel 1776, avanzarono a Maria Teresa la richiesta di costruire il nuovo teatro, che sarà la Scala. Fu inoltre uno dei fondatori della Società Patriottica di Milano (1776) insieme con Cesare Beccaria, Giuseppe Parini, Paolo Frisi, Agostino Litta e altri. Nel suo sontuoso palazzo di via S. Antonio (rifabbricato dal Piermarini) riceveva principi e alte personalità italiane e straniere, nonché artisti e musicisti.

Fra le lettere a lui dirette, che si conservano nell'Archivio di Stato di Milano, numerose sono quelle di persone appartenenti o gravitanti intorno al mondo del teatro: per esempio vi figurano Metastasio, l'impresario D'Afflizio, Teresa Angiolini Fogliazzi, Maddalena Marliani comica, Caterina Gabrielli, Marco Coltellini, Geltrude Allegretti Falchini, oltre ad Antonia Bernasconi.

Anche qualche particolare relativo al viaggio di Mozart a Milano nel 1771

---

[6] C. A. VIANELLO, *Teatri spettacoli musiche a Milano nei secoli scorsi*, Milano 1941, p. 237 e segg.

risulta dal carteggio Greppi, come ha rilevato Guglielmo Barblan[7]. Nel carteggio si trovano, per esempio, parecchie richieste di biglietti, rivolte a Greppi da varie persone, per assistere all'»*opera e Serenata*« (cioè il *Ruggero* di Hasse e l'*Ascanio in Alba* di Mozart), che si sarebbero eseguite il 16 e 17 ottobre 1771, in onore delle nozze dell'Arciduca d'Austria con Maria Beatrice d'Este. Quanto ai retroscena per cui, durante il precedente soggiorno a Milano di Mozart, l'interprete del *Mitridate re di Ponto* (26 dicembre 1770) fu Antonia Bernasconi e non Caterina Gabrielli (come era stato invece previsto), ne parleremo a proposito delle lettere della Bernasconi.

Antonio Greppi aveva a Vienna alcuni agenti, che lo informavano con regolarità (e cioè ad ogni »ordinario« o corriere postale, vale a dire in media una volta alla settimana) non soltanto intorno agli affari dei quali erano incaricati, ma anche intorno ai principali avvenimenti della Corte e perfino intorno alla politica estera: erano questi il banchiere Segalla, Giovanni Pietro de Soresina e D. Volpi. Si terrà conto anche delle loro lettere, quando contengano notizie riguardanti Calzabigi, la Bernasconi e altri avvenimenti musicali. Da esse risulta, fra l'altro, che quasi ad ogni »ordinario« Greppi spediva alla Corte di Vienna cassettine di musica: una testimonianza in più dei ben noti, stretti rapporti musicali e del costante interscambio di composizioni fra Milano e Vienna.

Per venire ora all'episodio dell'*Alceste* milanese, cui si riferiscono le lettere inviate dal Calzabigi sia al Padre Frisi che a Greppi, ricorderemo che lo storpiatore del libretto era nientemeno che Giuseppe Parini, il quale, in quegli anni, aveva l'incarico di poeta del Teatro Ducale, incarico che comportava anche l'obbligo di adattare libretti altrui alle esigenze dei cantanti e degli impresari. Le trasformazioni inflitte dal »Parrini« al libretto originario dell'*Alceste*[8] giustificano davvero la protesta dell'indignato autore. Né basta ad assolvere il correttore la richiesta di perdono avanzata alla fine dell'»*Argomento*« dell'*Alceste* milanese,

---

[7] In: *Mozart in Italia. I viaggi e le lettere*, a cura di G. Barblan e di A. Della Corte, Milano, 1956, p. 102 e segg. Va rettificato, in proposito, un piccolo errore di lettura di un nome che figura in due lettere a Greppi in data 12 e 13 ottobre 1771, lettere nelle quali si prega Greppi di invitare Caterina Gabrielli all'accademia che si sarebbe tenuta a Corte il 15 ottobre con l'intervento anche del giovane Mozart: insieme al marchese Moriggia chi scrive a Greppi è il conte Monti e non Nemi (come si legge invece nell'op. cit. a pag. 105 e 106). Potrebbe trattarsi di Gio. Battista Monti, nominato conte nel 1723 (cfr. *Storia di Milano* XII, 40, tav. VII).

[8] Ecco il frontespizio del libretto:
ALCESTE. Dramma tragico da rappresentarsi nel Regio-Ducal Teatro di Milano Nel Carnovale dell'Anno 1769. Dedicato a Sua Altezza Serenissima il Duca di Modena, Reggio, Mirandola ec. ec. [...] In Milano, MDCCLXVIII. Nella Regia Ducal Corte, per Giuseppe Richino Malatesta Stampatore Regio Camerale.
(La dedica è sottoscritta da Gl'Interessati nel Regio Appalto del Teatro. Personaggi e interpreti: Admeto: Guglielmo d'Ettore; Alceste: Antonia Maria Girelli Aguilar; Apollo sotto nome di Evandro: Giuseppe Nicolini; Ismene: Felicita Suardi; Gran Sacerdote d'Apollo: Gaspare Bassano. Scene dei Fratelli Galeari. Balli di Vincenzo Galeotti.)

non firmato, ma certo scritto da lui: »*Di ciò si spera perdono dall'applaudito Autore, non essendosi fatto per intendimento di migliorare, ma per accomodarsi alle presenti inevitabili circostanze del nostro Teatro* [...]«.

Il confronto fra il testo originale e quello rimaneggiato dà veramente un'immagine ben negativa del gusto italiano, ancorato alla più vieta *routine* operistica, mentre a Vienna si erano accolte con ammirazione sia l'*Orfeo ed Euridice* (1762), sia appunto l'*Alceste* (26 dicembre 1767), entrambe con musica di Gluck. Infatti le inserzioni pariniane, fatte per allungare l'opera e per accontentare alcuni cantanti, sono per lo più arie di stampo metastasiano, banali nell'espressione poetica e stucchevoli per contenuto: insomma riempitivi goffi e dannosi all'efficacia del dramma. È chiaro che queste arie furono volute soprattutto dai cantanti Giuseppe Nicolini e Felicita Suardi, poiché sono assegnate ai rispettivi personaggi di Evandro e di Ismene (una è anche di Alceste). Quanto alla musica di Pietro Alessandro Guglielmi, non si ha notizia di alcun esemplare della partitura che ci sia pervenuto.

Tralasciando la lettera a Greppi del 6 aprile 1768, perché riprodotta integralmente (anche se con alcune inesattezze) da C. A. Vianello nell'opera citata, inizierò la pubblicazione dalla lettera, pure a Greppi, del 18 aprile 1768, continuando poi, in ordine di data, con le successive indirizzate a Greppi e a Paolo Frisi. Includerò la riproduzione integrale anche delle quattro parzialmente pubblicate dal Vianello, e cioè: a Greppi 12 dic. 1768; a Frisi senza data (dicembre 1768); a Frisi 15 dicembre 1768; a Frisi 12 gennaio 1769. Le parti omesse dal Vianello contengono pure elementi interessanti. Per esempio, di particolare importanza è ciò che emerge dalla lettera del 12 dicembre 1768 circa la prefazione all'*Alceste,* pubblicata nell'edizione della partitura (Vienna, Trattner, 1769). Questa notissima prefazione, redatta in forma di dedica all'Altezza Reale l'Arciduca Pietro Leopoldo Granduca di Toscana, e contenente le linee programmatiche seguite dal librettista e dal musicista nei loro melodrammi di nuova concezione, è firmata, come si sa, da Gluck. Quasi tutti gli studiosi di Gluck avevano già supposto che, nonostante la firma, essa fosse stata stesa per lo meno in collaborazione con Calzabigi[9]. Alfred Einstein[10] l'attribuisce a Calzabigi. Ora questa lettera dà la prova documentaria dell'esattezza di questa logica supposizione, informando anche sui patti intercorsi fra librettista e musicista circa i diritti di stampa e di esecuzione dell'opera. »*Le nostre convenzioni fra Gluk e me* — scrive Calzabigi — *sono che non produrrà la sua Musica che a mia volontà, dovendo io premettere a quella stampa una Prefazione che spieghi il motivo,*

---

[9] Vedi per es.: Andrea DELLA CORTE, *Gluck e i suoi tempi*, Firenze 1948, p. 119. Non così Gustave DESNOIRESTERRES, che, senza nominare Calzabigi, l'attribuisce a Gluck, pur riportando, in nota, l'opinione di Brack, traduttore di Burney, che afferma essere stata scritta dall'abate Coltellini (*Gluck et Piccinni*, Paris 1875, p. 65—66).
[10] *Gluck*, trad. it., Milano 1946, p. 128.

anzi i motivi dell'enorme cambiamento da noi fatto in tali Drammatiche Composizioni. Ora questa Prefazione non l'ho fatta ancora . . .«
Altrettanto interessante è rilevare da questa lettera e da quella del 2 gennaio 1769 che Gluck era al corrente delle intenzioni del Teatro Ducale; si risponde così alla domanda posta da Della Corte: »*Ignorò Gluck le intenzioni del Teatro Ducale, la proposta del rifacimento del libretto, l'esclusione della sua musica, e l'incarico al Guglielmi?*«[11]
Spassoso è poi l'episodio del trafugamento di un esemplare della partitura appena stampata, ad opera dell'agente di Greppi D. Volpi, e del contemporaneo invio a Greppi dell'altro esemplare da parte del Consigliere aulico Valmagini; i due avevano agito all'insaputa l'uno dell'altro, per fornire a tutti i costi la partitura agli impazienti direttori del Teatro Ducale.
Quanto poi all'»assoluzione« concessa infine dal Calzabigi agli storpiatori milanesi della sua opera, bisogna anzitutto notare che nessuna legge proteggeva ancora i diritti di un autore; anzi nella lettera del 15 dicembre 1768 a P. Frisi il Calzabigi osserva: »*La stampa avendo resa propria l'Alceste di chiunque voglia mettervi l'ugna sopra sarebbe stravaganza la mia in pretendere che rimanesse intatta.*« Inoltre non bisogna dimenticare che il Calzabigi non poteva permettersi di essere troppo intransigente con Antonio Greppi, perché gli era debitore di un prestito, che per anni (come si vedrà dalle lettere) non fu in grado di rimborsare.
Le lettere al Padre Frisi sono naturalmente più vive e dense di argomenti rispetto a quelle a Greppi, data la qualità del destinatario. Anche nelle tre riprodotte parzialmente dal Vianello i brani omessi da questo contengono spesso notizie interessanti: per esempio, nella lettera del 12 gennaio 1769, accanto al giudizio sui compositori del tipo di Guglielmi, che sono ignoranti e »*appena sanno leggere*«, c'è l'osservazione che non si usava comporre »*passaggi*« sulla vocale i.
Fra gli altri libretti del Calzabigi, dei quali le lettere danno notizia, troviamo *Paride ed Elena* (rappresentato a Vienna con musica di Gluck nel 1769), e infine quell'*Amiti e Ontario, o I selvaggi*, ambientato nell'America del Nord, che aveva a protagonisti dei buoni selvaggi, un quacchero e altri colonizzatori anglicani: riflesso certo di idee libertarie e umanitarie che erano nell'aria, insieme con l'interesse per le vicende del Nuovo Mondo. Di questo libretto non si conosce alcuna musica; anzi si riteneva che non fosse mai stato musicato (»nicht aufgeführt«, scrive Anna Amalie Abert nella voce *Calzabigi* della MGG). Dalla lettera del 24 agosto 1772 apprendiamo invece che il Calzabigi dovette scriverlo in soli 25 giorni, perché »*si deve rappresentare a Sleppe Terra della Sig.ᵃ Principessa d'Aversperg*«. Si deve supporre dunque che una esecuzione ci sia stata, sebbene resti ancora ignoto l'autore della musica.

---

[11] op. cit. p. 122.

Dal canto loro le lettere a Greppi contengono spesso interessanti apprezzamenti e notizie su cantanti ed esecutori che, anche col tramite di Calzabigi, i teatri di Milano e di Vienna si scambiavano o si contendevano.

Nel loro complesso queste lettere offrono una buona testimonianza biografica sul Calzabigi; fra l'altro attestano che fino al 1772 egli si trovava sicuramente a Vienna (mentre A. Einstein, nell'op. cit., p. 160, scrive: *»La carriera di Calzabigi durante il periodo 1771—4 è oscura«*). È molto probabile che, seguitando ad esplorare lo sterminato carteggio Greppi, vengano alla luce altre sue lettere o notizie su di lui.

Passiamo ora alle lettere di Antonia Bernasconi o che la riguardano, conservate nell'Archivio Greppi.

Antonia Bernasconi era una cantante tedesca, figlia di un valletto del Duca di Württemberg, che aveva assunto il cognome del suo patrigno Andrea Bernasconi, compositore italo-francese attivo dapprima in Italia, poi a Vienna e infine a Monaco di Baviera. Il vero cognome di Antonia è indicato come Wasel[12] oppure Wagele[13]. Nell'Archivio Greppi la si trova nominata, oltre che Antonia Bernasconi, anche Antonia de Löwenturn o Löwenture[14]: forse il cognome del marito? Dopo aver iniziato come buffa a Vienna, fu scelta da Calzabigi e Gluck per impersonare la protagonista dell'*Alceste* a Vienna nel 1767. Da allora si affermò come prima donna di grido. La sua voce non era molto robusta: il Calzabigi, nella citata lettera a Greppi del 6 aprile 1768, scrive che se l'*Alceste* fu scorciata a Vienna *»ciò fu solo a motivo che si conobbe alle prove che la delicata voce della Signora Bernasconi difficilmente potrebbe reggere alla parte intera d'Alceste colla richiesta vibrazione ed energia«*. Mozart ne riconosceva il valore nelle parti tragiche, pur criticandone l'intonazione.

Le sue lettere a Greppi iniziano dal novembre 1770. In quei giorni la Bernasconi era a Milano, perché doveva cantare nel *Mitridate re di Ponto* del quattordicenne Mozart, che andò in scena il 26 dicembre. Vedremo particolareggiatamente, nelle lettere, i retroscena che portarono alla scrittura della Bernasconi per quest'opera al posto di Caterina Gabrielli, inizialmente prescelta. Per quel che riguarda i rapporti della cantante con Antonio Greppi, risulta dalle lettere che quest'ultimo non solo provvedeva, tramite i suoi agenti di Mantova, Venezia, Vienna ecc., a fornirle i servizi di banca (come faceva anche per altre cantanti), ma le assicurava un effettivo appoggio per i problemi pratici della vita quotidiana (fornitura di legna e di calze di seta, presa in consegna di bauli, vendita

---

[12] in *Enciclopedia dello Spettacolo* (voce di Emilia ZANETTI).
[13] G. BARBLAN, op. cit., p. 126 n.
[14] Cart. 68, 17 dic. 1770, e cart. 69, 1º genn. 1771.

della carrozza, ecc.) e soprattutto l'assisteva in un lungo e penoso affare di riscossione di un credito che la Bernasconi aveva imprudentemente accordato ad un certo conte Seriman e di cui non riusciva a rientrare in possesso.

Le lettere della Bernasconi (quasi tutte autografe, e piene di sbagli di grammatica e di ortografia italiana, a cominciare dal nome del destinatario, storpiato in »Creppi«) continuano ad essere inviate a Greppi anche quando la cantante è partita da Milano. La seguiamo dunque a Bologna, Venezia e Napoli.

Ma veniamo ai retroscena della scrittura per il *Mitridate*. Guglielmo Barblan, che per primo ha attinto all'Archivio Greppi la documentazione del motivo per cui Caterina Gabrielli non fu, come previsto, l'Aspasia nell'opera mozartiana a Milano, ha citato[15] la lettera della Gabrielli a Greppi (25 marzo 1770, da Palermo), nella quale questa cantante comunica di non potersi liberare da impegni col teatro di Palermo. Attraverso le lettere dell'agente di Greppi a Vienna possiamo ora seguire il corso delle trattative del Teatro Ducale per avere la Bernasconi a Milano: dapprima il diniego di Kaunitz (nonché il suo giudizio sulla Gabrielli: *»questa è sempre stata una pazza, et una bestia, e tale morirà«*), i tentennamenti dell'impresario Afflizio, finché, il 27 maggio 1770, scoppia la bomba, comunicata dal prudentissimo agente de Soresina: la Bernasconi è bandita non solo da Vienna, ma da ogni altro Stato tedesco dipendente da S.M. la Sovrana, *»e ciò per motivo di quanto alla detta Virtuosa gli è seguito in Venezia cioè di essersi sgravata di quel frutto, che qui aveva acquistato«*. La Sovrana l'ha fatto dire per mezzo del conte Wenzel Sporck, succeduto al conte Giacomo Durazzo, nel 1764, come intendente dei teatri di Vienna. Si deve probabilmente vedere in questo episodio un riflesso di quella contrapposizione di mentalità e di simpatie, che regnava a Vienna fra il conte Durazzo, aperto a nuove iniziative e a innovazioni musicali e teatrali, protettore di Gluck, Calzabigi e Angiolini (e dunque anche della Bernasconi, loro amica) e il partito più »codino« di Metastasio, Hasse, Giuseppe Scarlatti: partito, quest'ultimo, che riscuoteva le simpatie non solo del conte Sporck, ma anche di Giuseppe II (*»di questo monarca dottrinario, che non era nulla più che un burocrate incoronato«*, secondo Alfred Einstein[16]), nonché di Maria Teresa; in particolare, nel bando della Bernasconi per ragioni di »buon costume«, si rispecchia il filisteismo della sovrana. Per fortuna della Bernasconi, Antonio Greppi e gli altri amici milanesi non solo sono ben felici di averla senza altre difficoltà per il *Mitridate*, ma non l'abbandonano neppure in seguito: vediamo infatti, dalla lettera del 2 agosto 1771, che *»S.E. il Conte di Firmian mi à fatto un grande elogio apresso la Corte«*, dopo di che il bando, almeno parzialmente, sembra revocato, l'innocenza riconosciuta e i calunniatori (Sporck e Stampa) puniti.

---

[15] op. cit., p. 102—104.
[16] op. cit., p. 118.

Quanto alla sua partecipazione all'opera di Mozart, sappiamo, da una lettera di Leopold Mozart al Padre Martini in data 2 gennaio 1771 da Milano, che la Bernasconi si rifiutò di sostituire, nel *Mitridate*, alcune arie di Mozart con quelle dell'abate Gasparini di Torino, come qualcuno tentava di indurla a fare.

Ma ecco le lettere.

LETTERE DI RANIERI DE CALZABIGI
AD ANTONIO GREPPI E AL PADRE PAOLO FRISI

Le lettere sono riprodotte in ordine cronologico. Quelle a Greppi si trovano all'Archivio di Stato di Milano, Archivio Greppi: di volta in volta si indica il numero della rispettiva Cartella. Le lettere a Paolo Frisi sono conservate alla Biblioteca Ambrosiana di Milano, in un manoscritto miscellaneo che reca la segnatura: Y. 152 sup. Per ogni lettera si indica il numero da cui è contrassegnata.

A Greppi
Cart. 52

Vienna 18 Avril 1768

Amico, e P.ne Stim.mo

Lungamente fu da me supplito con mia precedente che sarà già in suo potere a quanto si degnò richiedermi sull'Alceste, e che si degna ripetermi in questa deg. del corrente, ora pervenutami.

Spedii ancora l'Alceste intiera come mi mostrò aver desiderio.

Esposi le mie riflessioni in proposito nella Recita che cotesti Suoi S.ri Direttori vorrebbero farne fare nel loro Teatro.

Finii con esibir quanto da me poteva farsi per secondare, e facilitare questa loro idea supposto che vi persistessero, come mi lusingo.

Aggiungo adesso che la Sig.ra Viziani meglio converrebbe Loro che ogni altra, e che il Sig. Tipaldi Tenore è l'unico che possino scegliere per il Rolo d'Admeto da lui sostenuto qui ammirabilmente.

Aspetterò adunque le sue e loro risoluzioni per tutto ciò che potrà occorrere.

Mi trovo in congiuntura d'essergli di bel nuovo importuno, profittando nuovamente del suo buon core verso di me con quella confidenza altre volte praticata, e da Lei autorizzata con tanta sua gentilezza; più volentieri affidandomi ad un amico come Lei, che ricorrendo qui a' miei conoscenti. Lo supplico dunque favorirmi in risposta del comodo di f. 600 e Ung.ri 150 al solito verso il Sig. Segalla con contentarsi di mia ricevuta, ed obligo che ne manderò a Lei direttamente ricevendo il danaro, quale sarà da me puntualmente restituito in dicembre.

Di grazia compatisca, e comandi anche a me che pronto (in qualunque cosa ch'io possa) a tutti i suoi comandi col solito ossequio mi dichiaro sempre tutto suo um.mo servit. e amico

De Calsabigi

A Greppi
Cart. 53

Vienna 12. Maggio 1768

Amico, e P.ne Riv.mo

Rispondo subito all'ultima sua de' 2 del corrente in cui mi richiede, sull'accennato motivo, un Primo Buffo, ed una Prima Buffa di quelli che sono all'attual servizio di questi Teatri.

Ne ho fatto pronte premure con Afflizio, ma finora senza speranza. È vero che abbiamo qui tutti primi Buffi, fra quali v'è ancora il Sig.r Laschi, e tutte prime Buffe, ma non però la Compagnia è sopraabbondante, poiché consiste solamente in 8 personaggi, obligati ad alternare distributivamente fra loro tutte le prime, e tutte l'ultime parti, di maniera che smembrandosene alcuno, rimarrebbe ella incompleta, inabile al servizio, e non possibile a supplirsi in Germania.

Non lascerò peraltro di vedere coll'Afflizio sud[detto] se può farsi disposizione tale di spettacoli che lo metta in grado di compiacerla, ed in ciò sarò esatto a porgergli ultimo, e decisivo ragguaglio Lunedì venturo.

Esigei la passata gli Ungheri Cento cinquanta dietro semplice ricevuta dal Sig. Segalla, quali mi obligo nuovamente restituirgli in dicembre prossimo. Manderò obligo se vuole, e lo farei in questa ma m'imbroglia il doppio documento, non parendomi proprio stendere in un obligo la dichiarazione d'averne fatto ricevuta, e che ambedue contengono un solo effetto. Ma se lo desidera così lo invierò subito, assicurandolo che questo non aggiunge nulla alla mia promessa che sarà da me puntualmente adempita. Intanto però li rendo distinte grazie di questa nuova prova della sua bontà, e amicizia per me.

Niente mi riesce ancora per la Campori, quantunque siasi licenziata la Lodi perché è inviluppata la Direzione con due impegni per la Fabris e Lolli a Stougard, aspettando se riuscirà loro rompere le catene contratte col Duca, come hanno promesso, ma subito si schiarirà questo punto penserò alla sua protetta, e ci penserò efficacemente. Mi creda intanto tutto suo, e finché vivrò Amico grato, e serv.re ob.mo

De Calsabigi

A Greppi
Cart. 53

Vienna 16. Giugno 1768

A. C.

Il Sig. Garibaldi opponendo alle offerte di cotesti Direttori gli Ungheri 400 che guadagna qui, e riflettendo a molti altri accidenti non accetta gli Ungheri 200 onde non servirà farne altro discorso.

In questa combinerò il consaputo obligo col Sig. Segalla. Non mi estendo per esser pieno di affari.

Gli rassegno la mia servitù e sono tutto suo di core

Um.mo Ob.mo Serv.
De Calsabigi

A Greppi
Cart. 54

                                                        Vienna 25. luglio 1768
Amico e P.ne stim.

Non posso dispensarmi di raccomandargli con tutta la premura il Sig. Giorgio Scotti celebre virtuoso di Contrabasso il quale doppo esser stato 3 anni al servizio del Duca di Wittemberg ritorna a cotesta sua Patria. L'eccellenza della sua abilità gli avrebbe fatto qui trovar luogo assolutamente ma impegni sopra impegni da non potersi disdire sono causa che a nostro sommo rammarico, per ora bisogna lasciarlo andare. S.A. il Sig. Principe di Kaunitz per cui ordine ha il detto Scotti sonato in questo Teatro alcune sere ha promesso di proteggerlo, ed assisterlo, ed io mi avanzo di raccomandarglielo quanto so, e posso, sperando dalla sua bontà che vorrà far comprendere allo Scotti suddetto che la mia raccomandazione ha presso di Lei qualche potere.

Mi conservi la sua grazia e mi comandi anche Lei, mentre al solito mi confermo col maggior ossequio suo vero amico, e servitore

                                                        De Calsabigi L'aîné

A Greppi
Cart. 56

                                                        Vienna 12. Dicembre 1768
Stim.mo e Riv.mo Amico

Mi prevenne due Ordinarj sono la signora Teresa[17] della fiera mutilazione da Loro ideata della mia *Alceste,* o più tosto ampliazione perché mi disse che doveva lavorarci sopra l'Ab.te Parrino; ed io non comprendo qual debba essere il suo lavoro se non ricordando che cotesti Signori Direttori vollero già per suo mezzo esigere da me che aggiungessi all'*Alceste personaggi interessanti.* Comunque sia deplorando non come Poeta, ma come *homme de gout* il *barbaro governo* che fanno adesso in Italia alle produzioni Teatrali più sensate a solo motivo di tirarle alla ridicola durata di cinque ore e di poter cenare mentre si rappresentano; e molto più compiangendo la barbarie nostra in quanto a me *Ego vos absolvo ab omni vinculo Excommunicationis,* e solo mi ristringo a desiderare una prossima emenda.

Non sarebbe stato naturale che storpiandosi la mia poesia si volesse lasciare intatta la musica e me l'ero pensata, quando capitò ieri da me il Sig. Gluk con un esemplare dell'*Alceste* parole e Musica finito di stampare nella settimana scorsa, chiedendomi permesso di spedirlo a Lor Signori per mezzo del Sig. Valmagini. Le nostre convenzioni fra Gluk e me sono che non produrrà la sua Musica che a mia volontà, dovendo io premettere a quella stampa una Prefazione che spieghi il motivo, anzi i motivi dell'enorme cambiamento da noi fatto in tali Drammatiche Composizioni. Ora questa Prefazione non l'ho fatta ancora, e manca alla stampa sud[dett]a Titolo, Dedica, e prefazione sud[dett]a necessarissima. Sarebbe pertanto questo il caso di non accordargli l'assenso per produrla, ma trattandosi di Lorsignori gli ho dato facoltà di far ciò che

---

[17] Teresa Fogliazzi, moglie del celebre coreografo Gaspare Angiolini ed ella stessa ballerina ammirata per la grazia e l'intelligenza. A Milano teneva circolo intellettuale, frequentato da eminenti personalità del mondo culturale.

stima, acciò in genere, numero, e caso si cucinino a Loro modo l'*Alceste*; ma quello che imploro dal sig. Greppi per ottenere da' suoi Signori è una qualche ampla generosità per il detto Maestro, e per la sua compiacenza per sollevarlo dalle spese della Stampa, il che decentemente si può fare con sottoscriversi per un *certo numero di Esemplari* quali potranno poi distribuire costì o altrove in Italia o in dono, o anche facendoli esitare per conto del Teatro da un Libraro. Per esempio: *S. Greppi per 10 Esemplari*. Non sarebbe un gran male, e ne saranno ricompensati con avere i primi le altre produzioni della nostra società una delle quali intitolata *Paride ed Elena,* compita per parte mia, e al lavoro per il Sig. Gluk. Tutto ciò sia detto senza voler far torto a maggiore rimunerazione che potessero aver pensata cotesti Sig. Direttori alla quale non intendo derogare con questa proposizione; lasciando fare al Sig. Greppi che so che farà bene anche sul riflesso che il Sig. Gluk dando a loro i primi la sua Composizione musica non potrà più farne uso *come di cosa novissima* verso altra Persona, come ne aveva intenzione.

Venendo a mie cose particolari, La supplico scrivere al Sig. Segalla che da me ritardandosi il pagamento del saputo Biglietto in questo mese pazienti a riceverlo che io sarò prontamente esatto al possibile al mio dovere; pregandolo di scusare queste mie soverchie confidenze come amico.

Alla suddetta Sig.ª Teresa dirà che lessi l'articolo della sua lettera alla consaputa persona che ne mostrò gradimento. Al P. Frisio che si è scordato di noi, tutti i miei complimenti. E in mentre protestandoli tutta la mia riconoscenza, e obligazione col desiderio che mi dia luogo a servirla in quanto posso col solito ossequio mi dichiaro tutto suo e vero amico e servitore

De Calsabigi

A Frisi
Nº 143
Vienna 15. Dicembre 1768
Stimat.ᵐᵒ P.ᵉ e Amico.

Quando mi fu scritto dal nostro amab.ᵐᵒ Sig. Greppi a nome di cotesti Sig. Direttori degli Spettacoli, che desideravano che io volessi aggiungere all'Alceste de' Personaggi interessanti; e quando con mia lunga lettera[18] fui obligato dare al suddetto Amico una dura ma giustificata negativa, mi dovevo naturalmente aspettare a ciò che si fa adesso dell'Alceste per altra mano. Fu quello il lampo di questo tuono. Io non ho saputo trovare nella favola d'Alceste altri personaggi importanti che Alceste, Admeto, e i loro figli, avendone esclusi il Padre, e la Madre d'Alceste da Euripide introdotti appunto perchè non interessavano: il Sig. Abbate Parrini sarà stato più acuto di me, e grato mi sarà di vedere come in mano di migliore ingegno possa crescer d'interesse un'azione, che da me fu riputata eccellente per la sua semplicità. So che sull'uso Metastasiano potevo, anzi dovevo fare Evandro amante di Alceste, e sfortunato; Ismene amante d'Admeto, e infelice, e aggiunger forse un Ercole pure innamorato d'Alceste come Quinault. In tal guisa tutti questi personaggi si sarebbero presentati sulla scena con parte interessante, secondo il pensare Italiano, e il mio Dramma non avrebbe abbisognato d'un secondo poeta per finirlo, e per perfezionarlo. Disgrazia-

---

[18] È la lettera del 6 aprile 1768, pubblicata da C.A. Vianello.

tamente io non ho trovato né in Aristotile né in Orazio legislatori della Poesia queste nuove regolette che ci procurano parti drammatici sublimi tanto, e tanto ingegnosi; e che tanta attenzione esigono dagli spettatori. Povera Italia! E tanto più da compiangere quanto che in un Milano si pensa così da chi dirige i Teatri. Io per me mi dichiaro insensibilissimo a questo pasticcio di cucina barbara pur troppo deplorabile. La stampa avendo resa propria l'Alceste di chiunque voglia mettervi l'ugna sopra sarebbe stravaganza la mia in pretendere che rimanesse intatta. Se ne fo con Lei questa o doglianza o risata ciò sicuro alla mia poetica superbia non appartiene, ma alla miserabile decadenza delle Lettere che di giorno in giorno va crescendo nella nostra Patria; decadenza deplorata fin dalle Nazioni che per emulazione desideran vederci avviliti.

Rendo grazie distinte all'amico P. Frisi d'avermi comunicato questo arcano, e lo prego di favorirmi del rifatto Dramma quando potrà averlo a solo titolo di curiosità. Ne ho già pronto un altro intitolato Paride ed Elena, che, contro mia credenza, mi figuro sarà anch'esso trovato incompleto, onde resta preparato nuovo lavoro a quelli che danno l'ultima mano agli aborti; e se la Provvidenza mi conserva in vita gli assicuro che non mancheranno mai d'impiego.

Son poi tenuto alle nuove che Ella mi dà. In proposito Ecclesiastico giusto i scorsi giorni scrissi ad amico a Berlino »Les Princes veulent que desormais nous nous torchions le C... avec du Parchemin; cela sera un peu dur, mais on y parviendra«. Saprà che S.S.ᵃ[19] avendo l'anno scorso ricusato a questa Imp. Corte di rinovare l'Indulto quindecennale per la Levée de quelques impôts sur les Biens Ecclesiastiques, se non a strane condizioni, le L.L.M. han creduto poter fare a meno dell'Indulto, onde senza Indulto fu ordinata la continuazione dell'esazione, e Mgr. Nunzio che (penetrata la risoluzione) si è fatto trovare pronto coll'Indulto senza pretensione, non sa a chi darlo, lo tiene in tasca, e vorrebbe pure che gli se ne dicessi una parola per subito regalarlo, ma nissuno gli ne discorre, e nissuno se ne cura. Egli perde in questo Regolamento 6 mila fiorini annui.

S.A. cui lessi la sua lettera molto si diffuse in lodi anzi elogi della sua persona riguardo a dottrina, ingegno, costume, e tante belle qualità sociabili che l'adornano e m'incaricò di fargli i suoi saluti, e di assicurarlo della sua stima. Mi rallegro con lei di questo pensare del Principe a suo vantaggio; pensare meritato, come facilmente converrà ognuno che sa pesare gli uomini, e che abbia avuto il piacere di godere della sua ambita compagnia. Appunto per leggere la sua lettera a S.A. ho trattenuto fino a oggi a spedirla quantunque già scritta in gran parte alcuni giorni sono. Mi conservi la sua amicizia, e mi comandi che io col più vero ossequio mi do l'onore di dichiararmi

Suo vero servo, e amico
De Calsabigi

Marco[20] la saluta caramente.
S.A. ha riso smisuratamente dell'idea di aggiungere all'Alceste, et ha compianto quel pensare sì strano, e sì poco a noi decoroso.

---

[19] Clemente XIII.
[20] Marco Coltellini, librettista.

A Frisi
N° 138

[senza data, ma fine dicembre 1768]

Rev.^{mo} P.re e Stim.^{mo} Amico.

Hanno fatto a Milano coll'Alceste quello che farebbe ad una sua dimostrazione Geometrica chi alla figura aggiungesse a capriccio delle linee inutili per attondarla, o riquadrarla, ad oggetto di renderla, a suo credere, più graziosa alla vista.

Il Poeta del mattino[21], non è niente proprio per la sera, al lume delle scene. Ella sa quanto sia diverso il parlare ex se, o sia fare il predicatore, dal far parlare gli altri. Il Parrini poi non conosce affatto né la concatenazione della frase Poetica Teatrale, né il vocabolario drammatico, tanto diverso da quello della Canzonetta, Poemetto, e Sonettino, che nulla più.

Hanno così ridotta la Tragedia d'Alceste in opera buffa: a me nulla importa di questa mascherata, perché i più amorosi padri veggono con piacere talvolta i loro figli vestiti da Arlecchino, o da Pulcinella nel Carnevale.

Prevveddi l'esito infelice della storpiata Alceste perché conoscevo il Poemetto del Mattino: Qui calza il nostro trito proverbio: Il buon dì si conosce dal *mattino*.

La morale letteraria insegna a non metter mano nelle cose altrui. Al più si può fare per scorciare, mai per allungare. Il prendersi poi l'ardire di aggiustar versi (cioè a dire di buoni farli cattivi) si può chiamare impertinenza Poetica e orgoglio imperdonabile. E questo basti sull'Alceste della cui rappezzatura, e nuova Poesia si sono fatte risate eterne.

La ringrazio del Libro mi ha spedito. Que' Signori Direttori non mi hanno creduto assai importante per mandarmelo, ne anche sul riflesso che n'ero l'autore.

Se non viene S.A. da me domani, o l'altro, avrò modo di fargli leggere l'articolo della sua lettera per il consaputo MS. E per Giovedì dirò il risultato: gli manderò la lettera a casa.

Coltellini la saluta ed io con vera stima e costante amicizia mi confermo suo vero amico e servitore

De Calsabigi

A Greppi
Cart. 57

Vienna 2 Gennajo 1769

Amico e P.^{ne} Stim.^{mo}

Insiste il Sig. Gluk avergli domandato a nome di cotesti Direttori Teatrali il Sig. Valmagini la Musica d'Alceste. Lei sa meglio di noi quel che ne sia, ma certo nulla si deve al Sig. Gluk, se nulla se gli è richiesto, come benissimo Ella osserva.

Ricevei i Tartufi e glie ne resto in estremo obligato, come della compiacenza per la dilazione per il consaputo pagamento.

Qualche incomodo sopraggiuntomi non mi permette dilungarmi; solo aggiungo i miei voti per le sue felicità, buona salute, e allegrezza nell'anno in cui entriamo, e

---

[21] Giuseppe Parini aveva pubblicato *Il Mattino* (prima parte del *Giorno*) nel 1763.

motivo a me di provargli efficacemente la verità di que' vivi sentimenti co' quali mi dichiaro per sempre suo vero amico e servo

RCalsabigi

A Greppi
Cart. 57
Lettera di D. Volpi, agente di Greppi a Vienna.

Vienna 2 Gennajo 1769

[...] Devo poi significarle che la somma insuperabile difficoltà da me incontrata allor quando, per di Lei commissione, ricercai qui l'opera intitolata l'*Alceste*, scritta dal Sig.ᵣ Calsabigi, e posta in musica dal Sig.ᵣ maestro Gluk, non in altro consistette sennonsé nel proposito in cui eransi fissati questi due soggetti di pubblicarla colla stampa, esitandola ad un prezzo proporzionato al Lavoro. La si sta dunque stampando e prima che termini il Carnovale verrà pubblicata e venduta dal Trattner. Per un accidente mi è riuscito di averne un esemplare, stato involato dalla stamperia medesima. Questo l'ò comperato per 4 ongheri. Vi è tutto lo spartito della musica nella più esatta forma. Il volume non è indifferente: quindi io ne ò fatto un involto, e col mezzo della Diligenza di Mantova l'ò spedito stamane al Sig.ᵣ Marliani, cui prego parimenti stassera di procurarlo, e inoltrarlo immediatamente a V.S. Ill.ᵐᵃ Io non sò per dir vero se m'abbia fatto né ben né male; ma visto che la spesa non è eccedente, mi sono presa la libertà di profittare d'un furto che non porta danno a nessuno, persuaso che non vorrà per ciò condannarmi [...]

A Greppi
Cart. 57
Lettera del Consigliere aulico Valmagini

Vienna 2. del 1769

Ill.ᵐᵒ Sig.ʳᵉ Sig.ʳᵉ P.ne Col.ᵐᵒ

Quando venni in cognizione del desiderio di V.S. Ill.ᵐᵃ di avere la musica dell'Alceste, si stava quella perfezionando. Onde prima d'ora non mi è stato possibile di servirlo. Il Signor Cavalier Gluk che ne è l'Autore me ne ha tosto dato un esemplare da lui corretto, ed ha desiderato che io fossi l'unico mezzo di presentarglielo. Così eseguisco con estremo piacere; e non essendomi capitata, come avrei desiderato, altra occasione più pronta, mi sono risoluto di rimettere il pacchetto per la Diligenza di Posta, partita or ora per Mantova [...]

A Greppi
Cart. 57

Vienna 12 Gennaio 1769

Am. e P. stim.

Nel rileggere a caso la sua ultima stim.ᵐᵃ veggo ciò che mi era sfuggito, cioè che scriveva al sig. Segalla di sospendere l'esazione del mio obligo a tutto Gennaio. Io veramente spero di compiere, ma se a sorte non fosse, dipendendo ciò da un fondo che entrar mi deve, supplico a scrivergli di bel nuovo di protrarre, che io sarò esatto subito che mi entrerà il fondo suddetto. Scusi di grazia questa dilazione e seccatura e comandi anche a me che son pronto ad ogni sua volontà. E confermandogli il mio più distinto ossequio con tutto il core sono il suo vero amico e serv.ᵉ

De Calsabigi

A Frisi
N° 144

Vienna 12. Gennajo 1769

Rev. P.ʳᵉ e stim.ᵐᵒ Amico.

Continuando a render grazie distinte a V.S. per l'accuratezza con cui si è degnata favorirmi le notizie della storpiata Alceste, sono d'altrove inteso della pessima Musica, colla quale vogliono scusare il Parrini. La Musica non poteva esser buona, cioè propria al libro, conoscendo io lo stile infelice del rappezzator di note Guglielmi[22]. Costui, e quasi tutti gli altri maestri di cappella fuori di sapere che alla tal nota ci vuol la tal altra, sono affatto ignoranti, e appena sanno leggere. Non mi maraviglio non abbia trovato musica sulle parole »sono al fin del viver mio«. Voleva trovar certo un passaggio su quel verso per la meschina Girelli[23], né lo trovava per causa del fi, vi, mi, attesoché sull'i non si costuma; ecco l'arcano.

Quanto poi al sig. Parrini tutto gli accordo fuori di aver cambiato i miei versi, e per spirito di correzione, giacché altro patente motivo non so vedere al mettere *orrore* per *paura*, malgrado la replica d'*orrore* poco sotto, e a troncare, sostituire, cambiare molti miei versi per (a parer suo bisogna) farli migliori. Quest'orgoglio poetico è insoffribile tanto più in lui, che non ha merito affatto per assumerlo, non avendo a' miei giorni veduto cosa più meschina, *plus plate,* che i suoi versi drammatici. Sono, per i miei peccati, ormai 35 anni che il mio stile poetico è noto e distinto in Italia, e non supponevo trovarmi ora sulle spalle un sì magro pedagogo. Ma s'egli è contento delle sue correzzioni perché invidiarli questa boria? Sarebbe un ricompensarlo malamente del suo *Chef d'Oeuvre.* Noti che tutto il merito del piano d'Alceste tende a far risaltare l'amore coniugale, e la gratitudine d'Admeto per l'atto (a proposito cambiò anche *atto grande s'adempia* il Sʳ Parrini, chi sa il perché) grande d'Alceste, ed egli tutto distrugge col meschino ritrovato del Dono d'Apollo, mediante il quale fa senza necessità abbandonare ad Admeto la memoria della pur troppo benefica Alceste. Io mi vado dilungando male a proposito in queste sciocchezze Parriniane che non vagliano la pena d'esser ponderate. Meglio farò a dirgli che S.A. lesse le due sue lettere, fece grandi elogi di Lei, e disse gli rispondeva oggi, onde io, se la mia lettera gli viene aperta la prima gli annunzio questo favore, e questo contento, e ratificandogli tutti i sentimenti più vivi miei per la sua amicizia mi confermo pronto ad ogni suo piacere con soscrivermi suo vero amico

e serv. Calsabigi

---

[22] Pietro Alessandro Guglielmi (Massa 1728 — Roma 1804).
[23] Antonia Maria Girelli Aguilar, interprete del personaggio di Alceste.

A Greppi
Cart. 57

Vienna 9. febbrajo 1769

Amico e P.ne Stim.mo

Rendo le più distinte grazie alla sua gentilezza per il ritardo fattomi per la consaputa obligazione, assicurandola che sarò puntuale a compire. Intanto se vaglio a servirla mi comandi, che procurerò dimostrargli la mia riconoscenza; avendo ancora in questi passati giorni ricevuto la Cioccolata, onde mi veggo ricolmo delle sue grazie per ogni verso.

La supplico salutare la S.ra Teresa, e dirle la gran nuova d'esser passato Novere a fare i Balli al Teatro Tedesco, Afflizio essendosi sbarazzato con un Dilettante di Teatri, e di quel Teatro e di Novere, onde io scrivo in questa settimana a Angiolini per l'anno venturo: che qui hanno in mira l'Epy, Boucqueton, e un certo D'Auvigny, senza contar Regina, ottimo facitore di Balli Pantomimi buffi, che già è in Vienna, ma che sarà mio pensiero di non far far torto al suo Marito. Fra due anni Novere certo sarà fuori di Vienna, terminando allora il suo contratto. Sono al solito con ossequi e gratit.ne tutto suo e vero amico

Calsabigi

A Frisi
N° 141

Vienna 27 feb.º 1769

A. e P.e Stim.º

Lessi l'articolo della sua gent.a del 10 a S.A. che mi disse non avere ancora ricevuto l'annunziato suo Ms. Ho stimato bene avvisarglielo: nel di più non cambia il Principe nella maniera di pensare a suo riguardo; né preveggo che possa alterarsi la stima da Esso per Lei concepita. Queste rivoluzioni succedono in persona di chi non ha lumi, verso chi non ha merito: allora le prime idee formate sono sorprese, e non durano.

Lei si diverte intanto colle sue matematiche che io me la passo con poca buona salute, motivo di non prolungar la lettera quanto vorrei; pochi essendovi più premurosi di me al trattenersi cogli amici della Sua categoria con lunghi discorsi, da' quali sempre qualche costrutto si cava.

I Turchi fanno il Diavolo in armamenti[24], e la Russia non giunge a capire, come *le cose che ha fatte per il bene della Porta* gli abbiano procurata la di lei inimicizia, e nega poi d'aver mai esercitato alcuna autorità in Polonia, e in ciò *si rapporta al detto di tutta l'Europa*. Questi Signori ci prendono per gli abitanti della Groenlandia; e questa loro Politica mi par degna di que' popoli che mangiano Olio di Balena. Vorrebbero far la pace ed anche non è cominciata la guerra. Gridano contro i francesi perchè non vogliono soffrire le loro Cabale; veramente hanno il torto questi di non lasciar la Polonia schiava della Russia!

Il P. Adami è una cogliaccia: questo è il nome che gli sta bene per eccellenza, con molti altri ancora. Io lo conosco di persona no ma di borsa per avere a me e a mio

---

[24] Caterina II di Russia era impegnata, nel 1768, nella guerra contro i Turchi; i Russi invasero le provincie turche di Moldavia e di Valacchia. Nel contempo la Russia esercitava una forte pressione sulla Polonia, riducendola quasi ad un suo protettorato.

fratello estorto, e mangiato 200 Zecchini col pretesto d'interessarci in una sua ruberia o stamperia, di cui doppo 15 anni non ha dato mai conto.

Se il nuovo Papa[25] non si terrà a ciò che dice il proverbio nostro, cioè a godersi il Papato, mi pare che il suo credito e influenza faranno f . . . Dio gli dia giudizio.

Col solito ossequio mi soscrivo suo buon serv.[re] e vero Amico

De Calsabigi

A Frisi
N° 140

Vienna 12. Giugno 1769

Stim.[mo] e Riv.[mo] Amico.

La mia salute par che vada ora prendendo buona piega, ma da qualche giorni sono assai doloroso nel pugno della mano dritta il che m'impedisce di scrivere. Se è gotta è ostinata perché non viene a gonfiezza, onde non può l'umore andarsi gentilmente traspirando, e dilatarsi. Pazienza anche in questo: ad hoc nati sumus; benché io dovrei bestemmiare in vedere che più che per qualsisia altro par scritto per me questo bel motto.

Ecco il Ganganelli diventato il Giove Capitolino della moderna Roma colla Tiara, e colle pianelle, vibrante fulmini di cartapecora. Il negozio però non cammina come ne' passati secoli di timore, onde il povero Giove sarà credo costretto a far la statua, e appigliarsi al silenzio Pitagorico. Qui (considerato quel che era il Ganganelli) ci va a puntino il motto d'Orazio:

Olim truncus eram ficulnus inutile lignum.

Col maluit esse decem che seguita. Lasciamolo evacuar benedizioni, e desideriamo che sia ridotto a non poter più maledire, come il Re d'Inghilterra che in vigor di quella ammirabil Costituzione può far del bene, e mai del male o vero, o finto.

Addio Corsi, e Paoli[26]. Il Ministro francese or potrà dire avere in coscienza guadagnati quegli alcuni milioni propinatigli dall'Ecc.[mo] Sorba a Parigi. Meravigliosa è la gloria che ne risulta alla Nazione francese che con tanti apparati, e forze terrestri, e marittime, e legioni e cannoni, e macchine incendiarie ha finalmente schiacciato un pidocchio.

Una Volpe coperta della pelle di Leone hanno per parte loro fugata, e costretta a rintanar pochi Turchi (dicono al più 40 m.) sotto Coczino, attaccati dalla grande Armata Russa. Artiglieria perduta, Niester ripassato, 36 leghe d'Alemagna indietro corse a furia sono le conseguenze della Vittoria insigne che decantano gli stampati di Petersburgo. Ci ritiriamo a Kiovca, né aspetteremo il gran Visir per evacuare la Polonia dove facevamo da padroni. Così va a chi vuole peter plus haut que le cul. Scusi la trivialità anzi immondizia del proverbio francese, ma non me lo sono potuto inghiottire perché va tanto bene a gentaglia che senza quattrini e senza truppe si cimentano a tutto e imposturano da tanti anni con bugie, e con liste di 628 o 28 soldati effettivi il globo Terraqueo. Queste sono le notizie fresche di quelle parti Pollacche ove non tarderanno a seguire gran rivoluzioni.

---

[25] Clemente XIV (Giovanni Vincenzo Ganganelli), che pontificò dal 1769 al 1774. Col suo breve *Dominus ac Redemptor noster* soppresse nel 1773 la Società di Gesù.

[26] Pasquale Paoli era riuscito a fare della Corsica una repubblica indipendente, divenendone presidente nel 1755. Ma nel 1768 Genova vendette alla Francia i propri diritti sull'isola e Paoli fu sconfitto nella battaglia di Pontenuovo (1769).

Ho letto la sua al Personaggio che mi ha d[ett]o scrivergli Essergli obligato della memoria che di lui conserva. Saluti Greppi, e la Sig.ª Teresa se li vede e mi creda suo in ogni maniera in ogni tempo amico vero e buon servitore

C.

A Greppi
Cart. 60

Vienna 10 Agosto 1769: [Si dice pronto a procurare a Greppi alcuni piatti e tazze e la ricetta per la colla in caso di rottura. Si scusa per non aver ancora potuto rimborsare il prestito.]

A Greppi
Cart. 60

Vienna 31 Agosto 1769: [Ha consegnato al Sig. Segalla i piatti e le tazze.]

A Frisi
Nº 139

Vienna 31. Ag. 1769

Rev.º e Stim.º Padre e Amico,

A buon conto non è poca la mia consolazione ch'ella si ricordi di me, e qualche volta mi faccia grazia di sue lettere; quando io sono così inesatto, e così laconico a rispondere. Convien scusarmi. Se i miei incommodi sono da qualche tempo minori, non sono però cessati. Ho poi degli affari, e finalmente de' rompimenti di capo. Bisogna mettere a calcolo tutte queste distrazioni, e pigliarmi come sono, e come vuol ch'io sia la mia situazione. È però vero che non manco all'amicizia, e non ho bisogno di stimolo, e di memorativo. Lo fo da me, perché son caldo, impegnoso, e efficace.

S.A. partì ieri per Austerlitz ove starà tutto 7bre. I miei incomodi mi privano da più anni di quella villeggiatura. Fino al suo ritorno non potrò passar quell'uffizio che mi raccomanda ma già spesso si è fatta commemorazione di Lei con suo sommo vantaggio, e tale che non saprei che aggiungere.

A proposito rileggendo l'Istoria Romana m'abbattei nell'Antonino Pio di Giulio Capitolino in cui trovai che il carattere di quell'umanissimo Imp[erato]re calzava giusto a quello del Principe col solamente toglierne una parola, onde ne feci un'Epigrafe sotto il suo ritratto. Ecco il testo. Lo troverà sicuro felicissimamente applicato.

Vir forma conspicuus, ingenio clarus, moribus clemens, nobilis vultu, et placidus ingenio. Singularis eloquentiae, nitidae literaturae, praecipue sobrius, diligens, mitis, largus, alieni abstinens, et omnia haec cum mensura, et sine jactantia. La somiglianza non può esser più esatta, ed è glorioso somigliare agli Antonini[27].

---

[27] Questa epigrafe si trova infatti riportata nella dedica a Sua Altezza Vinceslao Antonio di Kaunitz, che il Calzabigi pubblicò a pag. 3 del Tomo I delle sue *Poesie* (Livorno 1774); nello stesso volume è pure riprodotto il ritratto di Kaunitz in un medaglione.

Mi figuro che la mia lettera Lo ritroverà forse ancora armato di canocchiale a speculare la non calcolata cometa in Tauro. Se mai Ella pensasse a prefiggerle tempo di ritorno preciso, avverto sarà bene assegnarglielo lungo per non esser smentito da queste signore che non badano troppo (mi pare) alle prescrizioni degli astronomi.

Vatti veggendo, e che sì che questa Cometa predice (e lo sarà presso al volgo sicuramente) l'estinzione de' Gesuiti. Anche qui s'aspetta ed è preventivamente annunziata. Quando ciò succederà diremo: E Uno. L'imbroglio sarà per la cupidità di scoprire le accumulate e nascoste ricchezze. E che sì che qualche Jerofante dell'ordine la pagherà male. Prevedo qualche cosa di somigliante a' Templari in ragione però del più umano pensare del nostro secolo. Credo che alcuni di que' Padri, quando saremo a' tesori, dovrà però soffrire *la question*. Non penso d'ingannarmi.

Qui si dicono gran cose de' Certosini di Pavia già rimessi in pristinum per quello decantasi, del Sr *D'Aveiro* o *Averio*, costretto dicono a domandare sa demission, *a qualche altro personaggio* che non dovrà più mescolarsi in Cose Ecclesiastiche, all'Em.mo *Pozzobonelli* che sarà alla testa d'una Giunta per detti affari, del *P.re Frisio* che non se ne ingerirà più, e lo scrivano tutto di Roma; ho visto la lettera. Avvisi qualche cosa di vero. Sono tutto suo

A Frisi
N° 142

Vienna 22 Aprile 1770

Rev.mo P.re e Stim.o Amico.

Che dirà della mia impudenza, troppo filosofica in aver ardire di rispondere in Aprile ad una stim.a sua di novembre! È tale il mio peccato che non ardisco domandarne perdon. Lo confesso però, e tocca alla sua gentilezza a fare il di più. Volontario affatto non è perché il mio Inverno è stato de' più afflitti; non ho avuto un'ora di salute, né un momento di quiete. 5 o sei sole volte ho avuto l'onore di far la mia Corte a S.A. il nostro degnissimo Mecenate, hebbe fin la bontà di soffrirmi quasi storpiato in casa sua. In queste visite non ebbi luogo a parlar di Lei, come ora a primo incontro lo farò perché vorrei che facesse un'altra corsa a Vienna. Ma già S.A. non ha bisogno di rammemorazione degli uomini che stima, e seco questi tali uffici sono veramente superflui. Godo che Ella l'abbia esperimentato, e ne può avere tanta maggior sodisfazione, quanta più glie ne può derivare dal sapere che i nuovi benefizj di S.A. Ella non li deve che a lui medesimo. Non sollecitato, non stimolato.

La ringrazio del suo concetto del mio Orfeo fatto con strepito a Parma[28] che tornerà qui in scena fra 8 o 10 giorni, e l'Alceste in Autunno, e il Paride mio nuovo Dramma in questo stesso anno a Carnevale, e forse prima. Ella sa la somma stima che fo de' suoi giudizi letterari, stima dovuta al suo eminente merito, onde non le parrà strano che io nel voler dire qualche cosa di me per il mio Orfeo, premetta »L'approvò il P.e Frisi«. A suo tempo sottometterò il Paride alla sua censura dottissima; ma se mi resta qualche desiderio sarebbe di averlo qui a vederli tutti in Teatro, e ne discorrerò con chi può nelle vacanze procurargli questa passeggiata. Intanto si accerti che io son

---

28 Alla corte di Parma, in occasione delle nozze del Reale Infante di Spagna duca Ferdinando con l'arciduchessa d'Austria Maria Amalia, andò in scena, il 24 agosto 1769, uno spettacolo con musiche di Gluck, dal titolo *Le feste d'Apollo*, che comprendeva anche *L'atto di Orfeo*. Era questo l'*Orfeo* di Calzabigi e Gluck e fu rappresentato in un solo atto.

sempre il medesimo, scriva, o non scriva; che non cambio mai, che i miei sentimenti per lei derivano non da cerimoniosa finta maschera ma da vera affezione e stima delle sue amabili qualità, e che son tutto suo davero, e per sempre app.º Amico
de Calsabigi
Mi dia qualche Gesuitica nuova. Non ne sappiamo nulla qui. Così pure se vi sono notizie letterarie, me le favorisca. Ella è più in giorno di me, povero ignorante, e infermo.

A Frisi
Nº 146
Vienna 11. Ottobre 1770
Amico, e P.ne Stim.º e Riv.mo

Da' Giornali rilevai il premio da lei ottenuto a Copenaghen, e ne ebbi estrema consolazione, prendendo infinita parte a' vantaggi, e sopratutto alla celebrità degli amici. Stimerei moltissimo che Ella si degnasse mettermi in caso di legger la Dissertazione premiata, ma siccome m'immagino che ancora sarà Ms. così mi riserberò per allorquando la darà alle stampe; supposto sempre che non vi sieno imbarazzi grandi di calcoli perché è gran tempo che ho disimparate per disgrazia, tutte queste difficoltà astronomiche. Se dunque Ella crede che la dissertazione sia pane per i miei denti, mi annovererà (La supplico) fra quelli a' quali vorrà trasmetterla.

Vedrò ben volentieri il Suo stimato Libro de' Fiumi[29] coll'aggiunte fattevi, quando dal Sig. C. Crivelli mi sarà fatto consegnare il pacchetto, e subito scorso l'avrò, lo presenterò colla sua lettera a S.A. il Sig. Principe Kaunitz come ella m'impone. L'occhiata che io potrò darvi non sarà che per ammirare le sue profonde cognizioni, e per compiacermi d'aver, con sì debol merito, un amico di tanto lustro, e entità, nella Republica de' Letterati.

Non mi pare che pensi, almen per ora, a viaggiare il Sig. Duca di Braganza[30], per quanto posso io saperne. Molto bensì desidererei che Ella pensasse seriamente nel nuovo anno a far nuovo viaggio a Vienna; e mi lusingo che S.A. il suddetto S.r Principe volentierissimo l'accorderà perché so quanto valuti il suo sapere, e sue buone qualità. Per me poi, ricordevole della sua dolce compagnia l'altra volta da me goduta, non potrebbe succeder cosa più grata.

Il mio *Paride* doveva qui rappresentarsi alla metà di questo mese, ma S.A.R. il Granduca[31] mostrò desiderio di vedere ancora l'*Alceste*, onde prontamente se ne fecero le disposizioni, e sarà data il 21. ed il *Paride* la seguiterà subito e prima del 6. novembre giorno in cui par fissata la partenza di quel Principe. Publicato che sia il Dramma lo spedirò subito a Lei, ringraziandola della sua premura per queste bagattelle mie.

Conoscendo io pienamente il merito, ed il carattere di alcuni de' Virtuosi che hanno

---

[29] Il libro di Paolo Frisi s'intitola *Del modo di regolare i fiumi, e torrenti principalmente del Bolognese, e della Romagna.* Quest'opera, come c'informa Pietro Verri, ebbe varie edizioni: la prima e la seconda a Lucca (1762 e 1768), la terza a Firenze 1770. Quest'ultima (alla quale si riferisce evidentemente il Calzabigi) contiene un'aggiunta sui canali navigabili.

[30] Durante il suo soggiorno a Vienna il Padre Frisi aveva avuto modo di conoscere e frequentare il duca Don Giovanni di Braganza, il quale poi mantenne un'amichevole corrispondenza con lui. Molte di queste lettere si conservano alla Biblioteca Ambrosiana. A lui il Calzabigi dedicò il *Paride ed Elena*.

[31] Il Granduca Pietro Leopoldo di Toscana, al quale è dedicato il libretto dell'*Alceste*.

servito cotesti S.^{ri} Cavalieri nella loro ultima intrapresa non mi maraviglio che abbiano fatto voto di mai più imbarazzarsi di cose teatrali.

Viene costì nel Carnevale la Sig.^a Bernasconi[32] e se sanno metterla al suo fare avranno sommo piacere quelli che frequentano il Teatro. Io non la raccomando al P.^e Frisi, ma agli amici del P.^e Frisi: *la cosa è così più decente*. Ella è mia amica ed è quella da me scelta per rappresentar sempre le prime parti di donna nelle mie cose Drammatiche. L'accidente[33] ha fatto che ho dovuto vedermene privo con sommo rammarico, e con perdita irreparabile. Spero che non sarà lunga la privazione. Sono immutabilmente il suo buon amico

e vero serv.^{re}

De Calsabigi

A Frisi
N° 145

Vienna 20 Dicembre 1770

Amico, e P.ne Stim.°

A quest'ora Ella avrà ricevuto il riscontro gli diedi della consegna da me fatta a S.A. il Sig. Principe di Kaunitz della sua lettera, e del suo libro, consegnatomi dal Sig. C. Crivelli, e forse S.A. ne avrà dato a Lei qualche cenno. Intanto io altresì ricevei la sua stim.^a de' 12 del passato, alla quale protrassi la risposta perchè mi lusingavo di trovare occasione non solo di spedirgli il mio Paride, ma ancora la ristampa fatta di tutte e 3 le mie Cose Drammatiche. Questa non per anche è finita. L'occasione d'inviargli il solo Paride mi tardò fino a jeri che a un nipote di cotesto Sig. Galliari pittore per costì partito consegnai due libri del Paride da rimettersi a M.ª Bernasconi, cui oggi do avviso che uno di questi esemplari deve a Lei farlo avere. Arriverà il Galliari fra 15 giorni, onde, scorso questo tempo, potrà farlo dimandare alla suddetta Signora. Promesse il Sig. Coltellini darmi l'Ifigenia, ma finora non lo fece benché ne replicassi le premure; se l'avessi ottenuta, colla medesima congiuntura l'avrei mandata.

Favorisce avvisarmi che il mio Orfeo fu rappresentato in una Villa. Mi dice che la Musica per una cosa di campagna era assai buona. Dunque non fu eseguito colla musica di Gluk. Desidererei sapere chi ha fatta questa nuova Musica, per mia curiosità, e se vi ha messi de' passaggi. Mi consolo dell'idea che cotesti Cavalieri ne hanno concepita. Veggo così che il Vero si va facendo largo. Se il Sr C. Belgiojoso di cui mi parla è quello ch'io conobbi già 15 anni sono a Parigi La prego umiliargli il mio ossequio colle proteste della somma stima che per lui conservo fin da quel tempo.

So che costì e per l'Italia si fa correre de' discorsi ridicoli sopra il Paride, ma qui si mettono in ridicolo i Personaggi che spargono queste ridicolezze. In 8 recite Paride (senza Logge perché tutte affittate, e malgrado gran numero di abbonati all'anno che non si contano) ha fatto di pura porta 4000 f. il che è il massimo delle ricette per uno spettacolo che si replichi una, o due volte la settimana. Posso promettergli che anderà tutto il Carnevale colla stessa affluenza di Mondo; così resta *col calcolo* smentita la diceria, che a vero dire cade più sulla Musica che sul Dramma. Alceste poi in 3 prime volte che si è ora data di nuovo ha già fatto 1760 f. e continuerà anch'ella alternativamente col Paride tutto il Carnevale: cosa strana in questo Paese, ove ci vorrebbe

---

[32] Per cantare nel *Mitridate re di Ponto* di Mozart.
[33] L'»accidente« è quello ampiamente illustrato dalle lettere qui di seguito pubblicate.

novità ogni giorno per tirare gli spettatori. Ella vedrà il Paride, e me ne dirà poi il suo parere, e quello de' suoi amici. Questo è un nuovo genere tutto galante, senza Diavoli, che ho voluto provare per tâter le goût du Public.

Fu da me il Signor Lambertenghi che colla sua figura s'annunzia qual Ella me lo descrive. Oggi l'aspetto a pranzo meco. Il Libro de' fiumi suo non mi ha dato ancora. Di quello de' Canali navigabili gli scrissi già ciò che pensavo: sarebbe bene se ne facesse uso; nel di più Ella sa l'altissima, e ben dovuta stima che ho per Lei, e per le opere sue.

Mi conservi la sua grazia, ed amicizia e mi creda con que' sentimenti sinceri, e di stima, e d'amicizia e per sempre quale mi raffermo suo vero amico e buon servitore

De Calsabigi

A Frisi
Nº 148

Vienna 6. Maggio 1771

Rev.º P.e e Amico Stim.º

Veramente non mi supponevo che dietro la premura da me fatta alla Sig.ª Bernasconi dovesse Ella rimaner privo del mio Paride, ma giacché così è, ne consegnerò un altro al Sig. Lambertenghi per inoltrarglielo. Uno degli uomini de' quali mi sia più caro aver l'approvazione alle cose mie è certo Lei, onde sono col rammarico che tanto tardi debba pervenirgli quest'ultimo mio lavoro di Teatro. Dico ultimo in ogni senso perché inutile oramai sarebbe che prendessi pena di farne altri, quando in Italia non ponno i Drammi in quel mio gusto ed in quella mia invenzione adattarsi alla scena a motivo de' Cori, e de' Balli, e perché qui le cose del Teatro sono ridotte a tal forzosa parsimonia che convien per sempre sbandirne la spesa d'un'opera seria. Se costì dicono *poca cosa* il Ruggiero, e Bradamante[34], qui lo spacciano per *cattiva cosa*. Veramente la Poesia di più di 70. anni non può essere se non rimbambita. Stupisco che l'Autore in quell'età e in questo rigido clima che ceteris paribus raffredda tanto l'Estro poetico habbia lasciato la strada dell'Istoria Romana, nella quale si può andare avanti con que' sentimentoni, e quelle sentenzione che si trovano negli autori antichi, e che tradotte in volgare fanno poi un sì bello spicco ne' di lui Attilj, Catoni, Adriani &c. e che si sia impegnato in un soggetto in cui (salvo il pigliar tutto di peso dall'Ariosto) bisogna lavorar di Genie, trattandosi d'incanti, romanzesche avventure, e operazioni di Demonj e di Fate. Forse s'è egli imaginato di andar sul mio nuovo piano, ma questo esige troppa fantasia, e una tal fantasia non ammette vecchiaja. Vedremo. Qualora il Sig. Verri sia a favorirmi non mancherò fargli capire la haute estime que je fais d'un homme illustre comme le Rev.d Père Frisi, et que cette estime reflechit sur tout ce qui me vient de sa part. Je vous supplie Mon Tres Reverend Pere de presenter mes tres humbles respects à Monsieur le Comte Belgiojoso. J'ai admiré en lui lorsque j'eu l'honneur de le connoitre à Paris les belles qualités si rares dans les Italiens, qu'on pouvoit presenter aux François, pour les empecher de nous prendre tous pour des Ostrogots; Et vraiment hors le Comte Belgiojoso dans dix ans de demeure que j'ai fait à Paris je ne sache avoir vû nul autre Gentilhomme de mon Pays, che potesse servire a cosi

---

[34] *Il Ruggiero o vero l'Eroica gratitudine*, libretto di Metastasio con musica di Johann Adolf Hasse, rappresentato a Milano nel 1771.

reprimere le idee che hanno di noi i francesi, e che per Dio sono pur troppo giuste. Finisco con dichiararmi suo vero amico e buon servitore.

De Calsabigi

A Greppi
Cart. 75

Vienna 9 Gennajo 1772

Amico e P.ne Riv.^{mo}

Veramente confesso aver io abusato della lunga compiacenza d'un amico. Diversi accidenti ne son stati cagione, e spezialmente la mia poca salute che mi ha distolto d'occuparmi anche agli affari proprj. Avevo però destinato nella prossima Quaresima rimborsargli la partita che gli devo in mano del Sig.^r Segalla. Credo che il Sig. Greppi stim.^o si contenterà di questa mia disposizione, ma quando no, dietro suo nuovo ordine procurerò compire, restandomi in ogni caso a rendergli senza fine le grazie e della bontà, e della tolleranza per il che sono in obligo di stretta riconoscenza, e disimpegnerò l'obligo ad ogni incontro, e con piacere giacché è piacere servire il Sig. Greppi. Gli rendo frattanto gli augurj di felicità favoritimi, con bramargli ogni sodisfazione e contentezza, da quel sincero amico, e vero servitore che me gli dichiaro per sempre

De Calsabigi

A Greppi
Cart. 76

Vienna 2 Aprile 1772

Amico e P.ne Riv.^{mo}

È stata indiscretezza e ridicolezza imperdonabile la mia di tardare fino ad oggi a compire al mio debito verso di Lei di f. 635 sborsatimi dal Sig. Segalla, ed a lui di suo ordine sodisfatti. L'interesse di tanto tempo è già una somma, e cogli amici è soverchia confidenza tal dilazione, e cogli indifferenti è abuso. Resto colla confusione della sua straordinaria compiacenza, e col peso della gratitudine, peso che verso di Lei non ho modo di sollevare, perché in nulla poss'io essergli utile. Qualunque cosa però che dalla mia persona, mezzi, cognizioni può mai, o potrà da Lei esser stimata di sua convenienza in qualsivoglia incontro è in me a Sua intiera disposizione, né con quell'uso che Ella ne facesse intendo mai disimpegnar l'obbligazione. Questa mi resterà finché io viva. Gli domando in virtù di questi miei veri sentimenti, non di complimento, la continuazione della sua cara amicizia, e l'esercizio con me della sua Padronanza, mentre di core, e con umile ossequio e stima, e impegno, mi dichiaro qual sarò sempre suo um.^o dev.^o obbl.^{mo} Servo e amico

De Calsabigi

Ivi, lettera di Segalla:
... antecipo a raguagliarvi, che sulle nuove istanze fatte al Sig. Calzabigi, mi ha finalmente pagato li U. 150 che vi doveva...

A Greppi
Cart. 77

Vienna 4 Maggio 1772

A.º e P.ne Stim.º

Oltre il rinnovarle i miei vivi ringraziamenti, e la mia illimitata gratitudine per la sua somma bontà al ritardo da me fatto al consaputo rimborso verso di Lei, devo ora nuovi obblighi aggiungere a' suoi gentili sentimenti per me, e per la mia amicizia. Questi mi saranno in perpetuo presenti alla memoria, in ragione di che potrà Ella disporre di me come persona affatto sua, e che altro non desidera che dargli prove evidenti della sua maniera di pensare a suo riguardo.

Scrissi al Sig. D. Pio Fogliazzi, e volevo far presente a loro per la prima **uscita in** Italia della Sig.ª Caterina Schindlerin virtuosa già nota costì a ragione di que' tanti Signori Milanesi che la vedero recitare quando vennero per la partenza di S.A.R. l'arciduca. Mi rispose che per questo Carnevale erano impegnati, e già ella ancora lo era a Praga, e che terminavano quest'anno. Se dunque per l'anno venturo l'appalto Teatrale cade in suoi amici La prego ricordarsi della suddetta che potranno trattare per mezzo mio, restando in mano al suddetto Sig. D. Pio i dettagli da me datigli della di lei abilità e di quella della sua nipote che proposi per 2ᵈᵃ Donna, quale pure in tal qualità va ora a Praga. Mi farà grazia il g.ᵐᵒ Sig. D. Antonio di passarne anche uffici a S. Cav. di Torino in tempo debito che io di tutto a Lei sarò obligato, e quegl'Impresarj che faranno l'acquisto ne glie ne avranno altrettanto obligo sicuramente.

Mi confermo sempre con ossequio e stima, e riconoscenza vero amico e vero serv.ᵉ

De Calsabigi

A Frisi
Nº 147

Vienna 24. Agosto 1772

A.ᶜᵒ e P.ⁿᵉ Stim.º

Con piacere, e un qualche risentimento gustoso d'amor proprio ho letto il suo sentimento sul Paride. L'effetto della rappresentazione fu quasi disgraziato, mentre volevano proibirlo, e s'attribuì a grazia dell'Impressario il lasciarlo correre. Dissero esser troppo molle e inspirar volontà per la seduzione. E pure fu il brutto Millico che rappresentò Paride. Avevo abbandonato la Lira; ma impegno per bella Dama me l'ha fatta ripigliare doppo 4 anni. Ho auto somma pena ad accordarla, e tanto più che in 25 giorni ho dovuto trovarmi pronto. Ho dunque, su 3 personaggi di Carattere, e 2 serj che necessariamente fui costretto ad impiegare, composto un Dramma intitolato Amiti, e Ontario, o i Selvaggi, di mia pura idea ma semplicissima. Ho supposto un Quacchero Colono in una campagna della Pensilvania nell'America Settentrionale. A questo ho dato una cognata e una nipote di religione Anglicana, e la cognata vedova. Ho fatto suoi schiavi per ragion di guerra Amiti, e Ontario selvaggi, amanti, ma che per comodo, e per non insospettire si son dichiarati fratelli. Il Quacchero vorrebbe sposare Amiti perché in lei vede disposizioni all'entusiasmo. La sua cognata vuole Ontario che è un bel giovane; e la sua figlia ci pretende ancor lei. In questa vessazione fuggono i due Americani; ma Amiti è presa, Ontario che lo vede torna a correr la stessa fortuna della sua cara. Decide il Quacchero co' suoi principj, e gli assolve, e adotta. M'è riuscito (credo) toccar bene, e fortemente i Caratteri, e il Dramma (mi pare) è venuto interessante. Si deve rappresentare a Sleppe Terra della Sig.ª principessa d'Aversperg. Quando avrò occasione lo trasmetterò.

Mi consolo poi della sua buona salute, e averei desiderato il suo passaggio a Vienna per rivederla ed esser seco a qualche chiacchiera filosofica. Qui non v'è filosofia. Tutto è grossolano. La superficie è in onore. Lei pensi a star bene, a lavorar poco, e a riposarsi; e faccia conto d'avere a Vienna un vero amico, e un buon servitore.

De Calsabigi

LETTERE DI ANTONIA BERNASCONI O A LEI RELATIVE
AD ANTONIO GREPPI

Cart. 65

Vienna 17 maggio 1770

[...] Dispiacemi però di non poterle dare, in quest'ordinario, il pronto desiderato riscontro per rapporto al disimpegno della Sig.ª Bernasconi, la quale presentemente si ritrova in Venezia, e ciò per ritrovarsi S.A. Padrone a Laxemburgo, ma siccome questa stessa sera sarà qui di ritorno, così, in questi giorni procurerò di ritrovare il momento opportuno per umiliarle le di Lei premure, onde mi riservo di darlene, col prossimo ordinario, una distinta e genuina relazione di quanto mi sarà riuscito d'ottenere dalla benignità dell'A.I., dalla quale ne spero tutto il buon esito. [...]

Gio. Pietro de Soresina

Cart. 65

Vienna 21 maggio 1770

[...] Dalla qui annessa ostensibile V.S. Ill.ma rileverà la risposta, che con somma benignità mi ha data S.A. Padrone per rapporto al disimpegno della Sig.ra Bernasconi, assicurandola però d'avere l'A.S. attentamente il tutto letto, e dopo di avere finita di leggere quella della Sig.ra Gabrielli, che qui inclusa le rimando, giusto il di Lei comando, dissemi questa è sempre stata una pazza, et una bestia, e tale morirà. [...]

Gio. Pietro de Soresina

Lettera allegata:
In esecuzione dei sempre rispettabilissimi comandi di V.S. Ill.ma, avanzatimi con la stimatissima Sua dei 8 del corr.te, non ho mancato di prontamente portarmi presso S.A. il Sig. Principe di Kaunitz, nostro benignissimo Padrone, e Superiore, e dopo di avere allo stesso umiliate le premure di V.S. Ill.ma per potter avere la Sig.ra Bernasconi al servizio di codesto Teatro di Milano per il venturo Carnovale dell'Anno 1771, per mancanza della Sig.ra Gabrielli, l'A.S. mi chiese la lettera di V.S. Ill.ma, e dopo, che con somma attenzione l'ebbe letta, mi ha comandato di scriverle quanto segue. *Rispondete in mio nome al caro Greppi, che lo saluto caramente, e che mi dispiace di non potterlo secondare in questa sua premura, e ciò per il motivo, che trattandosi d'affari di particolari, con particolari per li due Teatri, io non pottevo, né dovevo*

mischiarmi per favorire l'uno in pregiudizio dell'altro. Vi do però la libertà di trattare voi quest'affare, con Afrizio, ch'è quanto posso dirvi.

Io non avrei avuto la minima difficoltà di parlare al detto Sig. Afrizio [...] ma ho stimato di astenermene sino a tanto, che da V.S. Ill.ma non ne ricevi il previo consenso, e comando. [...]

Gio. Pietro de Soresina

Cart. 65
Afflizio (Impresario)
Vienna 21 maggio 1770: [Lascia intravvedere la possibilità di concedere la Bernasconi al Teatro di Milano, nonostante la risposta di Kaunitz.]

Cart. 65

Vienna 27 Maggio 1770

[...] Sono due giorni, che qui si è sparsa una voce, che S.M. della Sovrana abbia fatto dire, per mezzo di S.E. il Sig.r Co. Sporck, Cavaliere sopra la Musica, a questo Sig.r Afrisio di dover fare in maniera di ritirare il di lui contratto con la Bernasconi, e di fargli intendere, che assolutamente non abbia la medesima più ardire di non solo portarsi in questa Residenza, ma eziandio tampoco in verun altro Stato della Germania alla M.S. appartenente, e ciò per motivo di quanto alla detta Virtuosa gli è seguito in Venezia cioè di essersi sgravata di quel frutto, che qui aveva acquistato. Io veramente a tali voci non volsi dare fede, che perciò informatomi da persona, che può essere al fatto della verità, ne ho ricevuta da ogn'uno la conferma; onde se così è, come ormai più non dubito, la detta Signora rimane al presente in libertà di accettare codesto Regio Ducal Teatro senza ulteriori impegni, et ho stimato mio dovere di avanzarne a V.S. Ill.ma la presente confidenziale notizia affinché possi prenderne le sue rissoluzioni in tempo opportuno. [...]

Gio. Pietro de Soresina

Cart. 65
Ill.mo Sig.re Sig.r e P.ne Col.mo

Le promisi colla precedente mia una final risposta sulla Sig.ra Bernasconi, e adempio alla promessa. Ho dunque il piacere di dirle che la detta Signora ha già ricevuto da me il riscontro d'esser messa in piena libertà d'accettare l'offerte che da V.S. Ill.ma le vengono fatte per il Carnovale venturo, restando affatto disciolta dal suo impegno con questo teatro. Gradisca la mia premura a servirla, e mi continui il vantaggio d'essere come con tutta la stima mi dichiaro

Di V.S. Ill.ma
Dev. D'Afflizio

Vienna 28. Maggio 1770

Cart. 65

[...] Per rapporto poi alla Sig.ra Bernasconi, non solo mi riporto a quanto ho avuto la sorte di sinceramente scriverle con le antecedenti mie, m'altresì le confermo quanto le partecipai con la seconda, mentre in oggi non solo è cosa certissima, m'è altresì publica in tutta la Città. Le avanzerò bensì la notizia, che questi regi Teatri non corrono più a conto d'Afrisio, ma bensì per conto del Sig.r Conte Kohary, il quale, mediante lo sborso di 160 m. Fiorini fatto al detto Afrisio, n'è rimasto il proprietario [...]

Vienna 4. Giugno 1770

                                                      Gio. Pietro de Soresina

Cart. 68

Molto stimato Sig.re Creppi

Non poco m'affligge, a sentire che il Suo incomodo sempre va continuando, e sono priva del piacere di vederla. Jeri sera credevo di poterla riverire[35], mà fu vana la mia speranza; stò atendendo con premura grande il di Lei statto, questa sera sono occupata con il Maestro Lampugnani, non essendo lui venuto questa mattina, altrimenti sarei venuta in persona a pregarla del favore di mandare 12 cigliati al Marchante Canna che io gli le devo per quella vesta richa che mandai al Conte Seriman, il marchante vuole cigliate, e io non ne ho, prego dunque V.S. di farmi il piacere di mandarglile che io saro debbatrice. Come anche li debbo il danaro per le calze di setta, asieme si farà il conto, prego però scusarmi l'ardire, ma essendomi notta la Sua grande bontà, sò che non prenderà in mala parte il disturbo che gli fò; fratanto gli auguro di vero cuore un presto ricuparamento di Sua salute [...]

                              Umiliss.ma Serva

                                                            Bernasconi

Di casa [Milano] li 26 novembre 1770

Cart. 68

Amabilissimo Sig.re Creppi

Non vengo in persona a portarci la lettera del Conte Seriman avendo io prova, e devo studiare; la prego il grazia di fargli rispondere e trovare una buona scusa per riavere il mio danaro, e per non farmelo enemico. Avanti mercoledì io spero già di avere il piacere di parlargli; la prego anche di fare insegnare al mio servo dove si può avere di quella istessa legnia che Lei mi favorì, come anche di dirci il prezzo. Fra tanto sono sua

                              Umilissima serva

                                                            Bernasconi

[Milano] 17 dicembre 1770

---

[35] Si era tenuta in casa Firmian un'accademia, alla quale aveva partecipato anche Mozart.

[Allegato un foglio col solo nome Antonia de Löwenturn, scritto d'altra mano.]
Antonio Greppi teneva l'amministrazione della Bernasconi tramite i suoi agenti Ca-
valli di Modena e Piccinini, come si rileva da un appunto sul verso di una lettera di
Cavalli da Modena 26 dic. 1770: »Il conto spese Bernasconi dato al S. Piccinini«.

Cart. 69
[Milano] 6 febbraio 1771

Antonia Bernasconi: [rinnova la preghiera di mandarle le calze di seta:] »per questa
sera son senza calze«.
[...] In questo punto mandò da me il Conte de Firmian con dirmi che venerdì sera
senza fallo io dovessi venire da lui [...]

Cart. 70

Bologna il 22 Marzo 1771

Stimatissimo Sig.re Creppi

   Sono arrivata felicemente a Bologna, ma la faticha di viaggiare alla corriera mi
causò un grantissimo dolore di rene, e dovete stare per forza alletto, fortuna che stò
in casa d'un buon amico, che è Cicogniani[36] il quale mi venne ad incontrare tre miglie
lontano da Bologna e a forza vuolse che io allogi in casa sua avendo lui sorelle, ed
altre donne che mi servono come fossi una regina. Il Sig.re Andriani fù già due volte da
me, come anche il cavaliere Farinello, il quale mi vuol un bene infinito. Jeri pranzai da
lui; oggi scrivo a Vienna e farò le mie gran lagnanze: Dio farà conoscere l'innocenza
mia ed il gran torto che mi vien fatto, spero che in poco tempo Lei vedrà il frutto
ch'averà fatto il mio scrivere per Vienna, Sporck mi vuole opressa ma li giuro che li
costerà caro, il torto che lui mi fece. Arivata che sarò a Venezia non mancherò di darci subito aviso, spero che da qui non sarò schaggiata; un caso simile
quale il mio, è incredibile, e mai sucesso, che una donna che non fà male alcuno, e che
stima tanto il suo onore, sia stata fatto tali schorni e torto così grande. Pazienza.
Amabilissimo Sig.re Creppi li rendo di nuovo mille grazie per tutte le finezze e grazie
fattomi, che non mi scorderò finché vivo, e in tutte le occasioni li farò vedere la mia gratitudine verso di Lei. La prego di continuarmi la di Lei buona amicizia. Essendo io
sicura di questo, mi chiamerò felice, avendo in Lei un amico incomparabile. La prego
ancora a diffendere il mio onore, in caso si mormorasse a Milano per la mia partenza
fretolosa, mi racomandi a S.E. il Conte de Firmian, assicurandola che io li averò
un'eterna gratitudine, e sempre mi darò il [piacere] di dirmi sua
                                    umilissima serva
                                                            Bernasconi
La prego di salutarmi il Sig.re Mambrini, e Castiglioni e tutti quelli che mi ànno
volsuto bene.

---

[36] Probabilmente il cantante Giuseppe Cicognani, che in quegli anni cantava spesso al Teatro
   Ducale di Milano.

Cart. 70

Bologna il 26 Marzo 1771

[. . .] Alli 8 d'Aprile parto da qui per Venezia [. . .]

Bernasconi

Cart. 70

Venezia li 27 Aprile 1771

Stimatissimo Signore

Le chiedo scusa, se prima d'ora non ho risposto alle sue stimat.^{me} per essere stata impegnata ad una Cantata in Cesena fatta in onore del Sig. Cardinale Pallavicini, dove sono stata vantaggiosamente rimunerata, e siccome collà m'ho dovuta trattenere molto tempo, è stato causa che sono giunta costà troppo tardi, ed ora mi trovo oppressa dalla fatica per angustia di tempo. [. . .]

[Seguita dando a Greppi incarichi vari, fra i quali quello di provvedere alla vendita della sua carrozza.]

Altre lettere di Antonia Bernasconi: Venezia   4 maggio 1771
          ”   25 maggio ”:
          ”   1° giugno   ”
          ”   8 giugno   ”

Cart. 72

Stimatissimo Signor

Perdoni che tanto tardi rispondo alla stimatiss. sua, la mi pervenne tardissimo essendo stata absente con la Impassatrice Durazzo. Ricevei anche l'interesse del mio capitale [. . .] Essendo conosciute a Lei queste cose, mi viene scritto da Vienna che S.E. il Conte di Firmian mi à fatto un grande elogio apresso la Corte, e per segnio tale mi fu dato piena permissione di andare a Milano quando io vorò, fu conosciuta tutta la falsità, a l'Imperatore dispiacque molto l'afronto che mi fu fatto inocentemente. Solo ho piacere che Stampa è stato ricompensato secondo il suo merito, ed io feci molto bene di fare sapere il tutto a S.M. Imperatore, in poco tempo sarà ricompensato anche il Conte Sporck: ò basta, mai e poi mai mi scorderò li favori ricevuti da Lei, ed averò un'eterna gratitudine [. . .]

Umilissima Serva

Bernasconi

Venezia adì 2 agosto 1771

Altra lettera: Venezia 30 agosto 1771

Cart. 76

Venezia 7 Marzo 1772: Antonia Bernasconi: [Chiede l'aiuto di Greppi per riavere la somma prestata al conte Seriman.]

Altra lettera sullo stesso argomento: Venezia 20 marzo 1772

Cart. 78

[...] Del mio incontro in questo Reale Teatro stimo inutile di parlarliene, essendo sicura, che ne avrà ricevuto li riscontri da Suoi amici [...]
[Il resto della lettera tratta del credito Seriman.]

Napoli a 14 Luglio 1772

                                                                    Bernasconi

Cart. 78

[...] Se non li scrivo di proprio pugno, non è mancanza di volontà, ma per ritrovarmi alquanto incommodata dalle forti fatighe sia per l'Opera dell'Achille in Sciro[37] che la sera de 13 andiede in scena con felice incontro, come anche per avere a studiare la mia parte di prima donna nella Cantata di Spagna, musica di Jommelli [...]
Napoli a 18 Agosto 1772

                                                                    Bernasconi

Cart. 79

[...] Seguito ad essere molto occupata ne' Concerti che ogni giorno si fanno per la Cantata di Spagna la quale anderà in scena il dì 14 del corr.te
Da varie parti mi scrivono ch'è corsa voce che io sia fermata in questo Teatro per 3 anni; ciò non è vero, bensì dovevo restarvi per il venturo anno, ma un forte maneggio della Deamicis non me lo ha permesso, e ne sarà persuaso quando gli trasmetterò la copia della sua epoca che per verità fa poco onore ad una prima Donna sua pari, pertanto per il Carnevale 74 mi trovo fin'ora libera, ed avrei piacere aver il Teatro di Turino, ma siccome non ho colà amici, perciò glielo partecipo, che se mai li riuscisse potermi favorire, glie ne sarei eternamente obligata [...]
Napoli 8 Settembre 1772

                                                                    Bernasconi

---

[37] Opera di Antonio Amicone.

CHERUBINI UND DER MUSIKALISCHE KLASSIZISMUS

von *Stefan Kunze* (Bern)

METHODISCHE VORBEMERKUNG

Der Begriff des Klassizismus ist mehrdeutig. In seiner Vielschichtigkeit spiegelt sich nicht nur gedankenlose Verwendung, sondern eine Aporie der empirischen Kunstwissenschaft: daß nämlich ihre Fach- und Begriffssprache nicht abzulösen ist vom allgemeinen Sprachgebrauch und daß terminologische Exaktheit utopisch anmutet, wenn sie erkauft ist durch die Unverbindlichkeit eines ausschließlich fachwissenschaftlichen Vokabulars. Die sprachliche Bezeichnung, das Begreifen von Sachverhalten des Geschichtlichen in weitestem Sinn ist zugleich Interpretation, d. h. ein Verstehen, das den eigenen Standort, die jeweils gegenwärtige Situation einbezieht. Sie artikuliert sich u. a. in sprachlicher Form. Interpretation ist demnach nicht möglich ohne ein bereits in der Sprache vorgegebenes Verstehen, welches zwar ausgeführt und erweitert werden kann, aber nicht ersetzbar ist durch ein System von Neologismen, die genau besehen doch wieder, wenn auch uneingestanden, auf begrifflich präformierte Inhalte zurückgehen. Etwa der Versuch, den mit naturwissenschaftlicher Exaktheit kaum fixierbaren Begriff der Klassik zu ersetzen durch einen unmißverständlichen neuen, der den gemeinten Sachverhalt restlos und nur ihn erfaßt, könnte — auch abgesehen davon, daß in historisch-empirischer Wissenschaft Sache und Bezeichnung zu eigentümlicher Einheit verschmelzen — gar nicht anders, als Inhalte einfließen zu lassen, die bereits in der Sprache als eingebürgerter Sprachgebrauch enthalten sind. Er bietet die Gewähr sowohl für die historische Kontinuität des Verstehens, somit für die Verbindlichkeit hier und jetzt, als auch, gerade durch Flexibilität der Bedeutungen, für einen Beziehungsreichtum, der Verstehenszusammenhänge sichtbar macht, sich definitorischer Festlegung entzieht und trotzdem zur Sache selbst gehört. Was Klassik sei, ist weniger definitorisch als vielmehr interpretatorisch zu beantworten. Definition und Interpretation schließen einander weitgehend aus. Mit Definition hat die interpretatorische Anstrengung nur dies gemein, daß sie Abgrenzungen gegen nichtssagende Verallgemeinerungen vornimmt, Bedeutungen aufklärt und konkretisiert. Sprachliche Begrifflichkeit ist nicht bloß das Instrument, um Sachverhalte, die eindeutig geworden sind, in einer Fachsprache zur Verständigung der Sachkenner untereinander festzulegen, sondern bestimmt auch die Grenzen und die Möglichkeiten der Interpretation. Dies schließt nicht aus, daß Inhalte wechseln, Bedeutungen sich verschieben oder gänzlich aufgegeben werden können. Der vorfindliche Sprachgebrauch ist Instrument zur Erkenntnis und zugleich ihr Grund, von dem sie ausgehen muß. Sobald sich Erkenntnis sprachlich artikuliert, ist nicht nur sie, sondern auch die Sprache in den »hermeneutischen Zirkel« einbezogen[1]. Die Forderung, man müsse die Interpretation nur auf die einer Epoche eigenen Begriffe stützen, ist methodisch ebenso anfechtbar wie die naive Meinung, man könne unabhängig vom gegebenen Begriffs- und Vorstellungsrepertoire zu einer »objektiven« Bestimmung von Begriffsinhalten gelangen. Es würde zusätzliche Verunklärung bedeuten, wollte man den Begriff des Klassizismus deshalb fallenlassen, weil sein Spezifisches nur schwer faßbar ist, und ihn durch einen neuen ersetzen, der doch stillschweigend vorgedachte Inhalte paraphrasiert[2]. Es gilt vielmehr, sich zunächst über die Gehalte klar zu werden, die sich mit dem Begriff des Klassizismus heute verbinden, weiterhin jedoch den Begriff zu legitimieren durch den Versuch, ihn am Gegenstand zu präzisieren.

Zwar ist die inhaltliche Bestimmung des Terminus, der erst dadurch zur Begrifflichkeit aufsteigt, unerläßlich, da sie zum Akt des Begreifens selbst gehört. Doch Begriffsgeschichte allein, die dabei stehenbleiben wollte, nur den (auch wissenschaftlichen) Sprachgebrauch zu ermitteln, die, um ein übriges zu tun, ihn bloß eingrenzen würde, wäre unzureichend. Diesem ersten Schritt müßte ein zweiter folgen: die Beschreibung des spezifischen Inhalts, den der Begriff bezogen auf seinen Gegenstand besitzt. Die Frage, was Klassik oder Klassizismus sei, d. h. nicht nur, was in Bezeichnungen wie Klassik und Klassizismus über eine Gegebenheit ausgesagt ist, dürfte kaum sinnvoll zu beantworten sein, wenn sie nicht Untersuchungen zur musikalischen Struktur einschließt. Das Reflektieren über den Begriff der »Klassik« geht ins Leere, solange nicht einigermaßen feststeht, was sich eigentlich in der Musik ereignet, die als die klassische verstanden wurde. Allerdings kann es sich aufgrund dieser über eine rein begriffliche Untersuchung hinausgehenden Fragestellung ergeben, daß Begriffe unbrauchbar werden, daß zumindest eine neue Inhaltsbestimmung zu erfolgen hat, die von der Sache her Gültigkeit beansprucht. Es scheint aber vertretbar, an einem Terminus festzuhalten, solange zwischen dem neuen Verständnis eines Begriffs und dem Terminus noch ein gemeinsamer Vorstellungsgrund vorhanden ist. Nicht Klärung der Begriffe, sondern der durch Begriffe erfaßten und erfaßbaren Sachverhalte sollte das Ziel terminologischer Bemühung sein.

---

[1] Vgl. zur Sprachlichkeit als Medium des Verstehens H.-G. GADAMER, *Wahrheit und Methode, Grundzüge einer philosophischen Hermeneutik*, Tübingen 1965 (2. Auflage), vor allem III. Teil, S. 361 ff.

[2] Im Grundsätzlichen übereinstimmend auch L. FINSCHER, *Zum Begriff der Klassik in der Musik*, Deutsches Jahrbuch der Musikwissenschaft für 1966, hrsg. v. R. Eller, Jg. 11 (1967), vor allem S. 24 f.

Zum Begriff des Klassizismus

»Klassizismus« gehört im Unterschied zur »Klassik« zu den in engerem Sinn kunstgeschichtlichen Termini. Er setzt Geschichtsbewußtsein voraus, doch auch Anerkennung eines Normativen, das dem Begriff der Klassik zugeordnet ist. Im Unterschied jedoch zum Klassikbegriff scheint von Klassizismus nicht vor dem 19. Jahrhundert die Rede zu sein[3]. Gegenüber »Klassik« in des Wortes ursprünglicher, normativer Bedeutung ist »Klassizismus« nicht nur eine historisch-relativierende, abgeleitete Bezeichnung. Sie impliziert vielmehr — dies nun analog zur »Klassik« — auch ein Werturteil. Dem Klassizismus haftet als Begriffsinhalt stets das Odium des Pejorativen an. Klassizismus setzt Erfahrung von Klassik voraus, von der Klassizismus sich als Abglanz, Nachklang abhebt. Stets schwingt in der Bezeichnung der Verdacht der leeren Nachahmung, des Künstlichen, Formalistischen, eines restaurativen Epigonentums mit und einer sich selbst beschränkenden Rückwendung zu einem als normativ Aufgefaßten[4]. Es ist freilich abzusehen, daß auch der Klassizismus den negativen Beiklang verliert, ähnlich wie andere Bezeichnungen (Gotik, Barock), als sie zu Stilbegriffen wurden, ihren pejorativen Sinn ablegten, der mit ihnen ursprünglich verbunden war. Denn auch diese Bezeichnungen bezogen sich zunächst auf die Norm der Klassik[5]. Die Verselbständigung und Reduzierung solcher Termini zu Stilbegriffen rührt daher, daß das historische Bewußtsein den normativen Begriff der Klassik zersetzte, der für Winckelmann und in der 2. Hälfte des 18. Jahrhunderts noch der maßgebende war. Winckelmann sah in der klassischen Antike noch das Vorbild jeder späteren Kunst. Bereits seit Herder finden die Historisierung des Klassikbegriffs sowie ein Ausgleich zwischen historischem und normativem Sinn statt. Aber erst durch

---

[3] Die Unterscheidung von Klassik und Klassizismus gilt in erster Linie für die deutsche Sprache. Im Italienischen ist »classicismo« gleichbedeutend mit »Klassik«. Der Unterschied zwischen »classicismo« und »classicità« ist nicht genau zu bestimmen. Vgl. N. Zingarelli, *Vocabolario della lingua italiana, Decima edizione,* Bologna 1970. Der Sprachgebrauch, der die Antike nicht abgrenzt von den Erscheinungen, die mittelbar oder unmittelbar an die Antike anknüpfen, mag mit der ununterbrochenen Tradition der Antikenrezeption auf italienischem Boden zusammenhängen. Aus der Sicht dieser Tradition erscheint Palladios Architektur nicht als Klassizismus im engeren, wissenschaftlichen Sinn. Das Grimmsche Wörterbuch verzeichnet zwar das Wort »Klassik« und »klassisch«, nicht jedoch »Klassizismus«. Es wäre aufschlußreich festzustellen, wann »Klassizismus« als eine von der Klassik abhebende Bezeichnung in Gebrauch kam.

[4] Bezeichnend für die negative Auffassung ist der Artikel *Klassizismus* von H. Cysarz im Reallexikon der Deutschen Literaturgeschichte, begründet von P. Merker und W. Stammler, 2. Aufl. hrsg. von W. Kohlschmidt und W. Mohr, Berlin 1958, Bd. I. Dogmatische Weiterführung der Formen, Isolierung des Formalen, epigonale *»Schwundstufe der Klassik«* u. a. kennzeichneten den Klassizismus.

[5] Vgl. dazu B. Snell, *Bemerkungen zu Theorien des Stils,* in: Wesen und Wirklichkeit des Menschen, Festschrift für Helmuth Plessner, hrsg. von Klaus Ziegler, Göttingen 1957, S. 333—339.

Hegel wird »Klassik« zum deskriptiven Stilbegriff, dessen normativer Gehalt nur noch uneingestanden wirksam ist[6]. »Klassik« wird zur Kennzeichnung von Stilen und Epochen. Dies führte zu einer Erweiterung des Begriffs und ermöglichte seine Anwendung auf verschiedene Epochen im Sinne einer Vollendung, eines Gelungenen, einer Leistung, in der es zwischen Absicht und Ergebnis keinen ungelösten Rest gibt. Allerdings ist diese Seite des Anwendungsbereichs keine bloße Folgeerscheinung des historischen Bewußtseins, wie man annehmen könnte, sondern läßt sich bereits in der römischen Antike nachweisen: Die Vollendung einer Gattung der Literatur galt als klassisch. Eine solche Anschauung setzt Anerkennung von musterhaften Phasen der Kunst bzw. der Literatur voraus und dokumentiert sich in einer Auswahl »klassischer« Schulautoren. Doch besteht ein wesentlicher Unterschied zwischen diesem zwar nicht zeitlich begrenzten Verständnis »klassischer« Autoren (Homer wurde für das Epos als ebenso klassisch angesehen wie Sophokles für die Tragödie) und dem gänzlich historisch relativierten Gebrauch, der, wie Finscher (a. a. O.) mit Recht bemerkte, einer Entleerung des Begriffs gleichkommt. Denn jene antike Vorstellung des klassischen Schriftstellers ist gebunden an eine geltende Tradition, deren »vollendete« Stufen als maßgeblich erachtet wurden. Außerhalb dieser Tradition (Kontinuität der Literatursprache) wäre ein »classicus scriptor« nicht denkbar gewesen[7]. Später, vermittelt durch historisches Bewußtsein, entfiel der Bezug auf eine das klassische Muster und eine an dieser Norm orientierte künstlerische Betätigung verbindende Tradition. Winckelmanns Klassikbegriff ist wie derjenige Hegels, auch wenn er auf das griechische Altertum fixiert blieb, unabhängig von dem Bestehen einer echten Tradition (einer Gattungstradition etwa). Der neue Begriff rechnet vielmehr damit, daß die Kontinuität im engeren Sinn nicht mehr existiert. Klassik wäre demzufolge — sobald auch die Verknüpfung des Begriffs mit der Antike aufgegeben ist — in verschiedenen Epochen und in verschiedenen Stilen möglich. Die Übertragbarkeit des Klassikbegriffs, man mag ihre Berechtigung bejahen oder bestreiten, rührt nicht etwa aus dem ursprünglichen, antiken Sprachgebrauch, der freilich bis heute weiterwirkt, sondern daher, daß dieser auf den historischen Begriff des Stils und auf Epochen projiziert wurde. »Klassik« ist seitdem untrennbar vom wissenschaftlichen Stilbegriff, der in erster Linie formal bestimmt ist, und somit auch mit dessen Problematik verknüpft. Erst jetzt konnte die Frage entstehen, wie der klassische »Stil« bzw. klassische Stile zu kennzeichnen seien. Nicht von ungefähr ist es dagegen nicht gelungen, den Begriff der Klassik an dem Kanon der antiken Schulschriftsteller als einheitlichen Stil zu erweisen[8].

---

[6] Ich folge hier in erster Linie den Ausführungen von GADAMER, *Wahrheit und Methode*, besonders S. 269—275.

[7] Vgl. dazu auch Johannes STROUX, *Die Anschauungen vom Klassischen im Altertum*, in: Das Problem des Klassischen und die Antike, hrsg. von W. Jaeger, Leipzig und Berlin, 1931.

[8] *Das Problem des Klassischen und die Antike*, hrsg. von W. Jaeger (siehe Anm. 7).

»Klassik« ist später ein Stilbegriff geworden, der sich aber von anderen Stilbegriffen (Renaissance, Barock u. a.) darin unterscheidet, daß er durch den normativen Anspruch der Geschichtlichkeit gleichsam entzogen ist[9]. Oft ausdrücklich, stets unausgesprochen trägt »Klassik« die Signatur eines für alle Zeiten, wenn nicht Vorbildlichen, so doch Geltenden. Der Zwiespalt eines ursprünglich unhistorischen, dann von Geschichtsbewußtsein getragenen Begriffs spiegelt sich in seinen Bestimmungen, jener Hegelschen, daß Klassik »*das sich selbst Bedeutende und damit auch sich selber Deutende*« sei, also ex definitione ein auch als Vergangenes doch stets Gegenwärtiges, die Erscheinung, die durch sich selbst einleuchtet und unabhängig von ihren besonderen Entstehungsbedingungen in die Geschichte wirkt, sowie jenen zahlreichen stilgeschichtlichen, also historischen Kriterien, die sich nicht stets mit den allgemeinen Inhalten decken. Die stilistischen Kriterien einer »klassischen Vokalpolyphonie« — die auszeichnende Benennung, mit der man das Werk Palestrinas belegte — stehen ohne Beziehung zum Postulat, daß in »Klassik« die Einheit von Allgemeinem und Besonderem stattfände. Die Kategorien der Bestimmung sind verschiedene. Aus dem erwähnten Zwiespalt erklärt sich, daß Heinrich Wölfflin, ausgehend vom Begriff des Klassischen, das im Grunde genommen ungeschichtliche Konzept der kunstgeschichtlichen Grundbegriffe entwickeln konnte (Entwicklung formaler Gegebenheiten)[10]. Es ist immerhin bemerkenswert, daß im Konzept der Stilgeschichte, in dem naturgeschichtliches und historisches Denken vereinbar schien, der Begriff der Klassik eine Schlüsselstellung einnahm.

Man könnte schematisch und vorläufig folgende Stadien der Begriffsgeschichte festhalten, zwischen denen Wechselwirkung besteht:

1. Das »Klassische« wird verstanden als anerkannter, in erster Linie literarischer Kanon antiker Schulschriftsteller von Homer bis zu den Rhetoren. Seitdem ist »Vollendung« in Werk und in der Gattung Kennzeichen des Klassischen, ebenso die Bindung an die griechische Antike. Später wird die römische Antike einbezogen.

2. »Klassik« wird Inbegriff eines maßgebenden Stils, der nicht nur zeitlich auf eine Epoche (»klassische Antike«), sondern auch durch stilistische Kriterien fixiert ist (Winckelmann).

---

[9] Th. W. ADORNOS Satz (*Ästhetische Theorie*, Gesammelte Schriften 7, Suhrkamp 1970, S. 242), »Klassizität« hieße »*soviel wie immanentes Gelingen*« und habe »*nichts mit Stil und Gesinnung zu tun*«, wäre dahingehend zu ergänzen, daß Klassik zwar eigentlich kein Stil ist, daß aber um so nachdrücklicher Klassik durch den Stilbegriff auf eine Epoche festlegbar wurde.

[10] Helmut KUHN allerdings nahm in einem speziellen Sinn »Klassik« als »*echt historischen Begriff*« in Anspruch, da er von der Situation des Auffassenden nicht trennbar sei (»*Klassisch*« *als historischer Begriff*, in: Das Problem des Klassischen und die Antike, S. 109). Zwar ist dies unbestreitbar. Doch bleibt die Frage, ob nicht das neue Geschichtsbewußtsein des 19. Jahrhunderts, das den Klassikbegriff aufgriff, nicht doch eine neuartige Situation entstehen ließ, die seitdem auch den Inhalt des Begriffs umdeutete.

3. Durch die Festlegung stilistischer und inhaltlicher Kriterien ließ sich das
Prädikat des »Klassischen« auch auf andere Epochen übertragen. »Klassik«
wurde in einen am naturwissenschaftlichen Denken orientierten entwicklungs-
geschichtlichen Begriff umgedeutet. Historische Relativierung ließ sich scheinbar
bruchlos mit dem normativen Inhalt des Begriffs vereinbaren. Die Möglichkeit
dazu ergab sich aus der Vorstellung von einer Sukzession der Stile, von denen
einige Stilstufen sich aufgrund gewisser Kriterien als klassische hervorheben ließen. Diese Kriterien jedoch hatten letztlich ihre Verbindung zur antiken Kunst
nicht verloren. Die klassische Kunst des 5. Jahrhunderts v. Chr. blieb stets das
Paradigma des klassischen Stils.

Der skizzierte begriffsgeschichtliche Vorgang ist bereits selbst Geschichte, somit
Gegenstand verstehender Interpretation, und weist zurück auf die Geschichts-
konzeption und auf den Kunstbegriff des 19. Jahrhunderts. Dies entbindet jedoch nicht von der Frage, von welcher Art jene Erscheinungen sind, die mehr
oder weniger reflektiert als klassische bezeichnet zu werden pflegen[11]. Nicht
darauf, was der Klassikbegriff meint, zielt die Fragestellung ab, sondern darauf, was in musikalischer Klassik vor sich geht. Voraussetzung ist allerdings,
die kaum haltbare und eher verunklärende Fusion des Klassikbegriffs mit dem
Stil- und Epochenbegriff einer kritischen Revision zu unterziehen.

Im Unterschied zu dem verabsolutierten Begriff der »Klassik« besagt »Klassizismus« engere Anknüpfung an die Antike. Dieser Gebrauch hat sich, wenn auch
im einzelnen umstritten, in Kunst- und Literaturgeschichte für verschiedene Bereiche eingebürgert: für die Kunst der römischen Kaiserzeit (Augustus-Hadrian),
für die Architektur Palladios im 16. Jahrhundert und für den französischen literarischen Klassizismus eines Corneille und Racine, für gewisse Züge der Malerei
von Poussin und Claude Lorrain[12]. Von solchen nur in eingeschränktem Sinne zu
verstehenden Klassizismen hebt sich ein eigentümlicher Klassizismus ab, der seit
etwa 1760 in der bildenden Kunst und Architektur zum Vorschein kommt und
sich zwischen ca. 1800 und 1820 durchsetzt. Erst jetzt war es möglich, den
Klassizismus als Epochenbezeichnung vorzuschlagen[13]. Rein klassizistische Werke

---

[11] Aus dem Grad der Reflektiertheit des Klassikbegriffs ist jedoch die Legitimität der Bezeichnung nicht abzuleiten. Es wäre vielmehr zu klären, wo »Klassik« primär zur Sache gehört
und wo Analogie zum Gebrauch des Terminus in einem erweiterten Sinn führte. Ersteres
dürfte für die »Wiener Klassik« in der Musik gelten, das Zweite für die »klassische Vokalpolyphonie« Palestrinas. Es käme darauf an, die jeweils verschiedenen Komponenten des Be-
griffsinhalts zu ermitteln. Erst dann ließe sich entscheiden, inwiefern die Hervorhebung einer
Klassik in der Musik — an sich bereits eine Übertragung, die den musikalischen Werkbegriff
voraussetzt — gerechtfertigt ist.

[12] Vgl. etwa *Lexikon der Kunst* in 4 Bänden, Leipzig 1971, Artikel *Klassizismus*.

[13] Neuerdings R. ZEITLER, *Die Kunst des 19. Jahrhunderts*, Propyläen Kunstgeschichte Bd. 11,
Berlin 1966, S. 34. Zur Orientierung seien noch genannt: S. GIEDION, *Spätbarocker und ro-
mantischer Klassizismus*, München 1922; G. PAULI, *Die Kunst des Klassizismus und der Romantik*, Berlin 1925; H. MEBES, *Klassizismus und Klassik in der Baukunst um 1800 als inter-*

wie A. R. Mengs »Parnass« (Deckengemälde in der Villa Albani, Rom) von 1761, und J. L. Davids »Schwur der Horatier« von 1784, die eine Wende herbeiführten, setzen sich einerseits programmatisch ab gegen den Barock (Mengs) und stehen andererseits in Verbindung mit der französischen Revolution. Daß der Klassizismus in den Projekten der französischen Revolutionsarchitekten Ledoux, Boullée u. a. zunächst revolutionäre Züge an sich hatte, bald jedoch restaurativ und die Revolution legitimierend auftrat, ist nur ein scheinbarer Widerspruch. Er ist im Begriff des Klassizismus angelegt: als Abbrechen geltender Tradition und als rigorose Wiederherstellung von Normen (Antike). Beides ist der Fall im deutschen Klassizismus um Schinkel und Klenze, aber auch in der Plastik Canovas und Thorwaldsens, deren Klassizismus exemplarisch zu sein scheint. Die dualistische Struktur des Klassizismus um 1800, die R. Zeitler gezeigt hat[14], könnte auch in diesem erweiterten Sinne gelten. Von Anfang an hat Klassizismus deshalb auch eine stark programmatische, kunsttheoretische Seite. Zwar nimmt die Antike als formaler Kanon im Klassizismus eine zentrale Stelle ein, doch läßt er sich nicht auf »formale Anlehnung ... an klassische Vorbilder« und deren »stilistische Nachbildung« reduzieren[15]. Im übrigen ist nicht die Klassik des 5. Jahrhunderts v. Chr. Vorbild, sondern die griechisch-römische Antike als Ganzes. Andererseits ist Adornos gelegentlich synonymer Gebrauch der Bezeichnungen »Klassizismus« und »Klassik« (bzw. »Klassizität«) eher geeignet, Verwirrung zu stiften[16]. Klassik und Klassizismus sind begrifflich wesentlich unterschieden: So wie Klassik Traditionszusammenhang im engen Sinne voraussetzt, der allerdings nicht auf die Antike zurückzugehen braucht, tendiert Klassizismus zum Bruch mit Traditionen. Aus diesem Grund lassen sich Erscheinungen wie die Architektur Palladios, aber auch die erwähnte Epoche römischer Kunst sowie das französische »klassische« Drama nur bedingt unter »Klassizismus« subsumieren. Die übliche Inhaltsbestimmung des Begriffs, seine Beschränkung aufs Formale (»Wiederholung der Einzelform«, Kuhn, a. a. O. S. 121), als beliebige Wiederholung klassischer Formen (Schadewaldt, a. a. O. S. 21) ist indessen leer. Zwar bedeutet Klassizismus Anlehnung an einen »klassischen« Kanon, doch zielt diese Anlehnung nicht auf Wiederherstellung ab, sondern meint Neues. Nicht zu übersehen ist dies in den Fällen, in denen klassizistische Vorstellung zugrundeliegt, ohne daß es zur Nachahmung antiker Bauformen kommt. Dies ist der Fall in der französischen Revolutionsarchitektur, hinter der die Emphase, das Pathos der reinen, nicht zufällig meist überdimensionierten Form steht. Das ideelle Mo-

---

nationale und nationale Erscheinungen, München 1931; U. CHRISTOFFEL, Klassizismus in Frankreich um 1800, München 1940. Außerdem: R. ZEITLER, Klassizismus und Utopia, Uppsala 1954.

[14] Die Kunst des 19. Jahrhunderts (Propyläen Kunstgeschichte), S. 39.

[15] Riemann Musik-Lexikon, Sachteil (Mainz 1967), Artikel Klassik (STEPHENSON).

[16] Vgl. z. B. Ästhetische Theorie, S. 240, 241 f., 243.

ment steht in der Bezugnahme auf Antikes, vorab Römisches im Vordergrund. Gegenüber früherer Antikenrezeption (Renaissance, Barock) scheint die Einstellung zur antiken Formenwelt, die nicht aufgehört hatte, gegenwärtig zu sein, sich grundsätzlich verschoben zu haben. Der Stellenwert übernommener Form (schon weil die Aufgaben bzw. Inhalte neu sind) könnte im Klassizismus vielleicht derart bestimmt werden, daß Formen prinzipiell austauschbar sind. Der »Stilpluralismus« des 19. Jahrhunderts, dessen erste Phase der Klassizismus ist, wäre die Bestätigung solcher Beliebigkeit der Form. Die Form wird Funktion der Idee und wird im Dienst von Ideen beliebig verfügbar.

In der Musik entfallen weitgehend die Möglichkeiten zu einem Klassizismus im strengen Sinn des Begriffs, solange musikalische Struktur in Rede steht. Trotzdem wird, etwa analog zur kunstgeschichtlichen Begrifflichkeit, Klassizismus, mit Vorbehalten allerdings, für die Musik von Mendelssohn, den Alfred Einstein als »romantischen Klassizisten« bezeichnete[17], und für Brahms in Anspruch genommen. Man sprach von einer klassizistischen Phase im Werk von Strawinsky. Ernst Bücken[18] brachte die Musik von Luigi Cherubini mit der »klassizistischen französischen Atmosphäre« in Verbindung. Es ist nicht sicher, ob man Glucks Bestrebungen einer Neuorientierung der Oper klassizistisch nennen kann. Der Begriff einer musikalischen Klassik, der ausschließlich der Wiener Klassik vorbehalten und aus ihr gewonnen werden sollte, scheint indessen auch den Begriff des Klassizismus in der Musik nach sich zu ziehen. Klassizistisch wäre demnach die Musik, die im Anschluß an die Wiener Klassik und nach ihrem Vorbild entstand, doch nicht im unmittelbaren Traditionszusammenhang mit ihr steht. Die erste Bestimmung wäre nichtssagend ohne Ergänzung durch die zweite. Doch auch die Kennzeichnung des Klassizismus als Nachfolge ohne Tradition, die Übernahme von Formen ohne deren Sinn ist kaum hinreichend. Es genügt nicht, Klassizismus allein von der musikalischen Struktur her zu verstehen. Auch ein anderes wesentliches Moment jedes Klassizismus ist in Betracht zu ziehen: die Art der Antikenrezeption. Es zeichnen sich somit drei Ansatzpunkte für die Bestimmung eines musikalischen Klassizismus ab: erstens aufgrund der musikalischen Bauweise, zweitens aufgrund der Situation, die zur Orientierung an einer Norm führten, drittens aufgrund der Stoffe, des Sujets, auf das sich Musik, musikalische Vorstellungen beziehen. Letzteres ist der Fall in der Oper. Seit ihrer Entstehung steht die Oper im Zeichen der Antikenrezeption. Die Oper von Monteverdis *Orfeo* (1607) bis einschließlich der Opera seria im 18. Jahrhundert als Phänomen eines Klassizismus zu beschreiben, wäre indessen grob vereinfachend; auch davon abgesehen, daß ein solcher Klassizismus musikalisch nicht zu begründen ist.

---

[17] *Die Romantik in der Musik*, München 1950, S. 150.
[18] *Die Musik des Rokoko und der Klassik*, Potsdam 1928, S. 236.

In die Nähe eines »dramatischen Klassizismus« rückt erst Glucks Opernreform. Er bekundet sich in der Absicht, die Oper an dramatischen Vorstellungen zu orientieren, die weder eindeutig auf der Tradition der italienischen, noch auf der der französischen Oper fußten, aber beide voraussetzen. Als Glucks *Iphigénie en Tauride* am 18. März 1779 in Paris in Szene ging, sprach man das Werk als »tragédie à la grecque« an. Glucks Idee vom wahren musikalischen Drama ging jedoch kaum direkt auf die antike Tragödie zurück als vielmehr auf das französische »klassische« Drama. Die Wirkung Glucks im 19. Jahrhundert nahm deshalb folgerichtig vor allem in Frankreich ihren Ausgang.

Daß die Oper des 19. Jahrhunderts die Tradition der beherrschenden Opera seria verließ, zeigte sich nicht zuletzt im Abrücken von den antiken Stoffen. Aber auch in den Werken um 1800, denen noch antike Stoffe zugrundegelegt wurden, zeichnet sich eine neue Situation ab. Über Méhul, Cherubini und Spontini, die Alfred Einstein »*ideale Schüler Glucks*« nannte[19], bahnte sich die »Große Oper« an[20]. Insbesondere an Cherubinis *Médée* läßt sich der Begriff des musikalischen Klassizismus genauer fassen.

CHERUBINIS MÉDÉE (1796)

Cherubinis im März 1797 am Théâtre Feydeau in Paris aufgeführte *Médée*, die Brahms für »*das Höchste in dramatischer Musik*«[21] hielt, ist ein nachrevolutionäres Werk. Es fiele nicht schwer, den Zusammenhang zwischen der politischen Indienstnahme des malerischen Klassizismus für die Legitimierung und Institutionalisierung der Revolution und des antikisierenden Tragödienbildes in Cherubinis Werk aufzudecken. Das antik und klassizistisch drapierte Sujet ist gegenüber der Seria-Dramatik Metastasios in neuem Sinn repräsentativ. Tragischer Stoff, klassizistisches Bühnenbild und die von François-Benoît Hoffman, dem Textdichter Méhuls, weitgehend nach dem Drama des Euripides konzipierte

---

[19] *Die Musik der Romantik*, S. 127.

[20] Der Verfall antiker Thematik hängt mit dem Zerfall einer allgemein verbindlichen höfischen Konvention zusammen, an der auch die späte Opera seria noch festhielt. Über die Stoffe der italienischen Oper zu Beginn des 19. Jahrhunderts vgl. den Überblick bei F. LIPPMANN, *Vincenzo Bellini und die italienische Opera seria seiner Zeit. Studien über Libretto, Arienform und Melodik*, Köln-Wien 1969 (Analecta musicologica 6), Kapitel 1. Die späte Phase der italienischen Opera seria sowie die französische Oper in der Nachfolge Glucks sind noch kaum erforscht. Die Metastasio-Bearbeitungen des späten 18. und des frühen 19. Jahrhunderts könnten die veränderte Situation beleuchten, durch die auch die antiken Stoffe neue Funktion erhalten.

[21] Vgl. Max KALBECK, *J. Brahms*, Bd. II, 2 (Berlin ²1910), S. 367.

straffe Handlung vermittelten Erhabenheit und Strenge. Es kann kein Zweifel sein, daß weniger das Geschehen selbst das integrierende Moment der Wirkung war, als vielmehr die antikisierende Attitüde und hinter ihr die Idee unnahbarer, beispielhafter Größe und Monumentalität, Züge, die der Metastasianischen Opera seria gänzlich fremd waren. Die aus der griechisch-römischen Geschichte oder Sage entnommenen Handlungen hatten nie den Charakter des allegorischen Festspiels abgelegt. Dies änderte sich vor 1800 bereits in der späten Seria: das antike Sujet ist nicht mehr selbstverständliche Konvention. Gemeint ist vielmehr die Idee eines Zeitlos-Verharrenden und Musterhaften. Sie trägt aber auch, wie zu zeigen ist, die Musik. Szene und Musik sind gleichermaßen bezogen auf die Wirkung dieses ideellen Momentes. Die »Naivität« früherer Antikenrezeption ist, um Schillers Kategorie zu gebrauchen, »sentimentalisch« geworden. Ähnlich wie Richard Wagner in seiner Bearbeitung der Gluckschen *Iphigénie en Aulide* schwebte Hoffman und Cherubini vor, die Oper durch Konzentration der Handlung auf den Hauptvorgang, das Umschlagen von Medeas Liebe in vernichtenden Haß, und auf die Person der Medea der Euripideischen Tragödie anzunähern, sich deren zusammengefaßte Wucht anzueignen. Cherubinis Oper ist reduziert auf die Darstellung der Katastrophe. Der zielstrebige, einsträngige Verlauf der Handlung, die Komprimierung des Geschehens auf wenige Schauplätze und seine Zusammenfassung in wenigen großen musikalischen Szenen nehmen Forderungen des dramatischen Baues vorweg, die später auch Wagner aufstellte und die allgemein für die Oper des 19. Jahrhunderts gelten. Auch die Funktion des Chores als einer bewegten und bewegenden musikalischen Staffage weist auf die Oper des 19. Jahrhunderts, desgleichen der Katastrophenschluß des Werks: die Vernichtung bringende Entrückung Medeas. Der Untergang durch Feuer ist ein universaler, er beschränkt sich nicht nur auf die Person Medeas. Es ist kaum abwegig, ihn mit Wagners *Götterdämmerungs*-Schluß in Parallele zu setzen. Klassizistisch könnte man indessen bei Cherubini die Eindeutigkeit der Lösung nennen. Sie hat nichts von jener für Wagner charakteristischen Konfiguration von Untergang und apotheotischer Verklärung (Erlösung). Noch weiter entfernt ist allerdings Cherubinis *Médée*-Schluß vom »lieto fine« der Opera seria im 18. Jahrhundert.

Es fällt schwer, Cherubinis Werk auf eine Tradition festzulegen, es sei denn auf eine spezifisch französische Form der Antikenoper, wie sie Cherubini durch seinen Generationsgenossen und späteren Freund Méhul vermittelt wurde. Ihm ist nicht von ungefähr *Médée* gewidmet. Doch die Ausgangsposition beider Komponisten unterscheidet sich erheblich. Die für Méhul selbstverständliche Tradition der französischen Oper und insbesondere der Opéra comique sowie die Nachfolge Glucks, mit dem Méhul auch persönlich in Berührung kam, ist für Cherubini nicht gegeben. Als Schüler von Giuseppe Sarti steht Cherubini in der Tradition der späten Opera seria. Die Wirkung, die von Glucks dramatischem

Werk, in erster Linie vom *Orfeo* ausging, erreichte Cherubini nur indirekt[22]. Die italienischen Opern aus der Frühzeit, die sämtlich vor seiner endgültigen Übersiedlung nach Paris im Jahr 1788 entstanden, gehören der Spätphase der Seria an, die freilich von Glucks Wirksamkeit nicht unberührt geblieben war[23].

Cherubinis *Médée* ist ihrem Typus nach eine Opéra comique. Gesprochene Dialoge, die später (1855) durch Franz Lachner in begleitete Rezitative umgewandelt wurden, trennen die musikalischen Nummern[24]. Dennoch schließen sich mehrere Nummern über die Dialoge hinweg zu musikalischen Szenen zusammen. Cherubini folgt damit eher Gluck und Tendenzen der späten Seria als den Gepflogenheiten der Opéra comique. Deutlich wird dies vor allem in der eröffnenden Szene, einem mehr beschaulichen Situationsbild, in dem die eigentliche Ursache für Medeas Haß, die bei Euripides lediglich erwähnt wird, musikalische und szenische Vergegenwärtigung erfährt: die Vorbereitungen zur Hochzeit von Kreusa (in der italienischen und deutschen Fassung des Werks Dirce)[25]. Die Soli-Chor-Nummer der Introduktion (Nr. 1) und die folgende, durch ein Accompagnato-Rezitativ mit der Introduktion zusammenhängende Arie der Kreusa, dann Marsch und Chor (Nr. 2) mit der Arie des Jason (Nr. 3) und dem zusammenfassenden Ensemble (Kreon, Kreusa, Jason und Chor) bilden zusammen, von der szenischen Konzeption her gesehen, ein großes musikalisch gegliedertes Tableau aus zwei Teilen. Jason-Arie (Nr. 3) und Ensemble (Nr. 4) sind ohnehin durch ein begleitetes Rezitativ verbunden. Allerdings ist keine tonart-

---

[22] Über die Jugendzeit Cherubinis in Italien vgl. M. Fabbri, *La Giovinezza di L. Cherubini*, in: L. Cherubini nel II Centenario della nascita. Contributo alla conoscenza della vita e dell'opera, hrsg. von A. Damerini, Florenz 1962 (»Historiae Musicae Cultores« Biblioteca XIX).

[23] Die Erforschung der späten Seria wäre dringend zu wünschen. Es käme u. a. darauf an, die Tendenzen aufzudecken, die für die Oper der 19. Jahrhunderts bedeutsam wurden, aber auch die vielzitierte Wirkung Glucks zu konkretisieren.

[24] Diese Fassung hat die Urgestalt gänzlich verdrängt und scheint der Intention eher zu entsprechen als die Trennung der musikalischen Nummern durch gesprochenen Dialog. — Das Autograph der Oper befindet sich in Stanford, Memorial Library (USA), ein Exemplar des Partitur-Erstdrucks Le Duc, Paris (1797) mit autographen Korrekturen in Brüssel (Bibliothèque du Conservatoire Royal de Musique). Ich benutzte den frühen Partiturdruck bei Imbault (1800), in den auch die gesprochenen Dialoge aufgenommen sind. (Bayer. Staatsbibl. München, Sign.: St.Th. 306, aus den Beständen der Münchner Hoftheater-Intendanz: Médée/ Opera en III actes/ Paroles d'Hoffmann. Musique de Cherubini/ Représenté sur le Théâtre de la rue faydeau le 23. Ventose/ L'Au 5. 13 Mars 1797. vieux style./ Propriété de l'Editeur./ Gravé par Huguet/ A Paris Chez Imbault. — Das Exemplar wurde als Aufführungspartitur benutzt und enthält auf hs. Blättern eingebunden die Lachnerschen Rezitative. Außerdem sind zahlreiche Striche eingetragen.) — Die angeblich von Cherubini selbst anläßlich der Wiener Aufführung — das stets zitierte Jahr 1809 ist fraglich — vorgenommenen Veränderungen der Originalfassung, die ebenfalls meist auf Kürzung hinauslaufen, können hier nicht berücksichtigt werden. Die wichtigsten Stellen der Bearbeitung sowie die vollständige spätere Fassung des abschließenden Duetts »Perfides ennemis« (»Ihr drohet mir umsonst«) im I. Akt sind im deutschen Klavierauszug des Werks bei C. F. Peters, Bureau de Musique, Leipzig & Berlin (Verlags-Nr. 1362, Pl.-Nr. 5607) wiedergegeben.

[25] Die erste Aufführung von Cherubinis *Médée* in Italien fand erst 1909 (30. 12.) an der Mailänder Scala, in der italienischen Übersetzung von C. Zangarini, statt.

liche Geschlossenheit angestrebt. Die Tonarten der erwähnten Stücke sind B-, C-,
ferner D-, G- und F-dur. Auch das folgende Tableau, dessen Mittelpunkt Medea ist, besteht aus mehreren nur scheinbar für sich stehenden Nummern: Auf
den furchterregenden Auftritt Medeas folgen die Arie des Kreon »*C'est à vous
à trembler*« (»*Zittre du*«, Nr. 5), die Arie der Medea »*Vous voyez de vos fils*«
(»*Sieh die Gattin vor dir*«, Nr. 6), die sich an Jason richtet, und das den Akt
abschließende Duett Medea-Jason »*Perfides ennemis*« (»*Ihr drohet mir umsonst*«,
Nr. 7). Die Folge h-moll, F-dur und e-moll ist durch die Tritonusbeziehung
zwischen den Arien Kreons und Medeas nicht zufällig, sondern spiegelt das
Feindschaftsverhältnis beider Personen. Stärker ist jedoch der szenische Zusammenhang. Kreusa und der Chor binden Kreons Arie an die übergeordnete Situation. Das Duett Medea-Jason ist die dramatische Konsequenz der Medea-
Arie. Die vier Nummern des zweiten Aktes sind annähernd symmetrisch angelegt und werden zentriert durch drei Ereignisse: durch Medeas Flehen um eine
Tagesfrist, bevor sie das Land verlassen muß (Ensemble Nr. 9), Medeas Verzweiflung und ihre Auseinandersetzung mit Jason (Arie der Neris Nr. 10, Duett
Jason-Medea Nr. 11), sowie durch den Hochzeitsaufzug mit Medeas Klage und
ihrem Entschluß zur Rachetat (Marsch und Chor Nr. 12). Am weitesten fortge-
schritten ist die Konzentration des Musikalisch-Szenischen im III. Akt. Er besteht
aus einer breit angelegten Orchester-Introduktion (Nr. 13) in d-moll und der
Arie der Medea »*De trouble affreux*« (»*Wie Zorn und Rache mich bewegen*«,
Nr. 14) in Es-dur, die sich trotz Trennung durch gesprochenen Dialog zu einer
monumentalen Szene zusammenschließen, ferner aus dem Finale (Nr. 15), das
die Katastrophe enthält. Die Schauplätze der Handlung sind auf eine Mindest-
zahl beschränkt. Die Bühnenbilder der drei Akte erscheinen dabei wie verschiedene Ausschnitte desselben großen Schauplatzes (I. Akt: Halle in Kreons Palast;
II. Akt: Flügel des Palastes, Freitreppe, Tempel der Juno; III. Akt: Gartenseite
des Palastes, gebirgige Gegend mit Tempel). Es entsteht der Eindruck einer
ideellen Einheit des Ortes. Als wesentliches Kriterium für den Zusammenschluß
von Einzelnummern zu szenisch geschlossenen Einheiten wäre anzuführen, daß
auch die Arien nicht mehr dramaturgisch isoliert stehen, wie dies in der älteren
Seriaoper der Fall war, sondern Teil einer Ensemblesituation werden, z. B. dadurch, daß etwa an der Kreon-Arie Nr. 5 der Chor und Kreusa sich beteiligen.
Diese Tendenzen begegnen allerdings nicht erstmals bei Cherubini, sondern bereits in der von Gluck nicht unberührten Spätphase der Seria. Sie ist unver-
kennbar auch für Cherubini Ausgangspunkt des Komponierens. Ebensowenig ist
andererseits zweifelhaft, daß er sich der Musik Haydns und in erster Linie Mozarts verpflichtet fühlte[26]. Er gehörte wohl zu den ersten Komponisten, die die

---

[26] Vgl. R. Hohenemser, *L. Cherubini. Sein Leben und seine Werke*, Leipzig 1913, S. 81; außerdem H. Kretzschmar, *Über die Bedeutung von Cherubinis Ouverturen und Hauptopern für
die Gegenwart*, Jahrbuch Peters 1906, S. 83.

Wiener Klassik als Norm des musikalischen Werkbegriffs anerkannten. Auf die
Entdeckung mehr oder weniger notengetreuer Reminiszenzen oder Anleihen
kommt es dabei nicht an. Gerade weil die Abhängigkeit tiefer greift, sind sie
selten. Unleugbar ist, daß diese Einstellung, mit der Cherubini um 1800 gerade in
Frankreich nicht alleinsteht (man denke z. B. an die Theoretiker J. J. de Momigny
und A. Reicha, die beide auch Kompositionslehren verfaßten), zu einer gewissen
akademischen Selbstbescheidung führte. Die Monumentalität als integrierende
Kategorie, die auch im antiken Tragödienstoff zutagetritt, ist nicht nur auf die
dramatische Intention zurückzuführen, sondern soll auch aus dem musikalischen
Gefüge selbst hervorgehen. Es darf nicht mehr als ein durch geläufige Satztypen
präformiertes erscheinen, sondern als das strukturell Außerordentliche. Unver-
kennbar steht hinter jenem Willen zu einer satztechnisch begründeten Monumentalität, die zugleich — und darin liegt ein wesentliches Kriterium für Cherubinis Klassizismus — den Anspruch allgemeiner Verbindlichkeit und Geltung erhebt und die sich nicht mit einer bloßen Tagesaktualität im Rahmen des Opern-
theaters begnügt, die Wiener Klassik. Im musikalischen Gefüge ist ebenso wie im
antiken Sujet Erfüllung einer Norm angestrebt, die den Werkcharakter garantiert. Als klassizistisch wäre die Haltung zu bezeichnen, die die Idee des Monumentalen, Normativen voraussetzt, um sie im Rückgriff auf Stoffe und Formen
zu verwirklichen, denen die Autorität des Maßgeblichen zuerkannt ist. Das
Verhältnis von Cherubinis *Médée* zum antiken Stoff ist nicht mehr das »naive«
der Opera seria zu ihren Stoffen, Cherubinis Satz ist nicht mehr begreifbar aus
einer ungebrochenen Tradition.

In der bedeutenden f-moll-Ouverture äußert sich der Wille zum Erhabenen im
Gestus, im Klangvolumen und in den zu symphonischer Breite erweiterten Di-
mensionen. Doch ließe sich zeigen, daß der Impetus, der an Beethoven gemahnt,
und die Agilität, die konstruktiv begründete Monumentalität klassischen Komponierens schon in der Exposition durch Wiederholung erstarren. Auch im durch-
führungsartigen, sehr ausgedehnten Mittelteil (T. 159—275) stagniert das musikalische Geschehen. Die Reihungs- und Wiederholungstechnik wirkt akademisch
(vgl. z. B. die Takte 199—269). Das konstant durchgehaltene Pathos scheint die
klassische Dialektik des musikalischen Satzes zu verhindern, von der andererseits
das Pathos sich ableitete und die nun gewissermaßen zur Institution wird.

Bereits in der Introduktion (B-dur), die im übrigen als beschauliches Zustands-
bild noch weitgehend von der Typik der italienischen Oper bestimmt ist, macht
sich der neue Anspruch bemerkbar. Die satzbeherrschende Wiederholungsfloskel,
die in den Rahmen zweier sich zur Dominante öffnenden Kadenzvorgänge ge-
spannt ist (4 + 4 Takte) und deren Moll-Wendung (T. 6 ff.) an Rossini erinnert,
erhält einen dreitaktigen Anhang, der den ausgewogenen Kadenzbau durchbricht,
die Dominante bestätigt und auch eine neue Bewegung und Satzart, nämlich

polyphon anmutendes Gewebe, einführt. Einheit erscheint hier nicht als präformierte, sondern als im individuellen Zugriff hergestellte:

1

Aus beiden Wendungen konstituiert sich im wesentlichen das musikalische Geschehen. Doch ihr Zusammenhang und ihre Funktion ändern sich im Verlauf des Stückes nicht. Die ständige Wiederkehr wirkt statuarisch, obwohl die zweite Wendung sich im Folgenden an zwei Stellen verselbständigt: Kreusa, *»Hélas, je l'avouerai l'avenir«* (*»Laßt ab, Ihr sucht umsonst«*) und *»Jason me dit!«* (*»Wie kann mein Herz Vertrau'n zu Jasons Treue fassen«*), dann vor dem Einsatz des Chors in die Kadenz einbezogen wird:

2

und sich schließlich mit der ersten Wendung verbindet:

3

Eine solche motivische Verknüpfungstechnik dürfte unmittelbar auf die Wirkung der Wiener Klassik zurückzuführen sein. Andererseits ist nicht zu übersehen, daß hier nicht auf diese Weise satztechnischer Zusammenhang hergestellt wird, sondern aufgrund der Wiederkehr und somit der Verfestigung der wesentlichen Bauglieder und der konstitutiven melodischen Floskeln. Satzvorstellungen, die für Cherubini den Rang des Maßgeblichen hatten, erscheinen in neuem Zusammenhang bzw. auf den Grundlagen italienischer Operntradition und dadurch auch in ihrem Sinn verändert. Die Aneignung vollzieht sich auf einer Ebene, die letztlich nicht die Konstruktion betrifft, sondern die Wirkung. Gerade die bedeutenden Stücke der Partitur beleuchten dies: etwa die Arie des Kreon Nr. 5 »C'est à vous à trembler (»Zittre du«). Als Aria con coro weist ihre dramatische Konzeption in die Zukunft. Der deklamatorische Duktus der Singstimme ist ohne Gluck nicht denkbar, die dreinfahrende, furiose Orchesterwendung bekundet einen Anspruch, eine Monumentalität, die Mozarts *Don Giovanni* voraussetzt:

4

Doch das Charakteristische dieses mächtigen und komprimierten orchestralen Gebildes wird durch die Konstruktion der Arie nicht eingelöst. Einmal aufgestellt, behält das Gebilde stets seine Proportionen bei. Gleichförmigkeit im engeren satztechnischen Sinne wird hier zu einem Mittel, um Monumentalität zu realisieren, die indessen trotz heftigster Bewegung zu statuarischer Größe erstarrt. Die Dynamik des erregten Bewegungsablaufs erscheint gebändigt, wird musikalisch nicht freigesetzt. In Kreons Arie findet die Konfrontation mit Medea statt. Sie wird des Landes verwiesen. Doch die ausgeglichenen musikalischen Proportionen verbinden die Vorstellung des Monumentalen mit der der Ruhe. Nur an einer, allerdings zentralen Stelle, am Schluß des Mittelteils, wird der Rahmen durch kadenzierende Ausweitung des Hauptmotivs durchbrochen:

5

Das Gleichgewicht stellt sich indessen durch mehrmalige Wiederholung des Kadenzvorgangs wieder her. Die Strenge, mit der Cherubini an den Verfahrensweisen festhält, die musikalisch die Vorstellung des Erhabenen hervorrufen, schlägt um in distanzierte Kühle. Dabei sind die Anlage von Kreons Ensemble-Arie und die deklamatorische Faktur alles andere als konventionell. Der musikalisch-dramatische Vorgang vollzieht sich in drei Teilen, von denen der aus zwei Abschnitten bestehende erste die Funktion einer Exposition hat (Abschluß in der Parallele D-dur), der zweite eine Wiederaufnahme mit Reprisencharakter ist und wieder zur Grundtonart h-moll zurückführt, und der dritte, wesentlich knappere Teil die Grundtonart kadenzierend bestätigt. Devisenartig, aber strukturell unverändert, tritt hier noch dreimal vor den Schlußkadenzierungen das Hauptmotiv auf. Cherubinis Intention, den als ein dramatisches Werden konzipierten Ablauf musikalisch autonom zu verankern, ist offenkundig. Die Lösung aber ist klassizistisch. Ihr liegt die Vorstellung statuarischer Monumentalität zugrunde[27].
Jene in der Kreon-Arie Nr. 5 konstatierte Gleichförmigkeit des Individuellen begegnet im e-moll-Duett Nr. 7 Medea-Jason »Perfides ennemis« (»Ihr drohet mir umsonst«) am Schluß des I. Aktes, das gleichwohl zu den bedeutendsten

---

[27] Musikalische Autonomie auf jeweils besondere Weise herzustellen, ist unleugbar auch in den übrigen Arien angestrebt. In der Arie der Kreusa nach der Introduktion (mit solistischer Flöte) überlagern sich Da capo- und Konzertsatz-Anlage mit Reprise (1. Teil: T—D^D D—D; 2. Teil: neue Bewegungsformen; Reprise des 1. Teils mit konzertanter Coda). Die Arie des Jason Nr. 3, ein lyrischer Larghetto-Typus, folgt einer differenzierten Reprisen-Anlage (ABA'), in der die einzelnen Teile motivisch eng aufeinander bezogen sind. Prinzipiell ähnlich ist die g-moll-Arie der Neris Nr. 10 gebaut. Deutlich setzt sich der Mittelteil durch eine musikalisch neue Wendung vom ersten ab, während die Reprise die Vorstellung einer motivisch reduzierten Zusammenfassung realisiert. Doch gerade in diesem zusammenfassenden Teil (»oui je te pleurerai sans cesse«; »Mir klage sicher deine Schmerzen . . .«), in dem die abschließenden Wendungen des ersten motivisch wirksam werden, zeigt sich Cherubinis Eigenart, aus klassischer Struktur abgeleitete Verfahrensweisen durch Wiederholungen gleichsam überdimensioniert erscheinen zu lassen. Die Arie Nr. 14, die den Höhepunkt von Medeas großem Monolog zu Beginn des III. Aktes bildet und gewiß — schon durch die Tonart Es-dur — mit den Ombra-Szenen der Opera seria in Verbindung steht, wird eröffnet durch einen ausgedehnten Largo-Teil (¢). Es folgt ein schneller Teil (Allegro moderato C) in der typischen Bewegungsform des Agitato. Auch hier ist musikalische Autonomie durch motivisch profilierte Vorgänge konzipiert.

Stücken der Partitur gehört[28]. Medea verkündet Jason, der eher passiv sekundiert, in höchstem Zorn Unheil. Das Duett ist gänzlich von Medea und ihrem Zustand her aufgebaut. Die Eindringlichkeit der Komposition läßt sich nicht zuletzt auf diese manisch anmutende und deshalb der Gemütsverfassung Medeas entsprechende Einseitigkeit zurückführen. Der eröffnenden zupackenden Sechzehntelfigur

7

ist als Bewegungsgrundlage des Duetts eine peitschende rhythmische Figur entgegengestellt:

8

Trotz ihrer Prägnanz und ihrer immanenten Dynamik bricht die erste Figur den Rahmen nicht, den ihr Cherubini zu Beginn zuwies, nämlich den einer stürmischen Eröffnung und einer Bestätigung. Auch die musikalische Komprimierung, die durch die sequenzierende Verkettung der Eröffnungsfigur hervorgerufen wird,

---

[28] Cherubinis für Wien vorgenommene Bearbeitung unterscheidet sich, abgesehen von einigen leichten Kürzungen, kaum von der ersten Fassung. Nur das abstürzende Hauptmotiv hat eine neutralere Fassung erhalten:

6

Die ursprüngliche Fassung dürfte deshalb vorzuziehen sein.

9

bringt zwar eine neue Wendung, doch der musikalische Vorgang fällt durch Wiederholung jener Verkettung in das statische Pathos des Anfangs zurück. Dynamik erscheint weitgehend neutralisiert zugunsten flächiger Überdimensionierung. Sie entsteht nicht in erster Linie etwa durch tatsächliche Ausdehnung, sondern mehr durch die auftreibende Wiederholung der Konstruktionsglieder. Die Überdimensionierung ist von der tatsächlichen Ausdehnung unabhängig. Cherubinis Verfahren zur Herstellung von flächiger und dadurch erhaben wirkender Größe, in der das Individuierte der musikalischen Substanz den statischen Charakter einer Norm annimmt, läßt sich auch an den orchestralen Vorspielen der einzelnen Akte beobachten. Die ungewöhnlich ausgedehnte Introduktion zum III. Akt, in deren Verlauf Medea auftritt und an die sich die »Szene und Arie« anschließt (Nr. 14), in der Medea den Tod ihrer Kinder beschließt, wird eröffnet durch ein orchestrales, zunächst unbegleitetes Motiv, das den d-moll-Dreiklang durchschreitet. Musikalisch kündigt sich gerade durch den geheimnisvollen, motivisch immer wieder innehaltenden Beginn ein bedeutendes Geschehen an:

10

Der zögernde Beginn (2 + 2 + 2 Takte) wird aufgefangen durch einen dominantisch schließenden Gang (4 Takte). Wirkt schon der wiederholte motivische Gestus abschwächend, oder besser gesagt in Richtung eines dekorativen Pathos, dem sich das Besondere des musikalischen Verlaufs unterordnet, so entsteht durch die Wiederholung des gesamten Vorgangs (diesmal von der Dominante ausgehend und in der Tonika schließend) der Eindruck eines Statuarischen. Auf dieses geht der Anspruch des Besonderen über. Auch der weitere Verlauf des Orchestervorspiels ist gekennzeichnet durch solche großflächigen Wiederholungen. Sie lassen sich zwar aus der kompositorischen Tradition der italienischen Oper des 18. Jahrhunderts zwanglos ableiten. Neu ist aber das vergrößerte innere und äußere Format des Einzelnen, das ohne Gluck und die Wiener Klassik kaum denkbar wäre. Daß in Cherubinis Musik das Motivische Gewicht erhält, wird deutlich etwa an dem aus der gleitenden Viertelwendung (T. 7 ff.) abgeleiteten Modulationsvorgang nach dem zweiten F-dur-Abschnitt der Introduktion. Auch die motivische Kombinatorik zu Beginn des d-moll-Schlußteils (Auftritt der Neris und dann der Medea) ändert nichts an der Regelmäßigkeit des Satzbaus, in den die motivischen Vorgänge gleichsam eingelassen sind. Dieselbe Gliederung der eröffnenden 10 Takte, die schon zu Beginn der Introduktion begegnete, tritt hier wieder auf, erweitert durch vier die Tonika (d-moll) bestätigende Takte. Die konstruktive Einheit, der feste Rahmen, der schon zu Beginn das motivische Geschehen band, wird im weiteren Verlauf nicht in Frage gestellt, sondern stets erneut bekräftigt. Es wäre nicht sinnvoll, etwa die besprochenen Teile des Ganzen mit der parataktischen Abfolge verschiedener Bewegungsgestalten, die sich anschließen, in konstruktive Beziehung zu bringen. In dieser Hinsicht gehört Cherubinis Komponieren noch gänzlich der »vorklassischen« Tradition präformierter Strukturen an, die gleichwohl den Wechsel der Bewegungen erlaubten.
Die Beweglichkeit und Vielgliedrigkeit des melodischen Baus weist die lyrische Medea-Arie Nr. 6 »*Vous voyez de vos fils*« (»*Sieh die Gattin vor dir*«, F-dur, Larghetto) eindeutig in die kompositorische Tradition des 18. Jahrhunderts. Neu ist indessen die Intention Cherubinis, dem musikalischen Einzelereignis Kontur und den Charakter individueller Aussage zu verleihen. Dies kommt auch in der Gesamtanlage der Arie, einer differenzierten Reprisenanlage, zum Ausdruck. Gerade in diesem Stück begegnen die Reminiszenzen an Mozart auf Schritt und Tritt. Wesentlicher ist jedoch, daß Cherubini Vorstellungen des klassischen Satzbaus übernimmt, etwa die spontane Zusammenfügung der einzelnen Glieder. Auf melodische Modelle läßt sich kaum eine Wendung zurückführen. Der satztechnische Pleonasmus, der sich bereits im Detail bemerkbar macht, ist allerdings vom klassischen Kompositionsbegriff denkbar weit entfernt: z. B. die dreimal ansetzende melodische Formel des Beginns:

11

Bezeichnend ist, daß in dem differenziert gegliederten periodischen Zusammenhang der ersten 19 Takte (2 + 3 + 2 + 1 + 2 + 2 + 2 + 2 + 3) sich auch die Deklamationsglieder wiederholen, so daß der Eindruck eines zwar individualisierten, aber additiven Verfahrens entsteht. Die neue, unvermittelte Wendung nach As-dur zu Beginn des Mittelteils, »... *toutes ses nuits étaient paisibles*« (»... *und ledig aller Liebesbande*«) verliert viel von ihrer Spontaneität dadurch, daß die ganze 7-taktige Phrase

12

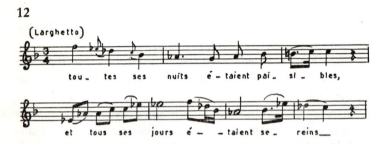

notengetreu wiederholt wird. Das satztechnisch Unregelmäßige, das seine Einheit aufhebt, um sie auf höherer Ebene wiederherzustellen, wird zum Ebenmaß stilisiert. Die Reprise wird eröffnet durch die Wiederaufnahme der ersten 4 Singstimmentakte (mit neuem Text) ohne die beiden Vorspieltakte, somit des Vordersatzes (Halbschluß). Der Nachsatz bringt eine neue, ausgeweitete melodische Phrasenkette, in der die Tonika F mehrmals bestätigt wird. Zum Abschluß dieses Abschnitts erscheint nun das Eröffnungsmotiv; doch diesmal fügt es sich in einen sehr kurzgefaßten periodischen Zusammenhang, der quintessenzartig wirkt:

13

Die Singstimme deklamiert lediglich dazu. Diese knappe Zusammenfassung wird jedoch neutralisiert durch die motivisch kombinatorische Weiterführung, die nicht mehr unter dem Aspekt der Konstruktion, sondern unter dem eines geistreichen motivischen Spiels begreifbar ist, zumal auch die beteuernden Wiederholungen abschwächend wirken. Nach den breit angelegten Kadenzierungen des anschließenden Abschnitts ist auch das letzte Auftreten des melodischen Hauptmotivs im Orchester mehr ornamentale Reminiszenz als konstruktive Zusammenfassung des Vorhergehenden:

14

Die »thematische Arbeit«, die Cherubini hier vorschwebt, gewinnt ihren Sinn aus dem satztechnischen Kontext. Es zeigt sich, daß sie akzidentiell, nicht primär ist. Ihr haftet ein Moment des Illustrativen an. Sie illustriert den Werkanspruch, indem sie das Bild der Wiener klassischen Musik beschwört. Jene Züge des Satzes, die ihm den Stempel des Individuierten und Bedeutenden aufdrücken, gehen auf in einer parataktisch-kadenzierenden Satzkonstruktion. Diese neutralisiert zwar den Einzelvorgang in seiner intendierten Individualität, ist aber die Voraussetzung für jene Idee des überdimensioniert Statuarischen, die auch im dramatischen Bau der Oper und in der Auffassung des Sujets wirksam ist. Weist die Art des parataktischen Kadenzbaus, die das mannigfaltig Wechselnde der Bewegungsformen innerhalb eines geschlossenen Stücks ermöglichte, auf die Oper des 18. Jahrhunderts zurück, so steht die Idee des Monumentalen bereits in engem Zusammenhang mit der Oper im 19. Jahrhundert.
Cherubinis Situation ist somit zwiespältig. Sie sei noch einmal in Stichworten zusammengefaßt: 1. Herkunft von der späten italienischen Seria-Oper; 2. die Hauptwerke jedoch französisch, in Frankreich entstanden und den Rahmen der Seria in Richtung auf die Oper im 19. Jahrhundert sprengend; 3. Vorbild der musikalischen Klassik; 4. Gluck als Vorbild für das ideale musikalische Griechendrama. — Man könnte, die Vielschichtigkeit der Herkunft, der Ansätze, der Tradition für jede Geschichtlichkeit in Anspruch nehmend, einwenden, daß eine Erscheinung wie etwa die Mozarts ebenfalls von verschiedenen Traditionen ausgehe. Cherubinis Klassizismus ist jedoch dadurch gekennzeichnet, daß er gelöst ist von einer unmittelbaren, selbstverständlichen handwerklichen Tradition. Cherubinis Verhältnis zu Gluck, zur Klassik und zur französischen Oper ist bereits ein viel-

fältig gebrochenes. Aus der Art dieses Verhältnisses scheint der Begriff des Klassizismus begründbar zu sein. Weder die Anerkennung der Wiener Klassik als Norm noch das antike, tragische Sujet machen Cherubinis Klassizismus aus, sondern die Idee, in deren Namen jene musikalisch-technische Berufung auf die Wiener Klassik und die dramatische Formung des Tragödienstoffes stattfinden. Diese Idee geht auch aus der musikalischen Struktur selbst hervor und manifestiert sich in dem mehrfach angesprochenen Zwiespalt zwischen dem Sinn des klassischen musikalischen Verfahrens und der Herstellung einer großflächigen Monumentalität, die auf Distanz zwischen Werk und Publikum angelegt ist. Der Zuschauer und -hörer soll sich der Wirkung eines »klassischen«, d. h. maßgeblichen, dem Werden, der Zeitlichkeit entzogenen Geschehens gegenübersehen, nicht die musikalischen Strukturen selbst rezipieren. Klassizistisch ist die Überlagerung der musikalischen Technik, des Kompositionsgerüsts durch Verfahrensweisen, die wegen ihrer spezifischen Wirkung zur Anwendung kommen. Sie verändern dadurch ihre ursprüngliche Funktion. Auf die Tendenz zur Überdimensionierung, die Analogien sowohl im deutschen Klassizismus (z. B. Klenzes »Befreiungshalle« bei Kehlheim) als auch in der französischen Revolutionsarchitektur hat, und auf die statuarische, Distanz schaffende Wirkung ist wohl auch jene Kühle von Cherubinis Musik zurückzuführen, die zwar Bewunderung zuließ, das Werk jedoch eigentlich heimatlos machte. Klassizistisch ist Cherubinis Medea-Drama, weil es mit seinem Publikum offensichtlich durch die Idee des autoritativen, erhabenen und deshalb statuarischen Kunstwerks kommuniziert. In diesem Punkt treffen sich Klassizismus und restaurativer Akademismus. Aber auch der Zusammenhang zwischen Cherubinis Komposition und seinem Wirken am Pariser Conservatoire wird greifbar. Cherubinis Klassizismus — vielleicht jeder Klassizismus — steht im Zeichen eines hemmenden Widerspruchs: daß sich nämlich das Außerordentliche, Erhabene zutragen soll, das außerhalb des durch Tradition Gegebenen steht, und daß dies doch durch die Unterwerfung unter eine Norm geschieht, die gewissermaßen ohne Zutun das Erhabene garantiert. Cherubinis *Médée* setzt ein bedeutendes und frühes Zeichen für den im 19. Jahrhundert in verschiedener Richtung unternommenen Versuch, den Anspruch des absoluten, reinen und von seinen gesellschaftlichen Bedingungen weitgehend isolierten Kunstwerks — einen Anspruch, der der Musik durch die Wiener Klassik zugewachsen war — durch musikalische Strukturen und durch dramatische Bilder einzulösen, in denen die Vorstellung des Denkmalhaften, des Statuarisch-Dauernden manifest wird. Möglich wird eine solche Einstellung durch eine tiefgreifende Veränderung des Standortes der Kunst im Gesellschaftsgefüge. Die aufsteigende Schicht eines neuen weltstädtischen Bürgertums bedurfte der Legitimation durch eine Kunst, die von ihrem Gesellschafts- und Traditionszusammenhang gelöst sein mußte, um solche Legitimation leisten und als Verkörperung der Idee einer erhabenen, unnahbaren Veranstaltung von Kunst erscheinen zu können.

Der Klassizismus ist weder Stil noch Epoche, sondern eine Intention, die verschiedene Lösungen zuläßt, in verschiedenen Bereichen möglich ist und die aufgrund der besonderen historisch-gesellschaftlichen Konstellation überkommene Gegebenheiten in neue von Tradition nahezu unabhängige Beziehung zueinander setzt. Allen Klassizismen scheint die Beschwörung eines Kanonischen, vom Stigma des Werdens und Vergehens scheinbar Befreiten gemeinsam zu sein, weiterhin die Bezogenheit auf eine Idee, von der die konkreten Formungen erst ihren Sinn erhalten. Im Dienste einer Idee, die sich selbst als Absolutes setzt, werden Formen (Stile) in neuer Weise verfügbar.

DER ITALIENISCHE VERS UND DER MUSIKALISCHE RHYTHMUS. ZUM VERHÄLTNIS VON VERS UND MUSIK IN DER ITALIENISCHEN OPER DES 19. JAHRHUNDERTS, MIT EINEM RÜCKBLICK AUF DIE 2. HÄLFTE DES 18. JAHRHUNDERTS

von *Friedrich Lippmann* (Rom)

II. Teil*

DER OTTONARIO

Der Ottonario ähnelt dem Senario im festgefügten Akzentsystem. Mit der größten Regelmäßigkeit fallen die Akzente auf die 3. und 7. Verssilbe. Zwei Beispiele:

METASTASIO, Szene II[10]
des *Adriano in Siria*,
Arie Emirena, 1. Strophe

Quell'amplesso e quel perdono,
Quello sguardo e quel sospiro
Fa più giusto il mio martiro,
Più colpevole mi fa.

ROMANI, Kultszene im
I. Akt der *Norma*, Gebet
Norma, 1. Strophe

Casta Diva che inargenti
Queste sacre antiche piante,
A noi volgi il bel sembiante
Senza nube e senza vel.

Jedoch fallen Nebenakzente gern — und auch in etlichen der zitierten Verse — auf die 1. und 5. Verssilbe. Der häufige Nebenakzent auf der 1. Verssilbe rechtfertigt die Existenz einer starken Gruppe von abtaktig beginnenden Melodien (Gruppe I)[61]. Der ebenfalls häufige Nebenakzent auf der 5. Verssilbe wird musikalisch dadurch unterstrichen, daß er bei zweitaktigen Gestalten auf die 3. Zählzeit des 4/4- oder die 4. Zählzeit des 6/8-Taktes fällt, bei viertaktigen Gestalten im 3/4- und 4/4-Takt sogar meistens auf die 1. Zählzeit.

---

* Der I. Teil steht in Analecta musicologica 12, 1973, p. 253—369. Der III. Teil wird in Analecta musicologica 15, 1974, erscheinen.

[61] »Rechtfertigen« allerdings nicht im Sinne, daß jede Melodie jener Gruppe auf einen Vers mit Nebenakzent auf der 1. Silbe komponiert worden wäre. Vielmehr gibt es nicht wenige Fälle, in denen auf musikalischer Seite ein kurzer Auftakt angemessener wäre.

Die Ottonario-Melodien gliedern sich in folgende Gruppen:

Gruppe I: Abtaktig beginnende Melodien aller Taktarten.
    Untergliederung:
    I A: Melodien aller Taktarten ohne Zäsur. Vgl. p. 330—338.
    I B: Melodien aller Taktarten mit Mittelzäsur. Vgl. p. 339—343.

Gruppe II: Auftaktig (mit Doppelauftakt) beginnende Melodien aller Taktarten (auftaktig meistens zur 1. Zählzeit, aber auch — im 4/4-Typ II A 1″ — zur genauen Taktmitte).
    Untergliederung:
    II A: Melodien aller Taktarten ohne Zäsur. Vgl. p. 343—360.
    II B: Melodien aller Taktarten mit Mittelzäsur. Vgl. p. 360—368.
    II C: Melodien aller Taktarten mit Synkopierung. Vgl. p. 368—370.

In den meisten Typen der Gruppe I werden mit der Vertonung eines Verses 4 musikalische Takte gefüllt (in zahlreichen auch drei). Die Typen der Gruppe II sind dagegen im großen Durchschnitt zweitaktig (der schon genannte Typ II A 1″ ist 1- bis 1½-taktig, die Typen II A 1′ und II A 3′ drei- und mehr als dreitaktig).
Die Typen II A stehen den Settenario-Typen der Gruppe II nahe, d. h. ein großer Teil der Ottonario-Melodien entspricht im Haupttakt dem Settenario-Haupttakt, und der einzige Unterschied der musikalischen Ottonario- zu den Settenario-Gestalten besteht dann im doppelgliedrigen Auftakt. Zwei und zwei häufig vertretene Typen:

Settenario   4/4
           6/8
Ottonario   4/4
           6/8

Die Ottonario-Typen II B (mit Mittelzäsur) und II C (mit Synkopen) hingegen stehen bestimmten Senario-Typen (I C und I D) nahe. Die in Ottonario II B und II C sinnfällige Gruppierung analogen, wenn nicht sogar ganz gleichen rhythmischen Geschehens um eine Mittelachse (in II B eine Pause) entspricht der Anlage des Ottonario-Verses, der sich genauso wie der Senario-Vers aus zwei gleichen Hälften aufbaut: ◡◡—◡   ◡◡—◡ .
Es fehlt eine Ottonario-Gruppe, die den Gruppen Quinario III, Senario II und Settenario III entspräche: Melodien, welche unbetont, quasi beiläufig (aber nicht

eigentlich »auftaktig«) innerhalb des Taktes nach Pause beginnen und in ihm alle Verssilben außer den beiden letzten präsentieren. Offenbar hängt das mit der Länge des Ottonario-Verses zusammen. (Dasselbe gilt für den Decasillabo.)

In seiner *Italienischen Metrik* operiert W. Theodor Elwert, wie grundsätzlich, so auch im Falle des Ottonario mit den Versfuß-Bezeichnungen der alten Griechen. Er spricht von einem »trochäischen« Typ des Ottonario (Beispiel: Chiabreras »*Belle rose porporine*«)[62]. Ob die griechischen Versfuß-Bezeichnungen zur Erklärung der rhythmischen Verhältnisse des italienischen Verses taugen, mögen die Romanisten unter sich ausmachen. Aber beim Ottonario gilt es zu konstatieren, daß die italienischen Komponisten in der Tat diesen Vers häufig so vertont haben, als ob er trochäisch sei:

199

a = Verdi, *Nabucco*, Presto-Ensemble mit Chor im I. Finale (Stimme Abigaille); b = Donizetti, *Anna Bolena*, Quintett im I. Akt, Cabaletta (Stimme Percy).

Die Verssilben 1 und 5 werden, vom Vers her gesehen, zu stark honoriert: durch Gleichstellung ihrer Nebenakzente mit den Hauptakzenten auf den Verssilben 3 und 7. Die zitierten Melodien gehören der Gruppe I an: abtaktig beginnend und oft im gleichen Rhythmus den ganzen Vers (und auch oft den zweiten) durchlaufend. Nun könnte man freilich die ganze Gruppe I als bloße Variante der Gruppe II betrachten: Variante darin, daß der Doppelauftakt zu $\frac{4}{4}$| ♪   ♪ | oder $\frac{3}{4}$| ♪   ♪ | verbreitert worden und darüber hinaus eine Dehnung des Gesamtgefüges (der zu einem Vers komponierten Musik) von 2 auf (meistens) 4 Takte erfolgt ist. Man könnte mit einiger Berechtigung so argumentieren. Nur machen die »verbreiterten«, abtaktig »gewordenen« Melodien einen so großen Prozentsatz der Ottonario-Kompositionen aus und haben ein so eigenes Gepräge (besonders in den soeben in Beispiel 199 gezeigten Typen), daß es sich empfiehlt, sie als eine eigene Gruppe zu betrachten. Zwischen einigen Typen der Gruppen I und II verläuft die Grenze jedoch sehr fließend, wie wir noch näher sehen werden[63].

---

[62] W. Theodor Elwert, *Italienische Metrik*, München 1968, p. 71.
[63] Vgl. p. 338.

Die Taktzahlen 2 und 4 triumphieren auch in der Vertonung dieser Versart, sei es in der Vertonung e i n e s Verses oder in der zweier benachbarter Verse. Zu ungeraden Taktzahlen kommt es, wie in allen Versarten, grundsätzlich durch Verbindung eines zweitaktigen Typs mit einem eintaktigen. Ferner durch partielle Dehnungen. Bloße Anfangsdehnung (z. B. im 4/4-Takt Verwandlung zweier Achtel in zwei Halbe)[64] führt meistens zur Dreitaktigkeit. Hier eine Dehnung der 3. Verssilbe, welche gleichfalls zur Dreitaktigkeit führt:

200

VERDI, *Giovanna d'Arco,* Coro di Borghigiani in Scena e Cavatina Carlo im Prolog (Sopran).

Und hier Dreitaktigkeit aufgrund von Dehnung der 3. und 4. Verssilbe:

201

VERDI, *Nabucco,* Introduktions-Chor des III. Aktes (Sopran).

Bellini dehnt im folgenden Beispiel die 7. Verssilbe so stark, daß die Versvertonung sogar auf vier Takte kommt:

202

BELLINI, *La Straniera,* Introduktions-Chor des I. Aktes (Tenor).

Die Dreitaktigkeit wird sehr häufig — besonders in der Zeit zwischen 1825 und 1875 circa — durch Wortwiederholung in Viertaktigkeit verwandelt:

---

[64] Vgl. die Beispiele auf p. 331 und 371.

203

a = Rossini, *L'Italiana in Algeri*, Arie Isabella im II. Akt, Cabaletta; b = Bellini, *Norma*, Cavatine Norma im I. Akt, 1. Tempo; c = Donizetti, *Belisario*, Cavatine Antonina im I. Akt, Cabaletta; d = Verdi, *Luisa Miller*, Duett Luisa/Rodolfo im III. Finale, Allegro (Stimme Rodolfo).

Eine fünftaktige Ausnahme, bezeichnenderweise aus dem Beginn des Jahrhunderts:

204

Rossini, *Tancredi*, Allegro-Ensemble mit Chor des I. Finales (Stimme Tancredi).

In der Frühzeit des Jahrhunderts (bis ca. 1825) sind auch die — besonders von Rossini geliebten — Melodien heimisch, die ich in meinem Bellini-Buch »offene« genannt habe[65]: im Kern deklamatorisch, aber mit Koloraturen weidlich behängt, wenn nicht überladen. Auch diese Melodien (sie sind meistens über Ottonario- und Settenario-Verse komponiert) sind oft ungeradzahlig in der Vertonung des einzelnen Verses. Aber Gerad- oder Ungeradzahligkeit zählen in ihnen kaum, da sie schlechthin zur Auflösung des musikalischen Metrums neigen. Beispiele:

---

[65] Friedrich Lippmann, *Vincenzo Bellini und die italienische Opera seria seiner Zeit*, Köln-Wien 1969 (Analecta musicologica 6), p. 154 ff.

205

a = P. Generali, *Argene e Alsindo*, Duett Clearco/Alsindo, Beginn (Stimme Clearco);
b = Donizetti, *Zoraide di Granata*, Cavatine Zoraide im I. Akt, 1. Tempo.

Raffungen, die das Maß von 1 Takt unterschreiten, sind selten. Meistens handelt es sich da um Fälle, in denen bewegte Figuren in langsamem Tempo notiert sind, wie hier:

206

a = Rossini, *L'Italiana in Algeri*, Quintett im I. Finale, aus dem Andantino (Stimme Isabella); b = Verdi, *Un Giorno di regno*, Sextett im I. Akt, aus dem 1. Teil (Stimme Barone di Kelbar).

Beide Melodien gehören dem Typ II A 1″ an, der normalerweise 1 Takt pro Vers füllt.
Beispiel für echte Raffung:

207

Rossini, *L'Italiana in Algeri*, Duett Lindoro/Mustafà im I. Akt (Stimme Lindoro).

Die Melodie gehört gleichfalls dem Typ II A 1″ an, der in der Regel im 2. Viertel beginnt.
Gleichfalls selten sind solche (in der »Großtakt«-Tradition stehende)[66] Gebilde,

---

[66] Vgl. *Analecta musicologica* 12, p. 264 f.

in welchen die Verskadenz (7. Verssilbe) in der 3. Zählzeit des 1. Taktes statt in der 1. Zählzeit des 2. Taktes beginnt, wie in folgendem Beispiel (Typ II A 3):

208

DONIZETTI, *L'Elisir d'amore,* aus Duett Adina/Nemorino im I. Akt (Stimme Adina).

Und wie auch hier (Typ II A 1)[67], wo nur die starke Enddehnung eine größere Länge, ein Sich-Hineinziehen in den 2. Takt bewirkt:

209

VERDI, *Attila,* Duett Odabella/Foresto im I. Akt, Cabaletta (Stimme Odabella).

Nun zu den einzelnen Gruppen und ihren Typen.

Gruppe I: Abtaktig beginnende Melodien aller Taktarten.

I A: Melodien ohne Zäsur.

I A 1: Zäsurlose Melodien im 4/4 (2/4)-Takt.
Wir beginnen mit Melodien, deren zweigliedriger Auftakt einen ganzen Takt einnimmt, während die folgenden 6 Silben, den meisten Typen der Gruppe II gemäß, auf 1½ Takte verteilt sind. Meistens hat der Auftakt die Gestalt

$\mathwidth$ (entsprechend beim 2/4-Takt).

Bsp. 211 →

a = ROSSINI, *Tancredi,* Arie Isaura im II. Akt; b = DONIZETTI, *Don Pasquale,* Duett Norina/Don Pasquale im III. Akt, 1. Tempo (Stimme Don P.); c = VERDI, *Un Giorno di regno,* Duett Marchesa/Cavaliere di Belfiore im II. Akt, 1. Tempo (Stimme Marchesa); d = id., *I Due Foscari,* Cavatine Lucrezia im I. Akt, 1. Tempo; e = id., *I Masnadieri,* aus Duettino Amalia/Massimiliano im I. Akt (Stimme Amalia).

---

[67] Vgl. auch Analecta musicologica 12, Beispiel 10b.

210

a = Donizetti, *Anna Bolena*, Duett Anna/Giovanna im II. Akt, aus der Cabaletta (Stimme Giovanna); b = Bellini, *Bianca e Fernando* (2. Fassung), aus Scena e Terzetto Fernando/Filippo/Viscardo im I. Akt (Stimme Filippo); c = id., *La Straniera*, Terzett Alaide/Arturo/Valdeburgo im I. Akt, Cabaletta (Stimme Arturo); d = Rossini, *La Cenerentola*, Sextett im II. Akt, Schlußteil (Stimmen Clorinda/Tisbe); e = Mayr, *Ginevra di Scozia*, Arie Lucanio im II. Akt.

Folgende — der »Großtakt«-Tradition verhaftete — Achtelmelodien bieten dasselbe rhythmische Verhältnis in anderer Notationsweise (2 bzw. 1½ Takte statt 3 bzw. 2½):

211

Manchmal rutscht die 1. Note des breiten Auftaktes auf das 2. Viertel:

212

a = DONIZETTI, *Gemma di Vergy*, Conte im Beginn des I. Finales; b = id., *Anna Bolena*, aus dem Allegro vivace des Quintetts im I. Akt (Stimme Anna); c = id., *Parisina*, Duett Parisina/Azzo im II. Akt, aus dem 1. Tempo (Stimme Azzo); d = ROSSINI, *La Cenerentola*, Vivace-Ensemble (mit Chor) des I. Finales (Stimmen Clorinda/Tisbe).

In den folgenden Melodien korrespondiert mit der Anfangsdehnung eine Schluß-dehnung; der Haupttakt (Silben 3—6) wird jedoch nicht gedehnt.

213

a = BELLINI, *Beatrice di Tenda*, Schlußteil des Quintetts im II. Akt (eröffnendes Solo Filippo); b = id., *I Capuleti e i Montecchi*, Beginn des Allegro-Ensembles im I. Finale (Stimme Giulietta); c = VERDI, *Giovanna d'Arco*, Chor im II. Finale (Sopran).

Den Löwenanteil an Gruppe I (sowohl an I A als auch an I B) haben jedoch solche Gestalten, deren sämtliche Glieder breit angelegt sind. Sie beanspruchen in der Regel 4 Takte pro Vers.

Es folgen von solchen (zäsurlosen) Gestalten im 4/4 (2/4)-Takt zuerst diejenigen, die im 1. Takt 2 Halbe- (oder, im 2/4-Takt, 2 Viertel-) Noten aufweisen.

214

a = ROSSINI, *L'Italiana in Algeri,* Introduktions-Chor (Tenor); b = id., *Otello,* das I. Finale eröffnender Chor (Tenor); c = DONIZETTI, *Il Furioso nell'Isola di S. Domingo,* die Introduktion eröffnendes Solo Marcella; d = id., *Anna Bolena,* Allegro-Teil des Quintetts (mit Chor) im I. Akt (Stimme Anna); e = VERDI, *Simon Boccanegra* (2. Fassung), aus Duett-Szene Gabriele/Fiesco im I. Akt (Stimme Fiesco).

Von einer eigenständigen »Gruppe I« — und in ihr von »I A« — zu sprechen, dazu berechtigen aber vor allem viertaktige Gestalten mit Beginn in der Relation lang-kurz.

Zäsurlose Melodien mit Beginn | ♩· ♩ | bzw. | ♩·· ♪ | :

215

a = ZINGARELLI, *Gli Orazi*, aus Arie Camilla im II. Akt; b = DONIZETTI, *Parisina*, aus Duett Parisina/Azzo im II. Akt, 1. Tempo (Stimme Azzo); c = BELLINI, *Il Pirata*, aus dem Schluß-Ensemble (mit Chor) des I. Finales (Stimme Imogene); d = VERDI, *Attila*, Solo Attila im II. Finale.

Vgl. auch die Beispiele 199a und 204.

Wie man sieht, ist die rhythmische Formel des Beginns konstitutiv für das ganze Gebilde. Dasselbe gilt für die folgenden Typen.

Melodien mit Beginn | 𝅘𝅥· 𝅘𝅥𝅘𝅥 | . (Es handelt sich um einen besonders stark vertretenen Typ.)

216

a = Rossini, *Mosè* (2. Fassung), Duett Anaide/Amenofi im I. Akt, Cabaletta (Stimme Amenofi); b = Donizetti, *Anna Bolena*, das schnelle Ensemble (mit Chor) des I. Finales eröffnendes Solo Anna; c = id., *Maria Stuarda*, Allegro-Ensemble (mit Chor) des II. Finales (Stimme Elisabetta); d = id., *Il Furioso nell'Isola di S. Domingo*, Allegro-Ensemble (mit Chor) des I. Finales, aus dem eröffnenden Solo Eleonora; e = id., *Roberto Devereux*, Duett Sara/Nottingham im III. Akt, Cabaletta (Stimme Nottingham); f = id., *Fausta*, Schluß-Ensemble des I. Finales, eröffnendes Solo Fausta; g = Bellini, *Beatrice di Tenda*, Ensemble (mit Chor) im Beginn des I. Finales (Stimme Agnese); h = id., *Il Pirata*, das Schlußensemble (mit Chor) des I. Finales eröffnendes Solo Imogene; i = Vaccai, *Giulietta e Romeo*, Terzett Giulietta/Tebaldo/Capellio im I. Akt, die Cabaletta eröffnendes Solo Giulietta; k = Verdi, *Nabucco*, Gran Sacerdote und Coro di Magi in Scena ed Aria Abigaille im II. Akt.
Vgl. auch Bsp. 199b.

Der Platzbeschränkung halber konnte nur immer die zu e i n e m Vers erfundene Melodie zitiert werden. Dabei findet sich, wie man schon von etlichen Beispielen ablesen konnte, keineswegs immer nach Takt 4 ein Einschnitt. Zahlreiche Melodien, gerade dieses Typs, stürmen in großem Schwung weiter, wie z. B. diese:

217

a = BELLINI, *Beatrice di Tenda*, Duett Agnese/Orombello im I. Akt, Cabaletta (Stimme Agnese); b = VERDI, *Il Corsaro*, Allegro-Ensemble (mit Chor) im I. Finale, eröffnendes Solo Seid; c = MERCADANTE, *Il Giuramento*, Stretta dell'Introduzione, Stimme Elaisa.

Melodien mit Beginn ... bzw. ... :

218

a = Rossini, *Tancredi*, Schluß-Ensemble der Introduktion (eröffnendes Solo Argirio);
b = id., *Semiramide*, Schluß-Ensemble der Introduktion (eröffnendes Solo Semiramide);
c = id., ibid., Duett Semiramide/Arsace im II. Akt, Cabaletta (Stimme Arsace); d =
id., *La Gazza ladra*, aus Terzett Ninetta/Podestà/Fernando im I. Akt (Stimme Podestà);
e = id., *Il Barbiere di Siviglia*, Schlußensemble (mit Chor) des I. Finales (Stimmen Ro-
sina/Marzellina); f = Donizetti, *L'Elisir d'amore*, Duett Nemorino/Belcore im II. Akt,
aus der Cabaletta (Stimme Nemorino).

I A 2: Zäsurlose Melodien im 3/4 (3/8)-Takt.
Sie beanspruchen in der Regel 4 Takte pro Vers.
Zunächst Melodien mit konstanten rhythmischen Figuren, die denen in den
Beispielen 216 und 218 entsprechen:

219

a = Verdi, *I Lombardi*, Arie Arvino im III. Akt; b = Donizetti, *Parisina*, Duett Pari-
sina/Azzo im II. Akt, Cabaletta (Stimme Parisina).

Folgende Gestalten könnte man ebensogut zusammen mit 6/8-Takt-Typen der Abteilung II A 3 betrachten (zumal in jener Abteilung nicht allein Melodien mit der Auftaktgestalt ♪ ♪ | , sondern auch mit der folgenden begegnen:

♪ ♪ | ; vgl. p. 359). Wenn sie hier ob ihres abtaktigen Beginns zitiert werden, so mit dem ausdrücklichen Hinweis darauf, daß die Grenzen zu II A 3 (bzw. II A 3′) fließend sind.

220

a = Donizetti, *Torquato Tasso*, Schlußensemble (mit Chor) des I. Finales (Stimme Roberto); b = id., *L'Ajo nell'imbarazzo*, Schlußensemble (mit Chor) des I. Finales (Stimme Leonarda); c = id., *Torquato Tasso*, Cavatine Eleonora im I. Akt, 1. Tempo; d = id., *Fausta*, Preghiera Fausta in der Introduktion.

I A 3: Zäsurlose Melodien im 6/8-Takt.
Auch sie sind im allgemeinen viertaktig pro Vers.

221

a = Bellini, *I Puritani*, Chor im I. Akt (Beginn: »*Ad Arturo onore*«), Sopran; b = Donizetti, *Maria Stuarda*, aus dem Introduktionschor (Sopr.); c = Verdi, *La Forza del destino*, Coro-Tarantella im III. Akt (Stimme Preziosilla).

I B: Melodien mit Mittelzäsur.

I B 1: Melodien im 4/4 (2/4)-Takt.

Mit Beginn $\mathbf{\frac{4}{4}}$| ♩ ♩ | (entsprechend im 2/4-Takt), sic oder mit figurativer Auflösung der beiden ersten Werte:

222

a = ROSSINI, *Semiramide*, Eingangschor des I. Finales (Sopran); b = id., *La Gazza ladra*, Cavatine Isacco im I. Akt; c = id., *Otello*, Introduktionschor (Tenor); d = DO-NIZETTI, *Zoraide di Granata*, Arie Ines im I. Akt; e = id., *Anna Bolena*, Duett Giovanna/Enrico im I. Akt, aus dem 1. Tempo (Stimme Enrico); f = id., *Linda di Chamounix*, Preghiera (Quintett) im III. Akt (Stimme Pierotto); g = VERDI, *Nabucco*, Preghiera Zaccaria im II. Akt; h = id., *Ernani*, Terzett Elvira/Ernani/Silva im II. Akt, Cabaletta (eröffnendes Solo Silva).
Vgl. auch Bsp. 14 (Analecta mus. 12).

Mit Beginn | 𝅘𝅥𝅭 𝅘𝅥 | bzw. | 𝅘𝅥𝅭𝅭 𝅘𝅥𝅮 | (entsprechend im 2/4-Takt):

223

a = ZINGARELLI, *Gerusalemme distrutta*, Arie Fanano im I. Akt; b = ROSSINI, *Il Barbiere di Siviglia*, Arie Basilio im I. Akt; c = BELLINI, *Norma*, Duett Adalgisa/Pollione im I. Akt, 1. Tempo (Stimme Pollione); d = DONIZETTI, *Lucia di Lammermoor*, Duett Lucia/Enrico im I. Akt, Cabaletta (Stimme Enrico); e = id., *Fausta*, Introduktions-Ensemble mit Chor (Stimme Fausta); f = VERDI, *Oberto*, Quartett im II. Akt, das 1. Tempo eröffnendes Solo Oberto.

Mit Beginn | 𝅘𝅥𝅭 𝅘𝅥𝅮𝅘𝅥𝅮 | bzw. | 𝅘𝅥𝅭 𝅘𝅥𝅮𝅘𝅥𝅮 | :

224

a = DONIZETTI, *Gemma di Vergy*, das Allegro-Ensemble (mit Chor) des I. Finales eröffnendes Solo Gemma; b = id., *Maria Stuarda*, Cavatine Leicester im I. Akt, 1. Tempo; c = id., *Linda di Chamounix*, Arie Carlo im III. Akt, 1. Tempo; d = VERDI,
Ernani, Terzett Elvira/Ernani/Silva im II. Akt, aus der Cabaletta (Stimme Elvira);
e = id., *Il Trovatore*, Duett Azucena/Manrico im II. Akt, 1. Tempo (Stimme Manrico).

Mit Beginn ![notation] oder ähnlich:

225

a = DONIZETTI, *Parisina*, Duett Parisina/Azzo im II. Akt, aus dem 1. Tempo (Stimme
Azzo); b = id., *L'Elisir d'amore*, Duett Nemorino/Dulcamaro, Cabaletta (Stimme
Nemorino); c = ROSSINI, *Semiramide*, Duett Arsace/Assur im I. Akt, 1. Tempo (Stim-
me Arsace); d = id., *Tancredi*, Arie Ruggiero im II. Akt.

I B 2: Melodien mit Mittelzäsur im 3/4 (3/8)-Takt.

226

a = ROSSINI, *Tancredi*, Arie Amenaide im II. Akt, 1. Tempo; b = id., *La Gazza ladra*, Preghiera Ninetta im II. Akt; c = DONIZETTI, *Maria di Rohan*, Duett Maria/Chalais im II. Akt, Cabaletta (Stimme Chalais); d = id., *Gemma di Vergy*, Duett Gemma/Guido im I. Akt, 2. Tempo (Stimme Gemma); e = id., *Fausta*, Coro di Donne im I. Akt (Sopran); f = BELLINI, *I Capuleti e i Montecchi*, Coro dei Capuleti im I. Akt (Tenor).

I B 3: Melodien mit Mittelzäsur im 6/8-Takt.

227

a = ROSSINI, *Semiramide*, Ensemble im I. Finale (Stimme Arsace); b = DONIZETTI, *Il Furioso nell'Isola di S. Domingo*, Duett Cardenio/Kaidamà im I. Akt, 1. Tempo (Stimme Cardenio); c = VERDI, *Un Giorno di regno*, Duett Tesoriere/Barone im II. Akt, Cabaletta (Stimme Barone).

Mit 7 statt 4 Takten:

228

BELLINI, *La Straniera,* Coro de' cacciatori im I. Akt (Tenor).

Gruppe II: Auftaktig beginnende Melodien aller Taktarten.

II A: Melodien ohne Zäsur.

II A 1: Zäsurlose Melodien im 4/4 (2/4)-Takt.

Zunächst Melodien der schlichten Gestalt $\frac{4}{4}$ ♪ ♪ | ♪ ♪ ♪ ♪ | ♪ ♪ ♪ |
(entsprechend im 2/4-Takt; der Auftakt weist oft Punktierung auf).

Hier einige legato oder jedenfalls überwiegend legato gesungene Melodien:

229

a = DONIZETTI, *Parisina,* Cavatine Azzo im I. Akt, aus der Cabaletta; b = id., ibid.,
Arie Ugo im II. Akt, Cabaletta; c = id., *Roberto Devereux,* Cavatine Nottingham im
I. Akt, Cabaletta; d = id., ibid., Cavatine Elisabetta im I. Akt, Cabaletta; e = BELLINI,

Norma, Duett Norma/Adalgisa im II. Akt, 1. Tempo (Stimme Norma); f = id., *I Capuleti e i Montecchi,* Duett Giulietta/Romeo im I. Akt, 1. Tempo (Stimme Romeo); g = Verdi, *Ernani,* Arie Don Carlo im II. Akt, Cabaletta; h = id., *La Forza del destino,* Duett Don Carlo/Don Alvaro im IV. Akt, 2. Tempo (Stimme Don Alvaro).

Im folgenden einige Staccato- bzw. pausendurchsetzte Melodien desselben Typs, wie sie von Rossini bis Verdi sehr beliebt waren:

230

a = Rossini, *Il Barbiere di Siviglia,* Aria finale Conte Almaviva, Cabaletta; b = id., *La Gazza ladra,* Chor innerhalb der Arie Podestà im II. Akt (Tenor); c = Pacini, *Amazilia,* 2. Arie Zadir, Cabaletta; d = Donizetti, *Torquato Tasso,* Coro de' Cavalieri innerhalb der Arie finale Tasso (Tenor); e = Verdi, *Ernani,* Coro de' Cavalieri innerhalb der Arie Don Carlo im II. Akt (Tenor); f = id., *La Battaglia di Legnano,* Cavatine Lida im I. Akt, Cabaletta; g = id., *Rigoletto,* Arie Gilda im I. Akt.

Einige 4/4 (2/4)-Melodien des soeben betrachteten Typs, deren Doppelauftakt statt ♪ ♪ | bzw. ♪˙ ♪ | folgendermaßen lautet: ♩ ♩ | bzw. ♩˙ ♪ | (entsprechend im 2/4-Takt).

231

a = DONIZETTI, *Don Pasquale*, Arie Ernesto im II. Akt, 1. Tempo; b = BELLINI, *Norma*, Duett Norma/Pollione im II. Akt, Cabaletta (Stimme Norma); c = VERDI, *Il Corsaro*, Solo Giovanni innerhalb der Arie Corrado im I. Akt; d = id., *La Battaglia di Legnano*, Romanze Rolando im I. Akt; e = id., *La Forza del destino*, aus dem Duett Leonora/Padre Guardiano im II. Akt (Stimme Leonora); f = id., ibid., Coro di Vivandiere im III. Akt (Sopr.); g = id., *Il Trovatore*, Introduktions-Chor des III. Aktes (Tenor).

In folgenden Gestalten ist der Haupttakt durch Melismen bereichert:

232

a = Donizetti, *Torquato Tasso*, Cavatine Roberto im I. Akt, Cabaletta; b = id., *Gemma di Vergy*, Cavatine Tamas im I. Akt, Cabaletta; c = Bellini, *La Sonnambula*, Arie Elvino im II. Akt, Cabaletta; d = id., ibid., Arie Amina im I. Akt, Cabaletta; e = id., *I Capuleti e i Montecchi*, Duett Giulietta/Romeo im I. Akt, 2. Tempo (Stimme Romeo).

Zahlreich sind punktierte Melodien.

Melodien mit Punktierung im 2. Viertel (meistens korrespondierend auch im Auftakt):

233

Melodien, die im Auftakt, im 2. und im 4. Viertel Punktierung aufweisen:

234

a = Donizetti, *Anna Bolena*, Cavatine Anna im I. Akt, Cabaletta; b = id., *Maria Stuarda*, Duett Maria/Leicester im II. Akt, Cabaletta (Stimme Maria); c = id., *Belisario*, Aria finale Antonina, 1. Tempo; d = Bellini, *I Capuleti e i Montecchi*, Cavatine Romeo im I. Akt, Cabaletta; e = S. Pavesi, *Arminio*, Cavatine Arminio im I. Akt, 1. Tempo; f = Verdi, *Ernani*, aus dem Coro de' Cavalieri innerhalb der Arie Don Carlo im II. Akt (Tenor).

← Bsp. 233

a = Bellini, *Beatrice di Tenda*, langsames Ensemble (mit Chor) im I. Finale (Stimme Beatrice); b = id., *I Puritani*, Duett Elvira/Giorgio im I. Akt, aus dem 1. Tempo (Stimme Elvira); c = Donizetti, *Anna Bolena*, Cavatine Percy im I. Akt, 1. Tempo; d = Verdi, *Un Giorno di regno*, Arie Edoardo im II. Akt, Cabaletta; e = id., *Luisa Miller*, Arie Miller im I. Akt, Cabaletta.

Punktierung in anderen Kombinationen:

235

a = Donizetti, *Lucia di Lammermoor*, Arie Raimondo im I. Akt, 1. Tempo; b = Bellini, *I Puritani*, Arie Elvira im II. Akt, Cabaletta; c = id., *Beatrice di Tenda*, das schnelle Ensemble (mit Chor) des I. Finales eröffnendes Solo Beatrice; d = Verdi, *La Battaglia di Legnano*, Cavatine Lida im I. Akt, 1. Tempo.

Eine 12/8-Takt-Parallele zu 235a:

236

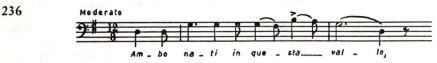

Donizetti, *Linda di Chamounix*, Romanze Antonio im I. Akt.

Bellini greift in folgenden Melodien zu totaler Punktierung:

237

a = Bellini, *Norma*, Cavatine Pollione im I. Akt, Cabaletta; b = id., *Beatrice di Tenda*, Aria finale Beatrice, Cabaletta; c = id., *Il Pirata*, Aria finale Imogene, 1. Tempo.

Dem so zahlreich vertretenen Settenario-Typ $\frac{4}{4}$ ♪ | ♩· ♪♩· ♪ | ♪ ♩ 𝄾 | entspricht der Ottonario-Typ $\frac{4}{4}$ ♪ ♪ | ♩· ♪♩· ♪ | ♪ ♩ 𝄾 | , der gleichfalls sehr häufig begegnet (oft mit doppelter Punktierung):

238

a = ZINGARELLI, *Gli Orazi,* Arie Camilla im I. Akt, 1. Tempo; b = ROSSINI, *Il Barbiere di Siviglia,* Duett Figaro/Conte im I. Akt, 1. Tempo (Stimme Figaro); c = id., ibid., Arie Bartolo im I. Akt, 1. Tempo; d = Giuseppe MOSCA, *Federico Secondo,* Arie Mansfeld im I. Akt, 1. Tempo; e = BELLINI, *I Puritani,* Arie Elvira im II. Akt, 1. Tempo; f = VERDI, *La Forza del destino,* Duett Leonora/Don Alvaro im I. Akt, 1. Tempo (Stimme Don Alvaro); g = id., *Il Trovatore,* Arie Leonora im IV. Akt, Cabaletta.

Eine 12/8-Takt-Parallele:

239

PACINI, *Gli Arabi nelle Gallie,* Arie Agobar im II. Akt, 1. Tempo.

Verwandt mit dem zuletzt gezeigten Typ — weil gleichfalls die 1. und 3. Zählzeit auf Kosten der zweiten und vierten betonend — ist der folgende mit abgerissenen Figuren arbeitende, leicht synkopische[68]:

240

a = DONIZETTI, *Anna Bolena*, Duett Giovanna/Enrico im I. Akt, aus dem 1. Tempo (Stimme Giovanna); b = id., ibid., Duett Anna/Giovanna im II. Akt, aus dem 2. Tempo (Stimme Giovanna); c = id., *Parisina*, Aria finale Parisina, aus der Cabaletta; d = BELLINI, *Il Pirata*, Arie Imogene im I. Akt, 1. Tempo.

1. und 2. Viertel laufen gleichmäßig durch, während das 3. Viertel gedehnt wird:

---

[68] Es gibt viel wenigere vergleichbare Settenario-Melodien. Hier sei genannt: VERDI, *La Forza del destino*, Don Alvaros »*Don Carlo, amico, il fremito*« im Duett Don Alvaro/Don Carlo im III. Akt. Vgl. den Decasillabo-Typ II A 1, Bsp. 325.

241

a = DONIZETTI, *Lucia di Lammermoor*, Arie Edgardo im III. Akt, Cabaletta; b = BEL-
LINI, *I Puritani*, Duett Enrichetta/Arturo im I. Akt, Cabaletta (Stimme Arturo); c =
VERDI, *Aida,* aus dem Duett Aida/Radames im III. Akt (Stimme Radames); d = id.,
ibid., aus dem Duett Amneris/Radames im IV. Akt (Stimme Amneris).
Vgl. auch Beispiel 3b (Analecta mus. 12).

Melodien, welche das 1. Viertel des Haupttaktes in das 2. Viertel hinein dehnen
und im 3. und 4. Viertel dann gleichmäßig ihren Gang gehen:

242

a = Giuseppe MOSCA, *Federico II*, Cavatine Quinto im I. Akt; b = BELLINI, *Beatrice di Tenda*, Cavatine Beatrice im I. Akt, Cabaletta; c = id., *Bianca e Fernando* (2. Fassung), Solo Filippo im I. Finale; d = DONIZETTI, *Lucia di Lammermoor*, Duett Edgardo/Enrico im II. Akt, 1. Tempo (Stimme Edgardo); e = id., *Anna Bolena*, Cavatine Percy im I. Akt, Cabaletta; f = VERDI, *Nabucco*, Preghiera Fenena im IV. Akt; g = id., ibid., Arie Abigaille im II. Akt, Cabaletta; h = id., *Il Trovatore*, Arie Conte di Luna im II. Akt, 1. Tempo; i = id., *Aida*, das Schlußensemble (mit Chor) des 1. Bildes des I. Aktes eröffnendes Solo Re.

12/8-Takt-Parallelen:

243

a = DONIZETTI, *Gemma di Vergy*, Arie Conte im II. Akt, 1. Tempo; b = id., *Parisina*, Cavatine Azzo im I. Akt, 1. Tempo.

Eher noch größer als die des entsprechenden Settenario-Typs scheint die Zahl derjenigen Ottonario-Melodien zu sein, deren 1. Viertel (nach Auftakt) über den Beginn der 3. Zählzeit hinaus gedehnt ist (entsprechend beim 2/4-Takt).

244

a = MAYR, *Ginevra di Scozia*, aus der Cavatine Ginevra im I. Akt; b = ROSSINI, *Mosè* (2. Fassung), Arie Anaide im IV. Akt, aus dem 1. Tempo; c = BELLINI, *Il Pirata*, Arie Gualtiero im II. Akt, 1. Tempo; d = DONIZETTI, *Lucrezia Borgia*, Aria finale Lucrezia (1. Fassung), Cabaletta; e = BELLINI, *La Straniera*, Aria finale Alaide, Cabaletta; f = VERDI, *Ernani*, Arie Don Carlo im II. Akt, 1. Tempo; g = id., *La Forza del destino*, aus dem Duett Leonora/Padre Guardiano im II. Akt (Stimme Padre G.); h = DONIZETTI, *Don Pasquale*, Quartett im II. Finale, 1. Tempo (Stimme Dottor Malatesta); i = VERDI, *La Forza del destino*, Arie Don Carlo im III. Akt, Cabaletta; k = id., *Aida*, Schlußteil des Duetts Aida/Radames im III. Akt, Unisono.

Beisp. 246 →

a = Rossini, *Il Barbiere di Siviglia*, Duettino Conte/Bartolo im II. Akt (Stimme Conte); b = id., *L'Italiana in Algeri*, aus dem II. Finale (Stimme Taddeo); c = id., *La Cenerentola*, Schlußensemble (mit Chor) der Introduktion, Stimme Tisbe; d = id., ibid., Sextett im II. Akt, Stimme Dandini; e = Donizetti, *La Regina di Golconda*, Quartett im I. Akt, aus dem letzten Tempo (Stimme Belfiore); f = id., *Linda di Chamounix*, Cavatine Marchese im I. Akt, Cabaletta; g = id., ibid., Duett Linda/Marchese im II. Akt, aus dem 1. Tempo (Stimme Marchese); h = Verdi, *I Lombardi*, Coro di Sgherri in der Arie Pagano im I. Akt; i = id., *Il Trovatore*, aus dem Duett Azucena/Manrico im II. Akt (Stimme Azucena); k = id., *La Traviata*, aus dem Ensemble mit Chor im I. Akt, das mit gleichen Worten beginnt (Stimmen Flora/Sopran).

II A 1': Breitere 4/4 (2/4)-Takt-Gestalten mit einer II A 1 entsprechenden rhythmischen Struktur.

Sie sind relativ selten. Die Komponisten des 19. Jahrhunderts bevorzugen es, breite Gestalten auch mit breitem Auftakt zu versehen, mit anderen Worten Melodien der Gruppe I zu schreiben.

Mit dem in Beispiel 238 gezeigten zweitaktigen Typ korrespondieren die folgenden breiten Gestalten:

245

a = Zingarelli, *Gli Orazi*, Arie Orazio im I. Akt; b = Rossini, *Semiramide*, Duett Semiramide/Assur im II. Akt, 1. Tempo (Stimme Semiramide); c = Bellini, *I Puritani*, Duett Elvira/Giorgio im I. Akt, Cabaletta (Stimme Elvira).

II A 1'': Schmalere 4/4-Takt-Gestalten mit einer II A 1 entsprechenden rhythmischen Struktur.

Sie sind, im Gegensatz zu II A 1', häufig zu finden.

Mit dem in den Beispielen 229/230 gezeigten zweitaktigen Typ korrespondiert der folgende 1—1¹/₂-taktige:

246

Mit dem in Beispiel 238 gezeigten zweitaktigen Typ korrespondiert der folgende 1—1½-taktige:

247

a = Rossini, *La Gazza ladra*, aus dem Terzett Ninetta/Podestà/Fernando im I. Akt (Stimme Ninetta); b = Donizetti, *Don Pasquale*, Duett Norina/Dottor Malatesta im I. Akt, aus der Cabaletta (Stimme Norina).

Eine 12/8-Takt-Parallele hierzu:

248

Si fi_gu_ri un ba_ri_lo_ne

VERDI, *Un Giorno di regno*, Duett Tesoriere/Barone im II. Akt, 2. Tempo (Stimme Tesoriere).

II A 2: Zäsurlose Melodien im 3/4-Takt.

Es handelt sich durchweg um Melodien, deren 1. Viertel (im Haupttakt) gedehnt ist.

249

Andante

a   U_na vo_ _ce po_co fa

Moderato

b   Di pia_cer_____ mi bal_za il cor,

Allegro moderato

c   Nel fu_ror del_le tem_pe_sto,

Larghetto sostenuto

d   Qual sa_rà do_lor che uc_ci_de

Larghetto

e   Co_me Pa_ _ri_de vez_zo_so

Larghetto

f   Chi mi fre_ _na in tal mo_men_to?

Larghetto

g   Ah, di pa_ dre ho l'al_ma in pet_to,

Andante maestoso

h   Giu_ri o_gnun que_sto ca_nu_to

Andante

i   Al_la vi_ ta che t'ar_ri_de

Eine 9/8-Takt-Parallele:

250

VERDI, *Un Giorno di regno*, Cavatine Cavaliere in der Introduktion.

II A 3: Zäsurlose Melodien im 6/8-Takt.

Die Hauptgestalt ist die folgende:

← Bsp. 249

a = ROSSINI, *Il Barbiere di Siviglia*, Arie Rosina im I. Akt, 1. Tempo; b = id., *La Gazza ladra*, Cavatine Ninetta im I. Akt, 1. Tempo; c = BELLINI, *Il Pirata*, Cavatine Gualtiero im I. Akt, 1. Tempo; d = id., *La Straniera*, Quartett im II. Akt (Stimme Alaide); e = DONIZETTI, *L'Elisir d'amore*, Cavatine Belcore im I. Akt, 1. Tempo; f = id., *Lucia di Lammermoor*, Sextett (mit Chor) im I. Finale, langsames Tempo (Stimme Edgardo); g = id., *Torquato Tasso*, Duett Roberto/Tasso im I. Akt, 2. Tempo (Stimme Tasso); h = VERDI, *I Masnadieri*, Carlo im III. Finale; i = id., *Un Ballo in maschera*, Solo Renato in der Introduktion.

251

a = Rossini, *La Gazza ladra,* Duett Ninetta/Giannetto im II. Akt, 1. Tempo (Stimme Ninetta); b = id., *La Cenerentola,* Solo Cenerentola in der Introduktion; c = id., ibid., Duett Cenerentola/Don Ramiro im I. Akt, 1. Tempo (Stimme Don R.); d = Mayr, *L'Amor conjugale,* Romanze Zeliska; e = Bellini, *I Puritani,* Romanze Arturo im III. Akt; f = Donizetti, *Linda di Chamounix,* Romanze Pierotto im I. Akt; g = id., *Parisina,* Duett Ugo/Ernesto im I. Akt, 2. Tempo (Stimme Ugo); h = Verdi, *I Due Foscari,* Barcarola im III. Akt (Sopran); i = id., *Alzira,* Cavatine Alzira im I. Akt, 1. Tempo; k = id., *La Traviata,* Arie Violetta im I. Akt, Cabaletta.

Wie beim Settenario gibt es auch hier 6/8-Takt-Melodien, welche im Haupttakt eine durchlaufende Achtel-Bewegung aufweisen:

252

a = DONIZETTI, *Maria di Rohan*, Preghiera Maria im III. Akt; b = id., *Il Furioso nell'Isola di S. Domingo*, Cavatine Fernando im I. Akt.

In etlichen Melodien erscheint — analog den Verhältnissen beim 4/4-Takt[69] — der Doppelauftakt ♪♪ | zu ♩ ♪ | gedehnt:

253

a = ROSSINI, *Semiramide*, Arie Idreno im II. Akt, 1. Tempo; b = BELLINI, *La Straniera*, aus dem Coro de' cacciatori im I. Akt (Tenor); c = id., *La Sonnambula*, Chor in der Introduktion (Sopran); d = VERDI, *Giovanna d'Arco*, Romanze Giovanna im I. Akt.

II A 3': 3/4 (3/8)-Takt-Melodien, die mit dem 6/8-Takt-Typ

6/8 ♪♪ | ♩ ♪♪ ♪ | ♩ ♪ 𝄾 eng verwandt sind.

Auch an dieser Stelle[70] sei betont, daß die Grenzen zwischen dem hier und dem in I A 2 gezeigten Typ fließend sind.

---

[69] Vgl. p. 344/345.
[70] Vgl. p. 338.

254

a = VERDI, *Il Trovatore*, aus dem Duett Azucena/Manrico im II. Akt (Stimme Azucena); b = DONIZETTI, *Parisina*, das Quartett des I. Finales eröffnendes Solo Parisina; c = id., ibid., Aria finale Parisina, 1. Tempo.

II B: Melodien aller Taktarten mit Mittelzäsur.

II B 1: Melodien im 4/4 (2/4)-Takt.

Da sind zunächst die Melodien von der Gestalt

4/4 (oder ähnlich):

255

a = MAYR, *Ginevra di Scozia*, aus der Arie Ariodante im Beginn des II. Aktes; b = ROSSINI, *L'Italiana in Algeri*, Duett Isabella/Taddeo im I. Akt, 1. Tempo (Stimme Isabella); c = id., *La Cenerentola*, Duett Dandini/Don Magnifico im II. Akt, 1. Tempo; d = id., ibid., Duett Don Ramiro/Dandini im Beginn des I. Finales (Stimme Don Ramiro); e = DONIZETTI, *Anna Bolena*, Arie Giovanna im II. Akt, Cabaletta; f = id., *Marino Falliero*, Arie Elena im III. Akt, Cabaletta; g = id., *Lucrezia Borgia*, Romanze Lucrezia im Prolog; h = id., *Gemma di Vergy*, Duett Gemma/Guido im I. Akt, aus dem 1. Tempo (Stimme Gemma); i = VERDI, *Un Giorno di regno*, Septett im II. Akt, Stimme Marchesa; k = id., *I Due Foscari*, Arie Lucrezia im III. Akt.

Eine 12/8-Takt-Parallele hierzu:

256

DONIZETTI, *La Regina di Golconda*, Duett Alina/Volmar im II. Akt, 2. Tempo (Stimme Alina).

In einem großen Prozentsatz auftaktiger Ottonario-Melodien mit Mittelzäsur sind die Endungen sowohl der ersten als auch der zweiten Vershälfte gedehnt:

257

a = Donizetti, *Il Furioso nell'Isola di S. Domingo*, Aria finale Eleonora, 1. Tempo;
b = id., *Marino Faliero*, Arie Faliero im II. Akt, Cabaletta; c = id., *L'Ajo nell'imbarazzo*, Aria finale Gilda, Cabaletta; d = Mercadante, *Il Giuramento*, Arie Man-
fredo im II. Akt, 1. Tempo; e = Verdi, *I Lombardi*, Arie Pagano im I. Akt, Cabaletta; f = id., ibid., Solo Giselda im III. Finale; g = id., *Macbeth* (2. Fassung),
aus dem Coro di profughi scozzesi im IV. Akt (Sopran).

Recht häufig begegnen Melodien mit »Auftakt« zum 4. Viertel des Haupttaktes.
Daß diese aus neun einzeln textierten Noten (die mit Melismen versehen sein
können) zusammengesetzten Gebilde sich mit einem Ottonario-Vers verbinden
können, beruht durchweg auf der Nichtbeachtung der Regel der »sinalefe«[71].

---

[71] Vgl. Analecta musicologica 12, p. 267—269.

258

a = MAYR, *Cora* (Neapel 1815), Solo Cora im I. Finale; b = ROSSINI, *L'Italiana in Algeri*, Cavatine Isabella im I. Akt, 1. Tempo; c = id., *Otello*, Duett Otello/Jago im II. Akt, 1. Tempo (Stimme Otello); d = DONIZETTI, *Lucia di Lammermoor*, Szene Raimondo/Chor im III. Akt (Stimme Raimondo); e = id., *Belisario*, Aria finale Antonina, Cabaletta; f = BELLINI, *Norma*, Duett Norma/Adalgisa im II. Akt, 2. Tempo (Stimme Adalgisa); g = id., *Beatrice di Tenda*, Quintett im II. Akt (vor dem geschlossenen Teil), Stimme Beatrice; h = VACCAI, *Giovanna d'Arco*, Cavatine Leonello im I. Akt, 1. Tempo; i = VERDI, *Nabucco*, Terzettino Abigaille/Fenena/Ismaele im I. Akt, Stimme Abigaille; k = id., *I Lombardi*, Arie Pagano im I. Akt, 1. Tempo.

Parallelen im 12/8-Takt:

a = BELLINI, *Zaira*, Arie Corasmino im I. Akt, 1. Tempo; b = id., *La Sonnambula*, langsames Ensemble (mit Chor) im I. Finale, Stimme Amina; c = id., *I Puritani*, Sortita Arturo (mit Ensemble und Chor) im I. Akt; d = DONIZETTI, *Marino Falliero*, Arie Israele im I. Akt, 1. Tempo; e = id., *Maria di Rohan*, Cavatine Maria im I. Akt, Cabaletta.

Letztgenannter Typ mit Dehnung der Endungen sowohl der ersten als auch der zweiten Vershälfte:

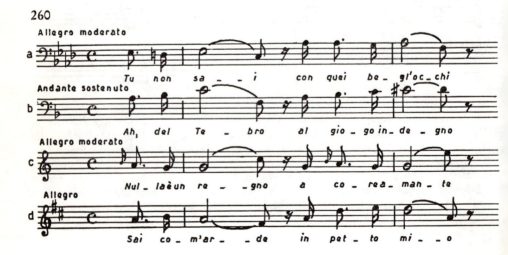

a = BELLINI, *La Sonnambula*, Cavatine Rodolfo im I. Akt, Cabaletta; b = id., *Norma*, Arie (mit Chor) Oroveso im II. Akt; c = id., *Beatrice di Tenda*, Duett Agnese/Orombello im I. Tempo, 1. Tempo (Stimme Agnese); d = BELLINI, *I Puritani*, Duett Elvira/Giorgio im I. Akt, 1. Tempo (Stimme Elvira); e = DONIZETTI, *Parisina*, Aria finale Parisina, aus der Cabaletta; f = id., *Lucrezia Borgia*, Duett Gennaro/Orsini im II. Akt, Cabaletta (Stimme Orsini); g = id., *Maria Stuarda*, Duettino Elisabetta/Cecil im III. Akt (Stimme Elisabetta); h = VERDI, *Un Giorno di regno*, Barone di Kelbar im I. Finale; i = id., *Nabucco*, Cavatine Zaccaria im I. Akt, Cabaletta; k = id., *Ernani*, Cavatine Silva im I. Akt, 1. Tempo.

Fallen in diesem durch die Mittelzäsur charakterisierten 4/4-Typ auf die 1. Zählzeit des Haupttaktes ein einsilbiges Wort oder ein einsilbiges Wortende ohne Diphthong, wird das 1. Viertel gern bis zur 2. Zählzeit gedehnt, oder der Komponist greift zu einer gleichfalls in der 2. (wenn nicht in der 3.) Zählzeit endenden Bindung:

261

a = ROSSINI, *L'Italiana in Algeri*, Solo Isabella im II. Finale; b = PACINI, *Medea*, Arie Medea im I. Akt, Cabaletta; c = BELLINI, *Norma*, Duett Norma/Pollione im II. Akt, 1. Tempo; d = id., *I Puritani*, Duett Giorgio/Riccardo im II. Akt, 1. Tempo (Stimme Giorgio); e = DONIZETTI, *Torquato Tasso*, langsames Ensemble im I. Finale, Stimme Eleonora; f = id., *Anna Bolena*, Duett Anna/Giovanna, 2. Tempo (Stimme Giovanna).

Weniger zahlreich scheinen die Fälle zu sein, in denen die Einsilbigkeit des Wortes oder der Endung dazu führt, daß der vor der Zäsur stehende Melodieteil mit der 1. Zählzeit endet (mit sofort nachfolgender Pause):

262

a = DONIZETTI, *Gemma di Vergy*, Duett Gemma/Tamas im II. Akt, 1. Tempo (Stimme Gemma); b = id., *Anna Bolena*, Arie Percy im II. Akt, 1. Tempo; c = ROSSINI, *Il Barbiere di Siviglia*, Duett Rosina/Figaro im I. Akt (Stimme Rosina).

Eine 12/8-Takt-Parallele:

263

Rossini, *Semiramide*, Arie Idreno im I. Akt, 1. Tempo.

II B 1′: Breitere 4/4-Takt-Gestalten sehr ähnlicher rhythmischer Struktur:

264

a = Mayr, *Medea*, Solo Creusa in der Introduktion; b = id., ibid., Arie Medea im II. Akt, 1. Tempo.

II B 2: Melodien mit Mittelzäsur im 3/4-Takt:

265

a = Donizetti, *Lucia di Lammermoor*, Duett Lucia/Edgardo im I. Akt, 2. Tempo; b = id., *Anna Bolena*, Quintett im I. Akt, langsames Tempo (Stimme Anna); c = id., ibid., Cavatine Smeton im I. Akt, Cabaletta; d = Rossini, *La Cenerentola*, Sextett im II. Akt, 2. Haupttempo (Stimme Cenerentola); e = Verdi, *Ernani*, aus dem Terzett Elvira/Ernani/Silva im I. Akt (Stimme Elvira).

9/8-Takt-Parallelen:

266

a = DONIZETTI, *Marino Falliero*, Arie Israele im III. Akt, 2. Tempo; b = BELLINI, *I Puritani*, Arie Riccardo im I. Akt, 1. Tempo; c = id., *I Capuleti e i Montecchi*, Cavatine Romeo im I. Akt, 1. Tempo.

II B 3: Melodien mit Mittelzäsur im 6/8-Takt:

267

a = DONIZETTI, *Gemma di Vergy*, das langsame Ensemble (mit Chor) des I. Finales eröffnendes Solo Tamas; b = VERDI, *La Traviata*, aus dem Duett Violetta/Germont im II. Akt (Stimme Violetta); c = BELLINI, *Bianca e Fernando* (2. Fassung), das langsame Ensemble (mit Chor) des I. Finales eröffnendes Solo Fernando.

II C: Melodien aller Taktarten mit Synkopierung.

II C 1: Melodien im 4/4 (2/4)-Takt.

Bsp. 269 →

a = BELLINI, *La Sonnambula*, Aria finale Amina, Cabaletta; b = DONIZETTI, *Gemma di Vergy*, Cavatine Gemma im I. Akt, Cabaletta; c = VERDI, *Giovanna d'Arco*, Romanze Giacomo im II. Akt; d = PACINI, *Saffo*, Arie Alcandro im I. Akt, Cabaletta.

268

a = DONIZETTI, *Parisina*, Duett Ugo/Ernesto im I. Akt, Cabaletta (Stimme Ugo); b = id., *Gemma di Vergy*, Cavatine Conte im I. Akt, Cabaletta; c = id., ibid., Cavatine Guido im I. Akt, Cabaletta; d = id., *L'Elisir d'amore*, Duett Nemorino/Belcore im II. Akt, 2. Tempo (Stimme Nemorino); e = VERDI, *I Masnadieri*, Arie Carlo im I. Akt, Cabaletta; f = id., *La Battaglia di Legnano*, Duett Arrigo/Rolando im II. Akt (Stimme Rolando).

In den folgenden, den soeben zitierten verwandten Melodien ist die 2. Note keine Halbe, sondern nur eine punktierte Viertelnote, weil das 4. Viertel einen Auftakt erhalten hat (bei Nichtbeachtung der Regel der »sinalefe«)[72]:

269

---

[72] Die Grenzen zu Typ 258 sind hinsichtlich des Höreindrucks mitunter fließend.

II C 2: Synkopische Melodien im 3/4-Takt:

270

BELLINI, *La Straniera,* Arie Isoletta im II. Akt, Cabaletta.

II C 3: Synkopische Melodien im 6/8-Takt (und synkopische 3/8-Takt-Melodien,
die dem 6/8-Haupttyp entsprechen)[73].

271

a = DONIZETTI, *Linda di Chamounix,* »Ballata« Pierotto im I. Akt; b = id., *L'Elisir
d'amore,* Cavatine Dulcamara im I. Akt, Schlußteil; c = VERDI, *Il Trovatore,* Terzett
Azucena/Conte Luna/Ferrando im II. Akt, Solo Azucena.

Bsp. 272 →

a = HASSE, *Ruggiero,* Arie Ottone II[1]; b = id., ibid., Arie Ruggiero III[5]; c = MOZART,
Idomeneo, Arie Idomeneo im I. Akt; d = id., *Don Giovanni,* Don Giovanni im Beginn
des II. Finales; e = id., ibid., aus dem Schlußensemble des I. Finales (Stimmen Anna/
Elvira/Zerlina); f = id., *Le Nozze di Figaro,* Contessa im II. Finale; g = id., *Così fan
tutte,* Duettino Fiordiligi/Dorabella im I. Finale (Stimme Fiordiligi); h = id., *La Cle-
menza di Tito,* Arie Tito im I. Akt; i = PAISIELLO, *Socrate immaginario,* Arie Don
Tammaro im I. Akt, 2. Tempo; k = CIMAROSA, *Il Matrimonio segreto,* Quintett im II.
Akt, eröffnendes Solo Carolina.

---

[73] Vgl. Typ 254.

RÜCKBLICK AUF DIE 2. HÄLFTE DES 18. JAHRHUNDERTS

I A 1.

Entsprechend Beispiel 210[74]:

272

---

[74] Genauso häufig wie die Auftaktsgestalt $\begin{array}{c}|\rho\cdot\rho|\end{array}$ erscheint im Settecento die Gestalt $\frac{4}{4}|\rho\rho|$, welche im Ottocento rar ist.

Entsprechend Beispiel 211:

273

a = MOZART, *Idomeneo*, Duett Ilia/Idamante im III. Akt, Stimme Ilia; b = id., *Don Giovanni*, Don Ottavio u. Donna Elvira im I. Finale; c = PAISIELLO, *Il Barbiere di Siviglia*, Terzett Rosina/Conte/Bartolo im I. Akt, letzter Teil (Stimme Rosina); d = CIMAROSA, *Il Matrimonio segreto*, aus dem Duett Carolina/Paolino im I. Akt (Stimme Carolina).

Während in den soeben zitierten Melodien und ihren Parallelen im Ottocento im 1. Takt 6 Silben »erledigt« werden, so hingegen in den folgenden — für die ich aus dem Ottocento keine Parallelen kenne — nur vier:

274

a = HASSE, *Arminio*, Terzett im I. Finale, Schlußabschnitt (Stimme Segeste); b = MOZART, *La Clemenza di Tito*, Rondo Sesto im II. Akt; c = CIMAROSA, *Il Matrimonio segreto*, Quartett im I. Akt, eröffnendes Solo Conte; d = id., *Il Matrimonio per raggiro*, aus dem Quartett im II. Akt (Stimme Babbione).

Die Folge einer solchen Kompositionsweise ist ein — besonders in Mozarts Melodie berückender — »level stress«, für den im italienischen Ottocento offenbar keine rechte Neigung mehr bestand.

Sich nahe sind Sette- und Ottocento hingegen wieder in folgenden Melodien[75], die durch »verrutschten« Auftakt gekennzeichnet sind:

275

a = Mozart, *Don Giovanni*, Arie Leporello im II. Akt; b = Paisiello, *La Molinara*, aus dem Quartett im I. Akt (Stimme Calloandro).

Entsprechend Beispiel 214:

276

a = Hasse, *Ruggiero*, Arie Bradamante I[9]; b = Paisiello, *Il Barbiere di Siviglia*, Arie Figaro im I. Akt; c = Mozart, *Don Giovanni*, Arie Donna Anna im II. Akt; d = id., *Così fan tutte*, Schlußensemble (Stimmen Fiordiligi/Dorabella).

---

[75] Vgl. Bsp. 212.

Entsprechend Beispiel 215:

277

a = HASSE, *Ruggiero*, Arie Leone I[6]; b = MOZART, *Le Nozze di Figaro*, Schlußensemble (Stimmen Susanna/Contessa); c = id., *Così fan tutte*, 3. Terzett Ferrando/Don
Alfonso/Guglielmo im I. Akt (Stimme Ferrando); d = id., ibid., schnelles Ensemble im
I. Finale (Stimme Ferrando); e = PAISIELLO, *La Molinara*, Beginn des II. Finales (Stimme Notaro); f = id., *Il Barbiere di Siviglia*, Schlußensemble (Stimme Rosina); g =
CIMAROSA, *Il Matrimonio segreto*, aus dem Duett Carolina/Paolino im I. Akt (Unisono);
h = id., ibid., aus dem Quartett im I. Akt (Stimme Carolina).

I A 2.
Entsprechend Beispiel 220:

Bsp. 279 →

a = MOZART, *Le Nozze di Figaro*, Duettino Susanna/Contessa im III. Akt (Stimme
Contessa); b = CIMAROSA, *Il Matrimonio segreto*, aus der Arie Carolina im I. Akt.

278

a = HASSE, *Arminio*, Arie Segimiro I[5]; b = id., ibid., Arie Marzia II[6]; c = id., *Ruggiero*, Arie Clotilde I[4]; d = id., ibid., Arie Ruggiero III[5]; e = GLUCK, *Orfeo* (1762), Schlußchor des II. Aktes (Sopran); f = TRAETTA, *Antigone*, aus dem Coro delle fanciulle im II. Akt (1. Sopran); g = MOZART, *Così fan tutte*, aus dem II. Finale (Stimme Fiordiligi).

Vgl. auch Beispiel 5a (Analecta mus. 12).

I A 3.

Entgegen den Verhältnissen im 19. Jahrhundert sind in der 2. Hälfte des 18. Jahrhunderts nur solche hier einschlägigen 6/8-Takt-Melodien beliebt, in denen die Verssilben 3—8 wie in II A 3 üblich vertont werden, der Doppel-Auftakt jedoch einen ganzen Takt beansprucht. Das bedeutet Zweieinhalb- bis Dreitaktigkeit.

279

Ganz ähnlich wie 279a in 3/8-Notierung:

280

HASSE, *Ruggiero*, Schlußchor (Sopran).

I B 1.
Entsprechend Beispiel 222:

281

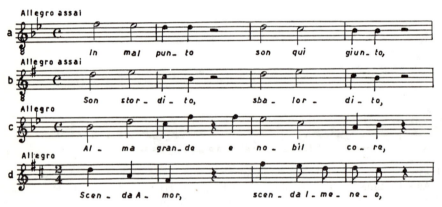

a = MOZART, *Le Nozze di Figaro,* Terzett des I. Aktes (Stimme Basilio); b = id., ibid., Ensemble in Schlußszene (Stimme Basilio/Don Curzio); c = id., Arie KV 578; d = id., *Idomeneo,* Schlußchor (Sopran).

Entsprechend Beispiel 223:

282

a = Mozart, *Idomeneo*, aus der Arie Idomeneo im I. Akt; b = id., *Le Nozze di Figaro*, Arie Bartolo im I. Akt; c = id., ibid., Cavatine Contessa im II. Akt; d = id., ibid., Arie Contessa im III. Akt; e = id., *Così fan tutte*, aus der Arie Fiordiligi im I. Akt; f = id., *La Clemenza di Tito*, Arie Tito im II. Akt.

I B 2.
Entsprechend Beispiel 226:

283

a = Mozart, *Idomeneo*, Arie Ilia im III. Akt; b = id., ibid., Arie Arbace im III. Akt; c = id., *Così fan tutte*, Duett Fiordiligi/Ferrando im II. Akt (Stimme Ferrando); d = id., *Don Giovanni*, aus der Arie Leporello im I. Akt; e = Paisiello, *Il Barbiere di Siviglia*, Duett Rosina/Bartolo im I. Akt (Stimme Rosina); f = Traetta, *Antigone*, Duett Ismene/Emone im I. Akt (Stimme Ismene); g = id., ibid., Arie Antigone im III. Akt.

II A 1.
Entsprechend den Beispielen 229/230:

284

a = Mozart, *Don Giovanni*, aus dem I. Finale (Stimme Zerlina); b = id., *Così fan tutte*, aus dem I. Finale (Stimmen Fiordiligi/Dorabella); c = Cimarosa, *Il Matrimonio segreto*, Duett Elisetta/Conte im II. Finale (Stimme Conte); d = Paisiello, *Il Barbiere di Siviglia*, Arie Bartolo im I. Akt.

Entsprechend Beispiel 231:

285

a = Mozart, *Don Giovanni*, Introduktion (Stimme Leporello); b = id., *Le Nozze di Figaro*, Arie Basilio im IV. Akt; c = id., ibid., aus dem II. Finale (Stimme Conte); d = id., *Così fan tutte*, Arie Guglielmo im II. Akt.

Entsprechend Beispiel 232:

286

a = Mozart, *Così fan tutte*, aus dem II. Finale (Stimme Don Alfonso); b = id., ibid., Duett Fiordiligi/Dorabella im II. Akt (Stimme Dorabella); c = id., *Don Giovanni*, Arie Elvira im II. Akt; d = id., *Così fan tutte*, 2. Terzett Ferrando/Don Alfonso/Guglielmo im I. Akt (Stimme Don A.).

Entsprechend den Beispielen 233—237 (viel seltener im Settecento):

287

a = Cimarosa, *Il Matrimonio segreto*, Arie Paolino im II. Akt; b = Mozart, *Così fan tutte*, Rondo Fiordiligi im II. Akt.

Überaus zahlreich dagegen ist der in Beispiel 238 gezeigte Typ im 18. Jahrhundert vertreten:

288

a = Mozart, *Le Nozze di Figaro*, Conte im IV. Finale; b = id., *Don Giovanni*, aus
dem I. Finale (Stimme Don Giovanni); c = id., ibid., Donna Anna in der Introduktion; d = id., *Così fan tutte*, Sextett im I. Akt (Stimme Don Alfonso); e = id., ibid.,
Arie Guglielmo im I. Akt (1. Fassung, KV 584); f = id., ibid., aus dem Rondo Fiordiligi im II. Akt; g = Hasse, *Arminio*, Arie Marzia II[6], Teil B; h = Gluck, *Orfeo*,
Orfeo im II. Akt; i = Cimarosa, *Il Matrimonio segreto*, Arie Carolina im I. Akt.

Entsprechend Beispiel 241:

289

a = Mozart, *Le Nozze di Figaro*, Sextett im II. Akt (Stimme Marzellina); b = id.,
Don Giovanni, Sextett im II. Akt (Stimme Don Ottavio); c = id., ibid., Arie Zerlina
im I. Akt.

Entsprechend Beispiel 242:

290

a = Gluck, *Orfeo*, Arie Orfeo im III. Akt; b = Mozart, *Così fan tutte*, Chor im I.
Akt (Sopran); c = id., *La Clemenza di Tito*, Duett Servilia/Annio im I. Akt (Stimme
Annio).

II A 1'.
Entsprechend Beispiel 245:

290 bis

Mozart, *Idomeneo*, Arie Arbace im II. Akt.

II A 1″.

Entsprechend Beispiel 246:

291

a = Mozart, *Le Nozze di Figaro*, Cherubino im IV. Finale; b = id., *Così fan tutte*, aus dem Quintett des I. Aktes (Stimme Fiordiligi); c = id., ibid., Despina im II. Finale; d = id., *Don Giovanni*, aus dem Quartett des I. Aktes (Stimme Don Ottavio); e = id., ibid., Don Ottavio im I. Finale; f = id., ibid., Don Giovanni im I. Finale; g = Paisiello, *Il Barbiere di Siviglia*, Terzett Giovinetto/Lo Svegliato/Bartolo (Stimme Bartolo); h = id., *Socrate immaginario*, Arie Mastr'Antonio im II. Akt.

Andere Notierung desselben Typs in langsamem Tempo[76]:

---

[76] Vgl. Bsp. 206.

292

a = Mozart. *Don Giovanni,* aus dem Quartett des I. Aktes, Stimme Don Giovanni;
b = Cimarosa, *Il Matrimonio segreto,* aus dem Terzett Carolina/Fidalma/Paolino im
II. Akt (Stimme Fidalma).

II A 2.
Entsprechend Beispiel 249:

293

a = Mozart, *Così fan tutte,* aus dem Sextett im I. Akt, Stimme Fiordiligi; b = id.,
Don Giovanni, Zerlina im I. Finale; c = Paisiello, *Il Barbiere di Siviglia,* Duett Con-
te/Bartolo im II. Akt (Stimme Bartolo).

II A 3.
Entsprechend den Beispielen 251—253:

294

a = MOZART, *Le Nozze di Figaro,* Chor im III. Akt (1. Sopran); b = id., *Don Giovanni,* Don Giovanni im II. Finale; c = id., ibid., Arie Zerlina im I. Akt; d = id., *Così fan tutte,* Arie Despina im II. Akt.

II A 3′.

Entsprechend Beispiel 254:

295

HASSE, *Arminio,* Arie Tusnelda I[7], Teil B.

II B 1.

Entsprechend Beispiel 255:

296

a = MOZART, *Don Giovanni,* Masetto im I. Finale; b = id., ibid., Don Giovanni im I. Finale; c = id., *Così fan tutte,* Don Alfonso im II. Finale; c = PAISIELLO, *Socrate immaginario,* Arie Don Tammaro im I. Akt.

Entsprechend den Beispielen 258 und 262:

297

a = MOZART, *Idomeneo*, Arie Idamante im I. Akt; b = CIMAROSA, *Il Matrimonio segreto*, Terzett Carolina/Fidalma/Paolino im II. Akt (Stimme Paolino); c = PAISIELLO, *Il Barbiere di Siviglia*, Conte im II. Finale.

II B 3.
Entsprechend Beispiel 267:

298

MOZART, *Le Nozze di Figaro*, Cavatine Barbarina im IV. Akt.

In der 2. Hälfte des Settecento sind mithin die meisten musikalisch-rhythmischen Typen des Ottocento ebenfalls gebräuchlich. Nicht begegnen im Settecento die breit angelegten Gestalten aus Gruppe I, die von den Rhythmen $\vert\,\cdot\,\cdot\,\vert$ oder $\vert\,\cdot\,\cdot\,\vert$ durchpulst werden; desgleichen kaum die breiten 6/8-Takt-Gestalten des Ottocento (I A 3, I B 3). Für den im Ottocento so beliebten Typ $\frac{4}{4}$ (II A 1, vgl. Beispiel 230) zeigt das Settecento (2. Hälfte) keine Liebe, obwohl es ihn kennt. Dasselbe gilt für die im 19. Jahrhundert so häufige Kombination Punktierung des Auftakts, des 2. und 4. Viertels (II A 1, vgl. Beispiel 234). Vor allem aber ist in Gruppe II das Fehlen zweier durch bestimmte Dehnungen charakterisierter Typen festzustellen: erstens des im Ottocento überaus geliebten Typs $\frac{4}{4}$

(II A I, vgl. Beispiel 244) und zweitens des im Ottocento auch sehr häufig be-
nutzten Typs 𝄴 ♩· ♪ | ♩ ♪ 𝄾 ♩· ♪ | ♩ ♪ 𝄾 (II B 1, vgl. Beispiel 257, auch
260). Desgleichen fehlt in der 2. Hälfte des 18. Jahrhunderts die forcierte Syn-
kopierung vom Schlage 𝄴 ♩· ♪ | ♩ ♩̄ ♩· ♪ | ♩ ♩̄ (II C).

DER DECASILLABO

An dieser Stelle wird nur vom eigentlichen Decasillabo gesprochen, dem mit starker metrischer Eigenart, und nicht vom Quinario doppio[77].
Der eigentliche Decasillabo ist charakterisiert durch feste Akzente auf der 3., 6.
und 9. Silbe.

> Metastasio, *Catone in Utica* I[6],
> Arie Cesare, 1. Strophe
>
> Nell'ardire che il seno ti accende
> Così bello lo sdegno si rende,
> Che in un punto mi desti nel petto
> Meraviglia, rispetto e pietà.
>
> Romani, *La Straniera*, Preghiera Alaide
> im II. Finale, 1. Strophe
>
> Ciel pietoso, in sì crudo momento
> Al mio labbro perdona un lamento.
> E' l'estrema favilla d'un foco
> Che fra poco più vita non ha.

In der italienischen Oper des Ottocento ähnelt ein guter Teil der musikalischen Decasillabo-Typen sehr stark bestimmten Ottonario-Typen. Heißt es in
Gruppe I A beim Ottonario z. B.:

𝄴 | ♩· ♫ | ♩· ♫ | ♩· ♫ | ♩ ♫ ♩ 𝄾 | (Rossini, *Mosè*, 2. Fassung, Duett
Do - v'e` mai quel co - re a - man - - te   Anaide/Amenofi im I. Akt, Ca-
baletta),

so beim Decasillabo:

𝄴 | ♩· ♫ | ♩· ♪ ♪ | ♩· ♪ ♪ | ♩· ♪ ♩ 𝄾 | (ibid., Schlußensemble des III. Fi-
Rad_dop - pia - te di ze - loe d'a - mo - - re   nales).

(Es müssen nur, um 2 Silben mehr unterzubringen, 2 Bindungen aufgelöst, d. h.
ihre Achtel einzeln textiert werden.)

---

[77] Vgl. Analecta musicologica 12, p. 274/275.

Heißt es beim Ottonario in Gruppe II A z. B.:

$\frac{4}{4}$ ♪· ♪ │♪ ♪·♪♪ ♪·♪ │♪ ♪

Da quel di che fin_no _ cen_te

(DONIZETTI, *Belisario*, Aria finale Antonina, 1. Tempo),

so beim Decasillabo:

$\frac{4}{4}$ ♪· ♪ │♪ ♪· ♪ ♪ ♪· ♪ │♪ ♪

V'e_ra un dì quan_do l'al_main_no_ cen_te

(id., *Parisina*, Cavatine Parisina im I. Akt, Cabaletta).

Ein anderes Beispiel aus Gruppe II A:
Heißt es beim Ottonario:

$\frac{4}{4}$ │ ♪ ♪ ♪ ♪ ♪ ♪ │♪ ♪

Ma nel_l'al_ma del_l'in _ gra_to

(VERDI, *Il Trovatore*, Azucena im Duett A./ Manrico im II. Akt),

so beim Decasillabo:

$\frac{4}{4}$ │ ♪ ♪ ♪ ♪ ♪ ♪ ♪ │♪♪ ♪

E sta l'o_dio che pre_pa_ra il fi _ o

(id., *Un Ballo in maschera*, Verschwörer in der Introduktion).

Übersicht über die Gruppen der Typen und ihre Gliederung:

Gruppe I: Abtaktig beginnende Melodien aller Taktarten.
    I A: Melodien ohne Zäsur. Vgl. p. 388 — p. 393.
    I B: Melodien mit Zäsur. Vgl. p. 393 — p. 394.

Gruppe II: Auftaktig beginnende Melodien aller Taktarten.
    II A: Melodien ohne Zäsur. Vgl. p. 395 — p. 403.
    II B: Melodien mit Zäsur. Vgl. p. 403.

Obwohl der Decasillabo sich nicht, wie Senario und Ottonario, aus zwei gleich-gestalteten Gliedern aufbaut, begegnen zahlreiche Melodien mit Zäsuren, so daß es sich, analog den Verhältnissen bei den Ottonario-Melodien, empfiehlt, die Unter-gliederung der Gruppen I und II vom Vorhandensein oder Fehlen der Zäsur ab-hängig zu machen. Es kann sich logischerweise nicht um eine »Mittelzäsur« han-deln, vielmehr um eine Zäsur nach der 4. Silbe.
Synkopik von der Vehemenz der in Senario und Ottonario beobachteten begegnet beim Decasillabo nicht.
Trotz seiner größeren Silbenzahl gilt genauso für den Decasillabo wie für den Ottonario: In der Gruppe I sind die Melodien meistens 4 Takte lang pro Vers, in der Gruppe II meistens 2 Takte (Ausnahmen: II A 1′ und II A 1″, vgl. p. 401; II A 3′, vgl. p. 402/403).

Partielle Dehnungen, gelegentlich Textwiederholungen sorgen auch bei den Decasillabo-Vertonungen für Abweichungen von der Regel, Abweichungen, die jedoch auch hier keineswegs so stark ins Gewicht fallen, daß nicht das Streben nach 2- und 4-Takt-Periodik deutlich bliebe. Hier ein Beispiel für partielle Dehnung. Es handelt sich um den Typ II A 3 (Beispiel 329). Seine normale Ausprägung ist die folgende: ♪♪♪│♪♪♪♪♪♪│♪♪ . Aus dieser Zweitaktigkeit wird aufgrund von Dehnung der 3. oder der 3. und 4. Silbe Dreitaktigkeit:

299

a = DONIZETTI, *Linda di Chamounix*, Arie Marchese im III. Akt, Cabaletta; b = VERDI, *Rigoletto*, Ballata Duca in der Introduktion.

Nun zu den einzelnen Gruppen und ihren Typen.

Gruppe I: Abtaktig beginnende Melodien aller Taktarten.

I A : Melodien ohne Zäsur.

I A 1: Melodien im 4/4 (2/4)-Takt.
Wie beim Ottonario, gibt es auch hier Melodien, deren zweigliedriger Auftakt einen ganzen Takt einnimmt, während die folgenden Silben auf 1½ Takte verteilt sind. Auch hier hat der Auftakt meistens die Gestalt │♪·   ♪ │ (entsprechend beim 2/4-Takt). (In der zweiten der in Beispiel 300 zitierten Melodien ist allerdings auch die Endung gedehnt[78].)

---

[78] Vgl. analoge Anfangs- und Schlußdehnungen beim Ottonario in Beispiel 213.

300

a = ROSSINI, *Semiramide*, Chor in der Arie Arsace im II. Akt (Tenor); b = DONI-
ZETTI, *La Regina di Golconda*, schnelles Ensemble (mit Chor) im I. Finale (Chor-
Tenor).

Meistens aber sind sämtliche Glieder des musikalischen Gebildes breit angelegt und
füllen gewöhnlich 4 Takte pro Vers.
Melodien mit 2 Halbe-Noten im 1. Takt (entsprechend beim 2/4-Takt; gelegentlich Auflösung einer der beiden ersten Noten in zwei):

301

a = VERDI, *Giovanna d'Arco*, Finale des Prologs, letztes Tempo (Stimme Giovanna);
b = DONIZETTI, *La Regina di Golconda*, Schlußchor der Introduktion (Sopran); c =
BELLINI, *Norma*, Kriegschor im II. Akt (Tenor); d = VERDI, *I Masnadieri*, Szene Car-
lo/Rolla/Chor im II. Finale (Stimmen Carlo/Rolla/Chor-Tenor).

In 6 Takten notiert, aber im selben Typ:

302

VERDI, *I Lombardi*, Schlußensemble (mit Chor) des I. Finales (Unisono).

Mit Beginn | ♪˙   ♪ | (sic oder figuriert; entsprechend im 2/4-Takt):

303

a = VERDI, *Oberto,* Quartett im II. Akt, das letzte Tempo eröffnendes Solo Leonora;
b = MERCADANTE, *L'Apoteosi d'Ercole,* die Stretta des I. Finales eröffnendes Solo Ercole; c = PACINI, *L'Ultimo giorno di Pompei,* Allegro-Ensemble (mit Chor) des I. Finales, eröffnendes Solo Ottavia; d = VERDI, *I Lombardi,* Inno de' Crociati im II. Akt (Tenor).

Mit Beginn | ♪˙   ♪♪ | :

304

a = ROSSINI, *La Gazza ladra,* Unisono Ninetta/Giannino im letzten Tempo des Quintetts (mit Chor) im II. Akt; b = DONIZETTI, *La Regina di Golconda,* Unisono Alina/Fiorina/Seide im letzten Tempo des I. Finales; c = VERDI, *Ernani,* Unisono Elvira/Ernani im Terzett Elvira/Ernani/Don Carlo des I. Aktes; d = id., *Alzira,* das letzte Tempo des I. Finales eröffnendes Solo Gusmano.

Sehr oft durchpulst, wie in den entsprechenden Ottonario-Vertonungen[79], die Figur | ♩· ♫ | das ganze Gebilde:

305

a = Rossini, *Mosè* (2. Fassung), Schlußensemble (mit Chor) des III. Finales (Stimme Mosè); b = id., *Ricciardo e Zoraide*, Terzett Zoraide/Zomira/Agorante im I. Akt, Cabaletta (eröffnendes Solo Agorante); c = id., *La Gazza ladra*, Arie Fernando im II. Akt, aus dem 1. Tempo; d = Donizetti, *Belisario*, das letzte Ensemble (mit Chor) des I. Finales eröffnendes Solo Antonina; e = id., *Lucrezia Borgia*, Duett Lucrezia/Duca im I. Akt, Cabaletta (2. Fassung), Stimme Lucrezia.

Gelegentlich tritt die Triole für die beiden Achtel ein:

306

a = Donizetti, *Fausta*, Solo Fausta in »Stretta dell'Introduzione«; b = Verdi, *Rigoletto*, Duett Gilda/Rigoletto im II. Akt, Cabaletta (Stimme Rigoletto).

---

[79] Vgl. Bsp. 216/217.

I A 2: (Zäsurlose) Melodien im 3/4 (3/8)-Takt.

Sind ihre beiden ersten Noten gleichlang, beanspruchen diese Melodien mehr als 4 Takte. Bei breitem Auftakt in der Relation lang-kurz dagegen ist Viertaktigkeit die Regel.

307

a = ROSSINI, *Semiramide*, Ensemble/Chor im I. Finale (Unisono); b = id., ibid., Unisono Semiramide/Arsace im I. Finale; c = BELLINI, *La Sonnambula*, Chor im II. Akt (Sopran); d = DONIZETTI, *Gemma di Vergy*, Coro di Arcieri im Beginn des I. Finales (Tenor); e = VERDI, *Ernani*, Unisono Ernani/Silva im II. Finale.

Es sei darauf hingewiesen, daß die in Beispiel 331 zitierten Melodien in ihrem Mittelstück den Melodien 307a—d strukturell ähnlich sind, sich grundsätzlich also nur durch die Auftakt-Gestalt von ihnen abheben. Die Grenzen, das gilt es auch an dieser Stelle zu betonen[80], sind durchaus fließend.

Melodien, die mit den von der Figur | 𝅘𝅥· 𝅘𝅥𝅮𝅘𝅥𝅮 | beherrschten 4/4-Takt-Gestalten korrespondieren:

---

[80] Vgl. p. 338.

308

a = DONIZETTI, *Anna Bolena*, Terzett Anna/Percy/Enrico im II. Akt, Cabaletta (Stimme Enrico); b = VERDI, *I Due Foscari*, Duett Lucrezia/Doge im I. Finale, Cabaletta (Stimme Lucrezia); c = id., ibid., Quartett im II. Akt, Unisono Lucrezia/Jacopo Foscari; d = id., *La Battaglia di Legnano*, Federico im II. Finale.

I A 3: (Zäsurlose) Melodien im 6/8-Takt.
Ich kenne nur e i n e Melodie:

309

DONIZETTI, *Lucia di Lammermoor*, schnelles Ensemble (mit Chor) im I. Finale (Unisono).

I B: Melodien mit Zäsur.
I B 1: Melodien im 4/4 (2/4)-Takt.

Mit Beginn $\frac{4}{4}$| ♪   ♪ | (sic oder mit figurativer Auflösung; entsprechend im 2/4-Takt):

310

a = BELLINI, *Il Pirata*, Chor im I. Akt (Tenor); b = DONIZETTI, *Gemma di Vergy*, Solo Guido in der Introduktion; c = id., *Anna Bolena*, Aria finale Anna, Cabaletta; d = VERDI, *Alzira*, »Brindisi« im II. Akt (Tenor).

Mit Beginn in der Relation lang-kurz:

311

a = DONIZETTI, *Parisina*, schnelles Ensemble (mit Chor) des I. Finales, Stimme Parisina; b = id., *Lucrezia Borgia*, Terzett Lucrezia/Gennaro/Duca im I. Finale, Schlußteil a 2 (Stimme Lucrezia); c = id., ibid., Duett Lucrezia/Duca im I. Akt, Cabaletta (1. Fassung).

I B 2: Melodien im 3/4 (3/8)-Takt.

Ich kenne keine einschlägigen Melodien.

I B 3: Melodien im 6/8-Takt.

Ich kenne nur eine Melodie:

312

VERDI, *Alzira*, Introduktions-Szene Otumbo/Chor (Stimmen Otumbo und Tenor).

Gruppe II: Auftaktig beginnende Melodien aller Taktarten.

II A: Melodien ohne Zäsur.

II A 1: Melodien im 4/4-Takt.

Melodien mit Gestalt $\frac{4}{4}$ ♪ ♪ | ♩ ♪ ♪ ♩ ♪ ♪ | ♩ ♩ (auch mit Verbreiterung

des Auftakts zu ♩ ♩ |):

313

a = VERDI, *Un Ballo in maschera*, Riccardo in der Introduktion; b = id., ibid., »Coro di Uffiziali e Gentiluomini« in der Introduktion (Tenor); c = id., *Aida*, Amonasro im II. Finale; d = DONIZETTI, *Parisina*, Chor im I. Finale (Tenor).

Mit durchgehender Achtelbewegung:

314

a = ROSSINI, *La Cenerentola*, Cavatine Dandini im I. Akt, Cabaletta; b = id., *La Gazza ladra*, das schnelle Ensemble (mit Chor) des I. Finales eröffnendes Solo Ninetta.

Die überwältigende Mehrheit der Melodien dieser Abteilung hat jedoch folgendes rhythmisches Gerüst: $\frac{4}{4}$ ♩. ♪ | ♩ ♩. ♪ ♩ ♩. ♪ | ♩ ♩ .

315

a = ROSSINI, *L'Italiana in Algeri*, Chor im I. Finale (Tenor); b = id., *Semiramide*, Schlußchor (Sopran); c = BELLINI, *Il Pirata*, Chor innerhalb der Arie Gualtiero im I. Akt (Tenor); d = id., *La Straniera*, Aria finale Alaide, 1. Tempo; e = DONIZETTI, *Lucrezia Borgia*, Orsini im Finale des Prologs; f = id., *Maria Stuarda*, Aria finale Maria, Cabaletta; g = id., *Parisina*, Cavatine Parisina im I. Akt, Cabaletta; h = VERDI, *Oberto*, Duett Cuniza/Riccardo im I. Akt, 1. Tempo (Stimme Cuniza); i = id., *Ernani*, Ernani im I. Finale; k = id., *Macbeth* (2. Fassung), Coro di Streghe in »Gran Scena delle Apparizioni« im III. Akt.

Des öfteren begegnet eine Pause im Gefüge (eine Pause, nicht eigentlich eine Zäsur):

316

a = DONIZETTI, *Fausta*, Aria finale Fausta, 1. Tempo; b = VERDI, *Nabucco*, Coro di Schiavi ebrei im III. Akt (Sopran).

Ja, nicht selten ist das ganze Gefüge mit Pausen durchsetzt. Das kann so aussehen:

317

a = VERDI, *I Due Foscari*, Eingangschor des III. Aktes (Sopran); b = id., *La Traviata*, Chor-Tenor im Beginn der 1. Szene.

Oder so:

318

a = DONIZETTI, *Maria Stuarda*, Cavatine Maria im II. Akt, Cabaletta; b = VERDI, *Un Giorno di regno*, Duett Edoardo/Cavaliere im I. Akt, Cabaletta (Stimme Edoardo); c = id., *Luisa Miller*, Arie Walter im I. Akt.

Eine 12/8-Takt-Parallele des soeben gezeigten Typs (315–318):

319

ROSSINI, *La Cenerentola*, Cavatine Dandini im I. Akt, 1. Tempo.

Gelegentlich wird die Punktierung noch weitergetrieben:

320

VERDI, *La Forza del destino*, Ballata des »Studente« im II. Akt.

Öfters bietet Verdi das 4. Viertel des Haupttakts statt in punktiertem Achtel und Sechzehntel in einer zweisilbig textierten Triole:

321

a = VERDI, *Ernani*, Congiura im III. Akt (Unisono Ensemble und Chor); b = id., *Un Ballo in maschera*, Renato (und Verschwörer) im III. Akt.

Melodien Verdis mit noch weitergehender Triolisierung (verbunden mit leichter Synkopierung):

322

a = VERDI, *Attila*, Duett Ezio/Attila im I. Akt, Cabaletta (Stimme Attila); b = id., *Giovanna d'Arco*, aus dem Introduktions-Chor (Unisono).

Melodien mit anderen Figuren im 3. und 4. Viertel:

323

a = VERDI, *Attila*, Cavatine Foresto im Prolog, Cabaletta; b = BELLINI, *La Sonnambula*, 2. Duett Amina/Elvino im I. Akt, 1. Tempo (Stimme Elvino).

Der beim Settenario und Ottonario so häufige Typ mit gleichmäßiger Dehnung des 1. und 3. Viertels des Haupttakts (Ottonario) ist beim Decasillabo selten:

324

VERDI, *Simon Boccanegra* (2. Fassung), Amelia im II. Finale.

Nicht selten ist jedoch die Hervorhebung des 1. und 3. Viertels des Haupttakts in einem leicht synkopischen Typ, der entsprechend auch beim Ottonario (seltener beim Settenario) vorkommt[81]:

---

[81] Vgl. Ottonario-Typ Beispiel 240.

325

a = ROSSINI, *Semiramide*, Arie Assur im II. Akt, 1. Tempo; b = DONIZETTI, *Roberto Devereux*, Duett Sara/Roberto im I. Akt, Cabaletta (Stimme Sara); c = id., *Gemma di Vergy*, Duett Gemma/Guido im I. Akt, Cabaletta (Stimme Gemma); d = VERDI, *Rigoletto*, Ensemble und Chor der Höflinge im I. Finale (Stimmen Borsa/Chor-Tenor); e = id., ibid., Arie Rigoletto im II. Akt.

Ausgesprochen wenig begegnet die beim Settenario und Ottonario so häufige Dehnung der 1. Note des Haupttakts in das 3. Viertel hinein (der Grund ist natürlich die dann unausbleibliche Zusammendrängung der Silben 4—8 auf sehr engem Raum). Ein Beispiel:

326

VERDI, *Aida*, Ramphis und Coro di Sacerdoti im IV. Akt.

II A 1': Breitere (auftaktige) 4/4-Takt-Gestalten mit einer II A 1 entsprechenden rhythmischen Struktur.

327

a = VERDI, *Giovanna d'Arco*, Giovanna im Finale des Prologs; b = id., *Nabucco*, »Profezia« Zaccaria im III. Finale.

II A 1'': Schmalere (auftaktige) 4/4-Takt-Gestalten mit einer II A 1 entsprechenden rhythmischen Struktur:

328

VERDI, *Un Ballo in maschera*, Verschwörer in der Introduktion.

II A 2: Auftaktige Melodien ohne Zäsur im 3/4 (3/8)-Takt.
Einschlägige Melodien mit Eigencharakter fehlen. Die vorhandenen auftaktigen 3/4-Takt-Melodien (ohne Zäsur), alle drei- und mehrtaktig[82], sind eher als strukturell mit II A 3 (6/8-Takt) zusammenhängend zu begreifen.

II A 3: Auftaktige Melodien ohne Zäsur im 6/8-Takt.
Die meisten Melodien gehorchen dem rhythmischen Schema

329

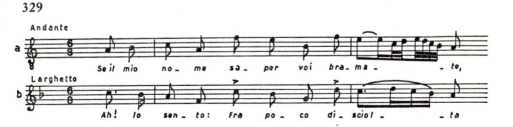

---

[82] Vgl. Beispiele 331 und 332 (II A 3').

a = ROSSINI, *Il Barbiere di Siviglia,* Canzone Conte im I. Akt; b = BELLINI, *Il Pirata,* Duett Imogene/Ernesto im II. Akt, 2. Tempo (Stimme Imogene); c = DONIZETTI, *La Regina di Golconda,* Duett Volmar/Belfiore im I. Akt, 2. Tempo (Stimme Belfiore); d = id., *Lucrezia Borgia,* Ballata Orsini im II. Akt; e = id., *Lucia di Lammermoor,* Normanno in der Introduktion; f = VERDI, *Luisa Miller,* Introduktion des II. Aktes (Unisono Laura/Chor); g = id., *Un Ballo in maschera,* Duett Amelia/Riccardo im II. Akt, 2. Tempo (Stimme Riccardo); h = id., ibid., Arie Amelia im II. Akt.

Im folgenden Beispiel ist der gleichmäßige Fluß zugunsten scharfer rhythmischer Prononcierung zerstört:

330

VERDI, *Un Ballo in maschera,* Terzett Amelia/Riccardo/Renato im II. Akt (Stimme Amelia).

II A 3': 3/4 (3/8)-Takt-Melodien, die mit den gezeigten 6/8-Typen eng verwandt sind.

Mit Beispiel 329 korrespondieren:

331

a = BELLINI, *I Puritani*, Duett Giorgio/Riccardo im II. Akt, 2. Tempo (Stimme Giorgio); b = VERDI, *Oberto*, Duett Leonora/Oberto im I. Akt, Cabaletta (Stimme Oberto).

Mit Beispiel 330 korrespondieren:

332

a = VERDI, *Ernani*, Duett Ernani/Silva im II. Finale, Cabaletta (Stimme Ernani); b = DONIZETTI, *Gemma di Vergy*, Duett Gemma/Tamas im II. Akt, Cabaletta (Stimme Tamas).

II B: Auftaktige Melodien mit Zäsur (nach der 4. Silbe).
An einschlägigen Melodien kenne ich nur solche im 4/4-Takt:

333

a = VERDI, *I Due Foscari*, Aria finale Doge, 1. Tempo; b = id., *I Masnadieri*, Massimiliano im III. Finale; c = id., *Rigoletto*, aus dem Duett Gilda/Rigoletto der Schlußszene (Stimme Gilda).

RÜCKBLICK AUF DIE 2. HÄLFTE DES 18. JAHRHUNDERTS

Der Decasillabo scheint in der 2. Hälfte des Settecento seltener als im Ottocento zu Libretto-Strophen benutzt worden zu sein. Auf der relativ schmalen Basis der durchgesehenen Opern wäre es wenig sinnvoll, die Melodien allzu stark aufzuschlüsseln. Die Melodien von Gruppe I werden in Bausch und Bogen zitiert, und nur die von Gruppe II werden etwas nach Typen sortiert. Eine Übersicht darüber, welche Typen des 19. Jahrhunderts in der 2. Hälfte des 18. Jahrhunderts fehlen, erscheint angesichts des geringen Materials zu gewagt.

Gruppe I:

334

a = MOZART, *Don Giovanni*, aus der Arie Leporello im I. Akt; b = PAISIELLO, *La Molinara*, »Canzoncina« im II. Akt (Stimme Calloandro); c = GLUCK, *Orfeo*, Introduktions-Chor des I. Aktes (Sopran); d = HASSE, *Arminio*, Arie Tullo III[13]; e = PAISIELLO, *Artaserse*, Arie Artabano I[3].

Gruppe II:

II A 1.

335

a = MOZART, *Le Nozze di Figaro*, Arie Cherubino im I. Akt; b = id., ibid., Antonio im II. Finale; c = id., *Don Giovanni*, aus der Arie Leporello im I. Akt; d = PAISIELLO, *Il Barbiere di Siviglia*, Conte im II. Finale; e = id., ibid., Figaro im III. Finale.

Mit weiter durchgeführter Achtelbewegung:

336

a = MOZART, *Così fan tutte*, Arie Ferrando im II. Akt; b = id., ibid., Ferrando im II. Finale.

Mit Punktierung (einer der Haupttypen im 19. Jahrhundert):

337

a = MOZART, *Le Nozze di Figaro*, Arie Figaro im I. Akt; b = PAISIELLO, *Socrate immaginaro*, Arie Donna Rosa im II. Akt.

II A 3:

338

a = MOZART, *Don Giovanni*, Szene Zerlina/Masetto/Chor im I. Akt, eröffnendes Solo Zerlina; b = id., ibid., Don Giovanni im I. Finale; c = id., *Le Nozze di Figaro*, Figaro im IV. Finale; d = CIMAROSA, *Giannina e Bernardone*, Bernardone im II. Finale.

DER ENDECASILLABO

Außer einem festen Akzent auf der 10. Silbe hat der Endecasillabo noch 1–3 Akzente in wechselnder Position, besonders gern entweder auf der 6. oder auf der 4. und 8. oder auf der 4. und 7. Silbe. Diesem Vers ist eine mehr oder weniger starke Zäsur eigen, die ebenfalls an keine bestimmte Stelle gebunden ist. Je nachdem, ob der erste Versteil der kürzere oder längere ist, spricht man von »endecasillabo a minore« oder »endecasillabo a maiore«.
Beispiel für den »endecasillabo a minore«:

> *Com'è gentil / la notte a mezzo april!*
>> (Donizetti und Giovanni Ruffini, *Don Pasquale*, Serenade im III. Akt)

Beispiel für den »endecasillabo a maiore«:

> *Da che tragge i suoi dì / Carlo sepolto*
>> (Domenico Gilardoni, *Bianca e Fernando*, komponiert von Bellini, Cavatine Filippo im I. Akt, 2. Tempo)

Vor der Zäsur können alle 3 Versendungen stehen, mit anderen Worten: Fällt beispielsweise ein starker Akzent auf die 4. Versilbe, so daß nach ihm die Zäsur eintritt, so kann der 1. Versteil ein Quinario tronco (besonders häufig und so

auch im zitierten *Don Pasquale*-Beispiel), Quinario piano oder (selten) Quinario sdrucciolo sein. Über die Zäsur hinweg ist jedoch (zum Unterschied von Quinario-, Senario-, Settenario-, Ottonario doppio) im Normalfall die Regel der »sinalefe« wirksam — was die Komponisten jedoch, wenn sie die Zäsur in der Melodie nachvollziehen, nicht beachten. (Auch gilt vor der Zäsur die tronco-Endung als einsilbig, die sdrucciolo-Endung als dreisilbig.)
Zwei Beispiele für Endecasillabo-Strophen (mit hinzugefügten Zäsurzeichen):

> Lorenzo Da Ponte, *Così fan tutte* II[13],
> Arie Don Alfonso, 1. Strophe
>
> Tutti accusan le donne, / ed io le scuso
> Se mille volte al dì / cangiano amore;
> Altri un vizio lo chiama / ed altri un uso:
> Ed a me par / necessità del core.

> »M. A.« [Giovanni Ruffini und Donizetti], *Don Pasquale*,
> Serenade im III. Akt, 1. Strophe
>
> Com'è gentil / la notte a mezzo april!
> E' azzurro il ciel, / la luna è senza vel:
> Tutt'è languor, / pace, mistero, amor!
> Ben mio, perchè / ancor non vieni a me?

Die musikalischen Themen, welche auf Endecasillabo-Verse komponiert sind, unterscheiden sich grundsätzlich dadurch, daß der Komponist einmal die Zäsur beachtet, das andere Mal nicht. Die Melodien mit Zäsur sind gewöhnlich länger (ab 2½ Takte) als die ohne Zäsur (meistens 2 Takte). Die musikalische Typik ist, im ganzen gesehen, geringer als die bei der Betrachtung der anderen Versarten festgestellte.

I. Melodien ohne Zäsur (in ihnen besonders vertont Verdi den Endecasillabo):

3 + 6 + 2 Silben (4/4- und 6/8-Takt; in e ein Sonderfall):

339

a = BELLINI, *I Puritani*, Romanze Giorgio im II. Akt; b = VERDI, *Aida*, Schlußduett
Aida/Radames (Stimme Aida); c = id., *I Masnadieri*, Coro de' Masnadieri im II. Akt
(Baß); d = id., *La Forza del destino*, Chor im III. Akt (Alt); e = id., *Aida*, Romanze
Aida im III. Akt.

2 + 7 + 2 Silben (mir nur im 4/4-Takt bekannt):

340

a = VERDI, *Il Trovatore*, »Racconto« Ferrando in der Introduktion; b = id., ibid.,
Chor innerhalb der Arie Leonora im IV. Akt (Tenor); c = id., *Aida*, aus dem Duett
Aida/Amonasro im III. Akt (Stimme Aida).

5 + 4 + 2 Silben:

341

VERDI, *Otello*, Preghiera Desdemona im IV. Akt.

II. Melodien mit Zäsur (»a maiore« in a und b, »a minore« in c und d):

342

a = ROSSINI, *Semiramide*, Chor in der Introduktion (Sopran); b = BELLINI, *Bianca e Fernando* (2. Fassung), Cavatine Filippo im I. Akt, 2. Tempo; c = DONIZETTI, *Don Pasquale*, Serenata Ernesto im III. Akt; d = VERDI, *Giovanna d'Arco*, Coro interno im Beginn des II. Finales (Sopran).

RÜCKBLICK AUF DIE 2. HÄLFTE DES 18. JAHRHUNDERTS

I. Ohne Zäsur:

343

a = MOZART, *Le Nozze di Figaro*, Arie Susanna im IV. Akt; b = CIMAROSA, *Giannina e Bernardone*, Canzone Giannina im I. Akt.

II. Mit Zäsur (»a maiore«):

344

a = MOZART, *Così fan tutte*, Arietta Don Alfonso im II. Akt; b = id., *Don Giovanni*, Canzonetta Don Giovanni im II. Akt.

Man sieht: Diese Melodien haben wieder einen ganz anderen Rhythmus als die aus dem Ottocento zitierten.

GAETANO DONIZETTI UND DER KAISERHOF ZU WIEN. NEUE DOKUMENTE

von *Lorenz Mikoletzky* (Wien)

Am Ende des Jahres 1841 begann Gaetano Donizetti diejenige Oper zu komponieren, die fünf Monate später in Wien begeisterten Beifall finden und ihrem Schöpfer den Weg zur Stellung des »Kammerkapellmeisters und Hofkompositeurs« ebnen sollte: *Linda di Chamounix*. Im März 1842 kam der Komponist in Wien an — dort alles andere als ein Unbekannter[1]. Am 4. Mai dirigierte er am Hofe Rossinis *Stabat Mater*, das er dann am 31. Mai im Redoutensaal einem weiteren Publikum zu Gehör brachte. Vorher jedoch, am 19. Mai, war die Premiere der Oper *Linda di Chamounix* (im Kärntnerthor-Theater). Die Wiener waren begeistert[2].

Der Hof suchte den berühmten und beliebten Komponisten an sich zu ziehen. Er entsann sich des Postens des kaiserlichen »Kammerkapellmeisters und Hofkompositeurs«, der nach dem Tode Franz Krommers (8. Januar 1831) 11 Jahre lang unbesetzt geblieben war. Am 2. Juli 1842 richtete Kaiser Ferdinand I. an seinen Oberstkämmerer Graf Johann Rudolph Czernin ein Kabinettsschreiben mit folgendem Wortlaut[3]:

> »Lieber Graf Czernin! Ich finde Mich bewogen, die seit einiger Zeit unbesetzt gebliebene Stelle eines Kammerkapellmeisters und Hofkompositeurs wieder zu besetzen. Mit dieser zum Oberstkämmererstabe gehörigen und Ihnen somit untergeordneten Stelle ist die Pflicht verbunden, in gewißen Perioden für die Hofkapelle, Hofoper oder sonstige Hoffeste geeignete Kompozitionen zu liefern, Kammer-Konzerte zu veranstalten oder zu leiten und in jenen Fällen, in welchen es erforderlich erkannt werden sollte, durch seine Einwirkung auf die Leitung des Hofopern-Orchesters deßen künstlerische Leistung in angemeßener Art zu befördern. Diese Stelle ver(leihe) Ich dem Gaetano Donizetti und (bewi)llige demselben hiefür nebst (der) siebenten Diäten-Claße jährlich (ei)nen Gehalt von zwey Tausend sechs (h)undert Gulden, ein Quartiergeld (von) vierhundert Gulden, dann eine (jähr)lich wiederkehrende Remu(n)erazion von Ein Tausend Gulden, (f)ür welche Letztere nach Verlan(ge)n periodisch für Meinen Hof entsprechende

---

[1] Vgl. Herbert WEINSTOCK, *Donizetti and the World of Opera in Italy, Paris, and Vienna in the First Half of the Nineteenth Century*, New York 1963, p. 178, ferner: Alfred LOEWEN-BERG, *Annals of Opera*, Genf ²1955, passim.

[2] In den Mai 1842 fällt auch die Komposition der *Ispirazioni viennesi* (vgl. H. Weinstock, a. a. O., p. 181).

[3] Finanzarchiv Wien, Präsidialakten 4846/1842, fol. 1 f. Der Akt ist etwas beschädigt; die in Klammern gesetzten Worte und Wortteile sind vom Verfasser sinngemäß ergänzt.

Musik-Komposizionen zu liefern seyn werden. Die Verpflichtung des Hof-Kom-
(po)siteurs zum Aufenthalte in (M)einer Residenz soll dem nicht (en)tgegenstehen,
daß derselbe von (Zei)t zu Zeit den zu einer Reise (in) das Ausland erforder-
lichen (l)ängeren Urlaub erhalte. Sie haben wegen sogleicher Vollziehung dieser
Meiner Entschliessung das Erforderliche zu veranlaßen, und hievon insbesondere
Meinen ersten Obersthofmeister und den Präsidenten Meiner allgemeinen Hof-
kammer die gehörige Mittheilung zu machen. Schönbrunn . . .«

Graf Czernin leitete das kaiserliche Schreiben an den ersten Obersthofmeister
Fürst Rudolph Colloredo-Mannsfeld weiter, der seinerseits, um die finanzielle
Seite der Ernennung zu regeln, ein Schreiben an den Hofkammerpräsidenten
Freiherr Carl Friedrich Kübeck von Kübau richtete, in welchem er den Vorna-
men des italienischen Maestro auf die deutsche Form Cajetan brachte. Er führte
unter anderem aus[4]:

»... Ich habe demnach die Ehre Eurer Excellenz dasselbe [das Kabinettsschrei-
ben] im Anbuge mitzutheilen, und wollen Dieselben es nach gemachtem Ge-
brauche an den kk. Herrn Oberstkämmerer zurückzuleiten belieben. Was die
Bezüge des Donizetti anbelangt, so weise ich demselben unter Einem den Gehalt
und das Quartiergeld vorschriftsmäßig bei dem kk. Hofzahlamte an; in Ansehung
der ihm bewilligten Remunerazion aber, sehe ich vorerst noch einer näheren Eröffnung des kk. Herrn Oberstkämmerers entgegen, da derselbe es angemessen
gefunden hat, über die Art der Flüßigmachung dieses Genußes sich allerhöchsten
Ortes anzufragen. Wien am 6ten Juli 1842«.

Acht Tage später, am 14. Juli, endete der Aktenlauf mit der Rückstellung des
Kabinettsschreibens durch Kübeck an Czernin.
Beide Teile hatten von dieser Ernennung ihren Vorteil. Der Kaiserhof, weil damit
ein Strahl des Ruhmes, der Donizetti in ganz Europa zuteil wurde, auf ihn
fiel. Donizetti, der sehr wohl wußte, daß sein großer Vorgänger im Amt — über
Krommer und Koželuch hinweg — Mozart gewesen war. Am 13. Juli 1842 schrieb
er an Antonio Vasselli[5]:

»... Tu mi volesti piazzato, ed eccomi *Imperial Regio Compositore di camera,
e direttore dei concerti privati di S.M.I.R. austriaca* con mille lire austriache al
mese, restando sei mesi a Vienna e sei a spasso: posto che avea Mozart. Eccomi
non più zingaro, ma in ispada e cappa ...«

Aus dem Brief geht auch hervor, wie hoch Donizetti die Freiheit — »*sei* [mesi] *a
spasso*« — zu schätzen wußte, die der Vertrag ihm zusicherte. Mit der Ernennung änderte sich an seinem Lebens- und Schaffensstil wenig. Im Grunde bedeutete ihm das Wiener Amt eine willkommene Auszeichnung, aber er war keineswegs, wie ein Krommer, darauf angewiesen.
Donizetti verließ Wien am 1. Juli 1842. Er sah es erst — nach dem triumphalen
Erfolg des *Don Pasquale* in Paris — im Januar des nächsten Jahres wieder. Am

---

4 Ebenda, fol. 2 f.
5 Zitat nach: Guido ZAVADINI, *Donizetti. Vita — Musiche — Epistolario*, Bergamo 1948, p. 618.

3. März dirigierte er in der Gesellschaft der Musikfreunde eines seiner *Ave Maria*[6]. Am 5. Juni leitete er die Premiere seiner neuen Oper *Maria di Rohan*. Wiederum ein großer Erfolg. Im Juli 1843 reiste er von Wien ab. In Paris fand unter seiner Leitung am 11. November 1843 die Premiere des *Dom Sébastien* statt. Die neapolitanische Premiere der *Caterina Cornaro* (12. Januar 1844) wurde hingegen nicht vom Komponisten betreut, der seit dem Dezember-Ende 1843 wieder in Wien weilte. Donizettis Schaffenskraft war nun erschöpft. Die Geschichte seiner Krankheit ist neuerdings von William Ashbrook und vor allem von Herbert Weinstock ausführlich erzählt worden[7]. Remo Giazotto hat interessante Dokumente vorgelegt[8]. Diese sollen hier durch ein Wiener Dokument ergänzt werden.

Am Wiener Hofe hatte man den in Paris weilenden kranken Donizetti nicht vergessen, man zeigte sich sehr besorgt um seinen Gesundheitszustand. Im Frühjahr 1846 wurde ein Arzt an die Seine geschickt, um *»verläßliche Nachrichten über den Gesundheits-Zustand des kk. Kammerkapellmeisters und Hofkompositeurs Donizetti zu erhalten«*[9]. Der Arzt Dr. (Anton) Weber kam mit der Nachricht zurück, daß der Fall hoffnungslos sei. Auch zu dieser Angelegenheit findet sich im Wiener Finanzarchiv ein Akt. Ein Schreiben des Oberhofmeisteramtes an den Hofkammerpräsidenten Kübeck informiert uns über die Kosten dieser Reise. Bezugnehmend auf eine kaiserliche Entschließung vom 30. Mai 1846, die lautet: *»Aus besonderer Gnade bewillige Ich, daß die hier angegebenen Auslagen zur Erforschung des Gesundheitszustandes Donizetti's nothwendig geworden sind, mittels einer außerordentlichen Dotation von den finanzen bedekt werden«*[10], ging am 3. Juni an Kübeck folgendes Schreiben ab[11]:

> »Mit dienstfreundlicher Berufung ... beehrt sich das kk. Oberbsthofmeisteramt Euere Excellenz um die gütige Beauftragung der kk. Staatszentralkasse zu ersuchen, dem kk. Hofzahlamte, gegen gehörige Empfangsbestättigung, den Betrag von Achthundert fünf und Siebzig Gulden CM. als eine extraordinäre Dotazion des kk. Hofzahlamtes, zur Bestreitung der Auslagen, auß Anlaß einer, auf a.h. Befehl stattgefundenen Reise des Doktor Weber nach Paris, um verläßliche Nachrichten über den Gesundheitszustand des kk. Kammerkapellmeisters und Hofkompositeurs Donizetti, zu erlangen, — ordnungsmäßig zu erfolgen.«

Der Auftrag an die Staatszentralkasse erfolgte bald darauf, und am 2. Juli 1846 wurde mit der Verständigung des Oberbsthofmeisteramtes, daß die Angelegenheit erledigt wurde, ein Schlußpunkt gesetzt*.

---

[6] Vgl. hierzu G. Zavadini, a. a. O., p. 660/661.
[7] William Ashbrook, *Donizetti*, London 1965; Herbert Weinstock: vgl. Fußnote 1.
[8] Remo Giazotto, *Donizetti ospite d'onore fra i dementi di Ivry*, in: Nuova Rivista Musicale Italiana II, 1968, p. 725—734.
[9] Finanzarchiv Wien, Präsidialakten 4848/1846, fol. 1.
[10] Ebenda.
[11] Ebenda, fol. 2.
* Für mannigfache Hilfe bin ich Dr. Friedrich Lippmann, Rom, und Otto Biba, Wien, verpflichtet.

DER BRIEFWECHSEL VERDI–NUITTER–DU LOCLE
ZUR REVISION DES *DON CARLOS*

von *Ursula Günther* (Paris)

Teil I

»Sul ›rifacimento‹ del 1883 esistono documenti numerosi del più alto interesse.«
Mit dieser vielversprechenden Feststellung beginnt im IV. Band der *Carteggi
verdiani* von Alessandro Luzio ein nur einseitiges Kapitel über die *Rifusione del
»Don Carlos«*[1]. Luzio verdanken wir in der Tat die frühesten Hinweise auf die
Zusammenarbeit Verdis mit Charles Nuitter und Camille Du Locle bei der Umformung des ursprünglich fünfaktigen *Don Carlos* in eine vieraktige Version.
Schon 1935, im II. Band der *Carteggi verdiani*, veröffentlichte Luzio einen Briefentwurf von 1882 aus den *Copialettere* Giuseppina Strepponis[2]. Er sprach dabei
vermutungsweise von einer Korrespondenz mit dem Librettisten Camille Du
Locle, bei der Giuseppina assistiert habe.
1947, im ersten Kapitel des IV. Bandes der *Carteggi*[3], enthüllte Luzio dann
selbst, daß es zwischen Verdi und Du Locle 1875 wegen einer finanziellen Affäre
zu einem ernsthaften Zerwürfnis gekommen war: 1870 hatte Verdi seinen
Freund gebeten, in Paris die ersten 50 000 Franken für die Komposition der
Aida für ihn entgegenzunehmen. 2000 Franken stiftete er unaufgefordert für
die Verwundeten des deutsch-französischen Krieges. Die restliche Summe sollte
Du Locle für den Ankauf von *»cartelle di rendita italiana«* verwenden. Um
seinem Freund, der seit kurzer Zeit an der Leitung der Opéra-Comique beteiligt
war, behilflich zu sein, überließ er ihm die Verwaltung dieser Papiere. Aber
1875, als Verdi das Geld dringend für eigene Zwecke benötigte, war Du Locle,
seinerzeit alleiniger Direktor der dem Ruin entgegensteuernden Opéra-Comique,
nicht in der Lage, Verdis Bitte um Übergabe der Effekten zu entsprechen. Der
Komponist sah sich daher gezwungen, einen Anwalt einzuschalten und schließlich die Gerichte bemühen zu lassen. Noch 1883 verkehrte deshalb Verdi mit seinem einstigen Freund verständlicherweise nur über einen »intermediario«, Charles Nuitter, den Archivar der Pariser Oper.

---

[1] Op. cit., Roma 1947, S. 207/208.
[2] Op. cit., S. 50/51; es handelt sich um einen Entwurf für Verdis Brief vom 9. Juni 1882, der
auf französisch formuliert ist.
[3] Op. cit., S. 5—27: *Come fu composta l'›Aida‹*; vgl. S. 26/27.

Luzio verfolgte mit dieser Veröffentlichung vor allem die Absicht, einer Publikation Prod'hommes[4] entgegenzuwirken, die den Anschein erweckt hatte, Verdi hätte sich gegenüber Du Locle und Nuitter ungerechtfertigt verhalten und dadurch den Bruch der seit 1866 freundschaftlichen Beziehungen verursacht[5]. Als Beweis für die stets großzügige Haltung Verdis und für die sich anbahnende Versöhnung zitierte Luzio zwei kurze Sätze aus Briefen Nuitters und Du Locles von 1883[6]. Im eingangs erwähnten Kapitel des gleichen Bandes gab Luzio dann zwei weitere Briefe Nuitters an Verdi und einen Antwortentwurf des Maestro bekannt, freilich ohne chronologisch und sachlich die richtigen Bezüge herzustellen[7].

Bis vor kurzem noch beschränkte sich das Wissen um die Revision des *Don Carlos*-Librettos auf diese sechs Zitate, aber da die beiden ersten Bände der *Carteggi verdiani* nur schwer zugänglich sind, wurden eigentlich nur die drei zuletzt erwähnten Dokumente bekannt, zumal Franco Abbiati nur diese in sein Standardwerk übernahm. Abbiati stützte sich dabei offenbar ausschließlich auf Luzios Publikation, verwandelte den »Vermittler Nuitter« aber in einen »*collaboratore letterario ... affiancato da Du Locle*«[8], so daß die Revision des Librettos seither stets beiden Franzosen gemeinsam zugeschrieben wird.

Diese weitverbreitete Ansicht entspricht aber keineswegs den Tatsachen, wie jeder feststellen wird, der die hier folgenden Dokumente zur Revision des *Don Carlos* genau studiert. Im August 1972 auf dem Kongreß der IGM in Kopen-

---

[4] Jacques Gabriel PROD'HOMME, *Lettres inédites de G. Verdi à Camille du Locle (1868—1874)*, in: La Revue Musicale X, 1928—29, Nr. 5, S. 97—112, und Nr. 7, S. 25—37. Diese von Luzio zitierte Auswahl der Briefe Verdis in französischer Übersetzung ist inhaltlich identisch mit der zuvor erschienenen englischen Version unter dem abweichenden Titel: *Unpublished Letters from Verdi to Camille Du Locle (1866—1876)*, in: The Musical Quarterly VII, 1921, S. 73—103. Beide Veröffentlichungen enden ohne nähere Erklärung mit Du Locles Schreiben vom 24. Februar 1874. Die Briefe von 1875 und 1876 werden ebensowenig erwähnt wie der wahre Grund des Zerwürfnisses. Stattdessen hat Prod'homme die Kopie eines Briefes beigefügt, in dem Du Locle seiner Frau die Entstehung des *Aida*-Librettos erklärt und sich beklagt: »*j'ai été mal récompensé. Moi qui trouve toujours que tout le monde a raison contre moi, com-[m]ent excuser Verdi d'avoir pris, par-dessus le marché, les droits de traduction du pauvre Nuitter?*« Vgl. zu diesem Schreiben das Postscriptum (nach Teil II).

[5] Verdi lernte Du Locle und Nuitter im Dezember 1865 in Paris kennen, als beide Librettisten sich um eine französische Fassung von *La forza del destino* bemühten, die eigentlich noch vor dem *Don Carlos* an der Pariser Oper zur Aufführung gelangen sollte. Vgl. hierzu Ursula GÜNTHER, *La genèse de Don Carlos, opéra en cinq actes de Giuseppe Verdi, représenté pour la première fois à Paris le 11 mars 1867*, in: Revue de Musicologie LVIII, 1972, S. 16—64, s. S. 35.

[6] *Carteggi verdiani*, vol. IV, S. 27.

[7] Luzio zitiert (ibidem, S. 207/208) nacheinander Briefe vom 7. und 2. Dezember sowie vom 11. Oktober 1882, interpretiert den letzten aber als Antwort auf den zweiten, obwohl unmißverständlich von zwei verschiedenen Szenen des *Don Carlos* die Rede ist.

[8] Franco ABBIATI, *Giuseppe Verdi*, Milano 1959, vol. IV, S. 201/202.

hagen habe ich bereits dargelegt, wie umfangreich das Material zu diesem Fra-
genkomplex wirklich ist[9]. Erhalten geblieben sind:

1. ein dreiseitiger Entwurf zur Umgestaltung des *Don Carlos* in eine vieraktige
   Oper, notiert von Charles Nuitter vermutlich bei der ersten Diskussion über
   dieses Projekt während einer Zusammenkunft mit Verdi im Hôtel de Bade
   im Mai 1882,
2. 21 Briefe Verdis an Charles Nuitter (zwei auch als Kopien von der Hand
   Nuitters), geschrieben zwischen dem 9. Juni 1882 und dem 23. Februar 1883,
3. 13 Briefe Nuitters an Verdi (einer davon nur als Entwurf), geschrieben zwischen dem 13. Mai 1882 und dem 21. März 1883,
4. ein Brief Du Locles an Nuitter vom 9. Februar 1883 sowie
5. 62 von Du Locle einseitig beschriebene Blätter mit einer ausführlichen Stel-
   lungnahme zu den Vorschlägen Verdis (17 Seiten), mit kurzen Notizen und
   mit den für die vieraktige Version neuerfundenen Versen. Nuitter hat dem
   Komponisten diese Mitteilungen Du Locles nach und nach in Form von Kopien zugestellt. Daher sind sie teilweise identisch mit dem Inhalt des 12. Heftes von Verdis Arbeitslibretto, das in seiner Bibliothek in Sant'Agata verwahrt wird[10].

Aus diesem Material geht eindeutig hervor, daß es sich um eine indirekte Korrespondenz zwischen Verdi und Du Locle gehandelt hat. Verdis Briefe gewäh-
ren Einblick in all das, was der Komponist dem Librettisten durch Nuitter hat
mitteilen lassen. Die von Du Locle an Nuitter übersandten Mitteilungen und
Verse sind in Paris kopiert und dem Komponisten in einer gut lesbaren Form
zugestellt worden. Nuitters Ansichten können allenfalls bei der Ausarbeitung des
von ihm notierten Entwurfes zur Umarbeitung eine Rolle gespielt haben. Anschließend hat sich der Archivar der Pariser Oper ganz bewußt auf die Rolle des
Vermittlers beschränkt und nie persönlich an der Diskussion beteiligt. Abgesehen
von wenigen Ausnahmen sind seine Briefe Begleitschreiben ohne Belang, nützlich
nur für die Datierung der von Du Locle übersandten Verse. Daher ist verständlich, daß Verdi nicht alle Briefe Nuitters aufbewahrt hat. Mindestens acht müssen
verlorengegangen sein.

Die meisten der oben unter 1, 2 und 5 erwähnten Dokumente stammen aus dem
von Charles Nuitter geordneten Archiv der Pariser Oper, befinden sich aber seit

---

[9] Der Vortrag *Zur Entstehung der zweiten französischen Fassung von Verdis Don Carlos* wird
im Kongreßbericht erscheinen.
[10] Genaue Angaben über die in Sant'Agata befindlichen Teile des Arbeitslibrettos enthält mein
Artikel über *Le livret français de »Don Carlos«* — *le premier acte et sa révision par Verdi*,
in: *Atti del II° congresso internazionale di studi verdiani*, Parma 1971, S. 91/92. Der Inhalt des 12. Heftes wird dort folgendermaßen beschrieben:

Note sur des projets de modification au livret de Don Carlos	9 Seiten
Akt I, Varianten zum Choeur de fête	1/2 Seite
Akt II, Varianten der Szenen 2 und 3	2 1/2 Seiten
Varianten für die Szene Philippe — Rodrigue	5 Seiten

1932 in den Archives Nationales[11]. Dadurch entgingen diese Schätze der Aufmerksamkeit Gattis und Abbiatis. Schon im Frühjahr 1971 stieß ich im Verlauf meiner vom Centre National de la Recherche Scientifique geförderten Arbeit[12] über die Frankreichaufenthalte Verdis bei Nachforschungen in den Archives Nationales auf eine Fülle neuen Materials zu den Aufführungen der Werke Verdis an der Pariser Oper. Bekannt wurde meine Entdeckung im April 1972 durch Pressemeldungen[13] und kurz darauf durch einen Vortrag Andrew Porters[14], der sich im Frühjahr 1972 das Material angesehen hatte. Im Juni 1972 auf dem III° congresso internazionale di studi verdiani in Mailand konnte ich dann selbst kurz über die »*Documents inconnus concernant les relations de Verdi avec l'Opéra de Paris*« berichten[15] und darauf hinweisen, daß es gerade zur Entstehungsgeschichte des *Don Carlos* sehr viel aufschlußreiches Material gibt. Die meisten Dokumente betreffen selbstverständlich den fünfaktigen *Don Carlos*, der am 11. März 1867 in bereits verkürzter Form seine Uraufführung erlebte[16]. Das den *Don Carlos* betreffende Dossier[17] enthält aber auch eine kleine Mappe mit der Aufschrift »*1882/1883*«, in der Charles Nuitter Belege zur Revision des Librettos gesammelt hat: seine selbstgeschriebenen Entwürfe und Kopien, die 21 Briefe Verdis und die 62 von Du Locle übersandten Blätter. Die Briefe Du Locles scheint Nuitter vernichtet zu haben bis auf einen einzigen, den er an Verdi weitergeleitet hat, ganz offensichtlich in der Absicht, eine Versöhnung der zerstrittenen Freunde herbeizuführen.

Die übrigen Dokumente, d. h. jenes Schreiben Du Locles und die Briefe Nuitters an Verdi[18] werden von den Erben des Komponisten in Sant'Agata verwahrt. Dott.ᵃ Gabriella Carrara Verdi war so liebenswürdig, mir für diese Publikation Kopien zur Verfügung zu stellen und ihre Mitarbeit bei der Entzifferung der

---

[11] Charles NUITTER, *Note relative aux Archives et à la Bibliothèque de l'Opéra*, Paris 1880; Et. GUILLEMOT, *Le versement des Archives de l'Opéra aux Archives Nationales*, in: Revue des Bibliothèques XXXIX (42), 1932, S. 385—391; J. G. PROD'HOMME, *Etat alphabétique sommaire des Archives de l'Opéra*, in: Revue de Musicologie XLVIII, 1933, 193—205; *Archives du Théâtre national de l'Opéra (AJ XIII 1 à 1466)*, Inventaire par Brigitte LABAT-POUSSIN, Paris 1972 (im Druck).

[12] Besonderen Dank für die Förderung meiner thèse de doctorat d'état ès-lettres schulde ich Herrn Prof. Jacques Chailley, Madame Nanie Bridgman und Madame Hélène Charnassée.

[13] Die Meldung erschien am 14. April 1972 in *Le Monde* und *Combat*; außerdem wurde sie über *Agence France Presse* weltweit verbreitet.

[14] Vgl. die Veröffentlichung des Vortrags vom 15. April 1972 über *The Making of »Don Carlos«* in: Proceedings of the Royal Musical Association, 98, 1972, S. 73—88.

[15] Im Druck in den *Atti del III° congresso internazionale di studi verdiani*.

[16] Die reich dokumentierte Entstehungsgeschichte des fünfaktigen *Don Carlos* von 1867 wird in meiner zweiteiligen Studie beschrieben, die in Anmerkung 5 zitiert ist.

[17] *AJ XIII 505* (Mise d'ouvrages 1865—1867).

[18] In Sant'Agata werden insgesamt 15 Briefe Nuitters an Verdi verwahrt, davon einer im *Copialettere* Verdis (vgl. Alessandro LUZIO, *I Copialettere di Giuseppe Verdi*, Milano 1913, S. 318); 13 Briefe gehören zur Korrespondenz der Jahre 1882/83, die beiden anderen datieren von 1892 und 1895.

Handschrift des Maestro zuzusagen. Zu danken habe ich den Doct.[es] Gabriella und Alberto Carrara Verdi ferner für Kopien sämtlicher Briefe Camille Du Locles und Léon Escudiers an Verdi sowie für Kopien aus den *Copialettere* Giuseppina Strepponis. Diese zum Teil unbekannten Unterlagen erlauben es, auch auf die noch ungeklärten Details der Vorgeschichte des Briefwechsels einzugehen.

Abbiati konnte bereits in groben Zügen klären, wie es zur finanziellen Affäre gekommen ist, die Verdi und Du Locle entzweit hat. Er veröffentlichte drei Mahnbriefe Verdis[19], aus denen hervorgeht, daß Du Locle nicht nur die oben erwähnten Papiere, sondern auch die Zinsen für 1875 und für das erste Halbjahr 1876 schuldig geblieben war. Durch ihn wissen wir, daß sich Verdi nach diesen erfolglosen Bemühungen während seines Pariser Aufenthaltes im Frühjahr 1876 brieflich an den Schwiegervater Du Locles wandte, an Emile Perrin[20], einst Leiter der Pariser Oper und nunmehr Direktor der Comédie-Française. Der vom Komponisten auf italienisch formulierte Brief, der auch in einer Übersetzung von Giuseppina erhalten geblieben ist[21], läßt erkennen, daß Verdi um eine gütliche Einigung bemüht blieb und jeden Skandal vermeiden wollte. Verdi berichtet Perrin von einem Brief, den Du Locle ihm am 24. Oktober 1870 »per ballon monté« aus dem belagerten Paris geschickt hatte und aus dem hervorgeht, daß »*les coupons au nombre de 77 et constatant 48.000 fr. de rente*« auf dem Konto einer Comtesse Mollien deponiert waren. Die »*Contessa M.*« wird auch in zwei Briefen erwähnt, die Verdi nach der Abreise aus Paris an seinen Verleger Léon Escudier gerichtet hat[22].

Offensichtlich hatte Verdi die Hoffnung gehegt, von jener Dame, einer alten Tante Du Locles, entschädigt zu werden, ohne einen Prozeß anstrengen zu müssen. Madame Du Locle war es jedoch gelungen, einen Brief Escudiers an die Comtesse abzufangen und sich direkt mit Verdis Anwalt in Verbindung zu setzen. Verärgert über das inkorrekte Verhalten der Frau Du Locles wie über die unwürdige Behandlung, die ihm deren Vater, Emile Perrin, zugemutet hatte, gab Verdi die Anweisung, nunmehr gerichtlich vorzugehen. Ein Jahr später äußerte Emanuele Muzio, Verdis Schüler und Freund, in einem von Abbiati zitierten Brief an Ricordi[23]: »*fu una fortuna per Verdi l'avere fatto il processo l'anno scorso, perché avrà il suo denaro avendo la garanzia della zia che è ricchissima e molto vecchia.*«

---

[19] ABBIATI, op. cit., vol. III, S. 778/779.

[20] Ibidem, S. 803/804.

[21] Abbiati gibt den italienischen Entwurf, der zusammen mit der Übersetzung lose im *Copialettere* Verdis liegen soll, unter dem Datum »23 maggio« wieder. Zur Kritik der Datierung vgl. die Darstellung auf S. 426.

[22] ABBIATI, op. cit., Vol. III, S. 802.

[23] *Verdi*, vol. IV, S. 41; der Brief Muzios vom 12. Juni 1877 wird im Archiv des Hauses Ricordi unter der Nummer 342 verwahrt. Für die Übersendung von Kopien einiger Briefe Muzios möchte ich Signora Luciana Pestalozza herzlich danken.

In der Verdi-Literatur sind keine weiteren Einzelheiten über die Affäre Du Locle bekannt geworden, obwohl mehrere Dokumente existieren, die in diesem Zusammenhang Erwähnung verdienten. Nur wer die Beweise ungetrübter Freundschaft und vollen Vertrauens aus der bewegten Kriegszeit 1870/71 kennt und weiß, wie sehr man in Sant'Agata um die Pariser Freunde gebangt hat, nur wer die diskreten Ermahnungen gelesen hat, die Giuseppina ihrem Freund Camille und seiner Frau Marie zukommen ließ, wird ermessen können, daß der Ruin Du Locles für Verdi wie für Giuseppina eine menschliche Tragödie war, die sie zutiefst getroffen hat, die zu verhindern beide aber nicht in der Lage waren. Die unbekannten Briefe und Briefentwürfe aus der Zeit von 1870—1876, die im folgenden zitiert werden, lassen die besonderen Qualitäten und schätzenswerten Charakterzüge, aber auch die menschlichen Schwächen jenes Künstlers erkennen, der Verdi und mehr noch Giuseppina unter allen französischen Freunden der liebste gewesen ist[24]. Zugleich machen sie verständlich, warum Du Locle gerne bereit war, einer indirekten Zusammenarbeit zuzustimmen, bei der er sich allenfalls bescheiden als »Autor dieser Zeilen« zu erkennen gab, und warum Nuitter sich während der Korrespondenz von 1882/83 bemühte, den Namen seines Freundes möglichst zu vermeiden. Erst nach Beendigung der Revision des *Don Carlos*-Librettos gelang es Nuitter, eine Aussöhnung der beiden Kontrahenten in die Wege zu leiten. Ab 1885 hat Verdi die Briefe Du Locles dann wieder gesammelt, wie in der Zeit engster Verbindung, von 1866 bis 1875[25].

»St Agata 5 Décem[bre] 1870

Cher ami

Vous pouvez bien penser avec quel bonheur ma femme et moi, nous avons reçu de vos nouvelles et comme nous désirons que les malheurs qui vous accablent, aient bientôt un terme! Vous n'ignorez pas combien nous vous aimons, et combien, quoique étrangers, nous aimons la France, et votre beau Paris!

Maintenant, veuillez me pardonner, si au milieu de vos graves préoccupations, j'ose vous dire un mot de mes affaires. — Vous me dites, que Mr Mariette est enfermé dans Paris. Je n'ai pas d'observations à faire à ce propos et s'il a voulu participer au sort de sa Patrie, je ne puis que l'admirer! Mais je trouve étrange, que la direction du Caire, ne m'ait jamais écrit un mot! Cette négligence me blesse, et je pourrais bien dire *»J'ai fini mon travail, j'ai rempli les conditions de mon traité, remplissez les vôtres. Si les décors et les costumes sont à Paris, cela ne me regarde pas.«*

Je ne désire pas en venir à ces déclarations, mais je répète, cette négligence de la direction du Caire, ne me satisfait nullement!. et d'autant plus elle me blesse, qu'ayant

---

[24] PROD'HOMME weist darauf hin, daß Du Locle einer von Verdis Wahlfreunden gewesen sei und der Komponist auch in rein geschäftlichen Briefen nie versäumt habe, einige herzliche Worte einfließen zu lassen (vgl. La Revue Musicale X, Nr. 5, S. 99, und MQ VII, S. 74).

[25] Die Korrespondenz der beiden Freunde erlosch erst nach 1896, wie aus Du Locles Briefen hervorgeht. Von Verdis Briefen aus der zweiten Periode wird nur einer in der Pariser Oper verwahrt: Es handelt sich um einen Brief von 1886, der irrtümlich unter die Briefe von 1866 geraten ist.

écrit à Mr Mariette (avec autorisation d'ouvrir la lettre, s'il n'était pas au Caire) on ne se donne même pas la peine, d'accuser réception de ma lettre! —

Pardon, pardon cher Du Locle de vous avoir occupé de moi. — Je désire, j'espère pouvoir vous embrasser bientôt. Madame Du Locle a écrit à ma femme qui s'unit à moi pour vous dire mille et mille choses pleines de sincère et chaude amitié. —

Addio addio
G. Verdi

Monsieur Camille Du Locle
   Rue Lafayette 36 Paris«

Mit diesem noch unveröffentlichten Brief aus der Sammlung der Pariser Oper[26] antwortete Verdi auf ein Schreiben, das Du Locle im November per Ballon aus der belagerten Hauptstadt schaffen konnte[27]. So warmherzige Formulierungen wie zu Beginn und am Schluß dieses Briefes hat Verdi nur selten verwendet, aber sie werden noch bei weitem übertroffen von den bewegten Worten, mit denen Verdi und seine Frau auf die Kapitulation und einen erschütternden Bericht Du Locles reagierten[28]. Am 4. Februar 1871 schrieb Joséphine Verdi unter anderem:

»Je vous vois d'ici avec vos éminentes qualités d'homme, et votre exquise délicatesse, presque féminine, secourir, encourager, consoler ces glorieuses victimes d'une guerre barbare, qui ont trouvé quelque baume à leur maux, sous votre toit hospitalier. Je dis encore: Soyez bénis!! ... vous avez à Gênes deux coeurs qui vous aiment, et deux amis!«

Verdi fügte diesem Brief seiner Frau noch eine ganze Seite hinzu[29], um seinem Schmerz und seinem Mitleid persönlich Ausdruck zu geben:

»Caro Du Locle
Voi mi conoscete, e so che mi credete se vi dico, che io soffro come Voi, e che il mio dolore eguaglia il vostro, per le grandi sventure toccate alla vostra patria. Noi lontani dai luoghi, vedevamo chiaramente le cose, e si prevedeva l'immensa catastrofe. Malgrado ciò, la notizia ci è venuta come inaspettata, perchè la speranza non abbandona mai, specialmente chi soffre! — Che posso io dirvi? ... Maledire con voi? ... Nò! Voi di Parigi tanto eroici nella resistenza, siate ora grandi e rassegnati nella sventura. Siate cauti, e l'avvenire, lo spero, vi sarà propizio. — È inutile vi dica, che avete in me un'amico che vi ama moltissimo, e su cui potete contare in tutto e per tutto. —

---

[26] Bibliothèque de l'Opéra, *Lettres autographes de Verdi à Camille Du Locle*, 1870, Nr. 14. Beim Zitieren der Dokumente wird die originale Schreibweise nur in der Akzentsetzung korrigiert.

[27] Vgl. ABBIATI, *Verdi*, vol. III. S. 410.

[28] Vgl. PROD'HOMME, op. cit., La Revue Musicale X, Nr. 7, S. 26/27, und die Übersetzung in MQ VII, S. 93.

[29] Die Zeilen Verdis sind von Prod'homme nur in französischer bzw. englischer Übersetzung veröffentlicht worden (ibidem, S. 27 bzw. 93). Die folgenden Briefe vom 4. und 14. Februar, die Prod'homme ohne Erwähnung überging, werden hier zitiert nach den Originalen der Sammlung der Pariser Oper, *Lettres autographes de Verdi à Camille Du Locle*, 1871, Nr. 1—3.

Vi stringo le mani e col cuore straziato vi dico addio

aff.

G. Verdi«

Dieses Freundschaftsbekenntnis mag Du Locle den Mut gegeben haben, Verdi um zeitweilige Überlassung jener Wertpapiere zu bitten, die er Anfang September 1870 für den Komponisten erworben hatte[30]. Der Brief mit der Bitte Du Locles scheint verlorengegangen zu sein, weil Verdi ihn später seinem Anwalt nach Paris geschickt hat[31]. Aber Verdis spontane und vorbehaltlos positive Antwort ist sogar in zwei Versionen erhalten geblieben:

»Genova 14 Feb[braio] 1871

Ca[ro] Du Locle

Ho ricevuto Jeri sera la vostra carissima lettera —

Appena seppi che le corrispondenze erano aperte, mi affrettai fino dai primi del mese, di mandarvi una lettera per la via di Bruxelles, e che spero avrete ricevuto. Voi potete ben immaginare, con quanta gioja sento le vostre nuove, e quanto desidero per Voi, e pei vostri un po' di bene. —

E prima di tutto, vi dico che potete disporre di quei tali titoli et[c.] et[c.], come voi mi domandate.

L'Aida, dietro un Carteggio fra me e Draneth [sic] Bey, sarà trasportata all'inverno prossimo e così pure alla Scala.

Quando io verrò a Parigi? Più presto forse che voi non pensate! Vi giuro, che se vi è stato mai momento in cui l'abbia desiderato, si è questo; e voi lo vedrete!

Il Monte Cenisio fù forato il giorno di Natale. L'incontro fù perfetto, e mi dicono, che non si può descrivere la gioja commovente di quel momento. Ora vi sta lavorando all'opera muraria, alle rotaje et[c.] et[c.] — e presto potremo, da Torino, venire a Parigi, senza moversi da sedere. —

Addio, mio caro Du Locle, vi abbraccio di tutto cuore! Vi auguro tutto il bene possibile. Ci vedremo presto

Ad. Af.   G. Verdi«

---

[30] Drei noch unveröffentlichte Briefe Du Locles geben genauen Aufschluß über den Ankauf der Papiere. Am 28. August 1870 versprach Du Locle, Verdis Bitte zu erfüllen, und dankte für jene 2000 Franken, die der Komponist den Verwundeten zugedacht hatte: »*Il sera fait comme vous le désirez et Merci pour mes pauvres blessés! Je reconnais bien là votre bon et grand coeur!*« Am 1. September berichtete er: »*Je viens de toucher (à 5 heures) vos cinquante mille francs. Je leur donnerai demain l'emploi que vous m'indiquez*...« Im Brief vom 2. September heißt es dann: »*J'ai immédiatement donné l'ordre à mon agent de change d'acheter pour vous 48 mille francs de Rente Italienne. Dès que j'aurais vos titres je les déposerai en lieu sûr, en attendant que vous veniez en France ou que j'aille en Italie.*« Der volle Wortlaut dieser Briefe erscheint in meinem Artikel *Zur Entstehung von Verdis Aida*, in: Studi Musicali II, 1973, Nr. 1, S. 15—71.

[31] In Verdis Brief vom 22. Juni 1876 an Léon Escudier, den Abbiati nicht vollständig veröffentlicht hat (*Verdi*, vol. III, S. 802/803), heißt es: »*Spero mandare in tempo quella lettera de Du Locle del Febbrajo 1871. Non la trovo qui, ma son quasi certo di trovarla a Genova, ove andrò ben presto.*« (Paris, Bibliothèque de l'Opéra, *Lettres autographes de Verdi à Léon Escudier*, 1876, Nr. 5.)

»Gênes 14 Février 1871

Mon cher Du Locle

Je viens d'envoyer à la poste une lettre pour vous: Mais, comme à l'ordinaire, je vous ai écrite [sic] en Italien; et dans la crainte qu'elle ne vous parvienne pas, je fais suivre ces peu de mots pour répéter, de vous servir des titres que vous m'avez demandé[s].

Tout à vous

G. Verdi«

Diese beiden Biefe aus der Bibliothek der Pariser Oper sind von Prod'homme offenbar in der Absicht übergangen worden, den wahren Grund für den Abbruch der Beziehungen beider Künstler zu verschleiern. Giuseppina hat dem italienisch formulierten Brief Verdis noch ergreifende Zeilen hinzugefügt, die ebenfalls nie publiziert worden sind:

»Cher Du Locle

Paris, ce grand Paris, que vous appelez le *grand cadavre,* je l'aime et je suis fière de l'aimer. Vous êtes, moralement, plus glorieux que vous ne l'avez jamais été! Je n'ai qu'un désir! C'est de venir m'agenouiller et baiser la poussière de ce grand pays, où mes amis ont tant souffert! Vous, qui me connaissez, vous savez que je dis vrai et que mes paroles partent du coeur!

Embrasser [sic] votre femme, vos enfants pour moi et laissez, que votre vieille amie vous embrasse aussi; dans l'effusion de tout ce qu'il [y] a de plus affectueux et de plus saint au monde.

Adieu adieu cher ami

Votre Aff^{ée} Josép[hi]ne Verdi«

Camille Du Commun Du Locle, 1832 in Orange geboren[32], war fast 20 Jahre jünger als Verdi. Daher ist verständlich, daß Giuseppina 1866/67, während der durch den *Don Carlos* bedingten Paris-Aufenthalte, ein fast mütterliches Verhältnis zu ihm und seiner Frau Marie entwickelt hatte[33] und sich um seine Familie mehr sorgte als um die anderen Pariser Freunde. Daher zögerte sie auch nicht, deutlich zu werden, als sich im Laufe des Jahres 1874 herausgestellt hatte, daß Du Locle weder nervlich noch finanziell in der Lage sein würde, seine

---

[32] Vgl. *Du Locle,* in *Enciclopedia dello spettacolo,* vol. IV, Firenze—Roma 1957, Sp. 1099.

[33] In der Pariser Bibliothèque de l'Opéra werden unter den Briefen Giuseppina Verdis auch einige an Marie Du Locle verwahrt. Im 15. Brief vom 17. November 1870 heißt es: »*Verdi très ému, très touché en lisant votre lettre, vous serre les mains avec effusion! — Il aime, il estime votre Camille … et il fera tout ce qu'il pourra pour lui. Il espère pouvoir lui faire parvenir une réponse, à ses lettres par ballon par un long détour diplomatique … mais réussira-t-il?*« Giuseppinas Brief vom 11. November 1873 (Nr. 23) endet folgendermaßen: »*Maintenant, je serre les pattes, de ce cher ami, qui s'appelle Camille Du-Locle, qui nous a comblé pendant notre séjour à Paris des plus exquises amabilités, et qu'on peut, à bon droit, appeler la fine fleur de la gentilhommerie. Quant à vous, ma belle chère et charmante Marie, je vous serre dans mes bras, comme si vous étiez ma Fille. C'est vous dire combien vous aime Joséphine Verdi*«

Träume als alleiniger Direktor der Opéra-Comique in die Tat umzusetzen[34]. 1874 und 1875 füllten die Aufführungen des *Requiems*, für die Verdi eigens nach Paris gekommen war, zwar vorübergehend die Kasse, aber die Uraufführung von Bizets *Carmen* (3. März 1875), in die Du Locle alle seine Hoffnungen gesetzt hatte, wurde ein Mißerfolg. Das konventionelle Pariser Publikum strömte in das neueröffnete Opernhaus im Palais Garnier, ins Théâtre Italien oder ins Théâtre Lyrique, wo man es nicht mit derart schockierenden Neuheiten konfrontierte. Krank und verbittert schloß Du Locle im Sommer 1875 für einige Zeit seine *petite boutique*, die Opéra-Comique. Giuseppina scheint diese Entwicklung geahnt zu haben, denn schon im Neujahrsbrief für 1875[35] machte sie diskret, aber unmißverständlich den Versuch, Du Locle zur Aufgabe des Theaters zu bewegen:

»Cher Monsieur Du Locle

Merci, de vos souhaits de bonheur pour la nouvelle année; et merci, de vous être rappelé aussi de moi, au milieu du hurl, des plaisirs, des folies parisiennes; malgré vos nombreuses occupations et malgré le chaos de cadeaux, de souhaits, plus ou moins sincères, de ces jours d'hipocrisie et de convoitise! … Moi, je prie le bon Dieu, qu'il vous donne, à tous deux, la santé, la paix, assez d'argent pour vivre honorablement… et si c'est possible, qu'il vous accorde tous ces biens, sans besoin, sans desir d'avoir une *boutique*, ni grande, ni petite!

À Paris et au milieu de ces maudits théâtres, on ne vit pas: on dévore la vie, et je desire que vous viviez longtemps heureux. — Quant à moi, je traîne ma vie en véritable colimaçon, mais j'aime si peu, si peu le monde, que je ne m'en plains pas. Je lis, j'écris, je travaille, je m'occupe de mon petit *chez-moi*, et je regarde la mer, qui est toujours la plus grande, la plus sublime manifestation de la puissance de Dieu!

Embrassez votre gracieuse femme et vos enfants pour moi, et vous, cher ami, agréez l'expression de ma sincère et constante amitié!

Gênes 30 x^bre 1874   Joséphine Verdi«

Obwohl der allzu optimistische Du Locle den besorgten Worten seiner mütterlichen Freundin keine Beachtung schenkte, blieb sein Verhältnis zu den Verdis weiterhin eng und herzlich. Dies bezeugen überschäumende Dankschreiben vom März 1875, die zwischen den Zeilen aber nicht verhehlen, wie schlecht es seinerzeit um die Einnahmen der Opéra-Comique bestellt gewesen sein muß. Du Locles Brief vom 17. März beginnt folgendermaßen:

»Cher et Illustre Maître,

Je vais faire graver en tête du papier sur lequel je Vous écris »*Merci*« car c'est le mot qu'il faut toujours que je vous dise.

---

[34] Die Situation der Opéra-Comique war schon 1872/73 durch Kürzung der Subventionen um 100 000 Franken schwieriger geworden, geriet aber völlig aus dem Gleichgewicht, als der reformfreudige Du Locle, der sich nicht an das überkommene Repertoire hielt, Alleinherrscher wurde: Am 20. Januar 1874 endete die vertraglich vereinbarte Sozietät mit de Leuven, an der Du Locle mit einem Barkapital von 250 000 Franken beteiligt gewesen war. Vgl. hierzu Albert SOUBIES und Charles MALHERBE, *Histoire de l'Opéra-Comique — La seconde Salle Favart 1860—1887*, Paris 1893, S. 154, 170/171, 188 und 213/214.

[35] Paris, Bibliothèque de l'Opéra, *Lettres de Joséphine Verdi*, Nr. 24.

La Messe est annoncée depuis ce matin, sans désignation de jour et déjà on vient demander des loges. Vous pouvez être assuré d'un succès plus grand s'il est possible que celui de l'an dernier.«

Die sieben Aufführungen der Messe konnten den Ruin Du Locles nur hinauszögern, nicht aufhalten. Verdis nüchterner, erfahrener Blick für die Realitäten des Pariser Theaterlebens muß dies deutlich erkannt haben, denn schon vor der Abreise aus Paris bat der Komponist seinen Freund um Aushändigung der »*Cartelle di rendita italiana*«[36], die er dringend für eine am 11. November fällige Zahlung benötigte. Du Locle sagte zu, die Papiere im Oktober persönlich nach Sant'Agata zu bringen, war aber nicht in der Lage, sein Versprechen einzuhalten. Sein verzweifeltes Bekenntnis, aus dem Luzio nur einen Satz zitiert hat[37], zeigt ihn bereits in tiefer Depression, psychisch und physisch zusammengebrochen unter der Last der Schulden:

»THÉÂTRE NATIONAL
          DE   Paris, le 5 oct[obre] 1875
L'OPÉRA-COMIQUE

Cabinet du Directeur

Cher et Illustre Maître, il m'arrive un vrai malheur et tel que nul autre je crois ne saurait m'être plus sensible. Je me trouve dans l'impossibilité de vous envoyer ce que je vous ai promis pour le 11. Une affaire sur laquelle je me croyais tout droit de compter me manque absolument, et les difficultés dont je vous ai parlé sont loin d'être terminées. Je tremble à la pensée de vous mettre dans l'embarras et de payer ainsi l'amitié que vous m'avez toujours temoignée et dont je sais bien tout le prix. Pour comble, j'ai depuis quelques jours un accident au coeur et je ne puis ni sortir ni même parler ni m'occuper de rien. Je me cache pour vous écrire ces quatre lignes vraiment désolés. C'est aujourd'hui le 5 et c'est demain 6 que toutes les affaires devaient être arrangées et partir à défaut de moi hors d'état de vous les porter. Je n'ose plus même penser à Madame Verdi et à vous et me réclamer de votre affection. Je suis bien désolé et bien malheureux!

                                                        C. Du Locle«

Schon wenige Tage später scheint Du Locle Verdi gebeten zu haben, die Zahlung noch etwas verzögern und statt der Papiere die entsprechende Geldsumme schicken zu dürfen. Diese Vorschläge lehnte Verdi in seiner bekannten Antwort

---

[36] Dies ist Verdis Brief an Perrin zu entnehmen. In dem von Abbiati (*Verdi*, vol. III, S. 803) zitierten Entwurf heißt es: »*L'anno passato prima di partire da Parigi io lo pregai di volermi restituire quelle Cartelle di rendita, di cui abbisognavo. Egli mi rispose con una sicurezza che pare ora incredibile che gl'indicassi l'epoca, ed Egli stesso in persona mi avrebbe portato le Cartelle nella mia campagna in Italia. Venne fissato la fine d'ottobre dell'anno scorso; ma Egli mancò alla sua promessa, cosa che mi mise in imbarrazzo non lieve.*«

[37] Vgl. *Carteggi verdiani*, vol. IV, S. 26. Mit diesem Schreiben endet die erste Serie von Briefen Du Locles. Die in den drei folgenden Briefen Verdis erwähnten Schreiben sind verlorengegangen.

vom 14. Oktober[38] ab mit dem Hinweis darauf, daß die *cartelle* in Italien mehr wert seien und er leider selbst einer finanziellen Verpflichtung nachkommen müsse. Der Ton dieses Briefes ist noch herzlich[39], und auch als daraufhin keine Zahlung erfolgte, hat Verdi weder gedrängt noch geklagt, vermutlich weil er wußte, wie schlecht es um die Gesundheit seines Freundes stand. Von Anfang November bis zum Weihnachtsfest mußte Du Locle auf einer Reise nach Ägypten Erholung suchen, während Charles Nuitter, offenbar einer seiner besten Freunde, vom Ministerium als Interimsdirektor der Opéra-Comique eingesetzt wurde, freilich ohne dabei irgendwelche Verantwortung in finanzieller Hinsicht zu übernehmen[40].

Erst am 15. Februar erinnerte Verdi erneut an die noch ausstehende Schuld, diesmal in kühlerem Ton, wie der Schluß des von Abbiati nur unvollständig wiedergegebenen Schreibens[41] zeigen möge:

> »Fra un mese circa io sarò a Parigi ed è necessario che mi rispondiate qualche cosa di netto su questo particolare. Vi prevengo anche che vi sono tre semestri d'*interessi* arretrati: due dell'anno 1875; uno del 1° Gen. 1876.
>
> Vogliate credermi
Vostro
G. Verdi«

Diesmal war Du Locle noch weniger in der Lage, Verdi zu befriedigen, denn er schuldete sogar den Künstlern seines Theaters die Gagen. Sein Gesundheitszustand hatte sich so sehr verschlechtert, daß er sich Anfang März zum Rücktritt gezwungen sah[42]. Am 9. März konnte man in *L'Art Musical*[43] lesen, daß Emile

---

[38] Vgl. ABBIATI, *Verdi*, vol. III, S. 778. Der von Abbiati nur unvollständig wiedergegebene erste Satz endet: »*per poterle realizzare in moneta ed essere pronto al giorno fissato a fare il detto pagamento.*« (Paris, Bibl. de l'Opéra, *Lettres de Verdi à Camille Du Locle*, 1875, Nr. 6).

[39] Dies beweist der Schluß des Schreibens: »*ma ahimè, io vorrei poterlo fare, che lo farei con tutto il cuore, ma voi capirete che dopo preso un impegno mi è impossibile non soddisfarlo. Mia moglie vi saluta ed io vi stringo di gran cuore le mani.*
Aff.
G. Verdi«

[40] Vgl. SOUBIES und MALHERBE, op. cit., S. 226, sowie Emile GENEST, *L'Opéra-Comique Connu et Inconnu — son histoire depuis l'origine jusqu'à nos jours*, Paris 1925, S. 195.

[41] Vgl. ABBIATI, *Verdi*, vol. III, S. 778/779. Es handelt sich um den Brief Nr. 1 von 1876 der mehrfach zitierten Pariser Sammlung.

[42] Vgl. SOUBIES und MALHERBE, op. cit., S. 227/228. *L'Art Musical* Nr. 9 vom 2. März 1876, S. 70, enthält folgende Meldung:
»*M. Camille du Locle, qui dernièrement avait fait un voyage en Egypte pour y rétablir sa santé, a trop présumé de ses forces en revenant à Paris. Les médecins viennent de lui intimer l'ordre de renoncer aux travaux fatigants que lui impose sa direction. Il va reprendre la route de l'Egypte. Le ministère, préoccupé de la situation du directeur de l'Opéra-Comique, est disposé à favoriser une combinaison qui, en sauvegardant les intérêts de M. du Locle, serait de nature à sauvegarder également les intérêts de l'art. Une conclusion est imminente. M. du Locle a donné sa démission.*«

[43] Nr. 10, S. 96.

Perrin, sein Schwiegervater, angeboten habe »*de solder une grande partie de la dette contractée envers les artistes, et de régir provisoirement le théâtre.*« Da auch Verdis dritte Mahnung vom 10. März[44] ohne Erfolg blieb, ist es verständlich, daß sich der Komponist gleich nach seiner Ankunft in Paris um eine diskrete Regelung der peinlichen Angelegenheit bemüht hat. Verdi und Du Locle scheinen einander aber nicht mehr begegnet zu sein. Die *Revue et Gazette Musicale* meldete am 26. März[45]:

»M. Du Locle, toujours souffrant, est parti la semaine dernière pour les îles d'Hyères.«

Verdi scheint am Mittwoch, dem 22. März, in Paris eingetroffen zu sein[46]. In Giuseppinas *Copialettere* datiert die erste Notiz unter der Überschrift »*Parigi Marzo 1876 Hôtel de Bâde App[artement] 77*« zwar erst vom 25., aber eine Seite davor steht bereits eine Eintragung mit dem Hinweis: »*Mr Perrin de Paris à Paris — Mars 1876.*« Es handelt sich dabei um den Anfang einer Übersetzung jenes Schreibens, das Abbiati[47] unter dem Datum »23 maggio« veröffentlicht hat, das aber ganz offensichtlich am »23 marzo« entstand, am Tag nach der Ankunft Verdis in der französischen Hauptstadt. Auch aus dem Inhalt des Briefes geht hervor, daß er zu Beginn des Paris-Aufenthaltes formuliert worden sein muß, bevor der Komponist andere Personen in die auch ihm äußerst unangenehme Affäre einweihte.

Wie mitfühlend das Ehepaar Verdi — trotz der Differenzen — seinerzeit den Schicksalsschlägen gegenüberstand, die ihre Freunde so hart getroffen hatten, enthüllt der letzte Brief Giuseppinas an Marie Du Locle, die ihren kranken Mann offenbar zunächst auf der Reise begleitet hatte. Der noch unveröffentlichte Brief[48] ist nicht datiert, wurde aber, wie aus dem Entwurf in Giuseppinas *Copialettere* hervorgeht, am 4. April geschrieben.

---

[44] Der von Abbiati (op. cit., vol. III, S. 779) nicht ganz korrekt und unvollständig wiedergegebene Schluß des Briefes Nr. 2 von 1876 lautet: »*Bisogna dunque me ne parliate ora chiaramente per dirmi cosa intendete fare, per restituirmi le Cartelle della Rendita Italiana, che io in buona fede vi ho lasciato nelle mani fino dal 1870. Oltre alle Cartelle vi sono pure i frutti di tre semestri che non m'avete pagato.*

Scrivetemi subito in proposito su tutto, e prima che io intraprenda il viaggio di Parigi che voi sapete imminente.

Vi saluto e mi dico
Vostro
G. Verdi«

[45] Nr. 13, S. 100.

[46] In der *Revue et Gazette Musicale* vom 2. April 1876 (Nr. 14, S. 109) heißt es: »*Verdi est arrivé mercredi dernier à Paris pour présider aux études d'A i d a dont la première représentation est fixé au 20 avril.*« Es ist anzunehmen, daß damit Mittwoch, der 22. (nicht der 29.) März gemeint war, denn Verdi spricht in seinem Brief an Léon Escudier vom 22. Juni 1876 (ABBIATI, *Verdi*, vol. III, S. 803) von einem Parisaufenthalt von über zwei Monaten.

[47] Ibidem, S. 803.

[48] Nr. 25 der bereits zitierten Pariser Sammlung.

»Chère Marie,

Avoir suivi votre mari, après les malheurs qui l'ont frappé et qui ont, peut-être, été cause de sa maladie, c'était le devoir d'une femme de coeur et vous l'avez toujours été. Dire que s'il ne vous avait pas épousée, il ne serait pas dans un pareil chagrin, c'est juger les choses dans un état d'exaltation douloureuse, état qui ne vous permet pas de les bien juger. Je n'irai pas chercher si au milieu de son enthousiasme et de ses illusions, votre mari n'a pas vu l'abime vers lequel il marchait à grands pas, sans vouloir écouter la voix de ceux qui lui criaient *gare* et qui auraient voulu l'arrêter sur la pente du précipice! ... Je ne veux pas savoir, si vous partagiez ses espérances, ses vues et ses erreurs en fait d'art, de spéculation, de direction et administration — ni si vous avez été sages et prévoyants, cachant (par fierté malentendue) vos blessures, quand il eut été encore temps de pouvoir les guérir ... Je sais que vous souffrez et je voudrais être puissante comme le bon Dieu, pour rendre la santé à votre mari, et le bonheur à vous tous! Je ne le puis pas, ma pauvre Marie! ... et mon coeur se serre, quand je pense à tout ce qui s'est passé dans un si court espace de temps, et dans quelle position pénible, difficile nous nous trouvons *tous* dans ce moment! ... Toutefois, vous qui avez eu tant de courage par le passé, tâchez de vous calmer et de ne pas désespérer de l'avenir ... surtout de l'avenir de vos enfants, qui ont des chances de fortune assez grandes, pour tranquilliser votre coeur de mère. Ne pensez pas au monde, ni à ses *on dit,* ma chère Marie ... Le monde est en général bien mauvais — c'est vrai — mais quelquefois, pas aussi mauvais qu'on veut bien le faire. Il n'est pas rare de trouver une grande justice et une grande indulgence, qui plane au-dessus des petites passions et du bavardage médisant de la foule.

Sur cela je prie Dieu qu'il veuille mettre un terme à vos souffrances et vous donner des jours calmes et meilleurs! — Je vous embrasse et vous prie d'agréer tous mes souhaits de bonheur! ...

Votre aff^{ée} Josephine Verdi«

Ernsthafte Vorwürfe klingen in diesen ergreifenden Worten des Trostes nur zwischen den Zeilen an. Dieser Brief der klugen und leidgeprüften Frau Verdis läßt keinen Zweifel: man hatte seit langem erkannt, daß Du Locle nicht die Eigenschaften besaß, die ein erfolgreicher Theaterdirektor mitbringen muß, man hatte versucht, den Freund vor dem Sturz in den Abgrund zu bewahren, und obwohl Du Locle den Warnungen kein Gehör geschenkt hatte, war man bereit, Nachsicht zu üben.

Seinerzeit glaubte Verdi offenbar noch an eine gütliche Beilegung der finanziellen Affäre durch den Schwiegervater Du Locles. Es war kein Geheimnis, daß Emile Perrin sofort die rückständigen Gagen für das Personal der Opéra-Comique bezahlt hatte[49]. Außerdem wußte Verdi, daß Du Locle, obwohl im Moment zahlungsunfähig, keineswegs unvermögend war: Er besaß das Aufführungsmaterial der Opéra-Comique, für das der zukünftige Direktor den von einer staat-

---

[49] Schon die *Revue et Gazette Musicale* vom 12. März 1876 meldete (Nr. 11, S. 85): »*M. Emile Perrin reste chargé de l'administration à titre provisoire; ayant pu enfin s'entendre avec le personnel, il a soldé intégralement tout l'arriéré dû à l'orchestre, aux choeurs, aux employés, et pris des arrangements. ... M. Du Locle est toujours souffrant et ne prend plus aucune part à la gestion du théâtre.*«

lichen Kommission festgesetzten Schätzpreis würde zahlen müssen. Genaue Angaben über den Wert des Materials wurden erst bekannt, als M. Carvalho wegen der Höhe der Forderung zögerte, die Nachfolge anzutreten, und deshalb der Ankauf durch staatliche Mittel sowie eine Erhöhung der jährlichen Subvention diskutiert wurden. In einem Artikel aus der *Revue et Gazette Musicale*[50] werden die mit dem Direktionswechsel zusammenhängenden finanziellen Probleme wie folgt dargestellt:

»En 1869, une expertise, faite suivant la forme ci-dessus prescrite, fixait la valeur du matériel à 217,000 francs. Des experts nommés, il y a quelques semaines, par le ministre des travaux publics, sur la demande du ministre des beaux-arts, ont procédé à un inventaire et fixé la valeur actuel du matériel appartenant à M. du Locle, à 316,000 francs. La plus-value de ce matériel se justifie par une dépense de plus de 600,000 francs, faite de ce chef par le directeur de l'Opéra-Comique, pendant six années d'exploitation. La pensée de l'acquisition du matériel par l'Etat est due à l'initiative intelligente de M. Waddington ... — En diminuant de 100,000 francs par an la subvention de l'Opéra-Comique, les prédécesseurs de M. Waddington ont commis une faute. L'exploitation est impossible dans de pareilles conditions. C'est la fortune personnelle de M. du Locle qui lui a permis de soutenir, depuis six ans, une lutte dans laquelle il devait nécessairement succomber et que personne ne se présente pour continuer. Une subvention insuffisante, l'acquisition d'un matériel d'exploitation, officiellement évalué à 316,000 francs, l'incertitude jetée tous les ans sur la quotité de la subvention par le vote annuel du budget: voilà, il faut bien l'avouer, des conditions qui ne sont pas bien tentantes pour le nouveau directeur.«

Abgesehen von den 316,000 Franken für das Aufführungsmaterial der Opéra-Comique hatte Du Locle offenbar eine größere Erbschaft zu erwarten. Seine Tante, die Comtesse Mollien, dürfte ein beachtliches Vermögen besessen haben, denn sie war die zweite Gemahlin jenes Nicolas-François Mollien, der als überaus fähiger Finanzberater Napoleons I. in die Geschichte eingegangen ist[51]. Der 1758 geborene Mollien war von 1806 bis 1814 und während der hundert Tage von 1815 *ministre du trésor publique* und wurde 1808 *comte de l'empire*. 1802 hatte er die sehr viel jüngere Adèle-Rosalie Collart-Dutilleul geheiratet, eine Ehrendame der Königin Marie-Amélie, Gemahlin von Louis-Philippe I. Mollien, der sich dank seines Vermögens schon 1815 zur Ruhe setzen konnte, verewigte seine Gemahlin in seinen *Mémoires d'un ministre du trésor public 1780—1815* mit folgenden Worten:

»Je dus au ciel une compagne, l'honneur et le charme de ma vie, uniquement occupée de mes sollicitudes au milieu de mes prospérités apparentes, et à qui la retraite n'a apporté aucune privation, parce que son caractère le met au-dessus de toutes les fortunes.«[52]

---

[50] Nr. 50 vom 23. Juli 1876, S. 238.

[51] Vgl. *Encyclopaedia Britannica*, vol. 15, 1968, S. 667, bzw. die ausführlichere Darstellung seines Lebens in der *Biographie Universelle* von MICHAUD, Bd. 28, S. 578—587.

[52] Zitiert nach der *Biographie Universelle* von MICHAUD, S. 585.

Als der Comte Mollien 1850 im Alter von 92 Jahren starb, hinterließ er keine Kinder[53], aber die Comtesse hat ihn noch 28 Jahre überlebt[54].

Schon 1873 mußte Camille Du Locle seine vermögende Tante um finanzielle Hilfe bitten. Ein Briefentwurf, erhalten in den Archives Nationales[55], beweist dies eindeutig:

»THÉÂTRE NATIONAL
　　　　　DE   Paris, le 3 Juin 1873
L'OPÉRA-COMIQUE

Cabinet du Directeur

　　　Ma chère Tante,
J'ai sauvé la patrie. On joue la Dame Blanche[56] dans un salon Louis XV. Et j'ai gardé 870 f. sur ma recette. (on a rendu 600 fr à peu près)
Cela n'empêche pas que Viltoz vient de venir me demander pour le 5 15.000 f de plus que je n'ai. Je suis obligé de recourir à vous, et il faudra que nous causions car j'ai bien peur de l'été ... malgré Verdi.
Je Vous envoie une carte qui vous permettra d'entrer dans la gare demain pour recevoir les jeunes époux (prière de ne pas la perdre!)
　　　　　　　　　　　Je Vous
　　　　　　　　　　　　　Camille«

Offensichtlich ist Du Locle schon damals in euphorischer Stimmung leichtfertig mit dem Geld von Freunden und Verwandten umgegangen. Aber er hat seiner Tante keinesfalls verschwiegen, daß Verdi ihm half und daß diese Mittel nicht mehr ausreichten, um die Opéra-Comique über Wasser zu halten. Er hatte offenbar grenzenloses Vertrauen in das Vermögen und die Großzügigkeit seiner Tante. Verdi und Giuseppina, die die alte Dame wohl persönlich kannten[57], scheinen dieses Vertrauen jahrelang geteilt zu haben, denn ohne die Garantie der reichen Comtesse Mollien[58] hätte Verdi seinem Freund wohl kaum für so lange Zeit ein

---

[53] Vgl. ibidem, S. 586.

[54] Die Comtesse Mollien starb am 26. Februar 1878 in Paris. Vgl. hierzu A. RÈVÉREND, *Armorial du premier empire*, t. III, Paris 1896, S. 256.

[55] Er befindet sich im Karton *AJ XIII 1135* unter den Papieren der Direktion de Leuven—Du Locle.

[56] Diese komische Oper von Scribe und Boieldieu, uraufgeführt am 10. Dezember 1825, hatte schon 1864 in Paris ihre 1000. Aufführung erlebt.

[57] Dies lassen noch unveröffentlichte Zeilen Giuseppinas an Du Locle vermuten. In ihrem Neujahrsbrief für 1869 heißt es u. a.: *»Mais avant tout, bon jour et bon an, à Vous, mon gracieux Poète, à votre belle Marie, à Mademoiselle Claire, à la famille Perrin, et me permettez vous aussi de souhaiter la bonne année à cette respectable Tante, que vous aimez tant? Que le bon Dieu vous bénisse tous, et vous accorde tous les bonheurs, que je vous souhaite de grand coeur!«* Der Schluß ihres Schreibens vom 9. Juni 1869 lautet: *»Embrassez pour moi la très aimable sympathique Madame Du Locle; un baiser à Mlle Claire et mes hommages réspectueux à Madame votre Tante.«*

[58] Vgl. hierzu die auf S. 5 zitierten Bemerkungen Muzios und Anm. 23.

Drittel jenes Geldes überlassen, das ihm die Partitur der *Aida* eingebracht hatte.
Die Tatsache, daß die Verwandten Du Locles Vermögen besaßen, macht auch verständlich, daß Verdi, der notleidende Freunde sonst stets bereitwillig unterstützt
hat, in diesem Fall nicht geneigt war, auf jene Summe zu verzichten, die ihm
rechtlich zustand und die er ganz offensichtlich schon anderweitig zugesagt hatte.

Trotz aller Schwierigkeiten scheint Verdi auch während seines Paris-Aufenthaltes
von 1876 noch an eine gütliche Einigung geglaubt zu haben. Hatte Perrin ihm
doch durch Charles Nuitter versichern lassen, daß er ihm vor der Abreise aus
Paris *»de l'argent beaucoup d'argent«* geben würde[59]. Erst als bis Anfang Juni
nichts dergleichen geschehen war, hat Verdi sich mit einem Anwalt in Verbindung gesetzt und seinen Pariser Verleger ins Vertrauen gezogen. Léon Escudier
schrieb daraufhin an die Comtesse. Verdis erste Reaktion auf diese Nachricht
zeigt deutlich, wie besorgt der Komponist nach der Abreise aus Paris war, daß
er aber immer noch nicht die Geduld verloren hatte[60].

»St Agata 20 Giug[no] 1876

Caro Leon

Sono a casa dall'altra sera un po' strapazzato dal viaggio e con un po' di mal di
gola ma ora stò meglio.

Ho ricevuto jeri la car[issi]ma vostra ed ho letto quanto avete scritto alla Contessa.
Stà bene e vi ringrazio, come vi ringrazio di tutto quello che farete intorno quest'affare. S'intende sempre che farete di tutte le spese anche le più piccole di quest'affare
una piccola nota che liquideremo in fine. Raccomando sopratutto di sollecitare il più
che sia possibile.

Stassera dunque è l'ultima d'Aida. Sarò ben contento nel sentire che tutto abbia
finito regolarmente senza malattie e disgrazie ... oh siete stato in questo ben fortunato! 26 recite di fila senza un'intoppo, un malanno che vi faccia perdere alcune recite
è una fortuna che non arriva una seconda volta! ...

La Peppina stà bene e saluta tutti. Io faccio lo stesso.

Scrivetemi e curatemi questo mio affare molto imbrogliato

Addio addio
Aff.
G. Verdi«

Erst als sich herausgestellt hatte, daß Léon Escudier sich weder brieflich noch
durch einen Mittelsmann mit der Comtesse Mollien in Verbindung setzen konnte,
erst als Madame Du Locle dem Anwalt Verdis unmißverständlich erklärt hatte,
daß sie in der Lage sei, jede Regelung der Angelegenheit über Madame Mollien
zu verhindern, riet man Verdi, nunmehr den Prozeß anzustrengen. Den Anstoß
zum Handeln gaben zwei noch unveröffentlichte Briefe aus der Sammlung des
Komponisten:

---

[59] Vgl. den von Abbiati (*Verdi*, vol. III, S. 802/803) veröffentlichten Brief Verdis vom 22. Juni
1876.

[60] Abbiati hat diesen Brief aus der Sammlung der Opéra (1876, Nr. 4) nur unvollständig und
nicht ganz korrekt wiedergegeben. Vgl. ibidem, S. 802, wo es irrtümlich heißt *»di tutta la
spiega anche la più piccola«*.

»THÉÂTRE ITALIEN
   Salle Ventadour   Paris, le 20 juin 1876
      Direction
         Cher maître et ami,

Rien de nouveau. La maison de la tante est cernée nuit et jour, et l'homme d'affaires, jusqu'à présent du moins est invisible. On m'avait assuré qu'il serait là hier; J'ai stationné une heure et demi sur le quai en face de l'hôtel et personne n'est venu; J'attendais une réponse d'étampes, et Mr Masson qui s'est chargé de me donner le nom de l'homme d'affaire n'a rien reçu à l'heure qu'il est. Hier j'ai reçu la lettre que je vous envoie de M. Cartier, qui m'a conté au long la visite de Mad. Du Locle. On n'est vraiment pas plus cynique. Comme cette situation menace de se prolonger, M. Cartier a envoyé aujourd'hui l'assignation. Peut-être prendra-t-on l'affaire au sérieux lorsque l'on sera bien convaincu que vous êtes décidé à agir vigoureusement. Cela n'empêchera pas de négocier amiablement et c'est ce que je continue de faire espérant toujours que je trouverai un point pour amener à votre satisfaction cette déplorable affaire.

Depuis hier il fait une chaleur insupportable. Ce soir, je le crois, le Théâtre sera plein; la location s'annonce du moins d'une façon très satisfaisante.

Je suis accablé de demandes de places par les journaux et les habitués *gratis*. On croirait vraiment que le théâtre italien est un dépot de mendicité.

Je suis forcé de quitter la plume pour recevoir une foule d'ennuyeux. Excusez-moi donc si je n'écris pas plus longuement.

Mes amitiés sincères à vous et à Mme Verdi de votre dévoué ami
                                         L. Escudier«

Der diesem Schreiben beigefügte Brief des Rechtsanwalts Ernest Cartier an Escudier hat folgenden Wortlaut:

                            »11bis Rue du Cirque
                               18 juin 1876

Je crains, monsieur, que vos démarches, si intelligentes et si actives qu'elles soient, ne demeurent sans effet. Mad^e la comtesse M ... est positivement chambrée. J'en ai eu l'assurance par Mad^e Du Locle elle-même. Elle est venue me voir hier. Elle n'a pas hésité à me dire qu'elle interceptait toute visite et toute lettre adressée à sa tante, que les gens avait le mot, et que tout passait par ses mains. Ceci concorde parfaitement avec ce que vous m'avez dit.

Ce n'était pas là, vous le pensez bien, le but ostensible de sa visite. Elle venait de la part d'un ami de son mari, qui est conseiller à la Cour, pour me demander si M. Verdi avait l'intention d'impliquer Mad^e M. dans le procès. J'ai dû lui répondre négativement. En effet il n'est pas possible, même à titre comminatoire, de diriger une action contre une personne qui n'a avec M. Verdi aucun lien de droit.

Mais l'explication que nous avons eue à ce sujet m'a permis de connaître le fond de la pensée de nos adversaires. C'est une fin de non-recevoir absolue.

Je ne crois pas que l'homme d'affaires puisse modifier cette résolution; je doute même, après ce qui m'a été dit, que vous puissiez arriver jusqu'à lui.

Mon avis serait donc de renoncer à la négociation, et de lancer immédiatement l'assignation. Voulez-vous en venir causer avec moi demain lundi à 4^h 1/2? Ou, sans vous déranger, si vous partagez mon opinion, veuillez me jeter un mot à la poste, j'agirai immédiatement.

Recevez, monsieur, l'assurance de ma parfaite considération
                                     Ernest Cartier«

Verärgert über dies Fiasko, über die »*bella commedia*«, der er Glauben geschenkt
hatte, wütend sowohl über die Dreistigkeit Mme Du Locles und deren Vaters als
auch über die zu freundlichen Auskünfte des Anwalts, gab Verdi seinem französischen Verleger im bekannten Brief vom 22. Juni 1876[61] die Anweisung: »*non
resta che a g i r e come ne ho il diritto ... a g i t e dunque e sarà che sarà*«. Inter-
essanter noch als die spontane Reaktion des Komponisten ist der wohlüberlegte
Brief an Cartier, den Giuseppina acht Tage später in ihrem *Copialettere* ent-
warf. Dieses bisher unbekannte Schreiben hat folgenden Wortlaut:

»Mr Cartier advocat à Paris   St Agata 30 Juin 1876

Mr Escudier m'a tenu au courant des inutiles démarches faites pour arriver jusqu'à
Mme Mollien. C'était un résultat prévu, qui ne m'a point étonné. Ce que je n'aurais
jamais imaginé et qui me dépasse, c'est la froide indifférence, l'impudente hardiesse de
Mme Du Locle. Comment Elle laisse son mari mourir, peut-être loin d'Elle — ayant
l'air de ne pas craindre un procès qui va le déshonorer! Mais ses enfants portent cependant son nom! ... Après cela elle couvre d'un masque hypocrite sa convoitise pour
l'héritage à venir et fait parade de sentiment pour empêcher à la vielle tante de son
mari le chagrin de savoir que l'honneur de son neveu (qu'elle aurait pu sauver) va
être publiquement compromis! Comme vous dites très bien, Monsieur: Elle préfère
la honte d'une condam. ...
    Singulière manière d'aimer les gens et de comprendre la dignité humaine! Je n'aurais
jamais cru que les affaires arrivassent à ce point. Cependant, Mr Cartier, malgré la manière indigne avec laquelle on a abusé de mon argent et on s'est joué de ma bonne foi,
j'aurais voulu éviter ce procès. J'ai attendu ... longtemps attendu, pour qu'on vint
à moi ... mais du moment qu'on a voulu me pousser à bout, soit: Agissez Monsieur,
selon la loi et mon droit, et à la grâce de Dieu advienne que pourra! Je désire aussi
que les choses finissent vite et je vous serai doublement obligé si vous réussirez à vous
opposer à toute délaition.« [sic]

Dieser Briefentwurf läßt keinen Zweifel: Verdi und Giuseppina hatten jede
Hoffnung auf eine Besserung Du Locles aufgegeben; der Prozeß richtete sich im
Grunde gegen Madame Du Locle, deren Heuchelei, kalte Gleichgültigkeit und
unverschämte Kühnheit alle Erwartungen übertroffen hatten. Nicht der unwürdige Mißbrauch seines Geldes und seiner Gutgläubigkeit hat Verdi zum Handeln
veranlaßt, sondern vielmehr die Tatsache, daß Marie Du Locle die Entehrung ihres Namens und die Schande einer Verurteilung ihres Mannes weniger zu fürch-
ten schien als die Minderung einer zu erwartenden Erbschaft.

---

[61] Der Schluß dieses von Abbiati (ibidem, S. 802/803) nicht ganz vollständig wiedergegebenen
Briefes aus der Sammlung der Opéra (1876, Nr. 5) lautet folgendermaßen:
»*Spero mandare in tempo quella lettera de Du Locle del F e b b r a j o 1871. Non la trovo
qui, ma son quasi certo di trovarla a Genova, ove andrò ben presto.
    Ora il Teatro è finito. E su questo non ho altro a ripetervi quello che dissi nell'altra
mia ...
    Scusate le noje che avete, e che avrete ... Ve ne ringrazio e mi dico
                                        Vostro
                                        G. Verdi*«

Über den Ausgang des Prozesses konnte nichts in Erfahrung gebracht werden, da alle Prozeßakten inzwischen vernichtet worden sind. Über den Prozeßverlauf hat Léon Escudier in zwei Zeitungsnotizen und in folgendem Brief an Verdi berichtet:

»THÉÂTRE ITALIEN　　　　　　　　　　　　　　Paris, le 14 juillet 1876
　　Salle Ventadour
　　　　Direction

　　　　　　　Cher Maître et ami,

　　à la hâte, je vous écris quelques lignes au dernier moment pour vous dire que l'affaire a été appelée hier et que M. Cartier a òbtenu qu'elle fut plaidée dans 15 jours vu la situation de Du Locle. M. de Vallée[62] insistait pour qu'elle ne revint devant le tribunal qu'après Vacation, c'est à dire au mois d'octobre. Tous les journaux ont reproduit la note de l'*Art Musical*. Je verrai M. Cartier lundi et prendrai des ordres. S'il juge à propos que j'aille en votre absence faire une visite au président, j'irai. On m'a assuré aujourd'hui que Du Locle devait arriver pour aller chez sa tante à la campagne. J'aurais des détails plus précis et vous écrirai à ce sujet. Vingt personnes au moins que j'ai vu sont très étonnées de ce que Perrin n'intervient pas pour arranger cette affaire. J'espère toujours.

　　J'ai reçu les corrections du quatuor; elles seront faites et je vous en enverrai l'épreuve.

　　Je voulais écrire à Muzio; je n'en ai plus le temps. J'ai engagé le baryton de Reszké[63] qui est excellent; il aura j'en suis sûr un grand succès à Paris. C'est Maini[64] en Baryton.

　　Milles amitiés à vous et à Mme Verdi. S'il fait chaud à St Agata, ici l'air est de feu; c'est à ne pas y tenir.

　　　　　　　　　　　　　Croyez-moi votre
　　　　　　　　　　　　　toujours dévoué
　　　　　　　　　　　　　ami
　　　　　　　　　　　　　　　L. Escudier«

Mit diesem Brief antwortete Escudier auf ein Schreiben vom 10. Juli, in dem Verdi von der Hitze in Sant'Agata, von Muzios Besuch sowie von einem Druckfehler im Quartett berichtet und angefragt hatte:

---

[62] Es handelt sich dabei um den gegnerischen Anwalt Oscar de Vallée, wohnhaft in Paris, rue de Vezelay, 12. Er ist wie Verdis Anwalt Ernest Cartier, rue du Cirque, 11 bis, als »*avocat à la cour d'appel*« verzeichnet im *Annuaire-Almanach du Commerce, 79e année, 1876,* Paris 1876, von Dɪᴅᴏᴛ-Bᴏᴛᴛɪɴ (S. 677 und 678).

[63] Jan de Reszké (1850—1925), polnischer Bariton, der über Venedig und London nach Paris kam und zwischen 1891 und 1901 an der Metropolitan in New York seine größten Erfolge feierte.

[64] Ormondo Maini, berühmter italienischer Bass, der sich unter den ersten Interpreten von *Aida* und Verdis *Requiem* befand.

»Come va l'affare Du Locle? Triste, triste, triste!

Ebbene, convenite anche voi ora di quello che vi dissi a Parigi, cioè che non ne avressimo cavato niente, e che non si faceva altro che sprecare il tempo ed aggiungere altre spese. Ne convenite ora voi?«[65]

Léon Escudier scheint die Lage anfangs also weniger ernst angesehen zu haben als Verdi. Auch die beiden Meldungen aus seiner Zeitschrift *L'Art Musical* bezeugen, daß er nie müde geworden ist, für eine gütliche Schlichtung der Angelegenheit einzutreten. Die in Escudiers Brief erwähnte Notiz[66] ist zudem von besonderem Interesse, weil sie eine klare Vorstellung von der Höhe des Streitwertes vermittelt:

»Divers journaux ont annoncé que M. Verdi intentait un procès à M. du Locle et réclamait à ce dernier une somme de 80,000 francs. Le fait est vrai. Nous avons jugé convenable, de ne point entretenir le public de cette délicate affaire, espérant qu'elle se dénouerait amiablement. Malheureusement notre espoir jusqu'à ce moment a été déçu.

M. Verdi a formé contre M. du Locle, une demande devant la 8me chambre tendant à une restitution de titres. C'est demain 14 juillet que cette affaire sera appelée.«[67]

Die erstaunliche Höhe des Streitwertes läßt sich vermutlich dadurch erklären, daß der Kurs der Papiere zwischen 1870 und 1876 erheblich gestiegen war und natürlich auch die versäumten Zinszahlungen berücksichtigt worden sein müssen. Am 10. August berichtete Escudier folgendermaßen über eine nochmalige Verschiebung der Urteilsverkündung[68]:

»Le jugement du procès pendant entre Verdi et M. du Locle a encore été remis à huitaine. L'avocat chargé des intérêts du maître n'a fait cette fois encore aucune difficulté pour accepter ce nouveau sursis. Une entente, voilà ce qui est désirable dans l'intérêt surtout de M. du Locle; voilà ce qui aurait déjà dû mettre fin à ce débat judiciaire excessivement pénible.

Nous n'en avons parlé qu'après plusieurs confrères, et nous n'en parlerions plus si nous ne savions que, malheureusement, les faits ont été mal interprétés par des amis trop zélés de l'ex-directeur de l'Opéra-Comique. Le silence est d'or, cela est bien vrai, et il est fâcheux qu'on ne sache pas saisir l'occasion de se taire quand elle se présente aussi favorablement que dans la circonstance qui nous occupe.

---

[65] Verdis Brief vom 10. Juli, ebenfalls aus der Sammlung der Opéra (1876, Nr. 6), ist von Jacques Gabriel PROD'HOMME veröffentlicht worden in *Lettres inédites de G. Verdi à Léon Escudier* in: Rivista Musicale Italiana XXXV, 1928, S. 551. Prod'homme hat den hier zitierten Abschnitt aber nicht ganz korrekt wiedergegeben und falsch interpretiert. Er bezieht die Frage nach dem *»affare Du Locle«* auf den Rücktritt des Direktors der Opéra-Comique, erwähnt den Prozeß mit keinem Wort und hat die voraufgehenden Briefe Verdis vom 20. und 22. Juni zwar erwähnt, aber nicht in seine Publikation aufgenommen, insgesamt also die gleiche verschleiernde Tendenz verfolgt wie bei der Edition der Briefe Verdis an Du Locle.

[66] Sie erschien am 13. Juli 1876 in *L'Art Musical* 28, S. 222.

[67] Das hier angegebene Datum läßt darauf schließen, daß der oben zitierte Brief Escudiers nicht am 14. sondern am 15. Juli geschrieben wurde.

[68] *L'Art Musical* 32, S. 255.

Verdi a prouvé par une longue patience tout ce qu'on pouvait attendre de sa courtoisie, disons même de son amitié. Il n'y a que des personnes n'ayant aucune con-
naissance des causes du procès qui puissent paraître en douter. Mais la solution est
prochaine. Attendons.«

Daß es in letzter Minute doch noch zu der von Escudier angedeuteten Verständigung gekommen ist, läßt sich nur vermuten. In der *Gazette des Tribunaux* findet
man zwar gelegentlich Berichte über die Sitzungen der 8. Kammer des *Tribunal
correctionnel de Paris*, aber der Prozeß Verdi gegen Du Locle wurde offenbar
mit äußerster Diskretion behandelt (vgl. das Postscriptum nach Teil II).
Sicher ist jedoch, daß Verdi mit dem von Cartier erzielten Ergebnis zufrieden
war. Dies geht nicht nur aus der von Abbiati zitierten Äußerung Muzios[69] hervor, sondern auch und noch deutlicher aus einem Briefentwurf von Giuseppinas
Hand. Diese bisher unbekannte Eintragung in ihrem *Copialettere* hat folgenden
Wortlaut:

»6 Novembre 1876 de St Agata à Paris   Monsieur Cartier

J'ai eu l'honneur de Vous écrire, il y a à peu près deux mois, pour Vous demander la
note de tout ce que je vous dois pour l'affaire Du Locle. Vous m'avez répondu, que
vous l'auriez envoyée plus tard, avec celle de Monsieur l'Avoué. N'ayant plus reçu
de réponse, il se pourrait bien, que ma lettre eut été perdue. C'est pourquoi je renou-
velle ma prière pour que vous vouliez bien m'envoyer cette note et que je puisse, au
moins matériellement, acquitter ma dette envers Vous, qui avez su m'arranger avec
tant de zèle et d'intelligence, une affaire très pénible et très délicate.
    Agréez l'expression des meilleurs sentiments de«

Zwei Monate zuvor, Anfang September also, hatte Verdi seinen Anwalt gebeten,
eine Rechnung zu schicken. Folglich dürfte der Prozeß noch im August beendet
worden sein, vermutlich durch einen Vergleich, denn schon im Oktober scheint
Verdi einen Teil der Entschädigung erhalten zu haben. Dies geht aus einem Briefentwurf hervor, den Giuseppina vermutlich während eines Aufenthaltes in Cremona in ihrem *Copialettere* niederschrieb. Frank Walker berichtet[70] über den
Inhalt dieser Eintragung u. a. folgendes:

»The rest is difficult to decipher fully from the draft, but the sense is clear. A former
friend, probably Du Locle, through whom Verdi had lost a considerable sum of money,
had offered to repay him, in whole or in part, or had suggested ways and means whereby
the money might be recovered. Giuseppina wished part of the interest on this money
to be given to the heads of six poor families in the vicinity. The details of these
charitable dispensations, however, are unimportant.«

---

[69] *Verdi*, vol. IV, S. 199; vgl. in diesem Artikel S. 418.
[70] Vgl. *The Man Verdi*, London 1962, S. 435.

Walker sieht in Giuseppinas Bitte um Erleichterung ihrer geistigen Qualen durch gute Taten[71] allein eine Reaktion auf Verdis intime Beziehungen zu Teresa Stolz. Aber dürfte nicht auch die Trauer über den Bruch der einst so engen Freundschaft mit Du Locle dazu beigetragen haben, Giuseppina die Freude am Leben und an dem rückerstatteten Geld zu rauben? Eine doppelte Motivation würde meines Erachtens besser erklären, warum Giuseppina ihrem Mann nahegelegt hat, einen Teil jener Mittel für wohltätige Zwecke auszugeben. Vermutlich litt diese feinfühlige und tiefreligiöse Frau mehr als Verdi unter der Vorstellung, einen notleidenden, todkranken Freund unter Druck gesetzt zu haben.

Zu den wenigen Menschen, die Camille Du Locle auch in der Phase größten Unglücks treu geblieben sind, gehört Charles-Louis-Étienne Truinet (1828-1899), der mit dem Anagramm Nuitter signierte, seit er der juristischen Laufbahn entsagt hatte, um sich ganz dem Pariser Theaterleben widmen zu können. Charles Nuitter, der seinen Freund während der Erholungsreise nach Ägypten in der Direktion der Opéra-Comique vertreten hatte, ist bekannt geworden als Librettist und Mitarbeiter von Offenbach, Sardou, Delibes und Lalo, sowie als Übersetzer eines breiten Opernrepertoires von Mozarts *Zauberflöte* und Webers *Oberon*, *Preziosa* und *Abu Hassan* bis zu Richard Wagners *Lohengrin*, *Tannhäuser*, *Fliegendem Holländer* und *Rienzi*. Für Verdi arbeitete er erstmals 1865 an den Übersetzungen von *Macbeth* und, zusammen mit Du Locle, *La forza del destino*. 1876 beendete er unter Verdis Aufsicht die mit Du Locle begonnene Übersetzung von *Aida*, 1883 lieferte er die französische Version von *Simon Boccanegra*. Als Archivar der Opéra hat Nuitter der Musikgeschichtsschreibung 30 Jahre lang unschätzbare Dienste geleistet: Er ordnete die unzählbaren Dokumente der Archive, katalogisierte die von ihm begründete Bibliothek und verfaßte einige wissenschaftliche Arbeiten zur französischen Operngeschichte[72].

Es ist schwer, sich vom Menschen Charles Nuitter eine Vorstellung zu machen, denn seine mit äußerster Akkuratesse geschriebenen Briefe verraten nichts Persönliches. Der am 25. Februar 1899 im *Figaro* erschienene Nachruf Nuitters schildert ihn als sehr großen Mann »*à figure rasée et souriante, d'une politesse ecclésiastique, d'une courtoisie extrème*«, der von allen geschätzt wurde, aber keinem Einblick in sein Privatleben gestattete:

»Il vivait absolument seul, 83, rue du Faubourg-Saint-Honoré, ayant pris pour devise le précepte du sage: Cache ta vie.

---

[71] Der Beginn der Eintragung lautet in der von Walker zitierten englischen Übersetzung: »*Since fate has willed that that which was my whole happiness in this life should now be irreparably lost, there may serve to alleviate the sufferings of my spirit the good that, through my suggestion and your natural generosity, you can do and will do, I am sure, especially to those who are your blood relations and bear, or bore, your name.*«

[72] Vgl. auch die *Nécrologie* in *Le Ménestrel* 3544 vom 26. Februar 1899 (Nr. 9, S. 72) sowie die Artikel *Nuitter* in der *Enciclopedia dello spettacolo*, vol. VII, Firenze-Roma 1960, Sp. 1256/7, und in *Grove's Dictionary of Music and Musicians*, vol. VI, London 1954, S. 140.

Il y était si fidèle que personne ne pénétrait dans le mystère de sa vie privée et qu'on ne sait même à qui envoyer les lettres de faire part pour ses obsèques.«

Verdi lernte Nuitters Qualitäten offenbar erst während seines Pariser Aufenthaltes von 1876 schätzen. Davon zeugen zwei kurze Briefe Verdis aus der Sammlung der Pariser Oper: Das von Abbiati[73] zitierte Schreiben vom 1. April 1876 bittet Nuitter zu einer ersten Unterredung im Hôtel de Bade. Das zweite, noch unveröffentlichte Schreiben lautet:

»2 Juin 1876

Mon cher Nuitter
Voilà trois jour[s] que je n'ai plus le plaisir de vous voir, malgré votre promesse de venir chez moi tous les matins à 10 heures.
Je sais che [sic] vous allez à l'Opéra-Comique vers une heure après midi, et je vous serai bien obligé de venir tout de suite chez moi.

Tout à vous
G. Verdi«

Die täglichen Zusammenkünfte Verdis mit Nuitter waren ohne Zweifel der gemeinsamen Arbeit an der *Aida*-Übersetzung gewidmet. Dies wissen wir aus Briefen Verdis an Ricordi, die Abbiati veröffentlicht hat[74]. In Verdis Brief vom 17. Mai 1876 heißt es:

»Desidero sapere positivamente da te e ben nettamente se Escudier ha diritto di fare una riduzione in francese per la stampa. Viste le infami traduzioni fatte delle altre mie opere, traduzioni che alteranno il senso drammatico e la frase musicale, io avevo in pensiero fin da quando stava scrivendo *Aida*, di riservarmi il diritto di fare la traduzione io stesso unitamente ad un poeta francese. Io faccio questo lavoro con Nuitter in ogni modo, ma mi dorrebbe assai di dare questa traduzione. Ripeto ancora di mandarmi a corsa di posta se Escudier ha diritto di stampare una traduzione francese...«

Im Brief vom 20. Mai stellte Verdi nochmals die gleiche Frage und erklärte anschließend ausführlich:

»Domando questo perché Nuitter aveva fatto qui una traduzione francese che è pessima per rapporto alla scena ed alla musica. Naturalmente il poeta che non è sorvegliato dal maestro non pensa che al suo verso, alla rima, alla frase etc. etc. Ma non è questo che ci vuole per fare una buona traduzione: bisogna principalmente dire quello che si deve dire, e che gli accenti siano giusti. Senza di ciò la frase musicale si altera e diventa altra cosa.
Ora io stesso, collo stesso Nuitter sto facendo la traduzione che deve servire per la rappresentazione che mi appartiene. Non sarà buona traduzione come stile, ma sarà buonissima dal lato scenico e musicale.«

In jenen Tagen glaubte sich Verdi von seinem französischen Verleger betrogen. Wegen der Autorenrechte und der *Aida*-Übersetzung war es zwischen beiden zu

---

[73] *Verdi*, vol. III, S. 795.
[74] Vgl. *Verdi*, vol. III, S. 798—800.

einem so heftigen Streit gekommen, daß Escudier zur Feder griff, um sich gegen die nach seiner Ansicht ungerechtfertigten Vorwürfe des Komponisten zu verteidigen. Verdis Antwort vom 19. Mai ist bekannt[75], wird jedoch erst verständlich, wenn man Escudiers noch nicht edierten Brief vom 18. liest: Er enthält zwar viele Details, die in diesem Zusammenhang überflüssig erscheinen mögen, ist zugleich aber der einzige Beweis für zwei wichtige Fakten:

1. dafür, daß auch Du Locle an jener Übersetzung beteiligt gewesen war, die Nuitter 1876 zusammen mit dem Komponisten überarbeitete,
2. dafür, daß Verdi auf Grund seiner Verträge nicht gezwungen und seinerzeit offensichtlich auch nicht geneigt war, die beiden Übersetzer an den Aufführungsrechten zu beteiligen.

Das vier Seiten lange Schreiben Escudiers hat folgenden Wortlaut:

»THÉÂTRE ITALIEN   Paris, le 18 mai 1876
SALLE VENTADOUR
———

DIRECTION   Mon cher Maître
———

J'ai été tellement accablé sous le poids de vos reproches que je n'ai pu justifier verbalement mes actes. Permettez-moi de les expliquer par écrit.

Je dois vous dire que le reproche le plus sanglant que m'ait péniblement frappé est celui que vous m'avez fait d'avoir touché vos droits à la Société des compositeurs et éditeurs, sans y avoir [été] autorisé par vous. C'est là une accusation grave et qui certainement vous a involontairement échappé. Je ne suis pas infaillible, mais en fait d'indélicatesse je suis à l'abri de toute atteinte.

Vous m'avez rappelé que j'avais à régler une somme de mille francs pour le solo de la Messe. Je ne l'ai pas oublié et si je ne vous en ai pas parlé, c'est que je comptais comprendre cette petite somme du[e] plutôt l'ajouter à celle de 25,000 francs pour vos droits-d'auteurs et à celle de 3,900 fr qui vous reviennent sur vos petits droits. Je sais trop ce que je vous dois de reconnaissance pour que ma mémoire me fasse défaut dans une question d'intérêt.

Ce qui vous a blessé, vous me l'avez dit, c'est mon arrangement avec Ricordi au sujet d'Aida. Mais en tractant avec Ricordi, c'était d'éditeur à l'éditeur / ignorant vos arrangements avec lui. A la vérité je me suis basé pour avoir les meilleures conditions sur les frais énormes de mon entreprise, et j'ai fait valoir les droits d'auteurs que je proposais de vous offrir. Je ne crois pas avoir commis un grand crime, mais Ricordi a commis une inconvenance. Ce que j'ai pu lui écrire était pour ainsi dire confidentiel. Si j'usais de représailles, il n'en serait pas je crois enchanté, mais jamais je me servirai de pareilles armes. Que le traité de Ricordi soit obscur, c'est possible. C'est la une affaire entre moi et Ricordi. Ce que j'ai toujours reconnu ce sont vos droits absolus sur les représentations des théâtres français. J'ai eu le tort peut-être de trop m'avancer envers M. M. du Locle [et Nuitter] en leur disant que je *pensais que vous les ferez*

---

[75] Ibidem, S. 801/802. Es handelt sich um den 3. Brief von 1876 aus der Sammlung der Opéra. Prod'homme hat auch dieses Schreiben nicht veröffentlicht, sondern nur in einer Anmerkung erwähnt, ohne auf die besondere Bedeutung hinzuweisen (vgl. RMI XXXV, S. 551).

participer aux droits d'auteurs, mais vous voudrez bien reconnaître je pense, que si je suis un peu coupable, c'est involontairement.

Ah, par exemple, le point sur lequel je suis en désaccord avec vous, c'est la publication de la partition en français! Lorsque j'ai traité avec Ricordi, il avait déjà annoncé une traduction française. Sur mon observation que cette partition n'était pas pour la France nous avons inséré cette clause dans notre traité:

»Je me réserve (c'est M. Ricordi) le droit de publier la partition *en français.*«

»Pour ce qui regarde la traduction en français que je me réserve de faire il est entendu *que ce ne sera que la traduction que je ferai faire moi-même.*«

Cette traduction annoncée était de M. Boito. Il ne pouvait entrer dans ma pensée pas plus que dans celle de Ricordi que cette traduction paraîtrait en France, car alors ma proprieté serait devenue une illusion.

Maintenant après ces explications toutes loyales que puis-je dire de plus, que puis-je faire? Dites et me voilà à vos ordres. Je resterai toujours votre reconnaissant et fidèle

Léon Escudier«

Die gemeinsamen Bemühungen Nuitters und Du Locles um eine französische Version der *Aida* lagen allerdings schon vier Jahre zurück. 1872 hatte Du Locle dem Komponisten mehrfach über seine Arbeit berichtet[76]; im April scheint er sie zunächst allein begonnen zu haben[77], aber im Brief vom 21. Mai schrieb er unmißverständlich:

»Nous travaillons, Nuitter et moi, à la traduction de la Forza, et nous préparons celle d'Aida. Ah comme je serais heureux si Aida pouvait être donné un jour et bientôt à Paris, comme je l'entendrais!«

Die Übersetzung scheint die beiden Librettisten bis in den Sommer hinein beschäftigt zu haben, denn Du Locle betonte in seinem Brief vom 19. Juli erneut: »*Nous travaillons toujours à la traduction d'Aïda.*« 1876 griffen Verdi und Nuitter offenbar auf jene in musikalischer Hinsicht unbefriedigende Übersetzung von 1872 zurück, an der Du Locle mitgewirkt hatte. Anders wäre kaum zu erklären, warum Verdi sich sechs Jahre später entschloß, zu Gunsten beider Librettisten auf die ihm gehörenden Rechte für die *Aida*-Aufführungen in französischer Sprache zu verzichten. Verdi hatte diesen Verzicht wohl im Mai 1882 während einer Zusammenkunft mit Charles Nuitter in Paris geäußert. Schriftlich fixiert wurde er nur in einem Brief Nuitters, den Verdi seinem *Copialettere* beigefügt hat. Das schon seit 1913 durch Luzios Veröffentlichung bekannte Schreiben[78] darf

---

[76] Die Briefe Du Locles von 1872 sind noch unveröffentlicht. In den bekannten Antworten Verdis vom 17. April und 22. Juni 1872 fällt der Name Nuitters nicht (vgl. PROD'HOMME, La Revue Musicale X, 7, S. 32/33, und ABBIATI, *Verdi*, vol. III, S. 567).

[77] Am 6. April schrieb Du Locle: »je veux seulement Vous dire que la traduction d'Aïda suit son cours«. Auf Verdis Anfrage vom 17. antwortete Du Locle am 26. April: »Oui, je travaille à traduire cette belle Aida. Cela est encore une manière d'être du moins un peu avec Vous. Une fois Aida traduite elle deviendra ce que Vous voudrez, et ce ne sera pas moi qui Vous tourmentera pour que Vous la confiez à la grande boutique — à moins cependant que par miracle elle ne devienne mienne —«

[78] Vgl. *Copialettere*, S. 318, und *Quaderni dell'Istituto di Studi Verdiani* 4, *Genesi dell'Aida con una documentazione inedita* a cura di SALEH ABDOUN, Parma 1971, S. 133/134.

in diesem Zusammenhang nicht fehlen, denn es dokumentiert die erste Versöh-
nungsgeste Verdis gegenüber Du Locle und ist zugleich wichtig für die Datierung
des Beginns der *Don Carlos*-Revision:

>>Paris. 13 Mai 1882

Cher et illustre maître

Vous étiez propriétaire de la traduction française d'*Aïda* faite par du Locle et moi.

Vous me faites savoir que vous renoncez volontairement et de votre propre mouve-
ment à vos droits sur cette traduction, et que, par conséquent, à partir du 1. Mai
1882 tous les droits d'auteur provenant de la représentation en langue française
d'*Aïda* seront partagés par moitié entre le compositeur d'une part et les auteurs de la
traduction de l'autre.

Je m'empresse de vous dire que cet arrangement est accepté par moi, en mon nom
et au nom de M. Camille du Locle dont j'ai la procuration, et j'ai l'honneur de vous
en remercier.

Veuillez recevoir, cher et illustre maître, l'assurance de mes sentiments les plus
distingués.

Ch Nuitter

89 F^{bg}. St Honoré.<<

Seinerzeit scheint Verdi also selbst das Bedürfnis verspürt zu haben, den finanziellen Erfolg der *Aida* in Frankreich mit jenen Männern zu teilen, die ihm bei
der Arbeit geholfen hatten. Nach Abklingen des Zornes über die finanzielle Auseinandersetzung mit Du Locle mag ihm in Erinnerung gekommen sein, daß sein
einstiger Freund ja nicht nur an der *Aida*-Übersetzung mitgearbeitet hatte, sondern auch an der Umformung des von Mariette Bey stammenden Vorwurfs in
ein brauchbares Libretto. Außerdem hatte Du Locle dazu beigetragen, daß der
Auftrag 1870 an Verdi fiel und nicht an Gounod oder Wagner[79]. Durch einige
bisher unbekannte Briefe von Auguste Mariette an Du Locle läßt sich dies eindeutig belegen[80]. Am 19. Mai z. B. schrieb Mariette seinem Freund Camille:

>>Le Vice-Roi brûle du désir de voir les choses se dessiner. Allons donc en avant. Si
Verdi ne peut pas, prenez Mr Gounod; au besoin voyez Wagner. Nous sommes autori-
sés à tout. Mais que bientôt je puisse dire au Vice-Roi que son opéra se fait, qu'il est
sur le chantier. Jusqu'à présent, malheureusement, nous n'en sommes encore qu'à un
échange de lettres, tandis que le compositeur devait déjà être à l'oeuvre.

En d'autres termes, faites choix au plus tôt d'un compositeur, entendez-vous avec
lui sur les conditions, prévenez-moi par le télégraphe, et par le télégraphe je vous
envoie l'ordre officiel du Vice-Roi de commencer, vos conditions acceptées.<<

---

[79] Vgl. ABBIATI, *Verdi*, vol. III, S. 370.

[80] Es handelt sich um fünf Briefe vom 27. April, 19. und 29. Mai sowie 4. und 21. Juni 1870,
die mit weiteren unveröffentlichten Dokumenten zur Vorgeschichte der *Aida* publiziert werden.
Vgl. meinen Artikel *Zur Entstehung von Verdis Aida*, in: Studi Musicali II, 1973, Nr. 1,
S. 15—71.

Im Nachwort des gleichen Briefes unterstreicht Mariette nochmals:

»Il faut que, par votre prochaine lettre, vous me disiez:
la musique de l'Opéra sera faite par M[r] ...
les paroles seront faites par M[r] Du Locle
les décors seront ...«

Die berechtigten Hoffnungen Du Locles wurden aber schon dadurch zunichte, daß sich Verdi von Anfang an das Eigentum des Librettos für alle Länder außer Ägypten vorbehielt[81]. Escudiers oben zitiertes Verteidigungsschreiben beweist, daß Verdi nicht verborgen geblieben sein kann, wie sehr Du Locle und auch Nuitter eine Beteiligung an den finanziellen Erträgen erhofft hatten. Beide waren offenbar von der zwar korrekten, aber wenig freundschaftlichen Haltung des Komponisten enttäuscht worden. Das spricht deutlich aus dem von Prod'homme veröffentlichten Schreiben Du Locles an seine Frau[82], aber auch aus einigen Briefen Du Locles an Nuitter, die aufbewahrt worden sind, weil sie den Ankauf zweier Bilder für die Sammlung der Opéra betreffen. Diese wenigen Briefe vom März und April 1880[83] lassen durchblicken, wie gut Nuitter und Du Locle einander kannten, wie eng sie befreundet waren. Von Bedeutung sind in diesem Zusammenhang nur die lakonischen Schlußworte eines langen Schreibens vom 5. April:

»il me reste juste la place de ne pas vous parler d'Aïda! pauvre ami! — Voilà tout ce que j'ai l'envie ... et la place de dire!
A vous
Camille«

Verdis Verzicht zu Gunsten der *Aida*-Übersetzer war wohl eine Art Wiedergutmachung, mit der zugleich der Weg für eine Zusammenarbeit am *Don Carlos* geebnet werden sollte. Andrew Porters Hypothese, nach der die ersten Pläne zur Umarbeitung des *Don Carlos* möglicherweise schon zwei Jahre zuvor entstanden seien, unabhängig von einer Anfrage des Intendanten der Wiener Hofoper, Hoffmann[84], hält einer kritischen Prüfung nicht stand. Die eben erwähnten Briefe Du Locles von 1880 sprechen nicht vom *Don Carlos*. Außerdem wissen wir durch Briefe Muzios an Ricordi[85], daß Verdi noch kurz vor seiner Parisreise von

---

[81] Vgl. vor allem Verdis Brief vom 2. Juni 1870, hrsg. von Luzio, *Copialettere*, S. 224/225, Abbiati, *Verdi,* vol. III, S. 372, und Abdoun, op. cit., S. 1. Interessant ist in diesem Zusammenhang auch Verdis Entwurf zu dem von Abdoun, ibidem, S. 8/9, edierten Kontrakt mit Mariette (Archives de l'Opéra — nouveau fonds). Vgl. Studi Musicali II, Nr. 1.

[82] Vgl. Anm. 4 und La Revue Musicale X, 7, S. 36/37.

[83] Sie werden in der Pariser Opéra verwahrt unter den *Papiers Nuitter I, 2214.*

[84] Andrew Porter sprach in dem in Anm. 14 erwähnten Londoner Vortrag von »*March 1880, when Verdi was in Paris for the first Opéra performance of Aida given in a translation by Nuitter and du Locle.*« Außerdem kritisierte er, daß »*the revision itself is apt to be attached too specifically to a projected Vienna production of 1883.*« Vgl. Proceedings of the Royal Musical Association, 98, S. 84 und 82.

[85] Hrsg. von Abbiati, *Verdi,* vol. IV, S. 198—200.

1882 nicht im entferntesten an eine erneute Zusammenarbeit mit Du Locle dachte, im Gegenteil, er hielt sie für unmöglich. Am 22. Februar 1882 ließ Muzio den Mailänder Verleger wissen, Verdi habe ihm auf seine Frage nach dem *Don Carlos* geantwortet: »*Ci vorrebbe un poeta sotto la mano, e questi dovrebbe essere naturalmente l'autore di prima. Ciò è impossibile.*« Muzio, der die Gedanken des Komponisten besser kannte als jeder andere, scheint selbst von der Unmöglichkeit eines solchen Planes überzeugt gewesen zu sein, denn er erklärte Ricordi ausführlich:

> »Tu sai cosa gli fece l'autore delle parole Du Locle. Per il D. Carlos non mi voglio dare per vinto, e col tempo voglio vedere se fosse possibile che Du Locle incaricasse, o vendesse i suoi diritti ad un altro poeta, ed in allora proporre questa combinazione a Verdi il quale veramente non ha a lodarsi delle persone colle quali ha fatto affari in Parigi, Du Locle, Escudier, Peragallo. Questi due ultimi gli hanno fatte tali bricconate, che disgustano!«[86]

Im Brief vom 23. Februar versprach Muzio dann[87]:

> »Per il D. Carlos io ne parlerò a Nuitter, e quando Verdi verrà a Parigi, che lo spero non più tardi della fine Aprile, lo farò assalire da ogni parte, affinché lo accorci e ne faccia un'opéra che gira il mondo sotto la nuova forma.«

Dieses Versprechen hat Muzio offenbar mit großem Geschick in die Tat umgesetzt. Am 19. Mai jedenfalls konnte er seinen Bericht über den Parisaufenthalt Verdis[88] schließen mit den Worten:

> »Riportò seco il D. Carlos coi tagli nel libretto ideati da Nuitter.«[89]

Verdi und Nuitter hatten sich in jenen Tagen offenbar mehrfach getroffen, um an der französischen Übersetzung der *Forza del destino* zu arbeiten und über das *Boccanegra*-Projekt zu diskutieren. Den Anstoß zu einem Gespräch über die Umformung des *Don Carlos* mag eine Anfrage des Wiener Hofoperntheaters gegeben haben, die ebenfalls von Muzio inszeniert worden sein könnte. Verdi selbst berichtete Maria Waldmann darüber folgendermaßen[90]:

> »In quanto a Vienna, venne da me, durante il mio soggiorno in Parigi, un signore incaricato dalla Direzione di quel Teatro per darvi il *Simone* od il *Carlos*. Nulla opposizione per Simone ma pel D. Carlos vorrei prima accorciarlo rifacendo naturalmente qua e là alcuni squarci.«

Verdi muß bei der Revision des *Don Carlos* tatsächlich anfangs eine Aufführung in Wien im Auge gehabt haben, wo sich nach seiner Ansicht das beste deutsche

---

[86] Brief Nr. 476 aus der Sammlung des Ricordi-Verlages.
[87] Brief Nr. 477.
[88] vom 1.—18. Mai 1882.
[89] Brief Nr. 508.
[90] Vgl. Luzio, *Carteggi Verdiani*, vol. II, S. 255. Es handelt sich um einen Brief aus Montecatini vom 25. Juni 1882.

Operntheater befand. Dies geht sehr deutlich aus einem oft zitierten Brief an Giuseppe Piroli hervor[91], dem Verdi in drastisch-humoristischer Sprache erklärte:

»Io lavoro ma lavoro in cosa pressochè inutile. Riduco in quattro atti il *Don Carlos* per Vienna. In questa città, voi sapete, che alle dieci di sera i portinai chiudono la porta principale delle case, e tutti a quell'ora mangiano e bevono Birra et *Gâteaux*. Per conseguenza il Teatro ossia lo spettacolo dev'essere allora finito. Le opere troppo lunghe si amputano ferocemente, come in un Teatro qualunque d'Italia. Dal momento che mi si dovevano tagliar le gambe, ho preferito affilare ed adoperare io stesso il coltello.«

Bereits im Oktober 1882 hat Verdi die an der Wiener Hofoper geplanten Aufführungen des *Don Carlos* auch mit Giulio Ricordi erörtert. Dies belegen drei Briefe Verdis vom 8., 13. und 23. 10. 1882. Sie befinden sich in einer im Sommer 1973 vom Musikantiquariat Hans Schneider in Tutzing zum Verkauf angebotenen Sammlung, über die mir Prof. Hans Busch (Bloomington/Indiana) freundlicherweise Auskunft gab.

Für den *Don Carlos* gilt also das gleiche wie für andere Opern Verdis[92]: Der Komponist entschloß sich zu Änderungen immer erst, wenn er überzeugt sein konnte, daß die neue Version binnen kurzem aufgeführt werden würde.

Die Geschichte des *Don Carlos* ist nur insofern besonders kompliziert, als sich Verdi schon vor der Pariser Uraufführung von 1867 gezwungen sah, wegen der Länge des Werkes drastische Kürzungen vorzunehmen[93]. Dadurch war dem Ablauf der Handlung an manchen Stellen die zwingende Logik geraubt worden: Im ersten Akt z. B. wurden die beiden Anfangsszenen ausgelassen, in denen Elisabeth eigentlich vor Augen geführt werden sollte, wie sehr ihr Volk unter dem Kriege litt und den Frieden herbeisehnte[94]. Dadurch bleibt fast unmotiviert, warum Elisabeth trotz ihrer Liebe zu Don Carlos so überraschend schnell in die Heirat mit König Philipp einwilligt. Im vierten Akt der Version von 1867 verstößt die Königin Elisabeth die Prinzessin Eboli allein wegen des an ihr begangenen Verrates, denn das ursprünglich vorhandene Bekenntnis Ebolis, die Maitresse des Königs zu sein, war gestrichen worden[95]. Besonders auffällig ist die

---

[91] Zuerst ediert von Luzio, *Carteggi verdiani*, vol. III, S. 158/159, Brief vom 3. Dezember 1882. Dem Wiener Intendanten gab Verdi schon am 31. Oktober 1882 eine Zusage betreffs des *Don Carlos*. Vgl. Luzio, *Copialettere*, S. 319.

[92] Vgl. z. B. die Arbeiten von Wolfgang Osthoff über *Die beiden »Boccanegra«-Fassungen und der Beginn von Verdis Spätwerk*, in: Analecta Musicologica I, 1963, S. 70—89, und über *Die beiden Fassungen von Verdis »Macbeth«*, in: Archiv für Musikwissenschaft XXIX, 1972, S. 17—44.

[93] Vgl. hierzu vor allem Andrew Porters Darstellung in *Proceedings of the Royal Musical Association*, 98, S. 73, sowie den zweiten Teil meiner in Anmerkung 5 zitierten Publikation.

[94] Der vollständige Text dieser Szenen und Angaben zur Musik befinden sich in meinem in Anm. 10 zitierten Beitrag zu den *Atti del II° congresso internazionale di studi verdiani*, S. 97—101.

[95] Den ursprünglichen Text und Angaben zur Musik enthält mein Beitrag zum Colloque de Saint-Germain-en-Laye (September 1970), vgl. Acta Musicologica XLIII, 1971, S. 184. Vgl.

Auslassung jenes Abschnittes aus dem ursprünglich zweiten Akt, in dem König
Philipp dem Marquis de Posa von der Zerrüttung seiner Ehe berichtet[96]. Dies muß
Verdi deutlich empfunden haben, denn schon 1872, für eine Aufführung in
Neapel, hat er Teile dieses Duetts neu komponiert und den Text dabei so ver-
ändert, daß die Zweifel des Königs an Sohn und Gemahlin zum Ausdruck
kommen. Außerdem hat Verdi 1872 das *Allegro marziale* aus dem Duett Elisa-
beth—Don Carlos des fünften Aktes gestrichen, einen Abschnitt also, der bei der
Revision von 1882/83 leicht verändert wieder eingebaut wurde[97].

Daß eine gründliche Umformung des *Don Carlos* von 1867 wünschenswert und
nützlich sein würde, erkannte Verdi offenbar erst drei Jahre später, und schon
damals wirkte eine Aufforderung aus Wien als treibende Kraft. Nach Angaben
Abbiatis[98] trat der Gesangspädagoge Salvatore Marchesi seinerzeit als Vermittler
des Wiener Impresarios Jauner auf und erhielt von Verdi folgende Antwort:

>»Non ho ancora risposto alla Casa Ricordi a proposito del *D. Carlos*; ciò nonostante
>me ne sono seriamente occupato. Trovo assai difficile farvi dei tagli, a meno di fare
>quanto si usa da molti maestri concertatori, che io chiamerei *scorticatori*!
>   Come capirete, io non devo e non voglio fare come costoro. Per ridurre quest'opera
>a proporzioni più ristrette, bisognerebbe aver tempo di studiarvi un po' sopra e fare
>quanto feci per la *Forza del Destino...*«

Auch Giuseppina schrieb in dieser Angelegenheit an Marchesi: Nach Angaben
Luzios[99] datiert die betreffende Eintragung in ihrem *Copialettere* vom 17. September 1875. Die damalige Anfrage aus Wien fiel also unglücklicherweise zusammen mit dem Beginn der Affäre Du Locle. Man darf demnach wohl vermuten, daß nur die unvermeidbare Auseinandersetzung mit dem Librettisten des
Don Carlos die Revision dieser Oper um fast sieben Jahre verzögert hat.

Dieser langen und komplizierten Vorgeschichte soll im nächsten Band der *Analecta musicologica* die Veröffentlichung all jener Dokumente folgen, die im engeren Sinne zur Revision des *Don Carlos* gehören.

---

außerdem Andrew PORTER, *A Note on Princess Eboli*, in: *The Musical Times*, August 1972,
S. 750—754.

[96] Die zuvor unbekannte Musik veröffentlichte David ROSEN in *Le quattro stesure del duetto
Filippo-Posa*, in: *Atti del IIº congresso internazionale di studi verdiani*, S. 368—388.

[97] Vgl. hierzu ROSENs Darstellung, ibidem, S. 370, Anm. 8.

[98] *Verdi*, vol. III, S. 777/778.

[99] *Carteggi verdiani*, vol. II, S. 45.

DAS DIARIUM DER SIXTINISCHEN SÄNGERKAPELLE IN ROM FÜR DAS JAHR 1594 (Nr. 19)

von *Herman-Walther Frey* †

Die Diarien der Sixtinischen Kapelle sind, obwohl sie eine der wichtigsten Quellen für die Geschichte dieser hochberühmten und einzigartigen Institution darstellen, bisher nur in geringem Umfang der Forschung zugänglich gemacht worden. Bei der Neuordnung der Kapelle zu Beginn des Pontifikats Pauls III. — mit der schriftlichen Fixierung ihrer Konstitutionen — wurden auch die Diarien eingerichtet. Zunächst in erster Linie als Bücher gedacht, in denen die für die Dienstversäumnisse der einzelnen Sänger verhängten Bußen notiert wurden, entwickelten sie sich bald zu einem wahren »Tagebuch«, zu einer — je nach dem Interesse und dem Pflichteifer des jahrweise zum Amt des »Punktators« bestimmten Sängers bald kurzen, bald ausführlichen — Niederschrift der täglichen Begebenheiten, mithin zu einer Fundgrube wertvollster Nachrichten über das Leben der Sänger, über die Vorgänge des täglichen Dienstes, über Wahl, Aufnahme oder Ausscheiden der einzelnen Mitglieder usw.

Raffaello Casimiri hat in der 1924 von ihm gegründeten Zeitschrift *Note d'Archivio per la Storia Musicale* in einzelnen Abschnitten die ersten fünf Diarien-Bände veröffentlicht (1924 ff.); sie sind später in einem Sammelbande zusammengefaßt worden[1]. Casimiris Publikation reicht vom Januar 1535 bis zum Februar 1560 und beschränkt sich auf den Abdruck des Textes der Bücher. Nur einige wenige Erläuterungen, in knappster Form, sind in Fußnoten beigefügt. Nach Casimiris Tode (1943) unterblieb zunächst die Fortsetzung. Meine 1959 veröffentlichte Ausgabe der Diarien der Jahre 1560 und 1561[2] war ein Versuch, durch die Hereinnahme zugehöriger Dokumente aus den Schätzen des Archivs der Kapelle und durch eine reichere Kommentierung den oft allzu kurzen und eintönigen Text der Aufzeichnungen lebendiger und anschaulicher zu gestalten. Diese Art der Edition, die ich besonders für die älteren Diarien für empfehlenswert halte, erscheint mir angesichts der Umfangsvergrößerung der späteren Diarien nicht mehr geraten. Ich habe daher hier von dieser Methode der Veröffentlichung abgesehen und beschränke mich auf den genauen Abdruck des

---

[1] R. CASIMIRI, *I Diarii Sistini, I primi 25 anni (1535—1559)*, Rom 1939, Edizioni »Psalterium«.
[2] *Die Diarien der Sixtinischen Kapelle in Rom der Jahre 1560 und 1561 (Diarium 5 fol. 156—192, Diarium 6)*, herausgegeben und erläutert von Herman-Walther FREY, Düsseldorf 1959, Schwann.

Buches mit nur wenigen erläuternden Fußnoten. Die Editionsgrundsätze sind dieselben, welche ich in meiner Ausgabe der Diarien von 1560/61 dargelegt habe (cfr. ibid. p. IX u. X). Das bedeutete die gelinde Modernisierung der Schreibweise an wenigen Stellen (z. B. *mancò* statt *manco*), die stillschweigende Auflösung nicht mehr geläufiger Abkürzungen (z. B. *Ottobre* statt *8bre*), die gelegentliche Setzung eines Interpunktionszeichens, die Vereinheitlichung etlicher Abkürzungen (z. B. *M.°* statt *m⁻*, *mʳᵒ*, *mᵒ* u. a.). Aber es wurde verzichtet auf schwerer wiegende Vereinheitlichungen, wie z. B. eine solche der verschiedenen Schreibweisen eines Sängernamens (z. B. *Santes, Santos, Sanctos*). Kurz, die »Modernisierung« griff nirgends an die Substanz, die Schreibeigentümlichkeiten des Punktators blieben erhalten.

Das vorliegende Diarium wurde vom Punktator Hippolito Gambocci geschrieben. Gambocci stammte aus Gubbio und war Priester; seit dem 3. Februar 1571 gehörte er der Cappella Sistina als Sänger an. Zum Punktator wurde er erstmalig für das Jahr 1584 gewählt. 1588 war er Camerlengo (auch Abbas genannt) und Giovanni Maria Nanino *»suo coadiutore et secretario«*; 1589 versah er das Amt des Kapellmeisters und wurde 1594 erneut zum Punktator ernannt. Sein Diarium zeigt ihn als einen gewandten und gebildeten Kleriker, als einen genauen, fast etwas weitschweifigen Darsteller der Ereignisse im täglichen Dienst der Kapelle.

Noch einige Worte zur äußeren Gestalt des Diariums. Es hat folgende Größe: 23 x 32,5 cm. Sein (originaler) Pergamenteinband ist in neuerer Zeit restauriert worden. Auf dem Einband vorn steht oben (original): *Ponti del anno 1594*, unten (wahrscheinlich von Gamboccis eigener Hand): *Hippollito Gamboccj*. Auf dem Einbandrücken: *Gamboccius*. Fol. 1r ist leer. Die originale Foliierung setzt erst mit fol. 2r (das sie 1 nennt) ein. Wir folgen der modernen Foliierung, die wohl etwa in den 1930er Jahren erfolgt ist. Mehrfach steht beim Beginn einer neuen Seite ein Kreuz oben in der Mitte, besonders im ersten Teil des Bandes; es wurde nicht übernommen. Die Wochentagsbezeichnungen sind im Original etwas in den Rand hinausgerückt; in unserer Ausgabe ist die Bemerkung zum einzelnen Tage dagegen durch Leerzeilen davor und danach herausgehoben. Das Zeichen / steht für Seitenwechsel; es fehlt, wenn der Beginn der Eintragungen zu einem neuen Tag mit dem Beginn einer neuen Seite zusammenfällt.

Wie auch andere Punktatoren hat Gambocci die ersten Bemerkungen zum Folgejahr noch im Diarium des Hauptjahres eingetragen (cfr. z. B. die Diarien für 1585 und für 1600: beide gehen bis zum 6. Januar des Folgejahres). Ein Diarium für 1595, das sich anschlösse, existiert in der Vaticana nicht mehr*.

---

* Nach dem Tode von H. W. Frey wurde das Manuskript von Herrn Dr. Klaus Fischer zum Druck vorbereitet, wofür ich ihm auch an dieser Stelle danke. F. L.

1594 GAMBOCCIUS
PONTI DEL ANNO 1594

Nel nome de Dio et della gloriosissima vergine Maria. Amen.   fol. 1v
Anno 1594.

Nota delli signori Cantori che al presente serveno nella Cappella di Nostro Sig.^{re} Clemente octavo l'anno secondo del suo Pontificato.

1	Il Rev.^{do} sig.^r Pietro Bartolomuccio decano	da Picinisco
2	Il sig.^r Alessandro Merolo	Romano
3	Il Rev.^{do} sig.^r Fran.^{co} Soto	Spagnolo
4	Il sig.^r Christiano Ameyden	Fiamengo M.^o di Cappella
5	Il sig.^r Paulo de Magistris	da Fumone
6	Hippolito Gambocci Puntator	da Gubbio
7	Il Rev.^{do} sig.^r Vincentio Musatti	Bolognese
8	Il sig.^r Agustino Martini	Romano
9	Il sig.^r Gio. Maria Nanini	Tibortino
10	Il sig.^r Horatio Crescenti	Napolitano
11	Il sig.^r Gio. Bap.^{ta} Martini	d'Aversa; remunerato d'un Canonicato al suo paese
12	Il Rev.^{do} sig.^r Archangelo Crivello	Bergamasco
13	Il sig.^r Thomasso Benigno Camerlengo	Romano
14	Il sig.^r Gio. Santes	spagnolo
15	Il sig.^r Diego Vasquez	spagnolo
16	Il sig.^r Paulo Facconio	Mantoano
17	Il sig.^r Luca Orfeo	da Fano
18	Il sig.^r Fra Oratio Malvicio	Romano
19	Il sig.^r Joseph Bianchi	Fiorentino
20	Il sig.^r Stefano Ugerio	Cremonese[3]
21	Il sig.^r Leonardo Crescenti	Bolognese
22	Il sig.^r G. Luca Conforti	Calabrese
23	Il sig.^r Horatio Griffi.	Romano
24	Il sig.^r Pietro Montoya	Spagnolo
25	Il sig.^r Franc.^{co} Spinosa	Spagnolo
26	Il sig.^r Antonio Manni	Forlivense
[27]	Il sig.^r Gio. Pier Luisci mastro di Cappella di San Pietro[4]	

Gio. Paulo Custode de libri di Cappella

Cappellani Il sig.^r Mario Corona Romano   fol. 2r
            Il sig.^r Pirro Alamanni
Scrittori   Il sig.^r Luca Orfeo da Fano
            Il sig.^r Gio. Luisci Mercato

---

[3] Der Name des Sängers Stefano Ugerio ist nachgetragen. Er ist in der Liste mit der Nummer 20 zwischen den Sängern Francesco Spinosa (Nr. 25) und Antonio Manni (Nr. 26) aufgeführt. Durch Verweiszeichen (doppelte Striche) hier und nach Nr. 19 (Joseph Bianchi) ist die Umstellung in der Reihenfolge der Liste kenntlich gemacht.

[4] Nach Pietro folgte: *Da Palestrino*, das gestrichen ist.

[GENNAIO]

Sabbato A di primo de Gennaro, la Circoncisione de Nostro sig.r, fu Cappella in Palazzo alla presentia de Nostro sig.r Papa Clemente ottavo, et l'ill.mo Cardinal Rusticuccio cantò la messa, come piu distintamente si vede per il libro del sig.r Vincentio Musatti puntatore del'anno prossimo passato.

Domenica A di 2 de Gennaro furno lette le constitutioni dal detto sig.r Vincentio Musatti e per questo fu ditto la messa legendo.

Lunedi A di 3 de Gennaro, il Rev.do sig.r Christiano Ameyden Mastro di Cappella fece congregare il Rev.do Collegio de Cantori del Papa in palazzo nella Cappella de Sisto per eleggere li novi officiali secondo il solito, cioe, Mastro di Cappella, Camerlengo et Puntatore, et prima il sig.r Fran.co Soto disse la messa legendo et di poi invocato il nome de Dio è ditta la oratione dello spirito sancto dal medesmo sig.r Soto tutti si misero per ordine a sedere alli suoi luochi, et il sig.r Christiano Ameyden mastro di Cappella fece un poco de oratione al detto Rev.do Collegio rengratiando tutti della molta amorevolezza et obedientia che haveva ricevuto dal Collegio et domandò perdono, se havesse mancato in qualche cosa quest'anno in questo suo offitio e se in alcuna cosa haveva mancato, non era stato per malitia, et molt'altre parole disse di sodisfatio- /

fol. 2v   ne del che il Collegio restò molto sodisfatto, e tutti per ordine lo rengratiorno et dissero che lui si era portato molto bene et che tutti laudavano et laudono la sua molta diligentia, et il detto renuntiò il detto offitio supplicando il Collegio a voler elegere un homo, che sia atto per questo peso del magistrato di Cappella e che ognuno havesse inanzi agli ochi il servitio de Dio, et se ben tutti, disse, son atti, non di meno ne proporrò doi delli piu vechi conforme alla bolla de Sisto quinto e sua signoria insieme col sig.r Decano proposero il sig.r Agostino Martini et il sig.r Gio. Maria Nanino; qual proposta fu accettata da tutti per buona et optima et nel discorrere con li voti a voce il sig.r Joseph Bianchi disse, che il sig.r Christiano si era portato tanto bene che a lui gli pareva, che si dovesse confirmar in questo offitio per quest'anno; il medesmo disse il sig.r Horatio Malvicio et d'alcuni altri anco confirmata questa opinione e poi tutti insieme dissero, che si proponesse il sig.r Christiano insieme con li doi soprannominati cioe il sig.r Agostino, e il sig.r Gio. Maria; et primo fu mandato fuora il sig.r Christiano per far il scrutinio et fu fatto il partito a voti secreti per fare bianche et nere et hebbe in favore quindici voti et nove in disfavore; di poi fu mandato fuora il sig.r Agostino, il quale hebbe diece voti in favore et quattordici in disfavore; terzo et ultimo fu mandato fuora il sig.r Gio. Maria Nanino, il quale hebbe otto voti in favore et sedici in disfavore, talche dal Collegio fu non sol confirmato il sig.r Christiano per Mastro di Cappella, ma di novo eletto, come si è visto per li voti, e tutti li cantori li resero ubedientia et l'albbracciorno come loro e nostro superiore. La medesma mattina il sig.r Archangelo Crivello camerlengo del anno prossimo passato 1593 renuntiò l'offitio, et se ben da molti del nostro Collegio fu pregato a volerlo esercitar anco per questo

fol. 3r   terzo anno, / non dimeno sua signoria con molte ragioni recusò farlo et con molta humiltà rengratiò tutto il Collegio de tanta amorevolezza et il Collegio per non disgustarlo non glie lo vuolse comandare, anzi da tutti fu rengratiato della buona administratione che haveva fatta in questi doi anni in questo offitio; et immediate il sig.r Mastro di Cappella propose per Camerlengo con consenso de tutto il Collegio il sig.r Thomasso Benigno et me Hippolito Gambocci, et perche li voti furno in favore quattordici per uno, fu ordinato, che di novo si votasse un'altra volta, nella quale il sig.r Thomasso hebbe tredici voti in favore et io undici, talche il detto sig.r Thomasso

fu eletto Camerlengo in[5] loco del sig.ʳ Archangelo et il[6] sig.ʳ Mastro gli dette il giuramento de administrar fidelmente il detto offitio, et anchorche il detto sig.ʳ Thomasso
per molte ragioni havesse prima recusato questo offitio con molta modestia, non dimeno
come figliol' d'ubedientia per ubedire al Collegio accettò volentieri questa fatica; et
sucessivamente la medesma mattina il molto Rev.ᵈᵒ sig.ʳ Vincentio Musatti Puntatore
del anno prossimo passato renuntiò l'offitio al Collegio et restituì il libro delli ponti in
mano del sig.ʳ Mastro di Cappella, et con quattro parole de complimento domandò
perdono a tutti, se non havesse fatto il debito suo, et da tutti fu rengratiato, che pur
troppo diligentemente l'haveva esercitato; et per questo offitio furno nominati dal
sig.ʳ Mastro et dal Collegio tre, cioe, il sig.ʳ Stefano Ugerio, il sig.ʳ Leonardo Crescentio
et me Hippolito Gambocci, et tutti tre ci mandorno fuora per far il scrutinio per voti
secreti, il sig.ʳ Leonardo hebbe nove voti in favore, il sig.ʳ Stefano n'hebbe diece et io
Hippolito n'hebbi undeci, per quanto me fu referto, talche il Collegio giudicò, che
io restassi puntatore per l'anno presente 1594 et giurai in mano del sig.ʳ Mastro, di
puntar fidelmente et giustamente, per quanto si estenderanno le mie debboli forze conforme alle nostre constitutioni, et me protestai / al detto Rev.ᵈᵒ Collegio, che nelle   fol. 3v
cappelle io puntarò rigorosamente, massime quando l'offitio si farrà alla presentia del
Papa et dell'Ill.ᵐⁱ sig.ʳⁱ Cardinali et particolarmente, quando non si osserverà il silentio a tempo e loco, e la medesma protesta feci anco inanzi che me proporressero per
tal offitio, et il sig.ʳ Mastro di Cappella me dette il libro delli ponti del sig.ʳ Vincentio
Musatti.
La medesma mattina il sig.ʳ Gio. Maria Nanino dette il libro delli decreti di Cappella
et il sigillo del nostro Collegio a detto sig.ʳ Mastro et renuntiò il secretariato dicendo,
che non essendoci per adesso piu faccende delle Abbatie non occorreva piu questo offitio
de secretario, ma se qualche cosa occorerà, alla giornata il puntatore la potrà scrivere, si
come era solito de scrivere tutte le congregationi, et detto sig.ʳ Mastro me consignò nelle
mani il detto libro de decreti et sigillo della Cappella. Di poi furno rese gratie a Nostro
Sig.ʳ Dio; in questa congregatione tutti li sig.ʳⁱ Cantori furno presenti eccetto il sig.ʳ
Horatio Crescentio, il qual sarà puntato un carlino, che cosi me l'ha dato in nota il
sig.ʳ Vincentio Musatti.
Il sig.ʳ Horatio Crescentio b 7¹/₂

Martedi A di 4 fu cantata la messa in Cappella de Sisto dal sig.ʳ Mario Corona cap-
pellano.
Il sig.ʳ Luca Conforto venne alla elevatione del corpus domini b 7
Il sig.ʳ Horatio Crescentio mancò in tutto b 7¹/₂
Questa mattina cantò la epistola il sottochierico, per che nessuno delli Clerici venne a
servire, et il detto sottochierico non è in sacris.

Mercordi A di 5 de Gennaro fu vespero in Cappella de Sisto, il Papa cominciò il
vespero et disse la oratione secondo il solito presente tutto il Collegio dell'Ill.ᵐⁱ et
Rev.ᵐⁱ Cardinali; tutti li sig.ʳⁱ Cantori furno presenti eccetto il sig.ʳ Alesandro Merlo
che è delli giubilati conforme alla bolla di Papa Sisto quinto.

Giovedi A di 6 Epiphania. L'Ill.ᵐᵒ et Rev.ᵐᵒ Cardinal Paleotto cantò la messa in san   fol. 4r
Pietro nella Cappella Gregoriana alla presentia del Papa et delli Ill.ᵐⁱ Cardinali; il

---

⁵ Cod.: *il.*
⁶ Cod.: danach ein zweites *il.*

Rev.^{do} Padre Procurator generale de san Marcello del ordine di santa Maria de Servi fece
il sermone, et Nostro Sig.^r dette 30 anni de indulgentia. Tutti li cantori furno presenti
eccetto il sig.^r Fran.^{co} Soto, che è giubilato.

Il sig.^r G. Luca Conforto venne mentre se diceva la gloria; però si punta in doi giulii
conforme alle constitutioni b 20

Venardi A di sette. Questa mattina si tornato a dir mattutino cantar prima et terza
secondo il solito, et ognuno si comincia a pigliar la sua giornata, et si punta un giulio
a tutto l'offitio, cioe, cinque baiochi, chi manca al primo salmo del mattuttino, un
baiocho a prima, un baiocco a terza et tre baiochi alla messa.

Il sig.^r Gio. Santes mancò a mattuttino prima e terza b 7
Il sig.^r Die[go] Vasquez [mancò] al mattutino b 5
Il sig.^r Paulo Faccone a matuttino prima, terza et venne al graduale, quando si cantava
il secondo verso b 9¹/₂
Il sig.^r Horatio Crescentio [mancò] al matuttino b 5
Il sig.^r Horatio Griffo mancò al matuttino b 5
Il sig.^r Pirro Alemani cantò la messa per il sig.^r Mario Corona.
Questa mattina fu concistorio. Il sig.^r Mastro di Cappella, il sig.^r Gio. Maria Nanino,
il sig.^r Thomasso Benigno hanno dato memoriali ad alcuni Ill.^{mi} Cardinali per far offitio de recuperar li quattro scudi, che li sig.^{ri} Cantori solevano haver dal sacro Collegio dell'Ill.^{mi} sig.^{ri} Cardinali ogni volta, che in cappella cantava messa alcuno di essi
signori Ill.^{mi}, et anco il sig.^r Leonardo fu con li sopradetti signori Compagni, et però
non è stato a matuttino ne lui nelli altri sopradetti.

fol. 4v   Sabbatho A di 8 il sig.^r Thomasso portò in cappella la resposta, di quanto era sucesso
per conto del memoriale dato hieri alli Ill.^{mi} sig.^{ri} Cardinali per conto delli quattro
scudi per le messe, et ha referto, che fu proposto in congregatione delli Ill.^{mi} sig.^{ri}
Cardinali il nostro memoriale e raccomandato dal Illmo nostro sig.^r Protettore Cardinal dal Monte, dal Illmo Paravicino[7], dal Illmo Aldobrandino e da tre altri Cardinali, ma la maggior parte delli Ill.^{mi} Cardinali cominciorno a replicar, che non si
doveva far niente di questo negotio, attento che il sacro Collegio è pur troppo aggra-
vato e che si dovria levar delli altri pesi che vi sonno et in questo era molto contrario
l'Illmo Cardinal de Camerino, e fu messo a partito per voti secreti il detto nostro
negotio et in conclusione fu perso, talche non havemo ottenuto niente. In questa mattina al offitio et messa non mancò nessuno se non quelli, che havevano il lor giorno.

Domenica A di 9 di Gennaro. Il sig.^r Paulo de Magistris venne alle laude, mancò al
matuttino b 3
Il sig.^r Horatio Malvicio mancò al matutino b 3
Il sig.^r Thomasso mancò al matutino b 3
Il sig.^r Gio. Luca Conforto mancò al matutino b 3
Il sig.^r Gio. Maria Nanino mancò al matuttino b 3
Il sig.^r Fran.^{co} Spinosa mancò al matutino e prima b 3¹/₂
Il sig.^r Giovan Santes per haver ditto il Capitolo al absolutione de prima, quel della
Epiphania in cambio per quel della dominica infra la octava di detta Epiphania, per
l'errore et lo scandalo, che ha dato per esser giorno di festa, l'ho pontato in cinque
baiochi b 5.

_____
[7] Cod.: *Paraccino.*

Il di medesmo a 9 di Gennaro cantò la messa il sig.ʳ Pirro Alamani Cappellano, et di   fol. 5r
poi la messa io Hippolito puntatore pregai il Collegio delli sig.ʳⁱ Cantori, che nello
offitio divino volessero observare il silentio et far il ponto nel salmegiare, et particolarmente observare il silentio nella messa, et pregai ancora tutti detti sig.ʳⁱ, che ognuno
attendesse a cantare, per che a questo effetto il papa ci tiene, et questo lo dissi, per
che c'è alcuno compagno che non canta; qual esortatione fu accettata da tutti et me
rengratiorno di questa amonitione, et me protestai, che io vedendo far il contrario non
mancharei del debito mio come puntatore, et a questo discorso furno tutti presenti
eccetto il sig.ʳ Fran.ᶜᵒ Soto, il sig.ʳ Decano et il sig.ʳ Alesandro Merlo, che sonno
giubilati.

Lunedi A di 10. Il sig.ʳ Paulo de Magistris mancò a tutto l'offitio et messa b 10
Il sig.ʳ Agostino mancò in tutto al'offitio et messa b 10
Il sig.ʳ Paulo Facconio [mancò] in tutto l'offitio et messa b 10
Il sig.ʳ Gio. Bap.ᵗᵃ Martino [mancò] al mattutino et prima b 6
Il sig.ʳ Vasquez mancò al mattutino b 5
Il sig.ʳ Horatio Malvicio fu trovato in habito corto in borgo et era tempo bellissimo
senza pioggia et senza fango, però conforme al capitulo decimo nono delle constitutioni
l'ho pontato un giulio b 10
Li sopradetti ponti meli dette in nota il sig.ʳ Antonio Manni sottopuntatore.

Martedi A di XI de Gennaro mancò il sig.ʳ Paulo Faccone al mattutino et prima e
terza b 7
Il sig.ʳ Gio. Bap.ᵗᵃ Martini mancò a mattutino, prima, terza et venne mentre se diceva
l'evangelio alla messa b 9¹/₂

Mercordi A di XII. Il sig.ʳ Horatio Crescentio mancò al matuttino b 5   fol. 5v
Il sig.ʳ Paulo Facconio mancò al matuttino e prima b 6
Il sig.ʳ Stefano Ugerio mancò al matuttino b 5
Il sig.ʳ Gio. Luca Conforto mancò al matuttino b 5.

Giovedi A di XIII. Questa mattina non mancò nessuno et il sig.ʳ Archangelo Crivello
Camerlengo del'anno passato 1593 distribuì la mancia de natale et de Capo d'anno
prossimo passato e dette quattro scudi d'oro in oro per uno, alli officiali doppia mancia et al sig.ʳ Mastro di cappella quadruplicata, cioe alli sig.ʳⁱ Cantori quattro, alli
officiali 8 et al mastro 16, che cosi è il solito.

Venardi A di XIIII. Il sig.ʳ Paulo de Magistris mancò matuttino e prima b 6
Il sig.ʳ Paulo Facconio mancò a matutti[no], prima e terza b 7
Il sig.ʳ Pietro Montoya mancò in tutto matuttino, prima, terza et messa b 10.

Sabbatho A di XV. Il sig.ʳ Gio. Luca Conforto mancò al matuttino b 5
Dominica A di XVI de Gennaro. Questa mattina si è fatto consecratione d'un vescovo
in Cappella de Sisto quarto in Palazzo e però non si è ditto offitio ne messa.

Lunedi A di 17. Questa mattina mancorno a tutto l'of[fi]tio et messa il sig.ʳ Gio. Bap.ᵗᵃ
Martini b 10
et il sig.ʳ Agostino in tutto b 10.

Martedi A di 18, la Cathedra Romana de san Pietro l'Illmo et Rev.^{mo} sig.^r Cardinal Montelpero cantò la messa in san Pietro nella Cappella de santo Andrea presente il sommo pontifice e il sacro Collegio delli Cardinali, non si fece sermone, sua santità dette vinti anni de indulgentia. Tutti li sig.^{ri} Cantori furno presenti eccetto il sig.^r Pietro Bartholmucci decano et il sig.^r Alesandro Merlo, che sonno delli giubilati.

fol. 6r   Mercordi A di 19. Il sig.^r Paulo Faccone mancò a matutino e prima b 7
Il sig.^r Horatio Crescentio mancò in tutto l'offitio et messa b 10
Il sig.^r Gio. Luca Conforto mancò in tutto l'offitio et messa b 10
Il sig.^r Joseph Bianco mancò in tutto l'offitio et messa b 10
Il sig.^r Thomasso Benigno mancò, per che prese la medicina.

Giovedi A di 20, San Fabiano e Sebastia[no], non se disse officio ne messa, per che tutti li Cappellani e Clerici di Cappella a[n]dorno a San Bastiano loro chiesa.

Venardi A di 21. Il sig.^r Paulo Facconio mancò il matutino b 5.

Sabbato A di 22. Il sig.^r Gio Bap.^{ta} Martini mancò al matutino prima b 6
Il sig.^r Gio. Luca Conforto mancò al matutino b 5
Il sig.^r Diego Vasquez mancò al matutino b 5.

Dominica A di 23. Il sig.^r Paulo de Magistris mancò al matutino b 3
Il sig.^r Paulo Facconio mancò al matutino, prima, terza et venne, ment[r]e si cantava il graduale b 7
Il sig.^r Battista Martini mancò al matutino b 3
Il sig.^r Horatio Malvicio mancò al matutino b 3
Il sig.^r Stefano mancò al matutino b 3
Il sig.^r Franc.^{co} Spinosa [mancò] al matutino b 3
Il sig.^r Diego Vasquez mancò a matutino e prima b 3:2
Il sig.^r Montoya mancò a matutino b 3
Il sig.^r Agostino Martini mancò al matutino b 3
Il sig.^r Gio. Luca Conforto mancò al matutino b 3.
Questa mattina Gio. Paulo custode de libri disse a me Ipolito puntatore, che lui andava a cantar fuora e che per lui serveria un chierico de san Pietro; quando poi fu tempo
fol. 6v   de mettere i libri mezzo la Cappella per cantar terza, non vi era quel / Chierico de san Pietro, ma in loco de Gio. Paulo custode de libri messe li libri in mezzo la Cappella il chierico del'altare, il quale haveva anco la chiave della Credenza delli libri della Cappella, il che parve molto stranio a molti de nostri Compagni, per che havevamo hauto una gran lite col detto chierico per canto di questo offitio, e di poi la messa il sig.^r G. Maria Nanino disse, che voleva dir doi parole in Congregatione et propose al nostro Collegio il pregiuditio, che poteva venire comportando, che questo Chierico dell'altare se cominciasse ad intromettere a far il servitio del Custode de libri, et che alla giornata ce potria dar delli travagli et metter in compromesso questo nostro offitio del Custode de libri, quale havemo littigato tanto tempo con tanta spesa, et sopra questo il sig.^r Mastro disse, che voleva ognuno dicesse il suo parere, et furno fatti molti discorsi, in ultimo fu resoluto da detto sig.^r Mastro di Cappella et Collegio, che M.^o Gio. Paulo Custode de libri havesse licentia d'andare a cantare dove gli pare per insino al primo giorno di quadragesima, che sarrà alli 23 de febraro prossimo d'avenire e che per lui faccia servire uno, ma che in nessun modo faccia servire per

lui quel chierico o vero servitor del'altare di Cappella per degni respetti, et finito questo tempo se revoca la licentia a detto Gio. Paulo, che non possa andare a nessun loco a cantare, mentre havrà da servire la Cappella, et se non puol stare in questo modo, che lo faccia intendere alli sig.ri Cantori, che se provederanno d'un altro custode de libri, et in plena Congregatione dal sig.r Mastro et Collegio me fu dato comissione, che io come puntatore scrivesse questa Congregatione e che facessi questa inbasciata al detto Gio. Paulo.

Questa medesma mattina fu dato ordine al sig.r Gio. Battista Martino, che solicitasse il nostro negotio della pensione, che ha la Cappella in testa del sig.r Fran.co Soto, et anco fu dato ordine al sig.r Mastro di Cappella, al sig.r Gio. Maria Nanino et a detto sig.r Gio. Bap.ta, / che debbiano sollicitare li nostri negotii dell'Abbatia de Mantoa per quel che restamo d'havere dal sig.r Nicolo Miniati, et hanno dato ordine esser tutti tre insieme domattina a 11 hore per parlar di questo negotio al sig.r Dottor Cepis avocato di Mantova, che al presente si trova in Roma et è molto informato di questo nostro negotio de Mantoa.   fol. 7r

Lunedi A di 24. Il sig.r Horatio Crescentio mancò a tutto l'offitio et messa b 10
Il sig.r Paulo Facconio mancò a matutino b 5
Questa mattina il sig.r Gio. Sanctos ha ditto parole ingiuriose al sig.r Antonio Manni sottopuntatore, quale parole sonno state: ›ingnorante, infame‹, et simili, delle quale io come puntatore ne devo dar querela al nostro Collegio; il quale ha da resolvere, se questo sig.r Sanctos si deve puntare o vero almeno farli una reprensione, che non si debba procedere di questa maniera con li offitiali, attento che la constitutione vuole che, chi si altera con il puntatore, faccia ingiuria a tutto il Collegio. Questa relatione l'ha fatto il detto sig.r Antonio Manni come sottopuntatore, che in loco mio puntava et me l'hanno anco referti alcuni altri de nostri compagni, però io alla prima congregatione ex officio ne darrò querela al nostro Collegio e mastro di Cappella.

Martedi A di 25 de Gennaro, Conversio santi Pauli, comune.
Il sig.r Paulo Faccone mancò al matutino, e per che non era suo giorno d'absentione, si ponta in[8] un grosso per il mattutino b 5
Il sig.r Gio. Luca mancò a tutto l'offitio et messa b 10
Questa mattina il sig.r mastro di Cappella, il sig.r Nanino et sig.r Gio. Bap.ta Martino sonno andati per parlar al sig.r Dottor Cepis Mantovano per li nostri negotij di Mantova e però non sonno stati in Cappella; et non hanno parlato, per che questo dottore si trovava indisposto et sonno restati parlarli domani. Questa / medesma mattina il sig.r Mattheo Argenti Cappellano per esser indisposto d'una mano fece cantar la messa per lui a M.o Gio. Paulo Cappellano de san Pietro.   fol. 7v[9]
In questa medesma mattina io Hipolito puntatore feci la imbasciata a Gio. Paulo Custode de libri, de quanto il Collegio haveva resoluto dominica prossima passata cioe, che gli dava licentia d'andare a cantar dove voleva per tutto Carnevale con questo patto, che lui facesse servire per lui uno in loco suo, ma non servisse questo servitore del'altare per il pregiuditio come di sopra, il qual Gio. Paulo accettò questo partito et promise de osservarlo, anzi soggionse, che non andaria piu a cantare, se cosi il Rev.do Collegio si contentava, e come figliolo d'obedientia faria sempre quanto dal Rev.do Collegio gli verrà comandato.

---

[8] Auf *si ponta in* folgte *un giulio*, diese Worte gestrichen, darüber *un grosso per il mattutino*.
[9] Unten am Rand eine (hinweisende) Hand gezeichnet.

Mercordi A di 26. Il sig.^r Gio Luca Conforto mancò al matuttino b 5
A di detto il sig.^r Thomasso Benigno mancò al matuttino b 5

Giovedi A di 27 fu concistorio publico in sala Regia per il serenissimo inbasciator del
Re de Pollonia, e per che fu impedita la Cappella, non si disse offitio ne messa.

Venardi A di 28 non si disse l'offitio, per che il sig.^r Mastro di Cappella fece congregatione et non fu intimata, ma solo se disse la messa cantata da M.º Gio. Paulo Cappellano
de san Pietro per il sig.^r Mattheo Argenti; di poi la messa se invocò il sig.^r Iddio per
la congregatione, il sig.^r Gio. Maria Nanino domandò al sig.^r Archangelo Crivello
Camerlengo del'anno passato, se haveva anco rescosso la messa de Monsig.^r Gimnasio,
respose, che da lui non era mancato, ma che dal Agente de detto Monsig.^r gli fu detto, che
non haveva anco potuto rescotere, ma che non mancaria, et il sig.^r Archangelo non
mancaria sollicitarlo.

Di poi io Hippolito Gambocci pontatore proposi al Rev.^{do} Collegio tre querele contro
il sig.^r Gio. Santos, la prima che haveva hauto / parole meco per haverlo io apuntato
una domenica per haver fallito il Capitolo del absolutione a prima, e che haveva portato poco respetto alli offitiali contro la constitutione. La seconda che un altra mattina
havendolo io represo, che dovesse far il ponto nel divino offitio et il sig.^r Vincentio
Musatti facendosi il segno di croce per modo di maraviglia di questo romore o poca
attentione, che si usava nel divino offitio, il detto sig.^r Gio Santos glie fece un atto
men che honesto con la bocca. Terzo et ultimo che essendo io alli 24 del presente mese
absente il detto sig.^r Gio. Santos se alterò con il sig.^r Antonio Manni sottopontatore et
glie disse molte parole poche honeste, et per che il detto sig.^r Gio. Sanctos se scusava,
che detto sig.^r Antonio glie dette qualche occasione de dir le quelle parole di ingiuria,
furno fatti di molti discorsi sopra dette querele e fu resoluto, che per questa volta se facesse una buona reprensione al detto sig.^r Gio. Santos et che per l'avenire portasse
respetto alli pontatori et alli altri officiali et vechi della Cappella, et fu dato ordine
al sig.^r mastro di Cappella, che è il sig.^r Christiano Ameyden, che la prima, che farrà
il detto sig.^r Gio. Santos o scandolo in Cappella o altro romore, che il detto sig.^r mastro
lo possa puntare senza remissione alcuna e senza dirne niente al collegio, et per che
tutti doi, cioe il sig.^r Gio. Santos et il sig.^r Antonio Manni, erano fuora absentati,
finche se ragionava di questo fatto, furno chiamati dentro in congregatione et prima
fattoli abbracciare insieme et repacificare, di poi il sig.^r Mastro di Cappella gli fece
a Sanctos l'ammonitione secondo haveva ordinato il Collegio, e gli fece anco la protesta, che mancando del debito suo non se gli havria piu respetto alcuno, et poi detto
mastro disse a me come pontatore, che, quando il detto sig.^r Gio. Sanctos non havesse
voluto ubedire e far il ponto nel divino officio salmegiando, che io lo pontasse rigorosamente non solo lui, ma anco li altri e che nel resto noi pontatori dovessemo procedere de modo, che / non diamo occasione alli sig.^{ri} Compagni, che facciano scandalo
e massime, mentre si celebrano li divini officij. La medesma mattina il sig.^r Mastro di
Cappella, il sig.^r Gio. Bap.^{ta} Martini, il sig.^r Gio. Maria Nanino et il sig.^r Paulo Faccone referimo in questa Congregatione, che havevano parlato mercordi prossimo pas-
sato al sig.^r Anibale dottor Cepis advocato Mantovano per le nostre cose de Mantoa,
il quale glie disse, che noi mettessemo in un foglio tutte le nostre pretensione, che
havemo per conto dell'Abbatia gia nostra di Mantoa e che facessimo, che il Cardinal

fol. 8r[10]

fol. 8v

---

[10] Am Rand vermerkt: *Querele del s.^r Gio: Santos.*

Cinthio alias de San Giorgio, che glie ne parlasse per modo di raccomandatione e che lui non mancaria de farci ogni favore et darci ogni aiuto in questa causa, et fu dato ordine al sig.ʳ Gio Bap.ᵗᵃ Martini, che formasse un'memoriale per darlo a detto sig.ʳ Cardinal San Giorgio et un'altro al sig.ʳ Cardinal del Monte come protettore ce voglia favorir in questa causa col detto sig.ʳ Dottor Cepis.

In questa medesma Congregatione il sig.ʳ Horatio Malvicio propose al collegio et domandò una fede per conto della lite, che verte tra lui et il sig.ʳ Don Stefano Ugerio, nella qual fede desidera, che per la verità il collegio dechiari, che, quando il detto sig.ʳ Stefano intrò in Cappella del Papa, si contentò de non pretendere piu cosa alcuna del tempo passato pertinente alla Cappella tanto della pensione quanto delli denari di Mantova et dogn' altra cosa passata sino a quel giorno, che lui intrò e se lui veramente accettò questo partito, avanti, che sottoscrivesse una poliza, che di questo fatto trattava; in questo fatto non furno fatti molti discorsi, perche tutti quelli, che ve si trovorno, quando il detto sig.ʳ Stefano fu ammesso nella cappella, si ricordino benissimo, che lui accettò questa con- / ditione, e però fu dato ordine al sig.ʳ Gio Bap.ᵗᵃ   fol. 9r
Martini, che facesse una narrativa sopra questa fede e poi la portasse a leggere in plena Congregatione del Collegio e inteso da tutti non si mancaria de sottoscriverla da tutti quelli, che a quel tempo si trovorno a questo fatto. In questa congregatione tutti furno presenti eccetto il sig.ʳ Gio Luca Conforto, imperò non si punta il detto sig.ʳ Conforto, che è sua giornata.

Il sig.ʳ Paulo Faccone venne di poi la messa b 10
Il sig.ʳ Diego Vasquez venne di poi la epistola, ma per che non fu fatto intendere, che se diceva la messa solo, si punta solo per il mattutino et non la messa, per che si è ditta un poco piu presto; però Vasquez b 5
Nella sopradetta Congregatione vi mancò il sig.ʳ Gio. Luca come di sopra; et vi mancorno anco il sig.ʳ Alesandro Merlo, il sig.ʳ Fran.ᶜᵒ Soto et il sig.ʳ Pietro Decano, che questi tre sonno iubilati; et finita detta Congregatione furno rese gratie al Nostro sig.ʳ Dio.

Sabbatho A di 29 de detto non mancò nessuno ne all'offitio ne alla messa se non quelli, che havevano la sua giorna de asentione.

Dominica A di 30, la Creatione de Nostro Sig.ʳ Clemente octavo, anno terzo. Fu Cappella in Palazzo, cantò la messa l'Ill.ᵐᵒ et Rev.ᵐᵒ Cardinal Salviati alla presentia del Papa et del sacro Collegio dell'Ill.ᵐⁱ Cardinali. Tutti li sig.ʳⁱ cantori furno presenti eccetto il sig.ʳ Fran.ᶜᵒ Soto et il sig.ʳ Pietro Bartholomuccio, che sonno iubilati; in questa mattina il Papa diede de indulgentia alla messa 25 anni et per nostre ragaglie doi scudi d'oro in oro per mancia, alli officiali quattro per uno et al sig.ʳ Mastro di Cappella otto ▽ d'oro in oro.

Lunedi A di 31. Il sig.ʳ Horatio Crescentio mancò al matuttino b 5   fol. 9v
Il sig.ʳ Diego Vasquez mancò a matuttino e prima b 6
Il sig.ʳ Paulo Facconio mancò in tutto b 10
Li ponti del mese prossimo passato sonno stati scudi tre e b settanta cinque et un quatrino; et partiti in vinti dui parte tocca per uno baiochi sedici e tre quatrini ▽ 3: 75: 1.
Al sig.ʳ Vincentio Musatti fu dato un giulio per haver letto le constitutioni il giorno che furno eletti li offitiali.

Li ponti del sig.ʳ Thomasso non si rescoteno, se non passano il numero delli 6 giorni, che gli vengono de iure per l'offitio, che questo anno tiene del Camerlengato, et de ragione per l'ordinario deve haver piu delli altri sei giorni.

Il ponto del sig.ʳ Horatio Malvicio d'un giulio non l'ho rescosso, per che me ha fatto vedere, che l'habito, che lui portava, quando fu apuntato, era d'un feraiolo longo, che passava mezza gamba, et veramente era habito piu presto clericale che seculare, ma questa volta glie servirà per amonitione si a lui come alli altri.

[FEBBRAIO]

fol. 10r   Martedi A di primo. Questa mattina non si offitiò in Cappella, per che M.º Tiburtio Clerico disse, che li falignami dovevano acconciare la Cappella per la beneditione delle Candele, ma questo non è solito lassar de offitiare, non dimeno li sig.ʳⁱ Cantori consentirno alla proposta di quel sopradetto Clerico.

Mercore A di 2, la Purificatione della madonna. Nostro Sig.ʳᵉ fece la beneditione delle Candele et le distribuì secondo il solito, et lo Ill.ᵐᵒ et Rev.ᵐᵒ Cardinal Terranova cantò la messa nella medesma Cappella in Palazzo; tutti li Rev.ᵈⁱ Cantori furno presenti eccetto il sig.ʳ Fran.ᶜᵒ Soto come giubilato.

Questa mattina[11] il sig.ʳ Giovanni Pier Loisci eccelentissimo musico nostro Compagno et mastro di Cappella in san Pietro passò di questa a miglior vita e a 24 hore fu portato in detta chiesa accompagnato non solo da tutti li musici di Roma, ma anco da una moltitudine de populo et secondo il nostro solito conforme alle nostre constitutioni cantammo il responsorio, libera me domine, tutti li nostri Compagni furno presenti eccetto il sig.ʳ Alesandro Merlo et il sig.ʳ Fran.ᵒᶜ Soto; et in questo giorno il sig.ʳ Thomasso Benigno pagò il mese presente.

Giovedi A di 3. Il sig.ʳ Horatio Griffi mancò al matuttino b 5
Il sig.ʳ Thomasso mancò al matuttino per andar a sollicitar le nostre Candele al sig.ʳ Mastro di Casa de Palazzo.
Il sig.ʳ Gio Battista Martini mancò a tutto l'offitio per andar a parlar al sig.ʳ Fran.ᶜᵒ Soto per la nostra pensione di Spagna.

Venardi A di 4. Il sig.ʳ Horatio Crescentio mancò a tutto l'offitio e messa b 10
Il sig.ʳ Diego Vasquez mancò al matuttino b 5
Il sig.ʳ Paulo Facconio mancò a tutto l'offitio et messa b 10
Il sig.ʳ Fran.ᶜᵒ Spinosa mancò al matuttino b 5.

Sabbato A di 5 non mancò nessuno. Questa mattina habbiamo ricevuto le candele dal palazzo, che sogliano darci, cioe le candele benedette.

fol. 10v   Domenica A di 6. Il sig.ʳ Mastro di Casa del sacro palazzo disse la messa in Cappella de Sisto quarto et comunicò la famiglia de detto palazzo et per questo impedimento non fu detto offitio ne messa dalli Cantori.

Lunedi A di 7. Il sig.ʳ Horatio Crescentio mancò al matuttino b 5
Il sig.ʳ Diego Vasquez mancò al matuttino b 5
Il sig.ʳ Josef mancò al matuttino b 5
Il sig.ʳ Gio. Sanctos mancò al matuttino b 5

─────────────────────
11 Am Rand: *morte del Palestrina*, darunter eine hinweisende Hand.

Questa mattina se fece congregatione, et fu proposto dal sig.ʳ Gio Bap.ᵗᵃ Martino, che
haveva cercato il registro per conto della nostra pensione et non si trova, che stia in
testa del sig.ʳ Soto, ma che quella pensione si trova messa in testa del sig.ʳ Cavallier
Girolimo Raynosa mastro di Cammera del Cardinal Alesandrino, il qual sig.ʳ Girolimo
dice non saper niente, che glie fusse messa in testa sua questa pensione, però in questo
negotio s'e concluso, che il detto sig.ʳ Gio. Bap.ᵗᵃ et il sig.ʳ Gioan Santos parlino et
trattino con detto sig.ʳ Gironimo per veder, se si potesse condurre, che facesse la procura di questa pensione in testa d'uno delli nostri compagni cantori di cappella, et
quando non si possa questo ottenere, ce resolveremo de pigliar la via del Papa con una
supplica, che la voglia permutare in testa d'un altro Spagnolo.

Questa medesma mattina il detto sig.ʳ Gio. Battista Martini domandò licentia al Collegio per andarsene al suo paese a far la residentia del Canonicato che ha obtenuto da
Nostro Signore in recompensa della sua servitù fatta in Cappella, et dice, che partirà
fra otto o dieci giorni, et per che anchora non ha il posesso de detto Canonicato et
non sa, quel che intorno a questo fatto possa succedere, ha supplicato il collegio, che
non lo voglia levar dal mandato della nostra provisione per un mese o doi d'avenire;
che havendo inteso il collegio la proposta, ha giudicato, che sia cosa giusta mantenerlo
in questo nostro mandato per il mese de Marzo prossimo d'avenire et darli la sua solita provisione, ma se il basso, che ha d'avenire, / serrà venuto in questo tempo, la   fol. 11r
provisione se intenda dare a quel basso, che intrarà in loco de detto sig.ʳ Gio. Bap.ᵗᵃ,
e di questo partito sene e fatto un decreto piu distesamente nel libro delli altri decreti
sottoscritto dal sig.ʳ Mastro di Cappella, et il detto sig.ʳ Gio. Bap.ᵗᵃ ha fatto passar un
breve de Nostro Sig.ʳᵉ in confirmatione della bolla de Papa Sisto quinto in favor della
nostra Cappella, del quale se ne farrà una Copia da metterla nel Archivio delle nostre scritture.

Questa medesma mattina il sig.ʳ Horatio Malvicio me dette in mano un foglio
scritto della Congregatione fatta dal nostro Collegio sotto il di 28 de Gennaro prossimo passato per conto della lite, che verte tra lui et il sig.ʳ Don Stefano Ugerio, et io
come secretario et puntatore lo lessi al Collegio et appena lettone la metà disse il sig.ʳ
Stefano »Signori, io me protesto, che non lo dovete sotto scrivere«, et havendo il
Collegio inteso tutta la narrativa di detto foglio, che esponeva la verità di quello era
occorso, quando intro di novo in Cappella il detto sig.ʳ Don Stefano, il sig.ʳ mastro di
Cappella disse al sig.ʳ Stephano et al sig.ʳ Horatio sopra detto, che andassero un poco
fora, che volevano discorrere sopra questo fatto, et uscirno fuora tutti doi; il sig.ʳ Stefano disse »signori, io me ne andarò a pranzo con vostra bona gratia«, et andò via;
fu fatto di novo discorso sopra questo fatto et giudicato, che quella narrativa stava
giustamente et veramente, come era intervenuto, quando il sig.ʳ Stefano fu de novo
accettato in Cappella, et per questo fu dato ordine al sig.ʳ Christiano, che sottoscrivesse
quel foglio approbando la congregatione fatta di sopra alli 28 de Gennaro, et fu dato
ordine, che si dicesse al sig.ʳ Fran.ᶜᵒ Soto mastro di Cappella di quel tempo, che ancora
sua signoria sottoscrivesse detto foglio approbando la verità del fatto, et a me fu dato
ordine, che mettesse il sigillo in detto foglio, si come ho eseguito et sottoscritto de mia
propria mano. A questa congregatio furno tutti presenti eccetto il sig.ʳ Fran.ᶜᵒ Soto, il
sig.ʳ Alesandro Merlo, il sig.ʳ Pietro Bartholmucci decano et il signor Luca da Fano.

Martedi A di 8. Il sig.ʳ Gio. Luca Conforto mancò al matuttino b 5   fol. 11v
Il sig.ʳ Mastro di Cappella questa mattina diede licentia al sig.ʳ Horatio Malvicio et
al sig.ʳ Leonardo Crescentio per andar a cantar alla Chiesa della Madonna della Val-
licella d instantia del sig.ʳ Fran.ᶜᵒ Soto et per questo non stettero alla Messa.

Mercordi A di 9, la Coronatione di Papa Clemente octavo. L'Illmo et Rev.^mo Cardinal de Fiorenza cantò la messa in Cappella de Sisto quarto in Palazzo alla presentia de Sua Santità et del sacro Collegio de Cardinali; per nostre regaglie havemo doi scudi d'oro in oro per uno, li officiali cioe pagatore et puntatore quattro per uno, et il sig.^r Mastro di Cappella otto ▽ d'oro in oro; tutti furno presenti eccetto il sig.^r Alesandro Merlo. Di poi la messa si andò a cantar il motetto al Papa mentre desinava e di poi intrammo dentro alla stantia dove desinava, et sua santità domandò al sig.^r Mastro di Cappella l'autore del motetto, che si era cantato questa mattina alla messa, glie respose, che era de M.° Gio. Maria Nanino nostro Compagno de Cappella, et il Papa disse non habbiamo inteso tropo bene le parole, il mastro disse, che erano parole della sacra scrittura, ma che non erano troppo in uso della chiesa et il motetto diceva In diademate Capitis; domandò anco, a chi erano restate le opere della bona memoria de M.° Gio. de Pelestrino, glie fu resposto, che erano restate al figliolo, et soggiense, che voleva dar ordine, che fussero di novo stampate e quelle anco, che non erano in luce, per utile delle chiese. Il sig.^r Mastro di Cappella tornò a recordare a sua santità, che ci haveva promessa una stantia in palazzo, e che ven'era una appresso la Cappella, qual teneva gia servitore de' Monsig.^r Bastone, che seria stata al proposito, il Papa disse, che se glie ne desse un poco de Memoriale, e ci dette una larga beneditione et ognuno se ne tornò a casa a desinare a 19 hore e mezzo; tutti furno presente eccetto il sig.^r Alesandro Merlo et il sig.^r Decano, che per esser molto tardo non potendo aspettar se n'andò.

fol. 12r   Giovedi A di X. Il sig.^r Archangelo Crivello non è stato al matuttino per esser andato a rescuotere la messa da Monsig.^r Gimnasio, qual la cantò la seconda Dominica del Advento prossimo passato et gli ha dato cinque scudi di moneta.
Il sig.^r Thomasso mancò al matuttino b 5

Venardi[12] A di 11. Il sig.^r Paulo Facconio mancò a tutto l'offitio et messa b 10
Questa mattina il sig.^r Gio. Bap.^ta Martini di novo domandò licentia al sig.^r Mastro di Cappella et Collegio de nostri Compagni per andar alla residentia del suo Canonicato al suo paese Aversa, et domattina vuol partire omnino col procaccio de Napoli.

Sabbato A di 12. Il sig.^r Paulo de Magistris mancò in tutto b 10
Il sig.^r Agostino Martini mancò in tutto b 10
Il sig.^r Gio. Maria Nanino mancò al matuttino b 5
Il sig.^r Gio. Luca Conforto mancò al matuttino b 5
Il sig.^r Pietro Montoya mancò al matuttino b 5
Questa mattina è partito per Aversa[13] il sig.^r Gio. Bap.^ta Martini, che va alla residentia del suo Canonicato hauto da Nostro Signore per recompensa come cantor di Cappella.

Domenica A di 13. Il sig.^r Paulo Facconio mancò a mattuttino, prima e terza b 4
Il sig.^r Gio. Luca Conforto mancò al matuttino b 3
Il sig.^r Vasquez mancò al matuttino b 3
Questa mattina il sig.^r Mastro di Cappella di poi la messa congregò il molto Rev.^do Collegio de Cantori e propose il negotio del sig.^r Gio Bap.^ta Martino, cioe che alli

---

[12] Am Rand eine hinweisende Hand.
[13] Vor *Aversa* ist *Napoli* gestr.

sette del presente glie fu fatto gratia dal Collegio, che per il mese de Marzo prossimo d'avenire glie si dovesse dare la paga come alli altri Cantori, et fatto di novo discorso sopra questo negotio fu resoluto dal Collegio, che questa gratia non la pol fare, essendo che questi sonno denari del Papa et noi non potemo disporre della borsa del Papa senza sua licentia, e tanto piu che se intende, che il detto sig.ʳ Gio. Bap.ᵗᵃ ha havuto gratia da Nostro Sig.ʳ de tutti li frutti del Canonicato, a die vacationis, et secondo che hanno referto alcuni compagni, il sig.ʳ Diego mastro di Camera del Papa ce amonisce, che avertiamo quel che facciamo in questo; et se ben tutto il Collegio era disposto a far ogni piacer al sig.ʳ Gio. Bap.ᵗᵃ, non di meno in questo / negotio fu   fol. 12v resoluto, che si spedisse il mandato delli Cantori senza la provisione che soleva venire al detto sig.ʳ Gio. Bap.ᵗᵃ Martini e questo per non fare errore, acciò al Collegio non venisse qualche disastro, et per che de questo a tutti pare il giusto; a questa congregatione tutti presenti eccetto il sig.ʳ Alesandro Merlo, il sig.ʳ Pietro Bartholmuccio decano et il sig.ʳ Fran.ᶜᵒ Soto.

Lunedi A di 14. Questa mattina habbiamo fatto l'esequie per la felice memoria del sig.ʳ Gio. Pierloisci da Pelestrina eccellentissimo musico et nostro Compagno in san Pietro nella Cappella Gregoriana, il sig.ʳ Vincentio de Gratis cantò la messa, il sig.ʳ Mario Corona l'epistola et il sig.ʳ Mattheo Argenti l'evangelio; tutti li nostri compagni furno presenti eccetto il sig.ʳ Alesandro Merlo et il sig.ʳ Fran.ᶜᵒ Soto, che sonno giubilati.
Il sig.ʳ Paulo Facconio venne con un ferraiolo a mezza gamba et senza sottana longa, però conforme alla nostra constitutione l'ho pontato un giulio. Il sig.ʳ Paulo sopradetto b 10.

Martedi A di 15. Il sig.ʳ Horatio Crescentio mancò al matuttino b 5
Questa mattina il sig.ʳ Thomasso Benigno ha destribuito la mancia della creatione et coronatione del Papa per l'anno terzo. Questa mattina fu dato ordine al detto sig.ʳ Thomasso da rescotere li denari delle 97 libbre de cera, che ci deve M.º Horatio Giani spetiale del'anchora in ponte.

Mercordi A di 16. Il sig.ʳ Facconio mancò al matuttino, prima, terza e messa b 10
A di detto il sig.ʳ Horatio Crescentio mancò ancor lui in tutto b 10

Giovedi A di 17. Il sig.ʳ Gio. Maria Nanino mancò in tutto b 10
Il sig.ʳ Thomasso Benigno mancò al matuttino e prima b 6
Il sig.ʳ Horatio Griffi mancò al matuttino e prima b 6.

Venardi A di 18. Per esser io amalato Hipolito puntatore feci far la scusa in Cappella per via del sig.ʳ Gio. Maria Nanino.
Giovedi prossimo passato il sig.ʳ Christiano Ameyden mastro de cappella venne per il sig.ʳ Gio. Maria Nanino, ma per che quel giorno non me disse niente, io lo puntai, però non deve esser pontato, e per questo quel punto e nullo.
Il sig.ʳ Paulo Facconio mancò in tutto b 10.

Sabbato A di 19. Il sig.ʳ Gio. Luca Conforto mancò matuttino, prima e terza b 7   fol. 13r
Il sig.ʳ Agostino Martini mancò in tutto b 10
Il sig.ʳ Diego Vasquez mancò a tutto l'offitio et venne passato la epistola alla messa b 9¹/₂

Dominica A di 20. Il sig.ʳ Paulo de Magistris mancò al matuttino b 3
Il sig.ʳ Gio. Luca Conforto mancò al matuttino b 3
Il sig.ʳ Montoya mancò al matuttino b 3
Il sig.ʳ Horatio Crescentio mancò in tutto b 7¹/₂
Il sig.ʳ Facconio per haver mancato a matuttino, prima e terza b 3:4

Lunedi A di 21 et Martedi a 22 non se disse offitio ne messa in Cappella, per che furno date le cotte al custode de libri per portarle a santa Sabina per la Cappella, che si farrà il primo giorno di quadragesima.

Martedi a 22. Vacanze per la causa sopradetta.

Mercordi A di 23. Il giorno delle Cennere fu Cappella a santa Sabina. Il Cardinal Santaseverina Maggior Penitentiario cantò la messa in detta Chiesa alla presentia de Nostro Sig.ʳᵉ et del sacro Collegio de Cardinali, et da sua santità fu data la cennere secondo il solito, il Tehologo del Cardinal Giustiniano fece il sermone et da parte de Nostro Sig.ʳᵉ anuntiò trent'anni de indulgentia. Tutti li nostri compagni furno presenti eccetto il sig.ʳ Pietro Bartholmuccio Decano, il sig.ʳ Alesandro Merolo et il sig.ʳ Fran.ᶜᵒ Soto, che sonno giubilati, et io Hipolito Gambocci tornai al servitio di Cappella et il sig.ʳ Antonio Manni me dette in nota li ponti sopradetti di questi tre giorni, che io non son stato in Cappella.

Giovedi A di 24. Questa mattina l'Ill.ᵐᵒ et Rev.ᵐᵒ Cardinal san Giorgio nepote del Papa ha pregato il nostro Collegio de Cantori, che cantassero la messa a detta Chiesa de san Giorgio, dove sua signoria Ill.ᵐᵃ ha preso il posesso del suo Titolo, a qual messa tutti li nostri compagni furno presenti eccetto il sig.ʳ Mastro di Capella, sig.ʳ Alesandro Merlo, il sig.ʳ Decano et il sig.ʳ Sotto; di poi la messa il sig.ʳ Luca Marentio invitò tutto il Collegio a desinare da parte del sopradetto sig.ʳ Cardinale in Palazzo, a qual desinare mancorno li giubilati, il sig.ʳ Horatio Crescentio, il sig.ʳ Archangelo Crivello et il sig.ʳ Pietro Montoya.

fol. 13v   Venardi A di 25. Il sig.ʳ Horatio Malvicio s'è scusato infermo.
Il sig.ʳ Faccone mancò a terza, sesta et messa b 5.

Sabbatho A di 26. Il sig.ʳ Horatio Malvicio questa mattina venne al servitio sano et salvo.

Dominica A di 27, la prima Dominica di Quadragesima, fu Cappella in Palazzo in Cappella de Sisto quarto. Monsig.ʳ Rev.ᵐᵒ Arcivescovo di Ravenna cantò la messa alla presentia de Nostro Sig.ʳᵉ et de tutto il Collegio dell Ill.ᵐⁱ et Rev.ᵐⁱ Cardinali, un frate della Minerva fece il sermone et da parte de Nostro Sig.ʳᵉ anuntiò diece anni de indulgentia; il sopradetto Monsig.ʳ Arcivescovo di Ravenna per esser la prima messa, che sua Signoria Rev.ᵐᵃ ha cantata in Cappella, ha donato di mancia al nostro Collegio de Cantori del Papa giulii settantaotto[14], che sonno sei ducati d'oro di camera novi; in questa messa tutti li compagni furno presenti eccetto il sig.ʳ Decano, il sig.ʳ Alesandro Merlo, il sig.ʳ Fran.ᶜᵒ Soto, che sonno giubilati.

Lunedi A di 28. Il sig.ʳ Paulo Faccone mancò a matuttino, prima, terza, sesta, nona et messa, ma venne al'Agnus dei, e per che la quadragesima per respetto del vespro, che se

---

[14] otto anstelle eines gestrichenen cinque.

dice la mattina in Cappella, si punta in tutto l'offitio doi carlini, cioe il matuttino cinque baiochi, prima, terza sesta et nona 4 baiochi, messa tre baiochi, et il vespro tre baiochi, talche il sig.ʳ Paulo Faccone per il ponto di questa mattina b 12.

Questa mattina il sig.ʳ Thomasso Benigno Camerlengo ha distribuito li settantaotto giulij hauti da Monsig.ʳ Rev.ᵐᵒ Arcivescovo di Ravenna come di sopra et partiti fra 25 Cantori.

Li ponti del mese de Febraro prossimo passato sonno stati giulij vintidoi e sette baiochi, quali sonno stati partiti fra 21 cantori, tocca per ciascheduno diece baiochi e quattro quatrini[15].

[MARZO]

Martedi A di primo mancò al matuttino, prima e terza il sig.ʳ Paulo Faccone b 7   fol. 14r
Il sig.ʳ Luca Conforto mancò al matuttino b 5
Il sig.ʳ Joseph Bianco mancò a matuttino e prima b 6

Mercordi A di 2. Il sig.ʳ Paulo Faccone mancò a matuttino, prima, terza, sesta, nona et venne di poi l'evangelio della messa b 12
Il sig.ʳ Horatio Crescentio mancò in tutto l'offitio messa et vespero b 15
Il sig.ʳ Benigno mancò al matuttino b 5

Giovedi A di 3. Il sig.ʳ Horatio Griffi mancò al matuttino b 5
Il sig.ʳ Gio Luca Conforto mancò al matuttino b 5
Il sig.ʳ Thomasso Benigno mancò al matuttino b 5

Venardi a di 4. Il sig.ʳ Paulo de Magistris mancò al matuttino b 5
Io Hipolito Puntatore mancai al matuttino et venni al terzo salmo b 5
Il sig.ʳ Paulo Facconio mancò a matuttino e tutte le hore b 9
Il sig.ʳ Horatio Malvicio mancò a matuttino e prima b 6
Il sig.ʳ Horatio Griffi mancò al matuttino b 5
Il sig.ʳ Joseffe Bianco mancò al matuttino e prima b 6
Il sig.ʳ Fran.ᶜᵒ Spinosa mancò al matuttino e prima b 6.
Questa mattina il sig.ʳ Mario Corona, cappellano che era de settimana, non venne e per questo non si cantò ne messa ne vespero.

Sabbatho A di 5. Non mancò nessuno questa mattina; il sig.ʳ Thomasso pagò il mese de Marzo e fece la distributione della paga della bona memoria del sig.ʳ Gio. da Pelestrino delli denari, che avanzorno per far l'esequie et toccano sette giulij e 12 quatrini per uno.

Domenica A di 6 de Marzo, Dominica seconda di Quadragesima, fu Cappella in Palazzo in Cappella de Sisto quarto, Monsig.ʳ Rev.ᵐᵒ Celso Vescovo di Castro cantò la messa alla presentia de Nostro Signore et del Collegio del Ill.ᵐⁱ sig.ʳⁱ Cardinali, un frate d'Ara Celi fece il sermone e da parte de Nostro Signore anuntiò diece anni de indulgentia, et il sopradetto Rev.ᵐᵒ Monsig.ʳ Rev.ᵐᵒ per esser la sua prima messa ditta

---

[15] Nach *quatrini* folgte: *per uno,* das gestrichen ist.

in Cappella donò di mancia al nostro Collegio de cantori scudi 6 d'oro in oro, che di moneta sonno ▽ 7:32. In questa Cappella tutti furno presenti eccetto il sig.ᵣ Pietro Bartholomucci decano, il sig.ᵣ Alesandro Merolo et il sig.ᵣ Fran.ᶜᵒ Soto giubilati.

fol. 14v Lunedi A di 7 de Marzo si fece cappella alla Minerva alla Cappella de san Thomasso d'Aquino, Monsig.ᵣ Rev.ᵐᵒ Vescovo della Scala cantò la messa alla presentia del Collegio dell Ill.ᵐⁱ et Rev.ᵐⁱ sig.ʳⁱ Cardinali numero 37, et ad instantia del Ill.ᵐᵒ et Rev.ᵐᵒ Cardinal di Ragona; tutto il nostro Collegio di cantori sonno stati a cantar detta Messa con le cotte; per nostro solito pagamento il detto Ill.ᵐᵒ Cardinal ci deve scudi diece di moneta. In questa Messa tutti furno presenti eccetto il sig.ᵣ Pietro Bartholmuccio Decano et il sig.ᵣ Alesandro Merolo; il sig.ᵣ Paulo Facconio intrava in coro, dove si cantava detta Messa di poi la epistola, quando se principiava il graduale e senza cotta, però de rigore ha perso il ponto et la participatione; participanti in questa messa 23. Il sig.ᵣ Paulo Faccone venuto di poi la Epistola b 15

Questa medesma mattina di poi la messa il sig.ᵣ Mastro di Cappella fece congregare il Collegio de cantori nel Claustro delli frati della Minerva et me dette una littera del sig.ᵣ Gio. Battista Martino venuto d'Aversa con una fede del Capitolo d'Aversa, nella quale fa fede, che detto sig.ᵣ G. Battista non ha ricevuto nessuna sorte de frutti del suo Canonicato dal giorno della morte del suo antecessore, si come era stato referto al nostro Collegio, et nella littera il detto sig.ᵣ Gio. Battista da avviso della posessione pigliata del suo canonicato et prega il Collegio, che voglia eleggere doi delli nostro Compagni per andar dal Ill.ᵐᵒ sig.ᵣ Diego mastro di Camera di Nostro Signore a far scusa per il detto sig.ᵣ Gio. Battista per conto della gratia, che se gli era fatta della paga per il mese di Marzo, che il tutto si era fatto per respetto, che non si sapeva se havesse possuto haver il posesso di detto Canonicato, et il tutto, acciò detto sig.ᵣ Diego restasse capace del fatto et anco cercar con questa diligentia, che il detto sig.ᵣ Gio. Bap.ᵗᵃ restasse nella bona gratia di detto sig.ᵣ Diego, et a questo offitio fu eletto il sig.ᵣ Gio. Sanctos, il sig.ᵣ Paulo Faccone et il Hipolito puntatore. Questa medesma

fol. 15r mattina fu dato ordine al sig.ᵣ Gio. Maria Nanino et al sig.ᵣ Gio. Sanctos per / sollicitar la pensione di cappella per suplicar, quando serrà tempo, che Nostro Sig.ᵣ commuti la persona de un Spagnolo, poi che il sig.ᵣ Girolimo Rainoto non la intende bene per noi. Questa medesma mattina il sig.ᵣ Mastro di Cappella et il sig.ᵣ Gio. Maria Nanino hanno referto in congregatione, che circa il Memoriale dato al Ill.ᵐᵒ Cardinal San Giorgio per le nostre cose de Mantoa, ha resposto, che prima che ce faccia la littera de favore al sig.ᵣ Duca de Mantoa, la vuol considerar molto bene, per che dubbita, che questa cosa non retorni in suo danno essendo lui patrone de quella Abbatia, et però disse il sig.ᵣ Cardinal, che se lasassero vedere, che glie darria resolutione. In questa Congregatione furno tutti presenti ecetto il sig.ᵣ Decano, il sig.ᵣ Alesandro Merlo et il sig.ᵣ Fran.ᶜᵒ Soto; et in questa ultima partita, dove si trattava della pensione e del interesso di Mantoa, non vi fu presente se non l'interressati.

In questa medesma mattina il sig.ᵣ Thomasso Benigno ha partito li sei scudi d'oro in oro riceuti dal Rev.ᵐᵒ Monsig.ᵣ Celso Vescovo di Castro, de quali denari se ne sonno levati diece giulij per le candele date al sig.ᵣ Cassier, che ci paga li denari del salario, et alli notarij, che spediscano il nostro mandato, del resto partiti in 25 parte ha dato a ciascheduno 25 baiochi et un quatrino.

Martedi A di 8. Il sig.ᵣ Horatio Crescentio mancò a tutto l'offitio, messa et vespero b 15

A di detto il sig.ᵣ Gio. Luca Conforto mancò al matuttino b 5

Mercordi A di 9. Il sig.ʳ Paulo Faccone mancò a mattutino e prima b 6

Il sig.ʳ Paulo de Magistris per relatione del sig.ʳ Paulo Faccone fa la scusa come infermo; ma per che lui non ha mandato detta scusa, si punta il detto sig.ʳ Paulo de Magistris. b 15

Il sig.ʳ Thomasso Benigno mancò a matuttino e prima b 6

Questa mattina il detto sig.ʳ Thomasso Benigno ha distribuito li scudi diece de moneta riceuto dal Ill.ᵐᵒ Cardinal de Ragona per la messa cantata alla Minerva il giorno de san Thomasso alli sette del presente mese et ha dato a 23 cantori giulij quattro, doi baiochi e tre quatrini per uno, ma se retiene la parte che toccaria al sig.ʳ Paulo Faccone per insino a tanto, che si dichiari dal Collegio, se gli viene di ragione essendo lui venuto tardo et se retiene doi giulij spesi per far portar la cassa delle cotte / il   fol. 15v
detto giorno de san Thomasso alla Minerva; in questo giorno a hore dicinove il sig.ʳ Paulo Facconio et io Hipolito puntatore mandati dal molto Rev.ᵈᵒ nostro Collegio siamo stati dal Ill.ᵐᵒ sig.ʳ Diego mastro di Camera de Nostro Sig.ʳ a farli saper da parte del Collegio, che quanto s'era fatto per conto de dar la paga di Marzo al sig.ʳ Gio. Bap.ᵗᵃ Martini recompensato da Nostro Sig.ʳᵉ del Canonicato; tutto si era fatto a bon fine pensando, che non havesse cosi presto consequito il posesso, et acciò non restasse senza l'uno e l'altro, si era fatto decreto de darli questa paga de Marzo, ma poi havendo considerato il Collegio, che non toccava a noi a metter la mano alla borsa dal Papa, l'habbiamo levato del mandato de Marzo e ce siamo appigliati al consiglio de sua signoria Ill.ᵐᵃ, che ci mandò avertire di tutto questo fatto per nostro utile; et il detto sig.ʳ Ill.ᵐᵒ restò molto sodisfatto di questa diligentia offerendosi a far sempre ogni servitio a tutto il Collegio in particolare et in generale a tutti, et parimente al sig.ʳ Gio. Bap.ᵗᵃ Martino, et ce disse, che glie scrivessemo, che non mancharia farli ogni servitio a tutte le sue ocorentie.

Giovedi A di 10. Il sig.ʳ Thomasso Benigno mancò al matuttino b 5

Venardi. Il sig.ʳ Horatio Crescentio mancò a matuttino e tutte l'hore b 9

Il sig.ʳ Thomasso Benigno mancò al matuttino b 5

Il sig.ʳ Fran.ᶜᵒ Spinosa mancò a matuttino, prima e terza b 7

Il sig.ʳ Paulo Facconio mancò a matuttino e tutte l'hore b 9.

Questa mattina sig.ʳ Thomasso Benigno partì la parte, che pretendeva il sig.ʳ Paulo Facconio della messa de san Thomasso d'Aquino, che per non esser stato a tempo, non glie ne tocca; questa medesma mattina il sig.ʳ Paulo Facconio et io Hipolito Gambocci habbiamo referto al collegio la imbasciata fatta al sig.ʳ Ill.ᵐᵒ mastro di Camera sig.ʳ Diego et ditto al Collegio da parte de sua Sig.ʳⁱᵃ Ill.ᵐᵃ, che se nessuno sapesse, dove fusse qualche bon Basso, glielo faccia intendere, che farrà scrivere da diversi sig.ʳⁱ, atteso che quello doveva venire in loco del sig.ʳ Gio. Bap.ᵗᵃ Martini, non se ne sa nova; et questa mattina si è dato risposta alla littera de detto sig.ʳ Gio. Bap.ᵗᵃ Martini letta da me Hipolito in collegio, e mancorno quelli del suo giorno asente.

Sabbato A di 12, San Gregorio. Questa mattina il sig.ʳ Horatio Malvicio, il sig.ʳ Horatio Griffi et il sig.ʳ Gio. Luca Conforto tutti tre giunti insieme non hanno mai fatto   fol. 16r
punto alli salmi delli noturni del matuttino con disturbo del coro, et anchor che io l'habbia avertiti, nondimeno non lo facevano, però li ho pontati tutti tre cinque baiochi per uno.

Il sig.ʳ Horatio Malvicio
Il sig.ʳ Horatio Griffi   } per la detta causa b 5
Il sig.ʳ Gio. Luca Conforto

Domenica A di 13 de Marzo, Domenica III de Quadragesima, cantò la messa in cappella de Sisto IIII alla presentia de Nostro Signore et del Collegio del Ill.mi sig.ri Cardinali Monsig.r Rev.mo Vescovo de Todi, un frate de sant' Agostino fece il sermone, et da parte de Nostro Signore diede X anni de indulgentia; tutti li sig.ri compagni furno presenti eccetto il sig.r Pietro Bartholmucci decano et il sig.r Alesandro Merlo iubilati.

Lunedi A di 14. Il sig.r Benigno mancò al matuttino b 5
Il sig.r Paulo Facconio mancò al matuttino b 5

Martedi A di 15. Il sig.r Paulo Facconio mancò a tutto l'offitio, messa et vespero b 15

Mercordi a di 16. niente. Il sig.r Gio. Luca Conforto mancò a matuttino e tutte le hore b 9
Il sig.r Horatio Malvicio mancò a matuttino e tutte l'hore b 9

Giovedi A di 17. Il sig.r Agostino Martini mancò al matuttino b 5
Il sig.r Thomasso Benigno mancò a matuttino b 5
Il sig.r Horatio Griffi mancò al matuttino e tutte l'hore b 9.

Venardi A di 18. Il sig.r Paulo de Magistris mancò a matuttino e tutte l'hore b 9
Il sig.r Benigno mancò a matuttino e prima b 6
Il sig.r Joseph Bianco mancò a matuttino e prima b 6
Il sig.r Paulo Faccone mancò a matuttino b 5
Il sig.r Diego Vasquez mancò al matuttino b 5
Il sig.r Fran.co Spinosa mancò a matuttino et prima b 6

Sabbatho A di 19. Il sig.r Horatio Malvicio mancò al matuttino b 5
Il sig.r Gio. Luca Conforto mancò al matuttino e prima b 6

fol. 16v Domenica A di 20, la Domenica IIII de Quadragesima. L'Ill.mo et Rev.mo Cardinal Pallotto cantò la messa in Palazzo della Cappella de Papa Sisto IIII alla presentia de Nostro Sig.r et del sacro Collegio del Ill.mi et Rev.mi sig.ri Cardinali, un frate del ordine de Carmelitani fece il sermone et anuntiò da parte de Nostro Sig.r Clemente VIII quindici anni de indulgentia; tutti li nostri Compagni et fratelli furno presenti eccetto il sig.r Pietro Bartholmuccio decano, sig.r Alesandro Merlo, et il sig.r Fran.co Soto, quali sonno giubilati.

Lunedi A di 21. Il sig.r Paulo Faccone mancò al matuttino e prima b 6
Il sig.r Thomasso Benigno mancò al matuttino b 5
Il sig.r Gio. Santes mancò al matuttino b 5
Il sig.r Diego Vasquez mancò al matuttino b 5

Martedi A di 22. Il sig.r Paulo Faccone mancò al matuttino, prima e terza b 7

Mercordi A di 23. Il sig.r Paulo Faccone mancò al matuttino e prima b 6
Il sig.r Thomasso mancò al matuttino b 5
Il sig.r Fran.co Spinosa mancò al matuttino b 5

Giovedi A di 24. Questo di se mandorno le cotte alla Minerva, però non si disse ne offitio ne messa.

Venardi A di 25 fu Cappella alla chiesa della Minerva. L'Ill.mo et Rev.mo Cardinal d'Ascoli cantò la messa alla presentia de Nostro Sig.re et del sacro Collegio de Cardinali et il Papa fece il maritaggio delle Zitelle della Anuntiata secondo il solito; tutti li Rev.di sig.ri Cantori furno presenti eccetto il sig.r Pietro Decano, il sig.r Alesandro Merolo et il sig.r Fran.co Soto, che sonno giubilati.

Sabbatho A di 26. Non si disse offitio ne messa in cappella, per che la maggior parte andorno a cantar la messa a san Nicola in Carcere ad instantia del Ill.mo et Rev.mo Sig.r Cardinal Aldobrandino nepote del Papa.

Domenica A di 27 Dominica de Passione cantò la messa Monsig.r Rev.mo Vescovo Mon-   fol. 17r
sig.r Montorio alla presentia del Papa et del sacro Collegio de Cardinali in Cappella de Sisto IIII. Un frate de santa Maria de Servi fece il sermone et anuntiò X anni de indulgentia da parte de Nostro Sig.re et il sopradetto Monsig.r Montorio per esser la prima messa, che ha cantata in Cappella, ha donato al nostro Collegio de Cantori scudi sei d'oro, cioe dodici giulij per scudo in tanti testoni, che di moneta sonno scudi sette e doi giulij; tutti li Rev.di sig.ri Cantori furno presenti eccetto il sig.r Pietro Decano, il sig.r Alesandro Merlo et il sig.r Fran.co Soto, che sonno giubilati. Di poi la messa fu dato ordine, che domattina a 13 hore e mezzo si cominciasse a provare le lamentationi per la settimana santa.

Lunedi A di 28. Si cominciò a provar le lamentationi per la settimana santa, il sig.r Luca Orfeo fece la scusa, che sta infermo.
Il sig.r Paulo Facconio non venne in tutta questa mattina, però si punt[a] il detto b 15.
Il sig.r Paulo Fumone domandò licentia per questa settimana et li fu concessa da tutto il Collegio esser absente.
Il sig.r Fran.co Soto questa mattina propose al collegio voler participare come giubilato del esequie, che furno fatte per il sig.r Gio. de Pelestrino dicendo, che è cosa ordinaria della Cappella, delle quali disse, che tutti li giubilati devono participare, sopra la qual proposta non fu data altra resolutione se non, che si faccia vedere per poter resolvere cosa giusta et honesta.
Questa medesma mattina il sig.r Thomasso Benigno ha partito li sette scudi e doi giulij receutj da Monsig.r Montorio per la messa de hier mattina et ha dato per ciascheduno baiochi 28 et quattro quatrini in 25 cantori, che tanti siamo adesso et ve se includeno anco li giubilati.

Martedi A di 29. Questa mattina, di poi che si sonno provate le lamentationi, fu esaminato M.o Fran.co Ceciliano basso di san Pietro et fu resoluto dal Collegio, che il sig.r Mastro di Cappella domandasse secretamente a ciascheduno cantore di Cappella, che gli pareva della voce et della sufficientia de detto M.o Fran.co, et secondo la relatione, che haveva dalli Cantori, referisse al Ill.mo sig.r Diego mastro di Camera di Nostro Sig.re, qual diligentia il sig.r Mastro di Cappella disse la faria un giorno di questa presente settimana; in questa medesma mattina il sig.r Paulo Facconio / portò una   fol. 17v
littera in Cappella, qual veniva da Baviera, che la mandava un certo M.o Jacomo Carlo, al quale fu scritto dal sig.r Paulo Belasio da parte del sig.r Diego mastro di Camera, che venisse per Basso nella Cappella di Nostro Sig.re essendo referto, che era buono per questo servitio del Papa; nella qual littera il detto M.o Jacomo responde a detto sig.r Paulo Belasio, che lui non ha hauto ardere de domandar licentia al duca di Baviera per alcuni respetti, et che non ardisce ancor domandar licentia sino a tanto,

che non habbia un breve qualmente lui sia gia accettato et aspettato a questo servitio de Nostro signore, e che allora si risolverà di venire. In questo fu resoluto, che il sig.ʳ Paulo Faccone portasse la detta littera al Ill.ᵐᵒ sig.ʳ Diego et vedesse e referisse, quanto gli respondeva, dicendo che non è solito mandar brevi a Cantori, che Nostro Sig.ʳᵉ non è solito di far tal brevi se non a Cardinali et altri principi, ma se il sig.ʳ Diego giudicarà, che se gli scriva una littera, la Cappella glie scriverà. In questa congregatione furno tutti presenti eccetto il sig.ʳ Decano, il sig.ʳ Alesandro et il sig.ʳ Luca Orfeo infirmi.

Mercordi A di 30 de Marzo. Di poi che furno provate le lamentationi, il sig.ʳ Stephano Ugerio propose al Collegio una fede dell'admisione del sig.ʳ Horatio Malevuitio et della provisione, che il detto ha riceuta come tutti l'altri cantori al tempo delle Abbatie et prega il Collegio, che gli faccia sottoscrivere la detta fede dal mastro di Cappella et havendo il Collegio considerato, che la domanda di detto sig.ʳ Stephano era giusta e vera, ha ordinato al sig.ʳ Christiano Ameyden mastro di Cappella, che in nome del Collegio sottoscriva detta fede, si come ha sottoscritto, et io Hipolito Gambocci come secretario ho sottoscritto de mandato la detta fede questo di 30 de Marzo 1594. Questa medesma mattina si è dato licentia al sig.ʳ Luca Orfeo, che possa uscir di casa, che cosi è il consiglio del medico. Questa medesma mattina si è dato licentia et resoluto, che li tre giorni seguenti cioe Giovedi, Venardi e sabbato ciascheduno attenda al esamine della sua conscidentia per confessarsi e poi con l'aiuto de Dio il giorno della Santa Pasqua de Resuretione si possa comunicare ognuno alla sua Parochia.

fol. 18r   Giovedi A di 31 de Marzo. ⎫
           Venardi A di primo d'Aprile ⎬   Questi tre giorni non si va in cappella per
           Sabato A di 2 d'Aprile   ⎭   attendere alla confessione.

[APRILE]

Li ponti de Marzo prossimo passato sonno stati scudi tre e baiochi quarantadoi a 21 parte e toccato baiochi sedici et un quatrino per uno; li ponti del sig.ʳ Thomasso Benigno non se rescoteno per esse lui Camerlengo se non passano però le sei giornate, che al lui prevengono per il detto offitio, e li 4 giubilati non participano delli ponti, avanza il pontatore tre quatrini.

Domenica delle Palme a di 3 d'Aprile. L'Ill.ᵐᵒ et Rev.ᵐᵒ Cardinal Borromeo cantò la messa in Cappella de Sisto IIII in Palazzo alla presentia de tutto il Collegio dell'Ill.ᵐⁱ et Rev.ᵐⁱ Cardinali. Nostro Sig.ʳ fece la beneditione e distributione delle palme secondo il solito e fu presente alla messa, il Passio lo cantò il Rev.ᵈᵒ sig.ʳ Archangelo il testo: il Rev.ᵈᵒ sig.ʳ Don Stefano, il Christo; et io Hipollito Gambocci le turbe. Nostro Sig.ʳ diede 25 anni de indulgentia; tutti presenti eccetto il sig.ʳ Decano, che sta male, il sig.ʳ Alesandro Merlo et il sig.ʳ Fran.ᶜᵒ Soto; questa mattina si è hauta la paga.
Questa[16] medesma mattina venne in Cappella de Sisto IIII nel coro il sig.ʳ Luca Cavalcanti mastro di Camera o cameriero secreto dello Ill.ᵐᵒ et Rev.ᵈᵒ Cardinal Aldobrandino nepote de Nostro Signore et disse al Collegio da parte del detto Ill.ᵐᵒ Cardinale Aldobrandino, che il Papa haveva fatto gratia a M.ᵒ Felice Anerio[17] del luoco,

---

[16] Am Rand: *Il sig.ʳ Felice Enerio accettato per compositore.*
[17] Cod.: *Enerio.*

che haveva la buona memoria del sig.ʳ Gio. Pierluisci da Pelestrino et che lo haveva accettato per compositore della Cappella et che gia haveva cominciato ad haver la provisione et però detto Ill.ᵐᵒ pregava il Collegio, che lo volesse accettare in detto loco et che fussero contenti tutti de far una fede di questa amissione, et se ben da alcuno fu resposto, che questo non era solito e che al sig.ʳ Gio. da Pelestrino non fu fatta questa fede, non dimeno fu ditto dal mastro e dalla maggior parte, che erano li, che si farria quanto sua signoria Ill.ᵐᵃ comanda.

Di poi la messa la medesma mattina comparse M.ᵒ Felice Anerio[18] in Cappella nel medesmo coro et rengratiò il Collegio de Sig.ʳⁱ Cantori della gratia, che gli havevano fatta d'haverlo accettato, si come anco Nostro sig.ʳ l'haveva accettato nel loco del sig.ʳ Gio. de Pelestrina et il sig.ʳ mastro di Cappella lo pregò, che se ingegnasse de componere qualche cosa di bono per cantar nelle Cappelle, e lui respose, che non mancaria con ogni diligentia.

Lunedi santo A di 4 d'Aprile	Non si è fatto niente in Cappella.
Martedi santo A di 5 d'Aprile	

fol. 18v

Mercordi santo A di 6 fu detto il matuttino delle tenebre in Cappella de Sisto IIII in Palazzo alla presentia del Papa et de tutto il Collegio del Ill.ᵐⁱ sig.ʳⁱ Cardinali; tutti li cantori furno presenti eccetto il sig.ʳ Decano et il sig.ʳ Alesandro Merlo. Il sig.ʳ Vincentio Musatti ha fatto hoggi la scusa, che sta male de febre.

Il sig.ʳ Gio. Luca Conforto è andato a cantar a san Giovanni de Fiorentini per comissione del Ill.ᵐᵒ sig.ʳ Cardinal Aldobrandini. Lo Ill.ᵐᵒ et Rev.ᵐᵒ sig.ʳ Cardinal Borrome ha donato al Collegio de Cantori de Nostro sig.ʳ scudi diece d'oro in oro e giulij diece per la messa, che sua signoria Ill.ᵐᵃ cantò in Cappella la domenica prossima passata delle palme, che fu la prima messa, che sua signoria Ill.ᵐᵃ ha cantata in Cappella.

Giovedi Santo A di 7. L'Ill.ᵐᵒ et Rev.ᵐᵒ Cardinal de Como cantò la messa in Cappella de Sisto IIII alla presentia de Nostro sig.ʳ Papa Clemente et del Ill.ᵐⁱ et Rev.ᵐⁱ Cardinali, di poi la messa fu portato da Nostro Sig.ʳᵉ il santissimo sacramento al sepulcro et di poi fu letto la bolla in Cena domini alla solita loggia; il Cardinal Sforza anuntiò la indulgentia plenaria da parte de Nostro Sig.ʳᵉ; tutti li sig.ʳⁱ Cantori furno presenti eccetto il sig.ʳ Pietro Decano et il sig.ʳ Alesandro et il sig.ʳ Fran.ᶜᵒ Soto giubilati et il sig.ʳ Vincentio Musatti et il sig.ʳ Gio. Luca Conforto infermi.

Questa mattina habbiamo hauto il pranzo in tinello, et il sig.ʳ Thomasso Benigno ha destribuito li denari della messa, che ha riceuti dallo Ill.ᵐᵒ Cardinal Borromeo, ha dato a ciascheduno 49 baiochi e doi quatrini in 18 cantori et alli altri sette ha dato baiochi sei e doi quatrini, perche se ne sonno levati sei giulij di spesa fatta per il nostro Collegio dati a Gio. Paulo custode de li libri e doi giulij dati al sig.ʳ Gio. Maria Nanino per haver fatto scrivere certe scritture per interesse dell'Abbatia de Mantoa.

La medesma sera fu fatto l'offitio solito in Cappella de Sisto alla presentia de Nostro Sig.ʳᵉ et del Ill.ᵐᵒ et Rev.ᵐᵒ Collegio de Cardinali. Il sig.ʳ Vincentio Musatti venne a servire, e tutti furno presenti eccetto il sig.ʳ Pietro Bartholmuccio decano et il sig.ʳ Alesandro Merlo giubilati et il sig.ʳ Gio. Luca Conforto, che è infermo.

Venardi santo A di 8 d'Aprile. L'Ill.ᵐᵒ et Rev.ᵐᵒ Cardinal Santa Severina in Cappella de Sisto IIII alla presentia del Papa et de tutto il Collegio del Ill.ᵐⁱ Cardinali ha

fol. 19r

---

[18] Cod.: *Enerio.*

cantato la messa, il passio l'hanno cantato il sig.ʳ Fran.ᶜᵒ Soto la turba, io Hipolito Gambocci il testo, et il sig.ʳ Vincentio Musatti il Christo; un padre Giesuita ha fatto il sermone et ha pronuntiato 30 anni de indulgentia; doppò la processione del Santissimo sacramento et finita la messa si è cantato il vespero secondo il solito, tutti furno presenti eccetto il sig.ʳ Decano, sig.ʳ Alesandro Merlo et sig.ʳ Gio. Luca Conforto. Questa mattina habbiamo hauto il pranzo in tinello secondo il solito.

Questa medesma sera a l'hora consueta si è cantato[19] l'offitio secondo il solito, ma le lamentationi sono state cantate in canto fermo per ordine del Cardinal Aldobrandino; tutti presenti eccetto il sig.ʳ Decano, sig.ʳ Alesandro Merlo et il sig.ʳ Gio. Luca Conforto; et per che il sig.ʳ Horatio Griffo è venuto di poi il primo psalmo, si è puntato cinque giulij conforme alla constitutione: Il sig.ʳ Horatio Griffi b 50.

Sabbatho santo A di 9 d'Aprile. Lo Ill.ᵐᵒ et Rev.ᵐᵒ Cardinal del Monte in cappella de Sisto alla presentia del Papa et del Collegio del Ill.ᵐⁱ et Rev.ᵐⁱ Cardinali ha cantato la messa et infine ha pronuntiato 30 anni de indulgentia; tutti presenti eccetto il sig.ʳ Alesandro Merlo, il sig.ʳ Decano et il sig.ʳ Fran.ᶜᵒ Soto et il sig.ʳ Gio. Luca Conforto.

Domenica Pasqua A di 10, Pasqua de Resurectione. Nostro sig.ʳ Papa Clemente octavo ha cantata la messa in san Pietro nella Cappella Gregoriana e di poi la messa si è mostrato la lancia de Christo et il volto santo in san Pietro et di poi si è andato alla loggia, dove sua santità ha dato la beneditione al solito, et data indulgentia plenaria, e di poi si è andato alle stantie del Papa a cantar il motetto al solito; del qual motetto io Hipolito fui absente con licentia de nostro Collegio; nella sopradetta messa tutti furno presenti eccetto il sig.ʳ Decano, il Alesandro Merlo, il sig.ʳ Fran.ᶜᵒ Soto et il sig.ʳ Gio. Luca Conforto. Per nostri emolumenti Nostro Signore ci da di mancia ▽ 2 d'oro in oro per uno.

Lunedi de Pasqua A di 11. Lo Ill.ᵐᵒ et Rev.ᵈᵒ Cardinal de Camerrino cantò la messa in Palazzo nella solita Cappella alla presentia de Nostro Sig.ʳ et del Ill.ᵐⁱ et Rev.ᵐⁱ Cardinali et anuntiò 30 anni de indulgentia. Il sig.ʳ Gio. Luca è venuto; il sig.ʳ Archangelo Crivello per esser venuto di poi li Kyrie si punta in doi giulij, il sig.ʳ Diego Vasquez per esser venuto di poi la epistola si punta in cinque giulij, tutti li altri sig.ʳⁱ Compagni furno presenti eccetto il sig.ʳ Decano, sig.ʳ Alesandro Merlo et il sig.ʳ Soto.

Il sig.ʳ Archangelo Crivello b 20
Il sig.ʳ Diego Vasquez b 50.

fol. 19v   Martedi de Pasqua A di 12 cantò la messa in Cappella de Sisto IIII in Palazzo lo Ill.ᵐᵒ et Rev.ᵐᵒ Cardinal Parravicino alla presentia de Nostro Signore et de tutto il Collegio dell'Ill.ᵐⁱ et Rev.ᵐⁱ Cardinali et pronuntiò 30 anni de indulgentia; tutti presenti eccetto il sig.ʳ Decano, il sig.ʳ Alesandro Merlo et il sig.ʳ Fran.ᶜᵒ Soto. Il sig.ʳ Diego Vasquez per esser venuto di poi li Kyrie si ponta doi giulij et il sig.ʳ Gio. Luca Conforto è venuto tardo di poi l'ultimo introito, però si punta anchor lui doi giulij.

Il sig.ʳ Vasquez b 20
Il sig.ʳ Gio. Luca Conforto b 20.

---

[19] Cod.: *cantò.*

Questa medesma mattina il collegio de Cantori ha supplicato il sig.ʳ mastro di Cappella, che voglia concederli vacantia per li tre giorni sequenti, cioe Mercordi, Giovedi et Venardi per respetto delle fatiche passate della settimana santa et per respetto della Canonizatione da farsi Dominica per il Beato Jacinto, e se bene alcuni erano di contraria opinione per esser la settimana di pasqua, nella quale almeno se poteva dir la messa solamente, non dimeno il sig.ʳ Mastro di Cappella si è contentato, che se reposino li detti tre giorni.

Mercordi A di 13
Giovedi A di 14   } Niente per ordine come di sopra.
Venardi A di 15 di Pasqua

Sabbatho in Albis A di 16 fu Cappella in palazzo. Lo Ill.ᵐᵒ et Rev.ᵐᵒ Cardinal Plata alla presentia di Nostro Sig.ʳ Clemente ottavo et del sacro Collegio de Ill.ᵐⁱ et Rev.ᵐⁱ Cardinali cantò la messa et in fine pronuntiò 25 anni de indulgentia; tutti furno presenti eccetto il sig.ʳ Decano et il sig.ʳ Alesandro Merlo, et per esser la prima messa, che il detto Monsig.ʳ Ill.ᵐᵒ Rev.ᵐᵒ Plata ha cantata in Cappella, ha donato al nostro Collegio de cantori scudi sei d'oro in oro e sei giulij.

Dominica in albis A di 17 d'Aprile fu fatta la Canonizatione de san Iacinto Pollacco, il Papa fece intimare tutto il Clero de Roma a 9 hore, et li Ill.ᵐⁱ Cardinali et altri sig.ʳⁱ prelati a X hore, e sua santità venne in Cappella a X hore e mezza, de dove partì processionalmente con l'Ill.ᵐⁱ Cardinali intonato da sua santità l'ymno Ave maris stella, qual fu seguitato dalli Cantori sino all'ingresso della chiesa di San Pietro et arri- / vato il Papa in San Pietro fece oratione al'altare e di poi si fece la obedientia, e di poi il sig.ʳ imbasciatore de Polonia fece la prima instantia per la Canonizatione di questo santo, qual fatta il sig.ʳ Silvio Troiani mastro di Camera del Papa et secretario de Brevi fece un oratione racontando li miracoli de detto Santo et finita si fece la seconda instantia et si cantorno le letanie da doi soprani cantori, et di poi se fece dal medesmo imbasciatore la terza instantia, qual finita il Papa intonò Veni creator spiritus tutto l'ymno, e di poi fu sonato l'organo, trombette et intonato dal Papa il Te deum laudamus, et finito tutto il papa dette la beneditione et disse la oratione del santo, et di poi il Papa cantò la messa solenne come è il solito con tutte le cerimonie secondo il pontificale, et finita la messa et data da sua santità la beneditione il Cardinal Gesualdo Decano anuntiò indulgentia plenaria; tutti li sig.ʳⁱ compagni Cantori furno presenti eccetto il sig.ʳ Pietro Bartholmuccio decano et il sig.ʳ Alesandro Merlo. Per nostre ragaglie havemmo una Candela per uno d'una libra de cera bianca et alli offitiali doi per uno, et dal imbasciator del Re di Polonia scudi vinticinque d'oro in oro.

fol. 20v

Questa medesma mattina il sig.ʳ Agostino Martini ha domandato licentia per andar alla Madonna de Loreto a Recanati per adimpire un suo voto per una infirmità, che haveva hauta gia doi anni sonno, qual licentia gli fu concessa della maggior parte delli compagni, et a questa licentia vi mancorno l'infrascritti, che non erano anco venuti da san Pietro: Il sig.ʳ Vincentio Musatti, il sig.ʳ Paulo de Magistris, il sig.ʳ Horatio Malvicio et il sig.ʳ Horatio Griffi.

Lunedi A di 18. Non fu ditto officio in Cappella ne messa per respetto della canonizatione fatta hieri de santo Jacinto, che fu de molta faticha ultimamente fu resoluto, che si dovesse dir la messa sola, qual non se disse, per che non venne il sig.ʳ Mattheo Argenti, al qual toccava a cantar la messa.

Martedi A di 19 fu ditto la messa sola, perche li chierici non erano venuti a metter in ordine l'altare e non vi era candelieri ne candele, per quanto me ha referto il sig.ʳ Gio. Maria Nanino, il quale questa mattina ha fatto scusa per me Hipolito Gambocci, che stavo male; il sig.ʳ Thomasso Benigno questa mattina ha destribuito la mancia de

fol. 20v   Pasqua et / ha dato a ciascheduno doi scudi d'oro in oro, al sig.ʳ Mastro di Cappella otto et alli altri officiali, cioe Camerlengo et puntatore quattro per uno. Questo giorno mancò a tutta la messa il sig.ʳ Paulo Faccone, che cosi me ha referto il sig.ʳ Antonio Manni sottopuntatore.

Il sig.ʳ Paulo Faccone mancò alla messa in tutto b 7¹/₂.

Mercordi A di 20 fu cantato la messa solamente, il sig.ʳ Paulo Faccone mancò il presente giorno, ma venne di poi la epistola, per quanto ha referto il sig.ʳ sottopontatore.

Il sig.ʳ Paulo Faccone venne di poi la epistola b 7

Questa mattina fu dato ordine de andar a cantar la messa al'oratorio de san Marcello, per che il Papa sta a Monte Cavallo, et fu ordinato dir detta messa a 13 hore.

Giovedi A di 21. Si portorno le cotte et libri al'horatorio de San Marcello e però questa mattina non si è cantata la messa; il sig.ʳ Agostino Martini partì per Loreto con licentia per 20 giorni.

Venardi A di 22. Si cominciò a cantar la messa a hore 13 al horatorio de san Marcello; et la cantò un frate de S. Marcello per non esserci don Mattheo.

Il sig.ʳ Paulo Facconio mancò in tutto b 7¹/₂.

Questa mattina il sig.ʳ Thomasso Benigno ha distribuito li 6 ducati, che ha riceuti dal Ill.ᵐᵒ Cardinal Plata per la sua messa prima cantata in Cappella il Sabbatho prossimo passato in Albis et ha dato per uno baiochi trentuno e tre quatrini. Questa medesma mattina il sig.ʳ Thomasso Benigno ha distribuito li vinticinque scudi d'oro in oro, che si sonno riceuti per la Canonizatione de san Hyacinto fatta la domenica prossima passata in Albis. Io Hipolito Gambocci son tornato al servitio questa mattina sano et salvo per gratia de Nostro Sig.ʳ Dio.

Sabbatho A di 23. Questa mattina non si è cantata la messa, per che il sig.ʳ Mattheo Argenti Cappellano ebdomedario non è venuto, ne anco ha mandato nessuno, che per lui la cantasse, et il medesmo fece hier mattina, ma il sig.ʳ Christiano Ameyden mastro di Cappella, per che non se restasse senza cantar la messa, fece chiamar un frate de san Marcello e però hier mattina fu cantata.

fol. 21r   Dominica A di 24 Dominica seconda post Pascha fu cantata la messa al'oratorio de san Marcello dal Rev.ᵈᵒ sig.ʳ Mario Corona Cappellano ebdomedario, tutti presenti ecceto il sig.ʳ Decano, sig.ʳ Alesandro Merlo, li sig.ʳ Soto et il sig.ʳ Agostino Martino, li primi tre giubilati et l'altro fuor di Roma con licentia. Questa mattina di poi la messa il sig.ʳ Paulo Faccone propose al Collegio, che si dovesse andar dal Ill.ᵐᵒ sig.ʳ Cardinal Gallo nostro protectore a suplicarlo, che quando andava da Nostro Sig.ʳ per la confirmatione della nostra bolla et privileggi, che fusse contento supplicar il Papa volesse aggiongere alla nostra bolla il privilegio, che li Cantori di Cappella non fusseno sottoposti al auditor della Camera per l'oblighi Camerali, cioe obligo informa camera, e de piu che detti Cantori per le criminalità non siano sottoposti se non al nostro protectore, a qual proposta il collegio ne propose anco un'altra, cioe, che detto Ill.ᵐᵒ

Cardinale domandasse a Nostro sig.^re, che li Cantori se potessino ordinare ad titulum Cappelle quelli, che si voranno far preiti, e a questo effetto mandorno il sig.^r Christiano mastro di Cappella, il sig.^r Paulo Fumone, Hipolito Gambocci, il sig.^r Gio. Maria Nanino et il sig.^r Paulo Faccone, quali andorno e per non haver potuto parlar al detto sig.^r Cardinal, lassorno questo carico de parlarli al sig.^r Paulo Faccone.

Lunedi A di 25, San Marco, fu comune, si cantorno le letanie maggiore in anzi la messa e di poi la messa; il sig.^r Paulo Faccone ha referto al nostro Collegio, che ha parlato al Illmo Cardinal Gallo, il quale dice che farrà, quanto dal Collegio si desidera, quando andarà dal Papa, cioe che nella Confirmatione delli privileggi domandarà anco le tre sopradette cose, cioe l'obligo in forma Camere, la Criminalità, et che si possino ordinare li Cantori ad titulum Cappelle; tutti presenti eccetto il mastro di Cappella, li giubilati et il sig.^r Agostino.

Martedi A di 26. Il sig.^r Fran.^co Spinosa fa scusa che sta male.
Il sig.^r Paulo Faccone mancò a tutta la messa b 7¹/₂
Il sig.^r Horatio Crescentio [mancò] a tutta la messa b 7¹/₂.

Mercordi A di 27. Il sig.^r Luca Orfeo per una medicina, che ha presa questa mattina, se scusa.
Il sig.^r Paulo Faccone venne, quando se diceva l'Evangelio, però perde b 7.

Giovedi A di 28. Il Luca Orfeo è venuto al servitio; tutti presenti eccetto quelli della   fol. 21v
sua giornata.

Venardi A di 29. Questa mattina il sig.^r mastro di Cappella et la maggior parte del Collegio hanno ordinato, che domenica prossima, che è il primo di Maggio, si dica la messa a 12 hore, et Gio. Paulo custode de libri ha supplicato il detto Collegio, che gli faccia gratia, che tutta questa state possa andare a cantare, dove gli pare le feste, atteso che desidera guadagnar qual che cosa per levarsi de certi debiti che si trova, et il Collegio considerando esser opera di Carità glie l'ha concesso gratiosamente per le feste, ma non per le cappelle, et che lui sia obbligato lassar uno, che metta e levi li libri per lui in sua absentia; tutti presenti eccetto quelli, che havevano il giorno. Il sig.^r Alesandro Merolo, il sig.^r Decano et il sig.^r Fran.^co Soto giubilati. Questa mattina il sig.^r Fran.^co Spinosa è guarito et tornato al servitio di Cappella.

Sabbatho A di 30 d'Aprile, Tutti presenti eccetto quelli della sua giornata.
Li ponti d'Aprile sonno doi scudi e 3 baiochi, tocca 12 [?] baiochi e 3 quatrini per uno in parte 20.

[MAGGIO]
Domenica A di primo Maggio, Santi Philippo et Jacobo Apostoli. Tutti presenti eccetto il sig.^r Fran.^co Soto, Alessandro Merlo et il sig.^r Decano iubilati.

Lunedi A di 2 de Maggio. Tutti presenti eccetto quelli della sua giornata.

Martedi A di 3, la inventione della Santa Croce fu cantata la messa a san Marcello secondo il solito; tutti furno presenti eccetto li sig.^ri Alesandro Merlo, il sig.^r Fran.^co

Soto et il sig.ʳ Decano iubilati, et il sig.ʳ Horatio Crescentio, il qual si ponta doi carlini.

Il sig.ʳ Horatio Crescentio mancò alla sopradetta messa b 15.

Mercordi A di 4. Il sig.ʳ Paulo Faccone mancò a tutta la messa b 7¹/₂.

Giovedi A di 5. Tutti presenti eccetto li iubilati.

Venardi A di 6, San Giovanni ante portam Latinam, Comune.
Il sig.ʳ Paulo Faccone mancò a tutta questa messa b 7¹/₂
Il sig.ʳ Gio. Luca Conforto mancò a questa messa b 7¹/₂
Il sig.ʳ Joseph Bianco se scusa infermo.

Sabbatho A di 7. Tutti presenti. Il sig.ʳ Joseph Bianco è comparso sano et salvo dio gratia.

fol. 22r   Dominica A di 8, Dominica quarta post pascha. Il sig.ʳ Thomasso Benigno Camerlengo distribuì la paga del presente mese de Maggio.
Il sig.ʳ Paulo de Magistris venne al principio del evangelio b 7
Il sig.ʳ Paulo Faccone venne al credo b 7
Il sig.ʳ Gio. Luca Conforto venne di poi la epistola b 7.
Questa medesma mattina il sig.ʳ Thomasso ha distribuito li denari, che si sonno rescossi da M.º Horatio Giani speciale incontro a san Celso in banchi per conto delle facole, che glie furno date alla sedevacante de Sisto quinto, et ha dato per ciascheduno sette giulij e 2 quatrini in parte 17, che tanti sonno l'interessati, et ha fatto bono scudi 5 al detto speciale per tante candele servite per dare a notarij et procuratori in nome de tutta la Cappella.
Questa medesma mattina io Hipolito Gambocci ho distribuito li ponti del mese d'Aprile prossimo passato e dato un giulio per uno et sonno 20 a participare, perche il sig.ʳ Agostino Martini non participa delli ponti de detto mese per esser stato absente X giorni d'Aprile del servitio della Cappella.

Lunedi A di 9. Il sig.ʳ Diego Vasquez venne di poi l'epistola b 7
Il sig.ʳ Stephano Ugerio fa scusa che non pol venire, perche ha pigliato la medicina.

Martedi A di 10. Il sig.ʳ Gio. Luca Conforto venne di poi la epistola b 7
Il sig.ʳ Stephano Ugerio è venuto al servitio.
Hoggi finisce la licentia delli 20 giorni, che ha hauta il sig.ʳ Agostino Martini per andar a Loreto.

Mercordi A di 11 de Maggio. Il sig.ʳ Agostino Martino non è tornato, ma hoggi è sua giornata de asentione, tutti li altri son stati presenti.

Giovedi A di 12. Il sig.ʳ Agostino Martini è mancato a tutta la messa b 7¹/₂.

Venardi A di 13. Tutti furno presenti.

Sabbato A di 14. Il sig.ʳ Agostino Martino mancò alla messa b 7¹/₂.

Domenica A di 15. Il sig.ʳ Agostino Martino mancò a tutta la messa b 7¹/₂.
Il sig.ʳ Paulo Faccone venne di poi l'Agnus Dei b 7.

Lunedi A di 16. Il sig.ʳ Agostino è tornato da Loreto et venuto hoggi al servitio al oratorio de san Marcello.
Il sig.ʳ Paulo Faccone mancò alla Messa b 7¹/₂.

A di 17. Non si cantò la messa, per che se mandorno le cotte et libri a palazzo per   fol. 22v
il vespero del Ascensione che sarrà domani.

Mercordi A di 18, la vigilia del Ascensione. L'Ill.ᵐᵒ et Rev.ᵐᵒ Cardina[l] Gesualdo cantò il vespero in Cappella de Sisto, PP. quarto in Palazzo alla presentia de tutto il Collegio del Ill.ᵐⁱ et Rev.ᵐⁱ sig.ʳⁱ Cardinali, ma in absenza del Papa; tutti li sig.ʳⁱ Cantori furno presenti, eccetto il sig.ʳ Pietro Bartholmuccio decano.
Il sig.ʳ Gio. Luca Conforto venne al secondo psalmo, però si punta il detto sig.ʳ Gio. Luca Conforto b 50.

Giovedi A di 19, il giorno del Ascensione. Lo Ill.ᵐᵒ et Rev.ᵐᵒ Cardinal Alessandrino cantò la messa in san Pietro nella Cappella Gregoriana in absentia de Nostro Signore Papa Clemente, ma alla presentia de tutto il sacro Collegio del Ill.ᵐⁱ et Rev.ᵐⁱ Cardinali, il sermone lo fece il sig.ʳ Benedetto Sansone Canonico de Catalogna et dette de indulgentia da parte de Nostro Sig.ʳ trent'anni[20], tutti li sig.ʳⁱ Cantori furno presenti eccetto il sig.ʳ Pietro Bartholmuccio decano et sig.ʳ Fran.ᶜᵒ Soto, quali sonno giubilati.

Venardi A di 20. Non fu ditto Messa, perche fu dato ordine da portar li libri e le cotte a san Marcello al Oratorio.

Sabbato A di 21. Non fu ditto la messa, che anchora non si erano portato li libri e cotte al oratorio.

Domenica A di 22. Il sig.ʳ Cristiano mastro di Cappella venne per il sig.ʳ Gio. Maria Nanino.
Questa mattina io Hippolito Gambocci puntatore ho referto al nostro Rev.ᵈᵒ Collegio, qualmente essendo stati eletti a reveder li conti et l'administratione del Camerlengato del Rev.ᵈᵒ Don Archangelo per l'anno passato il sig.ʳ Gio. Maria Nanino et io Hippolito Gambocci habbiamo visto et rencontrato tutte le partite delli libri del detto sig.ʳ Don Archangelo, tanto del ordinario, quanto dello estraordinario, et habbiamo trovato, che il detto sig.ʳ Don Archangelo Crivello si è portato fidelissimamente in questa sua administratione, et per segno di cio noi sopradetti deputati gli habbiamo fatto quietanza et saldo nelli suoi libri de detta sua administratione sottoscritta de nostro propria mano sotto il di 18 de Maggio 1594; et di questa relatione et esegutione il Rev.ᵈᵒ Collegio è restato molto sodisfatto. A questa relatione, che io Hipolito feci, furno tutti presenti eccetto il sig.ʳ Decano, sig.ʳ Alesandro Merlo, il sig.ʳ Fran.ᶜᵒ Soto et il sig.ʳ Gio. Maria Nanino.

Lunedi A di 23. Tutti furno presenti.   fol. 23r

---

[20] Nach *trent'anni* durchgestrichen: *de indulgentia.*

Martedi A di 24. Il sig.^r Paulo Faccone mancò a tutta la messa b 7¹/₂.
Questa mattina il sig.^r Archangelo Crivello ha servito per il sig.^r Gio. Maria Nanino.

Mercordi A di 25. Il sig.^r Paulo de Magistris mancò a tutta la messa b 7¹/₂.
Il sig.^r Fran.^{co} Spino[sa] fece far la scusa come amalato, ma di venne al evangelio.
Questa mattina il sig.^r Facco[ne] me consignò la bolla delli nostri privilegij alla presentia de tutto il Collegio, però mancavano quelli della sua giornata e li giubilati.

Giovedi A di 26. Il sig.^r Joseph Bianco ha servito per il Gio. Maria Nanino.

Venardi A di 27. Si è mandato la Cassa delle Cotte et li libri a palazzo.

Sabbato A di 28 fu vespero in Cappella de Sisto quarto in Palazzo. Nostro Sig.^{re} Papa Clemente fece l'offitio secondo il solito alla presentia de tutto il sacro Collegio delli Ill.^{mi} Cardinali. Tutti li Rev.^{di} Sig.^{ri} Cantori furno presenti, eccetto il sig.^r Pietro Bartholomuccio decano et il sig.^r Alesandro Merlo giubilati.

Domenica A di 29, la Pentecoste. L'Illmo et Rev.^{mo} Cardinal Paleotto cantò la messa in san Pietro nella Cappella Gregoriana alla presentia de Nostro Signore Papa Clemente et de tutto il Collegio del Ill.^{mi} et Rev.^{mi} Cardinali, fece il sermone il sig.^r Licentiato Cabrera Spagnolo et anuntiò trent'anni d'indulgentia da parte de Nostro Signore. Tutti presenti, eccetto il sig.^r Decano et il sig.^r Fran.^{co} Soto giubilati.

Lunedi A di 30. Questa mattina si è dato ordine, che si porti li libbri et cotte al oratorio de san Marcello, per che sua Santità è tornato a Monte Cavallo.

Martedi A di ultimo de Maggio fu cantata la messa al'Oratorio de san Marcello, tutti furno presenti.
Li ponti del presente mese sonno giulij sedici e 28 baiochi, a participare de detti ponti sonno 20, per che il sig.^r Agostino Martino non participa del sopradetto mese de Maggio, per che è stato absente piu de X giorni, e tocca otto baiochi per uno et un quatrino avanza al puntatore 13 quatrini.

[GIUGNO]

fol. 23v Mercordi A di primo de Giugno. Il sig.^r Gio. Maria Nanino ha servito per il sig.^r Archangelo Crivello, tutti li altri furno presenti eccetto quelli della lor giornata.

Giovedi A di 2. Tutti furno presenti eccetto quelli della sua giornata.

Venardi A di 3. Si mandò il forziero delle cotte et libri alla chiesa del Giesù, dove Nostro Sig.^r vuol far Cappella domani et Domenica.

Sabbato A di 4. Nostro Sig.^r cantò vespero secondo il solito, ma alla Chiesa del Giesu, dove intervenne tutto il Collegio dell'Ill.^{mi} sig.^{ri} Cardinali. Tutti li Rev.^{di} Sig.^{ri} Cantori furno presenti eccetto il Sig.^r Decano et il sig.^r Alesandro Merlo, che sonno giubilati. Questa medesma giornata il sig.^r mastro di Cappella propose al nostro Collegio, che il sig.^r Paulo Facconio deve dare a detto Collegio scudi cinque et vintinove baiochi per il resto delli 15 scudi, che detto sig.^r Paulo hebbe in Mantoa e che adesso per molti travagli, nelli quali si trova il detto sig.ʳ Paulo, non li puol pagare et ne desidera qualche poca de dilatione, et in questo caso il collegio rimese al sig.ʳ mastro, che gli facesse la dilatione che gli pareva, et restò d'accordo col detto sig.ʳ Paulo, che ne pagaria uno scudo il mese cominciando a pagarlo alla paga del mese de Luglio prossimo d' avenire.

Questo medesmo giorno il sig.ʳ Thomasso Benigno ha distribuito la paga per il presente mese de Giugno et ha dato 21 a Gio. Paulo Custode de libri per farsi aiutar a portar i libri da palazzo per il vespero della Trinità.

Dominica A di 5, la sanctissima Trinità fu Cappella alla Chiesa del Giesù. L'Ill.ᵐᵒ et Rev.ᵐᵒ Cardinal Pinella cantò la messa alla presentia de Nostro Sig.ʳᵉ et del Collegio dell'Ill.ᵐⁱ sig.ʳⁱ Cardinali; fece il sermone il sig.ʳ Cesare Amati et annuntiò 25 anni de indulgentia; tutti li Rev.ᵈⁱ Cantori furno presenti eccetto il sig.ʳ Decano et il sig.ʳ Fran.ᶜᵒ Soto, che sonno giubilati.

Lunedi A di 6 et Martedi a di 7 non si cantò messa, per che fu ordinato, che li libri et la cassa delle cotte fussero portati a palazzo per il vespero del Corpus Domini.

Mercordi A di 8, la vigilia del Corpus domini. Nostro Sig.ʳᵉ Papa Clemente cantò il vespero secondo il solito in palazzo nella Cappella de Sisto quarto alla presentia dell Ill.ᵐᵒ et Rev.ᵐᵒ Collegio de Cardinali, tutti li Rev.ᵈⁱ Cantori furno presenti eccetto il sig.ʳ Decano et il sig.ʳ Alesandro Merlo, et io Hippolito Gambocci hoggi ho distribuito li ponti del Mese di Maggio prossimo passato.   fol. 24r

Giovedi A di 9, la Festa del Corpus Domini. Nostro Sig.ʳᵉ disse la messa legendo in Cappella de Sisto IV alla presentia de tutto il Collegio dell'Ill.ᵐⁱ et Rev.ᵐⁱ Cardinali, et di poi sua santità portò il santissimo Corpo de Christo processionalmente secondo il solito et andò a piedi. In questa processione tutti li Rev.ᵈⁱ Cantori furno presenti eccetto il sig.ʳ Pietro Decano et il sig.ʳ Fran.ᶜᵒ Soto; il sig.ʳ Gio. Luca Conforto venne tardo a questa processione, comparse di poi che la croce, che va inanzi alli Vescovi, era fuor del palazzo del Papa, per il che deve esser puntato in cinque giulij conforme alla Constitutione. In questa medesma mattina fu ordinato dal sig.ʳ Mastro di Cappella, che si dovesse portar li libri et cassa delle Cotte al'Oratorio de San Marcello, e che Domenica si cominciasse a dir la nostra solita messa al'oratorio a hore XI.

Il sig.ʳ Gio. Luca Conforto per esser venuto tardo alla detta processione b 50.

Venardi A di X   }   Non si cantò messa, perche si portorno le cotte e libri a san
Sabbato A di XI   }   Marcello.

Dominica A di XII Dominica infra octava corporis Christi seconda post Pentecoste. Non fu cantata la Messa, per che il sig.ʳ Mattheo Argenti, che era hebdomedario, non venne.

Lunedi A di 13. Il sig.ʳ Faccone mancò a tutta la messa b 7¹/₂.

Martedi A di 14. Il sig.ʳ Paulo Faccone venne alla elevatione del corpus Domini b 7
Il sig.ʳ Horatio Malvezzi et il sig.ʳ Leonardo Crescentio andorno a cantar la messa a san Gio. de Fiorentino per ordine del Cardinal Gallo nostro Protettore; il sig.ʳ Mastro di Cappella me ha cosi referto.
Il sigʳ. Luca Orfeo mancò alla messa b 7¹/₂.

fol. 24v   Mercordi A di 15 non mancò nessuno.

Giovedi A di 16 mancò a tutta la messa il sig.ᵣ Luca Orfeo b 7¹/₂,
il sig.ᵣ Pietro Montoya mancò a tutta la messa b 7¹/₂.

Venardi A di 17 mancò il sig.ᵣ Diego Vasquez, ma venne di poi al santus b 7.

Sabbato A di 18. Il sig.ᵣ Horatio Malvicio venne di poi alla epistola b 7.
Questa medesma mattina il sig.ᵣ Vincentio Musatti disse da parte del sig.ᵣ Mastro di
Camera del Papa, che non si debba puntare il sig.ᵣ Luca Orfeo, per che non puol venire
al servitio di Cappella essendo occupato per scrivere alcune cerimonie, che si hanno
da fare per la consecratione del Altare de san Pietro, et per questo respetto fu occupato Martedi, Mercordi et Giovedi prossimi passati, e però non si faranno pagare
detti ponti.

Dominica A di 19, che è la III di poi la Pentecoste. Il sig.ᵣ Horatio venne, mentre
si cantava il verso del aleluya b 7
Il sig.ᵣ Santos venne, mentre si cantava l'evangelio b 7
Il sig.ᵣ Paulo Faccone [venne] mentre si cantava il credo b 7
Il sig.ᵣ Luca Conforto venne di poi l'Aleluja b 7
Il sig.ᵣ Diego Vasquez mancò a tutta la messa e non venne b 7¹/₂.

Lunedi A di 20. Il sig.ᵣ Joseph Bianco mancò in tutta la messa b 7¹/₂.

Martedi A di 21. Il sig.ᵣ Horatio Crescentio venne di poi l'epistola b 7.
Il sig.ᵣ Luca Orfeos, per che il sig.ᵣ Vincentio Musatti me dice, che le scritture, che
faceva per il Papa, sonno gia finite, però lo puntarò, perche non è venuto alla messa
b 7¹/₂.
Mercordi a di 22. Il sig.ᵣ Benigno mancò a tutta la messa b 7¹/₂
Il sig.ᵣ Horatio Griffi mancò a tutta la messa b 7¹/₂
Il sig.ᵣ Joseph Bianco mancò a tutta la messa b 7¹/₂
Il sig.ᵣ Gio. Santos mancò a tutta la messa b 7¹/₂
Il sig.ᵣ Diego Vasquez mancò a tutta la messa b 7¹/₂
Il sig.ᵣ Gio. Luca Conforto venne al'evangelio b 7
Il sig.ᵣ Luca Orfeo mancò a tutta la messa b 7¹/₂.
Questa mattina il sig.ᵣ Paulo Faccone fa scusa che sta male.

Giovedi Alli 23 de Giugno. Si è dato ordine de portar le cotte et libri a san Gio. Laterano per la messa de detta Festa, che Nostro Sig.ᵣ vi fa Cappella.

fol. 25r   Venardi A di 24 la Natività de San Gio. Battista fu Cappella a san Giovanni Laterano.
L'Ill.ᵐᵒ et Rev.ᵐᵒ Cardinal Sfondrato cantò la Messa in detta chiesa nel altar Maggiore
alla presentia Nostro Sig.ʳᵉ et de tutto il Collegio dell'Ill.ᵐⁱ et Rev.ᵐⁱ Cardinali; tutti
li Rev.ᵈⁱ Cantori furno presenti eccetto il sig.ᵣ Decano, il sig.ᵣ Alesandro Merlo et il
sig.ᵣ Fran.ᶜᵒ Soto, che sonno giubilati; et fu anuntiato 30 anni d'indulgentia. Il sig.ᵣ
Paulo Faccone doi giorni fu[21] escusato per infermo, questa mattina è venuto al servitio del Papa alla presente messa.

Sabbato A di 25 furno portate le cotte et libri a Palazzo.

---

[21] Cod.: *fa.*

Dominica A di 26 di Giugno. Nostro Sig.re Papa Clemente octavo consacrò l'altare di san Pietro con le cerimonie conforme al Pontificale alla presentia de tutto il Collegio dell'Ill.mi et Rev.mi Cardinali, tutti li Vescovi, che si trovavano in Roma, et tutto il Clero di Roma. Tutti li Rev.di Cantori furno presenti eccetto il sig.r Decano et sig.r Fran.co Soto, che sonno giubilati; di poi fatta la consacratione del altare Nostro Signore disse la messa in san Pietro nel medesmo altare et in fine di detta messa l'Ill.mo et Rev.mo Cardinal Gesualdo Decano anuntiò indulgentia plenaria da parte di sua Santità a tutti quelli, che quivi furno presenti. Questa mattina il sig.r Luca Conforto venne, che se dicevano le letanie, et gia si era cantata un'antiphona et un psalmo, si ponta b 20.

Lunedi A di 27 non si cantò messa.

Martedi A di 28 la Vigilia de san Pietro. La Santità di Nostro Sig.r Clemente ottavo cantò il Vespero pontificalmente in detta Chiesa alla presentia de tutto il Collegio dell'Ill.mi et Rev.mi Cardinali; tutti presenti eccetto il sig.r Alesandro Merlo giubilato.

Mercordi A di 29 festa de san Pietro e san Paulo. Nostro Sig.r Papa Clemente ottavo ha cantata la Messa in san Pietro alla presentia de tutto il sacro collegio de Cardinali, et infine de detta Messa l'Ill.mo Cardinal Gesualdo ha anuntiato indulgentia plenaria; tutti presenti eccetto il sig.r Decano et sig.r Soto jubilati.
Il sig.r Ioseph Bianco è venuto a terza di poi il gloria patri del primo psalmo, però si ponta in doi giulij b 20.
Di poi la messa se andò a cantar il mottetto a Sua Santità, mentre desinava, secondo il solito et per nostri emolumenti Nostro Sig.re ci da per mancia ▽ 4 d'oro in oro per uno secondo il solito.

Giovedi A di 30. Niente. Li ponti del presente messe de Giugno sonno ▽ 2:13 b.   fol. 25v

[LUGLIO]
Venardi A di primo de Luglio. Si portano le cotte et libri a san Marcello.

Sabbato A di 2 la Visitatione della Madonna Comune.
Il sig.r Horatio Crescentio mancò a tutta la messa b 7½
Il sig.r Thomasso mancò a tutta la messa b 7½
Il sig.r Pietro Montoya venne di poi la epistola, mentre si cantava l'Alleluia b 7.
Questa mattina il Collegio nostro dette comissione a me Hipolito puntatore, che devesse puntar doi giulij il sig.r Gio. Luca Conforto per esser venuto tardo alla Consacratione del altare de San Pietro, qual fece nostro Sig.re alli 26 del mese prossimo passato de Giugno, et parendomi, che questo fusse il giusto, gia l'haveva puntato, come si vede alla detta giornata.

Dominica A di 3 de Luglio Domenica quinta post pentecoste.
Il sig.r Agostino Martini b 7 ⎫
Il sig.r Thomasso Benigni b 7 ⎪ Tutti quattro comparsero di poi l'epistola.
Il sig.r Paulo Facconio b 7 ⎬
Il sig.r Diego Vasque[z] ⎭

Lunedi A di 4 de Luglio. Tutti furno presenti.

Martedi A di 5 non se cantò la messa, per che Gio. Paulo Custode de libri non venne, et noi non potemmo pigliar le cotte, per che lui tiene la chiave del forziero, e per questo desordine il sig.^r mastro di Cappella me ha comandato, che lo ponti in tre giulij, per che questa non è la prima volta che ha mancato.

Gio. Paulo Custode de libri b 30.

Mercordi A di 6. Il sig.^r Paulo Faccone mancò a tutta la messa b 7¹/₂.

Questa mattina il sig.^r Vincentio de Gratis ha domandato la bolla delli nostri privilegij al sig.^r Mastro di Cappella, et per che io la tengo detta bolla come secretario, l'ho prima detto al collegio che darla; il qual collegio ha resoluto, che non se li debba dare per bon respetto, ma che se dica al sig.^r Vincentio, che per suo servitio il nostro Collegio è tutto pronto in generale et in particulare sempre per giovarli; ma havendo M.º Tiburtio mostrato con parole haverce poco obligo di darli o non darli questa bolla dicendo, che in ogni modo la potranno haver dal registro, s'è risoluto, che se la vadi a pigliar al registro, poi che ne hanno de bisogno per il loro Collegio della sacristia.

fol. 26r   Giovedi A di 7. Il sig.^r Gio. Luca Conforto, mentre si cantava il gradual, comparse b 7.

Il sig.^r Thomasso Benigno questa mattina ha destribuito la paga del presente mese de Luglio.

Il detto sig.^r Thomasso ha retenuto uno scudo il sig.^r Paulo Faccone a bon conto delli cinque scudi e 29 baiochi, che deve al Collegio de Cantori.

Venardi A di 8. Non mancò nessuno, et io Hipolito Gambocci puntatore ho distribuito li ponti del mese prossimo passato de Giugno et dato a ciascheduno un giulio, cioe a queli, che non hanno perso niente. Il sig.^r Luca Orfeo non ha voluto accettare li quatrini delli ponti, poi che il mese passato de Giugno glie fu fatto gratia delli ponti, che haveva fatto per causa de scrivere per il Papa per la consecratione del Altar de san Pietro, però il giulio, che a lui toccava, lo metterò in comune per li ponti del presente mese.

Sabbato A di 9 non si cantò messa, perche al'oratorio de san Marcello si facevano le orationi delle 40 hore.

Domenica A di 10, che è la sesta di poi la pentecoste, fu cantata la nostra messa al'oratorio e di poi la messa si fece la processione et se rimese il sanctissimo sacramento; tutti furno presenti; e se ben il sig.^r Faccone venne al'evangelio, non si deve puntar, essendo che la messa fu cominciata un quarto d'hora prima di quel che fu ordinato.

Lunedi A di 11. Il sig.^r Paulo Faccone venne al'Evangelio b 7.

Martedi A di 12. Il sig.^r Horatio Malvicio venne al Agnus Dei b 7.
Il sig.^r Paulo Faccone mancò a tutta la messa b 7¹/₂.

Mercordi A di 13. Il sig.^r Thomasso Benigno mancò a tutta la messa b 7¹/₂
Il sig.^r Archangelo mancò a tutta la messa b 7¹/₂.

Giovedi A di 14 non mancò nessuno.

Venardi A di 15. Il sig.ʳ Benigno mancò a tutta la messa b 7¹/₂
Il sig.ʳ Paulo de Magistris mancò a tutta la messa b 7¹/₂
Il sig.ʳ Vasquez mancò a tutta la messa b 7¹/₂
Il sig.ʳ Paulo Faccone mancò a tutta la messa b 7¹/₂
Il sig.ʳ Horatio Crescentio b 7　　} comparsero al offertorio
Il sig.ʳ Horatio Malvicio b 7.　　}

Sabbato A di 16. Tutti furno presenti. Questa mattina il sig.ʳ Mastro di Cappella ha
dato ordine, che domani si cominci a cantar la messa a sant'Apostolo, per che il
Papa è andato a star al Palazzo del Cardinal Ascanio Colonna appresso detta chiesa.

Dominica VII Post Pentecoste A di 17 si cantò la messa in Santi Apostoli, tutti furno　　fol. 26v
presenti. Di poi la messa il sig.ʳ Mastro di Cappella propose al Collegio, che quelli
sig.ʳⁱ della natione Spagnola hanno mandato a pregar detto Collegio, che voglia andar
a cantar la messa in san Jacomo de detta Natione il giorno de detta Festa, et per che
l'anno passato non dettero se non tredici scudi, fu fatto discorso sopra questo fatto,
et secondo il parer della maggior parte fu resoluto, che si dovesse andar cantar detta
messa a san Jacomo de Spagnoli per 15 scudi e non per manco, et questa resolutione
da dare a detti sig.ʳⁱ Spagnoli furno eletti doi de nostri, il sig.ʳ Thomasso Benigno et
il sig.ʳ Gio. Santos Spagnolo.

Lunedi A di 18. Non mancò nessuno.

Martedi A di 19. Tutti furno presenti.

Mercordi A di 20. Il sig.ʳ Paulo de Magistris mancò a tutta la messa b 7¹/₂
Il sig.ʳ Paulo Faccone comparse al Agnus dei b 7
Il sig.ʳ Gio. Luca Conforto mancò a tutta la messa b 7¹/₂.

Giovedi A di 21. Non mancò nessuno. Il sig.ʳ Thomasso ha distribuito la mancia de
santi Pietro e Paulo.

Venardi A di 22. Mancò alla messa il sig.ʳ Diego Vasquez b 7¹/₂
Il sig.ʳ Paulo Faccone venne di poi l'evangelio b 7
Il sig.ʳ Thomasso Benigno venne al offertorio b 7.

Sabbato A di 23. Non mancò nessuno.
Dominica A di 24. Ottava post Pentecoste. Il sig.ʳ Thomasso Benigno venne al credo
b 7
Il sig.ʳ Pietro Montoia mancò a tutta la messa b 7¹/₂.

Lunedi A di 25, san Jacomo Apostolo. Tutto il Collegio de Cantori andò a cantar la
messa a san Jacomo de Spagnoli ad instantia de detta Natione, et per nostro emolumento ci diedero quindici scudi di moneta; tutti furno presenti eccetto il sig.ʳ Pietro
decano et il sig.ʳ Alesandro Merlo: parte 23.

Martedi A di 26, Sant'Anna. Tutti presenti eccetto quelli della sua giornata.

Mercordi A di 27. Tutti furno presenti.

Giovedi A 28. Tutti furno presenti. Questa mattina il sig.ʳ Thomasso Benigno ha destribuito li 15 scudi, che ha rescossi per la messa, che habbiamo cantata il giorno de san Jacomo della Natione Spagnola, et ha dato giulij sei per uno et 26 quatrini.

fol. 27r Venardi Alli 29. Il sig.ʳ Diego Vasquez venne al santus b 7
Il sig.ʳ Paulo Faccone venne al offertorio b 7.

Sabbato A di 30. Il sig.ʳ Agostino Martini venne al offertorio b 7
Il sig.ʳ Diego Vasquez venne al offertorio b 7
Il sig.ʳ Gio. Luca Conforto mancò in tutto b 7¹/₂.

Dominica IX post pentecoste A di ultimo de Luglio. Il sig.ʳ Thomasso Benigno venne di poi il credo b 7
Il sig.ʳ Paulo Faccone mancò in tutta la messa b 7¹/₂.
Questa mattina il sig.ʳ Christiano Ameyden mastro di Cappella domandò Congregatione al Collegio, nella stantia della Compagnia delli 12 Apostoli nella medesma chiesa, et invocato lo spirito santo con la sua oratione il sig.ʳ mastro di Cappella sopradetto propose al collegio un errore fatto nella chiesa de san Jacomo de Spagnoli il giorno de detta festa, nel motetto quale era a tre chori, del qual errore ne fu causa il sig.ʳ Gio. Sanctos Spagnolo per non haver fatto sapere al mastro il motetto, che si cantava, et per haver lui stesso spartito le parte alli cantori con non haver poco respetto al autorità del mastro di Cappella e de tutto il nostro Collegio. Però di questo fatto il detto mastro di Cappella ne dette querela al Collegio et il detto sig.ʳ Gio. Sanctos si scusò, che quel che haveva fatto, non l'haveva fatto con malitia e che in cio non pretendeva non solo castigo, ma non intendeva haver peccato pur venialmente; ma havendo il collegio fatto discorso sopra questo fatto, fu resoluto, che si mandasse fuora il detto sig.ʳ Gio. Sanctos, et fu proposto, che si votasse, si doveva puntarsi o no, et fu resoluto per voti bianchi e neri, che si dovesse puntare. Di poi fu proposto da detto sig.ʳ Mastro di Cappella, che si dovesse metter al partito, quanto si doveva puntare, et pregò il Collegio, che volesse in questo fatto moderato, ma che era bene farli qualche segno, acciò un'altra volta ne lui ne altri havesse a dire pigliar prosuntione dell autorità del mastro di cappella contra l'honor de tutto il Collegio, et misse il partito cinque o sei scudi, et sopra cio ognuno disse il suo parere, alcuni volevano fusse puntato cinque ▽, altri 4, alcuni 3, chi doi scudi, chi uno, et chi doi carlini, et per
fol. 27v che furno varie l'opinioni, fu remesso / al partito delli voti secreti, si doveva esser puntato cinque overo doi scudi, poi che la maggior parte teneva questi doi numeri. Et fu resoluto, che dovesse pagare cinque scudi, anchor che da molti fu detto, che questo era poco per lui, essendo suo solito esser poco ubediente al mastro di cappella come piu volte ha mostrato, che nella voce del tono che il mastro di cappella gli ha dato, sempre ha desobedito pigliando un tono piu basso o piu alto per gara. Li voti in favore del detto sig.ʳ Gio. Sanctos, che dovesse pagar solo doi scudi, furno sette, ma che dovesse pagarne cinque ▽, furno 12 voti. Il detto sig.ʳ Mastro di Cappella questa medesma mattina propose al detto Collegio, che il sig.ʳ Diego Vasquez Spagnolo la medes[ma] mattina in san Jacomo disse al detto mastro di Cappella, che il Collegio si faceva poco honore e però, disse, domandate 20, overo 25 scudi, che li meritamo, e cio disse si sprezzando il detto mastro et Collegio, alle quale parole furno presenti alcuni cappellani de san Jacomo et alcuni de nostri, che fanno fede di questo, et parendo al collegio, che questo fusse in offesa sua e del mastro di Cappella, comandò, che il detto sig.ʳ Vasquez andasse fuora, che si voleva trattar sopra questo negotio, et a

voce viva da tutti fu giudicato, che si dovesse puntare, accio un'altra volta portasse quella reverentia, che si deve al mastro di cappella et Collegio et che in presentia de forestieri non si dicesse parole, che potessero esser contra l'honor del detto Collegio, et fu resoluto per voti secreti, che il detto sig.ʳ Vasquez fusse puntato in doi scudi, li voti, che dovesse pagar doi scudi, furno 13, et in favore furno 6. Et nella medesma hora il detto collegio ordinò al sig.ʳ Thomasso Benigno, che dovesse pagare per il sig.ʳ Sanctos a bon conto della sua paga d'Agosto prossimo scudi cinque, et doi scudi per il sig.ʳ Diego Vasquez et che subbito si mettessero nella cassa delle eleemosine della Compagnia de San Apostolo, et ordinò a me Hipolito, che fussi presente, quando metteva detti denari in detta cassa, et prima che fussemo usciti della chiesa de santi Apostoli, il detto sig.ʳ Thomaso Benigno messe detti denari in mia presentia nella detta cassa. In detta congregatione tutti furno presenti eccetto il sig.ʳ Decano, sig.ʳ Alesandro Merlo et il sig.ʳ Soto, et il sig.ʳ Gio. Luca questa mattina scusato per infermo. Questa mattina di poi la congregatione il sig.ʳ Paulo Faccone hebbe licentia de poter cantar fuora hoggi, poi che non ce stato alla nostra messa.

Questa medesma mattina alla messa li soprani lassorno de cominciare un terzo, che   fol. 28r
fu il Benedictus qui venit, qual cominciava col contralto, e lassorno cantar quella parte del contralto circa 20 battute, prima che nessuno delli soprani volesse cominciare, però li pontarò cinque baiochi per uno, per che era giorno festivo e fu scandalo. Il sig.ʳ Gio. Santos haveva gia cantato un terzo, non toccava a lui a dire: ma li altri tre, uno aspettava l'altro; e però.
Il sig.ʳ Diego Vasquez b 5
Il sig.ʳ Pietro Montoya b 5
Il sig.ʳ Francesco Spinosa b 5.
Li ponti del presente mese de Luglio sonno stati scudi doi e baiochi sessanta, ma li ponti del sig.ʳ Thomasso Benigno per esser pagatore è asente de sei ponti il mese, però non ho rescosso li suoi, talche restano doi scudi e b 13; et un giulio metto fra detti punti, che il mese passato il sig.ʳ Luca Orfeo si contentò de lassarlo al comune, si che in tutto sonno giulij 22 e sette baiochi.
Questa mattina si è dato ordine dal mastro di Cappella e tutto il Collegio, che do-mattina se cominci a cantar la nostra messa alle dodici hore conforme al solito.
Nella predetta congregatione, quando fu penato il sig.ʳ Gio. Sanctos delli cinque scudi, il sig.ʳ Christiano Ameyden mastro di Cappella non volse votare; ma quando fu penato il sig.ʳ Diego Vasquez, votò anchor lui, et io Hipolito Gambocci come puntatore et secretario del sopradetto Collegio de mandato ho scritto la sopradetta Congregatione questo di ultimo de Luglio 1594.

[AGOSTO]
Lunedi A di Primo detto, San Pietro in Vincula, Comune. Questa mattina si cominciò   fol. 28v
a cantar la messa a 12 hore; tutti furno presenti.

Martedi A 2. Il sig.ʳ Horatio Crescentio mancò a tutta la messa b 7¹/₂.

Mercordi Alli 3. Il sig.ʳ Thomasso Benigno Camerlengo ha distribuito la paga del presente mese d'Agosto.
Il sig.ʳ Horatio Cresentio mancò a tutta la messa b 7¹/₂.

Giovedi Alli 4. Tutti furno presenti.

Venardi Alli 5, Santa Maria ad nives, Comune. Il sig.ʳ Paulo Faccone venne al credo b 7.

Questa mattina il sig.ʳ Christiano Ameiden ha congregato il Collegio nella stantia delli 12 Apostoli in detta chiesa et ha referto a detto collegio, che l'Ill.ᵐᵒ et Rev.ᵐᵒ Cardinal Gallo nostro Protettor l'altro giorno lo mandò a dimandar come mastro di Cappella et glie disse, che il ponto, che havevano dato de 5 scudi al sig.ʳ Gio. Sanctos Spagnolo, glie pareva troppo rigoroso e che detto sig.ʳ Gio. Santos se n'era appallato a lui et che lui come protectore non poteva far di manco non ascoltarlo, se ben haveva dato comissione per prima al detto mastro di Cappella, che lo ponisse e che di questo non occoreva, che gli andasse a parlare e che facesse il consueto della Cappella e che se facesse temere conforme alli privileggi et constitutioni de detta Cappella, et mentre detto sig.ʳ Cristiano stava dal detto sig.ʳ Cardinale narrando il fatto con il sig.ʳ Luca Orfeo et me Hipolito, venne il sig.ʳ Gio. Santos et il sig.ʳ Diego Vasquez, dove si stette un pezzo in contradittorie sopra il fatto di questa Congregatione fatta il di ultimo de Luglio prossimo passato, et havendo l'Ill.ᵐᵒ sig.ʳ Cardinal inteso molte ragioni da una parte e da l'altra, disse: io ve ho dato un giudice, che è Monsig.ʳ Ciuccolini, et si voltò a detti sig.ʳⁱ Gio. Sanctos et Diego Vasquez et glie disse: andate da Monsig.ʳ Ciuccolino et fate esaminar li vostri testimonij et poi farrete citar il mastro di Cappella, che dirrà

fol. 29r le ragioni del collegio, et se havete fallito, sarrete ben puntato, et havendo il / Collegio inteso la relatione, che ha fatta il mastro di Cappella, gli è molto dispiaciuto, perche è solito ab antiquo, che, quando un Cantore è punito dal collegio, non deve reclamare fuora, per che le nostre liti per conto delle punitioni sempre si sogliano finir tra noi, e non par bene al Collegio, che de ogni minima cosa si corra al protettore, e per che il Collegio intende diffendersi et mantener fermo la sua authorità et li privileggi et constitutioni della Cappella, ha eletto cinque de nostri compagni, che trattino col sig.ʳ Cardinal Protettore, col giudice da sua signoria Ill.ᵐᵃ eletto, et con chi bisognarà et in nome de tutto il Collegio respondere, a quanto la Cappella sarrà chiamata; li eletti cioe l'infrascritti cioe

> Il sig.ʳ mastro di Cappella,
> Don Hipolito Gambocci puntatore,
> Il sig.ʳ Gio. Maria Nanino,
> Il sig.ʳ D. Archangelo Crivello,
> Il sig.ʳ Luca Orfeo da Fano.

In questa Congregatione tutti furno presenti eccetto il sig.ʳ Pietro decano, il sig.ʳ Alesandro Merlo et il sig.ʳ Soto giubilati; et mancò anco il sig.ʳ Gio. Luca Conforto, che sta male. Gio. Sanctos fu mandato fuora della sopradetta Congregatione, per che con molte parole dava impedimento alla conclusione della Congregatione.

Sabbato[22] A di 6, la Transfiguratione de Nostro Sig.ʳ Comune.

Il sig.ʳ Joseph Bianco mancò a tutta la messa b 7¹/₂

Il sig.ʳ Luca Orfeo mancò a tutta la messa b 7¹/₂.

In questa medesma mattina il sig.ʳ Gio. Maria Nanino domandò Congregatione al Collegio et disse a detto collegio, che il sig.ʳ Horatio Griffi haveva scritto in favore del sig.ʳ Gio. Santes per conto della punitione, che il Collegio gli dette l'altro dj e per

---

[22] Fol. 29v am Rand: *licentia domandata da Gio. Paulo Custode de libri*; getrennt davon, aber gleichfalls am Rand: *electione del Custode de libri*.

che il detto sig.ʳ Gio. Maria l'haveva / ditto ad alcun delli Compagni, però in plena congregatione ha ditto il sig.ʳ Gio. Maria, che ha visto quello scritto e che veramente non ha ditto cosa, che sia in pregiuditio del Collegio; e questa relatione il detto sig.ʳ Gio. Maria l'ha fatta per sodisfatione del detto sig.ʳ Horatio Griffi. Questa medesma mattina il sig.ʳ Christiano Ameyden mastro di Cappella in ditta Congregatione disse, che Gio. Paulo Pellegrini custode de nostri libri della Cappella voleva dir doi parole al Collegio, et fu chiamato in congregatione et intrato dentro fece sua scusa col collegio, se in questo tempo, che l'haveva servitio, non haveva fatto il debito suo con quella diligentia, che si richiede, et supplicò tutto il Collegio, che gli volesse perdonare pregandolo, che gli volesse dar buona licentia, atteso che lui non voleva piu servire e però che il Collegio facesse electione d'un altro in loco suo. Havendo inteso il Collegio l'animo suo gli diede buona licentia però, che promettesse per una sicurtà idonea de pagar li debiti, che lui haveva fatte, de quali haveva promesso per lui il Collegio, et cosi promisse de eseguire.

In questa medesma mattina fu proposto per custode de libri Ottavio Portella raccomandato dal Ill.ᵐᵒ sig.ʳ Diego del Campo mastro di Camera de Nostro Sig.ʳᵉ et dal sig.ʳ Gio. Battista Sassatello Camerier secreto di Nostro Sig.ʳ parimente; et fatto discorso da tutto il Collegio sopra questa electione del novo Custode de libri fu[23] eletto a vive voci nessuno contradicente il sopradetto M.ᵒ Ottavio Portella et si chiamò dentro in Congregatione e per ordine de tutto il Collegio de Cantori il sig.ʳ M.ᵒ di Cappella gli dette il giuramento de servire fidelmente in detto offitio de Custode de libri et esser ubediente al sig.ʳ M.ᵒ di Cappella et a tutto il Collegio nel sudetto offitio, et in segno del possesso il detto sig.ʳ M.ᵒ di cappella gli diede un libro in mano, et basciando le mani al sig.ʳ mastro rengratiò tutto il Collegio di questa gratia, che gli haveva fatta, et promise / dar sicurtà di quanto maneggiaria de detta Cappella, et in quella medesma hora il sig.ʳ Pietro Paulo Portella aiutante di Camera di Nostro Sig.ʳᵉ et fratello del istesso Ottavio promise per lui , che si portarà fidelmente obligando se stesso per tutto quello, che il detto suo fratello maneggiarà de detta Cappella. Nel detta Congregatio tutti furno presenti eccetto il sig.ʳ Decano, il sig.ʳ Alesandro Merlo, il sig.ʳ Sotto giubilati; il sig.ʳ Gio. Luca Conforto infermo, il sig.ʳ Joseph Bianco et il sig.ʳ Luca Orfeo, che hanno mancato in questa messa, talche la electione de detto custode de libri è stata fatta da 19 cantori inclusovi il sig.ʳ Mastro et nessuno fu discrepante. Questa medesma mattina il sig.ʳ Gio. Maria Nanino ha portato un memoriale riceuto da Monsig.ʳ Ciecolini, quale ha dato il sig.ʳ Gio. Santos et Diego Vasquez, al quale memoriale responderanno li cinque deputati dal Collegio, poiche detto memoriale e tutto contra quello, che fu fatto nella Congregatione il di ultimo de Luglio prossimo passato.

Dominica A di 7 dominica decima post Pentecoste. Il sig.ʳ Mattheo hebdomedario cantò la messa.
Il sig.ʳ Paulo de Magistris venne alla fine del credo b 7
Il sig.ʳ Diego Vasquez mancò a tutta la messa b 7½.
Di poi la messa io Hipolito Puntatore pregai tutto il Collegio, che volessero osservare il silentio in choro et star attento alla messa si come si conviene, altramente io non mancarò de puntare secondo il costume della Cappella, et da tutti fu accetta questa amonitione. Il sig.ʳ Mastro di Cappella questa medesma mattina ha exortato tutto il

fol. 29v

fol. 30r

---

[23] Die Worte von *fu eletto* bis *contradicente* unterstrichen.

detto Collegio, che si voglino prepare alla santa Comunione, che si farrà in giorno
infra la octava del Assumptione della Madonna.

Lunedi Alli 8. Il sig.ʳ Josephe Bianco a tutta la messa mancò b 7¹/₂
Il sig.ʳ Archangelo Crivello mancò per esser occupato nella Congregatione delli cinque,
che hanno da respondere al memoriale, che ha dato Gio. Sanctos contro il Collegio.

fol. 30vᵉ²⁴ Martedi A di 9. Non mancò nessuno.

Mercordi A di 10, San Lorenzo. Non mancò nessuno. Il sig.ʳ Gio. Maria ha servito
per il sig.ʳ Joseph, et io Hip.ᵗᵒ Gambocci ho servito per il sig.ʳ Thomasso Benigno.
Questa mattina ho partito li ponti del mese prossimo passato de Luglio et dato a
quelli, che non hanno perso niente, undici baiochi e tre quatrini.

Giovedi A 11. Il sig.ʳ Arcangelo mancò a tutta la messa b 7¹/₂
Il sig.ʳ Agostino Martino mancò a tutta la messa b 7¹/₂
Il sig.ʳ Gio. Luca Conforto è guarito et venuto alla messa.
Il sig.ʳ Stefano Ugerio se scusa per infermo.

Venardi A di 12. Il sig.ʳ Paulo mancò a tutta la messa b 7¹/₂.

Sabbato A di 13. Tutti presenti eccetto quelli della sua giornata.
Il sig.ʳ Stephano Ugerio è guarito et venuto alla messa.

Dominica XI Post Pentecoste. A di 14. Non si canta messa, per che si mandano le
cotte et li libri a Santa Maria Maggiore, dove Nostro Sig.ʳᵉ farrà domani Cappella.

Lunedi A 15, l'Assumptione della Madonna fu Cappella a Santa Maria Maggiore.
L'Ill.ᵐᵒ et Rev.ᵐᵒ Cardinal Castruccio cantò la messa alla presentia della Santità de
Nostro Sig.ʳᵉ et de tutto il Collegio del Ill.ᵐⁱ sig.ʳⁱ Cardinali. Tutti li Rev.ᵈⁱ Cantori
furno presenti eccetto il sig.ʳ Decano et sig.ʳ Soto giubilati. Il sig.ʳ Paulo Faccone venne
di poi li Kyrie eleyson, però si punta in doi giulij. Il sig.ʳ Paulo Faccone b 20.

Martedi Alli 16. Non si è cantato messa per non esser anchor stato reportati li libri
et le cotte. Il sig.ʳ Mastro di Cappella hier mattina in santa Maria Maggiore recordò
alli sig.ʳⁱ cantori, che dominica prossima si farrà la santa Comunione, che ognuno si
debba preparare come si conviene.

Mercordi A di 17. Il sig.ʳ Horatio Griffi mancò a tutta la messa b 7¹/₂.
Il sig.ʳ Luca da Fano mancò a tutta la messa b 7¹/₂

---

²⁴ Zwischen fol. 30ᵛ (alt 29ᵛ) und fol. 31 (alt 30) findet sich ein Blatt eingeheftet, das mit
fol. 30 A (mit Blei) foliiert und von anderer Hand geschrieben ist, also nicht hierher gehört.
Es sei aber im folgenden mitgeteilt:
Instrumentum promissionum inter multum Rev.ᵈᵘᵐ Collegium Cappellae Pontificiae et ma-
gistrum D. Nicolaum Miniattum: In Christi nomine etc. Anno 1590. Die Lune 29 mensis
octobris Mantue in studio Magnifici Domini Anibalis Chieppis, Notarius rogatus Emilius
Righellus, pro seminationis idem Dominus Nicolaus obligatus fuit a di 2 d'ottobre fu dato
al sig.ʳ Paulo de Magistris, a di 9 il detto sig.ʳ Paulo dette il sopradetto instromento al
sig.ʳ Paulo Faccone, a di 16 de ottobre data la sopradetta scrittura al sig.ʳ Christiano ma-
stro di Cappella.

Il sig.ʳ Gio. Santos venne al evangelio b 7
Il sig.ʳ Vasquez mancò a tutta la messa b 7¹/₂.

Giovedi A di 18. Il sig.ʳ Archangelo Crivello mancò a tutta la messa b 7¹/₂.   fol. 31r

Venardi A 19. Non mancò nessuno. Il. sig.ʳ M.º di Cappella recordò la Comunion' per Domenica.

Sabbato A 20. Il sig.ʳ Antonio mancò a tutta la messa b 7¹/₂.

Dominica XII Post Pentecoste. A di 21 infra octava Assumptionis B. Marie, virginis. Il Rev.ᵈᵒ sig.ʳ Don Vincentio de Gratis cantò la messa in sant'Apostolo; tutti furno presenti eccetto li sig.ʳ[i] giubilati cioe il sig.ʳ Decano, il sig.ʳ Alesandro Merlo et il sig.ʳ Francesco Soto. Il sig.ʳ Agostino venne all'Aleluia b 7
Il sig.ʳ Gio. Luca Conforto venne al Evangelio b 7.
In questa messa fu fatta la santissima Comunion dal Collegio delli Cantori, il sopradetto sig.ʳ Don Vincentio de Gratis comunicò tutti quelli, che si vuolssero comunicare; quelli che son preiti, dissero la Messa, li altri tutti si comunicorno, eccetto il sig.ʳ Paulo de Magistris, il sig.ʳ Agostino Martini, il sig.ʳ Paulo Faccone, il sig.ʳ Horatio Griffi et il sig.ʳ Gio. Luca Conforto, e ben vero che alcuni di questi cinque disser esser comunicatj alla Festività del Assumptione della Madonna del presente mese e di poi la messa il sig.ʳ Mastro di Cappella fece cantar il Motetto O sacrum Convivium.

Lunedi Alli 22 d'Agosto. Il sig.ʳ Paulo de Magistris venne di poi il Graduale b 7.
Questa medesma mattina il sig.ʳ Mastro di Cappella di poi la messa domandò congregatione al Collegio et propose a detto Collegio, che volesse ratificare qualmente alli 5. del presente mese d'Agosto nella Congregatione fatta in sant'Apostolo il Collegio de detti cantori fecero elettione de 4 de nostri insieme col mastro, che respondessero a tutto quello faceva de bisogno nella lite, che verte fra il Collegio et tra Gio. Santos et Vasquez, et mandati fuora questi doi cioe Gio. Santos et Vasquez della Congregatione fu letta questa Narrativa da me Hipolito Gambocci secretario et puntatore: Noi infrascritti per la presente dechiaramo, qualmente alli 5. de Agosto 1594 in publica Congregatione fatta in Santi Apostoli furno eletti per sollicitar et respondere a tutto quel che faceva de bisogno nella causa, che verte tra il Collegio e mastro di Cappella contro Gio. Santos et Diego Vasquez cantori de detta Cappella.
E tutti quelli, che si trovorno in questa congregatione si sonno sottoscritti di propria mano et hanno concesso a me Hipolito puntatore, che per comissione del Collegio la faccia anco sottoscrivere alli altri, che si trovorno nella deputatione de detto Collegio. A questa Congregatione tutti furno presenti eccetto il sig.ʳ Pietro decano, il sig.ʳ Alesandro Merlo et il sig.ʳ Fran.ᶜᵒ Sotto giubilati, et lj sig.ʳ Horatio Griffi, Horatio Malvezzi, Luca da Fano et Gio. Luca Conforto, che sonno asenti per esser sua giornata.
Questa medesma mattina venne il sig.ʳ Felice Anerio[25] da parte del Ill.ᵐᵒ et Rev.ᵐᵒ   fol. 31v
Cardinal Aldobrandino a domandar l'infrascritti Cantori per cantar una messa domani a sant'Antonio da Padova, per che il mastro di Casa de detto Ill.ᵐᵒ Cardinal pigliarà la Croce dal sig.ʳ Imbasciator di Spagna, et li fu concesso licentia: Il sig.ʳ Gio. Luca Conforto, il sig.ʳ Horatio Griffi, sig.ʳ Horatio Malvezzi, sig.ʳ Paulo Faccone, sig.ʳ

---

²⁵ Cod.: *Enerio.*

Leonardo Crescentio, sig.^r Thomasso Benigno et il sig.^r Antonio Manni. Li deputati
sopra la lite, che verte tra il Collegio contro Gio. Santos et Diego Vasquez, hanno
scritto contro il memoriale dato da loro a Monsig.^r Ceccolini giudice deputato dal
sig.^r Cardinal Gallo Protettore et dato il detto scritto a Monsig.^r Ceccolino giudice;
et questa Mattina il sig.^r Gio. Maria Nanino ha portato il rescritto contra il nostro,
dato dalli detti Gio. Santos et Vasquez a detto sig.^r Giudice.

Martedi Alli 23 d'Agosto non mancò nessuno.

Mercordi Alli 24 Vigilia de san Bartholomeo. Il sig.^r Paulo Faccone mancò alla messa
b 7½.
Questa mattina il sig.^r Gio. Maria Nanino da parte del Illmo Cardinal Gallo Protettor
della Cappella ha detto al mastro, che dia licentia a l'infrascritti cantori per domani
per andar a cantar la messa a san Luisci della natione francese, et detto mastro me ha
data una poliza scritta di tutti questi per ordine de detto Illmo Cardinale cioe in
questa forma: Don Stephano, M.^o Joseph, M.^o Leonardo, M.^o Antonio, M.^o Thomasso,
M.^o Gio. Maria Nanino, M.^o Oratio basso.
Il sig.^r Horatio Crescentio ha mancato questa mattina a tutta la messa b 7½.

Giovedi A di 25, San Bartholomeo, Comune. Tutti furno presenti eccetto li sopradetti,
andati a san Loisci con licentia concessa dal Cardinal Protettore.

Venardi Alli 26. Tutti presenti.
Questa mattina di poi la messa il sig.^r Paulo de Magistris domandò Congregatione et
nel proprio Coro, dove si è cantato[26] la messa disse al Collegio nostro de Cantori da
parte del Cardinal Mont'Alto, che domattina si fanno l'esequie della felice memoria
de Papa Sisto in santa Maria Maggiore, e a questo effetto invita la Cappella si debba
trovare domattina in detta chiesa, et si dette ordine al custode de libri, che portasse
li libri et facesse portar la cassa con le nostre cotte.

fol. 32r   Sabbatho A di 27. In Santa Maria Maggiore fu fatto l'esequie della felice memoria de
Papa Sisto Quinto. Monsig.^r Rev.^{mo} Alacro cantò la Messa alla presentia de vint'un
Cardinali. Il Cardinal Mont'Alto, ad instantia del quale fu dette esequie, ha dato
per nostri emolumenti scudi 15 d'oro in oro. Tutti presenti eccetto il sig.^r Decano, il
sig.^r Alesandro Merlo et il sig.^r Francesco Soto, tutti tre giubilati. Parte 22.

Dominica XIII Post pentecoste A di 28. Questa mattina per ordine del Collegio s'e
cominciato a cantar la messa a 13 hore; tutti sonno stati presenti eccetto li quattro
infrascritti, che per ordine del Illmo Cardinal Gallo Protettore sonno andati a cantar la messa a sant'Agostino: il sig.^r Gio. Maria Nanino, il sig.^r Stephano Ugerio, il
sig.^r Leonardo Crescentio e il sig.^r Antonio Manni; e questa imbasciata me l'ha fatta
il sig.^r mastro di Cappella, al quale è venuto uno staffier da parte del detto Illmo
Cardinal con una poliza delli quattro cantori gia nominati.

Lunedi Alli 29 d'Agosto. Il sig.^r Agostino Martini mancò a tutta la messa b 7½.
Nella Causa, che verte tra Gio. Santos et Vasquez contra il mastro de Cappella et
Collegio de Cantori di Nostro Sig.^{re} il detto Gio. Santos ha ditto a Monsig.^r Cecolino

---

[26] Cod.: *cantanto*.

giudice della Causa, che li deputati a defender questa causa sonno suoi nemici, et li
ha allegati per sospetti; però ha pregato la sua signoria Rev.ᵐᵃ, che chiami doi Cantori
di Cappella di buona vita et fama e che li esamini, che trovarà che detto Gio. Santos
è stato mal penato, per la qual cosa il detto sig.ʳ Giudice ha fatto chiamare il Rev.ᵈᵒ
Don Stephano Ugerio et M.º Agostino Martini et li ha esaminati sopra detta Causa;
et per che detto sig.ʳ Giudice desidera finir la causa e venir a sententia, ha ditto a me
Hipolito puntatore et secretario, che se glie porti una fede della maggior parte del
Collegio, che il detto Gio. Santos et Vasquez siano ben penati, et fatto la narrativa di
questa forma: »Noi infrascritti Cantori della Cappella de Nostro Sig.ʳᵉ per la presente dechiaramo, qualmente che l'errore commesso et disturbo seguito nella chiesa di
san Jacomo de Spagnoli il giorno di detto santo per conto del mottetto cantato nel
offertorio è proceduto per conto de Gio. Santos et esso ne è stato causa. Però dicemo
che è stato ben penato.« Et il simile è stato ben penato Diego Vasquez per haver /
sparlato delli cantori dicendo »Cantori da quattro baiochi« et altre parole in dishonore   fol. 32ᵛ
del Collegio. Li sottoscritti a questa fede furno 12 cioe, il sig.ʳ Paulo de Magistris, sig.ʳ
Vincentio Musatti, sig.ʳ Oratio Crescentio, sig.ʳ Thomasso Benigno, sig.ʳ Paulo Facconio,
sig.ʳ Joseppe Bianco, sig.ʳ Stephano Ugerio, sig.ʳ Leonardo Crescentio, sig.ʳ Antonio
Manni, sig.ʳ Agostino Martini, sig.ʳ Francesco Spinosa et sig.ʳ Pietro Montoya. Li 4
deputati per questa causa col. sig.ʳ Mastro di Cappella non hanno sottoscritta la sopradetta poliza, poi che da detto Gio. Santos sonno stati allegati per sospetti et suoi
inimici.

Martedi Alli 30. Io Hippolito Gambocci puntatore questa mattina ho presentato la
sopradetta poliza sottoscritta come disopra a Monsig.ʳ Rev.ᵐᵒ Cecolino giudice, il qual
ha promesso spedir detta causa quanto prima. Questa mattina il sig.ʳ Paulo Faccone
mancò a tutta la messa b 7¹/₂.
In questa medesma giornata essendo il sig.ʳ Gio. Maria Nanino andato dal sig.ʳ Giudice
Monsig.ʳ Cecolini per conto della causa de Gio. Santos et Diego Vasquez, ha ditto, che,
se ben quelli quattro eletti per defendere la causa sonno stati allegati per sospetti et
inimici, non dimeno per questo sospetto non se gli ha da negare, che non possino dar
tutti il suo voto, et havendo considerato il detto sig.ʳ Giudice, che de ragione non
se gli deve negare il voto, ha dato licentia, che anco quelli 4 eletti possino sottoscrivere
la sopradetta poliza insieme col mastro di Cappella come Cantore, sicome l'hanno
sottoscritta cioe: il sig.ʳ Don Archangelo Crivelli, Jo, Don Hipolito Gambocci, il sig.ʳ
Gio. Maria Nanino, il sig.ʳ Luca Orfeo et il sig.ʳ Christiano Ameyden cantor et mastro
di Cappella, talche secondo la forma delle constitutioni il detto Gio. Santos ha perso
il partito, per che de 20 Cantori, che si trovorno nella sopradetta congregatione,
quando fu penato lui et Vasquez, dicesette hanno confirmato de manu propria, che
sonno stati ben penati.

Mercordi A l'ultimo d'Agosto fu cantata la messa de Requiem per l'anima della matre
del sig.ʳ Martio Colonna ad instantia della Compagnia de 12 Apostoli in detta chiesa;
tutti presenti. Li punti del presente mese d'Agosto sonno giulij 18 et un baiocco et
mezzo.
Il sig.ʳ Gio. Luca Conforto non participa delli ponti del presente mese d'Agosto, per
che stato diece giorni absente dal servitio, infirmitatis causa, e conforme alla constitutione non participa.

[SETTEMBRE]

fol. 33r Giovedi A di primo. Il sig.ʳ Gio. Maria Nanino s'escusato per infermo. Questa mattina habbiamo cominciato a cantar la messa nel oratorio de san Marcello, per che il Papa è tornato a Monte Cavallo, e tutti sonno stati presenti eccetto quelli della sua giornata; il sig.ʳ Joseph Bianco ha servito per il sig.ʳ Oratio Griffi.

Venardi A di 2. Il sig.ʳ Gio. Maria Nanino è venuto al servitio, e tutti li altri questa mattina sonno stati presenti.

Hieri²⁷ il sig.ʳ Giudice della Causa del Collegio contro Gio. Santos et Diego Vasquez mandò a chiamar il sig.ʳ Gio. Maria Nanino, et per che stava male, io andai da detto sig.ʳ Giudice, il qual me disse, che io dovese produrre in actis quella poliza della dechiaratione del error fatto in san Jacomo de Spagnoli il di de esso Santo nel mottetto cantato nel offertorio, et io Hippolito Gambocci come cantor, puntator et secretario de detto Collegio produssi in actis la predetta poliza overo dechiaratione sottoscritta dalli nostri Compagni, et M.º Ortentio notario pigliò quest'atto sotto il di primo de settembre 1594.

Sabbatho A di 3. Il sig.ʳ Joseph Bianco è venuto per il sig.ʳ Oratio Griffi, et il sig.ʳ Santos è venuto per Diego Vasquez.

Questa medesma mattina io Hip.ᵗᵒ puntator son andato col sig.ʳ Gio. Maria et col sig.ʳ Luca Orfeo dal nostro notario et ho fatto una protesta in actis contra Gio. Santos et Diego Vasquez protestandomi in nome del nostro Collegio, che volendo loro eseguire in anzi a quel, che ha fatto il Collegio della pena, che gli ha fatto giustamente pagare, che tutte le spese et danni vadano aconto di detti Gio. Santos et Vasquez et non del Collegio.

Dominica A di 4. Io Hippolito Puntator mandai a far la scusa per esser infermo di febre; tutto il resto presenti, per quanto m'e stato referto dal sig.ʳ Antonio Manni sottopuntatore.

Lunedi. A di 5. Non mancò nessuno.

Martedi Alli 6. Il sig.ʳ Paulo Faccone mancò a tutta la messa b 7¹/₂.
Questa mattina il sig.ʳ Thomasso Beningo ha distribuito la paga del presente mese.

Mercordi Alli 7. Il sig.ʳ Paulo Faccone venne di poi l'evangelio b 7.
Questa mattina il sig.ʳ Antonio sottopuntator ha distribuito li ponti d'Agosto prossimo passato.

Giovedi Alli 8. Tutti presenti. Comune per la Natività della Madonna.

Venardi Alli 9. Il sig.ʳ Horatio Basso mancò a tutta la messa b 7¹/₂.

fol. 33v Sabbato A di X. Io Hipolito son tornato al servitio per gratia de Dio sanato.
Il sig.ʳ Horatio Malvezzi mancò a tutta la messa b 7¹/₂.
Questa mattina il sig.ʳ Thomasso Benigno ha destribuito li 15 scudi d'oro in oro re-scossi dal Ill.ᵐᵒ Cardinal Mont'alto per l'esequie fatte per la felice memoria di Papa Sisto a santa Maria Maggior alli 27 d'Agosto. Questa mattina sig.ʳ Gio. Santos è venuto per il sig.ʳ Diego Vasquez.

---

²⁷ Am Rand eine hinweisende Hand.

Dominica XV. Post Pentecoste A di XI de settembre. Il sig.ʳ Paulo Faccone venne di poi l'epistola. b 7.

Questa medesma mattina di poi la messa Monsig.ʳ Rev.ᵐᵒ Cecolini comme Giudice deputato da Monsig.ʳ Ill.ᵐᵒ Cardinal Gallo nostro Protectore congregò il nostro Collegio de Cantori nella sacristia del Horatorio di San Marcello et disse, che il detto Monsig.ʳ Ill.ᵐᵒ lo mandava da noi et da sua parte ci faceva questa imbasciata, che dovessimo star uniti et in pace, da buoni fratellj, si come si deve, et che la pena pagata da Gio. Sanctos et Diego Vasquez per questa volta non voleva se venisse ad altra sententia, poi che a preghi di sua signoria Ill.ᵐᵃ li detti penati Gio. Santos et Diego Vasquez si contentano poner silentio et fine alla lite senza proceder piu oltre; et disse anco il detto Monsig.ʳ Cecolino, che di qua avanti, quando il Collegio ha da penare alcuno delli Compagni, il detto Ill.ᵐᵒ Monsig.ʳ Cardinal Gallo come Protectore datoci dal Papa vuol esserne fatto prima consapevole, per poter remediar all'inconvenienti, che possano occorere, et il sig.ʳ Mastro di Cappella in nome de tutti rengratiò Monsig.ʳ Cecolini di questa inbasciata et che non si mancarà metter ad escecutione, quanto comanda Monsig.ʳ Ill.ᵐᵒ Protettore. A questa Congregatione tutti furno presenti eccetto il sig.ʳ Pietro Decano, il sig.ʳ Alesandro Merlo et il sig.ʳ Fran.ᶜᵒ Soto giubilati.

Lunedi Alli XII. Il sig.ʳ Paulo de Magistris mancò a tutta la messa b 7¹/₂.

Martedi Alli XIII. Il sig.ʳ Paulo Faccone venne al Credo b 7.

Questa mattina Monsig.ʳ Cecolini me ha restituito la bolla et il libro delle Constitutioni.

Mercordi Alli 14, la exaltatione della Santa Croce habbiamo cantato la messa a san Marcello. Monsig.ʳ Rev.ᵐᵒ Robusterio ha cantata la messa alla presentia de Molti Ill.ᵐⁱ Cardinali, et si è fatto il maritaggio delle Zitelle.

Questa mattina il sig.ʳ Vasquez si è escusato per infermo, tutti li altri presenti.

Giovedi Alli 15. Non mancò nessuno.

fol. 34r

Venardi Alli 16. Il sig.ʳ Diego Vasquez è guarito et venuto alla messa; tutti presenti.

Sabbato A di 17. Non mancò nessuno.

Dominica XVI post pentecoste A di 18. Il sig.ʳ Pirro Allemani è hebdomedario; non è venuto a cantar la messa et ha mandato a dio, che sta male, e perche non vi era tempo de mandar a chiamar un'altro Cappellano, Hippolito Gambocci puntator ho cantato la messa de consenso de tutti li sig.ʳⁱ Compagni, che erano presenti; però l'ho cantata senza far pregiuditio al mio loco come cantore, et per che essendo festa non se restassi de cantar la messa.

Il sig.ʳ Paulo Faccone è venuto al evangelio b 7

Il sig.ʳ Agostino Martino è mancato in tutto b 7¹/₂.

Di poi la messa il sig.ʳ Horatio Griffi ha domandato licentia per pigliar li ordini sacri questa settimana, che le quattro tempora, et ha domandato perdono in publico, se lui havesse offeso nessuno delli compagni o in particular o in generale, che gli voglino perdonar et pregar Dio per lui, acciò possa pigliar questi sacri ordini per salute del'anima sua et servitio del Nostro sig.ʳ Dio, alla qual proposta tutti lo laudorno di questo bono offitio da Cristiano et gli dettero licentia d'andarsi a ordinare. In questa Congregatione tutti furno presenti, eccetto il sig.ʳ Agostino Martini et li 4 giubilati, cioe il sig.ʳ Decano, il sig.ʳ Christiano Ameiden M.º di Cappella, il sig.ʳ Alesandro Merlo et il sig.ʳ Fran.ᶜᵒ Soto.

Lunedi Alli 19. Il sig.ʳ Paulo Faccone mancò a tutta la messa b 7¹/₂.

Martedi Alli 20. Il sig.ʳ Luca Orfeo mancò a tutta la messa b 7¹/₂.

Mercordi Alli 21. San Mattheo Apostolo et evangelista, Comune. Tutti presenti eccetto li giubilati et il sig.ʳ Horatio Griffi, qual ha licentia per esser andato a piglia[r] l'ordini sacri.
Di poi la messa fu fatta congregatione dalli interessati nell'Abatia di Mantoa et nella pensione di Spagna: in quanto a Mantoa non fu resoluto niente, per che il sig.ʳ Paulo Faccone disse, che il Miniato, che ci doveva dar le semente, che noi pretendevamo, era fallito e che non si trovava piu in Mantoa. Della pensione di Spagna fu resoluto, che il sig.ʳ Gio. Santos facesse far una supplica et la desse al sig.ʳ Paulo de Magistris per dar la a Monsig.ʳ Vestri, che ne parli a Nostro Signore per commutar la pensione del sig.ʳ Gironimo Rainosa in testa d'un altro.

fol. 34v   Giovedi Alli 22. Questa mattina de Consenso de tutto il Collegio s'e cominciato a dir la messa a 13 hore e mezzo.
Il sig.ʳ Horatio basso²⁸ venne di poi l'epistola b 7
Il sig.ʳ Luca Orfeo mancò in tutta la messa b 7¹/₂.
Questa mattina ho dato la Cedola della pensione di Spagna al sig.ʳ Gio. Santos presente il sig.ʳ Mastro di Cappella.

Venardi Alli 23. Il sigʳ Gio Santos mancò per esser occupato per servitio della Cappella per la pensione di Spagna.
Il sig.ʳ Thomasso Benigno questa mattina non è venuto b 7¹/₂.

Sabbato A di 24. Tutti presenti eccetto il sig.ʳ Horatio Griffi, che è andato a pigliar l'ordini sacri.

Domenica XVII Post pentecoste. Alli 25. Il sig.ʳ Thomasso Benigno²⁸ non venne questa mattina b 7¹/₂.

Lunedi Alli 26. Il sig.ʳ Montoia mancò in tutto b 7¹/₂
Il sig.ʳ Fran.ᶜᵒ Spinosa mancò in tutto b 7¹/₂.

Martedi Alli 27. Il sig.ʳ Paulo Faccone venne al santus b 7
Il sig.ʳ Horatio Malvitio venne all'evangelio b 7.
Questa mattina il sig.ʳ Gio. Santos ha obtenuto licentia dal Collegio per andar fuor di Roma per 15 giorni, ma quando non sarrà comune per lui ha promesso farrà servire alcuno de suoi Compagni et parte domani. Il sig.ʳ Joseph Bianco mancò a tutta la messa b 7¹/₂.

---

²⁸ *basso — Benign*o über der Zeile eingefügt. Unter Horatio basso ist der Baß Fra Horatio Malvezzi gemeint, der am 15. I. 1590 in die Kapelle aufgenommen wurde und im Jubeljahr 1600 das Amt des Punktators versah.

Mercore A di 28. Il sig.ʳ Paulo de Magistris venne a l'Agnus dei b 7.
Questa mattina il sig.ʳ Horatio Griffi ha obtenuto licentia per il sig.ʳ Gio. Luca Conforto per domattina della messa.

Giovedi Alli 29. Il sig.ʳ Montoya mancò a tutta la messa b 7¹/₂.

Venardi Alli 30. Il sig.ʳ Thomasso Benigno venne al credo b 7¹/₂.
Questa mattina il sig.ʳ Mastro di Cappella ha presentato al Collegio una lettera del sig.ʳ Gio. Battista Martini et io Hipolito di poi la messa l'ho letta in publico, nella qual lettera il detto sig.ʳ Gio. Battista supplica il Collegio, che vogli deputar doi o tre Compagni, che parlino al Ill.ᵐᵒ Cardinal Camerlengo et obtenere, che li Cantori del Papa non paghino le decime quelli, che hanno benefitio, attento che li nostri priveleggi ci fanno asenti. Fu resoluto, che domenica, che sarremo tutti, si ordinarà quellj, che hanno da trattar questo negotio.
Li ponti del presente mese de settembre sonno giulij 13 e 3 baiochi.

Il sig.ʳ Gio. Santos è tornato et non ha voluto goder la licentia se non per 2 giorni.

[OTTOBRE]
Sabbato. Questa mattina de comune consensu de tutto il Collegio si è cominciato a cantar a 14 hore la messa al horatorio de san Marcello. Il sig.ʳ Paulo de Magistris mancò alla messa in totum b 7¹/₂.   fol. 35r
Questa mattina il sig.ʳ Agostino Martino ha preso il memoriale, che va al sig.ʳ Cardinal Gaetano per informarsi, se li familiari del papa pagono le decime, per poter dar resposta al sig.ʳ Gio. Battista Martini ad Aversa.

Domenica VIII Post Pentecoste, A di 2. Questa mattina tutti sonno stati presenti. Il sig.ʳ Agostino Martini ha dato il memoriale al sig.ʳ Ill.ᵐᵒ Cardinal Gaeta et ha referto per resposta, che in questo caso delle decime il Papa nella bolla, che ha fatto sopra di cio, ha derogato tutti li privileggi e che per tal facto il detto Cardinal non ci puol far gratia nessuna, a talche si è resoluto de respondere al sig.ʳ Gio. Battista, che in questo caso bisogna, che insieme con noi habbia pacientia, poi che il Papa ha derogato in questo caso alli privileggi.
Questa mattina il sig.ʳ Joseph ha obtenuto licentia dal Collegio poter esser absente da Roma per X giorni per alcune sue faccende de importanza, et parte domattina.
Questa medesma mattina ho dato al sig.ʳ Paulo de Magistris lo stromento delle semente, che il collegio pretende dal sig.ʳ Nicolo Miniati per conto della abbatia de Mantoa, et glie l'ho dato alla presentia del sig.ʳ Mastro di Cappella et del sig.ʳ Horatio Crescentio.

Lunedi Alli 3. Tutti sonno stati presenti.

Martedi Alli 4. Tutti furno presenti. Questa mattina il sig.ʳ Thomasso Benigno ha destribuito la paga del presente mese d'ottobre.

Mercordi Alli 5. Il sig.ʳ Paulo Faccone venne al principio del prefatio b 7.
Questa matti[na] ho destribuito li ponti del mese prossimo passato de settembre.

Giovedi Alli 6. Tutti presenti. Il sig.ʳ Gio. Luca Conforto ha obtenuto licentia dal Collegio ad instantia del Ill.ᵐᵒ sig.ʳ Cardinal Gallo Protettore per andar fuor di Roma al servitio del Ill.ᵐᵒ Cardinal Santi Quattro per tutto il presente mese.

Venardi Alli 7. Il sig.ʳ Thomasso Benigno non è venuto questa mattina b 7¹/₂.
Il sig.ʳ Paulo de Magistris non è venuto questa mattina b 7¹/₂.
Questa mattina io Hipolito ho letto in publico la resposta della lettera, che si manda domattina al sig.ʳ Gio. Battista Martini, et il sig.ʳ mastro di Cappella l'ha sottoscritta.

Sabbato A di 8. Tutti sonno stati presenti.

fol. 35v   Dominica 19 post Pentecoste. A di 9. Tutti furno presenti eccetto il sig.ʳ Joseph Bianchi et il sig.ʳ Gio. Luca Conforti, che sonno fuor di Roma con licentia.
Di poi la messa il sig.ʳ Mastro di Cappella domandò Congregatione al Collegio et exortò tutti a volersi preparare alla santa Comunione per la solemnità della festa de tutti li santi, sicome conviene, et ultra propose al Collegio, che essendo la parte delli contralti assai in numero gli pareva, che fusse bene metterne doi di essi alla parte del Tenore, essendo che in quella ce ne sonno doi asenti dal servitio, e qualche volta viene a restar debole, e propose metter in detta parte delli Tenori Il sig.ʳ Luca Orfeo et me Hipolito Gambocci; qual proposta fu comendata da tutti et accettata, et anco da noi per obedire a tutto il Collegio fu accettata, però senza pregiuditio della nostra admissione et antiquità del loco di Cappella, et senza pregiuditio di qual si voglia giurisditione nostra, et in conclusione da tutti fu consentito in questo modo sopradetto.

Lunedi Alli X. Tutti furno presenti.

Martedi Alli XI. Il sig.ʳ Agostino venne di poi il graduale b 7
Il sig.ʳ Horatio Crescentio non venne questa mattina b 7¹/₂.

Mercore A di XII. Il sig.ʳ Gio. Santo[s] venne al evangelio b 7.

Giovedi Alli XIII. Non mancò nessuno; hieri finnirno li X giorni della licentia del sig.ʳ Joseph Bianco, et hoggi è sua giornata d'assentione.

Venardi Alli XIIII. Il sig.ʳ Joseph Bianchi mancò in totum b 7¹/₂
Il sig.ʳ Paulo Faccone comparse questa mattina di poi la messa b 7¹/₂
Il sig.ʳ Diego Vasquez non è venuto b 7¹/₂
Il sig.ʳ Horatio Malvicio venne al alleluia dipoi la epistola b 7
Il sig.ʳ Thomasso venne alla elevatione del Corpus Domini b 7.
Questa mattina il sig.ʳ Vincentio Musatti ha obtenuto licentia dal Collegio per domattina per certe sue faccende d'importantia non portà venire.

Sabbato A di XV. Il sig.ʳ Vincentio Musatti è venuto et deferisce la licentia di questo giorno per Lunedi. Il. sig.ʳ Paulo Faccone venne per il sig.ʳ Paulo de Magistris, ma venne di poi la epistola, mentre se diceva l'alleluia, e si contenta, che io ponti lui, poi che haveva promesso de venire. Però il sig.ʳ Paulo Faccone b 7.

Dominica XX Post pentecoste A di 16. Tutti furno presenti; et de consensu de tutto il Collegio et mastro di Cappella questa mattina si è cominciato a dir la messa a 14 hore e mezza.

Il sig.^r Horatio Griffi ha supplicato tutto il Collegio, che lo voglia favorire Martedi, che sarrà il giorno de san Luca, andar a cantar la messa a san Giovanni de Fiorentini, dove lui con l'aiuto de Dio dirrà la sua prima Messa, il che ha obtenuto e tutti hanno accettato, et si andarà alle 15 hore, et sarà Comune per la festa de san Luca.

Lunedi Alli 17. Tutti furno presenti.   fol. 36r
Martedi Alli 18. Il sig.^r Horatio Griffi cantò la sua prima messa in san Giovanni de Fiorentini, et tutto il nostro Collegio fu a cantar detta messa, et vi mancò il sig.^r Gio. Luca Conforto, che è fuora di Roma con licentia; et vi mancorno li tre giubilati, cioe il sig.^r Pietro Decano, il sig.^r Alesandro Merlo et il sig.^r Fran.^{co} Soto.
Il sig.^r Horatio Griffi è stato ordinato ad titulum Cappelle et spedito il breve o suplica del mese de Settembre del presente anno 1594.

Mercordi Alli 19. Il sig.^r Vincentio Musatti venne di poi il vangelio b 7
Il sig.^r Paulo de Magistris venne di poi l'alleluia b 7
Il sig.^r Paulo Faccone venne al prefatio b 7
Il sig.^r Luca Orfeo venne al evangelio b 7.

Giovedi Alli 20. Il sig.^r Horatio Malvezzi s'escusò per infermo; questa mattina il sig.^r Luca Orfeo non comparse a niente b 7½.

Venardi Alli 21. Il sig.^r Vasquez è venuto al santus b 7
Il sig.^r Paulo Faccone venne al Agnus dei, ma non si mise la cotta b 7½.

Sabbato A di 22. Tutti presenti.

Dominica XXI Post pentecoste Alli 23. Il sig.^r Luca Orfeo venne di poi l'epistola al graduale b 7
In sig.^r Gio. Luca Conforto è tornato et venuto questa mattina al evangelio.
Di poi[29] la messa il sig.^r Thomasso Benigno domandò Congregatione al Collegio et propose al Collegio, che per utile delli nostri compagni defunti benefattori et pro quelli che mancranno sarria bene instituire un obligo, che ogni mese il primo Lunedi non impedito da Concistorio o cappella il collegio facesse un'aniversario o in cappella o in un'altra chiesia comoda secondo parà al Collegio, e che di questa ne haveva parlato al Illmo Cardinal Gallo protettor, il qual glie respose, che questa era un opera molto laudabile e che ne parleria al papa, ma voleva, che li cantori la domandassero loro stessi con una poliza sottoscritta da tutti del Collegio, alla qual proposta fu resposto da tutti, che era cosa molto santa et bona, ma che si reserbava de resolverla per un altra Congregatione, che fussero intimati tutti li Compagni.

Lunedi Alli 24. Il sig.^r Paulo Faccone mancò a tutta la messa b 7½   fol. 36v
Il sig.^r Antonio Manni venne di poi l'epistola b 7.

Martedi Alli 25. Il sig.^r Joseph Bianco venne di poi l'epistola e se diceva il graduale b 7.

Mercordi Alli 26. Per non esser venuto il sig.^r Vincentio de Gratis non s'è cantata la messa, ma il Rev.^{do} sig.^r Horatio Griffi ha detto la messa bassa e tutti li Compagni presenti eccetto li giubilati.

---

[29] Am Rand: *Proposta del sig.^r Thomasso Benigno.*

Il sig.^{r} Paulo de Magistris non è comparso in tutta questa messa b 7½.

Giovedi Alli 27. Il sig.^{r} Horatio Malvezzi venne al servitio della messa, et per che si trovava molto fiacco et debile, ha domandato gratia al Collegio, che per alcuni giorni possa venir con comodità et quando potrà, et essendo cosa giusta il collegio et il sig.^{r} Mastro glie l'ha concesso, e che venendo tardo o non venendo per alcuni giorni non sia puntato. Tutti furno presenti eccetto tre giubilati e quelli della sua giornata

Venardi Alli 28. Santi Apostoli Simone et Juda, Comune. Questa mattina di poi la messa fu dato ordine, che domani si mandino li libri e la cassa delle Cotte a Palazzo, dove il Papa torna per habitare secondo il solito.
Questa medesma mattina il sig.^{r} Mastro di Cappella ha di novo recordato, che ognuno si prepari alla santa Comunione per questa solemnità de tutti li santi; tutti sonno stati presenti eccetto il sig.^{r} Horatio Malvitij.

Sabbato Alli 29. Non fu fatto niente per il trasportar le robbe a palazzo, cioe libri et cotte.

Dominica 22 post pentecoste. Alli 30. Non fu fatto niente.

Lunedi Alli 31. In Cappella de Sisto IIII la Santità di Nostro Sig.^{re} Clemente ottavo ha fatto il vespero secondo il solito, alla presentia del Collegio dell' Ill.^{mi} et Rev.^{mi} Cardinali. Tutti presenti eccetto Fra Oratio Malvitio escusato et il sig.^{r} Alesandro Merlo giubilato. Di poi il Vespero il sig.^{r} Christiano Ameyden mastro di Cappella dette ordine, che per la Dominica prossima ognuno si preparasse di far la santissima Comunione. Li ponti del presente mese d'ottobre sonno giulij 15 e quattro baiochi. Il sig.^{r} Josef Bianco et il sig.^{r} Gio. Luca Conforto non participano de detti ponti, perche sonno stati absenti dal servitio di Cappella piu che diece giorni.

[NOVEMBRE]

fol. 37r   Martedi. Il primo. La Festa de tutti li santi. Nell'altare delli Apostoli in san Pietro l'Illmo et Rev.^{mo} Cardinal Gesualdo ha cantato la messa alla presentia de Nostro Sig.^{re} Clemente ottavo et de tutto il sacro Collegio de l'Ill.^{mi} Cardinali, et secondo il solito si è fatto il sermone da uno del Collegio Germanico con la indulgentia de 30 anni. Tutti presenti eccetto il sig.^{r} Pietro Decano, il sig.^{co} Sotto giubilati et il sig.^{r} Fra Horatio Malvitio infermo. Di poi la messa habbiamo hauto il pranzo in tinello secondo il solito.
La sera medesma la santità di Nostro Sig.^{re} Clemente ottavo fece il vespero et mattutino de morti secondo il solito nella Cappella de Sisto IIII in Palazzo alla presentia del Collegio del Ill.^{mi} Cardinali. Tutti presenti eccetto il sig.^{r} Decano, il sig.^{r} Fran.^{co} giubilati et il sig.^{r} Fra Oratio Malvitio infermo.

Mercordi Alli 2. In Cappella de Sisto in palazzo l'Illmo et Rev.^{mo} Cardinal Santa Severina cantò la messa de tutti li morti per esser maggior penitentiario alla presentia della santità de Nostro Sig.^{re} Clemente ottavo et de tutto il Collegio delli Ill.^{mi} sig.^{ri} Cardinali. Tutti presenti eccetto il sig.^{r} Decano, il sig.^{r} Fran.^{co} Soto et il sig.^{r} Fra Oratio Malvezzi infermo. Di poi la messa s'è dato ordine, che domatti[na] si dica la messa a XV hore, et chi ha il suo giorno, sia absente da detta messa, et non si dirrà offitio.

Giovedi Alli 3. Il sig.ʳ Mattheo Argenti ebdomedario cantò la messa; tutti presenti.

Venardi A di 4. In Cappella Sisto si è fatto l'aniversario dell'Ill.ᵐⁱ sig.ʳⁱ Cardinali in absentia del Papa, il Cardinal de Medici Arcivescovo di Fiorenza ha cantata la messa alla presentia del Collegio delli Ill.ᵐⁱ sig.ʳⁱ Cardinali; tutti presenti eccetto il sig.ʳ Decano, Fran.ᶜᵒ Soto et sig.ʳ Alesandro Merlo giubilati, et il sig.ʳ Horatio Malvitij infermo.
Il sig.ʳ Paulo de Magistris venne alla fine della sequentia di poi l'epistola, però si punta il detto sig.ʳ Paulo de Magistris b 50.
Il sig.ʳ Spinosa questa mattina si è scusato per infermo.

Sabbato A di 5. Non si canta messa, per che li Compagni attendono alle reconciliationi per far domattina la santa Comunione in Cappella.

Dominica 23 post Pentecoste[30] Alli 6, Dominica infra l'octava de tutti li santi, in cap-   fol. 37v
pella de Sisto III in Palazzo il sig.ʳ Rev.ᵈᵒ Don Archangelo Crivello ha ditto la messa bassa et ha comunicato il sig.ʳ Mastro di Cappella et collegio de cantori, et il sig.ʳ Paulo de Magistris, il sig.ʳ Paulo Faccone, il sig.ʳ Joseph Bianco, il sig.ʳ Horatio Malvitij non si sonno comunicati, li preiti dicano haver ditto missa altrove, il sig.ʳ Don Vincentio Musatti ne il sig.ʳ Don Horatio Griffi non sonno comparsi, però io li puntarò secondo l' ordinario, che havevano licentia de dir messa, dove gli pareva, ma non de non comparire in Cappella.
Il sig.ʳ Vincentio Musatti b 7¹/₂   ⎫   per non esser comparsi; fu dechiarato, che non
Il sig.ʳ Horatio Griffi b 7¹/₂   ⎭   si puntassero.
Di poi la comunione finita la messa si cantò il motetto »O sacrum convivium«.
Il sig.ʳ Paulo Faccone comparse di poi il motetto.
Il sig.ʳ Horatio Malvezzi et il sig.ʳ Spinosa, che stavano male, questa mattina sonno venuti in Cappella.
Il sig.ʳ Thomasso Benigno questa mattina ha portata et distribuita la paga del presente mese de novembre.
Il sig.ʳ Paulo Faccone ha finito di pagare questa mattina in mano del sig.ʳ Thomasso Benigno li cinque scudi e 29 baiochi, che doveva dare al Collegio per resto delli scudi 15, che hebbe in Mantoa.

Lunedi A 7. Non se disse l'offitio, il sig.ʳ Mario Corona cantò la messa solita.
Il sig.ʳ Paulo Faccone venne di poi l'epistola, mentre si cantava alleluia b 7.

Martedi Alli 8. Il sig.ʳ Paulo Faccone mancò per servitio del Collegio, tutti li altri presenti.

Mercordi Alli 9. A hore 16 si è cantata la messa nostra solita alla chiesa de san Gregorio per li nostri compagni defuncti, il sig.ʳ Pirro Allemani ha cantato la messe, il sig.ʳ Pirro Chiachi [?] il vangelio et io Hipolito Gambocci l'epistola per non esserci altro che la dicesse; il sig.ʳ Paulo Faccone è venuto di poi l'epistola b 15.

---

[30] Am Rand: *Comunione.*

Il sig.^r Horatio Malvezzi è venuto tardo, ma secondo la sua licentia de convalescentia non si ponta.

Il sig.^r Gio. Luca Conforto è venuto con un feraiolo corto e senza sottana longa b 10

Il sig.^r Thomasso Benigno è venuto con feraiolo corto senza sottana longa b 10, et questa mattina è stata bellissima giornata, che non vi è scusa di pioggia, et conforme alla Constitutione, Capitolo 19 li ho pontati ut supra.

Questa mattina ho distribuito li ponti del mese prossimo passato d'ottobre.

fol. 38r Giovedi A di 10. Si cominciò a dir il mattutino secondo il solito alle Laude di san Pietro, il sig.^r Mario Corona cantò la messa, tutti presenti.

Il sig.^r Horatio Malvezzi si scusa, che per X giorni non puol venir al mattuttino per respetto, che la mattina pigliò li siroppi, ma che alla messa verrà.

Venardi A di 11, san Martino. Tutti presenti; questa mattina il sig.^r Mastro di Cappella et Collegio han dechiarato, che il ponto del sig.^r Vincentio Musatto et del sig.^r Horatio Griffi sia nullo, poi che quel giorno, che si fece la comunione, loro andorno a dir messa, ma per un'altra congregatione si dechiararà se tutti devono comparire in cappella il giorno, che si fa la comunione, ancor che non si canti la messa. Però il ponto delli sopradetti, sotto il di 6 del presente non si rescoterà.

Sabbato A di 12. Non mancò nessuno.

Dominica 24 Post pentecoste A di 13. Il sig.^r Vincentio Musatto s'escusa per infermo.

Il sig.^r Paulo de Magistris b 3
Io Hipolito Gambocci puntatore b 3
Il sig.^r Paulo Faccone b 3
Il sig.^r Stefano Ugerio b 3   } Tutti sonno mancati al matuttino.
Il sig.^r Horatio Griffi b 3
Il sig.^r Vasquez b 3

Questa mattina di poi la messa il sig.^r Mastro di Cappella ad instantia de alcuni sig.^{ri} Cantori ha proposto, se si deve cantar a cominciar l'offitio alla Campana delle Laude di san Pietro overo deputar un hora congrua a tutti; è stato discorso a voce, e per che vi fu contraversie di pareri, non si è resoluto niente, se non che se seguiti le Laude de san Pietro conforme alla constitutione sino a tanto, che se risolverà altramente per un'altra congregatione.

Lunedi A di 14. Il sig.^r Paulo Faccone mancò a matuttino e prima b 6.

Martedi Alli 15 fu Concistorio publico, Comune. Fece l'intrata l'Illmo et Rev.^{mo} Cardinal Sega, et mentre stette in Cappella, fu cantato il motetto exaltabo te domine; tutti presenti eccetto il sig.^r Decano et sig.^r Alesandro Merlo guibilati.

Mercordi Alli 16. Il sig.^r Paulo Faccone mancò al matuttino b 5.

Giovedi Alli 17. Il sig.^r Agostino Martini mancò a tutto et la messa b 10.

Venardi Alli 18. Il sig.^r Paulo de Magistris mancò al matuttino b 5
Il sig.^r Diego Vasquez mancò al matuttino b 5.
Questo di ad instantia del sig.^r Diego mastro di Camera del Papa mancorno sei can-

tori alla messa con licentia del Collegio per andar a san Pietro: il sig.ʳ Paulo Faccone, Antonio Manni, Leonardo Crescentio, Stefano Ugerio, Archangelo Crivelli et Josef Bianco.

Sabbato A di 19. Il sig.ʳ Paulo de Magistris mancò a tutto l'offitio et messa b 10   fol. 38v
Il sig.ʳ Gio. Luca Conforto mancò a tutto l'offitio et messa b 10
Il sig.ʳ Agostino Martini mancò a matutino solo b 5
Il sig.ʳ Horatio Griffi mancò al matutino solo b 5
Il sig.ʳ Pietro Montoya mancò al matutino b 5
Il sig.ʳ Diego Vasquez mancò al matutino b 5.

Dominica ultima Post Pentecoste A di 20. Il sig.ʳ Horatio Crescentio mancò al matutino b 3
Il sig.ʳ Joseffe Bianco [mancò] al matutino b 3.

Lunedi Alli 21, la presentatione della Madonna, Comune.
Il sig.ʳ Gio. Luca venne di poi il credo b 7.
Di poi la messa il Cardinal Sfondrato ha mandato un cappellano ad invitare tutto il nostro Collegio, che voglia andar a cantar domani la messa et vespero alla Chiesa di santa Cecilia suo titulo; glie fu resposto dal mastro di Cappella, che alla Messa si anderà per servire a sua signoria Ill.ᵐᵃ, ma il vespero non è solito che la Cappella del Papa collegialiter lo canti mai in nessun loco; et fu detto al detto Cappellano, che il Cardinal Mont'alto e il Cardinal Matthei hanno donato altre volte alla Cappella, cioe per li cantori scudi quindici per una messa sola; però con li padroni non si fa patti.
Questa[31] medesma mattina il sig.ʳ Thomasso Benigno ha partito li trenta ducati, che ha rescossi del Cappello del Cardinal Sega. Tutti presenti eccetto il sig.ʳ Decano, il sig.ʳ Alesandro Merlo et il sig.ʳ Soto giubilati. Questa medesma mattina il sig.ʳ Stefano Ugerio propose al Collegio, che havendo lui servito, quando il Cardinal Sernano et Alano pigliorno il cappello, gli pareva cosa giusta participar come li altri del Cappello, et havendo intesa la proposta il sig.ʳ M.º di Cappella lo pregò, che andasse un poco fuora, che se discorreria questo negotio con li sig.ʳⁱ Compagni; et fatto molti discorsi sopra questo fatto la maggior parte teneva, che il sig.ʳ Stefano non dovesse a guardare a queste minutie, poi che il collegio s'era portato con lui amorevolmente in donarli 125 scudi, che doveva pagar alla Cappella per una sentenza de Monsig.ʳ Orfino, et che anco detto sig.ʳ haveva hauto diece scudi per un mese, che non l'haveva servito Stefano, quando se ne andò in Baviera, et detti diece scudi erano denari appartinenti alle intrate delle Abbatie, che pervenivano alli cantori et non alla Camera Apostolica, et essendo chiamato il detto / sig.ʳ Stefano gli fu detto dal sig.ʳ M.º di Cappella il discorso, che si era fatto nel suo negotio; hora detto sig.ʳ Stefano cominciò a gridar tanto forte et intrò in tanta collora, che messe sotto sopra tutto il Collegio chiamandoli tutti Turchi, iniqui et ingiusti, et con tutto cio che il sig.ʳ mastro lo pregava, che stesse quieto e che dicesse le sue ragioni con altro modo; non era possibile quietarlo et in questo modo fu finita la Congregatione senza altra resolutione con grandissimo disturbo de tutti.   fol. 39r

Martedi Alli 22, Santa Cecilia. Questa mattina ad instantia del Ill.ᵐᵒ et Rev.ᵐᵒ Cardinal Sfondrato siamo andati a cantar la messa a detta chiesa de Santa Cecilia

---

[31] Am Rand: *Cardinal Sega parte 21.*

suo titulo; tutti presenti eccetto il sig.ʳ Decano, sig.ʳ Alesandro Merlo et il sig.ʳ Soto.
Detto Ill.ᵐᵒ sig.ʳ Cardinal ci dette da pranzo a casa sua e di poi pregò il Collegio, che
andasse a dir Vespero alla medesma chiesa, et per piu comodità ci mandò tutti in cochio,
et cantammo Vespero, al quale oltra le tre sopradetti mancò. In detto Vespero il sig.ʳ
Horatio Crescentio, il qual questa mattina di poi la messa me disse, che non se sentiva
troppo bene e che haveva anco un poco da fare a casa che se voleva andare. Il detto
Ill.ᵐᵒ Cardinal questo medesmo giorno mandò al nostro Collegio scudi quindici di
moneta.

Mercordi Alli 23, Il sig.ʳ Paulo Faccone mancò al matuttino b 5
Il sig.ʳ Diego Vasquez mancò a matuttino e prima b 6.
Questa mattina il Collegio ha resoluto, che delli 15 scudi che ha dato lo Ill.ᵐᵒ Cardinal Sfondrato per santa Cecilia il sig.ʳ Horatio Crescentio non debba participar se
non de diece scudi, che si sonno attribuitj alla messa, delli altri cinque scudi si sonno
atribuitj per il vespero della medesma giornata hanno resoluto, che non debba parti-
ciparne il detto sig.ʳ Horatio Crescentio, perche non se ci trovò presente.

Giovedi Alli 24. Il sig.ʳ Thomasso ha destribuito li sopradetti 15 scudi receuiti dal
Ill.ᵐᵒ Cardinal Sfondrato, b 68 per uno parte 21, et al detto sig.ʳ Horatio Crescentio,
b 46, et ha dato al custode de libri 28 baiochi.
Questa[32] medesma mattina il sig.ʳ Antonio sottomastro di casa del Papa è venuto in
Cappella, ha ditto al nostro Collegio, che il Papa metterà l'oratione delle 40 hore Dominica prossima, che sarrà la prima del Advento et che ha uno da asistere sempre doi
cantori con le cotte per ordine de Nostro Sig.ʳᵉ dalle 14 hore per insino a doi hore di
notte.

fol. 39v   Venardi Alli 25. Il sig.ʳ Paulo de Magistris s'è scusato per infermo.
Il sig.ʳ Gio. Santos ha ottenuto [licentia] per questa mattina per andar a san Sebastiano
per pigliar delle reliquie de santi.
Il sig.ʳ Diego Vasquez mancò al mattutino b 5
Il sig.ʳ Paulo Faccone ha mancato al matuttino b 5.
Il[33] Molto Rev.ᵈᵒ nostro Collegio questa mattina ha resoluto et ordinato, che il can-
tore, che mancarà nella sua oratione secondo la lista per le quarant hore, sarà puntato
in tutto quattro giulij, cioe per ogni quarto d'hora un giulio. Tutti furno presenti,
eccetto il sig.ʳ Paulo de Magistris, Gio. Santos et li quattro della giornata.
Il sig.ʳ Vincentio Musatti ha ottenuto licentia del hora de oratione, che gli toccarà martedi, che per esser molto a bon hora per sua indispositione non l'ha può fare.
Questa[34] medesma mattina il sig.ʳ Thomasso Benigno ha proposto un memoriale al
Rev.ᵈᵒ Collegio per dar al Papa per conto de far celebrar una messa ogni mese in
Cappella per li nostri Compagni et benefattori defunti; fu discorso sopra questo fatto
et fu resoluto dalla maggior parte, che potendo far da noi in Cappella si debba fare
questo bene e dir la messa de defunti in Cambio della messa corrente, ma che per
questo conto non si debba dar fastidio a Nostro Sig.ʳ, per che havemo bisogno de supplicar sua Santità per aiuto delli vinj.

---

[32] Am Rand: *comandamento delle 40 hore.*
[33] Am Rand: *Decreto per le 40 hore.*
[34] Am Rand: *Il memoriale proposto dal sig.ʳ Thomasso Benigno.*

Sabbato 26 novembre. Questa mattina non s'è ditto offitio ne cantato la messa, ma il sig.^r Vincentio de Gratis ha ditto una messa bassa, per che il sig.^r Mastro di Cappella voleva far Congregatione.

Di poi[35] la Messa il sig.^r Mastro congregò il Rev.^{do} Collegio de Cantori nella Cappella de Papa Sisto IIII et disse, che hieri lo Illmo et Rev.^{mo} sig.^r Cardinal Gallo Protettor delli Cantori de Cappella lo mandò a chiamar et glie disse da parte de Nostro Sig.^{re}, che mettesse in Cappella nel numero de Cantori M.^o Hercole Ferruzzi et che lo mettesse hoggi in ogni modo con quelli cantori, che si trovavano presenti et se non erano tutti, non importava, per che il detto Monsig.^r Illmo haveva hauto un memorial mandatoli da Nostro Sig.^r col rescritto, che dovesse mettere il detto M.^o Hercole in Cappella per la prima Domenica dello Advento, che sarrà domani; et havendo inteso il Collegio la proposta del sig.^r Mastro di Cappella et la comissione del'Illmo et Rev.^{mo} Cardinal Gallo nostro Protettor da parte de Nostro Sig.^{re}, con ogni debita reverentia ha obedito, et tutti hanno dato il suo voto vive vocis giudicando, che il detto M.^o Hercole[36], ha buona voce de Basso, canta bene et è sufficiente et meritevole de loco de Cappella, et in questa medesma hora il sig.^r Mastro di Cappella gli dette la cotta conforme alle nostre constitutioni. Tutti presenti eccetto il sig.^r Decano, il sig.^r Alesandro Merlo, il sig.^r Paulo de Magistris, il sig.^r Paulo Faccone, il sig.^r Stefano Ugerio, il sig.^r Horatio Crescentio et il sig.^r Joseph Bianco; li presenti a questa actione siamo stati dicidotto.

Domenica prima del Advento. A di 27. Monsig.^r Illmo Arcivescovo Silvio Savello ha cantato la Messa in Cappella de Sisto quarto in Palazzo alla presentia del Collegio dell Ill.^{mi} sig.^{r[i]} Cardinali in absentia de Nostro Sig.^{re}, un frate ha fatto il sermone et ha pronuntiato da parte del Papa X anni de indulgentia. Il detto Monsig.^r Illmo, che ha celebrato, per esser la prima messa, che ha cantata in Cappella, ha donato al nostro Collegio de Cantori otto scudi di moneta; tutti presenti eccetto il sig.^r Decano, il sig.^r Alesandro Merlo et il sig.^r Soto giubilati.

fol. 40r

Di poi la messa s'è fatta la processione dalla Cappella de Sisto alla Cappella Paulina, dove si è portato il santissimo Sacramento et si è cominciato l'horatione delle 40 hore.

Questa Mattina il sig.^r Paulo de Magistris, che stava male, è venuto alla Messa.

Lunedi A di 28 de novembre. Non si è ditto ne offitio ne messa, perche li Cantori asisteno all'horatione del santissimo sacramento sempre doi con la cotta per ordine cominciando dalli piu antichi.

Questa mattina il sig.^r Thomasso Benigno ha distribuito li otto scudi, che ha donato de Mancia l'Illmo Arcivescovo Savello in parte 25.

Questa matti[na] il sig.^r Gio. Luca Conforto ha mancato una mezz'hora per la sua hora delle 40 hore dell'oratione, però si punta in doi giulij secondo l'ordine dato, il sig.^r Gio. Luca Conforto b 20.

La sera medesma il sig.^r Gio. Luca Conforto mancò tutta la sua hora della horatione, che gli toccava a un hora de notte. Però il detto si ponta b 40.

Martedi Alli 29. Monsig.^r Sacrista ha detto la messa nella Cappella Paulina, dove stava il santissimo sacramento per fine delle horatione delle 40 hore, et noi habbiamo can-

---

[35] Am Rand: *Amissione del sig.^r Hercole Ferruzzo Ro.*
[36] Die Worte von *tutti hanno . . .* bis *Hercole* unterstrichen.

tato[37] il motetto O sacrum convivium alla elevatione del santissimo sacramento; tutti presenti eccetto il sig.ʳ Decano, il sig.ʳ Merlo e il sig.ʳ Soto giubilati.

Questa mattina il sig.ʳ Thomasso Benigno me ha dato un foglio delle spese fatte dal sig.ʳ Gio. Santos per la pensione de Spagna del Collegio, fatto per Comissione de nostro Collegio, quale spese inportano in tutta somma scudi dodeci e 3 giulij, delli quali il sig.ʳ Thomasso sopradetto ne ha pagati scudi cinque e 3 giulij, quali haveva rescossi dal sig.ʳ Paulo Faccone per altri tanti, che ne doveva dar al nostro Collegio.

Mercordi Sant'Andrea apostolo Alli 30. Il sig.ʳ Paulo Faccone mancò al matuttino b 5.

Li ponti del presente mese de novembre sonno doi scudi e 55 baiochi, in parte 20, tocca per uno baiochi dodeci, avanzano quindici quatrini al puntatore.

[DICEMBRE]

fol. 40v   Giovedi A di primo de dicembre. Il sig.ʳ Archangelo Crivello mancò al matuttino b 5
Il sig.ʳ Agostino Martini mancò al matuttino b 5.

Venardi Alli 2. Il sig.ʳ Paulo de Magistris si scusa per infermo.
Il sig.ʳ Paulo Faccone mancò al matuttino b 5
Il sig.ʳ Horatio Griffi mancò al matuttino b 5.
Questa[38] mattina il sig.ʳ Hercole Ferruzzo ha pagato il suo introito in mano del sig.ʳ Thomasso Benigno Camerlengo, et detto sig.ʳ Thomasso l'ha destribuito alli Compagni secondo il solito et ha dato anco il ducato al sig.ʳ Pietro Bartholmuccio Decano conforme alla constitutione et ha retenuto 39 b per uno all'interressati della pensione de Spagna et ha pagato sette scudi al sig.ʳ Gio. Santos per resto della spesa di detta pensione.

Sabbato A di 3. Non mancò nessuno.

Dominica II Adventus A di 4. Monsig.ʳ Rev.ᵐᵒ Vescovo d'Aversa ha cantato la messa in Cappella de Sisto quarto alla presentia de Nostro Sig.ʳᵉ et del Collegio dell'Ill.ᵐⁱ Cardinali, un frate de sant'Apostolo ha fatto il sermone et ha pronuntiato sette anni de indulgentia. Tutti presenti eccetto il sig.ʳ Decano et il sig.ʳ Fran.ᶜᵒ Sotto giubilati. Questa mattina il sig.ʳ Paulo de Magistris, che stava male, è guarito e venuto alla messa sopradetta.

Lunedi Alli 5 de dicembre. Monsig.ʳ Ill.ᵐᵒ Cardinal Aldobrandino ha mandato il sig.ʳ Felice Anerio[39] a pregar il Rev.ᵈᵒ Collegio de Cantori, che domattina vada a cantar la messa a san Nicolò in Carcere suo Titolo.
Il sig.ʳ Paulo de Magistris mancò al matuttino b 5
Il sig.ʳ Paulo Faccone mancò a Matuttino e prima b 6
Il sig.ʳ Stefano Ugerio mancò a Matuttino b 5
Il sig.ʳ Thomasso Benigno [mancò] b 5
Il sig.ʳ Josef Bianco [mancò] in tutto b 10.

---

[37] Cod.: *canto.*
[38] Am Rand: *il sig.ʳ Hercole ha pagato il suo introito.*
[39] Cod.: *Nerio.*

Questa[40] medesma mattina il sig.ᵣ Paulo de Magistris di poi la Messa congregò il Molto Rev.ᵈᵒ Collegio, al quale espose, qualmente lui haveva in questa medesma mattina finito li vinticinque anni del suo servitio in Cappella, del che ne rengrantia sommamente la Maestà de Dio benedetto et lo prega, che tutti li suoi sig.ʳⁱ et Compagni habbino questa medesma gratia de venir a questo termine; et però bona gratia de tutto il detto Rev.ᵈᵒ Collegio comincierà domattina a godere la giubilatione conforme al nostro privileggio et la bolla della santa Memoria de Papa Sisto Quinto. Gli fu resposto da detto Collegio, che tutti si rallegravano di questa sua bona gratia et pregarano Dio benedetto glie faccia anco gratia, che possa godere questo dono della giubilatione per molti anni con sanità et consolatione dell'anima e del corpo.

Martedi Alli 6. Al instantia dello Ill.ᵐᵒ Rev.ᵐᵒ Cardinal Aldobrandino tutto il Collegio è andato questa mattina a cantar la messa a san Nicolo in Carcere; tutti presenti eccetto il sig.ᵣ Decano, sig.ᵣ Alesandro Merlo et il sig.ᵣ Fran.ᶜᵒ Soto giubilati; et il sig.ᵣ Gio. Maria Nanino, al quale per esser hieri la sua giornata, non ha saputo niente, che si andava a san Nicolo, et se ben Ottavio custode de libri ha lassato la imbasciata in casa sua, non dimeno non gli è stata fatta, et per segno di cio il detto sig.ᵣ G. Maria questa mattina è andato a Palazzo per andar al officio secondo il solito, et questo io l'ho saputo dal sig.ᵣ Lelio de Bolis padrone del fondaco de san Marco in Panico, il qual fa fede, che lui è andato a Palazzo. Però a giuditio mio secondo la diligentia del detto sig.ᵣ Gio. Maria non si deve puntare anzi si deve mettere presente, se ci sarrà qualche donativo del sudetto Ill.ᵐᵒ Cardinal Aldobrandino.

fol. 41r

Mercordi Alli 7[41]. La santità de Nostro Sig.ᵣ prese il Giubileo et andò processionalmente[42] dalla Minerva, dove sua santità disse la messa bassa, andò alla chiesia de santa Maria dell'Anime, per la strada si cantorno le letanie da doi soprani et il choro respondeva il medesmo; tutti furno presenti eccetto il sig.ᵣ Decano, il sig.ᵣ Alesandro Merlo et il sig.ᵣ Soto giubilati.

Giovedi Alli 8, la Conceptione della Madonna Comune: ma questa mattina non si è fatto niente in Palazzo, per che il forziero delle cotte si è mandato a santa Maria delli Angeli a termini per la processione, che farrà la Santità di Nostro Sig.ʳᵉ domani.

Venardi Alli 9. La Santità de Nostro Sig.ᵣ ha fatta la processione da santa Maria delli Angeli alli termini per insigno a santa Maria Maggiore, il sig.ᵣ Gio. Santos et Diego Vasquez hanno cantato le litanie et il resto delli Rev.ᵈⁱ sig.ʳⁱ Cantori hanno reposto; tutti presenti eccetto il sig.ᵣ Decano et il sig.ᵣ Fran.ᶜᵒ Soto giubilati.

Sabbato Alli X. Non si fece niente in cappella, per che si attende alla confessione per pigliar questo santo Giubileo. Piaccia a sua divina Maestà exaudirci.
Hoggi il sig.ᵣ Thomasso Benigno ha destribuito la paga del presente mese et ha retenuto dodeci quatrini per uno per sei giulij, che lui dette del elemosina alla chiesa de san Gregorio il giorno, che dal nostro Collegio fu fatto l'esequie per li nostri Compagni defuncti, che fu alli 9 de novembre prossimo passato.

---

⁴⁰ Am Rand: *Giubilatione del sig.ᵣ Paulo de Magistris.*
⁴¹ Am Rand: *Giubileo.*
⁴² Cod.: *precissionalmente.*

fol. 41v   Domenica terza dell'Advento Alli XI. Monsig.^r Illmo Cardinal Montalpero[43] ha cantata la messa in cappella de Sisto quarto alla presentia di sua Santità et del Collegio
dell'Ill.^{mi} Cardinali, un frate de sant'Agostino ha fatto il sermone et pronuntiato 15
anni de indulgentia. Tutti presenti eccetto il sig.^r Decano et il sig.^r Fran.^{co} Soto giubilati.
Questa[44] mattina il sig.^r Thomasso Benigno Camerlengo ha destribuito scudi quindici de
moneta, quali ha hauti dal Illmo Cardinal Pietro Aldobrandino per la messa, che habbiamo cantata a san Nicolo in Carcere, ha dato b 68 per uno, parte 22.
Questa mattina di poi la messa il sig.^r Gio. Santos me ha dato il transunto del Motu-
proprio della pensione di Spagna, che è in testa del sig.^r Soto, et me ha dato la supplica signata dal Papa sotto il di 14 d'ottobre 1594, et me ha dato anco la cedola
vechia della medesma pensione.

Lunedi Alli XII. Il sig.^r Paulo Faccone mancò a matuttino prima e terza b 7
Il sig.^r Josef Bianco mancò a matuttino e prima b 6
Il sig.^r Thomasso Benigno mancò a matuttino prima e terza b 7.
Questa mattina il sig.^r mastro domandò Congregatione di poi la messa et propose al
Collegio, che erano molti de dettj, che si lamentavano, che il sig.^r Thomasso Benigno
Camerlengo havesse destribuito li 15 scudi dati dal Cardinal Aldobrandino e che ne
havesse dato la parte al sig.^r Gio. Maria Nanino non essendosi trovato alla Messe de
santo Nicola in Carcere, per il che si era dato li detti denari, et se ben il sig.^r Gio.
Maria haveva qualche ragione de participare secondo la relatione fatta da alcuni Compagni, nondimeno la maggior parte del Collegio non voleva, che il sig.^r Thomasso
l'havesse partiti senza farne una parola in congregatione essendo il Caso dubbioso,
sopra il qual fatto fu discorso assai et resoluto dal sig.^r Mastro, che quello, che non
voleva, che il sig.^r Gio. Maria participasse de detta messa andasse da detto sig.^r Thomasso, che glie darrebbe la sua parte, e tutto questo fu fatto acciò il Camerlengo non
debba destribuire de suo Capo senza farne consapevole il Collegio.
Et in questa sopradetta Congregatione furno tutti presenti eccetto li giubilati et
quelli della sua giornata.

Martedi Alli 13 santa Lucia. Questa mattina si fece una Consacratio d'un Vescovo in
cappella, et però non si è fatto altr'offitio.

Mercordi Quattro tempora Alli 14. Il sig.^r Horatio Crescentio mancò al matuttino b 5
Il sig.^r Paulo Faccone mancò a tutto l'offitio e messa b 10
Il Diego Vasquez mancò matuttino prima, terza e sesta b 8
Il sig.^r Gio. Luca Conforto mancò al matuttino b 5.
Questa mattina io Hipolito Gambocci. Puntatore ha distribuito li ponti del mese di no-
vembre prossimo passato.

fol. 42r   Giovedi Alli 15 non mancò nessuno.

Venardi a 16. Il sig.^r Diego Vasquez mancò a matuttino b 5
Il sig.^r Paulo Faccone mancò a matuttino e prima b 6

---

[43] Gregorius (Petrochini) de Montalbero, Generalprior des Eremitenordens des hl. Augustin, von
Sixtus V. am 20. Dezember 1589 zum Kardinal promoviert und am 23. III. 1590 zum Car-
dinalpresbyter erhoben.
[44] Am Rand: ▽ *15 hauti dal Cardinal Aldobrandino.*

Sabbato Alli 17. Questa mattina il sig.ʳ Luca Orfeo con licentia del Collegio è mancato all'offitio per andar al'ordinatione et ha pigliato l'Accolitato, tutti li altri presenti.

Domenica 4 del advento Alli 18. Monsig.ʳ Rev.ᵐᵒ San Giorgio Vescovo di Vegevena ha cantato la messa in Cappella de Sisto quarto alla presentia de Nostro Sig.ʳᵉ et de tutto il Collegio dell Ill.ᵐⁱ et Rev.ᵐⁱ Cardinali, un frate del Carmine ha fatto il sermone et ha pronu[n]tiato X anni de indulgentia; tutti presenti eccetto il sig.ʳ Decano et il sig.ʳ Fran.ᶜᵒ Soto giubilati. Il detto Rev.ᵐᵒ Monsig.ʳ per esser la sua prima messa cantata in Cappella ha donato al nostro Collegio otto scudi di moneta da partire in 25.

Lunedi A 19. Il sig.ʳ Paulo Faccone mancò a matuttino, prima, terza et messa, compar di poi la elevatione del corpus domini b 9.

Martedi A 20. Il sig.ʳ Paulo Faccone mancò a matuttino, prima, terza, sesta et messa b 10.

Mercordi A 21 San Thomasso Apostolo Comune; ma questa mattina, per che fu una Consacratione d'un Vescovo, non fu ditto altr'offitio in Cappella, et il sig.ʳ mastro disse hieri alli sig.ʳⁱ Cantori, che questi doi gior[ni] inanzi la vigilia della Santissima Natività si faccia vacantia dell'offitio et messa in Cappella per attendere alla preparatione, come si deve per questa Santissima Festività.

Giovedi a 22. Niente.

Venardi a 23. Niente.

Sabbato Alli 24, la Vigilia della Santissima Natività del Nostro Sig.ʳᵉ. La Santità di Nostro Sig.ʳ Clemente octavo cantò il Vespero nella Cappella Gregoriana in san Pietro alla presentia del Collegio del Ill.ᵐⁱ sig.ʳ[ⁱ] Cardinalj; tutti presenti eccetto il sig.ʳ Pietro Bartholomuccio decano; di poi [il] vespero Monsig.ʳ Mastro di Casa ci dette la solita colatione.
Il sig.ʳ Thomasso Benigno hoggi ha portata et distribuita la paga del mese de Gennaro prossimo d'avenire 1595; et ha destribuito li otto scudi, che ha riceuti dal Rev.ᵐᵒ Monsig.ʳ San Giorgio Vescovo di Vegevena et ha retenuta 4 giulij per la sopraviventia del sig.ʳ Fran.ᶜᵒ Soto per mandarla in Spagna per conto della nostra pensione, et ha retenuto anco sette giulij spesi dal custode de libri per portar il nostro Forziero con le cotte a santa Maria dell'anime et a Santa Maria Maggiore per il Giubileo.
La sera de Natale La santità de Nostro Sig.ʳ Clemente ottavo cantò il matuttino et cominicò a 4 hore di notte alla presentia de 10 Cardinali, cantò la messa l'Ill.ᵐᵒ et Rev.ᵐᵒ Cardinal Gaetano Camerlengo in Cappella de Sisto IIII; tutti presenti eccetto li sig.ʳⁱ Decano, Alesandro Merlo, Soto et Paulo de Magistris; il sig.ʳ Horatio Griffi et Gio. Luca Conforto andorno questa notte a san Giovanni de Fiorentino con licentia del Collegio et mastro di Cappella ad instantia del Ill.ᵐᵒ sig.ʳ Cardinal Aldobrandino.

fol. 42v

Natale Domenica alli 25, la Natività del Sig.ʳᵉ: il Papa cantò la messa nella Cappella Gregoriana in san Pietro alla presentia del Collegio delli Ill.ᵐⁱ Cardinali, il Cardinal Gesualdo pronuntiò in fine della detta messa indulgentia plenaria da parte di nostro Sig.ʳᵉ; tutti presenti eccetto il sig.ʳ Decano, Alesandro Merlo et il Soto.

Lunedi A 26 San Stefano. Lo Illmo et Rev.^{mo} Cardinal Castruccio cantò la Messa in Cappella de Sisto IIII in Palazzo alla presentia della santità di Nostro Sig.^{re} et del Collegio delli Ill.^{mi} sig.^{ri} Cardinali, un giovine del Collegio del'Inglesi fece il sermone et pronuntiò 30 anni de indulgentia; tutti presenti eccetto il sig.^r Decano et sig.^r Soto.
Il sig.^r Paulo Faccone venne al primo Kyrie eleyson e si ponta b 20.

Martedi A 27 san Giovanni. L'Illmo et Rev.^{mo} Cardinal Antonio Maria Gallo cantò la Messa alla presentia della Santità di Nostro sig.^{re} et del Collegio del Ill.^{mi} sig.^{ri} Cardinali in Palazzo. Uno Spagnolo fece il sermone et pronuntiò 30 anni de indulgentia; tutti presenti eccetto il sig.^r Decano et il sig.^r Fran.^{co} Soto jubilati.

Mercordi A di 28. La festa delli Innocenti, Comune. Non si da giorno di vacantia a nessuno per in sino al giorno della Epiphania, e non si dice matuttino.
Questa mattina mancorno l'infrascritti
Il sig.^r Paulo Faccone venne a l'Agnus dei b 7
Il sig.^r Horatio Crescentio b 7$^1/_2$
Il sig.^r Gio. Santos b 7$^1/_2$
Il sig.^r Horatio Griffi b 7$^1/_2$ } questi 4 non son comparsi.
Il sig.^r Pietro Montoya b 7$^1/_2$.
Questa mattina il sig.^r Paulo Faccone ha domandato licentia al Collegio per lui e per il sig.^r Antonio Manni per domani per andar a cantar al Collegio dell'Inglesi et l'ha ottenuta; tutti presenti eccetto li 4 sopradetti, il sig.^r Mastro et li giubilati.

fol. 43r   Giovedi Alli 29. Il sig.^r Horatio Crescentio non è comparso b 7$^1/_2$.
Tutti li altri sig.^{ri} Compagni presenti eccetto li sig.^{ri} giubilati et il sig.^r Paulo Faccone et il sig.^r Antonio Manni, che con licentia del Collegio sonno andati a cantar alla Chiesia delli Inglesi, et nella licentia, che gli fu data alli sopradetti, il sig.^r Vincentio Musatti non fu presente, per che, quando la domandorno, gia era partito di Cappella.

Venardi Alli 30 fu fatto l'esequie de Papa Inocentio VIIII felice memoria. Cantò la Messa l'Illmo et Rev.^{mo} Cardinal Sega alias de Piasenza in absentia della Santità di Nostro Sig.^{re} alla presentia de tutto il Collegio del Ill.^{mi} et Rev.^{mi} sig.^{ri} Cardinali in Cappella de Sisto IIII in Palazzo, et fu la prima messa, che sua signoria Illma ha cantata in Cappella, et ha donato di Mancia al nostro Collegio dieci scudi d'oro in oro: Parte 25.
Tutti presenti eccetto il sig.^r Pietro Bartholmuccio decano, il sig.^r Alessandro Merlo et il sig.^r Fran.^{co} Sotto, che sonno giubilati,
Il sig.^r Horatio Malvicio è venuto alli Kyrie eleison, perde doi giulij b 20.

Sabbato A di Ultimo de dicembre 1594 la Vigilia della Circoncisione del Nostro sig.^r Jesu Christo. In Cappella de Sisto quarto in Palazzo l'Illmo et Rev.^{mo} Cardinal Sfondrato ha intonato et finito il Vespero in absentia della santità di Nostro Sig.^{re} alla presentia del Collegio dell Ill.^{mi} et Rev.^{mi} Cardinali; tutti li Rev.^{di} sig.^{ri} Cantori presenti eccetto il sig.^r Pietro Decano et il sig.^r Alesandro Merlo giubilati.
Li ponti del presente mese de dicembre sonno uno scudo e baiochi novanta uno e mezzo, in vinti parte tocca nove baiochi per uno e tre quatrini.

Finis
　　Laus Deo et Beate Marie Virginj.
Io Hippolito Gamboccj Puntator et Secretario del sopradetto anno 1594 ho scritto ut supra manu propria.

Ohne Eintragungen.　　　　　　　　　　　　　　　　　　　　　　　　　　fol. 43v

In nomine Domini Nostri Jesu Christi Amen. Anno a Nativitate eiusdem　　fol. 44r
　　Domini MD. LXXXXV.

[GENNAIO 1595]

Domenica A di primo de Gennaro 1595. L'Ill.mo et Rev.mo Cardinal Sfondrato ha cantato la Messa in Cappella de Sisto IIII in Pallazzo in absentia della santità di Nostro Signore, alla presentia del Collegio dell Ill.mi sig.ri Cardinali. Tutti presenti eccetto il sig.r Decano et il sig.r Fran.co Soto giubilati; il sig.r Pompeo Ugonio ha fatto il sermone e pronuntiato 30 anni de indulgentia da parte de Nostro Sig.re. Per nostre regaglie il Papa ci da quattro scudi d'oro in oro per mancia, cioe doi per Natale e doi per la festa de hoggi.

Questa mattina il sig.r Thomasso Benigno Camerlengo ha destribuito li X scudi d'oro in oro, che ha riceuti dal Ill.mo Cardinal Sega per la messa, che cantò alli 30 de dicembre prossimo passato, et ha retenuto giulij 26 per darne tredici alli ministri della pannattaria et tredici alli ministri della Cantina in nome del nostro Collegio per mancia, e del resto ne ha dato trent'otto baiochi per uno: in parte 25.

Di poi la messa il sig.r Christiano Ameyden mastro di Cappella ha intimato il Collegio delli Rev.di sig.ri Cantori per domattina alle laude de san Pietro per far la nova electione delli nostri offitiali secondo il solito. Questa medesma Mattina tutto il nostro Collegio è andato disopra alle stantie del Papa per Cantarli il motetto secondo il solito per darli il buon principio del anno; et di poi, che siamo stati un pezzo aspettar, che ci fusse comandato de Cantare: Nostro Sig.r ce mandò a dir, che andassemo a Pranzo, che era tardo, et senza cantar il motetto ognuno andò a casa sua; tutti furno presenti eccetto il sig.r Decano, il sig.r Alesandro Merlo et il sig.r Fran.co Soto jubilati.

BIBLIOGRAPHIE DER AUFSÄTZE ZUR MUSIK IN AUSSERMUSIKALISCHEN ITALIENISCHEN ZEITSCHRIFTEN VIII

von *Klaus Fischer* (Rom)

LA BIBLIOFILIA
Firenze
Anno I, 1899-1900 — LXXI, 1969

1. [Rezension:] VANBIANCHI, Carlo: Raccolta e raccoglitori di autografi in Italia. Milano, Hoepli, 1901. — Rez. G. de Lunis. — II (1900-1901), 282-286. [U. a. Hinweise auf Autographe Mayrs, Paers, Portas.]

2. JADART, H.: Les dessins de Jacques Cellier artiste rémois du XVIᵉ siècle. — III (1901-1902), 117-133. [Manuskripte von Zeichnungen: a) Paris, Bibl. Nationale, manuscrits français, n° 9152, fol. 75 (Orgeln), b) Ms. der Bibl. Reims, dem.-rel.mar.vert. du Levant, fol. 29-36, Régles de musique et figures, fol. 33: Handzeichnung des Orgelprospekts der großen Orgel der Reimser Kathedrale mit Anfangstakten einer Orgeltabulatur, fol. 64: Zeichnungen verschiedener Musikinstrumente, 1 fotogr. Wiedergabe von fol. 33 des Reimser Ms.]

3. OLSCHKI, Leo S[amuele]: Una visita alla Collezione del Comm. C. Lozzi di autografi e documenti riguardante la Musica e il Teatro in tutte le loro appartenenze e ogni sorta di pubblico spettacolo. — III (1901-1902), 231-259. [U. a. Fotos von autographen Notizen, Briefen und Kompositionen Horatio Vecchis, Giulio Caccinis, Monteverdis, Cimarosas, Gaffurios, Chopins Arcangelo Corellis, Giovanni Guidettis, Gomberts.]

4. LOZZI, C[arlo]: Di alcune scoperte riguardanti la storia del liuto e i liutai con la mostra de' relativi autografi e documenti. — VI (1904-1905), 13-19.

5. [Rezension:] LOZZI, Carlo: Cecco d'Ascoli e la musa popolare. Ascoli Piceno. 1904. — Rez. [Olschk]i. — VI (1904-1905), 241-243.
   [Das Buch enthält außer Beschreibungen des Volksgesangs eine Titelsammlung von ca. 400 Liedern der Marche.]

6. [Rezension:] LEVI, Eugenia: Lirica italiana antica: novissima scelta di rime dei secoli XIII, XIV, XV: illustrate con sessanta riproduzioni di pitture, miniature, sculture, incisioni e melodie del tempo e con note dichiarative. Firenze, 1905. — Rez. [Olschk]i. — VI (1904-1905), 340-349.

[Behandlung zahlreicher Laudenvertonungen, u. a. Serafino Razzi, Laudi spirituali, 1563. 343: vierst. Laude »Laudata sempre sia la vergine Maria«, 346: photogr. Wiedergabe einer Laude in Mensuralnotation.]

7. Lozzi, C[arlo]: Edizione del 1538 sconosciuta o non bene descritta, d'una festa e commedia »degl'Intronati« senesi. — VII (1905-1906), 33-36.

8. Spadolini, Ernesto: L'arte della stampa in Ancona dal 1574 al 1660. — VII (1905-1906), 78-90.
   [89: Melodrammi von Prospero Bonarelli, 1647.]

9. Celani, Enrico: Dediche, postille, dichiarazioni di proprietà ecc. nei libri a stampa della R. Biblioteca Angelica di Roma. — VII (1905-1906), 138-150 [140 Giov. Batt. Doni, 147 Horatio Griffi, päpstl. Kapellsänger Ende des 16. Jh.]; VII, 258-263 [258 Athanasius Kircher, 259 Stefano Landi]; VIII (1906-1907), 96-105 [103 Fortunato Santini]. Die Fortsetzungen VII, 91-104, 366-372; VIII, 154-164, enthalten keine Namen von Komponisten, Musikern oder Musiktheoretikern.

10. Lozzi, C[arlo]: Le Feste dei Comuni italiani e in ispecie del Santo patrono di Ascoli e del tremuòto. — VII (1905-1906), 225-248, 321-343. [Mit zahlreichen Abb.]

11. Vajna De Pava, E[ugenio]: Di un Codice della Collez. del Comm. Leo S. Olschki contenente la Sfera del Dati e altre opere italiane dei secoli XIV e XV e di un codice Laurenziano contenente la Sfera di Andalò di Negro. — VIII (1906-1907), 16-21. [18 eine Laude, 19 ein weihnachtl. Hirtenstück, Anf. des 16. Jh.] VIII, 70-85. [71 über eine geistl. Laude.] Die Fortsetzungen VII (1905-1906), 343-355, u. VIII, 164-168, enthalten über Musik nichts.

12. Olschki, Leonardo: Lorenzo Da Ponte libraio e bibliofilo. — VIII (1906-1907), 41-49.

13. Olschki, Leo S[amuele]: Contribution à la bibliographie de la Musique vocale italienne du genre profane des XVIe et XVIIe siècles. — VIII (1906-1907), 241-253. [Fotogr. Wiedergabe von 3 Titelblättern. 2 Notenbeisp.]

14. Bonaventura, Arnaldo: Di un Codice Musicale del Secolo XVII. — VIII (1906-1907), 321-335. [Privatbesitz Leo S. Olschkis. 26 Kompositionen, u. a. von Alessandro Scarlatti, Domenico Zazzera, Giuseppe Celani, Giuseppe De Sanctis, Giovan Carlo Amaltei. 8 Notenbeisp., 1 Foto des Einbandes.]

15. Riemann, Hugo: Breviarium Benedictinum Completum IX.-X. Saeculi. — VIII (1906-1907), 441-446. [2 Fotos.]

16. Olschki, Leo S[amuele]: Découverte du manuscrit autographe de la dixième sonate de L. van Beethoven. — IX (1907-1908), 1-4. [Über die Sonate (G-dur) für Klavier und Violine, op. 96. Mit zwei Faksimiles in

Originalgröße: erste Seite des ersten Satzes, erste Seite des zweiten Satzes. 1 Notenbeisp.]

17. Lozzi, C[arlo]: Saggio di Cimeli marchegiani. — IX (1907-1908), 90-103. Die Folge IX, 34—54, enthält nichts über Musik. [101-103 u. a. über Ottaviano Petrucci, Gioacchino Rossini, Pasquale Bini (Schüler Tartinis), die Sängerin Maria-Felicità Malibran. Mit zwei Abb., darunter ein Foto Rossinis nebst Widmung.]

18. Olschki, Leo S[amuele]: Contribution à la bibliographie de la Musique vocale italienne du genre profane des XVIe et XVIIe siècles. — IX (1907-1908), 153-173. [Mit fotogr. Wiedergaben mehrerer Titelblätter.]

19. Bonaventura, Arnaldo: Un Breviarium del Secolo XIII. — IX (1907-1908), 251-262. [Ein Faksimile, 12 Fotografien von Text und Neumen.]

20. Bonaventura, Arnaldo: Antiche Suites orchestrali francesi. — IX (1907-1908), 289-294. [Handschriftensammlung aus der Landesbibliothek Kassel, mehrere Notenbeisp.]

21. B[onaventura], A[rnaldo]: Ancora del Codice Scarlattiano. — IX (1907-1908), 327-329. [Ergänzung zum Aufsatz in Bibl. VIII, 321-335. 2 Notenbeisp.]

22. Bonaventura, Arnaldo: Una importante collezione di Lieder. — IX (1907-1908), 361-378. [Über »Das deutsche Lied geistlich und weltlich bis zum 18. Jahrhundert«, herausgegeben von Martin Breslauer, Berlin, 1908. Zahlreiche Notenbeisp. Unmittelbar vor 361 Faks. der ersten Seite einer Partitur-Abschrift von Beethovens Streichtrio op. 3 mit autographen Eintragungen aus dem Antiquariat Paul Gottschalk in Berlin. Seit 1950 in Privatbesitz Frankfurt/M. Vgl. Kinsky-Halm S. 10.]

23. Sabelli, F.: L'anima intima di Beethoven. — IX (1907-1908), 392-395. [Übernahme eines Art. aus der »Tribuna« vom 15. 1. 1908.]

24. Bonaventura, Arnaldo: Un esemplare eccezionale dei Flores Musicae. — X (1908-1909), 6-16. [Über Hugo von Reutlingens »Flores Musicae omnis cantus gregoriani«. Mit 7 fotogr. Wiedergaben.]

25. Lozzi, Carlo: Giovanni Guidetti e le sue opere musicali. — X (1908-1909), 87-97. [8 Fotografien von Noten u. Dokumenten.]

26. Vatielli, Francesco: Una mostra bibliografica del Liceo Musicale di Bologna. — X (1908-1909), 187-202. [Mit 15 fot. Wiedergaben von Musikalien, Porträts u. Titelblättern.]

27. [Rezension:] Levi, Eugenia: Lirica italiana nel Cinquecento e nel Seicento fino all'Arcadia. Firenze, Leo S. Olschki, 1909. — Rez. Arnaldo Bonaventura. — X (1908-1909), 474-479. [Das Buch beschreibt zahlreiche Musikdrucke des 16. u. beginnenden 17. Jahrhunderts. In die Rez. sind mehrere Notenbeispiele eingestreut.]

28. MITJANA, Rafael: Una visita bibliográfica á la Sección de Música del la Real Biblioteca Universitaria de Uppsala. — XI (1909-1910), 1-23. [Mit 4 fotogr. Wiedergaben.]

29. BONAVENTURA, Arnaldo: Nuovi ricordi di Niccolò Paganini. — XI (1909-1910), 127-132. [Abb. einer Violine, vermutlich Instrument Paganinis.]

30. BONAVENTURA, Arnaldo: L'Associazione dei Musicologi Italiani e la bibliografia musicale. — XI (1909-1910), 285-293. [Mit 2 fotogr. Wiedergaben aus Traktaten Fr. Gaffurios.]

31. ZAMBRA, Luigi: Manoscritti editi e inediti di Pietro Metastasio nella biblioteca del Museo Nazionale di Budapest. — XI (1909-1910), 402-410.

32. BONAVENTURA, Arnaldo: Gli autografi musicali di N. Paganani. — XII (1910-1911), 1-31 [1: Bildnis u. Fotografien von Autographen; 13—31: Werkverzeichnis.]

33. ZAMBRA, Luigi: I manoscritti italiani nella Biblioteca Széchényi del Museo Nazionale Ungherese di Budapest. — XII (1910-1911), 94-102. [100 u. 101: Metastasio, 101: Oct. ital. 12 (Ms. mit Text und Musik einiger Kanzonen), die hdschr. Kopie eines Duetts aus Verdis »Attila« und des Librettos von Donizettis »Lucia di Lammermoor«.]

34. C[ELANI] E[nrico]: Alcuni rari Cataloghi di Biblioteche vendute. — XII (1910-1911), 241-247. [Kataloge aus dem 16. u. 17. Jh., u. a. Collectio in unum corpus ... Pars tertia, Frankfurt/M. 1592, die auch Musikdrucke enthält.]

35. ROCCO, Lorenzo u. Emanuele: Anonimi e pseudonimi italiani. Supplemento al Melzi ed al Passano di Emanuele Rocco (Opera postuma). — XII (1910-1911), 249-261. [259 u. a. eine Ode an Rossini von Filippo Martinelli.] In der Forts. XII, 419-429 ist über Musik nichts enthalten.

36. OLSCHKI, Leo S[amuele]: Quelques Manuscrits fort précieux. — XII (1910-1911), 274-280. [Mit 8 Fotos, darunter Choralnotation zweier verschiedener Antiphonarien aus dem 15. Jh., ital. Herkunft, eines weiteren Antiphonariums mit dem Porträt des Miniaturmalers und eines dritten, das wahrscheinlich gegen 1425 in Verona entstand.]
Die Forts. XII (1910-1911), 341-349, XIII (1911-1912), 13-19, 134-137, 216-222, 412-421, 462-468, XVI (1914-1915), 48-50, 113, 276-277, XVII (1915-1916), 453-462, XXIV (1922-1923), 306-307, 336-337, 374-375 u. XXV (1923-1924), 15, 163 enthalten über Musik nichts.

37. PICOZZI, G[iovanni] B[attista]: Cristoforo Preda il celebre miniatore della Corte ducale sforzesca era milanese e sordomuto. (Aus »Unione«, Milano). — XII (1910-1911), 313-318. [2 fot. Wiedergaben von Choralhandschriften.]

38. DI COCCO, Giovanni: I Corali miniati di Monteoliveto Maggiore conser-

vati nella Cattedrale di Chiusi. — XII (1910-1911), 365-389. [10 Fotos von Choralhandschriften.]

39. BONAVENTURA, Arnaldo: Le esumazioni della musica antica. — XII (1910-1911), 445-459. [6 fotogr. Wiedergaben, davon 4 von Choralhandschriften u. -drucken in Hufnagelnotation.]

40. BONAVENTURA, Arnaldo: Una grande pubblicazione di Bibliografia musicale. — XIII (1911-1912), 117-123. [Über F. Pedrells Cat. de la Bibl. mus. de la Diputació de Barcelona, 2 Bde., Barcelona, 1908-09. 4 Abb. aus span. Musiktraktaten.]

41. TENNERONI, Annibale: Il Libro di una Fraternità di San Sebastiano. Regola, Preci e Laudi. — XIII (1911-1912), 165-171. [Kodex aus dem 15. u. 16. Jh., wahrscheinlich aus den Marken. Enthält c. 32^b-45^b 21 Lauden. 1 Abb.]

42. BONAVENTURA, Arnaldo: Cimeli bibliografici e Strumenti musicali all'Esposizione del R. Istituto Musicale di Firenze. — XIV (1912-1913), 46-60. [Mit 7 Abb. von Musikinstr.]

43. D'ANCONA, Paolo: Di alcune opere inedite di Nicolò di Giacomo da Bologna. — XIV (1912-1913), 281-284. [Miniaturenmaler des 14. Jh., 4 faks. Tafeln aus der Samml. Olschki, auf denen Choralnotation sichtbar ist.]

44. BONAVENTURA, Arnaldo: Di un Codice Musicale Mediceo. — XV (1913-1914), 165-173. [Libreria Olschki, Pergament-Kodex Anf. des 16. Jh., 2 Faks.-Tafeln: Zwischen 164 u. 165 »Virgo gloriosa« von Adrian Willaert. Chorbuchnotation, Alt-, Tenor-, Tenor-, Baßschlüssel. Zwischen 168 u. 169 »Nimphes des bois deesses des fontaines« (auf den Tod Ockeghems) von Josquin Desprez. Im Tenor: Requiem aeternam. Chorbuchnotation.]

45. RONDEL, Auguste: La Bibliographie dramatique et les Collections de Théâtre en France. — XV (1913-1914), 257-262, 345-354, 374-382.

46. ZAMBRA, L[uigi]: La barzelletta »Lassa far a mi« in un codice della Biblioteca Comunale di Budapest. — XV (1913-1914), 410-413. [Kodex Zichy, carta 376. Diese Barzelletta auch von Josquin vertont.]

47. D'ANCONA, Paolo: Don Simone Camaldolese miniatore fiorentino della fine del secolo XIV. — XVI (1914-1915), 1-4. [2 Faks. von Choralhandschriften.]

48. ZAMBRA, L[uigi]: Il codice Zichy della Biblioteca Comunale di Budapest. Contributo allo studio della lirica italiana del quattrocento. — XVI (1914-1915), 5-16.

49. HEVESY, André de: Le Psautier des Dominicains de Santa Maria di Castello à Gênes. — XVI (1914-1915), 41-47. [Samml. Olschki, Ms. Choralnotation in roter Schrift. 6 Fotos, 6 Faks.-Tafeln.]

50. MAZZI, C[urzio]: Una sconosciuta compilazione di un libro quattrocentistico di balli. — XVI (1914-1915), 185-209. [Biblioteca Comunale di Siena, Cod. L. V. 29. Mit fotogr. Wiedergabe einer Textseite.]

51. Mazzi, C[urzio]: Il »libro dell'arte del danzare« di Antonio Cornazano. — XVII (1915-1916), 1-30. [Mit 11 fotogr. Wiedergaben und Text des Traktats.]

52. Zambra, L[uigi]: Il codice Zichy della Biblioteca Comunale di Budapest. Tavola e indici. — XVII (1915-1916), 184-213, 278-288. [Enthält u. a. die Texte zahlreicher canzoni, sonetti, barzellette und strambotti.]

53. Manacorda, Giuseppe: Libri scolastici del Medioevo e del Rinascimento. — XVII (1915-1916), 397-421. [406 Martianus Capella: De nuptiis Philologiae et Mercurii. Kodex des 15. Jh. Rom, Bibl. Ap. Vat. Codice Urbinate latino 329 (già 532).]

54. Soriga, Renato: Prime ricerche bibliografiche sulla Massoneria italiana nella età napoleonica. — XVIII (1916-1917), 99-106. [37. Stanze da cantarsi nella pompa funebre del F∴ Cartier 1°∴ Sovr. della R∴ L∴ Reale Gioseffina. — (S. L. et anno) Raccolta Bertarelli.

42. Tavole per la musica da eseguirsi nel g∴ 24 del 7 m∴ 5807 pe' trav∴ delle R R∴ LL∴ Real Gioseffina e Real Eugenio dell O∴ di Milano. — (S.d. et loco) Ambrosiana S.S.H. 12.

45. Versi da cantarsi nella R∴ L∴ Reale Augusta all'Or∴ di Milano celebrandosi il giorno onomastico, le nozze ed il parto della Regia Intitolatrice nel g∴ 23 dell' 8∴ m∴ dell'anno della V∴ L∴ 5807. — Milano, Stamperia del G∴ O∴ 1808. Ambrosiana. S. S. H. IX.

46. Versi da cantarsi nel trav∴ mass∴ del g∴ 20 del m∴ 4 an∴ 5811 consacrato della R∴ L∴ R∴ Gioseffina alla nascita del Re di Roma proclamato luweton dal Pot^mo∴ G∴ O∴ d'Italia. — (Milano, 1811) Brera. 14.16.D.14.4.]

55. Faloci-Pulignani, D. M[ichele]: L'arte tipografica a Foligno nel XVII secolo. — XVIII (1916-1917), 106-133.
[72. Cirocchi, Lodovico: Prologo recitato in musica con gli argomenti a ciaschedun atto della commedia intitolata »La fede costante«, rappresentata dagli Accademici Ardenti di Foligno, l'anno 1639.
128. Unti, Ovidio: Il tradimento per l'honore. Capriccio tragico in musica recitato in Foligno l'anno 1655.
134. Unti, Ovidio: I trionfi dell'ira. Scherzo tragico in musica recitato in Foligno l'anno 1656.]

56. Clerici, Graziano Paolo: Una copiosa raccolta manoscritta di musica e poesia del Cinquecento. — XVIII (1916-1917), 305-328.
[Die Sammlung wurde 1589 von Graf Jo. Alessandro Tarasconi, Parma, erworben. Sie enthält 211 Madrigale bedeutender Meister aus der 2. Hälfte des 16. Jh., Privatbesitz. Verz. der Kompositionen. 3 fot. Wiedergaben von Madrigalen Cipriano de Rores.]

57. Faloci-Pulignani, M[ichele]: L'arte tipografica a Foligno nei sec. XVII

e XVIII. – XIX (1917-1918), 51-67. [52 Unti, Ovidio: La S. Messalina Vergine e Martire. Dramma musicale. Foligno, Antonio Mariotti, 1677. 55 Lazzarini, S.: S. Giovanni Battista, oratorio a quattro voci da cantarsi in S. Giacomo di Foligno. Foligno, Ant. Mariotti, 1690. 56 Montemellini, N.: Decio in Foligno, melodramma, Ant. Mariotti, 1697. 57 Boccolini, G. B.: Il martirio di S. Messalina Vergine Promartire di Foligno. Musica del sig. D. Pietro Benedetti. Antonio Mariotti, 1708. 64 Lazzarini, S.: S. Luigi Re di Francia. Oratorio a 5 voci da cantarsi in S. Feliciano. Foligno, Gaetano Zenobi, 1692. 64 Lazzarini, S.: S. Filippo Neri. Oratorio a sei voci da cantarsi in S. Feliciano. Gaetano Zenobi, 1692. 65 Lazzarini, S.: S. Filippo Neri. Oratorio cantato per la Festa di S. Feliciano. Gaetano Zenobi, 1693. 65 La vita humana mascherata da musica rappr. in Fuligno l'anno MDCLXXXXIV. Foligno, Carlo Zenobi, 1694. 67 La Giuditta. Oratorio. Foligno, Fratelli Antonelli, 1713.]

58. TESTI, Laudedeo: I Corali miniati della chiesa di S. Giovanni Evangelista in Parma. – XX (1918-1919), 1-30. [16 fotogr. Wiedergaben im Text.] Die Forts. XX, 132-152 enthält Dokumente über die Fam. Da Moile. Da Moile als Miniaturenmaler an der Ausgestaltung zahlreicher Choralhandschriften beteiligt.

59. RONDEL, Auguste: Origines et Développement du Théâtre en Europe du XV\ au XVII\ siècle d'après les textes imprimés. – XX (1918-1919), 161-174.

60. MONTI, Gennaro Maria: L'incunabolo Casanatense 818. – XX (1918-1919), 267–268. [Buch mit Laudentexten aus dem 15. Jh. Roma, Bibl. Casanatense.]

61. VITALETTI, Guido: Un inventario di codici del secolo XIII e le vicende della Biblioteca, dell'archivio e del tesoro di Fonte Avellana. – XX (1918-1919), 297-315. [302 Hieronymus: Liber legum de musica, lib. 1.] XXI (1919-1920), 117-156. [134 über Musik Lib. VI, Ep. 23 Dilectissimo fratri Guilelmo.] Die Forts. XX (1918-1919), 249-264, XXI (1919-1920), 42-76, 117-156, 291-338, XXII (1920-1921), 30-41 enthalten über Musik nichts.

62. LAMBERTINI, Michelangelo: Les Bibliothèques musicales portugaises. Essai de classement d'une Bibliothèque générale de la Musique. – XXI (1919-1920), 11-26.

63. MONTI, Gennaro Maria: Bibliografia della Laude. – XXI (1919-1920), 241-257, XXII (1920-1921), 288-299, XXIII (1921–1922), 260-267, XXIV (1922-1923), 29-40, XXV (1923-1924), 71-75, 256-265, XXVII (1925-1926), 38-46.

64. ROMERO, Francesco Garcia: Algunas correcciones y adiciones à la Bibliografia Ibérica del siglo XV del Dr. K. Haebler. – XXII (1920-1921),

138-149. [U. a. 142—143 Missale der Benediktiner von Valladolid, gedr. v. Johannes Luschner, Montserrat, 1499.]

65. VITALETTI, Guido: Le stampe popolari della Miscellanea Malfatti nella Riccardiana di Firenze. — XXII (1920-1921), 299-315. [306-315 Abdruck mehrerer Frottoletexte.]

66. FRATI, Carlo: Bibliografia degli scritti di Léon Dorez (1890-1921). — XXIV (1922-1923), 88-95. [U. a. 89 über Antonio Blado, Musikdrucker des 16. Jh., 89, 90 über Jean de Baif.]

67. FERRARI, Vincenzo: La Miniatura dei Corali della Ghiara e di altre Chiese di Reggio Emilia. — XXV (1923-1924), 57-70. [Mit Fotos vorwiegend aus Choralhandschriften des 15. Jh.]

68. LUSTIG, Renzo: Saggio di Catalogo della Collezione di Melodrammi della R. Biblioteca Marucelliana in Firenze. — XXV (1923-1924), 239-247, 305-312, XXVI (1924-1925), 67-74. [Nur Libretti.]

69. La Direzione: Elenco delle pubblicazioni del dott. Lodovico Frati (1883-1923). — XXV (1923-1924), 360-374. [Auch Aufs. über verschiedene Gebiete der Musik mit Schwerpunkt Musikgesch. Bolognas.]

70. VITALETTI, Guido: Intorno alla Canzonetta »A caso un giorno mi guidò la sorte« e ad altri documenti di letteratura popolare. — XXVI (1924-1925), 179-188. [U. a. Sonette, Villanellen, Stanzen, Madrigale des 16. Jh.; Anmerkungen dazu von Lodovico Frati XXVI, 357—359, der auch auf Canzoni napoletane und Madrigaldrucke (Musikaliendrucke) hinweist.]

71. [Rezension:] BALCKE, Curt: Bibliographie zur Geschichte der Preußischen Staatsbibliothek, Leipzig 1925. — Rez. Max Husung. — XXVII (1925-1926), 171-172. [U. a. über die Musik- u. Lautabteilung, auch die Riv. mus. italiana als Quelle zur Geschichte dieser Institution herangezogen.]

72. DREI, Giovanni: I Viotti stampatori e librai Parmigiani nei secoli XVI-XVII. — XXVII (1925-1926), 218-243. [Mit 2 genealogischen Tafeln, Seth u. Erasmo Viotto auch als Musikdrucker hervorgetreten.]

73. TIRABASSI, A[ntonio]: La parabole des Vierges sages et des Vierges folles d'après un Office noté du XIe siècle. — XXVII (1925-1926), 257-262.

74. WAGNER, P[eter]: Fragments liturgiques neumés du XIIe siècle. — XXVIII (1926-1927), 1-13. [Mit 2 fotogr. Wiedergaben von Fragm. aus einer Samml. Privatbes. Olschki: 9 Messe de S. Martin, 12 Sequenz »Christo inclita candida«.]

75. MARTINI, Mario Augusto: La vita di S. Giovanni Gualberto in una antica lauda inedita. — XXVIII (1926-1927), 161-185 [Firenze, Biblioteca Nazionale Centrale, Sign. II, IV, 67. Mit dem Text der Laude.]

76. RONDEL, Auguste: Les livres et gravures relatifs aux Fêtes de Cour et aux Cérémonies publiques. — XXVIII (1926-1927), 321-331. [Auch Hinweise

auf die frz. Oper.] XXVIII (1926-1927), 433-453. [Deutschland, England, Spanien und Italien.] XXIX (1927), 20—26. [Übrige Länder.]

77. PASERO, Carlo: Un prezioso Missale Bresciano. — XXVIII (1926-1927), 331-333. [Missale Carmelitarum. Brescia, Bonini, 1490. Mailand, Biblioteca di Brera, A.K.XIII.22.]

78. CASTELBARCO ALBANI DELLA SOMAGLIA, M[aria]: La Biblioteca Angelica e il suo Fondatore. — XXVIII (1926-1927), 382-393. [Mit Bildnis Angelo Roccas. 391 Antiphonarium S. Gregorii mit Choralnotation, 9.-14. Jh.]

79. MARIANI, Valerio: Miniature del Rinascimento ad Aquila. — XXIX (1927), 81-92. [Auch Choralhandschriften einbezogen. Fotogr. Wiedergaben.]

80. TIRABASSI, A[ntonio]: Introduction à l'étude de la Parabole des Vierges Sages et des Vierges Folles d'après un Office noté du XIme siècle (mss. 1139 fond latin de la Bibliothèque Nationale de Paris). — XXIX (1927), 108-117. [3 Fotografien.]

81. SALMI, Mario: Jacopo di Casentino Miniatore. — XXX (1928), 369-382. [Mehrere fotogr. Abb. von Miniaturen aus Choralhandschriften.]

82. [Rezension:] COHEN, Gustave: Le Théâtre au moyen âge. I. Le Théâtre religieux. (Bibliothèque générale illustrée, VI). Paris, Edition Rieder, 1928. — Rez. L. P. — XXXI (1929), 318-320. [U. a. über Liturgische Dramen.]

83. [Rezension:] MILAR, Eric G.: La Miniature anglaise du XVe siècle. Paris et Bruxelles, G. van Oest, 1928. — Rez. L. P. — XXXI (1929), 377—382.

84. GUALANDI, Enea: Carlo Frati (1863—1930). — XXXII (1930), 89-112. [Mit Bibliographie seiner Schriften, unter denen sich auch solche über mus. Themen befinden.]

85. [Rezension:] ZAMBRINI, F[rancesco]: Le Opere volgari a stampa dei secoli XIII e XIV. Supplemento con gli indici generali dei capoversi dei manoscritti, dei nomi e soggetti a cura di S. Morpurgo. Bologna, Nicola Zanichelli, 1930. — Rez. Emilio Lovarini. — XXXII (1930), 169—171. [U. a. auch über Lauden.]

86. BERNARD, C.: Expositions du Livre en Belgique, à l'occasion du Centenaire de l'Indépendance. I. Les manuscrits. — XXXIII (1931), 89-106. [100 Band von 1617 aus dem Convent des Croisiers in Lüttich mit Orgelkomp. von Gabrieli, Philips, Bruhns u. Sweelinck, Universitätsbibl. Lüttich; Musikalbum, dat. 1511, mit lat., franz. und flämischen Chansons, signiert von Louis Bloc; Brügge, Bibl. de la ville.] — II. Les Livres imprimés. — XXXIII (1931), 383-406. [393-394 Wichtige Musikmanuskripte und -drucke vorwiegend des 16. Jh. Mus. Sektion der Ausstellung von Antwerpen; 397 Konservatorium Lüttich, Manuskripte, Part. oder Autographe u. a. von A. Scarlatti, W. Fr. Bach, Ph. Em. Bach, Gretry, Gossec, Beethoven, César Franck.].

87. SALMI, Mario: Intorno al miniatore Neri da Rimini. — XXXIII (1931),

265-286. [15 Fotos von Miniaturen aus Choralhandschriften des frühen 14. Jh.]

88. [Rezension:] ALCARI, Cesare: Parma nella musica. Parma, M. Fresching, 1931. — Rez. A. Boselli. — XXXIII (1931), 470—471.

89. RUGGIERI, Jole: Manoscritti italiani nella Biblioteca dell'Escuriale. — XXXIV (1932), 127-139. [134-137 Texte von Canzoni musicali. (ms.a. IV.24.)] Die Fortsetzungen XXXII (1930), 421-441, XXXIII (1931), 138-149, 201-209, 308-318, XXXIV (1932), 52-61, 245—255, 381-392 enthalten über Musik nichts. — XXXV (1933), 20-28. [20-21 Texte von Laude della Vergine (ms.d.IV.32, ff. 122ᵛ-125ʳ.)]

90. Spectator: L'esposizione d'arte francese a Londra. — XXXIV (1932), 173-179. [175 Brevier des hl. Stephan aus Chalons-sur Marne von mus. Interesse.]

91. PAGNIN, Beniamino: Della miniatura padovana dalle origini al principio del secolo XIV. — XXXV (1933), 1-20. [14 Padova, Bibl. Capitolare B. 16, Choralhandschrift.]

92. [Rezension:] Les Trésors des Bibliothèques de France. Tome III, 1930. — Rez. A[médée] B[oinet]. — XXXV (1933), 110-113. [Enthält einen Aufs. von M. Robert Caillet über Porträts berühmter Musiker von Bonaventure Laurens in der Bibl. Inguimbertine zu Carpentras.]

93. SIMHART, Max: Stampe popolari italiane del sec. XVI nella Biblioteca Bavarese di Stato. — XXXV (1933), 129—149. [Texte von Canzoni, So-netti, Stanze, Villanelle, Frottole, Canzoni napoletane enthaltend. Mit 14 Abb.]

94. [Rezension:] GRAHAM, Bessie: The Bookman's Manual. A guide to Litera-ture. Third edition. New York, R. R. Bowker. — Rez. Vittorio Camerani. — XXXV (1933), 252-253. [Auch Kapitel über Musik enthaltend.]

95. SALVONI-SAVORINI, Grazia: Di alcuni codici miniati della Biblioteca Ca-sanatense. — XXXVI (1934), 61—78. [Cod. 1394 »Messale Certosino«, Ende des 14. Jh.]

96. PERROTT, Emilia: Un Messale umbro del Quattrocento. — XXXVI (1934), 173-184. [Bibl. Olschki. 181 ff. 1 Faks. u. Hinweise auf die Choralhand-schrift M, San Pietro de' Cassinesi, Perugia, 1472.]

97. BRESCIANO, Giovanni: Neapolitana II. Nuovi contributi alla storia della tipografia napoletana nel secolo XVI. — XXXVI (1934), 184-193. [192 Romano, Francesco Antonio: Nuove Laudi spirituali, prima parte, 1594. Nicht bei Vogel.] — Nichts über Musik enthalten die Fortsetzungen XXVIII (1926-1927), 14-31, 126-141, 280-290, XXXI (1929), 284-295, XXXIII (1931), 49-57, 210-225, XXXIV (1932), 70-76, 179-188, XXXV (1933), 69-78, 233-244, XXXVI (1934), 387-397, XXXVII (1935), 225-233, XXXVIII (1936), 194-201.

98. WITTGENS, Fernanda: Cristoforo De Predis. — XXXVI (1934), 341-370. [Miniaturenmaler, dem die Mitarbeit an der Choralhandschrift der Kapelle Ercoles I. zugeschrieben wird, die in der Biblioteca Estense zu Modena unter der Sign. cod. lat. P.I.6 aufbewahrt wird. Zahlr. fotogr. Wiedergaben.]

99. [Rezension:] The Pierpont Morgan Library. Exhibition of illuminated Manuscripts held at the New York Public Library. New York [1934.] — Rez. L[eonardo] O[lschki]. — XXXVII (1935), 34—36. [Auch Choralhandschriften des 15. Jh.]

100. O[LSCHKI], L[eonardo]: Il retaggio del mondo antico. Bibliografia dell'Istituto Warburg di Londra. — XXXVII (1935), 102-105. [Auch Musik enthaltend.]

101. [Rezension]: Les Tresors des Bibliothèques de France. Tome IV (fasc. XIII-XVI), 1933. — Rez. A[médée] B[oinet]. — XXXVII (1935), 106-111. [Enthält eine genaue Beschreibung des Kodex Montpellier H 196 von M. Dean Malo-Renault.]

102. CORBARA, Antonio: Due Antifonari miniati dal riminese Neri. — XXXVII (1935), 317—331. [2 Antiphonarien mit Choralnotation. Antiphonarium I u. III Archivio Capitolare del Duomo di Faenza. II Bibl. Olschki, von Salmi in Bibl. XXXIII (1931) beschrieben. 9 Faks.]

103. PASERO, Carlo: Giacomo Franco, editore, incisore e calcografo nei secoli XVI e XVII. — XXXVII (1935), 332-356. [3 Tanzsammlungen: 1) Caroso da Sermoneta, Fabrizio: Il Ballarino ... Venezia, Francesco Ziletti, 1581. 2) Nobiltà di Dame del S. Fabritio Caroso da Sermoneta, Venezia, Muschio, 1600. 3) Raccolta di varii Balli. Roma, Guglielmo Faciotti, 1630.]

104. [Rezension:] DE BOOM, Ghislaine: Marguerite d'Autriche-Savoie et la Pré-Renaissance. Paris, E. Droz, u. Brüssel, Falk fils, 1935. — Rez. Amédée Boinet. — XXXVIII (1936), 206—209. — [Brüssel, Bibliothèque Royale de Belgique, Sign. n° 10572 ein Buch mit Balladen; Sign. n°. 228 ein Album mit franz., lat. u. flämischen Chansons.]

105. [Rezension:] CAPORALI: Storia della musica e critica musicale. (1921-1935) Roma, 1935. — Rez. Vittorio Camerani. — XXXVIII (1936), 213-214.

106. EINSTEIN, Alfred: Una ignota stampa musicale torinese. — XXXVIII (1936), 229-233. [Il secondo libro de Madrigali a cinque voci von Gio. Pietro Cottone, gedr. bei Gio. Domenico Tarini, Torino, 1581. 231 Foto des Titelblatts der Altstimme.]

107. [Rezension:] Les Trésors des Bibliothèques de France. Tome V. Paris, Editions d'Art et d'Histoire, 1935. — Rez. Amédée Boinet. — XXXVIII (1936), 279-282. [U. a. Chansonnier de Jean de Montchenu (zwischen 1460 u. 1477) mit Werken von Ockeghem, Busnoys, Hayne van Ghizeghem, Dufay u. a.]

108. BOINET, A[médée]: Expositions du Livre à Bruxelles, à l'occasion de l'Exposition Universelle et Internationale. — XXXVIII (1936), 347-382. [361-363 über Bücher u. Mss. die Musik betreffend.]

109. LUIN, E[lisabet] J[eannette]: Repertorio dei Libri musicali di S.A.S. Francesco II d'Este nell'Archivio di Stato di Modena. — XXXVIII (1936), 418-445.

110. [Rezension:] GHISI, Federico: Canti Carnascialeschi nelle fonti musicali del XV e XVI secolo, Firenze, Leo S. Olschki, 1937. — Rez. [Olschk]i. — XXXVIII (1936), 463-465. [1 Faks.]

111. BOINET, A[médée]: Le Livre et les arts graphiques à l'exposition internationale de Paris. — XXXIX (1937), 404-430. [422 ff. über Mss. liturgischer Dramen und Mysterienspiele, 430 über Codices, die Musik des 15. Jh. enthalten.] — Die Forts. XL (1938), 113-131 enthält über Musik nichts.

112. OLSCHKI, Leo S[amuele]: Une nouvelle collection de musique du XVIIᵉ siècle contenant plusieurs ouvrages uniques et inconnus de bibliographes. — XL (1938), 1-16. [Samml. Olschki, 4 Fotos von Titelblättern u. Noten.]

113. EINSTEIN, Alfred: Un libro di canzoni spirituali di Orfeo Vecchi. — XL (1938), 38-46. [O. Vecchi: La Donna vestita di sole ... in 21. Madrigali ... Milano, S. Tini & Gio. Franc. Besozzi, 1602. Samml. Olschki, Firenze. 3 Fotos.]

114. [Rezension:] MAGRIEL, Paul David: A bibliography of dancing; a list of books and articles on the dance and related subjects. New York, H. W. Wilson Comp. 1936. — -A i-. — XL (1938), 225.

115. JANSEN, Franz: Il Messale Salisburghense del 1605. — XL (1938), 455-459. [Missale Salisburgense juxta ritum et consuetudinem S. Romanae ecclesiae restitutum. Conrad Kürner, 1605. Mit 2 Fotos.]

116. [Rezension:] WEISSENBÄCK, Andreas: Sacra Musica. Lexikon der Katholischen Kirchenmusik. Klosterneuburg bei Wien, 1937. — Rez. A[lfred] E[instein]. — XL (1938), 468-469.

117. BECHERINI, Bianca: Giovanni Francesco Anerio ed alcune sue Gagliarde per cembalo. — XLI (1939), 159-164. [Mit 2 fotogr. Wiedergaben.]

118. KRISTELLER, Paul Oskar: Un documento sconosciuto sulla Giostra di Giuliano de' Medici. — XLI (1939), 405-417.

119. SANTORO, Caterina: La collezione degli autografi della Biblioteca Trivulziana. — XLII (1940), 1-41. [19 Rossini, 31 Metastasio, 36 Apostolo Zeno.]

120. MORAZZANI, G[iuseppe]: La Mostra Paganiniana a Genova. — XLII (1940), 195-202. [3 Abb.]

121. [Rezension:] Ellinwood, Leonard: The Work of Francesco Landini. The Mediaeval Academy of America, Cambridge/Massachusetts, 1939. — Rez. F[ederico] Ghisi. — XLII (1940), 208—209.

122. [Rezension:] VERNARELLI, Gerardo: Nicolò Paganini nei disegni di un impressionista contemporaneo. Roma, 1940. — Rez. Re[nato] Mariani. — XLII (1940), 380—381.

123. BOFFITO, G[iuseppe]: Bibliografia delle bibliografie. Bilancio annuale (1940-XVIII). — XLIII (1941), 30-49. [U. a. 33 Paganini, 35 Girolamo Cavazzoni.]

124. [Rezension:] MOLINARO, Simone Genovese: Intavolatura di liuto. Libro primo. Trascritto in notazione moderna ed interpretato da Giuseppe Gullino con presentazione di Piero Jahier. Firenze, Edizioni Musicali, 1940. — Rez. Amol. — XLIII (1941), 49-50. [Mit Foto des Titelblatts.]

125. BECHERINI, Bianca: Due canzoni di Dufay del Codice Fiorentino 2794. — XLIII (1941), 124-135. [Firenze, Bibl. Riccardiana Cod. 2794. Mit Transkriptionen.]

126. [Rezension:] KEPLER, Johannes: Gesammelte Werke. Bd. VI, Harmonia Mundi, herausgegeben von Max Caspar. München, C. H. Beck'sche Verlagsbuchhandlung, 1940. — Rez. G[iuseppe] B[offito]. — XLIV (1942), 60-61.

127. BONAVENTURA, Arnaldo: Il Poliziano e la musica. — XLIV (1942), 114-131. [3 Faks. u. 2 Notenbeisp.]

128. PIATTOLI, Renato: Frammenti di antichi messali. — XLIV (1942), 185-194. [Missale aus der 2. Hälfte des 12.Jh. mit Choralnotation. Aus Benevent. 2 Faks.]

129. BECHERINI, Bianca: Il »Cortegiano« e la musica. — XLV (1943), 84-96. [Baldassare da Castiglione, »Il Cortegiano«, 1528.]

130. SCARDIN, Giampiero: Il codice Laudario Marciano IX it. 182. — XLV (1943), 109-137. [Venezia, Biblioteca nazionale Marciana.]

131. PINTO, O[LGA]: Enciclopedie vecchie e curiose. — XLVI (1944), 53-66. [59 J. La Combe de Prezels »Dictionnaire portatif des beaux-arts« (Paris, 1752) und seine it. Übers. »Dizionario portatile delle belle arti« (Venedig, 1758) schließen auch Musik ein; 60: weitere bekannte Enzyklopädien und Dictionnaires über Musik und Tanz.]

132. SARTORI, Claudio: Le 7 edizioni delle Toccate di Girolamo Frescobaldi (1614-1637). — L (1948), 198-214. [Mit 7 Fotos der Titelblätter.]

133. BECHERINI, Bianca: Mostre italiane. Cimeli musicali alla »Mostra d'arte Fiamminga e Olandese« in Firenze. — L (1948), 219-235. [Mit 4 Notenbeisp. u. Tavole folgender Codices: Cod. Banco Rari 229 (Magl. XIX, 59), Firenze, Biblioteca Nazionale Centrale, u. Cod. Laurenziano Ashb. 1085, Firenze, Bibl. Mediceo-Laurenziana, nebst Tavole einiger Attaignant-Drucke.]

134. [Rezension:] Katalog der Musikbibliothek Paul Hirsch. Herausgegeben von

Kathi Meyer und Paul Hirsch. Bd. IV. Cambridge, University Press, 1947. — Rez. E[dward] Lowinsky. — L (1948), 261-262.

135. Poli, Liliana: Contributi sopra Bartolomeo de' Libri. — LI (1949), 9-27. [Drucker aus Florenz Ende des 16. Jh. U. a. mehrere Drucke von weltl. u. geistl. Lauden verzeichnet.]

136. Becherini, Bianca: Poesia e Musica nel codice Laurenziano Ash. 1085. — LI (1949), 166-184. [Firenze, Biblioteca Laurenziana. Frz. Chansons des 16. Jh. Mit 2 fotogr. Wiedergaben.]

137. Ferrara, Mario: Il codice Venturi Ginori di rime antiche. (Descrizione, notizie, indici dei capoversi e dei nomi). — LII (1950), 41-102. [Kodex des 15. Jh. Sonette, Ballate, Canzoni. Bei Nr. 460 Hinweis auf gesangl. Ausführung.]

138. [Rezension:] Van Moé, Émile: La lettre ornée dans les Mss. du VIIIe au XIIe siècle. Paris, Edition du Chêne, 1949. — Rez. Paolo Collura. — LII (1950), 277-278. [Auch Psalterien u. Gradualien einbezogen.]

139. [Rezension:] British Museum, Catalogue of additions to the Manuscripts, 1921-1925. London, 1950. — Rez. Anna Saitta Revignas. — LIII (1951), 164-166.

140. [Rezension:] Davidsson, Åke: Catalogue critique et descriptif des Imprimés de Musique des XVIe et XVIIe siècles conservés dans les Bibliothèques suèdoises. Upsala, 1952. — Rez. C[laudio] S[artori]. — LV (1953), 165.

141. [Rezension:] Annales Musicologiques. Moyen-âge et renaissance. Tome I. Société de Musique d'autrefois, Paris, 1953. — Rez. αoi. — LVI (1954), 52-53.

142. [Rezension:] Albrecht, Otto E.: A census of autograph music of European Composers in American Libraries. Philadelphia, University of Pennsylvania Press, 1953. — Rez. αoi. — LVI (1954), 53—54.

143. Donati, Lamberto: Passio Domini nostri Jesu Christi. Frammento tipografico della Biblioteca Parsoniana. — LVI (1954), 181-215. [Typograph. Bedeutung dieses Drucks und Textkonkordanzen nebst Aufführungsform der Passion im Vordergrund stehend, auch Hinweise auf dt. Kirchengesangbücher. 25 Abb.]

144. Sartori, Claudio: Una dinastia di editori musicali. Documenti inediti sui Gardano e i loro congiunti Stefano Bindoni e Alessandro Raverii. — LVIII (1956), 176-208. [Genealogischer Stammbaum Gardanos, Bindonis und Raveriis. 7 fotogr. Wiedergaben.]

145. Donati, Lamberto: Le fonti iconografiche di alcuni manoscritti urbinati della Biblioteca Vaticana. Osservazioni intorno ai cosiddetti »Tarocchi del Mantegna«. — LX (1958), 48-129. [Mit Abb. von Musikinstrumenten 82, 98, 99, 100, 103, 107, 108, 109.]

146. D'Ancona, Mirella Levi: Zanobi Strozzi reconsidered. — LXI (1959), 1-38. [Miniaturenmaler des 15. Jh. Mehrere fotogr. Wiedergaben von Miniaturen aus Choralhandschriften.]

147. [Rezension:] Krohn, C. Ernst: The history of music. An index to the literature available in a selected group of musicological publications. St. Louis, Baton Music Co., 1958. — Rez. Vittorio Camerani. — LXII (1960), 179-180.

148. [Rezension:] Donà, Mariangela: La Stampa Musicale a Milano fino all'anno 1700. Firenze, Leo S. Olschki, 1961. — Rez. Claudio Gallico. — LXIII (1961), 91-92.

149. Lodi, Teresa: Il »Catalogus Scriptorum Florentinorum« di Giambattista Doni. — LXIII (1961), 125-156. [Mit einem Bildnis des bekannten Musiktheoretikers und 3 Fotogr. des hds. Kat.]

150. Parronchi, Alessandro: La prima rappresentazione della Mandragola. Il modello per l'apparato. — L'allegoria. — LXIV (1962), 37-86. [Komödie von Machiavelli, 81 über die Mitwirkung von Musikinstr. Zahlreiche Abb.]

151. [Rezension:] Sartori, C[laudio]: La Cappella della Basilica di S. Francesco. Catalogo del fondo musicale nella Biblioteca Comunale di Assisi. Milano, Istituto Editoriale Italiano, 1962. — Rez. Aoi. — LXIV (1962), 197-198.

152. [Rezension:] Davidsson, Åke: Bibliographie der musiktheoretischen Drucke des 16. Jahrhunderts, Baden-Baden, Heitz, 1962. — Rez. Giuseppe Massera. — LXIV (1962), 324.

153. [Rezension:] Meyer-Baer, Kathi: Liturgical Music Incunabula. London, The Bibliographical Society, 1962. — Rez. Giuseppe Massera. — LXV (1963), 87-88.

154. Bianchi, Dante: Un trattato inedito di Domenico da Piacenza. — LXV (1963), 109-149. [Bibl. Nat. de Paris (Ms. italien 972). De arte saltandi et choreas ducendi. De la arte di ballare et danzare MCCCCXVI. Zahlreiche Notenbeisp. u. Abdruck des Traktats.]

155. [Rezension:] Vaccaro, Sofia: Emerenziana. Catalogo delle edizioni di Antonio Blado asolano ed eredi (1516-1593) ... Fasc. IV. Roma, Istituto Poligrafico dello Stato, 1961. (Ministero della Pubblica Istruzione. »Indici e cataloghi«, XIV). — Rez. Francesco Barberi. — LXV (1963), 200-203. [Aus seiner röm. Offizin gingen zahlreiche Musikdrucke hervor.]

156. Ridolfi, Roberto: Del Machiavelli, di un codice di Lucrezio e d'altro ancora. — LXV (1963), 249-259. [2 Fotos. 258 über den Gebrauch von Musik in Machiavellis »Mandragola«.]

157. De Gregori, Giorgio: Vittorio Camerani, bibliotecario e bibliografo. — LXV (1963), 263-297. [Mit Bibliographie, die auch Rez. u. Bemerkungen über Musikbibliographien umfaßt.]

158. BECHERINI, Bianca: I Manoscritti e le stampe rare della Biblioteca del Conservatorio »L. Cherubini« di Firenze. Nuova catalogazione e reintegrazione. — LXVI (1964), 255-299. [Mit 3 Abb.]

159. BARBERI, Francesco: I Dorico, tipografi a Roma nel Cinquecento. — LXVII (1965), 221—261. [Auch als Musikdrucker hervorgetreten. Zahlreiche fotogr. Wiedergaben von Titelblättern. Im Anhang ein Kontrakt vom 10. 2. 1543 über einen Messendruck von Christobal Morales.]

160. CAULA, Giacomo Alessandro: Una rarità bibliografica del Cinquecento francese. Il »Solitaire second ou prose de la musique« di Pontus de Tyard. — LXVII (1965), 297-302. [1 Bildnis Tyards, der zu der frz. Dichtergruppe der Pléiade gehörte.]

161. SANTORO, Caterina: Tipografi milanesi del secolo XVII. — LXVII (1965), 303—349. [308, 313, 316, 337, 344, 345, 347, 349 Hinweise auf Musikdrucke. Zahlreiche fotogr. Wiedergaben von Titelblättern.]

162. GARRISON, E. B.: Notes on Certain Italian Mediaeval Manuscripts. — LXVIII (1966), 1—30. [Auch Choralhandschriften einbezogen, u. a. ein Graduale von 1256 aus Parma. 4 Fotos, auf einem Choralnot. sichtbar.]
Die Forts. LXIX (1967), 1-67 mit 11 fotogr. Wiedergaben.

163. BOTASSO, Enzo: I paleotipi alla ricerca del frontespizio. — LXX (1968), 217-281. [237-240 Erwähnung von Gaffurios »Theoricum opus musicae disciplinae«, gedr. bei Francesco di Dino, Napoli.]

164. OLSCHKI, Cesare: Ricordo di Benvenuto Disertori. (1887-1969). — LXXI (1969), 281—287. [Zu ital. Drucken des 16. u. 17. Jh.]

165. [Rezension:] MORANTI, Luigi: L'arte tipografica in Urbino (1493—1800) con appendice di documenti e annali. Firenze, Leo S. Olschki, 1967, »Biblioteca di Bibliografia Italiana XIX«. — Rez. Luigi Balsamo. — LXXI (1969), 289-290. [Sorgfältige Nachforschungen auch über das Material der Kapelle von Urbino.]

RIVISTA ITALIANA DEL DRAMMA

Roma

Anno I, 1937 — V, 1941

166. [Rezension:] INGUANEZ, D. Mauro: Un dramma della Passione del secolo XII. Badia di Montecassino, 1936. (Miscellanea Cassinese, n. 12). — Rez. G[iuseppe] De Luca. — I,1 (1937), 103-105.

167. RONGA, Luigi: Idee sulle origini del Melodramma. — I,1 (1937), 144-157.

168. BRUNELLI, Bruno: Un commediografo dimenticato: S.A. Sografi. — I,1 (1937), 171-188. [Enth. häufige Hinweise auf Komponisten seiner Libretti nebst dazugehörigen Aufführungsdaten ihrer Werke.]

169. [Rezension:] Matsudaira, N.: Les fêtes saisonnières au Japon (province de Mikawa). Étude descriptive e sociologique. Paris, Librairie orientale et américane G. P. Maisonneuve, 1936. — Rez. Paolo Toschi. — I,1 (1937), 234—236. [In Verbindung mit den Festbeschreibungen Bemerkungen über Musik und Tanz.]

170. Toschi, Paolo: Narrazione e Dramma nel nostro antico teatro religioso. — I,2 (1937), 158—180. [Über Dramma liturgico u. Dramma sacro in volgare in Italien.]

171. Mariani, Lucilla: »La Natività di Christo« di autore incerto. — I,2 (1937), 354-364. [Neapolitanisches Geistl. Drama des 16. Jh. Fotogr. Wiedergabe des Titelblatts.]

172. [Rezension:] Mistero della Natività, Passione e Resurrezione di Nostro Signore (tratto da laudi dei secoli XIII e XIV). Edizioni »Roma«, Collezione »Repertorio«, 1937. — Rez. Aldo Vannucci. — I,2 (1937), 368-369.

173. [Rezension:] Curiel, Carlo L.: Il Teatro S. Pietro di Trieste. Milano, 1937. — Rez. Aldo Vannucci. — I,2 (1937), 369-371. [Im Anhang Übersicht über veranstaltete Bälle, das Orchester und Repertoire verschiedener Schauspieltruppen.]

174. Liuzzi, Fernando: Un »cantare« del secolo XV sulla Passione. — II,1 (1938), 3—22. [Paris, Bibliothèque dell'Arsénal, cod. 8521, f. 182-194ᵛ.]

175. Toschi, Paolo: Ugo Foscolo critico drammatico. — II,1 (1938), 178-196. [191 ff. über Foscolos Essay »Dell'impresa di un teatro per musica«.]

176. De Luca, Giuseppe: Il »veleno wagneriano«. — II,1 (1938), 379-384.

177. Salzer, Elisabetta Carlotta: Teatro italiano in Vienna Barocca. — II,2 (1938), 47-70. [Über den Kaiserl. Hofpoeten und Librettisten Niccolò Minato.]

178. [Rezension:] De Angelis, Alberto: Scenografi di ieri e di oggi. Roma, Cremonese, 1938. — Rez. Virgilio Marchi. — II,2 (1938), 235-240. [Behandelt auch den Einfluß des Wagnerschen Gesamtkunstwerks auf die moderne Inszenierung.]

179. [Rezension:] Nicholl, Allardyce: Stuart Masques and the Renaissance Stage. London, Harrap & Co., 1937. — Rez. Mario Praz. — II,2 (1938), 241-245.

180. Toschi, Paolo: L'origine romana del dramma liturgico. — II,2 (1938), 257-268.

181. Salzer, Elisabetta Carlotta: Commediografi italiani a Vienna. — II,2 (1938), 269-296. [Enthält u. a. kurze Beschreibungen des Handlungsablaufs mehrerer Opern Antonio Draghis und Ausführungen über Niccolò Minato.]

182. Mariani, Valerio: Nota di Regìa Giottesca. — II,2 (1938), 324-331. [Giottos Bild »Istituzione del Presepe di Greccio«, Assisi, Chiesa superiore di

San Francesco, als Dokument zur Aufführung des Liturgischen Dramas gedeutet. 1 Foto dieses Gemäldes.]

183. [Rezension:] Crocioni, Giovanni: L'Alidoro o dei primordi del melodramma. Bologna, L. Parma, 1938. — Rez. Luigi Ronga. — II,2 (1938), 355-358.

184. Bona, Emma: La prima della »nave« in quattro lettere inedite di Gabriele d'Annunzio. — III,1 (1939), 55-64. [Ein Brief D'Annunzios an den Baron Rodolfo Kanzler v. 21. 11. 1906 kündigt die bevorstehende Zusammenkunft mit Ildebrando Pizzetti in Parma an. Ein anderer Brief an denselben Empf. v. 29. 12. 1906 gibt die Zufriedenheit mit der Musik Pizzettis wieder.]

185. Salzer, Elisabetta Carlotta: Il Teatro allegorico italiano a Vienna. — III,1 (1939), 65—84. [Die Allegorie in den Serenate, Sacre Rappresentazioni und Balletti der 2. Hälfte des 17. Jh. 79 ff. das allegorische Motiv in den Opernlibretti Niccolò Minatos.]

186. [Rezension:] De Silvestri, Ludovico: Civico teatro Fraschini di Pavia, 1938. — Rez. Achille Fiocco. — III,1 (1939), 109-111. [Ca. 550 Opern und Opernaufführungen, vorwiegend aus d. 19. Jh., erwähnt.]

187. Scontenti, Pietro: Riflessioni sull'interpretazione. — III,1 (1939), 129-142. [Auch die mus. Interpretation berücksichtigt.]

188. Salzer, Elisabetta Carlotta: Epoca aurea del teatro italiano a Vienna. — III,1 (1939), 161-187. [U. a. ausführl. Beschreibungen der Auff. des Balletts »La Contesa dell'Aria e dell'Acqua« mit der Musik von Marc'Antonio Bertoli (1667) u. der Oper »Il Pomo d'oro« von Marc'Antonio Cesti (1668), 4 Abb.]

189. [Rezension:] Škerlj, Stanko: Italijanske prestave v Ljubljani od XVII do XIX stoletja. Ljubljana, Natismila Uciteljska Tiskana, 1936. — Rez. Enrico Damiani. — III,1 (1939), 221-225. [Zahlreiche Hinweise auf Aufführungen von Opern der berühmtesten ital. Komponisten des 18. u. 19. Jh.]

190. Bizzarri, Edoardo: Il teatro italiano in Cile (1803-1850). — III,1 (1939), 248-256. [251-255 über ital. Opern, Sänger und Musiker. 255—256 Bibliographie der Auff. ital. Opern in Chile von 1844-1850.]

191. Franceschini, Ezio: Un »ludus scenicus de Nativitate Christi« del secolo XII. — III,1 (1939), 292-317. [Geistliches Drama, ursprünglich Abtei Benediktbeuern, jetzt Bayer. Staatsbibl. München, Clm. 4660, ff. 99-106.]

192. Quarti, G. A.: Francesco Maria Piave Poeta melodrammatico. — III,1 (1939), 318-336. [337-340 Tabellarische Übersicht seiner Libretti.]

193. A[rtoni], G.: Le Raccolte teatrali della Società italiana degli autori ed editori. I. La Biblioteca »Roberto Forges Davanzati«. — III,1 (1939), 341-358.

194. Costa, Orazio: La regia teatrale. — III,2 (1939), 12-27. [18 »Didone abbandonata« von Metastasio als Bsp. angeführt, 19 über Vaudeville und Drama im allgemeinen.]

195. A[RTONI], G.: Le Raccolte teatrali della Società italiana degli autori ed editori. II. La Collezione »Luigi Rasi«. — III,2 (1939), 95-108.

196. [Rezension:] D'Amico, Silvio: Storia del teatro drammatico (vol. I). Milano, Rizzoli, 1939. — Rez. Valerio Mariani. — III,2 (1939), 111-117. [U. a. auch über die Lauda, das Liturgische Drama, Metastasio.]

197. SALZER, Elisabetta Carlotta: Le grandi rappresentazioni del teatro italiano a Vienna Barocca. — III,2 (1939), 155-190. [U. a. Inhaltsangaben von Opernlibretti und Daten zu Opernaufführungen aus der Zeit Ferdinands III. (1637—57) u. Leopolds I. (1658-1705).]

198. [Rezension:] GUELETTE, Thomas Simon: Notes et souvenirs sur le théâtre italien au XVIIIe siècle. Paris, Droz, 1938. — Rez. Enrico Fulchignoni. — III,2 (1939), 200-201.

199. CONTINI, Ermanno: Casanova uomo di teatro. — III,2 (1939), 230-249. [U. a. Erwähnung von Libretti u. einer Kantate.]

200. [Rezension:] APOLLONIO, Mario: Storia del teatro italiano, Vol. I: La Drammaturgia Medievale: dramma sacro e mimo. Firenze, Sansoni, 1938. — Rez. G. A[rtoni]. — III,2 (1939), 260—265.

201. RONGA, Luigi: Ritorno ad Alessandro Scarlatti. — IV,1 (1940), 21-38.

202. BILLANOVICH, Giuseppe: Uffizi drammatici della Chiesa Padovana. — IV,1 (1940), 72-100. [Über Liturgische Dramen vermutlich zu Beginn des 15. Jh. Bibl. Capitolare Padovana C 55 und C 56.]

203. [Rezension:] Il libro della Musica. Firenze, Sansoni, o. J. — Rez. Lele d'Amico. — IV,1 (1940), 109-114.

204. MARCHESINI, Cesare G.: Una rappresentazione popolare dell'episodio dell'Epifania. — IV,1 (1940), 126-128. [Chiesa San Giovanni Calanosco bei Bologna.]

205. [Rezension:] APOLLONIO, Mario: Storia del Teatro italiano. Vol. II: Il Teatro del Rinascimento. Commedia, tragedia, melodramma. Firenze, Sansoni, 1940. — Rez. G. A[rtoni]. — IV,1 (1940), 220-226.

206. [Rezension:] D'AMICO, Silvio: Storia del Teatro drammatico, Vol. II (parte III: Il Teatro Europeo dal Rinascimento al Romantismo), Milano, Rizzoli, 1940. — Rez. Valerio Mariani. — IV,1 (1940), 227-231.

207. MARCHESINI, Cesare G.: Il Teatro Comunale di Imola. — IV,1 (1940), 251-256. [254-256: Namen berühmter ital. Sänger des 19. Jh., die in Imola bei Opernaufführungen mitwirkten, ferner Aufführungsdaten.]

208. BONACCORSI, Alfredo: Il Melodramma di Alessandro Manzoni. — IV,1 (1940), 272-279. [Manzonis »Promessi Sposi« in ihrer Eignung als Libretto. 276-278 Hinweise auf Opern dieses Titels.]

209. FRANCESCHINI, Ezio: Un dramma latino del secolo XII: Il »Ludus de Antichristo«. — IV,1 (1940), 328-352. [Mysterienspiel aus Tegernsee, Bayer. Staatsbibl. München, clm. 19411.]

210. Pannain, Guido: Il Cinquantenario di un successo (»Cavalleria rustica-na«). — IV,1 (1940), 353-358.

211. Marchesini, Cesare G.: Una dinastia di architetti teatrali: i Bibiena. — IV,1 (1940), 377-382. [Auch bei zahlreichen Opernaufführungen des 18. Jh. beteiligt.]

212. Brunelli, Bruno: Grandezza e decadenza della riforma Metastasiana. — IV,2 (1940), 30-54.

213. Della Corte, Andrea: Gli elementi drammatici nella musica di Paisiel-lo. — IV,2 (1940), 77-88.

214. Costa, Orazio: Regia dell'»Attilio regolo«. — IV,2 (1940), 89—111. [Me-tastasio. Mit 9 Abb., 101—105.]

215. [Rezension:] Toschi, Paolo: Dal dramma liturgico alla rappresentazione sacra. Firenze, Sansoni, 1940. — Rez. Achille Fiocco. — IV,2 (1940), 112-114.

216. Vagniluca, Vittoria: La Lauda drammatica e la devozione. — IV,2 (1940), 155-202, 269-287. [Umbrien: Perugia, Orvieto.] 269-287. [U. a. über die Beziehungen zwischen Liturgischem Drama und Geistlichem Dra-ma in italienischer Sprache. Verz. von laude drammatiche 279-287.]

217. Gavazzeni, Gianandrea: La musica di scena di Pizzetti. — IV,2 (1940), 213-238, 288-308.

218. De Angelis, Alberto: Giulio Gatti-Casazza. — IV,2 (1940), 252-256. [Di-rektor der Mailänder Scala u. später der Metropolitan Opera in New York, 1869-1940.]

219. Scaravaglio Laiatico, Gabriella: Rappresentazioni drammatiche alla corte dei Montefeltro (1488-1513). — IV,2 (1940), 309-326. [Hof von Ur-bino, Erwähnung von Musik 321, 324, 327, 328. 4 fotogr. Wiedergaben von Gemälden. 326—329 Brief von Baldassare Castiglione an den Conte Ludovico Canossa.]

220. Rocca, Enrico: Indicazioni di un referendum. — IV,2 (1940), 330-340. [Statistische Erhebungen des Ente italiano audizioni radiofoniche. 334-336 über die einzelnen Sparten der gesendeten Musik und ihren Hörerkreis.]

221. Costa, Orazio: Regia d'un »Mistero« medioevale. — IV,2 (1940), 341-363. [Mit Abb. 355-363.]

222. [Rezension:] D'Angeli, Andrea: Benedetto Marcello. — Vita e opere. Mi-lano, 1940. — Rez. Gastone Rossi-Doria. — IV,2 (1940), 364-367.

223. Pieri, Antonio Aldo: Salvatore Viganò, coreografo della »Scala«. — IV,2 (1940), 378-382. [Viganò 1769-1821.]

224. Montalto, Lina: Fra virtuosi e musici nella corte del Card. Benedetto Pamphilj. — V,1 (1941), 83-97. [Benedetto Pamphilj, Neffe Papst Inno-zenz X. (1653—1730).] Forts. V,1 (1941), 193-209. [8 Karikaturen P. Leone Ghezzis von Mitwirkenden am Hofe Benedetto Pamphiljs.]

225. ARAGNO, Riccardo: I teatri italiani di prosa. Il teatro Carignano di Torino. — V,1 (1941), 121-128. [Enthält auch Daten von Opernaufführungen u. Konzerten aus dem 18. u. 19. Jh.]

226. SAUER, Kurt: Il teatro nazionale della nuova Germania. — V,1 (1941), 152-162. [NS-Kulturpolitik im Musikleben, 158-161.]

227. TRANQUILLI, Vittorio: Il teatro a Trieste e il suo museo. — V,1 (1941), 210-224. [215 Hinweis auf Tausende Sparten geistl. u. weltlicher Musik, zahlreiche Libretti (vorw. Erstdrucke), Dokumente zur Theatergeschichte u. zu G. Verdi.]

228. D'A[MICO], L[ele]: »Affè, Barilli«. — V,1 (1941), 251-256. [Gegen einen Anti-Wagner-Artikel gerichtet.]

229. BRUNELLI, Bruno: L'Impresario in angustie. — V,1 (1941), 311-341. [Über den Impresario Mario Faustini, der 1657 das Theater San Cassiano in Venedig übernahm. Zahlreiche Hinweise auf die von 1657-1667 aufgeführten Opern u. Abdruck von Briefen Cavallis u. Cestis.]

230. LUCIANI, S. A.: La più antica reliquia di musica scenica. Lo Stasimon dell'Oreste di Euripide. — V,1 (1941), 342-346. [Mit 3 Notenbeisp.]

231. [Rezension:] a) RONCAGLIA, Gino: L'ascensione creatrice di Giuseppe Verdi. Firenze, Sansoni, o. J. b) CAPRI, Antonio: Verdi uomo e artista. Milano, Moltrasio, o. J. c) VERDI, Giuseppe: Autobiografia dalle lettere, Milano, Mondadori, o. J. — Rez. L[ele] d'A[mico]. — V,1 (1941), 361-364.

232. A[RTONI], G.: Due progetti ottocenteschi per un Teatro d'Opera a Roma. — V,1 (1941), 379-382.

233. ROSSI-DORIA, Gastone: Avviamenti della coltura verdiana in Italia. — V,2 (1941), 24-51.

234. LUCIANI, S. A.: La Juditha triumphans di Antonio Vivaldi. — V,2 (1941), 349-355.

AUTORENREGISTER ZUR BIBLIOGRAPHIE

PERSONEN- UND SACHREGISTER ZUR BIBLIOGRAPHIE

Analecta musicologica

Veröffentlichung der musikgeschichtlichen Abteilung des Deutschen Historischen Instituts in Rom

ARNO VOLK VERLAG HANS GERIG KG · KÖLN

Concentus musicus

Veröffentlichung der musikgeschichtlichen Abteilung des Deutschen Historischen Instituts in Rom — Eine kritische Notenedition.

Band 1: *Johann Adolf Hasse: »Ruggiero«*

Herausgeber: Klaus Hortschansky
454 S. Noten, 32 S. Vorwort u. Kritischer Bericht (deutsch), 4 Tafeln
AV 230, Leinen DM 220.—
Subskriptionspreis: DM 187.—

Band 2: *Giovanni Priuli: »Sacrorum Concentuum Pars I«*

Herausgeber: Albert Biales
262 S. Noten, 6 S. Vorwort u. Kritischer Bericht (englisch), 2 Faksimilia
AV 231, Leinen DM 160.—
Subskriptionspreis: DM 136.—

Band 3: *Domenico Mazzocchi: »Cantiones sacrae«*

Herausgeber: Wolfgang Witzenmann
221 S. Noten, 16 S. Vorwort u. Kritischer Bericht (deutsch), 4 Faksimilia
AV 232, Leinen DM 110.—
Subskriptionspreis: DM 93.50

Der Subskriptionspreis gilt nur bei Verpflichtung zur Abnahme der Gesamtreihe.

In Vorbereitung:

Dietrich Kämper: Werke Giovanni Battista Confortis
Ludwig Finscher: Italienische Streichquartette
Pierluigi Petrobelli: Konzerte Tartinis
Howard E. Smither: Italienische Oratorien des Barock
Günther Massenkeil: Kantaten Carissimis

ARNO VOLK VERLAG HANS GERIG KG · KÖLN